Lecture Notes in Artificial Intelligence   8109

Subseries of Lecture Notes in Computer Science

LNAI Series Editors

Randy Goebel
University of Alberta, Edmonton, Canada
Yuzuru Tanaka
Hokkaido University, Sapporo, Japan
Wolfgang Wahlster
DFKI and Saarland University, Saarbrücken, Germany

LNAI Founding Series Editor

Joerg Siekmann
DFKI and Saarland University, Saarbrücken, Germany

Concha Bielza   Antonio Salmerón
Amparo Alonso-Betanzos
J. Ignacio Hidalgo   Luis Martínez
Alicia Troncoso Emilio Corchado
Juan M. Corchado (Eds.)

Advances in Artificial Intelligence

15th Conference of the Spanish Association
for Artificial Intelligence, CAEPIA 2013
Madrid, Spain, September 17-20, 2013
Proceedings

 Springer

Volume Editors

Concha Bielza
Universidad Politécnica de Madrid
28660 Madrid, Spain
E-mail: mcbielza@fi.upm.es

Amparo Alonso-Betanzos
Universidad de A Coruña
15071 A Coruña, Spain
E-mail: ciamparo@udc.es

Luis Martínez
Universidad de Jaén
23071 Jaén, Spain
E-mail: luis.martinez@ujaen.es

Emilio Corchado
Universidad de Salamanca
37008 Salamanca, Spain,
E-mail: escorchado@usal.es

Antonio Salmerón
Universidad de Almería
04120 Almería, Spain
E-mail: antonio.salmeron@ual.es

J. Ignacio Hidalgo
Universidad Complutense de Madrid
28040 Madrid, Spain
E-mail: hidalgo@dacya.ucm.es

Alicia Troncoso
Universidad Pablo de Olavide
41013 Sevilla, Spain
E-mail: ali@upo.es

Juan M. Corchado
Universidad de Salamanca
37008 Salamanca, Spain
E-mail: corchado@usal.es

ISSN 0302-9743
ISBN 978-3-642-40642-3
DOI 10.1007/978-3-642-40643-0

e-ISSN 1611-3349
e-ISBN 978-3-642-40643-0

Springer Heidelberg New York Dordrecht London

Library of Congress Control Number: 2013946545

CR Subject Classification (1998): I.2, F.1, I.4, H.3-4, F.2, C.2

LNCS Sublibrary: SL 7 – Artificial Intelligence

© Springer-Verlag Berlin Heidelberg 2013

Typesetting: Camera-ready by author, data conversion by Scientific Publishing Services, Chennai, India

Printed on acid-free paper

Springer is part of Springer Science+Business Media (www.springer.com)

Preface

This volume contains a selection of the papers accepted for oral presentation at the 15th Conference of the Spanish Association for Artificial Intelligence (CAEPIA 2013), held in Madrid (Spain), during September 17-20, 2013. This was the 15th biennial conference in the CAEPIA series, which was started back in 1985. Previous editions took place in Madrid, Alicante, Málaga, Murcia, Gijón, Donostia, Santiago de Compostela, Salamanca, Seville, and La Laguna. This edition of CAEPIA was coordinated with various independent conferences: IX Spanish Congress on Metaheuristics, Evolutive and Bioinspired Algorithms (MAEB 2013), IV Symposium of Fuzzy Logic and Soft Computing (LFSC), VII Symposium of Data Mining Theory and Applications (TAMIDA 2013), Information Fusion 2013 (FINO 2013) and Agent and Multiagent Systems: From Theory to Practice (ASMas). This is why this time the conference is called Multi-Conference CAEPIA, as a sign of the strong tie between all Spanish artificial intelligence (AI) researchers. Moreover, this year CAEPIA was held within the IV Spanish Congress on Informatics (CEDI 2013).

CAEPIA is a forum open to worldwide researchers to present and discuss their last scientific and technological advances in AI. Its main aims are to facilitate the dissemination of new ideas and experiences, to strengthen the links among the different research groups, and to help spread new developments to society. All perspectives –theory, methodology, and applications– are welcome.

Apart from the presentation of technical full papers, the scientific program of CAEPIA 2013 included two invited lectures, a Doctoral Consortium and, for the first time, a special session on outstanding recent papers (Key Works) already published in journals or forums of renowned reputation.

With the permanent goal of making CAEPIA a high-quality conference, and following the model of current demanding AI conferences, the CAEPIA Program Chairs organized the review process as follows. The Scientific Committee was structured in two levels. At the first level the AI knowledge was distributed in 11 areas and a Track Chair was assigned for each one. These Track Chairs are well-known members of the AI community affiliated to Spanish universities and research centers. At the second level there was a Program Committee with 116 members (37 non-Spanish institutions). All papers were carefully peer-reviewed, sometimes with the support of additional reviewers. There were 19 additional reviewers (eight non-Spanish institutions). The reviewers judged the overall quality of the submitted papers, together with their originality and novelty, technical correctness, awareness of related work, and quality of presentation. The reviewers stated their confidence in the subject area in addition to detailed written comments. Each paper was assigned to at least three Program Committee members who made the reviews (following the double-blind model), and to a Track Chair who supervised these reviews. On the basis of the reviews, the Track Chairs recommended paper acceptance or rejection to the CAEPIA Program Chairs, who made the final decisions. The CAEPIA Program Chairs chose the Best CAEPIA Paper and the Best Reviewer, both awards acknowledged by AEPIA.

CAEPIA received 66 submissions. Authors were requested to mark their paper as candidate to be published in the LNAI volume. Out of the 66 submissions, 48 had this mark. After the review process, 27 out of these marked papers were accepted for oral presentation and publication in this volume. Also, there were submissions for this volume from the other associated conferences: 17 from MAEB 2013 (six accepted), 10 from LFSC (four accepted), eight from TAMIDA 2013 (two accepted), one from FINO 2013 (0 accepted) and two from ASMas (one accepted). These papers were reviewed under the same process and Scientific Committee as the previous CAEPIA papers. The Program Chairs of these conferences and the Chairs of the most related CAEPIA track also contributed to the review process. As a result, this volume contains 40 papers, each presented in a 20-minute oral presentation during the conference. The papers were organized according to their topics.

The two distinguished invited speakers were Francisco Herrera (ECCAI Fellow, University of Granada, Spain) and Tom Heskes (Editor-in-Chief of the scientific journal *Neurocomputing*, Radboud University Nijmegen, The Netherlands). Francisco Herrera presented the most relevant aspects of big data, the characteristics of current libraries, and the challenges in the development of new scalable algorithms. Tom Heskes showed how Bayesian machine learning techniques can lead to a novel paradigm for brain–computer interfaces, the reconstruction of images based on fMRI activation, and network analysis from diffusion tensor imaging.

The Doctoral Consortium was specially designed for the interaction between PhD students and senior researchers. A scientific panel of 12 Spanish professors in AI interacted orally with the students on their plans and preliminary results. The Doctoral Consortium was a joint activity with all the conferences coordinated with CAEPIA, receiving 29 submissions. The Campus de Excelencia BioTICs of the Granada University sponsored the best PhD work with the GENIL prize, whereas AEPIA granted the next two best PhD proposals.

The session on Key Works, also jointly held with the other five conferences, had 14 submissions. Recent works published in journals or forums of renown reputation during the period 2011-2013 were allowed so as to spread them among a wide audience from the AI community. Three senior members shaped the Selection Committee.

The editors would like to thank everyone who contributed to the Multi-Conference CAEPIA 2013: the authors of the papers, the members of the Scientific Committee together with the additional reviewers, the invited speakers, and the Doctoral Consortium and Key Works session organizers. Thanks are also due to Luis Guerra, who designed the website of the CAEPIA conference, managed the free EasyChair conference web system (http://www.easychair.org/), and compiled this volume. Final thanks go to the Organizing Committee (that of CEDI included), the Complutense and Technical Universities of Madrid, the Springer team, our sponsors, and AEPIA for their support.

June 2013

Concha Bielza
Antonio Salmerón
Amparo Alonso-Betanzos
Multi-Conference Organising
J. Ignacio Hidalgo
Luis Martínez
Alicia Troncoso
Emilio Corchado
Juan M. Corchado

Organization

Executive Committee

Concha Bielza — Technical University of Madrid, Spain
Antonio Salmerón — University of Almería, Spain
Amparo Alonso-Betanzos — University of A Coruña, Spain

Senior Program Committee

Enrique Alba, Spain
Ismael García Varea, Spain
Francisco Herrera, Spain
Pedro Larrañaga, Spain
Serafín Moral, Spain
Filiberto Plá, Spain

Emilio Corchado, Spain
Lluis Godó, Spain
Juan Huete, Spain
Pedro Meseguer, Spain
Sascha Ossowski, Spain

Program Committee

Enrique Alegre, Spain
Alessandro Antonucci, Italy
Carlos Beltran, Italy
Christian Blum, Spain
Daniel Borrajo, Spain
Vicent Botti, Spain
Humberto Bustince, Spain
Fidel Cacheda, Spain
Borja Calvo, Spain
Andrés Cano, Spain
Enric Cervera, Spain
Francisco Chicano, Spain
Carlos Coello, Mexico
Oscar Cordón, Spain
Inés Couso, Spain
Sergio Damas, Spain
Arjen de Vries,
    The Netherlands
S. Irene Díaz, Spain
Richard Duro, Spain

Cesare Alippi, Italy
Rubén Armañanzas, Spain
Alexandre Bernardino, Portugal
Blai Bonet, Venezuela
Juan Botía, Spain
Alberto Bugarín, Spain
Pedro Cabalar, Spain
José M. Cadenas, Spain
José L. Calvo Rolle, Spain
Pablo Castell, Spain
Carlos Chesñevar, Argentina
Francisco Chiclana, UK
Juan M. Corchado, Spain
Carlos Cotta, Spain
Fabio Crestani, Italy
Andre C.P.L.F. de Carvalho, Brazil

María J. del Jesús, Spain
Bernabé Dorronsoro, France
Marcelo Federico, Italy

Additional Reviewers

Carlos Agüero, Spain
Diego Fernández, Spain
Shima Gerani, Italy
Giacomo Inches, Italy
Henrique Lopes, Portugal
Francisco Martín, Spain
Luis Matías, Portugal
Jonathan
   Ortigosa-Hernández, Spain
Josep Puyol-Gruart, Spain
Ana Paula Rocha, Portugal

Hanen Borchani, Spain
Vreixo Formoso, Spain
Daniel Gutiérrez, Spain
Monica Landoni, Italy
Parvaz Mahdabi, Italy
Vicente Matellán, Spain
Manuel Mucientes, Spain

Antonio Pereira, Portugal
Alejandro Rituerto, Spain

Organizing Committee

Multiconference CAEPIA 2013 was held within the Spanish Congress on Informatics (CEDI 2013), which was hosted by the Complutense University of Madrid and the Technical University of Madrid.

Sponsors

– Asociación Española para la Inteligencia Artificial (AEPIA)

Table of Contents

Constraints, Search and Planning

An Evaluation of Best Compromise Search in Graphs................ 1
 Enrique Machuca, Lawrence Mandow, and Lucie Galand

Intelligent Web and Information Retrieval

Compressing Semantic Metadata for Efficient Multimedia Retrieval..... 12
 *Mario Arias Gallego, Oscar Corcho, Javier D. Fernández,
 Miguel A. Martínez-Prieto, and Mari Carmen Suárez-Figueroa*

Time-Aware Evaluation of Methods for Identifying Active Household
Members in Recommender Systems 22
 *Pedro G. Campos, Alejandro Bellogín, Iván Cantador, and
 Fernando Díez*

Comments-Oriented Query Expansion for Opinion Retrieval in Blogs ... 32
 Jose M. Chenlo, Javier Parapar, and David E. Losada

A Contextual Modeling Approach for Model-Based Recommender
Systems 42
 *Ignacio Fernández-Tobías, Pedro G. Campos, Iván Cantador, and
 Fernando Díez*

Identifying Overlapping Communities and Their Leading Members in
Social Networks.. 52
 Camilo Palazuelos and Marta Zorrilla

Fuzzy Systems

Permutability of Fuzzy Consequence Operators and Fuzzy Interior
Operators.. 62
 Neus Carmona, Jorge Elorza, Jordi Recasens, and Jean Bragard

A Fuzzy Filter for High-Density Salt and Pepper Noise Removal 70
 *Manuel González-Hidalgo, Sebastià Massanet, Arnau Mir, and
 Daniel Ruiz-Aguilera*

A New Class of Functions for Integrating Weighting Means and OWA
Operators   80
    Bonifacio Llamazares

Attitude-Driven Web Consensus Support System for Large-Scale GDM
Problems Based on Fuzzy Linguistic Approach   91
    Iván Palomares and Luis Martínez

Knowledge Representation, Reasoning and Logic

Decidability of a Logic for Order of Magnitude Qualitative Reasoning
with Comparability and Negligibility Relations   101
    Alfredo Burrieza

Machine Learning

Applying Resampling Methods for Imbalanced Datasets to not so
Imbalanced Datasets   111
    *Olatz Arbelaitz, Ibai Gurrutxaga, Javier Muguerza, and
    Jesús María Pérez*

Scaling Up Feature Selection: A Distributed Filter Approach   121
    *Verónica Bolón-Canedo, Noelia Sánchez-Maroño, and
    Joana Cerviño-Rabuñal*

Experiments on Neuroevolution and Online Weight Adaptation in
Complex Environments   131
    *Francisco José Gallego-Durán, Rafael Molina-Carmona, and
    Faraón Llorens-Largo*

Learning Conditional Linear Gaussian Classifiers with Probabilistic
Class Labels   139
    Pedro L. López-Cruz, Concha Bielza, and Pedro Larrañaga

Exact Incremental Learning for a Single Non-linear Neuron Based on
Taylor Expansion and Greville Formula   149
    *David Martínez-Rego, Oscar Fontenla-Romero, and
    Amparo Alonso-Betanzos*

Augmented Semi-naive Bayes Classifier   159
    Bojan Mihaljevic, Pedro Larrañaga, and Concha Bielza

Automatic Ontology User Profiling for Social Networks from URLs
shared   168
    *Paula Peña, Rafael Del Hoyo, Jorge Vea-Murguía,
    Carlos González, and Sergio Mayo*

Multiagent Systems

A Common-Recipe and Conflict-Solving MAP Approach for Care
Planning in Comorbid Patients 178
*Gonzalo Milla-Millán, Juan Fdez-Olivares, and
Inmaculada Sánchez-Garzón*

An Argumentation-Based Multi-agent Temporal Planning System Built
on t-DeLP 188
Pere Pardo and Lluís Godó

Engineering the Decentralized Coordination of UAVs with Limited
Communication Range... 199
*Marc Pujol-Gonzalez, Jesús Cerquides, Pedro Meseguer,
Juan Antonio Rodríguez-Aguilar, and Milind Tambe*

Multidisciplinary Topics and Applications

Concurrent CPU-GPU Code Optimization: The Two-Point Angular
Correlation Function as Case Study 209
*Miguel Cárdenas-Montes, Miguel Ángel Vega-Rodríguez,
Ignacio Sevilla, Rafael Ponce, Juan José Rodríguez-Vázquez, and
Eusebio Sánchez Álvaro*

.Cloud: Unified Platform for Compilation and Execution Processes in a
Cloud 219
*Fernando De la Prieta, Antonio Juan Sánchez, Carolina Zato,
Sara Rodríguez, and Javier Bajo*

A SIR e-Epidemic Model for Computer Worms Based on Cellular
Automata.. 228
Ángel Martín del Rey

A Common Framework for Fault Diagnosis of Parametric and Discrete
Faults Using Possible Conflicts 239
*Noemi Moya Alonso, Anibal Bregon,
Carlos J. Alonso-González, and Belarmino Pulido*

Metaheuristics

Impact of the Production Mix Preservation on the ORV Problem 250
Joaquín Bautista, Alberto Cano, Rocío Alfaro, and Cristina Batalla

Sustainable Internet Services in Contributory Communities............ 260
*Guillem Cabrera, Hebert Pérez-Rosés, Angel A. Juan, and
Joan Manuel Marquès*

A Study of the Combination of Variation Operators in the NSGA-II
Algorithm... 269
    Antonio J. Nebro, Juan J. Durillo, Mirialys Machín,
    Carlos A. Coello Coello, and Bernabé Dorronsoro

A New Heuristic for the Capacitated Vertex p-Center Problem......... 279
    Dagoberto R. Quevedo-Orozco and Roger Z. Ríos-Mercado

Reducing Gas Emissions in Smart Cities by Using the Red Swarm
Architecture... 289
    Daniel H. Stolfi and Enrique Alba

Heuristic Optimization Model for Infrastructure Asset Management 300
    Cristina Torres-Machí, Eugenio Pellicer, Víctor Yepes, and
    Alondra Chamorro

Uncertainty in Artificial Intelligence

Learning more Accurate Bayesian Networks in the CHC Approach by
Adjusting the Trade-Off between Efficiency and Accuracy 310
    Jacinto Arias, José A. Gámez, and José M. Puerta

Approximate Lazy Evaluation of Influence Diagrams 321
    Rafael Cabañas, Andrés Cano, Manuel Gómez-Olmedo, and
    Anders L. Madsen

Learning Recursive Probability Trees from Data 332
    Andrés Cano, Manuel Gómez-Olmedo, Serafín Moral,
    Cora Beatriz Pérez-Ariza, and Antonio Salmerón

On Using the PC Algorithm for Learning Continuous Bayesian
Networks: An Experimental Analysis 342
    Antonio Fernández, Inmaculada Pérez-Bernabé, and
    Antonio Salmerón

Learning from Crowds in Multi-dimensional Classification Domains 352
    Jerónimo Hernández-González, Iñaki Inza, and José A. Lozano

Learning Mixtures of Polynomials of Conditional Densities
from Data 363
    Pedro L. López-Cruz, Thomas D. Nielsen, Concha Bielza, and
    Pedro Larrañaga

A Dynamic Bayesian Network Framework for Learning
from Observation 373
    Santiago Ontañón, José Luis Montaña, and Avelino J. Gonzalez

Approximate Counting of Graphical Models via MCMC Revisited 383
    José M. Peña

Multidimensional *k*-Interaction Classifier: Taking Advantage of All the
Information Contained in Low Order Interactions 393
    Aritz Pérez Martínes, José A. Lozano, and Iñaki Inza

Author Index 403

An Evaluation of Best Compromise Search in Graphs

Enrique Machuca[1], Lawrence Mandow[1], and Lucie Galand[2]

[1] Univ. Malaga, Spain
{machuca,lawrence}@lcc.uma.es
[2] Univ. Paris-Dauphine, France
lucie.galand@dauphine.fr

Abstract. This work evaluates two different approaches for multicriteria graph search problems using compromise preferences. This approach focuses search on a single solution that represents a balanced tradeoff between objectives, rather than on the whole set of Pareto optimal solutions. We review the main concepts underlying compromise preferences, and two main approaches proposed for their solution in heuristic graph problems: naive Pareto search (NAMOA*), and a k-shortest-path approach (kA*). The performance of both approaches is evaluated on sets of standard bicriterion road map problems. The experiments reveal that the k-shortest-path approach looses effectiveness in favor of naive Pareto search as graph size increases. The reasons for this behavior are analyzed and discussed.

1 Introduction

Multicriteria optimization problems involve the consideration of different objectives that need to be optimized simultaneously. These problems seldom have a single optimal solution, and in general, many optimal trade-offs between the different objectives can be considered. The set of *rational* decisions to the problem is defined by the set of non-dominated (*Pareto-optimal*) solutions. A nondominated solution cannot be improved by other solution in one objective without worsening in at least another one.

However, choosing one among the set of nondominated solutions is a subjective decision particular to each decision maker. Several approaches have been proposed to tackle this question. These include goal satisfaction, multiattribute utility theory, or compromise programming [1]. One of the most popular approaches in multicriteria decision making is based on the use of *achievement scalarizing functions*. These functions evaluate a solution according to its *distance* to a reference point in the objective space [12]. The most preferred solution is then the closest one to the reference point. Such a solution is called hereafter a *best compromise solution*. The reference point can be specified by the decision maker as her aspiration level on each objective [10]. Otherwise, the reference point can be the *ideal point*, defined as the cost of an ideal (but generally unreachable) solution that would achieve the scalar optimal value for all objectives [14].

In this paper, we consider the problem of determining a *best compromise* path from an initial node to a goal node in a graph where the arcs are valued by several objective functions. In this setting, the value of a path is the componentwise sum of the value of its arcs. Since a best compromise solution is Pareto optimal (for any rational decision maker), a simple approach could be a two-step procedure: 1) generate the set of Pareto

C. Bielza et al. (Eds.): CAEPIA 2013, LNAI 8109, pp. 1–11, 2013.

optimal paths, and 2) select the best compromise path among them. Efficient algorithms have been proposed to generate the whole set of Pareto optimal paths [7]. Contrary to the single objective case, several distinct paths can be (Pareto) optimal on a node. The number of Pareto optimal paths can even be exponential in the size of the instance [4].

Pareto dominance tests have to be performed to compare subpaths reaching each node, requiring significant computation times. More specific approaches have been proposed to directly focus the search on a preferred path with respect to a specific preference model without generating the whole set of Pareto optimal solutions ([8,2,3]). Among these, kA* relies on an ordered enumeration of the paths (*k-shortest-path* algorithm) according to a linear scalarizing function, until one obtains the guarantee that the best compromise path has been found (i.e. already enumerated). Thanks to the use of a linear scalarization, this approach does not require costly Pareto dominance tests.

In this paper, we compare two different heuristic algorithmic strategies for best compromise search in multiobjective graphs. The first one is a two-step procedure based on standard Pareto search algorithms, like NAMOA* [7]. The second one explores the use of *k*-shortest-path algorithms to avoid evaluating all Pareto optimal paths in the graph, as well as performing computationally costly Pareto dominance tests. Preliminary results [2] showed an advantage in performance for kA* against the naive Pareto search (NAMOA*) on random graphs with an artificially calculated heuristic. This paper performs a more systematic evaluation of both approaches on sets of standard bicriterion route planning problems [9,6,5]. The algorithms are provided with the precalculated Tung-Chew heuristics [11]. The experiments reveal that the *k*-shortest-path approach looses effectiveness in favor of naive Pareto search as graph size increases.

Section 2 reviews relevant concepts and previous work that are used in this paper. After the presentation of the instances in Section 3, the results obtained are shown in Section 4. Then they are analyzed in Section 5 to exhibit the advantages and the drawbacks of the two approaches. Finally, some conclusions are summarized in Section 6, leading us to further research perspectives.

2   Related Work

2.1   Preliminaries

Let us consider a decision problem where X denotes the set of feasible alternatives and each feasible alternative $x \in X$ is evaluated according to a set of q objective functions to be minimized $f_i : X \to \mathbb{R}$, $i \in \{1..q\}$. Each alternative x is represented in the objective space by an evaluation vector (vector cost) $\boldsymbol{f}(x) = (f_1(x), \ldots, f_q(x))$. Let $Y = f(X)$ denote the set of images of the feasible alternatives of X in the objective space. The comparison of the elements of X boils down to the comparison of their vector costs in Y. Let us define the dominance relation ($\prec$) between vectors as follows,

$$\forall \boldsymbol{y}, \boldsymbol{y}' \in \mathbb{R}^q \quad \boldsymbol{y} \prec \boldsymbol{y}' \quad \Leftrightarrow \quad \forall i \quad y_i \leq y_i' \land \boldsymbol{y} \neq \boldsymbol{y}' \tag{1}$$

where y_i denotes the i-th element of vector $\boldsymbol{y}$.

Given a set of vectors Y, we shall define $\mathcal{N}(Y)$ the set of non-dominated (Pareto-optimal) vectors in set Y in the following way,

$$\mathcal{N}(Y) = \{\boldsymbol{y} \in Y \mid \nexists \boldsymbol{y}' \in Y \quad \boldsymbol{y}' \prec \boldsymbol{y}\} \tag{2}$$

The set $\mathcal{N}(Y)$ is bounded by the *ideal point* $\boldsymbol{\alpha} = (\alpha_1 \ldots \alpha_q)$ and the *nadir point* $\boldsymbol{\beta} = (\beta_1 \ldots \beta_q)$, where $\alpha_i = min_{\boldsymbol{y} \in \mathcal{N}(Y)}\{y_i\}$ and $\beta_i = max_{\boldsymbol{y} \in \mathcal{N}(Y)}\{y_i\}$ [1].

2.2 Scalarizing Functions

Resorting to scalarizing functions amounts to modifying the multiobjective optimization problem into a single objective one. Preferential information is taken into account through parameters used in the scalarizing functions (e.g. weights to define the importance of the objectives). An adequate scalarizing function s is required to have the following properties: (1) any non-dominated solution can be optimal with respect to s (with an appropriate choice of parameters); and (2) any optimal solution with respect to s has to be non-dominated. These requirements ensure that, for any rational decision maker, the preferred solution can be reached optimizing some scalarizing function.

One of the simplest multicriteria approaches is to define the scalarizing function as a linear weighted combination of the evaluation vector. Given a set of weights w_i, the goodness or *utility* of a solution is given by,

$$u(\boldsymbol{y}) = \sum_i w_i \, y_i \tag{3}$$

Any solution minimizing $u(\boldsymbol{y})$ will be non-dominated (second requirement). However, in general only a subset of all non-dominated solutions can be obtained (the so-called *supported* solutions). Some non-dominated solutions cannot be obtained regardless of the chosen weights. The first requirement is thus not satisfied.

Achievement scalarizing functions are widely used in multicriteria decision making. They estimate the distance of a solution to a reference point using Minkowski's distance, or ℓ_p-norm, defined by:

$$\ell_p(\boldsymbol{y}) = \|\boldsymbol{y}\|_p = \left(\sum_i |y_i|^p\right)^{1/p} \qquad (p \geq 1) \tag{4}$$

Different norms are obtained for different values of p. The case for $p = 1$ is called *Manhattan* distance, $p = 2$ is the *Euclidean* distance, and $p = \infty$ is the *Chebyshev* distance, which measures the maximum component.

In the absence of further preferential information, and without loss of generality, we may consider that the preferred solution is the one that minimizes distance to the ideal point. For example, the Manhattan and Chebyshev distances from a vector $\boldsymbol{y}$ to the ideal point $\boldsymbol{\alpha}$ are defined respectively as,

$$\|\boldsymbol{y} - \boldsymbol{\alpha}\|_1 = \sum_i |y_i - \alpha_i| \tag{5}$$

---

[1] For $q = 2$ these points are easily obtained by the heuristic precalculation procedure [11].

$$\|\boldsymbol{y} - \boldsymbol{\alpha}\|_\infty = \max_i |y_i - \alpha_i| \tag{6}$$

Notice that any solution that minimizes ℓ_p distance to the ideal point for some p is a non-dominated solution (second requirement), except for the case $p = \infty$ [13]. In the latter case, there is at least one ℓ_∞-optimal solution that is non-dominated, but this may dominate other ℓ_∞-optimal ones. However when $p = \infty$, any non-dominated solution can minimize ℓ_p distance. The first requirement is then satisfied. Actually, there does not exist any scalarizing function satisfying simultaneously the two requirements [13]. Chebyshev distance appears thus as an adequate achievement function which enables to reach any potentially preferred solution. We define therefore in the following a *best compromise solution* as a solution that minimizes Chebyshev distance to the ideal point. We use the following scalarizing functions for Manhattan and Chebyshev norms[2],

$$s^1(\boldsymbol{y}) = \sum_i w_i(y_i - \alpha_i) = \sum_i w_i y_i - \sum_i w_i \alpha_i \tag{7}$$

$$s^\infty(\boldsymbol{y}) = \max_i w_i(y_i - \alpha_i) \tag{8}$$

where for all i, $w_i = \frac{\delta_i}{\beta_i - \alpha_i}$ and δ_i is the relative importance of objective i.

2.3 Compromise Search with Chebyshev Norm

We consider the problem of determining a best compromise path from an initial node to a goal node in a multiobjective graph with respect to the Chebyshev norm. Notice that partial solutions evaluated according to the Chebyshev norm do not satisfy Bellman's optimality principle [2]. We compare two main general approaches. The first (*naive*) approach consists in calculating the set of all nondominated solution costs using a label setting algorithm like NAMOA* [7], and then identifying the optimal solution among them. This approach is simple, but: (a) requires the calculation of the full Pareto set, (b) costly Pareto dominance tests must be performed during the search to compare the current subpaths and keep only the optimal ones. The second approach is an alternative algorithm based on single-objective k-shortest paths search [2]. The major insight is that it is possible to devise a weighted linear function that minorates the Chebyshev distance [2]. For any vector cost $\boldsymbol{y} \in \mathbb{R}^q$, it can indeed be easily shown that,

$$\frac{s^1(\boldsymbol{y})}{q} \leq s^\infty(\boldsymbol{y}) \tag{9}$$

The linearity of the scalarizing function s^1 makes it possible to determine the optimal path with respect to s^1 from optimal (w.r.t. s^1) subpaths (exploiting Bellman's principle). However, the optimal path with respect to s^1 is not necessarily a path which minimizes the Chebyshev norm. The principle of this approach is then to enumerate the k best paths with respect to s^1 until we are sure to have found the optimal path with respect to s^∞. The procedure can be summarized as follows,

---

[2] Note that if we are evaluating *solutions* (not partial solutions), then by definition we have that $\forall i, 0 \leq \alpha_i \leq y_i$.

1. Use a k-shortest paths algorithm to generate a sequence of solutions according to s^1. Let us denote by $\boldsymbol{y}_n$ the vector cost of the n-th solution found.
2. For each new solution found, calculate its value according to the Chebyshev norm s^∞, keeping the best value found so far, i.e $p^* = min_n s^\infty(\boldsymbol{y}_n)$.
3. Stop searching as soon as a newly found solution $\boldsymbol{y}_m$ satisfies $\frac{s^1(\boldsymbol{y}_m)}{q} > p^*$.
4. Return the solution that achieved the optimal value of p^*. Path p^* is optimal since for any $r > m$, $\frac{s^1(y_r)}{q} \geq \frac{s^1(y_m)}{q} > p^*$ and by (9) we have $s^\infty(y_r) \geq \frac{s^1(y_r)}{q}$.

Since the k-best search is performed on a single objective version of the problem, no Pareto dominance tests are performed during the search. In the following, we evaluate this approach using kA*, a variant of A* that calculates k-shortest paths [2]. More precisely, we improve kA* to avoid cyclic paths, which can obviously never lead to non-dominated solutions. Otherwise, performance would be quite poor in our test sets.

3   Experiments

The algorithms have been tested on different classes of problem sets taken from the multiobjective search literature: bidimensional grids with random costs, and random route planning problems on road maps. In all cases, the algorithms were provided with pre-calculated heuristic functions as described by Tung and Chew [11]. These are obtained from ideal optimal values for both objectives calculated with reverse scalar searches, which are computationally much less costly than subsequent multicriteria searches [6].

The first test set involves square grids, like those described in [6]. A vicinity of four neighbours is used. Bidimensional costs are random integers in the range $[1, 10]$. Start node is placed at the center of the grid. For a grid of size $d \times d$, the goal is placed at depth d. Depth varies from 10 to 100 in steps of 10 with 10 problems for each size, i.e., there are 100 problem instances. Thus, the total number of nodes and arcs for the largest-sized grids (200×200) is 40000 and 159200 respectively. The average number of Pareto-optimal solution paths for the ten largest problems (200×200) is 124.8.

The second test set is taken from the work of Raith and Ehrgott [9]. This consists of three modified road maps from the '9th DIMACS Challenge on Shortest Paths': Washington DC (DC), Rhode Island (RI), and New Jersey (NJ). These include integer cost values for two different objectives: time and distance. The maps include a Hamiltonian cycle that guarantees all nodes are connected. Nine random problems are defined for each map. The size of the maps and the average number of distinct Pareto-optimal costs are displayed in table 1.

The final test set consists of fifty random problems over the unmodified New York City (NY) map from the DIMACS Challenge presented at [5]. The hardest road map problems tested for the algorithms appear in this problem set, as reflected in the average number of distinct Pareto (see table 1).

In all cases, problem instances were solved with a 1h time limit. The algorithms were implemented in ANSI Common Lisp using LispWorks 6.0 Enterprise 64 bits. The first and third test sets were run on a Sun Fire X4140 server with 2 six-core AMD Opteron 2435 @ 2.60GHz processors and 64 Gb of RAM, under Windows Server 2008 R2 Enterprise (64-bits). In the second test set, the algorithms were run on a Windows 7 64-bit platform, with an Intel Core2 Quad Q9550 at 2.8Ghz, and 4Gb of RAM.

Table 1. Size of road maps used in the test sets, and average number of nondominated solution costs (DC, RI, and NJ as taken from [9], NY as taken from [5])

Name	Location	Nodes	Arcs	Avg. nondom. costs
DC	Washington D.C.	9,559	39,377	3.33
RI	Rhode Island	53,658	192,084	9.44
NJ	New Jersey	330,386	1,202,458	10.66
NY	New York City	264,346	730,100	198.62

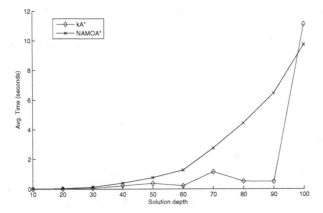

Fig. 1. Average execution times for the square grid problem set, as a function of goal depth

4   Results

Regarding the grid test set, figure 1 shows average execution times as a function of solution depth (averaged for the ten random problems available for each depth). NAMOA* displays a steady growth of time requirements. In general kA* provides better results except for the hardest problems. Table 2 details the execution times for each of the ten problems at depth 200. Most of the problems are solved rather quickly. However, two of them have very large time requirements referred to their actual nondominated solutions.

Regarding the modified road map test sets (DC, RI, and NJ) maps, each problem was solved in ten different runs. Figure 2 shows average execution times in logarithmic

Table 2. Data of kA* for each problem instance of the grid test set (200 × 200 grids)

Problem	Time (sec.)	k	Sol. vector costs	Avg. paths per sol. cost	Nondom sol. vector costs
1	0.1560	164	81	2.02	23
2	1.0140	382	101	3.78	41
3	57.6270	3280	168	19.52	44
4	0.0940	40	24	1.66	16
5	0.5460	101	36	2.80	16
6	0.8890	530	141	3.75	37
7	0.7800	160	51	3.13	37
8	43.0090	2992	160	18.70	33
9	0.1720	75	35	2.14	17
10	6.8320	808	65	12.43	27

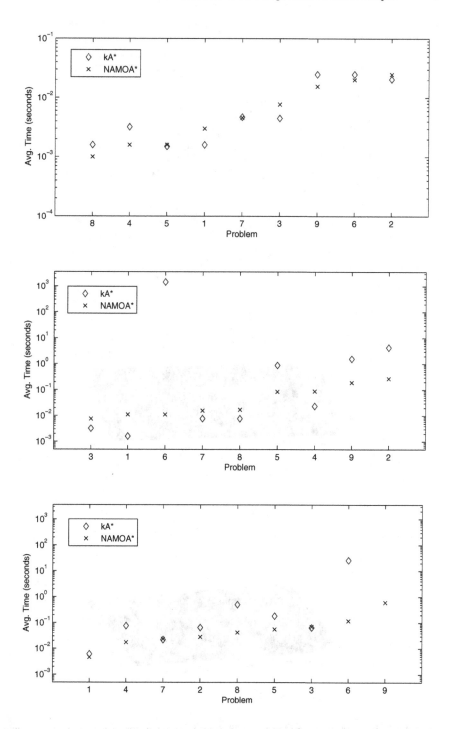

Fig. 2. Time results on modified DIMACS road map problems (DC - top, RI - center, NJ - bottom)

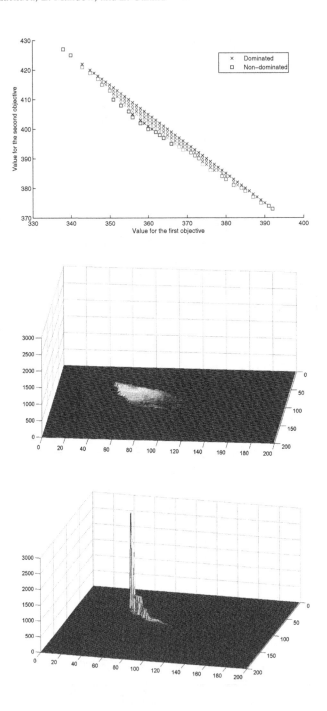

Fig. 3. Analysis of 200×200 grid instance #8: (top) Solution vector costs in cost space; (center) Label expansions in search space (NAMOA*); (bottom) Label expansions in search space (kA*)

scale. Problem instances in the abscissa axis are ordered by increasing value of ordinate for NAMOA*. Values not displayed exceeded 1h time limit. In the NY City map, NAMOA* was able to solve all 50 instances, against only 15 of them by kA* under the time constraints. Algorithm kA* was faster than NAMOA* only in 3 of them (Fig. 4).

5 Discussion

The execution time of kA* is much less predictable than that of NAMOA*. This is quite evident from the grid data set, where solution depth can be easily controlled for experimental purposes. In the ten 200×200 grid instances, differences of three orders of magnitude in execution time can be observed for different problems. Table 2 provides valuable information regarding the performance of kA*. For example, in the hardest instances (#3 and #8), the number k of solution paths examined grows to 3280 and 2992 respectively. The number of distinct *solution* vector costs found was 164 and 154. Therefore, the average number of solution paths for each distinct vector cost raises to 20, which makes the algorithm much less competitive in these instances. The table also shows the number of nondominated solution vector costs among those explored by kA*.

The number of labels explored by kA* at each node can increase sharply. This can be attributed to the exponential worst case behavior of the algorithm, i.e. in some problem instances there can be a combinatorially large number of paths with the same vector cost. All of them are explicitly explored by the k-shortest-path approach. In contrast, NAMOA* can be guaranteed to explore the same label for each node only once [7].

Let us analyze instance #8 in more detail. Figure 3(top) displays a portion of cost space with the distinct solution vector costs explored by kA*. Figures 3(center) and 3(bottom) show the number of label expansions for each node in the bidimensional grid for NAMOA* and kA*. NAMOA* explores a larger portion of the grid. The number of nondominated vector costs grows polynomially with depth and, since NAMOA* explores each one only once, the overall number of label expansions is much lower. On the other hand, kA* explicitly explores many different paths with the same vector costs or the same value with respect to s^1 (some of them dominated). The explored

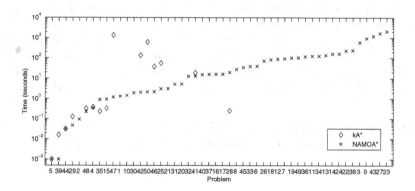

Fig. 4. Time results (in seconds) on the NY City map

portion of the grid is much smaller, and the number of dominated solution vector costs is marginally larger. However, the overall search effort is much higher. This indicates that kA* could be improved if only a single label were explored at each node for each different vector cost, as happens in NAMOA*.

The inability of kA* to solve instance 9 in the NJ map in the given time is also an example of this unpredictability. Results on the NY City map provide further confirmation. Finally, results on road map problems indicate that the performance of kA* is worse than that of NAMOA* in the hardest instances.

6   Conclusions and Future Work

This paper compares two approaches described in the literature for the calculation of a best compromise path in a multiobjective graph. The first one uses NAMOA*, a multiobjective generalization of A*, to calculate the Pareto set and then determine the best compromise solution. The second one relies on kA*, a k-shortest-paths variant of A*, improved here to avoid cycles. This approach needs to consider dominated paths, but avoids Pareto dominance checks. Earlier tests on small sized problems showed and advantage for the second approach [2]. We perform a more systematic evaluation on a variety of standard problem sets taken from the literature. These comprise random grids as well as realistic route planning problems in road maps. An analysis of the results shows that kA* can indeed be faster in the simpler instances, but looses effectiveness in favor of the full Pareto approach as graph size (and hence, problem difficulty) increases. The data also show that the time performance of kA* can be quite unpredictable. This is attributed to the combinatorial nature of the problem, since in some problems there can be a large number of paths with the same vector cost.

Another linear function different to s^1/q could be used to lower bound s^∞. Indeed $1/q$ is not the only weight that could be used. Actually we have $\sum_i \lambda_i w_i(y_i - \alpha_i) \leq s^\infty(y)$ for any nonnegative λ such that $\sum_i \lambda_i = 1$. The number of enumerated solutions depends on the choice of λ. A further study should take this issue into account.

A better understanding on performance of the two very different approaches (kA* and NAMOA*) would make it possible to design a more efficient and more robust algorithm. In particular, cycle avoidance allows effective pruning of some dominated paths on grids and road maps. Other new enhancements of the k-shortest-paths approach should be further investigated. In particular, a variant that only explores the k shortest paths with *different* vector costs is an interesting avenue of future reseach. Our results suggest that a k-shortest-path approach where each label is explored only once for each node, as happens in standard Pareto search, could yield a much more effective algorithm.

Acknowledgments. Partially funded by P07-TIC-03018, Cons. Innovación, Ciencia y Empresa (Junta Andalucía), and Univ. Málaga, Campus Excel. Int. Andalucía Tech.

References

1. Chankong, V., Haimes, Y.Y.: Multiobjective Decision Making: Theory and Methodology. North-Holland (1983)
2. Galand, L., Perny, P.: Search for compromise solutions in multiobjective state space graphs. In: Proc. of ECAI 2006, pp. 93–97 (2006)
3. Galand, L., Spanjaard, O.: Owa-based search in state space graphs with multiple cost functions. In: FLAIRS Conference 2007, pp. 86–91 (2007)
4. Hansen, P.: Bicriterion path problems. Lecture Notes in Economics and Mathematical Systems (LNEMS), vol. 177, pp. 109–127. Springer (1980)
5. Machuca, E., Mandow, L.: Multiobjective heuristic search in road maps. Expert Systems with Applications 39, 6435–6445 (2012)
6. Machuca, E., Mandow, L., Pérez-de-la-Cruz, J.L., Ruiz-Sepúlveda, A.: A comparison of heuristic best-first algorithms for bicriterion shortest path problems. European Journal of Operational Research 217, 44–53 (2012)
7. Mandow, L., Pérez de la Cruz, J.L.: Multiobjective A* search with consistent heuristics. Journal of the ACM 57(5), 27:1–27:25 (2010)
8. Perny, P., Spanjaard, O.: On preference-based search in state space graphs. In: Proc. Eighteenth Nat. Conf. on AI, pp. 751–756. AAAI Press (July 2002)
9. Raith, A., Ehrgott, M.: A comparison of solution strategies for biobjective shortest path problems. Computers & Operations Research 36(4), 1299–1331 (2009)
10. Steuer, R.E., Choo, E.: An interactive weighted Tchebycheff procedure for multiple objective programming. Mathematical Programming 26(1), 326–344 (1983)
11. Tung, C., Chew, K.: A multicriteria Pareto-optimal path algorithm. European Journal of Operational Research 62, 203–209 (1992)
12. Wierzbicki, A.P.: The use of reference objectives in multiobjective optimisation. In: Fandel, G., Gal, T. (eds.) LNEMS, vol. 177, pp. 468–486. Springer (1980)
13. Wierzbicki, A.P.: On the completeness and constructiveness of parametric characterizations to vector optimization problems. OR Spektrum 8, 73–87 (1986)
14. Zeleny, M.: Multiple criteria decision making. LNEMS, vol. 123. Springer (1976)

Compressing Semantic Metadata
for Efficient Multimedia Retrieval

Mario Arias Gallego[1], Oscar Corcho[2], Javier D. Fernández[3,4],
Miguel A. Martínez-Prieto[3], and Mari Carmen Suárez-Figueroa[2]

[1] DERI, National University of Ireland, Galway, Ireland
[2] Ontology Engineering Group (OEG), Universidad Politécnica de Madrid, Spain
[3] DataWeb Research, Dept. of Computer Science, Universidad de Valladolid, Spain
[4] Dept. of Computer Science, Universidad de Chile, Chile
mario.arias@deri.org, {ocorcho,mcsuarez}@fi.upm.es,
{jfergar,migumar2}@infor.uva.es

Abstract. The growth in multimedia production has increased the size of audiovisual repositories, and has also led to the formation of increasingly large
metadata collections about these contents. Deciding how these collections are
effectively represented is challenging due to their variety and volume. Besides,
large volumes also affect the performance of metadata retrieval tasks, compromis-
ing the success of multimedia search engines. This paper focuses on this scenario
and describes a case study in which semantic technologies are used for addressing metadata variety, and advanced compression techniques for dealing with the
volume dimension. As a result, we obtain a multimedia search prototype that consumes compressed RDF metadata. This approach efficiently resolves a subset of
SPARQL queries by implementing representative multimedia searches, and also
provides full-text search in compressed space.

1 Introduction

Nowadays, an increasing amount of multimedia contents are produced, processed, and
stored in digital form. We continuously consume multimedia in different formats (text,
audio, video, or images), in diverse languages, and from different provenances. Recent
statistics published by YouTube[1] give a real-world evidence of this growth. These numbers report that 72 hours of new video are uploaded every minute, accumulating a total
monthly production which exceeds the combined production of the three major U.S.
television networks during 60 years. This comparison is a clear example of multimedia
production in the WWW with respect to traditional mass media.

Managing huge multimedia collections involves efficient information retrieval systems [1] enabling storage, retrieval, and browsing of text documents, but also images,
audios, and videos. Technologies commonly used in such systems are based on the
analysis and processing of textual resource descriptions, which are typically generated
manually by the user. These data, commonly referred to as **metadata**, annotate different
features about multimedia resources, providing the clues by which a multimedia search
engine decides whether a resource is or not relevant to a particular query.

---

[1] www.youtube.com/t/press_statistics

C. Bielza et al. (Eds.): CAEPIA 2013, LNAI 8109, pp. 12–21, 2013.

Metadata *volume* grows proportionally with the amount of multimedia production, so its effective storage is the first concern to be addressed. However, it is not the only problem in this scenario. Metadata used for describing different types of multimedia resources vary both in semantics and structure. For instance, metadata used for describing a video differ from that used for audio, text, or image descriptions. This metadata *variety* is even more important when compound multimedia resources are managed because their description comprises metadata from each resource type within it. In this case, flexible data models are required to manage this lack of a strict metadata structure.

This paper deals with the infrastructure underlying a multimedia search engine built on top of (i) semantic technologies used for metadata modelling and querying, and (ii) compressed data encoding using the binary RDF/HDT (Header-Dictionary-Triples) format [4]. On the one hand, RDF [9] provides a flexible graph-based data model which enables metadata **variety** to be effectively managed, whereas SPARQL [12] sets the basic querying operators used for lookup purposes. It is worth noting that the use of these semantic technologies also enable data to be released and linked with other datasets within the Web of Data. This global space of knowledge (pushed by projects like Linked Data) comprises an increasing number of data providers whose scalability is compromised by data volume, but also by the *velocity* at which their information is queried. On the other hand, the use of HDT for serializing RDF enables drastic spatial savings to be achieved. It is an obvious improvement for addressing volume issues, but also allows efficient indexes to be built on compressed space. These spatial savings allow indexes to be loaded and queried in the main memory, achieving fast SPARQL resolution and also full-text search in the aforementioned compressed space. These three V's (variety, volume, and velocity) comprise a widely accepted *Big Data* description, and our ability to address all of them places our current approach in a highly competitive solution.

The rest of the paper is organized as follows. Section 2 introduces Linked Data foundations, reviews its two main standards (RDF and SPARQL), and analyzes multimedia datasets released within the Web of Data. Then, we introduce the binary HDT format and Section 3 describes our approach for its indexing. Section 4 studies how our approach performs (in space and querying time) for a real-world experimental setup in which it is also compared with respect to a general RDF store. Finally, Section 5 relates our current achievements and devises our future lines of research.

2   Preliminaries

The amount of semantic data published on the Web has experienced an impressive growth in the last few years. Inititatives like the **Linked Open Data**[2] project (LOD) are behind this technological movement which materializes the Sematic Web foundations. LOD focuses on linking data on the Web, turning it into a "global database" which connects things and facts about them. Public administrations (such as the USA and the UK governments) pioneered this initiative which has spread to other areas like multimedia (the New York Times or the BBC), educative and scientific projects, geography, etc.

The LOD philosophy has turned the Web into a global data space [8] in which data are directly connected, and these links can be consumed following a pattern similar

---

[2] http://linkeddata.org/

to that used between web pages. Thus, LOD moves the Web from a document-centric perspective (in which human users are the main target) to a data-centric one in which any kind of software application can publish, browse, visualize, or consume data in an automatic way. Semantic data are published and linked using RDF, enabling their effective value and utiliy to be improved with their interconnection in the LOD cloud.

Linking data involves four main principles [2]: (1) use URIs for naming resources; (2) use HTTP URIs so that people can look up those names; (3) use standard technologies (RDF, SPARQL) to provide useful information about the URI; (4) include links to other URIs. When data are published as Linked Data, their RDF features can be browsed using the corresponding labelled hyperlinks between them and the URIs can be dereferenced following the aforementioned principles.

2.1 Linked Data Description and Querying

RDF [9] is a logical data model designed for *resource* description. These resources model any kind of data as RDF expressions which are referenced through URIs. Moreover, *properties* define relationships or descriptive attributes about a resource. Finally, the *statements* assign value to a property of a given resource in the form of **triples** (*subject, predicate and object*). Thus, an RDF collection comprises a triple set shaping a directed and labelled graph structure. Figure 1 (left)[3] illustrates an RDF graph modelling an excerpt of multimedia metadata. The vertex m3:t5-21-10 describes a *video* resource (note that this is modelled by the arc rdf:type the vertex m3:t5-21-10 to m3mm:Video) in *MPEG2* and with dimensions *720 x 576*. Moreover, the vertex m3:individual1310128095945 describes a video fragment about the resource dbpedia:Andres_Iniesta which describes *Andrés Iniesta* in DBpedia.

The **SPARQL Protocol** [12] is the W3C recommended query language for RDF. It is built on top of conjunctions and disjunctions of *triple patterns* (TPs). These TPs are RDF triples in which each subject, predicate or object may be a variable. Thus, a given TP matches an RDF subgraph when variables are replaced by results from the RDF collection. In the previous example, the TP (m3:individual1310128095945, m3:shows, ?O) retrieves the result dbpedia:Andres_Iniesta in the variable **?O**.

2.2 Multimedia in Linked Data

The last report[4] about the LOD cloud points out that it comprises more than 31 billion triples from 295 different sources, and more than 500 million links establish cross-relations between datasets. A more focused analysis reports that 29 of these collections belong to multimedia providers, and they expose 2 billion triples. Examples of these multimeda providers are: *BBC Music*, which exposes semantic metadata about music contents on the BBC, *Event Media*, which publishes multimedia descriptions about events, and *LinkedMDB*, which provides information about movies and actors.

LOD enhances data value through their interconnection with other datasets in the Web. For instance, movies and actors described in LinkedMDB are also linked to their

---

[3] Note that prefixes are depicted at the bottom: m3 means http://www.buscamedia.es/ontologies/M3/# and m3-prefixed resources/properties are identified in its scope.

[4] www4.wiwiss.fu-berlin.de/lodcloud/state/ (September, 2011)

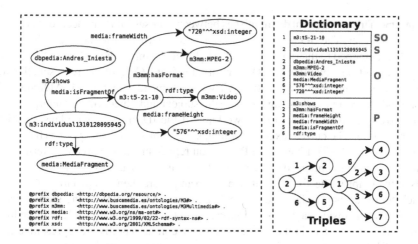

Fig. 1. RDF graph describing multimedia metadata and its HDT-based representation

corresponding descriptions in DBpedia, enhancing the amount of information which can be accessed from each one. However, an important issue that is not currently covered, is how more fine-grained semantic descriptions are handled; following the example, how an actor and his appearances in specific time frames of a video can be effectively interlinked [13]. This kind of problems, and scalability related ones, will be more pronounced according to the reported growth in multimedia production and semantic metadata describing these new contents in the web of data.

2.3   Header-Dictionary-Triples (HDT)

The HDT binary format [4] addresses the current needs of large RDF datasets for scalable publishing and exchanging in the Web of Data[5]. HDT describes a binary serialization format for RDF that keeps large datasets compressed while maintaining search and browse operations. It is worth noting that traditional RDF formats (N3[6], RDF/XML[7] or Turtle[8]) are dominated by a document-centric perspective of the Web, resulting in verbose textual syntaxes expensive to parse and index.

HDT integrates the data-centric and machine understandability perspectives to provide a data model for RDF. An HDT-encoded dataset is made up of three logical components: (i) the **Header (H)** holds metadata describing the collection (provenance, statistics, etc.) acting as an entry point for the consumer; (ii) the **Dictionary (D)** is a catalog comprising all the different terms used in the dataset, such as URIs, literals and blank nodes, while a unique identifier (ID) is assigned to each term; and (iii) the **Triples (T)** component models the RDF graph after ID substitution, *i.e.* represented as tuples of three IDs. The *Dictionary* and *Triples* components implement the main goal of HDT compactness. Figure 1 (right) illustrates them for the aforementioned RDF graph.

---

[5] www.w3.org/Submission/2011/03/
[6] www.w3.org/DesignIssues/Notation3/
[7] www.w3.org/TR/REC-rdf-syntax/
[8] www.w3.org/TeamSubmission/turtle/

Dictionary. This component distinguishes between four sets of terms according to their role in the dataset. The **SO** partition represents those terms acting both as subject and object: $|SO|$, mapped to the range $[1, |SO|]$. In the example, only m3:t5-21-10 satisfies this condition, obtaining the ID 1. In turn, the **S** and **O** partitions represent the non common subject and objects respectively. They are mapped from $|SO|+1$. Although this decision produces an overlapping between the subject and object ID, the interpretation of the correct partition is trivial once we know if the ID in the graph plays a subject or an object role. The current example contains one subject: m3:t5-21-10 (ID 2) and six objects (range 2-7). Finally, the **P** partition represents all the predicate terms: $|P|$, and are independently mapped to the range $[1, |P|]$ (no ambiguity is possible as they are labels in the graph). The six predicates in the example are then mapped to 1-6.

Each set of terms is independently encoded as a subdictionary of the global dictionary component. Inside each subdictionary, the IDs are assigned in a lexicographical order. Thus, terms with a similar role and sharing a common prefix are represented contiguously. This property allows better compression ratios to be achieved by applying differential encoding to the terms, *i.e.* each term is encoded compared to its predecessor, avoiding prefix repetitions. The implementation proposal makes use of *Front-Coding* [14] inside each subdictionary [3].

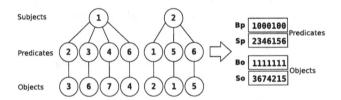

Fig. 2. Implementation of the *Triples* component

Triples. This comprises the pure structure of the underlying RDF graph. Figure 1 (right) shows that this structure respects the original graph, avoiding the noise produced by long labels and repetitions.

The implementation of this component deserves a deeper analysis. The left side of Figure 2 draws an alternative representation of the ID graph as a forest of trees, one per subject. Each subject is the root of its associated tree, representing the ordered list of predicates reachable from the subject in the middle level. The objects for each (subject, predicate) pair are listed in the leaves.

The final implementation of the *Triples* component is shown on the right side of Figure 2. Each predicate and object level stores a *bit sequence* and an *ID sequence*. The bit sequence $\mathcal{B}_p$, in the predicate level, is a binary representation of the number of predicates associated with each subject. The 1 bits mark the beginning of a new subject in the list and its cardinality is given by the number of the following 0 bits (before the next 1 bit). For instance, the representation of the first subject starts in the first position of $\mathcal{B}_p$, and the next three 0 bits denote that a total of four predicates are associated with this subject. The IDs of these predicates can be retrieved from the sequence $\mathcal{S}_p$ from the initial position of the subject (in our example, *predicates 2,3,4,6*). The object level is represented in the same way. In this case, $\mathcal{B}_o$ models the number of objects for each (subject, predicate) pair and the IDs are retrieved from S_o. For instance, the *subject 1* is associated with the *predicate 3* in the second position of S_p, then the list of related objects starts from the same second position of B_o and S_o. In this case, the list consists of a single object, the *object 6*.

3   HDT for Semantic Metadata Retrieval

Triple patterns are the SPARQL query atoms for basic RDF retrieval. That is, all triples matching a pattern (s, p, o) where each term may be variable.

The *Triples* in an HDT-encoded dataset are sorted by subject *(subject-predicate-object)*, hence SPARQL patterns with a given subject can be directly resolved in compressed space (as stated in the original proposal [4]). This conception has been recently extended [10] in order to resolve all kinds of triple patterns. The novel representation, referred to as **HDT-FoQ**: *HDT Focused on Querying*, enhances the original data structure with an additional index built at loading time. All this infrastructure enables basic triple patterns to be resolved very efficiently in compressed space.

This section describes the use of HDT-FoQ as the basis for efficient multimedia retrieval. We detail the indexes in *Dictionary* and *Triples* as well as a proposed mechanism for integrating SPARQL resolution and the *full-text* search, commonly used in multimedia.

3.1   Dictionary Indexing

The original HDT proposal encourages the use of differential encoding of the terms of the dictionary. Although this decision, in general, achieves compact representations and provides efficient retrieving (*ID-to-term* and *term-to-ID*), it fails to adapt to the peculiarities of the different terms in the RDF collection. Whereas URIs and *blank nodes* are compacted due to the presence of large common prefixes [11], literals are mostly stored in plain as they do not share this property. In addition, *full-text* search resolution is not directly supported.

Our proposal reviews the implementation of this component. Its compartmental organization allows us to propose a modification exclusively on the partition of the literal objects. We implement the subdictionary of the literals using a *self-indexing* structure called *FM-Index* [5]. A previous study [11] shows that the *FM-Index* achieves more compact representations for the literals at the expense of slightly lower retrieving operations (*ID-to-term* and *term-to-ID*). However, this technique directly supports efficient *full-text* search resolution over the literals, as it implements substring retrieval. Given a literal substring, the proposal generalizes the *ID-to-term* algorithm [3]: we search the substring in the structure and, for each occurrence, we retrieve the associated ID.

3.2   Triples Indexing

As stated, the original HDT proposal provides fast subject-based retrieval. This operation is implemented by mapping the bit sequences in an additional small structure [6] that ensures constant time resolution for some basic bit-operations, such as locating a certain 1 bit or 0 bit and counting the number of 1 bits or 0 bits up to a given position.

However, the implicit subject order hinders the access by predicate and object. HDT-FoQ [10] includes two additional indexes providing this access in compressed space.

Predicate Index. The *Triples* component lists all predicates in $\mathcal{S}_p$, but an additional index should group all the occurrences of each predicate in this sequence.

HDT-FoQ loads $\mathcal{S}_p$ into a succinct structure called *wavelet tree* [7]. This structure organizes a sequence of integers, in a range $[1, n]$, to provide some access and seek operations to the data in logarithmic time. In our case, n is the range of different predicates ($|P|$), which is commonly small. Thus, it provides access to all the occurrences of a given predicate in $O(log|P|)$, at the expense of $o(n)log|P|$ additional bits for $\mathcal{S}_p$.

Object Index. The *Triples* component is enhanced with an additional index that is responsible for solving accesses by object.

This index gathers the positions where each object appears in the original $\mathcal{S}_o$, as this information allows us to climb up the tree and retrieve the associated predicate and subject in the previous indexes. The index of the positions is also built as a pair of sequences; $\mathcal{B}_{oP}$ is the bit sequence marking the beginning and number of positions for each object and the integer sequence ($\mathcal{S}_{oP}$) holds the positions.

4   Experiments

This section analyzes how our approach performs when it is used as the heart of a multimedia search engine. We design an heterogenous setup comprising multimedia metadata obtained from five real-world dumps published in the LOD cloud: event media[9] (multimedia descriptions about events), yovisto[10] (videos about conferences and masterclasses), linkedmdb[11] (films and actors), freebase[12] (only metadata about TV), and dbtune[13] (music compilations). In addition, we concatenate all these collections in a single mashup referred to as all. This decision aims to analyze the numbers obtained when a heterogenoeus collection is represented and queried.

All collections are organized and encoded following the aforementioned HDT-FoQ decisions, and their results are compared to the ones reported by Virtuoso[14]. This RDF store is chosen because it is massively used in semantic scenarios, and also provides efficient *full-text* search facilities.

Table 1 shows, in the first column, the original collection size (in NTriples); the second and third columns report, respectively, storage requirements for each technique (note that Virtuoso sizes also include the space required by their full-text indexes). HDT-FoQ representations use $\approx 9 - 11\%$ of the original size for the largest collections, whereas the numbers increase for the smallest ones: 22.16% (yovisto) and 38.66% (event media). Finally, the all mashup is represented in 10.49% of its

---

[9] http://www.eurecom.fr/~troncy/ldtc2010/2010-06-15-N3_Events.zip
[10] http://www.yovisto.com/labs/dumps/latest.ttl.tar.gz
[11] http://queens.db.toronto.edu/~oktie/linkedmdb
[12] http://download.freebase.com/datadumps/2012-07-26/
[13] http://km.aifb.kit.edu/projects/btc-2011/
[14] http://www.openlinksw.com/

Table 1. Storage requirements *(in MB)*

	Original	HDT-FoQ	Virtuoso
event media	187.75	72.59	328.02
yovisto	708.35	156.95	778.02
linkedmdb	850.31	89.30	570.02
freebase	3354.09	302.80	3516.02
dbtune	9733.06	862.23	4220.02
all	14833.56	1555.35	8054.03

Table 2. Querying times

	HDT-FoQ	Virtuoso
Q_1	0.18 ms	2.60 ms
Q_2	42.51 s	86.54 s
Q_3	5.63 s	5.90 s
Q_4	5.21 s	11.95 s

original size, demonstrating that our approach reports effective numbers for all classes of audiovisual metadata. On the other hand, Virtuoso only achieves compression for linkedmdb and dbtune. It is worth mentioning that, in the worst case, Virtuoso full-text indexes take up to 25% of the total representation size, but these only represent 3% of the size used for representing the all mashup. Thus, Virtuoso uses ≈ 5 times more space than HDT-FoQ for the mashup representation. This comparison gives an idea of the storage savings which a multimedia search engine can benefit if our approach is chosen for metadata storage instead of a general RDF store.

```
Q₁:                    Q₂:                         Q₃:                       Q₄:
SELECT ?p ?o WHERE     SELECT ?s ?p ?o WHERE       SELECT ?s ?o WHERE        SELECT ?s ?p ?o WHERE
{                      {                           {                         {
<content> ?p ?o.       ?s rdf:type <type>.         ?s <pred> ?o.             ?s <pred> ?oo.
}                      ?s ?p ?o.                   FILTER regex(?o, "txt").  ?s ?p ?o.
                       }                           }                         FILTER regex(?oo, "txt").
                                                                             }
```

Q_1: retrieves all data related to the content provided as subject.
Q_2: retrieves all data related to the subject of a given *type*.
Q_3: retrieves all resources where a property value matches the *text pattern*.
Q_4: retrieves all associated data to resources where a property value matches the *text pattern*.

Then, we analyze retrieval performance using a set of generic queries which represent four typical searches in multimedia applications: a) Q_1 and Q_2 focus on pure SPARQL resolution, whereas b) Q_3 and Q_4 also involve full-text searches for regex filtering. We run all experiments on an AMD-Opteron™270@2Ghz, Dual Core, 4GB DDR2@800MHz, running 2.6.30-gentoo-r4. Our prototype is built on top of the C++ HDT library publicly available[15].

Querying experiments[16] were performed by running 50 queries of each type against the mashup all (we use 125,000 queries for Q_1 in order to obtain more precision). Each experiment was preceded by a *warm-up* stage running the same number of queries. This decision is made to load Virtuoso caches and obtain a more realistic comparison. Table 2 summarizes these experiments. Each cell contains the mean execution times per query of the whole batch; e.g. HDT-FoQ takes on average 0.18ms to evaluate each query of type Q_1, whereas Virtuoso takes 2.60ms for the same operation.

---

[15] http://code.google.com/p/hdt-it/
[16] http://dataweb.infor.uva.es/multimedia-setup.tgz

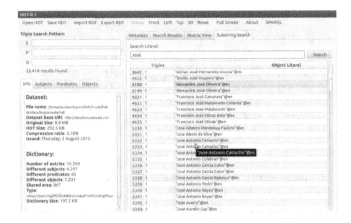

Fig. 3. Prototype of our multimedia search engine

HDT-FoQ largely overcomes Virtuoso for the pure structural queries: Q_1 and Q_2 (it is worth noting that evaluation times for Q_1 are more than 1 order of magnitude faster than the remaining queries). Both techniques report similar numbers for Q_3 due to the need for full-text searching, but HDT-FoQ overcomes Virtuoso again for Q_4. It is worth mentioning that searches involving full words were executed using Virtuoso's `bif:contains` because it improves `regex` peformance. Even so, HDT-FoQ reports better overall times for all queries in our setup, complementing our spatial achievements and endorsing its efficiency as the heart of a multimedia search engine.

5   Conclusions and Future Work

This paper describes a case study of multimedia metadata management and querying using semantic technologies. We have introduced RDF compression as the basis of a lightweight indexing technique: HDT-FoQ, which reports excellent numbers in a real-world setup involving some datasets from the Linked Data cloud. HDT-FoQ reduces spatial requirements up to 5 times with respect to a typical RDF store and also overcomes its performance for a set of common multimedia searches. These results support HDT-FoQ as basic technology for building a multimedia search engine which consumes semantic metadata. These facts make it an ideal solution for projects like Buscamedia.

Buscamedia[17] aims to develop an innovative multimedia semantic search engine, based on a) the new M3[18] ontology which represents multimedia knowledge in several domains and taking into account a multilingual context; b) a natural language search that allows direct interaction with the search system. Additionally, metadata collections following M3 are also being generated. These metadata describe Formula 1, soccer, and basketball TV videos in Spanish and Catalan languages.

Figure 3 shows our first prototype of semantic a search engine built on top of the HDT-FoQ proposal and managing data from Buscamedia. It represents the Buscamedia

---

[17] http://www.cenitbuscamedia.es/

[18] http://www.oeg-upm.net/files/m3/M3-v2.3.rar

data in $\approx 5\%$ of its original size, while providing SPARQL resolution and full-text search in compressed space. Moreover, it implements an efficient data browser which allows data to be traversed as pages in the WWW. Our future work focuses on building a complete semantic search engine enhancing the current prototype with more advanced searching capabilities. Achieving these goals is directly related to our research in how HDT-FoQ can efficiently resolve SPARQL constructs.

Acknowledgments. This work has been funded by the Science Foundation Ireland: SFI/08/CE/I1380, Lion-II, the Buscamedia Project: CENIT 2009-1026, and the Ministry of Economy and Competitiveness (Spain): TIN2009-14009-C02-02.

References

1. Baeza-Yates, R., Ribeiro-Neto, B.A.: Modern Information Retrieval - the concepts and technology behind search, 2nd edn. Pearson Education Ltd. (2011)
2. Berners-Lee, T.: Linked Data: Design Issues (2006),
   http://www.w3.org/DesignIssues/LinkedData.html
3. Brisaboa, N.R., Cánovas, R., Claude, F., Martínez-Prieto, M.A., Navarro, G.: Compressed String Dictionaries. In: Pardalos, P.M., Rebennack, S. (eds.) SEA 2011. LNCS, vol. 6630, pp. 136–147. Springer, Heidelberg (2011)
4. Fernández, J.D., Martínez-Prieto, M.A., Gutiérrez, C., Polleres, A., Arias, M.: Binary RDF representation for publication and exchange. Journal of Web Semantics 19, 22–41 (2013)
5. Ferragina, P., Manzini, G.: Opportunistic Data Structures with Applications. In: Proc. of FOCS, pp. 390–398 (2000)
6. González, R., Grabowski, S., Mäkinen, V., Navarro, G.: Practical Implementation of Rank and Select Queries. In: Proc. of WEA, pp. 27–38 (2005)
7. Grossi, R., Gupta, A., Vitter, J.S.: High-order entropy-compressed text indexes. In: Proc. of SODA, pp. 841–850 (2003)
8. Heath, T., Bizer, C.: Linked Data: Evolving the Web into a Global Data Space. Morgan & Claypool (2011), http://linkeddatabook.com/
9. Manola, F., Miller, E. (eds.): RDF Primer. W3C Recommendation (2004),
   http://www.w3.org/TR/rdf-primer/
10. Martínez-Prieto, M.A., Gallego, M.A., Fernández, J.D.: Exchange and Consumption of Huge RDF Data. In: Simperl, E., Cimiano, P., Polleres, A., Corcho, O., Presutti, V. (eds.) ESWC 2012. LNCS, vol. 7295, pp. 437–452. Springer, Heidelberg (2012)
11. Martínez-Prieto, M.A., Fernández, J.D., Cánovas, R.: Querying RDF Dictionaries in Compressed Space. ACM SIGAPP Applied Computing Reviews 12(2), 64–77 (2012)
12. Prud'hommeaux, E., Seaborne, A. (eds.): SPARQL Query Language for RDF. W3C Recommendation (2008), http://www.w3.org/TR/rdf-sparql-query/
13. Schandl, B., Haslhofer, B., Bürger, T., Langegger, A., Halb, W.: Linked data and multimedia: the state of affairs. Multimedia Tools Appl. 59(2), 523–556 (2012)
14. Witten, I.H., Moffat, A., Bell, T.C.: Managing Gigabytes: Compressing and Indexing Documents and Images. Morgan Kaufmann (1999)

Time-Aware Evaluation of Methods for Identifying Active Household Members in Recommender Systems

Pedro G. Campos[1,2], Alejandro Bellogín[2], Iván Cantador[2], and Fernando Díez[2]

[1] Departamento de Sistemas de Información
Universidad del Bío-Bío
4081112, Concepción, Chile
[2] Escuela Politécnica Superior
Universidad Autónoma de Madrid
28049 Madrid, Spain
pgcampos@ubiobio.cl,
{pedro.campos,alejandro.bellogin,
ivan.cantador,fernando.diez}@uam.es

Abstract. Online services are usually accessed via household accounts. A household account is typically shared by various users who live in the same house. This represents a problem for providing personalized services, such as recommendation. Identifying the household members who are interacting with an online system (e.g. an on-demand video service) in a given moment, is thus an interesting challenge for the recommender systems research community. Previous work has shown that methods based on the analysis of temporal patterns of users are highly accurate in the above task when they use randomly sampled test data. However, such evaluation methodology may not properly deal with the evolution of the users' preferences and behavior through time. In this paper we evaluate several methods' performance using time-aware evaluation methodologies. Results from our experiments show that the discrimination power of different time features varies considerably, and moreover, the accuracy achieved by the methods can be heavily penalized when using a more realistic evaluation methodology.

Keywords: household member identification, time-aware evaluation, evaluation methodologies, recommender systems.

1 Introduction

Many online services providers offer access to their services via user accounts. These accounts can be seen as a mechanism to identify the active user, and track her behavior, letting e.g. build a personalized profile. A user profile can be used afterwards to provide personalized services, e.g. recommendation. However, user accounts can be shared by multiple users. An example of shared account is a household account, that is, an account shared by several users who usually live in the same house. In general, it is hard to detect whether a user account is being

C. Bielza et al. (Eds.): CAEPIA 2013, LNAI 8109, pp. 22–31, 2013.

accessed by more than one user, which raises difficulties for providing personalized services [1,2].

Users sharing a household do not necessarily access the service together. Consider for instance a four members family (formed e.g. by a father, a mother, a son and a daughter), sharing a household account of video-on-demand service. Each member of the family has distinct viewing interests and habits, and thus each of them watches video differently. If one member of the family asks for video recommendations, it is likely that those recommendations do not fit the user's interests, because the account profile contains a mixture of preferences from the four family members.

Two main strategies can be adopted in order to overcome such problem [3]. The first strategy is to increase the diversity of delivered recommendations [4], aiming to cover the heterogeneous range of preferences of the different members in a household. The second strategy is to identify the active household members for which recommendations have to be delivered. In this paper, we focus on the second strategy since it lets make more accurate recommendations, by only using preferences of active members, and discarding preferences of other, non-present members [1].

Previous work on the task has shown that the analysis of temporal patterns on historical data of household accounts provides important information for the discrimination of users, letting accurately identify active members [3,5,6]. Nonetheless, it is important to note that proposed methods have been assessed using evaluation methodologies based on the random selection of test cases. In a recent study on evaluation methodologies for recommender systems [7] it has been argued, however, that using randomly selected test data may not be fair for evaluation, particularly when temporal trends are being considered by the evaluated methods. We question whether this is also applicable for the task at hand, and in such case, which accuracy for active user identification would be achieved by using a more realistic evaluation methodology.

Using different evaluation methodologies, in this paper we perform an empirical comparison of methods for active household member identification in recommender systems. The tested methods are based on exploiting time information, and thus, we include some stricter time-aware evaluation methodologies. Results obtained from experiments on a real dataset show that the contribution of time features vary considerable when assessed by different methodologies, and moreover, the accuracy achieved by the methods can be heavily penalized when using a more realistic evaluation methodology.

The reminder of the paper is structured as follows. In Section 2 we describe related work. In Section 3 we detail methodologies employed in recommender systems evaluation that can be applied for assessing accuracy of methods used for identifying active household members. In Section 4 we present the methods evaluated. In Section 5 we describe the experiments performed, and report the results obtained. Finally, in Section 6 we present some conclusions and lines of future work.

2   Related Work

The convenience of identifying users in households for recommendation purposes has been addressed in the recommender systems (RS) literature. Several proposals of RS on the TV domain consider the knowledge of which users are receiving the recommendations by means of explicit identification of users. For instance, Ardissono et al. [8] propose a personalized Electronic Programming Guide for TV shows, requiring the user to log in the system for providing personalization. Vildjiounaite et al. [9] propose a method to learn a joint model of users subsets in households, and use individual remote control devices for identifying users. The methods considered in this work, in contrast, aim to identify the user who is currently interacting with the system, by analyzing temporal patterns of individual users, without requiring to log in or to use special devices at recommendation time.

Specific methods for the identification of users from household accounts have been proposed in the RS research field. Goren-Bar and Glinansky [10] predict which users are watching TV based on a temporal profile manually stated. In [10] users indicate the time lapses in which they would probably be in front of the TV. Oh et al. [11] derive time-based profiles from household TV watching logs, which model preferences for viewing of time lapses instead of individual users. In this way, the target profile corresponds to the time lapse at which recommendations are requested. These methods assume that users have a fixed temporal behavior through time.

Recently, the 2011 edition of the Context-Aware Movie Recommendation (CAMRa) Challenge [2] requested participants to identify which members of particular households were responsible for a number of events –interactions with the system in the form of ratings. The contest provided a training dataset with information about ratings in a movie RS, including the household members who provided the ratings, and the associated timestamps. The challenge's goal was to identify the users who had been responsible for certain events (ratings), and whose household and timestamp were given in a randomly sampled test dataset. This task is assumed to be equivalent to the task of identifying active users requesting recommendations at a particular time.

The winners of the 2011 CAMRa challenge [6] and some other participants (e.g. [5,12]) exploited several time features derived from the available event timestamps. Such features showed different temporal rating habits of users in a household, regarding the day of the week, the hour of the day, and the absolute date when users rate items. In subsequent work [3], additional time features were investigated, as well as classification methods that enable an easy exploitation of such features, achieving a very high accuracy in the task (~ 98%). In this paper we use some of the best performing methods and time features presented in [3], and assess them using stricter evaluation methodologies, in order to test the reliability of the methods.

As a matter of fact, researchers in the RS field have questioned the suitability of some evaluation methodologies used for assessing RS that exploit temporal patterns in data [13,14]. Their main objection is that data used for test purposes is not always more recent than data used for training, and this may be unfair for methods exploiting time knowledge. In [7] we compared several RS using different evaluation methodologies, and found that measured performance and relative ranking of methods may vary considerably among methodologies. Extrapolating findings obtained in that work to the task at hand, we can expect to find differences in the accuracy of methods by utilizing methodologies that do not use randomly sampled test data.

3   Evaluation Methodologies for Recommender Systems

The evaluation of recommender systems can be performed either *online* or *offline* [15]. In an *online evaluation* real users interactively test one or more deployed systems, and in general, empirical comparisons of user satisfaction for different item recommendations are conducted by means of A/B tests [16]. In an *offline evaluation*, on the other hand, past user behavior recorded in a database is used to assess the systems' performance, by testing whether recommendations match the users' declared interests. Given the need of having deployed systems and a large number of people using them in online evaluations, and the availability of historical users' data, most work in the RS field –and the one presented here– have focused on offline evaluations.

From a methodological point of view, offline evaluation admits diverse strategies for assessing RS performance. In general, a recommendation model is built (trained) with available user data, and afterwards its ability to deliver *good[1]* recommendations is assessed somehow with additional (test) user data. From this, in an offline evaluation scenario, we have to simulate the users' actions *after* receiving recommendations. This is achieved by splitting the set of available ratings into a *training set* –which serves as historical data to learn the users' preferences– and a *test set* –which is considered as knowledge about the users' decisions when faced with recommendations, and which is commonly referred to as *ground truth* data. As noted in [15], there are several ways to split data into training and test sets, and this is a source for differences in evaluation of RS. Moreover, in case that the data is time stamped –the case for RS exploiting time information– differences in evaluation can be meaningful, and may affect relative ranking of the algorithms' performance [7].

Several offline evaluation methodologies had been employed in measuring recommender system performance. In [7] several time-aware (and time-unaware) methodologies are described, by means of a methodological description framework that is based on a number of key methodological conditions that drive a RS evaluation process. These methodological conditions include: a) the *rating order* criterion (σ) used for split data. For instance, we may use a time-dependent ordering of data (σ_{td}), assigning the last (according to timestamp) data to the test set. Or, we may assign a random subset of data (i.e. time-independent ordering, σ_{ti}) to the test set; b) the *base set* ($\mathscr{b}$) on which the rating order criterion is applied. For instance, the ordering criterion can be applied on the whole dataset (a community centered base set, $\mathscr{b}_{cc}$), or can be applied independently over each user's data (a user-centered base set, $\mathscr{b}_{uc}$). In

---

[1]   There is no general definition of what *good* recommendations are. Nonetheless, a commonly used approach is to establish the quality (goodness) of recommendations by computing different metrics that assess various desired characteristics of RS outputs.

the latter case, the last data from *each user* is assigned to the test set. This case, despite its popularity due to its application in the Netflix Prize competition [17], is not the best choice to mimic real-world evaluation conditions [7]; and c) the *size* condition (s), i.e., the number of ratings selected for the test set. For instance, a proportion-based schema can be used (s_{prop}), e.g. assigning 20% of data to the test set and the remaining 80% to the training set, or a fixed number q of ratings per user can be assigned to the test set ($s_{fix,q}$), assigning the remaining ratings from each user to the training set.

The above evaluation conditions and related methodologies can be easily extrapolated to the task at hand, in order to test the reliability of the existent methods for household member identification. The only condition that requires a special treatment is the base set condition. In this case, as available data includes the household at which each user belongs to, it is possible to define a *household-centered* base set (b_{hc}). That is, the application of rating order and size conditions on each household's data.

4 Methods for Identifying Active Household Members

Following the formulation given in [3], we treat the identification of the active household members as a classification problem, aiming to classify user patterns described by feature vectors that include time context information. This approach can be formalized as follows. Let us consider a set of events $E = \{e_1, e_2, \dots, e_m\}$ and a set of users $U_h = \{u_{1,h}, u_{2,h}, \dots, u_{n,h}\}$ within a household h, such that event e_i is associated to one, and only one, user $u_{j,h}$. Also, let us consider that each of these events is described by means of a feature vector, called X_{e_i}. The question to address is whether it is possible to determine which user is associated to an event e_i once (some) components x_{e_i} of its feature vector X_{e_i} are already known. In this paper, events correspond to instances of user ratings, and feature vectors correspond to time context representations of the events. Based on findings in [3], the time features considered in this work are the **absolute date** (D), the **day of the week** (W) and the **hour of the day** (H), as they are the best performing features reported in that paper for this task.

The first method considered is the *A priori* model described in [3]. This method computes probability distribution functions, which represent the probabilities that users are associated to particular events, and uses computed probabilities to assign a score to each user in a household given a new event. More specifically, we compute the probability mass function (PMF) of each feature given a particular user, restricted to the information related with that user's household, that is, $\{p(X = x_i|u_j)\}_{u_j \in U_h}$, where U_h is the set of users in the household h. Then, for each new event e, we obtain its representation as a feature vector $\hat{X}_e$, and identify the user who maximizes the PMF, that is, $u_j^*(e) = \arg\max_{u_j \in U_h} p(\hat{X}_e|u_j)$. When more than one feature is used, we assume independence and use the joint probability function, i.e., the product of the features' PMFs.

We also evaluate Machine Learning (ML) algorithms described in [3], that are able to deal with heterogeneous attributes. Specifically, we have restricted our study to the following methods: Bayesian Networks (BN), Decision Trees (DT), and Logistic Regression (LR). These methods provide a score $\left\{s\left(\hat{X}_e, u_j\right)\right\}_{u_j \in U_h}$ based on different statistics from the training data, and select the users with highest scores.

The above methods use a fixed set of time features in the classification task, i.e., they use the same set of features over all the households. It is important to note, however, that data from only one household is used for classifying events of that household, i.e., the methods do not use data from other households for identifying members of a given household.

5   Experiments

In this section we report and discuss results obtained in experiments we conducted to evaluate the methods presented in Section 4, by means of different evaluation methodologies. Using some time-aware methodologies, we aim to test the reliability of the methods for identification of active household members in a realistic scenario. We begin by describing the used dataset, followed evaluation methodologies, and assessed metric.

5.1   Dataset

We use a real movie rating dataset made publicly available by MoviePilot[2] for the 2011 edition of the CAMRa Challenge [2]. This dataset contains a training set of 4,546,891 time stamped ratings from 171,670 users on 23,974 movies, in the timespan from July 11, 2009 to July 12, 2010. A subset of 145,069 ratings contains a household identifier. This subset includes a total of 602 users from 290 different households, who rated 7710 movies. The dataset also includes two test sets that also contain ratings with household identifier. Test set #1 contains 4482 ratings from 594 users on 811 items in the timespan from July 15, 2009 to July 10, 2010, and Test set #2 contains 5450 ratings from 592 users on 1706 items in the timespan from July 13, 2009 to July 11, 2010. We merged all the ratings with household identification, obtaining a total of 155,001 unique ratings (the *household dataset*). These ratings were then used for building several training and test sets according to different evaluation methodologies, as described below.

5.2   Evaluation Methodologies and Metrics

Aiming to analyze differences on accuracy of the methods presented in Section 3, we selected three different evaluation methodologies. Two of them use a time-dependent rating order condition, and the other one use a time-independent order condition.

The first methodology (denoted as $\mathcal{B}_{cc}\sigma_{td}\mathcal{S}_{fix}$) consists of a combination of a community-centered base set ($\mathcal{B}_{cc}$), a time-dependent rating order (σ_{td}), and a fixed size ($\mathcal{S}_{fix,q=5450}$) condition. Specifically, all ratings in the household dataset are

---

[2] www.moviepilot.com

sorted according to their timestamp, and the last 5,450 ratings are assigned to the test set (and the first 149,551 are assigned to the training set). In this way, a test set of similar size to test set #2 is built. The second methodology (denoted as $\mathcal{B}_{hc}\sigma_{td}\mathcal{S}_{fix}$) is equivalent to $\mathcal{B}_{cc}\sigma_{td}\mathcal{S}_{fix}$ with a household-centered base set condition ($\mathcal{B}_{hc}$). Specifically, the ratings of each household are sorted according to timestamp, and the last 19 ratings from each household are assigned to the test set. We chose 19 ratings aiming to build a test set of similar size to the one built with $\mathcal{B}_{cc}\sigma_{td}\mathcal{S}_{fix}$. The third methodology (denoted as $\mathcal{B}_{hc}\sigma_{ti}\mathcal{S}_{fix}$) is similar to $\mathcal{B}_{hc}\sigma_{td}\mathcal{S}_{fix}$ with a time-independent rating order condition (σ_{ti}). That is, 19 ratings are randomly selected from each household, and assigned to the test set.

We computed the accuracy of the evaluated methods in terms of the correct classification rate by household ($acc_{\mathbb{H}}$), i.e., the number of correct active member predictions divided by the total number of predictions, averaged by household, as proposed by CAMRa organizers. Formally, let $\mathbb{H}$ be the entire set of households in the dataset, and let $f(\cdot)$ be a method under evaluation. The metric is expressed as follows:

$$acc_{\mathbb{H}} = \frac{1}{\mathbb{H}}\sum_{h\in\mathbb{H}}\frac{1}{h}\sum_{(e_i,u_i)\in h} L\big(u_i, f(e_i)\big)$$

where $f(e_i) = \hat{u}$ is the user predicted by $f(\cdot)$ as associated to e_i, $L(u,\hat{u}) = 1$ if $u = \hat{u}$, and 0 otherwise, and (e_i, u_i) are the pairs of events and users of household h in the test set.

5.3   Results

Table 1 shows the $acc_{\mathbb{H}}$ results obtained by the evaluated methods using the three methodologies detailed in Section 5.2. The table also shows the results obtained on the test set #2, proposed by CAMRa organizers for the task (column titled CAMRa).. The table shows the results obtained by using individual time features, grouped by method.

In the table, we observe similar results when using methodologies based on a time-independent (random) rating order condition (CAMRa and $\mathcal{B}_{hc}\sigma_{ti}\mathcal{S}_{fix}$). Much worse results are observed when using methodologies employing a time-dependent rating order condition ($\mathcal{B}_{cc}\sigma_{td}\mathcal{S}_{fix}$ and $\mathcal{B}_{hc}\sigma_{td}\mathcal{S}_{fix}$). Particularly lower accuracies are achieved when using $\mathcal{B}_{cc}\sigma_{td}\mathcal{S}_{fix}$. We note that this methodology provides the evaluation scenario most similar to a real-world situation: data up to a certain point in time is available for training purposes, and data after that (unknown at that time) is then used as ground truth. In our case, this methodology provides a small number of training events for some households, which affect the methods' ability to detect temporal patterns of users. In fact, for some households, there is no training data at all. In this way, $\mathcal{B}_{cc}\sigma_{td}\mathcal{S}_{fix}$ represents a hard, but realistic evaluation methodology for the task. On the contrary, methodologies using a time-independent rating order condition provide easy, but unrealistic evaluation scenarios, because they let the methods use training data that would not be available in a real-world setting. The $\mathcal{B}_{hc}\sigma_{td}\mathcal{S}_{fix}$ methodology provides an intermediate scenario, in which an important part of data is available for learning temporal patterns of each household's members.

We also observe in Table 1 that the discrimination power of the different time features varies among methodologies. In the case of the A priori method, the best results on time-independent methodologies and $\mathcal{B}_{hc}\sigma_{td}\delta_{fix}$ are obtained with **hour of the day** (H) feature, while **absolute date** (D) achieves the best results among ML methods –we note that results are similar across features. However, when using the stricter $\mathcal{B}_{cc}\sigma_{td}\delta_{fix}$, the best results among methods are obtained with **day of the week** (W) feature, nearly followed by the **hour of the day** feature. On the contrary, the **absolute date** feature performs the worst consistently. This highlights how unrealistic the less strict methodologies are for the task, because they let the methods exploit a temporal behavior (the exact date of interaction) that in a real situation would be impossible to learn. This also shows that **hour of the day**, and more strongly **day of the week**, features describe a consistent temporal pattern of users through time.

Table 1. Correct classification rates obtained by the evaluated methods using the different time features and evaluation methodologies. Global top values in each column are in bold, and the best values for each method are underlined.

Method	Time Feature	$\mathcal{B}_{cc}\sigma_{td}\delta_{fix}$	$\mathcal{B}_{hc}\sigma_{td}\delta_{fix}$	$\mathcal{B}_{hc}\sigma_{ti}\delta_{fix}$	CAMRa
A priori	H	0.6087	<u>0.8163</u>	0.9468	<u>0.9457</u>
	W	<u>0.6167</u>	0.8069	0.9299	0.9310
	D	0.4947	0.8152	0.9461	0.9413
BN	H	0.6533	0.8232	0.9539	0.9442
	W	<u>0.6907</u>	0.8189	0.9412	0.9438
	D	0.6506	**0.8575**	**0.9574**	**0.9538**
DT	H	0.6637	0.8229	<u>0.9541</u>	0.9459
	W	**0.6963**	0.8223	0.9417	0.9435
	D	0.6506	<u>0.8544</u>	0.9535	<u>0.9472</u>
LR	H	0.6674	0.8256	0.9537	0.9432
	W	<u>0.6908</u>	0.8132	0.9381	0.9405
	D	0.6147	<u>0.8307</u>	<u>0.9555</u>	<u>0.9515</u>

Table 2 shows the acc_H results obtained by the evaluated methods using combinations of time features, and the same methodologies reported in Table 1. The results show that using less strict methodologies, combinations including the **absolute date** feature perform better. On the contrary, using $\mathcal{B}_{cc}\sigma_{td}\delta_{fix}$ the best results are achieved by the combination of **hour of the day** and **day of week**.

All these results show that correct classification rate is prone to major differences depending on the evaluation methodology followed. The discrimination power of time features varies considerably when assessed by different methodologies. Moreover, the accuracy achieved by the methods is much lower when using the more realistic $\mathcal{B}_{cc}\sigma_{td}\delta_{fix}$ methodology.

Table 2. Correct classification rates obtained by the evaluated methods using combinations of time features, on different evaluation methodologies. Global top values in each column are in bold, and best values for each method are underlined.

Method	Time Feature	$\vartheta_{cc}\sigma_{td}\delta_{fix}$	$\vartheta_{hc}\sigma_{td}\delta_{fix}$	$\vartheta_{hc}\sigma_{ti}\delta_{fix}$	CAMRa
A priori	HW	0.6496	0.8421	0.9688	0.9652
	HD	0.4947	0.8205	0.9739	0.9727
	WD	0.4947	0.8152	0.9470	0.9426
	HWD	0.4947	0.8205	0.9746	0.9720
BN	HW	0.6876	0.8325	0.9721	0.9690
	HD	0.6262	0.8287	0.9773	0.9740
	WD	0.6529	0.8127	0.9534	0.9484
	HWD	0.6809	0.8401	0.9770	0.9744
DT	HW	**0.7188**	0.8644	0.9773	0.9750
	HD	0.6389	0.8648	0.9753	0.9709
	WD	0.6932	0.8417	0.9526	0.9470
	HWD	0.6950	0.8599	0.9777	0.9752
LR	HW	0.6635	0.8652	0.9768	0.9701
	HD	0.6515	0.8650	**0.9824**	**0.9769**
	WD	0.6636	**0.8697**	0.9553	0.9564
	HWD	0.6591	0.8670	0.9808	0.9759

6   Conclusions and Future Work

In this paper we have presented an empirical comparison of methods for active household member identification, evaluated under different methodologies previously applied on recommender systems evaluation. Given that the methods are based on exploiting temporal patterns, we included some time-aware evaluation methodologies in order to test the reliability of previously reported results. We also analyzed the contribution of each time feature and combinations of features to the task.

The results obtained show that the discrimination power of time features, alone and combined, varies considerably when assessed by different methodologies. We observed that less strict methodologies provide unrealistic results, due to the exploitation of temporal information that are hard to obtain in a realistic evaluation scenario. Moreover, the accuracy achieved by all the methods was much worse when using a strict time-aware evaluation methodology. This findings show that stronger methods are required to provide accurate identification of active household members in real-world applications.

Next steps in our research will consider the development of methods able to improve accuracy in the task on the stricter time-aware evaluation methodologies, as a previous step towards obtaining better results on real-world applications. One way to accomplish this goal may be to exploit patterns found across several households that may be useful to use in cases where little information about user's temporal behavior is available. Furthermore, we plan to test additional time features that can be derived from timestamps, and use a combination of time features and other type of features, e.g. based on demographic data, aiming to increase the discrimination power of the feature set.

References

1. Kabutoya, Y., Iwata, T., Fujimura, K.: Modeling Multiple Users' Purchase over a Single Account for Collaborative Filtering. In: Chen, L., Triantafillou, P., Suel, T. (eds.) WISE 2010. LNCS, vol. 6488, pp. 328–341. Springer, Heidelberg (2010)
2. Berkovsky, S., De Luca, E.W., Said, A.: Challenge on Context-Aware Movie Recommendation: CAMRa2011. In: Proceedings of the 5th ACM Conference on Recommender Systems, pp. 385–386 (2011)
3. Campos, P.G., Bellogin, A., Díez, F., Cantador, I.: Time feature Selection for Identifying Active Household Members. In: Proceedings of the 21st ACM International Conference on Information and Knowledge Management, pp. 2311–2314 (2012)
4. Zhang, M., Hurley, N.: Avoiding Monotony: Improving the Diversity of Recommendation Lists. In: Proceedings of the 2nd ACM Conference on Recommender Systems, pp. 123–130 (2008)
5. Campos, P.G., Díez, F., Bellogín, A.: Temporal Rating Habits: A Valuable Tool for Rater Differentiation. In: Proceedings of the 2nd Challenge on Context-Aware Movie Recommendation, pp. 29–35 (2011)
6. Bento, J., Fawaz, N., Montanari, A., Ioannidis, S.: Identifying Users from Their Rating Patterns. In: Proceedings of the 2nd Challenge on Context-Aware Movie Recommendation, pp. 39–46 (2011)
7. Campos, P.G., Díez, F., Cantador, I.: Time-Aware Recommender Systems: A Comprehensive Survey and Analysis of Existing Evaluation Protocols. User Modeling and User-Adapted Interaction (in press, 2013)
8. Ardissono, L., Portis, F., Torasso, P., Bellifemine, F., Chiarotto, A., Difino, A.: Architecture of a System for the Generation of Personalized Electronic Program Guides. In: Proceedings of the UM 2001 Workshop on Personalization in Future TV (2001)
9. Vildjiounaite, E., Kyllönen, V., Hannula, T., Alahuhta, P.: Unobtrusive dynamic modelling of TV program preferences in a household. In: Tscheligi, M., Obrist, M., Lugmayr, A. (eds.) EuroITV 2008. LNCS, vol. 5066, pp. 82–91. Springer, Heidelberg (2008)
10. Goren-Bar, D., Glinansky, O.: FIT-recommending TV Programs to Family Members. Computers & Graphics 24, 149–156 (2004)
11. Oh, J., Sung, Y., Kim, J., Humayoun, M., Park, Y.-H., Yu, H.: Time-Dependent User Profiling for TV Recommendation. In: Proceedings of the 2nd International Conference on Cloud and Green Computing, pp. 783–787 (2012)
12. Shi, Y., Larson, M., Hanjalic, A.: Mining Relational Context-aware Graph for Rater Identification. In: Proceedings of the 2nd Challenge on Context-Aware Movie Recommendation, pp. 53–59 (2011)
13. Lathia, N., Hailes, S., Capra, L.: Temporal Collaborative Filtering with Adaptive Neighbourhoods. In: Proceedings of the 32nd International ACM SIGIR Conference on Research and Development in Information Retrieval, pp. 796–797 (2009)
14. Campos, P.G., Díez, F., Sánchez-Montañés, M.: Towards a More Realistic Evaluation: Testing the Ability to Predict Future Tastes of Matrix Factorization-based Recommenders. In: Proceedings of the 5th ACM Conference on Recommender Systems, pp. 309–312 (2011)
15. Shani, G., Gunawardana, A.: Evaluating Recommendation Systems. In: Ricci, F., Rokach, L., Shapira, B., Kantor, P.B. (eds.) Recommender Systems Handbook, pp. 257–297. Springer US (2011)
16. Kohavi, R., Longbotham, R., Sommerfield, D., Henne, R.M.: Controlled Experiments on the Web: Survey and Practical Guide. Data Mining and Knowledge Discovery 18, 140–181 (2008)
17. Bennett, J., Lanning, S.: The Netflix Prize. In: Proceedings of KDD Cup and Workshop (2007)

Comments-Oriented Query Expansion
for Opinion Retrieval in Blogs

Jose M. Chenlo[1], Javier Parapar[2], and David E. Losada[1]

[1] Centro de Investigación en Tecnoloxías da Información (CITIUS)
Universidad de Santiago de Compostela, Spain
{josemanuel.gonzalez,david.losada}@usc.es
[2] IRLab, Computer Science Department
University of A Coruña, Spain
javierparapar@udc.es

Abstract. In recent years, Pseudo Relevance Feedback techniques have
become one of the most effective query expansion approaches for document retrieval. Particularly, Relevance-Based Language Models have
been applied in several domains as an effective and efficient way to enhance topic retrieval. Recently, some extensions to the original RM methods have been proposed to apply query expansion in other scenarios,
such as opinion retrieval. Such approaches rely on mixture models that
combine the query expansion provided by Relevance Models with opinionated terms obtained from external resources (e.g., opinion lexicons).
However, these methods ignore the structural aspects of a document,
which are valuable to extract topic-dependent opinion expressions. For
instance, the sentiments conveyed in blogs are often located in specific
parts of the blog posts and its comments. We argue here that the comments are a good guidance to find on-topic opinion terms that help to
move the query towards burning aspects of the topic. We study the role
of the different parts of a blog document to enhance blog opinion retrieval through query expansion. The proposed method does not require
external resources or additional knowledge and our experiments show
that this is a promising and simple way to make a more accurate ranking of blog posts in terms of their sentiment towards the query topic. Our
approach compares well with other opinion finding methods, obtaining
high precision performance without harming mean average precision.

Keywords: Information retrieval, opinion mining, blogs, comments, relevance models, pseudo relevance feedback, query expansion.

1 Introduction and Motivation

The blogosphere is one of the most important sources of opinion in the Internet
[1]. Given a query and a collection of blogs, several methods have been proposed
to retrieve opinions related to the query topic [1]. The most popular choice is
to consider this task as a two-stage process that involves a topic retrieval stage
(i.e., retrieve on-topic posts), and a re-ranking stage based on opinion features [2].

C. Bielza et al. (Eds.): CAEPIA 2013, LNAI 8109, pp. 32–41, 2013.

The first stage usually involves ad-hoc search with popular Information Retrieval (IR) models (e.g., BM25). The second stage is a more complex task with many unresolved issues (e.g., irony, off-topic opinions, mixed polarity). Most successful approaches search for documents that are both opinionated and on-topic by considering positional information as the best guidance to find on-topic opinions [3,4]. Pseudo Relevance Feedback (PRF) combined with external opinion resources has also been proposed to support opinion finding [5]. However, most studies ignore the structural aspects of a blog post to determine opinions. This is unfortunate because sentiments often appear in specific locations of the text. For instance, in the study of blog comments presented in [6], Mishne and Glance found that comments constitute a substantial part of the blogosphere, accounting for up to 30% of the total volume of blog data.

In this paper we present a simple PRF strategy that exploits the potential opinions provided in the comments to improve opinion finding in blogs. In particular, we use one of the most robust and effective PRF techniques: Relevance-Based Language Models (RM) [7]. Several estimations for RM have been proposed in the literature, being the so-called RM3 [8] the approach that performs best [9]. In this work we present an alternative RM3 estimation for selecting expansion terms from comments. We estimate the relevance model from these highly opinionated parts of the blogs with the objective of selecting opinionated and on-topic expansion terms. We compare the performance of our comments-based approach against the standard RM3 formulation. Our experiments show that the new expansion method is promising when compared to global approaches that consider the whole document to do expansion.

2   Background

Nowadays, advanced search tasks need to go beyond a ranked list of relevant documents. One of these tasks is opinion retrieval [10,1], where opinions need to be integrated within the retrieval task. For instance, in the TREC Blog Track [2] the participants are asked to search for blog pages that express an opinion about a given topic. This task can be summarised as: *What do people think about X?* [2] and is often addressed in two stages. First, a ranking of documents related to the topic (X) is obtained and, next, the initial list is re-ranked using opinion-based features. The output is a ranking of documents in decreasing order of their estimated subjectivity with respect to the query.

Relevance Models explicitly introduced the concept of relevance in the Language Modeling (LM) framework [7]. In RM, the original query is considered a very short sample of words obtained from a relevance model R and relevant documents are larger samples of text from the same model. From the words already seen, the relevance model is estimated. If more words from R are needed then the words with the highest estimated probability are chosen. The terms in the vocabulary are therefore sorted according to these estimated probabilities. After doing some assumptions the RM1 method is defined as:

$$P(w|R) \propto \sum_{d \in \mathcal{C}} P(d) \cdot P(w|d) \cdot \prod_{i=1}^{n} P(q_i|d) \tag{1}$$

Usually, $P(d)$ is assumed to be uniform. $\prod_{i=1}^{n} P(q_i|d)$ is the query likelihood given the document model, which is traditionally computed using Dirichlet smoothing. $P(w|d)$ accounts for the importance of the word w within the document d. The process follows four steps:

1. Initially, the documents in the collection ($\mathcal{C}$) are ranked using a standard LM retrieval model (e.g., query likelihood with Dirichlet smoothing).
2. The top r documents from the initial retrieval are taken for driving the estimation of the relevance model. In the following, this pseudo relevant set will be referred to as RS.
3. The relevance model's probabilities, $P(w|R)$, are calculated from the estimate presented in Eq. 1, using RS instead of $\mathcal{C}$.
4. The expanded query is built with the e terms with highest estimated $P(w|R)$.

RM3 [8] is a later extension of RM that performs better than RM1. RM3 interpolates the terms selected by RM1 with a LM computed from the original query:

$$P(w|q') = (1 - \lambda) \cdot P(w|q) + \lambda \cdot P(w|R) \tag{2}$$

Negative cross entropy with the expanded query is used to get the final ranking.

3   Comments-Biased Relevance Model

As we discussed in Section 1, people tend to express opinions related to the topic of the blog post when they write comments. We argue that the comments of a blog post are more densely populated by opinions than other parts of the document. Therefore, we hypothesize that terms in comments are highly opinionated and on-topic and therefore, a simple PRF technique that takes advantage of these specific words to expand the original query will be a very promising tool to improve opinion finding in blogs. We have designed an alternative RM3 estimation in which Eq. 1 is modified to promote terms that appear in the comments of the blog post:

$$P(w|R) \propto \sum_{d \in \mathcal{RS}} P(d) \cdot P(w|d_{comm}) \cdot \prod_{i=1}^{n} P(q_i|d) \tag{3}$$

where w is any word appearing in the set of comments associated to documents in RS and $P(w|d_{comm})$ is computed as the probability of w in the set of comments of document d. In this way, the comments act as proxies of the documents in terms of opinion. Observe that the estimation of the query likelihood remains at document level because the effect of topic relevance on the estimation of the relevance model is better encoded using the whole document.

Finally, both $P(w|d_{comm})$ and $P(q_i|d)$ are estimated using Dirichlet smoothing:

$$P(w|d_{comm}) = \frac{f_{w,d_{comm}} + \mu \cdot P(w|C_{comm})}{|d_{comm}| + \mu} \qquad (4)$$

$$P(q_i|d) = \frac{f_{q_i,d} + \mu \cdot P(q_i|C)}{|d| + \mu} \qquad (5)$$

where $f_{q_i,d}$ is the number of times that the query term q_i appears in document d, and $f_{w,d_{comm}}$ is the number of times that the word w appears in the document that is constructed by concatenating all the comments associated to d (d_{comm}). $|d|$ and $|d_{comm}|$ are the number of words in d and d_{comm}, respectively. $P(q_i|C)$ is the probability of q_i in the collection of documents C and $P(w|C_{comm})$ is the probability of w in the collection of comments. μ is an smoothing parameter that we have to train.

4   Experiments

In our experiments we used the well-known BLOGS06 test collection [11]. We considered the TREC 2006, TREC 2007, and TREC 2008 blog track's benchmarks, all of which have the BLOGS06 as the reference collection. One of the core tasks in these tracks is the opinion finding task, i.e., given a query topic, systems have to return a ranking of subjective blog posts related to the query. As usual in TREC, each query topic contains three different fields (title, description, and narrative). We only used the title field, which is short and the best representation of real user web's queries [2]. Documents were pre-processed and segmented into posts and comments following the heuristic method proposed in [12]. We also removed 733 common words from documents and queries.

Documents were judged by TREC assessors in two different aspects: i) Topic relevance: a post can be relevant, not relevant, or not judged, ii) Opinion: whether or not the on-topic documents contain explicit expression of opinion or sentiment about the topic. In this paper we are interested in this second level of judgements, focusing our attention on retrieving documents that express an explicit opinion about the query (regardless of the polarity of the opinion).

4.1   Baselines

In TREC 2008, to promote the study of the performance of opinion-finding methods against uniform retrieval rankings, a set of five topic-relevance retrieval runs was provided. These standard baselines use a variety of retrieval approaches, and have varying retrieval effectiveness[1].

It is a standard practice to use these baselines as initial input for the opinion retrieval stage. We followed this evaluation design and applied the proposed RM estimation to re-rank the baselines. The measures adopted to evaluate the

---

[1] Baselines were selected from the runs submitted to TREC Blog Retrieval Task 2008.

opinion retrieval effectiveness are mean average precision (MAP), Precision at 10 (P@10), and the Reliability of Improvement (RI) [13], which is a commonly used robustness measure for PRF methods:

$$RI(q) = \frac{n_+ - n_-}{|q|} \qquad (6)$$

where q is the set of queries tested, $n+$ is the number of improved queries, n_- the number of degraded queries and $|q|$ is the total number of queries in q. Observe that the gold-standard is obtained from the documents that were assessed as subjective with respect to the query topic.

4.2   Query Formulation

We used the Indri retrieval platform for both indexing and retrieval[2]. In order to apply our RM estimation under this framework, Equation 2 is implemented in the Indri's query language as follows:

$$\#weight\ (\lambda\ \#combine(\ q_1\ \cdots\ q_{|n|})$$
$$(1-\lambda)\ \#weight(\ P(t_1|R)\cdot t_1\ \cdots\ P(t_e|R)\cdot t_e)) \qquad (7)$$

where $q_1\cdots q_{|n|}$ are the original query terms, $t_1\cdots t_e$ are the e terms with highest probability according to Equation 3, and λ is a free parameter to control the trade-off between the original query and the expanded terms. We selected Dirichlet [14] as the smoothing technique for our experiments.

4.3   Training and Testing

We trained our methods with the 100 topics provided by TREC 2006 and TREC 2007 blog track (optimising MAP) and then we used the 50 TREC 2008 topics as the testing query set. The parameters trained were the following: the smoothing parameter of Dirichlet μ ($\mu \in \{10, 100, 1000, 2000, 3000, 4000, 5000, 6000\}$), the number of documents in the pseudo relevant set $r = |RS|$, ($r \in \{5, 10, 25, 50, 75, 100\}$), the number of terms selected for expansion e ($e \in \{5, 10, 25, 50, 75, 100\}$) and the interpolation weight λ ($\lambda \in \{0, .1, .2, .3, .4, .5, .6, .7, .8, .9, 1\}$). The parameters were tuned (independently for each baseline) for both the classical $RM3$ estimated from the whole documents (post and comments) and for our proposal (labelled as $RM3_C$) following an exhaustive exploration process (grid search).

4.4   Results

Table 1 and Table 2 report the experimental results. Each run was evaluated in terms of its ability to retrieve subjective documents higher up in the ranking. The best value for each baseline and performance measure is underlined. Statistical

---

[2] http://www.lemurproject.org/indri.php

Table 1. Opinion finding MAP results for the TREC 2008 dataset. The symbols ▲(▼) and △(▽) indicate a significant improvement(decrease) over the original baselines and the $RM3$ method respectively.

Baseline	orig. MAP	$RM3$ MAP	RI	$RM3_C$ MAP	RI
baseline1	.3239	.3750▲ (+16%)	.60	.3653▲ (+13%)	.56
baseline2	.2639	.3117▲ (+18%)	.36	.3244▲ (+23%)	.52
baseline3	.3564	.3739 (+5%)	.08	.3753 (+5%)	.12
baseline4	.3822	.3652 (−4%)	-.04	.3688 (−4%)	-.08
baseline5	.2988	.3383▲ (+13%)	.44	.3385▲ (+13%)	.48
average	.3251	.3528▲ (+8%)	.29	.3545▲ (+9%)	.32

Table 2. Opinion finding P@10 results for the TREC 2008 dataset. The symbols ▲(▼) and △(▽) indicate a significant improvement(decrease) over the original baselines and the $RM3$ method respectively.

Baseline	orig. P@10	$RM3$ P@10	RI	$RM3_C$ P@10	RI
baseline1	.5800	.6140 (+6%)	.18	.6360 (+10%)	.20
baseline2	.5500	.5560 (+1%)	.04	.6340▲△ (+15%)	.18
baseline3	.5540	.5800 (+5%)	-.02	.6460▲△ (+17%)	.30
baseline4	.6160	.6140 (−0%)	-.04	.6560 (+6%)	.18
baseline5	.5300	.5940 (+12%)	.18	.6660▲△ (+26%)	.54
average	.5660	.5916 (+5%)	.07	.6476▲△ (+14%)	.28

significance was estimated using the Wilcoxon test at the 95% level. The symbols ▲ and ▼ indicate a significant improvement or decrease over the original baselines and the symbols △ and ▽ indicate a significant improvement (resp. decrease) with respect to the standard $RM3$ method.

Opinion Retrieval Performance. Both $RM3$ and $RM3_C$ outperform the original baselines but $RM3_C$ performs the best. In terms of MAP, $RM3$ is able to achieve improvements that are similar to those found with $RM3_C$. However, in terms of $P@10$, $RM3_C$ shows significant improvements with respect to the baselines and with respect to $RM3$. Furthermore, $RM3_C$ shows higher values of RI. This indicates that the improvements obtained using queries expanded with terms from comments are more consistent than those obtained with terms from the whole document. These results also highlight the importance of comments to enhance precision without harming recall (MAP is roughly the same with either RM methods). This suggests that subjective words estimated from comments lead to a more accurate query-dependent opinion vocabulary. Furthermore, the independence of our method of any external lexicon is important because, in many domains and languages, there is a lack of good opinion resources.

Table 3. Average opinion finding MAP performance over the 5 different baselines re-ranked by TREC 2008 systems against the results achieved by $RM3_C$ on top of those systems. The symbols ▲(▼) indicate a significant (resp. decrease) improvement over the TREC systems. TREC systems that were able to outperform the original 5 topic-retrieval baselines are in bold.

TREC Run	orig. MAP	TREC run+$RM3_C$ MAP	RI
uicop1bl1r	.3614	.3524 (−2%)	-.18
B1PsgOpinAZN	.3565	.3558 (−2%)	.10
uogOP1PrintL	.3412	.3510 (+3%)	.10
NOpMM107	.3273	.3532▲ (+8%)	.38
UWnb1Op	.3215	.3538▲ (+10%)	.33
FIUBL1DFR	.2938	.3520▲ (+20%)	.61
UniNEopLRb1	.2118	.2121 (+0%)	.18
uams08b1pr	.1378	.3347▲ (+43%)	.93

Table 4. Average opinion finding P@10 performance over the 5 different baselines re-ranked by TREC 2008 systems agains the results achieved by $RM3_C$ on top of those systems. The symbols ▲(▼) indicate a significant (resp. decrease) improvement over the TREC systems. TREC systems that were able to outperform the original 5 topic-retrieval baselines are in bold.

TREC Run	orig. P@10	TREC run+$RM3_C$ P@10	RI
uicop1bl1r	.6020	.6264 (+4%)	.14
B1PsgOpinAZN	.6204	.6512▲ (+5%)	.30
uogOP1PrintL	.5964	.6320▲ (+6%)	.25
NOpMM107	.5744	.6432▲ (+12%)	.37
UWnb1Op	.6068	.6500 (+7%)	.25
FIUBL1DFR	.4804	.6392▲ (+33%)	.76
UniNEopLRb1	.6156	.6464 (+5%)	.29
uams08b1pr	.1284	.6100▲ (+375%)	1.0

Comparison against TREC Systems. Our technique does not use any specific opinion lexicon. It simply re-ranks documents based on a comments-oriented query expansion method that works from an initial ranked set of documents. This brings us the opportunity to apply our methods on top of effective opinion finding methods. To test this combination we considered the systems proposed by teams participating in the last TREC blog opinion retrieval task (TREC2008) [2]. Observe that this subjective task was quite challenging: half of TREC systems failed to retrieve more subjective documents than the baselines [2]. In Table 3 and Table 4 we report the mean performance (over the five baselines) of the TREC systems against the average performance achieved by applying $RM3_C$ on top of those systems' runs. Observe that our methods and these TREC systems were evaluated under the same testing conditions (i.e., re-ranking performance against the 5 topic-retrieval baselines). The systems in bold were the only ones able to show improvements with respect to the original five retrieval baselines in terms of MAP. We can observe that our $RM3_C$ approach is often able to improve the performance of these methods, showing usually significant improvements in terms of $P@10$, as well as good RI scores. This demonstrates that our method is able to improve strong subjective rankings. Table 3 and Table 4 also show that our expansion approach is robust because $RM3_C$ is able to outperform all types of opinion retrieval systems regardless of their original performance. Observe also that the average $P@10$ of our method in Table 2 (.6476) is clearly higher than the $P@10$ obtained by any TREC participant.

5 Related Work

Relevance Feeedback and Query Expansion techniques have been considered as an efficient, effective and natural way to enhance the effectiveness of retrieval systems [15]. RF methods use the information provided by relevant documents from an initial retrieval to rewrite and improve the quality of the original query [16]. However, in many scenarios, the applicability of RF is limited because of the lack of relevance judgements. In order to deal with the absence of judgements, Pseudo Relevance Feedback strategies were proposed [17,18]. These methods do not need explicit relevance judgements because they assume that some of the documents retrieved by an IR system are relevant to the original query. How to select the pseudo-relevance documents and also how to use them to improve the original query varies from one PRF method to another.

Relevance Models have emerged as one of the most effective and efficient PRF approaches. As a result of this, different estimations have been proposed [9] and applied in all sorts of IR problems. In particular, for the opinion retrieval task, Huang and Croft [5] proposed a RM estimation based on a mixture with external opinion resources. This approach showed satisfactory results. However, the information provided by the documents' structure to search for opinions is often ignored. This is unfortunate because the comments supply valuable information, as demonstrated in ad-hoc IR retrieval tasks [19,20], summarisation [21] and snippet generation problems [22].

Several blog opinion retrieval methods have been proposed in the literature. The most successful studies in this subject are those focused on finding documents that are both opinionated and on-topic [4,3,23]. To meet this aim, some papers consider term positional information to find opinionated information related to the query. Santos et al. [4] applied a novel opinion mining approach that takes into account the proximity of query terms to subjective sentences in a document. Gerani et al. [3,23] proposed proximity-based opinion propagation methods to calculate the opinion density at the position of each query term in a document. These two studies led to improvements over state of the art baselines for blog opinion retrieval. The main concern for applying these methods is their computational cost. For example, in [3,23], it is necessary to apply a kernel function at each opinion term to propagate their sentiment scores to every query term in the document. Furthermore, these methods are dependent on external opinion resources. These resources might not be available for a particular domain or language. We designed here a simple PRF method that, focusing the query expansion process on comments, performs well without the need of any external information. Moreover, as we explained in section 4, our proposal is complementary to other opinion finding techniques.

6   Conclusions and Future Work

In this paper we have proposed a RM estimation focused on the comments of the blog posts to support opinion finding. Under this framework, the original query is expanded with salient words supplied by a relevance model constructed from the comments of the blog posts. The proposed method significantly outperforms the classical $RM3$ estimation for an opinion finding task. We provided experimental evidence showing that the comments are very useful to move the query towards opinionated words. This novel expansion approach is particularly consistent as a high precision mechanism.

One of the characteristics of our approach is that we apply an homogeneous treatment for all types of queries. However, in some cases this could be not desirable. In this respect, we would like to study methods to dynamically adapting our expansion techniques depending on the quality of the initial query [13]. In the near future, we also want to study the effect of spam comments on our expansion approach.

Acknowledgments. This work was funded by *Secretaría de Estado de Investigación, Desarrollo e Innovación* from the Spanish Government under project TIN2012-33867.

References

1. Santos, R.L.T., Macdonald, C., McCreadie, R., Ounis, I., Soboroff, I.: Information retrieval on the blogosphere. Found. Trends Inf. Retr. 6(1), 1–125 (2012)
2. Ounis, I., Macdonald, C., Soboroff, I.: Overview of the TREC 2008 blog track. In: Proc. of the 17th Text Retrieval Conference, TREC 2008. NIST, Gaithersburg (2008)
3. Gerani, S., Carman, M.J., Crestani, F.: Proximity-based opinion retrieval. In: Proc. 33rd International ACM SIGIR Conference on Research and Development in Information Retrieval, SIGIR 2010, pp. 403–410. ACM Press, New York (2010)
4. Santos, R.L.T., He, B., Macdonald, C., Ounis, I.: Integrating proximity to subjective sentences for blog opinion retrieval. In: Boughanem, M., Berrut, C., Mothe, J., Soule-Dupuy, C. (eds.) ECIR 2009. LNCS, vol. 5478, pp. 325–336. Springer, Heidelberg (2009)
5. Huang, X., Croft, B.: A unified relevance model for opinion retrieval. In: Proc. of the 18th ACM Conference on Information and Knowledge Management, CIKM 2009, pp. 947–956. ACM, New York (2009)
6. Mishne, G., Glance, N.: Leave a reply: An analysis of weblog comments. In: Third Annual Workshop on the Weblogging Ecosystem (2006)

7. Lavrenko, V., Croft, W.B.: Relevance based language models. In: Proc. of the 24th Annual International ACM SIGIR Conference on Research and Development in Information Retrieval, SIGIR 2001, pp. 120–127. ACM, New York (2001)

8. Abdul-jaleel, N., Allan, J., Croft, W.B., Diaz, O., Larkey, L., Li, X., Smucker, M.D., Wade, C.: UMass at TREC 2004: Novelty and HARD. In: Proc. of TREC-13. NIST Special Publication, National Institute for Science and Technology (2004)

9. Lv, Y., Zhai, C.: A comparative study of methods for estimating query language models with pseudo feedback. In: Proc. of the 18th ACM Conf. on Information and Knowledge Management, CIKM 2009, pp. 1895–1898. ACM, New York (2009)

10. Pang, B., Lee, L.: Opinion mining and sentiment analysis. Foundations and Trends in Information Retrieval 2(1-2), 1–135 (2007)

11. Macdonald, C., Ounis, I.: The TREC Blogs 2006 collection: Creating and analysing a blog test collection. Technical Report TR-2006-224, Department of Computing Science, University of Glasgow (2006)

12. Parapar, J., López-castro, J., Barreiro, A.: Blog posts and comments extraction and impact on retrieval effectiveness. In: 1st Spanish Conference on Information Retrieval, CERI 2012, Madrid, pp. 5–16 (2010)

13. Sakai, T., Manabe, T., Koyama, M.: Flexible pseudo-relevance feedback via selective sampling. ACM Transactions on Asian Language Information Processing (TALIP) 4(2), 111–135 (2005)

14. Zhai, C., Lafferty, J.: A study of smoothing methods for language models applied to information retrieval. ACM Trans. Inf. Syst. 22(2), 179–214 (2004)

15. Rocchio, J.: Relevance feedback in information retrieval. In: Salton, G. (ed.) The SMART Retrieval System: Experiments in Automatic Document Processing, pp. 313–323. Prentice Hall, Inc. (1971)

16. Croft, B., Harper, D.J.: Using Probabilistic Models of Document Retrieval without Relevance Information. Journal of Documentation 35, 285–295 (1979)

17. Ruthven, I., Lalmas, M.: A survey on the use of relevance feedback for information access systems. Knowl. Eng. Rev. 18(2), 95–145 (2003)

18. Lu, X.A., Ayoub, M., Dong, J.: Ad Hoc Experiments Using EUREKA. In: Proc. of TREC-5, pp. 229–240. NIST Special Publication, National Institute for Science and Technology (1996)

19. Weerkamp, W., de Rijke, M.: Credibility improves topical blog post retrieval. In: Proc. of ACL 2008: HLT, pp. 923–931. Association for Computational Linguistics, Columbus (2008)

20. Mishne, G.: Using blog properties to improve retrieval. In: International Conference on Weblogs and Social Media 2007 (2007) (retrieved February 29, 2008)

21. Hu, M., Sun, A., Lim, E.P.: Comments-oriented blog summarization by sentence extraction. In: Proc. of the Sixteenth ACM Conference on Information and Knowledge Management, CIKM 2007, pp. 901–904. ACM, New York (2007)

22. Parapar, J., López-Castro, J., Barreiro, A.: Blog snippets: a comments-biased approach. In: Proc. of the 33rd International ACM SIGIR Conference on Research and Development in Information Retrieval, SIGIR 2010, pp. 711–712. ACM, New York (2010)

23. Gerani, S., Keikha, M., Crestani, F.: Aggregating multiple opinion evidence in proximity-based opinion retrieval. In: SIGIR, pp. 1199–1200 (2011)

A Contextual Modeling Approach
for Model-Based Recommender Systems

Ignacio Fernández-Tobías, Pedro G. Campos, Iván Cantador, and Fernando Díez

Escuela Politécnica Superior
Universidad Autónoma de Madrid
28049 Madrid, Spain
{i.fernandez,pedro.campos,ivan.cantador,fernando.diez}@uam.es

Abstract. In this paper we present a contextual modeling approach for model-based recommender systems that integrates and exploits both user preferences and contextual signals in a common vector space. Differently to previous work, we conduct a user study acquiring and analyzing a variety of realistic contextual signals associated to user preferences in several domains. Moreover, we report empirical results evaluating our approach in the movie and music domains, which show that enhancing model-based recommender systems with time, location and social companion information improves the accuracy of generated recommendations.

Keywords: context-aware recommendation, contextual modeling, model-based recommender systems.

1   Introduction

Recommender Systems (RS) are software tools that provide users with suggestions of items that should be the most appealing based on personal preferences (tastes, interests, goals). Main strategies of RS are *content-based filtering* (CBF), which recommends items similar to those preferred by the user in the past, and *collaborative filtering* (CF), which recommends items preferred in the past by people who are similar-minded to the user. To overcome particular limitations, CBF and CF are commonly combined in the so-called *hybrid filtering* (HF) strategies [3,7].

For any of the above strategies, recommendation approaches can be classified as *heuristic-based* or *model-based* [3,6]. Heuristic-based approaches utilize explicit heuristic formulas that aggregate collected user preferences to compute item relevance predictions. Model-based approaches, in contrast, utilize collected user preferences to build (machine learning) models that, once built, provide item relevance predictions. In this way, model-based approaches lead to faster responses at recommendation time.

In its basic formulation, recommender systems do not take into account the *context* –e.g. time, location, and social companion– in which the user experiences an item. It has been shown, however, that context may determine or affect the user's preferences when selecting items for consumption [9]. Those RS that somehow exploit contextual information are called context-aware recommender systems (CARS). Adomavicius et

C. Bielza et al. (Eds.): CAEPIA 2013, LNAI 8109, pp. 42–51, 2013.

al. [2,4], classify them as *contextual pre-filtering*, *contextual post-filtering*, and *contextual modeling* approaches. Contextual pre- and post-filtering approaches are based on context-unaware recommendation methods, which are applied on pre-processed preference data, or are used to generate recommendations that are post-adjusted, in both cases according to the user's current context. Contextual modeling, on the contrary, extends the user-item preference relations with contextual information to compute recommendations.

Researchers have shown that CARS provide more accurate recommendations than context-unaware RS [5,11]. Nevertheless, context-aware recommendation is a relatively unexplored area, and still needs a much better comprehension [4]. For instance, analyzing which are the characteristics and values of distinct contextual signals –alone or in combination– that really influence recommendation performance improvements is an important open research issue. Some researchers have conducted studies on context-aware recommendation comparing different approaches [13,14,15], but little work has been done at the contextual signal level. Moreover, in general, reported studies have focused on individual domains, without analyzing the generalization of the proposed approaches for several domains.

A major difficulty to address the above issues is the current lack of available real context-enriched data. A method for obtaining contextual data is to automatically infer the context in which the user experiences an item, e.g. by capturing time and location signals. In general, this approach has been used in CARS research to capture context data (usually timestamps) when users rate items. However, it is important to note that if a system collects ratings instead of consumption/purchase records, the captured contexts do not necessarily correspond to the real contexts that affect or determine the user's (contextualized) preferences for items.

In this paper we present a *contextual modeling* approach for *model-based RS* that integrates both user preferences and contextual signals in a common vector space, and, being a *hybrid recommendation* approach, exploits content-based user preferences in a collaborative filtering fashion. Differently to previous work, we conduct a user study acquiring and analyzing a variety of realistic contextual signals associated to user preferences in several domains. Moreover, we report empirical results evaluating our approach in the movie and music domains, which show that enhancing model-based recommender systems with time, location and social companion information improves the accuracy of generated recommendations.

The remainder of the paper is structured as follows. In Section 2 we discuss related work. In Section 3 we present our contextual modeling approach for integrating user preferences and contextual signals. In Section 4 we describe the user study and analysis performed, and in Section 5 we report the recommendation results obtained. Finally, in Section 6 we provide some conclusions and future research directions for our work.

2   Related Work

Quoting Dey [8], "context is any information that can be used to characterize the situation of an entity." In information retrieval and filtering systems, an entity can be a user, an (information) item, or an experience the user is evaluating [5], and any signal –such as device, location, time, social companion, and mood– regarding the situation in which a user interacts with an item can be considered as context.

Context-aware recommender systems exploit contextual information to provide differentiated recommendations according to the user's current situation. Based on how such contextual information is exploited, three types of context-aware recommendation approaches can be distinguished [4]: *contextual pre-filtering approaches* –which prune, split and/or group available user preference data according to the target context, before applying a context-independent recommendation algorithm–, *contextual post-filtering approaches* –which apply a context-independent recommendation algorithm on the original user preference data, and afterwards adapt the generated recommendations according to the target context–, and *contextual modeling* –which incorporate contextual information into the algorithm that generates recommendations.

In this paper we focus on contextual modeling, since it lets effectively extend and exploit the user-item relations with several contextual signals, without the need of discarding (valuable) data or adapting generated recommendations for providing contextualized recommendations.

One of the first contextual modeling approaches was presented in [12], where Oku et al. incorporated several contextual signals –including time, social companion, and weather– into a Support Vector Machine model for restaurant recommendation. Yu et al. [16] modeled situation context (in which the user utilizes/consumes an item) and capability context (in which the current capacity of the utilized device is specified) to provide media recommendations in smart phones. These contexts are incorporated into content-based Bayesian and rule-based recommendation approaches. Abbar et al. [1] proposed a conceptualization of context-aware recommendation based on an architecture composed of various context-based personalization services, including context discovery, binding and matching services. In the proposed architecture, context clusters are formed by analyzing user activity logs to describe regular contexts or situations, such as "at home" and "at work." Koren [11] extended the Matrix Factorization model incorporating temporal context information for movie rating prediction. The time signal was indeed argued as a key factor by the winning team of the well-known Netflix Prize competition. Finally, Karatzoglou et al. [10] used Tensor Factorization to model n-dimensional contextual information. The approach was called multiverse recommendation because of its ability to bridge data pertaining to different contexts (universes of information) into a unified model.

In the literature, most of the work on context modeling for recommendation focuses on individual domains, exploits a single contextual signal, and/or evaluates approaches in terms of performance recommendation improvements due to the consideration of contextual signals, without analyzing and characterizing the context values that really determine such improvements. Differently, in this paper we conduct a user study aimed to acquire and evaluate a variety of realistic contextual signals associated to the users' preferences in several domains, and present an analysis of recommendation improvements for the different values of the contextual signals when they are exploited alone or in combination.

3   Contextual Modeling in Model-Based Recommender Systems

We address the contextual modeling problem from a machine learning perspective. Specifically, we propose to represent both user preferences and contextual signals in a common vector space. The dimensions of the considered vector space are content-based attributes associated to user preferences and item features, and context-based attributes associated to user-item preference relations. Hence, as shown in Figure 1, a preference relation $p(u, i)$ between user $u \in \mathcal{U}$ and item $i \in \mathcal{I}$ is defined as a pattern:

$$p(u, i) \equiv \langle f_1(u), \dots, f_M(u), g_1(i), \dots, g_N(i), h_1(u, i), \dots, h_K(u, i); r \rangle$$

where $f_m(u): \mathcal{U} \to \mathbb{R}$ gives a numeric value that indicates the preference of user u for (items with) a content attribute a_m; $g_n(i): \mathcal{I} \to \mathbb{R}$ gives a numeric value that indicates the importance of a (content) attribute a_n for describing item i; $h_k(u, i): \mathcal{U} \times \mathcal{I} \to \{0,1\}$ is 1 if a contextual signal c_k is active in the preference of user u for item i, and 0 otherwise; and $r \in \{0,1\}$ is the preference relevance of user u for item i, being 1 if user u prefers/likes item i (for the context values $h_1(u, i), \dots, h_K(u, i)$), and 0 otherwise.

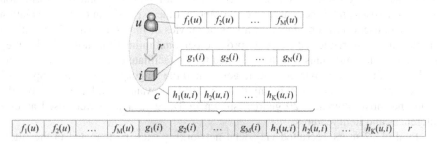

Fig. 1. A user-item preference relation as a pattern of content- and context-based attributes

In the user study presented in this paper, for the movie and music domains, we considered the content- and context-based attributes shown in Table 1. For each user u, the value $f_m(u)$ of a content-based attribute a_m was the number of u's liked/preferred items with a_m. For each item i, the value $g_n(i)$ of a content-based attribute a_n was 1 if i had the attribute, and 0 otherwise.

Table 1. Attributes in the movie and music domains considered in the user study

Domain	Attribute type		Attributes
movies	content-based (f, g)	a user's preferred/liked genres	action, adventure, animation, comedy, crime, drama, family, fantasy, futuristic, historical, horror, melodrama, musical, mystery, neo noir, parody, romance, sci-fi, thriller, war
		a movie's genres	
	context-based (h)	day of the week	work day, weekend day, indifferent
		time of the day	morning, afternoon, night, indifferent
		social companion	alone, with my partner, with my family, with friends, indifferent
music	content-based (f, g)	a user's preferred/liked genres	60s, 70s, 80s, 90s, acoustic, ambient, blues, classical, electronic, folk, hip hop, indie, jazz, latin, metal, pop, punk, rnb, rock, soul
		a musician's genres	
	context-based (h)	day of the week	work day, weekend day, indifferent
		time of the day	morning, afternoon, night, indifferent
		location	at home, at work, at the car/bus, at the bar/disco, indifferent

The set of attribute patterns (collected in the user study) was then used to build and evaluate a number of well-known classifiers, namely Naïve Bayes, Random forest, Multilayer Perceptron, and Support Vector Machine. In this way, preferences of individual users were exploited in a collaborative way, and the classifiers can be considered as model-based hybrid recommender systems.

Analyzing the collected patterns, in Section 4 we present relations existing between user preferences for movie/music genres and the considered contexts. Next, in Section 5 we present an evaluation on the effect of exploiting or discarding contextual information by the recommender systems.

4   Analyzing Contextualized User Preferences

To evaluate our contextual modeling approach with realistic context information associated to user preferences at item consumption time, we built an online evaluation tool[1], where users were presented with sets of movies or musicians (no combinations of both), and were requested to freely provide personal ratings for those movies they had watched and musicians they had listened to. To facilitate the evaluation, the users could select preferred movie and music genres and the language –English or Spanish– of the online evaluation, and skip any item they did not want to evaluate. For both the movie and music domains, 20 genres (shown in Tables 2 and 3) were used as user preferences and item features.

A total of 72 users, recruited via social networking sites, participated in the study, evaluating 178 movies and 132 musicians, generating 713 evaluation cases. In each evaluation case, a target user assigned to an item (movie or musician) an integer rating in the range [1, 10], and specified the context (h attribute values in Table 1) in which she preferred to consume the item. In the offline analysis, the preference relevance $r \in \{0,1\}$ of an evaluation case was set in two ways: a) r was set to 1 if the rating was greater or equal than 7, taking into account that the average ratings of all users (*community*) in the movie and music domains were 7.26 and 7.48, respectively; and b) r was set to 1 if the rating was greater or equal than the target *user*'s average rating.

4.1   Analysis of Contextualized User Preferences in the Movie Domain

Table 2 depicts the distribution of contextualized movie preferences of the users who participated in our study. The table relates the considered 20 movie genres with the time and social companion contexts. Each cell in the table has a numeric value that is the number of users who liked (i.e., assigned a rating greater or equal to 7) a movie belonging to the corresponding genre in a particular context, discarding cases in which a movie genre was preferred by only one user in the given context. The green/red arrows indicate the most/least liked movies in work and weekend days. The circles reflect the relative popularity of the genres in the *time of the day* (morning/afternoon/night) context.

From the table, interesting observations can be made. Regarding the *day of the week* context, comedy, adventure and fantasy movies are watched in any day, showing the users' majority like for movies evoking positive emotions. In contrast,

---

[1] Online evaluation tool, http://ir.ii.uam.es/emotions

science-fiction, futuristic and thriller genres are preferred in work days, and family and romance genres are preferred in the weekends (when kids, couples and whole families tend to watch movies together at home or at the cinema). This may mean that people tend to like tense, brainy and sophisticated movies in the work days, and more calm, easy-going and emotional movies in the weekends. Regarding the *time of the day* context, some genres show quite significant differences. Science-fiction and thriller movies are preferred in the morning and afternoon; action and drama movies, in the afternoon; and adventure, musical and romance movies, at night. Finally, regarding the *social companion* context, it is worth noting that the users preferred to watch movies alone in work days, while seem to watch movies with relatives and friends in the weekends. This may be of special interest in the design of time-aware group recommender systems.

Table 2. Summary of the users' preference distribution for movie genres in the considered time and social companion contexts

MOVIES	action	adventure	animation	comedy	crime	drama	family	fantasy	futuristic	historical	horror	melodrama	musical	mystery	neo noir	parody	romance	sci-fi	thriller	war
Work day	⇒	⇑	⇒	⇑	⇓	⇒	⇒	⇑	⇒	⇓	⇓	⇓	⇓	⇓	⇓	⇓	⇓	⇑	⇒	⇓
Morning	◑	●	◑	◕	○	◔	◑	●	◑	○	○	○	○	○	○	○	○	●	◔	○
Alone	39	58	27	41	2	18	28	48	28	2	5	4	4	7	6	5	12	52	20	4
With my partner	3	3	2	2			2											2		
With my family		11	8	12			10	11									2	4		
With friends		2		3				3	4							2		6	3	
Afternoon	◕	◑	○	◕	◕	◑	○	◑	◕	○	○		○	◕	○		○	●	◕	
Alone	15	20	5	9	11	20	3	18	18		3		2	12	5		4	30	18	
With my partner	4	2		2			4	6	3								6	4		
With my family	5	4	3	3	2	3	3	3												3
With friends	6	2			5			3	9	2	2			4	3			12	11	
Night	◔	●	◑	◕			○	●	●				○	○			○	○	○	
Alone	6	10	5	6		4	8	11					3	2				2	5	
With my partner				2													2			
With my family		8	6	7			8	8									3	3		
With friends		2		2			2	2												
Weekend day	⇒	⇑	⇒	⇑	⇓	⇓	⇑	⇑	⇓	⇓	⇓	⇓	⇓	⇓	⇓	⇓	⇒	⇓	⇓	⇓
Morning	○	●			○		◕	○	○											
Alone	2	3					3													
With my family		2		2			2	2												
Afternoon	●	●	◕	◕	○	◕	◕	◕	◑	○	○		○	○	○	○	◕	◕	◑	○
Alone	7	9	2	3		6	2	7	5	3	2						2	7	3	3
With my partner	17	18	4	11	2	5	3	16	10	4	5		3	4		2	6	12	8	3
With my family	5	10	6	7			6	6	2								6			
With friends	5	5		6	5	4		4	3					2	2		7	4	7	
Night	○	●	◑	◕	○	○	●	●	○	○		○	◕	○		○	◕	○	○	○
Alone	7	16	6	6		8	8	13	2	6		3	3	2			3	4		6
With my partner	7	30	28	26	2		30	25					10			4	12	3	2	
With my family	4	50	36	43		6	50	45	3	4		4	15			9	18	6		2
With friends		4	3	3			3	4									2	4		

4.2   Analysis of Contextualized User Preferences in the Music Domain

Analogously to Table 2 for the movie domain, Table 3 depicts the distribution of contextualized music preferences of the users who participated in our study. The table relates the considered 20 music genres with the time and location contexts. The meaning of numeric values, arrows and circles is the same as in Table 2.

In the music domain, we can make the following observations. Regarding the *day of the week* context, it can be seen that people stated their music preferences mostly for work days. The diversity of liked music genres is also higher in work days than in the weekends, when 80s-90s, electronic, rock, pop and Latin (American) music genres are the most preferred. Regarding the *time of the day* context, as one may expect, people mostly prefer listen to music during the morning (in work days, at work), and during the afternoon (in the weekends, at home). In general, for a particular music genre, and without taking the listening frequencies into account, no significant preference differences are observed among day time periods. Finally, regarding the *location* context, apart from the fact that people tend to listen to music at work in work days, and at home in the weekends, we could highlight that at a bar/disco, people prefer listening to indie, pop and rock music than other music genres.

Table 3. Summary of the users' preference distribution for music genres in the considered tim and location contexts

MUSIC	60s	70s	80s	90s	acoustic	ambient	blues	classical	electronic	folk	hip hop	indie	jazz	latin	metal	pop	punk	rnb	rock	soul
Work day	⇓	⇒	⇒	⇒	⇓	⇓	⇓	⇓	⇓	⇓	⇓	⇒	⇓	⇓	⇓	⇑	⇓	⇓	⇑	⇓
Morning	○	◑	◑	●	○	○	○	○	○	○	○	◑	○	◑	○	●	○	○	●	○
At home			3	3											2	6	2		6	
At work	7	26	36	39	4	11	15	5	12	2	5	26	5	21	12	61	3	3	60	7
At the car/bus		2	5	5		3			3			3				8		3	4	
At the bar/disco	2		3	7	2	2			6	3		4				9		3	7	
Afternoon	○	◑	○				◑		○			○		○		◑			●	
At home			2												2	2			3	
At work		2						2								3			3	
At the bar/disco	2	4							3			2		3		3			7	
Night	○	○	○				○		○			●	○			◑			●	◑
At work		2										2				2			2	2
At the car/bus												2							2	
At the bar/disco			3	3					2			2		4	2	4			4	2
Weekend day	⇓	⇒	⇑		⇓				⇒		⇓	⇓		⇓		⇑		⇓	⇒	⇓
Afternoon	○	◑	●		○				◑		○	○		◑		●		○	◑	○
At home		5	23	34	7				18		3	3		12		35		7	21	3
At work																2			2	
At the bar/disco					2				2			3				3			3	
Night			○	◑								◑				●			◑	
At the bar/disco			2	3								3				5			4	

5   Evaluating Contextualized Recommendations

In this section we report results from an offline evaluation of a number of machine learning algorithms –namely Naïve Bayes, Random forest, Multilayer Perceptron (MLP), and Support Vector Machine (SVM) classifiers– built with user (movie/music) genre preferences, item (movie/music) genres, and (time, location, social companion) context values integrated by the contextual modeling approach presented in Section 3.

The classifiers were built with patterns associated to user-item preference relations. The attributes of a pattern corresponded to a user's favorite genres, an item's genres, and, in some configurations, the time and/or location/social companion context of the user-item preference relation. The pattern's class label was 1 if the user "liked" the item in the given context, and 0 otherwise, where "liked" means the user assigned to the item a rating equal or greater than 7 (*community average*), or a rating greater or equal than the user's average rating (*user average*).

The tables of this section show the best average (10-fold cross validation) performance values of the classifiers for the distinct user profile types. As commonly done in machine learning, we computed accuracy (percentage of patterns correctly classified) as the main measure for recommendation performance. Additionally, in order to take the pattern's class distribution into account, we also computed the geometric mean $g = \sqrt{acc^+ \cdot acc^-}$ (being acc^+ and acc^- the accuracy values on the majority/like and minority/dislike classes respectively), and the Area Under the ROC Curve (AUC).

5.1 Evaluation of Contextualized Recommendations in the Movie Domain

Table 4 shows the performance results of the recommendation models for the different user profile types in the movie domain. It can be seen that in general incorporating contextual information into the classifiers improves the overall acc and g values. In this case, the time context was the most influential to obtain better performance, and Random Forest was the best performing algorithm.

Table 4. Performance values of the model-based recommender systems built with the different user profile types (attribute configurations) in the movie domain. Global top values are in bold, and best values for each profile type are underlined.

Profile type	Classifier	Community average					User average				
		acc	acc+	acc-	g	AUC	acc	acc+	acc-	g	AUC
-	*Majority class*	71.4	100.0	0.0	0.0	49.3	57.2	100.0	0.0	0.0	49.2
genres	*Naïve Bayes*	73.6	96.3	16.8	40.2	62.8	54.8	83.6	16.3	36.9	50.8
	Random forest	76.9	90.6	42.9	62.3	71.9	59.6	68.5	47.8	57.2	60.7
	MLP	73.3	91.6	27.7	50.4	67.1	53.4	60.5	43.8	51.5	52.1
	SVM	70.4	82.2	41.2	58.2	61.7	55.5	75.6	28.7	46.6	52.1
genres + time contexts	*Naïve Bayes*	73.8	96.3	17.6	41.2	63.5	55.5	81.5	20.8	41.2	52.7
	Random forest	77.4	91.2	42.9	62.5	74.5	63.9	70.2	55.6	62.5	66.3
	MLP	74.0	90.9	31.9	53.9	68.5	57.2	62.2	50.6	56.1	58.1
	SVM	70.7	80.5	46.2	61.0	63.3	55.5	74.8	29.8	47.2	52.3
genres + companion context	*Naïve Bayes*	73.3	96.0	16.8	40.2	62.9	53.6	80.3	18.0	38.0	51.0
	Random forest	74.0	89.2	36.1	56.8	70.9	60.1	69.7	47.2	57.4	61.6
	MLP	72.8	90.2	29.4	51.5	66.7	56.0	60.9	49.4	54.9	57.4
	SVM	69.5	79.1	45.4	59.9	62.3	55.0	73.9	29.8	46.9	51.9
genres + all contexts	*Naïve Bayes*	73.8	95.3	20.2	43.8	63.6	54.8	80.3	20.8	40.8	52.6
	Random forest	75.5	90.6	37.8	58.5	73.6	62.3	67.6	55.1	61.0	61.3
	MLP	73.8	89.9	33.6	55.0	68.1	53.8	61.3	43.8	51.8	54.4
	SVM	71.4	81.1	47.1	61.8	64.1	56.0	74.8	30.9	48.1	52.8

5.2   Evaluation of Contextualized Recommendations in the Music Domain

Table 5 shows the performance results of the recommendation models for the different user profile types in the music domain. Similarly to the movie domain, it can be seen that in general incorporating contextual information into the classifiers improves the overall acc and g values. In this case, location context is more influential than time context to obtain better performance, and is the combination of both contextual signals what leads to the best performance. Random Forest is again the algorithm that achieves the highest performance values.

Table 5. Performance values of the model-based recommender systems built with the different user profile types (attribute configurations) in the music domain. Global top values are in bold, and best values for each profile type are underlined.

Profile type	Classifier	Community average					User average				
		acc	acc+	acc-	g	AUC	acc	acc+	acc-	g	AUC
-	*Majority class*	75.9	100.0	0.0	0.0	46.5	56.0	100.0	0.0	0.0	47.6
genres	*Naïve Bayes*	70.7	82.8	32.6	51.9	53.5	50.3	60.7	36.9	47.3	47.2
	Random forest	73.3	85.5	34.8	54.5	58.7	<u>59.2</u>	66.4	50.0	<u>57.6</u>	<u>60.4</u>
	MLP	72.8	83.4	39.1	57.1	60.8	52.9	55.1	50.0	52.5	50.6
	SVM	<u>73.8</u>	83.4	43.5	<u>60.2</u>	<u>63.5</u>	52.9	58.9	45.2	51.6	52.1
genres + time contexts	*Naïve Bayes*	71.7	83.4	34.8	53.9	55.8	53.9	61.7	44.0	52.1	51.0
	Random forest	<u>75.4</u>	87.6	37.0	56.9	<u>69.8</u>	<u>60.7</u>	60.7	60.7	<u>60.7</u>	<u>62.3</u>
	MLP	74.9	83.4	47.8	63.2	68.8	59.7	59.8	59.5	59.7	58.5
	SVM	<u>75.4</u>	83.4	50.0	<u>64.6</u>	66.7	56.5	58.9	53.6	56.2	56.2
genres + location context	*Naïve Bayes*	71.2	82.8	34.8	53.7	54.3	53.9	61.7	44.0	52.1	49.7
	Random forest	<u>75.9</u>	87.6	39.1	58.5	64.2	61.8	65.4	57.1	61.1	61.0
	MLP	74.3	83.4	45.7	61.7	65.4	56.0	58.9	52.4	55.5	57.4
	SVM	74.3	81.4	52.2	<u>65.2</u>	<u>66.8</u>	<u>63.4</u>	63.6	63.1	<u>63.3</u>	<u>63.3</u>
genres + all contexts	*Naïve Bayes*	70.2	81.4	34.8	53.2	56.3	54.5	62.6	44.0	52.5	52.6
	Random forest	**79.6**	90.3	45.7	**64.2**	**74.4**	**63.9**	64.5	63.1	**63.8**	**65.0**
	MLP	76.4	85.5	47.8	64.0	65.3	60.2	64.5	54.8	59.4	59.9
	SVM	77.5	82.8	60.9	71.0	71.8	59.2	61.7	56.0	58.7	58.8

6   Conclusions and Future Work

On realistic context-enriched user preference data in the movie and music domains, we have analyzed the influence of several (isolated and combined) contextual signals –namely time, location and social companion–, and have empirically shown that a proposed contextual modeling approach lets improve the performance of a number of model-based recommender systems.

In the future we should increase the size of the dataset by collecting additional user evaluations. With a larger dataset we could build heuristic-based collaborative filtering strategies, and integrate them with pre- and post-filtering contextualization approaches. As stated by Adomavicius et al. [4], one of the main current challenges on context-aware recommendation is the investigation and comprehension of which contextualization approaches perform better, and under which circumstances.

References

1. Abbar, S., Bouzeghoub, M., Lopez, S.: Context-aware Recommender Systems: A Service-oriented Approach. In: Proceedings of the 3rd International Workshop on Personalized Access, Profile Management, and Context Awareness in Databases (2009)
2. Adomavicius, G., Sankaranarayanan, R., Sen, S., Tuzhilin, A.: Incorporating Contextual Information in Recommender Systems Using a Multidimensional Approach. ACM Transactions on Information Systems 23, 103–145 (2005)
3. Adomavicius, G., Tuzhilin, A.: Toward the Next Generation of Recommender Systems: A Survey of the State-of-the-art and Possible Extensions. IEEE Transactions on Knowledge and Data Engineering 17, 734–749 (2005)
4. Adomavicius, G., Tuzhilin, A.: Context-Aware Recommender Systems. In: Ricci, F., Rokach, L., Shapira, B., Kantor, P.B. (eds.) Recommender Systems Handbook, pp. 217–253. Springer (2011)
5. Baltrunas, L., Ricci, F.: Experimental Evaluation of Context-dependent Collaborative Filtering Using Item Splitting. User Modeling and User-Adapted Interaction (in press)
6. Breese, J., Heckerman, D., Kadie, C.: Empirical Analysis of Predictive Algorithms for Collaborative Filtering. In: Proceedings of the 14th Conference on Uncertainty in Artificial Intelligence, pp. 43–52 (1998)
7. Burke, R.: Hybrid Web Recommender Systems. In: Brusilovsky, P., Kobsa, A., Nejdl, W. (eds.) Adaptive Web 2007. LNCS, vol. 4321, pp. 377–408. Springer, Heidelberg (2007)
8. Dey, A.K.: Understanding and Using Context. Personal and Ubiquitous Computing 5, 4–7 (2001)
9. Gorgoglione, M., Panniello, U., Tuzhilin, A.: The Effect of Context-aware Recommendations on Customer Purchasing Behavior and Trust. In: Proceedings of the 5th ACM Conference Recommender Systems, pp. 85–92 (2011)
10. Karatzoglou, A., Amatriain, X., Baltrunas, L., Oliver, N.: Multiverse Recommendation: N-dimensional Tensor Factorization for Context-aware Collaborative Filtering. In: Proceedings of the 4th ACM Conference on Recommender Systems, pp. 79–86 (2010)
11. Koren, Y.: Collaborative Filtering with Temporal Dynamics. In: Proceedings of the 15th ACM SIGKDD International Conference on Knowledge Discovery and Data Mining, pp. 447–456 (2009)
12. Oku, K., Nakajima, S., Miyazaki, J., Uemura, S.: Context-Aware SVM for Context-Dependent Information Recommendation. In: Proceedings of the 7th International Conference on Mobile Data Management, p. 109 (2006)
13. Panniello, U., Gorgoglione, M.: Incorporating Context into Recommender Systems: An Empirical Comparison of Context-based Approaches. Electronic Commerce Research 12, 1–30 (2012)
14. Panniello, U., Gorgoglione, M., Palmisano, C.: Comparing Pre-filtering and Post-filtering Approach in a Collaborative Contextual Recommender System: An Application to E-commerce. In: Di Noia, T., Buccafurri, F. (eds.) EC-Web 2009. LNCS, vol. 5692, pp. 348–359. Springer, Heidelberg (2009)
15. Panniello, U., Tuzhilin, A.: Experimental Comparison of Pre- vs. Post-filtering Approaches in Context-aware Recommender Systems. In: Proceedings of the 3rd ACM Conference on Recommender Systems, pp. 265–268 (2009)
16. Yu, Z., Zhou, X., Zhang, D., Chin, C.-Y., Wang, X., Men, J.: Supporting Context-Aware Media Recommendations for Smart Phones. IEEE Pervasive Computing 5, 68–75 (2006)

Identifying Overlapping Communities and Their Leading Members in Social Networks

Camilo Palazuelos and Marta Zorrilla

Dept. of Mathematics, Statistics, and Computer Science, University of Cantabria
Avenida de los Castros s/n, 39005, Santander, Spain
{camilo.palazuelos,marta.zorrilla}@unican.es

Abstract. With the recent increasing popularity of social networking services like Facebook and Twitter, community structure has become a problem of considerable interest. Although there are more than a hundred algorithms that find communities in networks, only a few are able to detect *overlapping* communities, and an even smaller number of them follow an approach based on the evolution dynamics of these networks. Thus, we present FRINGE, an algorithm for the detection of overlapping communities in networks, which, based on the ideas of friendship and leadership, not only returns the overlapping communities detected, but also specifies their leading members. We describe the algorithm in detail and compare its results with those obtained by CFinder and iLCD for both synthetic and real-life networks. These results show that our proposal behaves well in networks with a clear social hierarchy, as seen in modern social networks.

Keywords: community detection, graph algorithms, overlapping communities, social influence, social networks.

1 Introduction

Various types of complex networks like biological, social, and technological can be effectively modeled as graphs by considering each entity as a vertex and each relationship as an edge. It has been shown that many real-world networks have a community structure that is characterized by groups of densely connected vertices [4]. Although there is not a universally accepted definition, a community is understood as a subgraph whose vertices are more tightly connected to each other than to vertices belonging to other communities [3].

Despite the fact that there is a large amount of algorithms that detect communities appropriately, most of them do not take into account the specific characteristics that social networks present, such as (i) the small-world property, (ii) power-law degree distributions, and (iii) network transitivity. The first shows that the average distance among vertices in a network is short, usually scaling logarithmically with the total number of vertices; the second states that there are typically many vertices in a network with low degree and a small number of them with high degree; finally, the third expresses that two vertices that are

C. Bielza et al. (Eds.): CAEPIA 2013, LNAI 8109, pp. 52–61, 2013.
© Springer-Verlag Berlin Heidelberg 2013

neighbors of the same third vertex are likely to be neighbors. We think that it is necessary to include part of the complexity of these underlying phenomena for the proper detection of groups with similar interests and their leading members in social networks.

Following this idea, we designed and implemented FRINGE (acronym for *FRIendship Networks with General Elements*), an algorithm for the discovery of overlapping communities, which is based on the intuitive idea of friendship among members of a community in which some of them act as leaders of the group. A modified version of FRINGE was used for measuring the correlation between the popularity of the set of photos uploaded by a user in Flickr and his or her influence [12]. In this paper, we explain FRINGE and compare it with two other algorithms: (i) CFinder and (ii) iLCD. The former is frequently used for testing community detection algorithms [1], whereas the latter is a recent algorithm that follows a social approach different from ours [2]. We test these algorithms with both synthetic and real-life networks. This paper is an updated and extended version of [11].

The paper is organized as follows. In Sect. 2, we review the existing research work related to the detection of overlapping communities in graphs, and, in particular, those applied to social networks. Section 3 defines the concepts and terminology on which the algorithm is based. Section 4 explains in detail the mode of operation of the algorithm. Section 5 gathers the results obtained by FRINGE with both synthetic and real-life networks in comparison to CFinder and iLCD. Finally, Sect. 6 summarizes and draws the most important conclusions of our proposal.

2   Related Work

Detecting communities in complex networks is one of the most interesting and still open problems in the field of network theory. Its application continues to be very useful in disciplines in which systems are represented as graphs. The amount of algorithms developed for community detection has grown since 2002, when Girvan and Newman (GN) proposed their divisive hierarchical algorithm [4]. Nevertheless, most of these algorithms are focused on detecting nonoverlapping communities, so they are not suitable for the detection of communities in social networks (for a comprehensive review article, see [3]).

An adapted version of the GN algorithm for discovering overlapping communities, named CONGA, was proposed by Gregory [5]. It is similar to the GN algorithm, except for the addition of a vertex splitting step that supports overlapping communities. Since the performance of the algorithm was not good, the same author proposed an improved version of his algorithm, called CONGO, based on a local form of betweenness that yields good results and is much faster [6].

CPM is another interesting and well-known algorithm, proposed by Palla et al. [13], for the detection of overlapping communities. CFinder [1] is a fast algorithm based on CPM that locates and visualizes overlapping, densely interconnected groups of vertices in undirected graphs, and allows the user to navigate through the graph and the set of communities detected. This algorithm is used in Sect. 5 for comparing our results to its output.

Regarding algorithms focused on detecting communities in *social* networks, we found the following works, which do not embrace the universal approach based on the optimization of the modularity quality function [4]. The importance of the modularity quality function seems to have recently vanished because of two shortcomings: (i) its resolution limit and (ii) the structural diversity of high-modularity partitions [3]. In short, the former refers to the impossibility of detecting clusters that are comparatively small with respect to the graph as a whole; the latter states that the optimal partition may not coincide with the most intuitive partition. This has led researchers to search for other approaches to the detection of communities, trying to incorporate in their algorithms how these communities are formed and evolve.

Finally, Cazabet et al. [2] proposed a new algorithm for community detection, called iLCD, using a new approach based on two notions: (i) intrinsic nature of communities and (ii) longitudinal detection. The former states that the detection of a community should not be limited to a certain size, i.e., the algorithm can find big and small communities in the same network; the latter aims to gather the dynamics of the network, i.e., the moment when a vertex or an edge is created. Cazabet et al. showed that the results obtained by iLCD are equal to or better than those obtained by CFinder in most cases. This algorithm is used in Sect. 5 for comparing our results with its output.

3   Definitions

3.1   Basic Terminology

Following the same notation as Fortunato [3], a *graph* $G = (V, E)$ is a pair of sets, where V is a set of *vertices* or *nodes* and E is a set of unordered pairs of elements of V, called *edges* or *links*; this type of graph is said to be *undirected*, but if E was a set of ordered pairs of vertices, the graph would be considered to be *directed*. Sometimes, it may be necessary to assign real numbers, i.e., *weights*, to each element of E; this type of graph is said to be *weighted*. Such weights might represent, for example, lengths or capacities. All the graphs in this paper are considered to be undirected, unweighted, and containing no self-loops.

A graph $G' = (V', E')$ is a *subgraph* of $G = (V, E)$ if $V' \subseteq V$ and $E' \subseteq E$. We denote the number of vertices and edges of a graph with n and m, respectively. The *density* of a graph G is defined as

$$\rho_G = \frac{2m}{n(n-1)} \ . \tag{1}$$

Since the maximum number of edges is $n(n-1)/2$, the maximal density of a graph is 1, whereas the minimal density is 0. Two vertices are *neighbors* if they are connected by an edge. The set of neighbors Γ_v of a vertex v is called *neighborhood*. The *degree* k_v of a vertex v is the number of its neighbors.

3.2   Extended Degree and General Elements

The *extended degree* of a vertex in a graph is a centrality measure—proposed by the authors of this paper—that aims to estimate the impact of a member in a social network by taking into consideration not only its direct neighbors, but also the neighbors of these. Generally, in social networks, people with more connections, i.e., with greater degree, are influential, but if the connections with other neighbors were taken into account, the prominence of these neighbors might be better modeled.

Thus, the extended degree k_v^+ of a vertex v is the number of edges attached to it plus the number of edges attached to each of its neighbors. In mathematical terms, it is defined as

$$k_v^+ = k_v + \sum_{w \in \Gamma_v} k_w \ . \tag{2}$$

The *leading member* of a community is the vertex that has the greatest extended degree among the vertices belonging to that community; it is precisely the most important member in a community. A *first-order friend* in a community is a vertex that connects directly to the leading member of that community, whereas an *nth-order friend* is a vertex whose minimum distance to the leading member equals $n \geq 2$, running only through the vertices belonging to that leading member's community.

3.3   Community

There is no universally accepted definition of community beyond the notion that there must be more internal than external edges in the community [3]. As a matter of fact, it strongly depends on the context of the phenomenon under study. Most algorithms developed for the identification of communities in graphs have their own definition, which makes it even more difficult to establish a formal definition of community. As a consequence, some researchers focused their work on establishing common features that held the members of a community together. We pay attention to the works of Wasserman and Faust [14], and Moody and White [10], and redefine the definition of community with their criteria.

Our notion of community is based on the intuitive idea of friendship among members of current social networking services like Facebook and Twitter, and the concept of leadership of some members, as seen in some classical networks in the scientific literature, e.g., Zachary karate club [15]. Thus, a community A detected by this version of the algorithm must be at least composed of a leading member, all vertices connecting directly to it, i.e. its first-order friends, and any nth-order friend v, $\forall n \geq 2$, that satisfies the following condition

$$\left| \bigcup_{C \in \mathcal{C}} \Gamma_v^C \right| - \max_{C \in \mathcal{C}} \left\{ |\Gamma_v^C| \right\} \geq \max_{C \in \mathcal{C}} \left\{ |\Gamma_v^C| \right\} - |\Gamma_v^A| \ , \tag{3}$$

where $\left| \bigcup_{C \in \mathcal{C}} \Gamma_v^C \right|$ is the number of neighbors of the vertex v already classified in any community (from first- to $(n-1)$th-order friends), $\mathcal{C}$ is the set of identified communities, $\max_{C \in \mathcal{C}} \left\{ \left| \Gamma_v^C \right| \right\}$ is the maximum value of the number of neighbors of the vertex v in each community of $\mathcal{C}$, and $\left| \Gamma_v^A \right|$ is the number of neighbors of the vertex v belonging to A, which is the community under study.

Two interesting criteria for subgraph cohesion by Wasserman and Faust are complete mutuality and reachability. Complete mutuality states that communities are defined as subgraphs whose vertices are all adjacent to each other—cliques in graph terms. However, this is a very strict definition of community. The other criterium, reachability, makes it possible to lessen the notion of clique and introduces a similar structure: k-cliques. A k-clique is a maximal subgraph such that the distance of each pair of its vertices is not larger than k. Let n be the largest minimum distance from an nth-order friend to the leading member, then our communities are always $2n$-cliques.

In [10], one useful feature of community arises. It states that the elimination of a member cannot dissolve the community. This restriction is true for our definition of community, except for the removal of leading members, which are the glue that binds communities together. Thus, we permit the removal of any member of a community, except for its leading member, which ensures that the definition of reachability above is satisfied. According to Fortunato [3], "a required property of a community is connectedness. We expect that, for C to be a community, there must be a path between each pair of its vertices, running only through vertices of C," which is true for our definition of community.

Thus, we define a community as a subgraph that meets the constraints of reachability, connectedness and nondissolution of the community when removing a vertex—except for its leading member—and highlight the importance of leading members and their neighbors in our intuitive approach based on leadership.

4   FRINGE

The FRINGE algorithm runs in four steps. The first step consists in detecting the initial set of communities, the second classifies first-order friends, the third classifies nth-order friends according to (3), and the fourth checks if any community is a subset of any of the rest and, if so, merges them. For a deeper understanding of the algorithm, a description of each step is provided.

The first question that must be clarified by the algorithm is, given a graph, how many communities are required to classify all its vertices? Since this information is not known in advance, this first phase of the algorithm is to identify the initial set of communities in which to classify vertices of the graph. Before any other operation is performed by the algorithm, all vertices must be arranged into a list L from largest to smallest extended degree. Since we want to detect at least two communities, the first two vertices in L are automatically selected to be the leading members of two different communities to form the initial set of communities $\mathcal{C}$; note that if these two vertices actually belonged to the same community, the last phase of the algorithm would eventually classify them into a sole community. Intuition says that if subsequent vertices in L want to be considered as leading members of new communities, the difference in extended degree between the last vertex selected and the candidate to be the leading member of a new community should be less than or equal to the difference in extended degree between the last two vertices selected. In mathematical terms, it is

$$k_{\ell_{i-2}}^+ - k_{\ell_{i-1}}^+ \geq k_{\ell_{i-1}}^+ - k_{\ell_i}^+ \ , \tag{4}$$

where ℓ_i is the current candidate to be the leading member of a new community, and ℓ_{i-1} and ℓ_{i-2} are the last two vertices selected as leading members. However, this is a very strict condition, hence we shall try to apply a more optimistic approach to the aforementioned condition. Thus, the authors of this paper introduce the concept of *restriction factor* of a graph as the factor to be applied to the left-hand side of (4) in order to make it easier to meet the condition. In mathematical terms, the restriction factor of a graph G is defined as

$$R_G = 2 - \rho_G \ , \tag{5}$$

where ρ_G is the density of G. For dense graphs (e.g., cliques), in which the extended degree of all vertices is very similar, i.e., it is not crucial to lessen the strictness of (4), the restriction factor is close to 1—since the density of dense graphs is very close to 1—and barely has effect. On the other hand, for sparse graphs (e.g., most social networks), in which the extended degree of all vertices is quite different, the restriction factor is closer to 2 than to 1—since the density of sparse graphs is close to 0—and makes it easier to meet the condition. Thus, the right condition to be met for every vertex to be considered as the leading member of a new community is defined as

$$\left\lfloor \left(k_{\ell_{i-2}}^+ - k_{\ell_{i-1}}^+ \right) R_G \right\rfloor + 1 \geq k_{\ell_{i-1}}^+ - k_{\ell_i}^+ \ . \tag{6}$$

After calculating the initial set of communities $\mathcal{C}$, the algorithm is able to classify first-order friends. For each vertex v of the graph (except for vertices already considered to be leading members), the algorithm classifies v into the communities in $\mathcal{C}$ in which v connects directly to the leading members.

For each vertex v that remains unclassified, the algorithm classifies v into the communities in $\mathcal{C}$ in which v satisfies (3). This is an iterative process that does not stop while there is a vertex that remains unclassified and the number of unclassified vertices after the ith iteration is smaller than the number after the $(i-1)$th iteration, which does not ensure that all vertices are classified into, at least, one community at the end of this step.

The last phase performed by the algorithm consists in finding all possible subsets among the communities in $\mathcal{C}$. For each community A, the algorithm checks if all its members belong to another larger community B, i.e., if A is a subgraph of B, and, if so, merges them.

The computational complexity of the algorithm is O $\left(u^2 \langle k \rangle \right)$, which highly depends on two factors: (i) the average degree $\langle k \rangle$ of the graph and (ii) the number of vertices that remain unclassified after the second phase of the algorithm, whose impact on the computational complexity is much deeper than the former's because $\langle k \rangle \ll n$ for sparse graphs, e.g., social networks.

5   Experimental Results

When a new method for the detection of communities is proposed, it is paramount to test its performance and compare it to other algorithms. In this section, we study the effectiveness of our proposal with both synthetic and real-life networks, for which the communities to be detected are known in advance, comparing FRINGE results to those obtained by CFinder and iLCD.

5.1   Synthetic Networks

Currently, one of the most acclaimed works published on the issue of comparing community detection algorithms is the paper written by Lancichinetti and For-tunato [7], in which they introduced an extension to the original version of their LFR benchmark [8] for directed and weighted graphs with overlapping commu-nities. Given a graph generated by the LFR benchmark, every vertex shares a fraction $1 - \mu$ of its edges with the other vertices of its community and a frac-tion μ with the vertices of the other communities, being μ the so-called mixing parameter. If $\mu \leq 0.5$, then the number of neighbors of every vertex inside its community is higher than or equal to the number of its neighbors belonging to other communities. The smaller μ is, the clearer the leadership hierarchy of the graph is. Therefore, FRINGE should recover most of the community structure of the graph for small values of μ.

The networks for this case study were generated using the LFR benchmark. These consist of 512 vertices, i.e., medium-sized networks, where every vertex has an average degree of 16 and a maximum degree of 64. In order to compare FRINGE to CFinder and iLCD, two different scenarios were established: (i) one in which the mixing parameter varies and (ii) another in which the density of the graph is varied. In the first case, 60 different networks were generated for values of μ ranging from 0 to 0.5, i.e., 10 different networks for each value of μ, adding 0.1 to μ in each step. In the second case, 40 different networks were generated for values of density ranging from 0.1 to 0.4, i.e., 10 different networks for each value of density, adding 0.1 to density in each step.

Normalized mutual information was the measure chosen to indicate the simi-larity between real partitions and those detected by the algorithms under study. In [7], an extension to normalized mutual information for overlapping communi-ties was presented, which is used in this case study. Once the normalized mutual information value of every network generated is calculated, the *best* value of all the networks with either the same mixing parameter or the same density—depending on the parameter to be represented—is chosen.

Figure 1 depicts normalized mutual information values when the mixing pa-rameter μ increases from 0 to 0.5. The figure indicates that FRINGE is able to recover almost 80% of the community structure for very low values of μ, i.e., for networks with a very clear leadership hierarchy. Furthermore, it shows that FRINGE results are slightly better than those obtained by CFinder and iLCD in most cases. As can also be seen in Fig. 1, the higher the density is, the better defined communities are. In this case, FRINGE provides better results than both

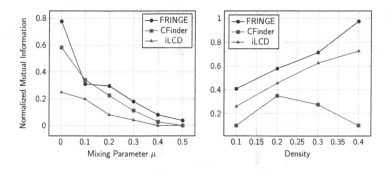

Fig. 1. Comparison of FRINGE, CFinder, and iLCD with synthetic networks

CFinder and iLCD in all cases. Note that the mixing parameter value chosen to measure the normalized mutual information when the density of the network is varied is a very low value, i.e., close to 0. This value is chosen because communities detected in social networks usually are formed by a relatively small number of members with a dense network of connections between them.

5.2 Real-Life Networks

As in other scientific disciplines, there are some experimental results that are considered to be reliable for measuring the effectiveness of the methods developed in the field of community detection. We now show the application of FRINGE on three real-life networks: (i) Zachary karate club, (ii) Bottlenose dolphins, and (iii) American college football.

Zachary karate club [15] is classically used as a standard benchmark in community detection. This network shows 78 social ties between 34 members of a karate club at an American university in the 1970s. Accidentally, the administrator and the instructor had an unpleasant argument, and as a consequence, the club eventually split into two smaller groups, centered on the administrator and the instructor, respectively. For this network, four overlapping communities were detected by FRINGE, with vertices 1, 34, 3, and 33 as leading members.

Bottlenose dolphins [9] describes the 159 associations between 62 dolphins living in Doubtful Sound (New Zealand) compiled by Lusseau et al. after seven years of research. This network can be split naturally into two groups. For this network, two overlapping communities are detected by FRINGE, with dolphins called Grin and SN4 as leading members.

The number of communities detected by FRINGE for the two networks above matches those reported by Lancichinetti and Fortunato in [7], whose algorithm optimizes the modularity quality function, though their communities do not include exactly the same members detected by FRINGE.

Finally, American college football [4] is also used as a standard benchmark for community detection. This network represents the Division I games during the 2000 season, where nodes denote football teams and edges show season games. The teams can be split into 12 conferences. The network consists of 115 vertices and 616 edges. For this network, eight overlapping communities are detected by FRINGE. To the best of our knowledge, this network has not been used for testing overlapping community detection algorithms.

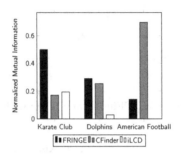

Fig. 2. Comparison of FRINGE, CFinder, and iLCD with real-life networks

To conclude, Figure 2 shows the good performance of FRINGE with Zachary karate club, which has a clear leadership hierarchy, as well as the bad performance with American college football, which is a perfect example of a network with vertices with similar *influence*, i.e., vertices with similar extended degrees, where clique-based algorithms like CFinder gather very good results. Furthermore, the bad results showed by iLCD seem to confirm that the algorithm does not work properly with small and medium-sized networks.

6   Conclusions

The aim of this paper was to provide a new algorithm, called FRINGE, for the detection of overlapping communities and the identification of their leading members in social networks. Unlike most techniques based on the optimization of the modularity quality function, FRINGE is based on the intuitive idea of friendship among members of current social networking services and the concept of leadership of some of these members.

To evaluate our proposal, we compared FRINGE to CFinder, a well-known algorithm widely used in the literature, and iLCD, a recent algorithm that follows a social approach different from ours. The experimentation performed showed that FRINGE adequately works on networks with a clear leadership hierarchy, obtaining better results than those gathered by CFinder and iLCD in most cases.

Currently, FRINGE works with undirected and unweighted graphs, but future research shall aim to update the algorithm in order for the detection of overlapping communities in all types of graphs. Since FRINGE is focused on social networks, we wish to extend it to be able to identify leadership hierarchies according to the actions that leaders perform in these social networks and the moment when these actions are carried out.

Acknowledgments. This work is partially supported by the Ministry of Education, Culture, and Sport of the Government of Spain, under grant Beca de colaboración (2012–2013).

References

1. Adamcsek, B., Palla, G., Farkas, I., Derényi, I., Vicsek, T.: CFinder: Locating Cliques and Overlapping Modules in Biological Networks. Bioinformatics 22(8), 1021–1023 (2006)
2. Cazabet, R., Amblard, F., Hanachi, C.: Detection of Overlapping Communities in Dynamical Social Networks. In: Proceedings of the 2nd IEEE International Conference on Social Computing, pp. 309–314 (2010)
3. Fortunato, S.: Community Detection in Graphs. Physics Reports 486(3-5), 75–174 (2010)
4. Girvan, M., Newman, M.: Community Structure in Social and Biological Networks. Proceedings of the National Academy of Sciences 99(12), 7821 (2002)
5. Gregory, S.: An Algorithm to Find Overlapping Community Structure in Networks. In: Kok, J.N., Koronacki, J., Lopez de Mantaras, R., Matwin, S., Mladenič, D., Skowron, A. (eds.) PKDD 2007. LNCS (LNAI), vol. 4702, pp. 91–102. Springer, Heidelberg (2007)
6. Gregory, S.: A Fast Algorithm to Find Overlapping Communities in Networks. In: Daelemans, W., Goethals, B., Morik, K. (eds.) ECML PKDD 2008, Part I. LNCS (LNAI), vol. 5211, pp. 408–423. Springer, Heidelberg (2008)
7. Lancichinetti, A., Fortunato, S.: Benchmarks for Testing Community Detection Algorithms on Directed and Weighted Graphs with Overlapping Communities. Physical Review E 80(1), 016118 (2009)
8. Lancichinetti, A., Fortunato, S., Radicchi, F.: Benchmark Graphs for Testing Community Detection Algorithms. Physical Review E 78(4), 046110 (2008)
9. Lusseau, D., Schneider, K., Boisseau, O., Haase, P., Slooten, E., Dawson, S.: The Bottlenose Dolphin Community of Doubtful Sound Features a Large Proportion of Long-lasting Associations. Behavioral Ecology and Sociobiology 54(4), 396–405 (2003)
10. Moody, J., White, D.: Structural Cohesion and Embeddedness: A Hierarchical Concept of Social Groups. American Sociological Review 68, 103–127 (2003)
11. Palazuelos, C., Zorrilla, M.: FRINGE: A New Approach to the Detection of Overlapping Communities in Graphs. In: Murgante, B., Gervasi, O., Iglesias, A., Taniar, D., Apduhan, B.O. (eds.) ICCSA 2011, Part III. LNCS, vol. 6784, pp. 638–653. Springer, Heidelberg (2011)
12. Palazuelos, C., Zorrilla, M.: Analysis of Social Metrics in Dynamic Networks: Measuring the Influence with FRINGE. In: Proceedings of the 2012 EDBT/ICDT Workshops, pp. 9–12 (2012)
13. Palla, G., Derényi, I., Farkas, I., Vicsek, T.: Uncovering the Overlapping Community Structure of Complex Networks in Nature and Society. Nature 435(7043), 814–818 (2005)
14. Wasserman, S., Faust, K.: Social Network Analysis: Methods and Applications. Structural Analysis in the Social Sciences. Cambridge University Press (1994)
15. Zachary, W.: An Information Flow Model for Conflict and Fission in Small Groups. Journal of Anthropological Research 33(4), 452–473 (1977)

Permutability of Fuzzy Consequence Operators and Fuzzy Interior Operators

Neus Carmona[1], Jorge Elorza[1], Jordi Recasens[2], and Jean Bragard[1]

[1] Departamento de Física y Matemática Aplicada,
Facultad de Ciencias, Universidad de Navarra, Pamplona, Spain
ncarmona@alumni.unav.es, {jelorza,jbragard}@unav.es
[2] Secció Matemàtiques i Informàtica, ETS Arquitectura del Vallès,
Universitat Politècnica de Catalunya, Sant Cugat del Vallès, Spain
j.recasens@upc.edu

Abstract. In this paper we study the permutability of the composition of fuzzy consequence operators (fuzzy closings) and fuzzy interior operators (fuzzy openings). We establish several characterizations and we show the relation of permutability with the fuzzy closure and fuzzy interior of a fuzzy operator. We also study the connection between permutability and the preservation of the operator type through the composition. More precisely, when the composition of two openings is an opening and the composition of two closings is a closing.

Keywords: Permutability, Fuzzy closing, Fuzzy Consequence Operator, Fuzzy Opening, Fuzzy Interior Operator.

1 Introduction

Composition of fuzzy operators often appears in fields like fuzzy mathematical morphology or approximate reasoning. These two fields are closely related and several results can be transfered from one field to the other [6].

In fuzzy mathematical morphology, fuzzy closings and openings act as morphological filters used for image processing [3,4]. These operators and their generalization to algebraic fuzzy closings and openings (which do not necessary need a structuring element) have been extensively studied in several contexts [2,7,10]. It seems natural to ask about the permutation of the usual composition of these operators, that is when the order of application does not change the result.

In approximate reasoning, fuzzy closings are called fuzzy consequence operators and they play the role of deriving consequences from certain premises and relations [5,8]. Fuzzy interior operators (fuzzy openings) appear as a dual notion of fuzzy consequence operators in the lattice of truth values [1]. Therefore, it is also natural in this context to wonder when these operators permute. Permutability of fuzzy indistinguibility relations, which are closely related to fuzzy interior and consequence operators, has already been studied [9]. The aim of this paper is the study of the permutability of fuzzy consequence operators (fuzzy closings) and fuzzy interior operators (fuzzy openings). We will work in the chain $[0,1]$, but all the results still hold if $[0,1]$ is replaced by any complete lattice L.

C. Bielza et al. (Eds.): CAEPIA 2013, LNAI 8109, pp. 62–69, 2013.

In Section 2 we recall the main definitions and results that will be used throughout the paper. In Section 3 we study the permutability of fuzzy consequence operators. In Section 4 we study the dual case of the permutability of fuzzy interior operators. Finally, in Section 5 we present the conclusions.

2 Preliminaries

In this paper, X will denote a non-empty classical universal set, $[0,1]^X$ will be the set of all fuzzy subsets of X and Ω' the set of fuzzy operators defined from $[0,1]^X$ to $[0,1]^X$.

Definition 1. *[8] A fuzzy operator $C \in \Omega'$ is called a **fuzzy consequence operator** (FCO for short) or **fuzzy closing** when it satisfies for all $\mu, \nu \in [0,1]^X$:*

1. *Inclusion $\mu \subseteq C(\mu)$*
2. *Monotonicity $\mu \subseteq \nu \Rightarrow C(\mu) \subseteq C(\nu)$*
3. *Idempotence $C(C(\mu)) = C(\mu)$*

Ω *will denote the set of all fuzzy consequence operators of $[0,1]^X$.*

The inclusion of fuzzy subsets is given by the pointwise order, i.e. $\mu \subseteq \nu$ if and only if $\mu(x) \leq \nu(x)$ for all $x \in X$.

Given two fuzzy operators C_1, C_2 we say that $C_1 \leq C_2$ if $C_1(\mu) \subseteq C_2(\mu)$ for all $\mu \in [0,1]^X$.

Definition 2. *[1] A fuzzy operator $C \in \Omega'$ is called a **fuzzy interior operator** (FIO for short) or **fuzzy opening** when it satisfies for all $\mu, \nu \in [0,1]^X$:*

1. *Antiinclusion $C(\mu) \subseteq \mu$*
2. *Monotonicity $\mu \subseteq \nu \Rightarrow C(\mu) \subseteq C(\nu)$*
3. *Idempotence $C(C(\mu)) = C(\mu)$*

Λ *will denote the set of all fuzzy interior operators of $[0,1]^X$.*

In the mathematical morphology context, properties 1 from Definitions 1 and 2 are usually called extensive and anti-extensive properties respectively.

For any fuzzy operator C, one can define the smallest FCO which is greater than or equal to C and the greatest FIO which is smaller than or equal to C.

Definition 3. *Let $C : [0,1]^X \longrightarrow [0,1]^X$ be a fuzzy operator. We define the **fuzzy closure** $\overline{C}$ of C as the fuzzy operator given by*

$$\overline{C} = \inf_{\substack{\phi \in \Omega \\ C \leq \phi}} \{\phi\} . \tag{1}$$

Note that the fuzzy closure is actually a fuzzy consequence operator. This property derives from the fact that the infimum of FCO is also a fuzzy consequence operator.

Definition 4. *Let* $C : [0,1]^X \longrightarrow [0,1]^X$ *be a fuzzy operator. We define the **fuzzy interior** $\overset{\circ}{C}$ of* C *as the fuzzy operator given by*

$$\overset{\circ}{C} = \sup_{\substack{\phi \in \Lambda \\ C \geq \phi}} \{\phi\} . \qquad (2)$$

Note that the fuzzy interior of a fuzzy operator is actually a fuzzy interior operator, since the supremum of FIO is also a fuzzy interior operator.

Using the usual composition, one can define the power of a fuzzy operator.

Definition 5. *Let* $C : [0,1]^X \longrightarrow [0,1]^X$ *be a fuzzy operator. We define* C^k *for* $k \in \mathbb{N}$ *as the fuzzy operator defined recursively as:*

$C^1 = C$ *i.e.* $C^1(\mu)(x) = C(\mu)(x)$ $\forall \mu \in [0,1]^X$ *and* $\forall x \in X.$
$C^k = C(C^{k-1})$ *i.e.* $C^k(\mu)(x) = C(C^{k-1}(\mu))(x)$ $\forall \mu \in [0,1]^X$, $\forall x \in X$ *and* $k \geq 2.$

That is, C^k *is the usual composition of the operator* C *with itself* k *times.*

To study the permutability of fuzzy consequence operators and fuzzy interior operators, we need some previous results about the properties of C^k. The following lemmas are easy to prove.

Lemma 1. *Let* $C : [0,1]^X \longrightarrow [0,1]^X$ *be a fuzzy operator. If* C *is inclusive, then* C^k *is inclusive for all* $k \in \mathbb{N}.$

Lemma 2. *Let* $C : [0,1]^X \longrightarrow [0,1]^X$ *be a fuzzy operator. If* C *is antiinclusive, then* C^k *is antiinclusive for all* $k \in \mathbb{N}.$

Lemma 3. *Let* $C : [0,1]^X \longrightarrow [0,1]^X$ *be a fuzzy operator. If* C *is monotone, then* C^k *is monotone for all* $k \in \mathbb{N}.$

3   Permutability of Fuzzy Consequence Operators

Consider the sequence of fuzzy operators given by $\{C^k\}_{k \in \mathbb{N}}$. It directly follows that if C is inclusive, the sequence is increasing.

Proposition 1. *Let* $C : [0,1]^X \longrightarrow [0,1]^X$ *be a fuzzy operator. If* C *is inclusive, then the sequence* $\{C^k\}_{k \in \mathbb{N}}$ *is increasing and convergent. That is,* $C^k \leq C^{k+1}$ *for all* $k \in \mathbb{N}$ *and there exists a fuzzy operator* $U \in \Omega'$ *such that* $U = \lim_{n \in \mathbb{N}} C^n.$

Proof. Since 1 is an upper bound for $C^k(\mu)(x)$ for all $\mu \in [0,1]^X$, all $x \in X$ and all $k \in \mathbb{N}$, the sequences $\{C^k(\mu)(x)\}_{k \in \mathbb{N}}$ are increasing and bounded, thus they converge. Hence, the limit operator exists and it is defined by

$$U(\mu)(x) = \lim_{n \to \infty} C^n(\mu)(x) . \qquad (3)$$

$\square$

Remark 1. Note that in this case, $U = \lim_{n \to \infty} C^n = \sup_{n \in \mathbb{N}} C^n$.

Theorem 1. *Let $C : [0,1]^X \longrightarrow [0,1]^X$ be an inclusive and monotone fuzzy operator. Then, $\lim_{n \to \infty} C^n = \overline{C}$.*

Proof. To show that $\lim_{n \to \infty} C^n \leq \overline{C}$ we shall prove that $C^k \leq \overline{C}$ for all $k \in \mathbb{N}$ by induction on k.

- For $k = 1$ it is clear that $C \leq \overline{C}$.
- Assume that $C^k \leq \overline{C}$ for a certain k. Then, $C^k(\mu) \subseteq \overline{C}(\mu)$ for all $\mu \in [0,1]^X$. Since $C \leq \overline{C}$ and $\overline{C}$ is monotone and idempotent, it follows that

$$C(C^k(\mu)) \subseteq \overline{C}(C^k(\mu)) \subseteq \overline{C}(\overline{C}(\mu)) = \overline{C}(\mu) .$$

Since $C^n \leq \overline{C}$ for all $n \in \mathbb{N}$, it follows that $\lim_{n \in \mathbb{N}} C^n \leq \overline{C}$.

To prove that $\lim_{n \to \infty} C^n \geq \overline{C}$ let us show that $\lim_{n \to \infty} C^n$ is a closure operator. Since C is inclusive and monotone, Lemmas 1 and 3 ensure the inclusion and monotonicity of $\lim_{n \to \infty} C^n$. For the idempontence, it is straightforward that

$$\lim_{n \to \infty} C^n (\lim_{n \to \infty} C^n(\mu))(x) = \lim_{n \to \infty} C^n(\mu)(x) .$$

Therefore, $\lim_{n \to \infty} C^n = \sup_{n \in \mathbb{N}} C^n = \overline{C}$. □

Let us recall the definition of permutability of fuzzy operators:

Definition 6. *Let C, C' be fuzzy operators. We say that C and C' are **permutable** (or that C and C' permute) if $C \circ C' = C' \circ C$.*

To characterize when two fuzzy consequence operators permute we need the following lemmas.

Lemma 4. *Let $C, C' : [0,1]^X \longrightarrow [0,1]^X$ be fuzzy consequence operators. Then,*

$$C \circ C' \geq \max(C, C') .$$

Proof. It directly follows from the inclusion and monotonicity properties. Since C is inclusive $C'(\mu) \subseteq C(C'(\mu))$ for all $\mu \in [0,1]^X$ and $C \circ C' \geq C'$. Since C' is inclusive $\mu \subseteq C'(\mu)$ and adding the monotonicity of C we get that $C(\mu) \subseteq C(C'(\mu))$ for all $\mu \in [0,1]^X$ and $C \circ C' \geq C$. Therefore, $C \circ C' \geq \max(C, C')$. □

Lemma 5. *Let $C, C' : [0,1]^X \longrightarrow [0,1]^X$ be two fuzzy consequence operators. Then, $\max(C, C')$ is an inclusive and monotone fuzzy operator.*

Proof. The proof is straightforward. As C and C' are inclusive, $\max(C, C')$ is also inclusive. For the monotonicity, note that $\mu_1 \subseteq \mu_2$ implies $C(\mu_1)(x) \leq C(\mu_2)(x)$ and $C'(\mu_1)(x) \leq C'(\mu_2)(x)$ for all $\mu \in [0,1]^X$ and $x \in X$. Hence, $\max(C, C')(\mu_1)(x)) \leq \max(C, C')(\mu_2)(x))$ for all $\mu \in [0,1]^X$ and $x \in X$. □

At this point, we are ready to prove that there is only one case where the composition of two fuzzy consequence operators is also a fuzzy consequence operator.

Proposition 2. *Let C, C' be fuzzy consequence operators. Then, $C \circ C'$ is a fuzzy consequence operator if and only if $C \circ C' = \max(C, C')$.*

Proof. It is sufficient to prove that if $C \circ C'$ is a FCO then $C \circ C' = \overline{\max(C, C')}$. The other implication follows from the the fact that the closure of an operator is a FCO.

Assume that $C \circ C'$ is a FCO. From Lemma 4, $C \circ C' \geq \max(C, C')$. Therefore, $C \circ C' \geq \overline{\max(C, C')}$.
In addition, we have

$$C \circ C' \leq \max(C, C') \circ \max(C, C') = \max^2(C, C') \leq \overline{\max(C, C')}$$

where the last inequality holds due to Theorem 1 and Lemma 5. Hence, $C \circ C' = \overline{\max(C, C')}$. $\qquad\square$

For two fuzzy consequence operators to permute it is necessary and sufficient that their composition gives a FCO in both directions.

Theorem 2. *Let C, C' be fuzzy consequence operators. Then, C and C' permute if and only if $C \circ C'$ and $C' \circ C$ are fuzzy consequence operators.*

Proof. First, let us show that if C and C' permute, then $C \circ C'$ and $C' \circ C$ are FCO.

- Inclusion: From Lemmas 4 and 5, $C \circ C' \geq \max(C, C')$ which is inclusive.
- Monotonicity: Suppose $\mu_1 \subseteq \mu_2$. From the monotonicity of C' it follows that $C'(\mu_1) \subseteq C'(\mu_2)$ and from the monotonicity of C, $C(C'(\mu_1)) \subseteq C(C'(\mu_2))$.
- Idempotence:

$$(C \circ C')((C \circ C')(\mu))(x) = (C \circ C')((C' \circ C)(\mu))(x) = C(C'(C'(C(\mu))))(x)$$
$$= C(C'(C(\mu)))(x) = C(C(C'(\mu)))(x) = C(C'(\mu))(x) = (C \circ C')(\mu)(x).$$

The same arguments hold for $C' \circ C$.

The other implication directly follows from Proposition 2. $\qquad\square$

Remark 2. Note that there are cases of fuzzy consequence operators C and C' such that $C' \circ C$ is a FCO (and therefore $C' \circ C = \overline{\max(C, C')}$) but C and C' do not permute.

Example 1. Let X be a non empty classical set and let $\alpha, \beta \in \mathbb{R}$ such that $0 < \beta < \alpha < 1$. Let C' and C be FCO defined as follows:

$$C'(\mu)(x) = \begin{cases} 1 \ \ if \ \mu(x) > \beta \\ \beta \ \ if \ \mu(x) \leq \beta \end{cases} \qquad\qquad C(\mu)(x) = \begin{cases} 1 \ \ if \ \mu(x) > \alpha \\ \alpha \ \ if \ \mu(x) \leq \alpha. \end{cases}$$

Note that $C' \circ C = \overline{\max(C,C')} = X$ where $X(x) = 1$ for all $x \in X$, but $C' \circ C \neq C \circ C'$. Indeed, one has

$$(C \circ C')(\mu)(x) \begin{cases} 1 \; if \; \mu(x) > \beta \\ \\ \alpha \; if \; \mu(x) \leq \beta \end{cases}$$

which is not a FCO.

4   Permutability of Fuzzy Interior Operators

One can prove analogous results for the fuzzy interior operators. From Lemma 2 the following proposition is easy to show.

Proposition 3. *Let $C : [0,1]^X \longrightarrow [0,1]^X$ be a fuzzy operator. If C is antiinclusive, then the sequence $\{C^k\}_{k \in \mathbb{N}}$ is decreasing and convergent. That is , $C^{k+1} \leq C^k$ for all $k \in \mathbb{N}$ and there exists a fuzzy operator $L \in \Omega'$ such that $L = \lim_{n \in \mathbb{N}} C^n$.*

Proof. Since 0 is a lower bound for $C^k(\mu)(x)$ for all $\mu \in [0,1]^X$, all $x \in X$ and all $k \in \mathbb{N}$, the sequences $\{C^k(\mu)(x)\}_{k \in \mathbb{N}}$ are decreasing and bounded, thus they converge. Hence, the limit operator exists and it is defined by

$$L(\mu)(x) = \lim_{n \to \infty} C^n(\mu)(x) \ . \tag{4}$$

$\square$

Remark 3. Note that in this case, $L = \lim_{n \to \infty} C^n = \inf_{n \in \mathbb{N}} C^n$.

Theorem 3. *Let $C : [0,1]^X \longrightarrow [0,1]^X$ be an antiinclusive and monotone fuzzy operator. Then, $\lim_{n \to \infty} C^n = \overset{\circ}{C}$.*

Proof. The proof is dual to Theorem 1, therefore we will only give a sketch of the demonstration. By induction on k, it can be proved that $C^k \geq \overset{\circ}{C}$ for all $k \in \mathbb{N}$. Thus, $\lim_{n \to \infty} C^n \geq \overset{\circ}{C}$.

To prove the other inequality we need to show that $\lim_{n \to \infty} C^n$ is an interior operator. Lemmas 2 and 3 ensure the antiinclusion and monotonicity properties. The idempotence is obtained using the definition of limit as done in Theorem 1.

Hence, $\lim_{n \to \infty} C^n = \inf_{n \in \mathbb{N}} C^n = \overset{\circ}{C}$. $\square$

The following lemmas are analogous to the ones of section 3. They are necessary to characterize when two fuzzy interior operators permute.

Lemma 6. *Let $C,C' : [0,1]^X \longrightarrow [0,1]^X$ be fuzzy interior operators. Then,*

$$C \circ C' \leq \min(C,C') \ .$$

Lemma 7. *Let $C,C' : [0,1]^X \longrightarrow [0,1]^X$ be fuzzy interior operators. Then, $\min(C,C')$ is an antiinclusive and monotone fuzzy operator.*

For fuzzy interior operators we obtain the dual result of Proposition 2. The composition of fuzzy interior operators is a FIO only in the following case:

Proposition 4. *Let C, C' be fuzzy interior operators. Then, $C \circ C'$ is a fuzzy interior operator if and only if $C \circ C' = \min(\overset{\circ}{C, C'})$.*

Proof. The proof is analogous to Proposition 2. It is sufficient to prove that if $C \circ C'$ is a FIO then $C \circ C' = \min(\overset{\circ}{C, C'})$. The other implication follows from the fact that the fuzzy interior of an operator is a FIO.

Suppose that $C \circ C'$ is a fuzzy interior operator. From Lemma 6, we know that $C \circ C' \leq \min(C, C')$. Therefore, $C \circ C' \leq \min(\overset{\circ}{C, C'})$.

In addition, one has,

$$C \circ C' \geq \min(C, C') \circ \min(C, C') = \min^2(C, C') \geq \min(\overset{\circ}{C, C'})$$

where the last inequality holds due to Theorem 3 and Lemma 7. Hence, $C \circ C' = \min(\overset{\circ}{C, C'})$.   □

Now we are ready to characterize when two fuzzy interior operators permute. The result is dual to the one obtained for FCO in section 3.

Theorem 4. *Let C, C' be fuzzy interior operators. Then, C and C' permute if and only if $C \circ C'$ and $C' \circ C$ are fuzzy interior operators.*

Proof. The proof is analogous to the proof of Theorem 2. First of all, let us show that if C and C' permute, then $C \circ C'$ and $C' \circ C$ are fuzzy openings. Monotonicity and idempotence are proved exactly in the same way than in Theorem 2. Inclusion follows from Lemmas 6 and 7. Since $C \circ C' \leq \min(C, C')$ and $\min(C, C')$ is antiinclusive, so is $C \circ C'$. The same argument holds for $C' \circ C$.

The other implication directly follows from Proposition 4.   □

5   Conclusions

We have shown that given two fuzzy consequence operators (fuzzy closings), they permute if and only if their composition is a FCO in both directions. In this case, their composition is the closure of their maximum.

We have obtained an analogous result for fuzzy interior operators (fuzzy openings). Two FIO permute if and only if their composition is a fuzzy interior operator in both directions. In this case, their composition is the interior of their minimum.

In addition, we have shown that the composition of two fuzzy closings is a fuzzy closing if and only if it is the closure of their maximum. Moreover, we have proved the dual result for fuzzy openings. That is, the composition of two fuzzy openings is a fuzzy opening if and only if it is the interior of their minimum.

Acknowledgements. We ackowledge the partial support of the project FIS2011-28820-C02-02 from the Spanish Government and N.C. acknowledges the financial support of the "Asociación de Amigos de la Universidad de Navarra".

References

1. Bělohlávek, R., Funioková, T.: Fuzzy interior operators. International Journal of General Systems 33(4), 415–430 (2004)
2. Bloch, I.: Lattices of fuzzy sets and bipolar fuzzy sets, and mathematical morphology. Information Sciences 181, 2002–2015 (2011)
3. De Baets, B., Kerre, E., Gupta, M.: The fundamentals of fuzzy mathematical morphology part 1: Basic concepts. International Journal of General Systems 23(2), 155–171 (1995)
4. Deng, T.Q., Heijmans, H.J.A.M.: Grey-scale morphology based on fuzzy logic. J. Math. Imaging Vision 16, 155–171 (2002)
5. Elorza, J., Burillo, P.: Connecting fuzzy preorders, fuzzy consequence operators and fuzzy closure and co-closure systems. Fuzzy Sets and Systems 139(3), 601–613 (2003)
6. Elorza, J., et al.: On the relation between fuzzy closing morphological operators, fuzzy consequence operators induced by fuzzy preorders and fuzzy closure and co-closure systems. Fuzzy Sets and Systems 218, 73–89 (2013)
7. Maragos, P.: Lattice image processing: a unication of morphological and fuzzy algebraic systems. J. Math. Imaging Vision 22, 333–353 (2005)
8. Pavelka, J.: On Fuzzy Logic I. Zeitschr. f. Math. Logik und Grundlagen d. Math. 25, 45–52 (1979)
9. Recasens, J.: Permutable indistinguishability operators, perfect vague groups and fuzzy subgroups. Information Sciences 196, 129–142 (2012)
10. Ronse, C., Heijmans, H.J.A.M.: The algebraic basis of mathematical morphology: II. Openings and Closings. CVGIP: Image Understanding 54(1), 74–97 (1991)

A Fuzzy Filter for High-Density Salt and Pepper Noise Removal

Manuel González-Hidalgo, Sebastià Massanet,
Arnau Mir, and Daniel Ruiz-Aguilera

Department of Mathematics and Computer Science,
University of the Balearic Islands, E-07122 Palma de Mallorca, Spain
{manuel.gonzalez,s.massanet,arnau.mir,daniel.ruiz}@uib.es

Abstract. In this paper, a novel filter for high-density salt and pepper noise removal based on the fuzzy mathematical morphology using t-norms is proposed. This filter involves two phases, namely, a detection step of the corrupted pixels and the restoration of the image using a specialized regularization method using fuzzy open-close and close-open sequences. The experimental results show that the proposed algorithm outperforms other nonlinear filtering methods both from the visual point of view and the values of some objective performance measures for images corrupted up to 90% of noise.

Keywords: Mathematical morphology, t-norm, residual implication, high density salt and pepper noise, noise reduction, open-close filter.

1 Introduction

In transmission or recording processes, digital images can be affected by noise. This can be considered as a problem, as the image processing techniques do not work properly in a noisy environment. Therefore, a preprocessing step to deal with this fact is necessary.

For example, in artificial vision, many techniques of interpretation, measurement, segmentation or detection of structures require the removal, reduction or smoothing of noise in order to improve their performance. However, the noise removal techniques must be applied looking for a compromise between the effective suppression of the noise while preserving the fine texture and edges. Different noise types can affect an image. Our contribution deals with the removal of the salt and pepper impulsive noise in high-density corrupted images.

In general, impulsive noise removal has been a recurring topic in last years. In addition of the classical median filter, several approaches have been proposed to remove this noise type. In [1], a decision-based algorithm was presented for restoration of images that are highly corrupted by impulsive noise, replacing the noisy pixel value by the median of its neighbour pixel values. Moreover, another approach was introduced in [2], where an impulsive noise detector using mathematical residues is proposed. This method tries to identify pixels that are corrupted by the salt and pepper noise and afterwards, the image is restored

C. Bielza et al. (Eds.): CAEPIA 2013, LNAI 8109, pp. 70–79, 2013.

using a sequence of open-close algorithms that it is applied only to the noisy pixels. Beyond all the previous methods, some recent algorithms based on fuzzy logic have been proposed (see [3,4]).

Among the fuzzy logic based theories, fuzzy mathematical morphology is the generalization of the binary morphology [5] using techniques of fuzzy sets (see [6,7]). This morphology has shown a great potential in image processing. In particular, fuzzy mathematical morphology plays an important role in many applications like segmentation and edge detection (see [8,9]) and filtering (see [10,11]). In particular, a novel filtering method for salt and pepper noise removal was proposed in [12] by extending the method presented in [2] to fuzzy mathematical morphology. This new method showed a better behaviour of the performance of the algorithm with respect to an increase of the amount of noise compared with the algorithm presented in [2]. In addition, it outperformed the non-fuzzy one for low amounts of noise while its performance was similar for images corrupted with high amounts of noise. However, its performance decreased sharply for images corrupted with more than 80% of noise. In this paper, we propose a modification of the algorithm presented in [12] based on a new detection function of the noisy pixels and an improved Block Smart Erase with an adaptive window size. This new version of the algorithm is able to remove the noise from images corrupted up to 90% of noise preserving the edges and details.

The communication is organized as follows. In Section 2, the definitions and properties of the fuzzy morphological operators are recalled. In Section 3 the proposed novel algorithm is explained. Then, in Section 4, the objective performance comparison based on PSNR and SSIM among our method and some noise filtering algorithms is performed. Finally, in the last section, some conclusions and future work are pointed out.

2   Fuzzy Logic Morphological Operators

Fuzzy morphological operators are defined using fuzzy operators such as fuzzy conjunctions, like t-norms, and fuzzy implications. More details on these logical connectives can be found in [13] and [14], respectively.

Definition 1. *A t-norm is a commutative, associative, non-decreasing function* $T : [0,1]^2 \to [0,1]$ *with neutral element 1, i.e.,* $T(1,x) = x$ *for all* $x \in [0,1]$.

Next we recall the definition of fuzzy implications.

Definition 2. *A binary operator* $I : [0,1]^2 \to [0,1]$ *is a* fuzzy implication *if it is non-increasing in the first variable, non-decreasing in the second one and it satisfies* $I(0,0) = I(1,1) = 1$ *and* $I(1,0) = 0$.

A well-known way to obtain fuzzy implications is the residuation method. Given a t-norm T the binary operator

$$I_T(x,y) = \sup\{z \in [0,1] \mid T(x,z) \le y\}$$

is a fuzzy implication called the *residual implication* or *R-implication* of T.

Using the previous operators, we can define the basic fuzzy morphological operators such as dilation and erosion. We will use the following notation: T denotes a t-norm, I a fuzzy implication, A a grey-level image, and B a grey-level structuring element.

Definition 3 ([15]). *The fuzzy dilation $D_T(A, B)$ and the fuzzy erosion $E_I(A, B)$ of A by B are the grey-level images defined by*

$$D_T(A, B)(y) = \sup_x T(B(x - y), A(x))$$
$$E_I(A, B)(y) = \inf_x I(B(x - y), A(x)).$$

From the fuzzy erosion and the fuzzy dilation, the fuzzy opening and the fuzzy closing of a grey-level image A by a structuring element B can be defined as follows.

Definition 4 ([15]). *The fuzzy closing $C_{T,I}(A, B)$ and the fuzzy opening $O_{T,I}(A, B)$ of A by B are the grey-level images defined by*

$$C_{T,I}(A, B)(y) = E_I(D_T(A, B), -B)(y),$$
$$O_{T,I}(A, B)(y) = D_T(E_I(A, B), -B)(y).$$

A more detailed account on these operators, its properties and applications can be found in [7,8,15]. In particular, when I is the residual implication of T, most of the usual properties of a mathematical morphology hold.

3   The Proposed Algorithm

The proposed algorithm is an improved version of the algorithm FMMOCS presented in [12] which was an extension to the fuzzy mathematical morphology of the algorithm presented in [2]. The method is divided in two main steps. The first one is a preliminary identification of corrupted pixels in an effort to avoid the processing of pixels which are not corrupted by impulse noise. In the second one the filtering method is applied only to those pixels identified as noise in the first step.

3.1   A Morphological Salt and Pepper Noise Detector

In [12], the noise detection function was based on the fuzzy mathematical morphological residues of Top-Hat and Dual Top-Hat operators. Although its performance was quite good, when the amount of noise was higher than 80% it failed to detect all the noisy pixels and consequently, the quality of the filtered results decreased both from the visual point of view and the values of the performance objective measures. In this paper, we propose to use the detection function presented in [16] specially introduced for images corrupted up to 90% of noise. This algorithm is based on the fuzzy morphological alternate filters. In particular, it follows the following steps for each pixel of the image:

1. Find out the maximum ($S_{\max}$) and minimum ($S_{\min}$) values of a 7×7 window centred at the current pixel.
2. Compute the following function

$$d(i,j) = \left| \frac{C_{T,I_T}(O_{T,I_T}(A,B),B)(i,j) + O_{T,I_T}(C_{T,I_T}(A,B),B)(i,j)}{2} - A(i,j) \right|$$

3. Finally, the detection function is given by

$$b(i,j) = \begin{cases} 1 \text{ if } (A(i,j) = S_{\max} \text{ or } A(i,j) = S_{\min}) \text{ and } d(i,j) \geq t, \\ 0 \text{ otherwise,} \end{cases}$$

where t is a predefined threshold and we conclude that $A(i,j)$ is a corrupted pixel if, and only if, $b(i,j) = 1$.

3.2   Fuzzy Open-Close Sequence Algorithm

In this second step, in order to remove the noise, two filters, namely the fuzzy open-close filter (FOCF) and the fuzzy close-open sequence filter (FCOF) are applied only to the corrupted pixels. FOCF is defined as follows:

$$FOCF_{T,I_T}(A, (B_1, B_2)) = C_{T,I_T}(O_{T,I_T}(A, B_1), B_2)$$

where B_1 and B_2 are two structuring elements. The main target of this filter is to remove the salt noise pixels. In particular, the size of B_1 must be small enough to preserve the details of the image and the size of B_2 must be larger than of B_1 in order to eliminate powerfully the pepper noise pixels which have been not removed by the fuzzy opening.

In the same way, FCOF is defined as follows:

$$FCOF_{T,I_T}(A, (B_1, B_2)) = O_{T,I_T}(C_{T,I_T}(A, B_1), B_2)$$

where B_1 and B_2 are again two structuring elements. Analogously to the previous filter, this filter is applied to remove the pepper noise pixels.

However, the noises whose size is larger than the size of B_1 will not be removed and in fact, they are propagated in the image. This fact leads to the generation of some undesired white (or black) blocks in the filtered image. To avoid this behaviour, the so-called Block Smart Erase (BSE) algorithm, which is based on the median of the surrounding pixels, is applied. The second modification we propose is included in this BSE algorithm. In [12], a fixed window size $N = 7$ was considered. This fact was good enough for images corrupted up to 80% of noise, however when the amount of noise was higher the BSE algorithm was not able to remove properly some undesired white and black blocks. The main reason is because when the amount of noise is higher than 80% some blocks are larger than 7×7 and consequently, a fixed window size of $N = 7$ does not remove them. Consequently, in order to remove them and preserve as much as possible the fine details of the image, we propose an adaptive window size for the BSE algorithm, which is specified as follows:

Table 1. PSNR for various filters for Lenna image at different noise densities

Noise	PSNR								
	DBA	SMF5	AMF17	OCS	OCSflat	FMMOCS*	FMMOCSflat*	FMMOCS	FMMOCSflat
10	30.2896	29.2999	37.1820	31.6873	29.7633	33.5973	32.2427	38.3735	38.3204
20	29.7204	28.2710	34.7001	31.1085	31.0747	31.5054	31.5612	33.7895	33.0919
30	29.0282	26.0472	32.8216	29.6786	31.1533	30.5352	31.1954	32.0707	31.6896
40	28.0453	25.5084	30.7554	28.3672	30.4075	29.9621	30.3865	30.9451	30.5128
50	26.8784	22.4622	29.2463	27.3714	29.3507	29.2843	29.3425	29.7788	29.3753
60	25.1899	18.4381	27.4294	26.5269	28.4292	28.2932	28.4284	28.5054	28.4224
70	23.7784	13.8772	25.7660	25.7700	27.4667	27.1356	27.4667	27.1802	27.4567
80	21.5853	10.1319	23.7004	24.8901	26.0970	25.1708	26.0963	25.3627	26.1346
90	18.7213	7.2976	18.3076	23.7672	21.8158	17.4673	21.8158	21.6633	23.7761

1. Consider an $N \times N$ window centred at the test pixel, starting by $N = 5$.
2. If $A(i,j) \in \{0, 255\}$ then we have an absolute extreme value and step 3 must be applied. Otherwise, the pixel is not altered.
3. If an extreme value is detected, assign the median value of the window as its gray-level value. If the median value is again an extreme value, go to step 1 and consider a larger window size N' with $N' = N + 2$.

Finally, the FMMOCS filter can be defined as the arithmetic mean of the two previous fuzzy open-close and close-open sequence filters after applying the BSE algorithm, that is,

$$FMMOCS_{T,I_T}(A,(B_1,B_2)) = \frac{BSE(FOCF_{T,I_T}(A,(B_1,B_2)))}{2} + \frac{BSE(FCOF_{T,I_T}(A,(B_1,B_2)))}{2}.$$

4 Simulation Results

In this section the performance of the proposed method will be evaluated and compared with other well-known methods for filtering noisy images which are corrupted by impulsive noise. In particular, we will compare the FMMOCS filter with some other nonlinear filtering algorithms such as the Decision-Based algorithm (DBA), a nonlinear filter designed by Srinivasan and Ebenezer in [1]; the standard 5×5 median filter (SMF5); an adaptive median filter with a maximum allowed size of the adaptive filter window (S_{max}) of 17 (AMF17); the open-close sequence algorithm (OCS) presented in [2] and based on the classical grey-level mathematical morphology; and the previous version of the FMMOCS filter (FMMOCS*) presented in [12]. These algorithms will be tested with two well-known gray-level images such us "lenna.tif", which is an image with homogeneous regions and low details, and "baboon.tif" which is an image with high activity. In the experiments, both images are corrupted by salt and pepper noise, where 255 represents salt and 0 represents the pepper noise with equal probability, with levels varying from 10% to 90% with increments of 10%.

In addition to a visual comparison of the filtered images obtained by these algorithms, the restoration performance is quantitatively measured by two widely

Table 2. SSIM for various filters for Lenna image at different noise densities

Noise	SSIM								
	DBA	SMF5	AMF17	OCS	OCSflat	FMMOCS*	FMMOCSflat*	FMMOCS	FMMOCSflat
10	0.998941	0.9933	0.9989	0.9940	0.9951	0.9975	0.9966	0.9992	0.9992
20	0.997221	0.9915	0.9981	0.9955	0.9965	0.9960	0.9960	0.9976	0.9972
30	0.995024	0.9887	0.9970	0.9956	0.9967	0.9950	0.9957	0.9965	0.9961
40	0.991075	0.9840	0.9952	0.9948	0.9960	0.9942	0.9948	0.9954	0.9949
50	0.985619	0.9680	0.9932	0.9933	0.9949	0.9933	0.9933	0.9940	0.9934
60	0.974659	0.9219	0.9897	0.9918	0.9933	0.9915	0.9917	0.9919	0.9917
70	0.961453	0.7976	0.9851	0.9897	0.9914	0.9889	0.9897	0.9890	0.9897
80	0.930712	0.5979	0.9758	0.9858	0.9850	0.9825	0.9858	0.9833	0.9859
90	0.856297	0.3976	0.9186	0.9617	0.8745	0.8996	0.9617	0.9607	0.9756

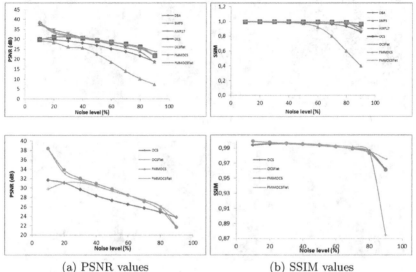

(a) PSNR values   (b) SSIM values

Fig. 1. PSNR and SSIM values for different filters operating on the "Lenna" image. Top: plot for all filters. Down: plot for the OCS and FMMOCS with the two types of structuring elements.

used performance objective measures, namely PSNR (see [1,2]) and SSIM (see [17]). Larger values of PSNR and SSIM are indicators of better capabilities for noise reduction and image recovery.

Following [12] and [2], we have fixed two different sequences of structuring elements: a flat sequence of squares of sizes 5, 3 and 7, respectively, and a binary sequence of diamonds with the same sizes. These structuring elements with sizes 5, 3 and 7 correspond to the structuring elements B, B_1 and B_2, respectively, of the algorithm explained in Section 3. When the flat squares are used, we will denote the algorithm by "FMMOCSflat" and simply by "FMMOCS" when binary diamonds are considered. The same structuring elements and notation are used for the OCS algorithm proposed in [2] and the old version of the FM-MOCS, denoted by FMMOCS*. For the FMMOCS and its old version we have

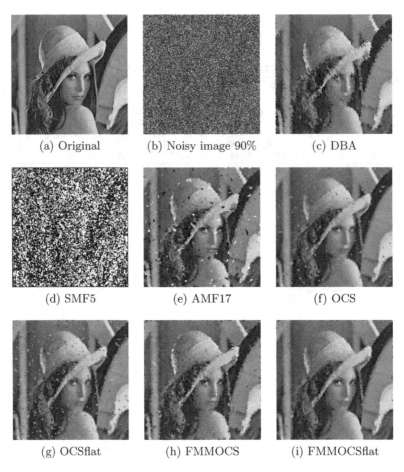

(a) Original   (b) Noisy image 90%   (c) DBA

(d) SMF5   (e) AMF17   (f) OCS

(g) OCSflat   (h) FMMOCS   (i) FMMOCSflat

Fig. 2. Filtered images for the Lenna image corrupted with 90% noise. See Tables 1 and 2 for the PSNR and SSIM values, respectively

considered the Łukasiewicz t-norm given by $T_{LK}(x,y) = \max\{x + y - 1, 0\}$ and its residual implication defined as $I_{LK}(x,y) = \min\{1, 1-x+y\}$ for all $x, y \in [0,1]$ as conjunction and fuzzy implication respectively, for the fuzzy morphological operators.

In Section 3, we have proposed a noise detection function depending of a threshold value. Obviously, this threshold value affects the performance of the proposed method and by choosing the appropriate value, we can effectively reduce the number of misclassified noise-free pixels. It is clear that as we increase the amount of noise, the threshold value must decrease to classify more pixels as corrupted ones. In particular, the following values have shown a great detection and classification performance: $t = 210$ (10%), $t = 85$ (20%), $t = 60$ (30%), $t = 30$ (40-50%) and $t = 0$ for higher amounts. For the implementation of an

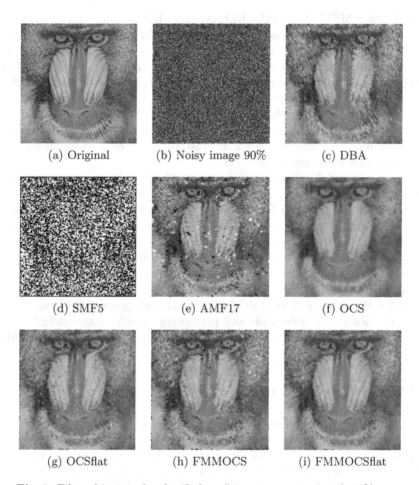

(a) Original   (b) Noisy image 90%   (c) DBA

(d) SMF5   (e) AMF17   (f) OCS

(g) OCSflat   (h) FMMOCS   (i) FMMOCSflat

Fig. 3. Filtered images for the "baboon" image corrupted with 90% noise

unsupervised version of the algorithm, the threshold value t could be automatically determined through a proper estimation of the density of the salt and pepper noise of the image. Finally, for the FMMOCS* noise detection function we have considered $t = 90$ as in [12] and $t = 0$ for the OCS filter as in [2].

The quantitative performance comparison of our method versus the other considered algorithms for the Lenna image is collected in Tables 1 and 2. In these tables, we display the values of the PSNR (dB) and SSIM measures, respectively, for the Lenna image corrupted from 10% to 90% of salt and pepper noise. In Figure 1, we can see graphically the evolution of the measures for each algorithm depending on the amount of noise. Note that we omit the curves of the old versions of FMMOCS since from Tables 1 and 2, their performances are worse than the new version presented in this paper. From these measures we can infer that FMMOCSflat and OCS obtain the best results at 90%, but FMMOCSflat obtains much higher performance values for the other amounts of noise. At 20 and 30%, the AMF17 obtains the highest values but its performance decreases drastically for high-density corrupted images. In addition, FMMOCS and FM-MOCSflat filters perform robustly over all the noise range. They represent a slowly decreasing curve even when the noise ratio significantly increases. Other filters fall down abruptly generating worse results when the noise ratio is high. It is worthy to note the undesirable behaviour of the OCSflat which obtains lower values of the measures for the images corrupted with 10% and 20% than the value obtained for the 30% amount of noise. We do not include the measures for the baboon image because of the space constraint and the similar behaviour of the measures for each filtering method.

In Figures 2 and 3, we present the restoration results for the two images considered in this section corrupted with 90% of salt and pepper noise. Note that the FMMOCSflat algorithm gives the best performance in terms of noise suppression and detail and edge preservation, as it was already suggested by the two measures. Some filtering methods, specially SMF5 and AMF17, are not able to remove the noise while DBA removes the noise but it does not preserve the edges and fine details of the image. In addition, most of the filtered images present some undesired black and white regions, which are successfully removed by the BSE algorithm of the FMMOCSflat. Thus, the proposed filter can remove most of the noise effectively while well preserving the edge image details of the image improving drastically the performance of the first version of this algorithm presented in [12].

5 Conclusions and Future Work

In this paper, we have presented a novel filtering method for high-density salt and pepper noise corrupted images based on the fuzzy mathematical morphology using t-norms. The algorithm is an improved version of the one presented in [12] by using a new noise detection function and an adaptive window size in the Block Smart Erase algorithm. The obtained results show that the new algorithm outperforms its predecessor and other well-established nonlinear filtering methods from both the visual point of view and the PSNR and SSIM values. As future work, we want to deal with random values impulse noise since we hope that the fuzzy approach can be very competitive for its removal. In addition, the performance of the fuzzy mathematical morphologies based on uninorms could be worthy to study.

Acknowledgements. Supported by the Government Spanish Grant MTM2009-10320, with FEDER support.

References

1. Srinivasan, K.S., Ebenezer, D.: A new fast and efficient decision-based algorithm for removal of high-density impulse noises. IEEE Signal Processing Letters 14(3), 189–192 (2007)

2. Ze-Feng, D., Zhou-Ping, Y., You-Lun, X.: High probability impulse noise-removing algorithm based on mathematical morphology. IEEE Signal Processing Letters 14(1), 31–34 (2007)
3. Schulte, S., De Witte, V., Nachtegael, M., Van der Weken, D., Kerre, E.E.: Fuzzy two-step filter for impulse noise reduction from color images. IEEE Transactions on Image Processing 15(11), 3567–3578 (2006)
4. Wang, X., Zhao, X., Guo, F., Ma, J.: Impulsive noise detection by double noise detector and removal using adaptive neural-fuzzy inference system. Int. J. Electron. Commun. 65, 429–434 (2011)
5. Serra, J.: Image analysis and mathematical morphology, vol. 1, 2. Academic Press, London (1982)
6. Bloch, I., Maître, H.: Fuzzy mathematical morphologies: A comparative study. Pattern Recognition 28, 1341–1387 (1995)
7. Nachtegael, M., Kerre, E.E.: Classical and fuzzy approaches towards mathematical morphology. In: Kerre, E.E., Nachtegael, M. (eds.) Fuzzy Techniques in Image Processing. STUDFUZZ, vol. 52, pp. 3–57. Springer, Heidelberg (2000)
8. González-Hidalgo, M., Mir-Torres, A., Ruiz-Aguilera, D., Torrens, J.: Fuzzy morphology based on uninorms: Image edge-detection. Opening and closing. In: Tavares, J., Jorge, N. (eds.) Computational Vision and Medical Image Processing, pp. 127–133. Taylor & Francis Group (2008)
9. Papari, G., Petkov, N.: Edge and line oriented contour detection: State of the art. Image and Vision Computing 29(2-3), 79–103 (2011)
10. Lerallut, R., Decenciére, É., Meyer, F.: Image filtering using morphological amoebas. Image and Vision Computing 25(4), 395–404 (2007)
11. Maragos, P.: Morphological filtering. In: Bovik, A. (ed.) The Essential Guide to Image Processing, pp. 293–321. Academic Press, Boston (2009)
12. González-Hidalgo, M., Massanet, S., Mir, A., Ruiz-Aguilera, D.: High-density impulse noise removal using fuzzy mathematical morphology. Accepted in EUSFLAT (2013)
13. Klement, E.P., Mesiar, R., Pap, E.: Triangular norms. Kluwer Academic Publishers, London (2000)
14. Baczyński, M., Jayaram, B.: Fuzzy Implications. STUDFUZZ, vol. 231. Springer, Heidelberg (2008)
15. De Baets, B.: Fuzzy morphology: A logical approach. In: Ayyub, B.M., Gupta, M.M. (eds.) Uncertainty Analysis in Engineering and Science: Fuzzy Logic, Statistics, and Neural Network Approach, pp. 53–68. Kluwer Academic Publishers, Norwell (1997)
16. Singh, A., Ghanekar, U., Kumar, C., Kumar, G.: An efficient morphological salt-and-pepper noise detector. Int. J. Advanced Networking and Applications 2, 873–875 (2011)
17. Wang, Z., Bovik, A.C., Sheikh, H.R., Simoncelli, E.P.: Image quality assessment: From error visibility to structural similarity. IEEE Transactions on Image Processing 13(4), 600–612 (2004)

A New Class of Functions
for Integrating Weighting Means
and OWA Operators

Bonifacio Llamazares

Departamento de Economía Aplicada, Instituto de Matemáticas (IMUVA),
Universidad de Valladolid, Avda. Valle de Esgueva 6, 47011 Valladolid, Spain
boni@eco.uva.es

Abstract. In this paper we introduce the semi-uninorm based ordered
weighted averaging (SUOWA) operators, a new class of aggregation functions that integrates weighted means and OWA operators. To do this we
take into account that weighted means and OWA operators are particular cases of Choquet integrals. So, the capacities associated to SUOWA
operators are defined by using the values of the capacities associated to
these functions and idempotent semi-uninorms.

Keywords: Weighted means, OWA operators, SUOWA operators, Choquet integrals, Semi-uninorms.

1 Introduction

Weighted means and ordered weighted averaging (OWA) operators (Yager [16])
are functions widely used in the aggregation processes. Although both are defined
through weighting vectors, their behavior is quite different: Weighted means
allow to weight each information source in relation to their reliability while
OWA operators allow to weight the values according to their ordering.

Some authors, such as Torra [13] and Torra and Narukawa [15], have reported
the need for both weightings. For instance, suppose we have several sensors to
measure a physical property. On the one hand, sensors may be of different quality
and precision, so a weighted mean type aggregation is necessary. On the other
hand, to prevent a faulty sensor alters the measurement, we might take a OWA
type aggregation where the maximum and minimum values are not considered.

Different aggregation functions have appeared in the literature to deal with
this kind of situations. Special attention deserve the weighted OWA (WOWA)
operators, introduced by Torra [13]. WOWA operators integrate weighted means
and OWA operators in the sense that one of these functions is obtained when
the other one has a "neutral" behavior, that is, its weighting vector is that of the
arithmetic mean (the behavior of WOWA operators and other similar functions
has been analyzed by Llamazares [10]).

The aim of this work is to introduce a new class of aggregation functions,
the semi-uninorm based ordered weighted averaging (SUOWA) operators, that

C. Bielza et al. (Eds.): CAEPIA 2013, LNAI 8109, pp. 80–90, 2013.

integrate the weighted means and the OWA operators in the above sense. To do this we take into account that weighted means and OWA operators are particular cases of Choquet integrals. So, the capacities associated to SUOWA operators are defined by using the values of the capacities associated to these functions and idempotent semi-uninorms.

The paper is organized as follows. In Section 2 we recall some basic properties of aggregation functions and the definitions of weighted means, OWA operators and Choquet integrals. Section 3 is devoted to the construction of capacities by means of which we can integrate weighted means and OWA operators in a new class of operators, the SUOWA operators. Finally, some concluding remarks are provided in Section 4.

2 Preliminaries

Throughout the paper we will use the following notation: $N = \{1, \ldots, n\}$; given $A \subseteq N$, $|A|$ will denote the cardinal of A; vectors will be denoted in bold; $\boldsymbol{\eta}$ will denote the vector $(1/n, \ldots, 1/n)$; $\boldsymbol{x} \geq \boldsymbol{y}$ will mean $x_i \geq y_i$ for all $i \in N$; given $\boldsymbol{x} \in \mathbb{R}^n$, $x_{[1]} \geq \cdots \geq x_{[n]}$ and $x_{(1)} \leq \cdots \leq x_{(n)}$ will denote the components of $\boldsymbol{x}$ in decreasing and increasing order, respectively.

In the following definition we present some well-known properties usually demanded to the functions used in the aggregation processes.

Definition 1. *Let $F : \mathbb{R}^n \longrightarrow \mathbb{R}$ be a function.*

1. *F is symmetric if $F(x_{\sigma(1)}, \ldots, x_{\sigma(n)}) = F(x_1, \ldots, x_n)$ for all $\boldsymbol{x} \in \mathbb{R}^n$ and for all permutation σ of N.*
2. *F is monotonic if $\boldsymbol{x} \geq \boldsymbol{y}$ implies $F(\boldsymbol{x}) \geq F(\boldsymbol{y})$ for all $\boldsymbol{x}, \boldsymbol{y} \in \mathbb{R}^n$.*
3. *F is idempotent if $F(x, \ldots, x) = x$ for all $x \in \mathbb{R}$.*
4. *F is compensative (or internal) if $\min(\boldsymbol{x}) \leq F(\boldsymbol{x}) \leq \max(\boldsymbol{x})$ for all $\boldsymbol{x} \in \mathbb{R}^n$.*
5. *F is homogeneous of degree 1 (or ratio scale invariant) if $F(\lambda \boldsymbol{x}) = \lambda F(\boldsymbol{x})$ for all $\boldsymbol{x} \in \mathbb{R}^n$ and for all $\lambda > 0$.*

2.1 Weighted Means and OWA Operators

Weighted means and OWA operators are defined by vectors with non-negative components whose sum is 1.

Definition 2. *A vector $\boldsymbol{q} \in \mathbb{R}^n$ is a weighting vector if $\boldsymbol{q} \in [0, 1]^n$ and $\sum_{i=1}^{n} q_i = 1$.*

Definition 3. *Let $\boldsymbol{p}$ be a weighting vector. The weighted mean associated to $\boldsymbol{p}$ is the function $M_{\boldsymbol{p}} : \mathbb{R}^n \longrightarrow \mathbb{R}$ given by*

$$M_{\boldsymbol{p}}(\boldsymbol{x}) = \sum_{i=1}^{n} p_i x_i.$$

Weighted means are continuous, monotonic, idempotent, compensative and homogeneous of degree 1 functions.

OWA operators were introduced by Yager [16] as a tool for aggregation procedures in multicriteria decision making.

Definition 4. *Let w be a weighting vector. The OWA operator associated to w is the function $O_w : \mathbb{R}^n \longrightarrow \mathbb{R}$ given by*

$$O_w(x) = \sum_{i=1}^{n} w_i x_{[i]}.$$

OWA operators are continuous, symmetric, monotonic, idempotent, compensative and homogeneous of degree 1 functions.

2.2 Choquet Integrals

Choquet integrals (see Choquet [2] and Murofushi and Sugeno [11]) are based on the notion of capacity. A capacity is similar to a probability measure but by replacing additivity by monotonicity (see also fuzzy measures in Sugeno [12]). Games are obtained when we drop the monotonicity property.

Definition 5

1. *A game v on N is a set function, $v : 2^N \longrightarrow \mathbb{R}$ satisfying $v(\varnothing) = 0$.*
2. *A capacity (or fuzzy measure) μ on N is a game on N satisfying $\mu(A) \leq \mu(B)$ whenever $A \subseteq B$. Therefore, $\mu : 2^N \longrightarrow [0, \infty)$. The capacity is said to be normalized if $\mu(N) = 1$.*

The Choquet integral can be defined in a general context (see Choquet [2] and Murofushi and Sugeno [11]). However, we only consider the Choquet integral in the framework that we are dealing with here (see Grabisch *et al.* [8, p. 181]).

Definition 6. *Let μ be a capacity on N. The Choquet integral with respect to μ is the function $C_\mu : \mathbb{R}^n \longrightarrow \mathbb{R}$ given by*

$$C_\mu(x) = \sum_{i=1}^{n} \mu(B_{(i)})(x_{(i)} - x_{(i-1)}),$$

where $B_{(i)} = \{(i), \ldots, (n)\}$ and, by convention, $x_{(0)} = 0$.

It is worth noting that we have defined the Choquet integral for all vectors of $\mathbb{R}^n$ instead of nonnegative vectors because we are actually considering the asymmetric Choquet integral with respect to μ (on this, see Grabisch *et al.* [8, p. 182]). In addition to this, note that the Choquet integral can be defined with respect to games instead of capacities (see again Grabisch *et al.* [8, p. 181]). In this case, the Choquet integral satisfies the following properties (Grabisch *et al.* [8, p. 193 and p. 196]):

Remark 1. If v is a game on N and $\mathcal{C}_v$ is the Choquet integral with respect to v, then

1. $\mathcal{C}_v$ is continuous.
2. $\mathcal{C}_v$ is homogeneous of degree 1.
3. $\mathcal{C}_v$ is monotonic if and only if v is a capacity.
4. $\mathcal{C}_v$ is idempotent when $v(N) = 1$.
5. $\mathcal{C}_v$ is compensative when v is a normalized capacity.

For the sake of similarity with OWA operators, in the sequel we show an equivalent representation of Choquet integral by means of decreasing sequences of values (see Torra [14]). Given $\boldsymbol{x} \in \mathbb{R}^n$, we can consider $[\cdot]$ and $(\cdot)$ so that $[i] = (n + 1 - i)$ for all $i \in N$. In this case,

$$\mathcal{C}_\mu(\boldsymbol{x}) = \sum_{i=1}^{n} \mu(A_{[i]})(x_{[i]} - x_{[i+1]}),$$

where $A_{[i]} = \{[1], \ldots, [i]\}$ and, by convention, $x_{[n+1]} = 0$.

From the previous expression, it is straightforward to check that the Choquet integral can be written as

$$\mathcal{C}_\mu(\boldsymbol{x}) = \sum_{i=1}^{n} \big(\mu(A_{[i]}) - \mu(A_{[i-1]})\big)x_{[i]},$$

with the convention $A_{[0]} = \varnothing$. From this formula we can easily see that weighted means and OWA operators are specific cases of Choquet integral (see also Fodor *et al.* [3] and Grabisch [6,7]).

Remark 2. Let μ be a capacity on N.

1. $\mathcal{C}_\mu$ is the weighted mean $M_{\boldsymbol{p}}$ if $\mu(A_{[i]}) - \mu(A_{[i-1]}) = p_{[i]}$ for all $i \in N$, or, equivalently, $\mu(A_{[i]}) = \sum_{j=1}^{i} p_{[j]}$ for all $i \in N$. Therefore $\mu(A) = \sum_{i \in A} p_i$ for all $A \subseteq N$.
2. $\mathcal{C}_\mu$ is the OWA operator $O_{\boldsymbol{w}}$ if $\mu(A_{[i]}) - \mu(A_{[i-1]}) = w_i$ for all $i \in N$, or, equivalently, $\mu(A_{[i]}) = \sum_{j=1}^{i} w_j$ for all $i \in N$. Therefore $\mu(A) = \sum_{i=1}^{|A|} w_i$ for all $A \subseteq N$.

3   Integrating Weighting Means and OWA Operators

Our aim is to find new functions based on the Choquet integral, $F_{\boldsymbol{p},\boldsymbol{w}}$, that integrate weighted means and OWA operators in the following sense: $F_{\boldsymbol{p},\boldsymbol{\eta}} = M_{\boldsymbol{p}}$ and $F_{\boldsymbol{\eta},\boldsymbol{w}} = O_{\boldsymbol{w}}$ (see WOWA operators in Torra [13]).

If we represent the function $F_{\boldsymbol{p},\boldsymbol{w}}$ as

$$F_{\boldsymbol{p},\boldsymbol{w}}(\boldsymbol{x}) = \sum_{i=1}^{n} \big(\mu_{\boldsymbol{p},\boldsymbol{w}}(A_{[i]}) - \mu_{\boldsymbol{p},\boldsymbol{w}}(A_{[i-1]})\big)x_{[i]},$$

with $A_{[0]} = \varnothing$, then, according to Remark 2, $F_{p,w}$ integrates weighted means and OWA operators when the capacity $\mu_{p,w}$ satisfies

$$\mu_{p,\eta}(A) = \sum_{i \in A} p_i \quad \text{and} \quad \mu_{\eta,w}(A) = \sum_{i=1}^{|A|} w_i, \tag{1}$$

for all $A \subseteq N$.

In the next subsection we show a procedure for constructing capacities satisfying the conditions given by (1).

3.1 Constructing Capacities by Using Semi-uninorms

Given $A \subseteq N$, weighted means and OWA operators are generated through normalized capacities defined by the values $\sum_{i \in A} p_i$ and $\sum_{i=1}^{|A|} w_i$, respectively. Therefore, our first intention is to consider a game on N given as a function of these values; that is,

$$\nu_{p,w}^f(A) = f\left(\sum_{i \in A} p_i, \sum_{i=1}^{|A|} w_i\right).$$

However, conditions given by (1) implies that, if $|A| = j$, then

$$\nu_{\eta,w}^f(A) = f\left(\frac{j}{n}, \sum_{i=1}^{|A|} w_i\right) = \sum_{i=1}^{|A|} w_i \quad \text{and} \quad \nu_{p,\eta}^f(A) = f\left(\sum_{i \in A} p_i, \frac{j}{n}\right) = \sum_{i \in A} p_i;$$

that is, j/n should be a neutral element of the function f. Since the neutral element of a function is unique, we should use different functions according to the cardinality of the set A. To avoid this, we make a transformation of the values $\sum_{i \in A} p_i$ and $\sum_{i=1}^{|A|} w_i$ taking into account the cardinality of the set A. So, when the set A is non-empty, we consider the set function

$$\nu_{p,w}^f(A) = |A| \cdot f\left(\frac{\sum_{i \in A} p_i}{|A|}, \frac{\sum_{i=1}^{|A|} w_i}{|A|}\right).$$

In this way, conditions given by (1) are satisfied when f is a function with neutral element $1/n$. When we look for functions with neutral elements, uninorms, introduced by Yager and Rybalov [17], appear in a natural way (see also Fodor *et al.* [5], and Fodor and De Baets [4]).

Definition 7. *A function $U : [0,1]^2 \longrightarrow [0,1]$ is a uninorm if it is symmetric, associative ($U(x, U(y,z)) = U(U(x,y), z)$ for all $x, y, z \in [0,1]$), monotonic and possesses a neutral element $e \in [0,1]$ ($U(x,e) = x$ for all $x \in [0,1]$).*

Nevertheless, for our purposes we can dispense with the symmetry and associativity properties. In this case we obtain semi-uninorms functions, introduced by Liu [9].

Definition 8. *A function $U : [0,1]^2 \longrightarrow [0,1]$ is a semi-uninorm if it is monotonic and possesses a neutral element $e \in [0,1]$ ($U(e,x) = U(x,e) = x$ for all $x \in [0,1]$).*

The set of semi-uninorms with neutral element $e \in [0,1]$ will be denoted by $\mathcal{U}^e$. Notice that semi-uninorms satisfy the following boundary conditions: $U(0,0) = 0$ and $U(1,1) = 1$.

Taking into account the above considerations, we can now define the game associated to two weighting vectors and a semi-uninorm.

Definition 9. *Let p and w be two weighting vectors and let $U \in \mathcal{U}^{1/n}$. The game associated to p, w and U is the set function $v_{p,w}^U : 2^N \longrightarrow \mathbb{R}$ defined by*

$$v_{p,w}^U(A) = |A| \cdot U\left(\frac{\sum_{i \in A} p_i}{|A|}, \frac{\sum_{i=1}^{|A|} w_i}{|A|}\right)$$

if $A \neq \varnothing$, and $v_{p,w}^U(\varnothing) = 0$.

It is easy to check that $v_{p,w}^U$ satisfies the conditions given by (1) and that $v_{p,w}^U(N) = 1$. However, the game $v_{p,w}^U$ may not be a capacity; that is, it may not be monotonic as we show in the following example.

Example 1. Let $p = (0.5, 0.2, 0.1, 0.1, 0.1)$ and $w = (0.6, 0.2, 0, 0, 0.2)$. Given $U \in \mathcal{U}^{0.2}$, we have

  - If $A = \{2\}$, then $v_{p,w}^U(A) = U(0.2, 0.6) = 0.6$.
  - If $B = \{2, 3, 4, 5\}$, then $v_{p,w}^U(B) = 4\,U(0.5/4, 0.2) = 0.5$.

Therefore, $A \subseteq B$ but $v_{p,w}^U(A) > v_{p,w}^U(B)$; that is, $v_{p,w}^U$ is not monotonic.

Nevertheless, it is relatively easy to obtain a capacity $\hat{v}$ from a game v. To do this, for each subset A of N we consider the maximum value of the set function over the subsets contained in A.

Definition 10. *Let v be a game on N. The capacity associated to v is the set function $\hat{v} : 2^N \longrightarrow [0, \infty)$ given by*

$$\hat{v}(A) = \max_{B \subseteq A} v(B).$$

Some basic properties of $\hat{v}$ are given in the sequel.

Remark 3. Let v be a game on N. Then:

1. If v is a capacity, then $\hat{v} = v$.

2. If $v(A) \leq 1$ for all $A \subseteq N$ and $v(N) = 1$, then $\hat{v}$ is a normalized capacity.

In addition to the previous properties, it is worth noting that if a game on N fulfils the conditions given by (1), then the capacity associated to the game also satisfies these conditions.

Proposition 1. *Let p and w be two weighting vectors and let $v_{p,w}$ be a game on N such that $v_{p,\eta}(A) = \sum_{i \in A} p_i$ and $v_{\eta,w}(A) = \sum_{i=1}^{|A|} w_i$ for all $A \subseteq N$. Then, $\hat{v}_{p,\eta}(A) = \sum_{i \in A} p_i$ and $\hat{v}_{\eta,w}(A) = \sum_{i=1}^{|A|} w_i$ for all $A \subseteq N$.*

Proof. Given $A \subseteq N$,

$$\hat{v}_{p,\eta}(A) = \max_{B \subseteq A} v_{p,\eta}(B) = \max_{B \subseteq A} \sum_{i \in B} p_i = \sum_{i \in A} p_i,$$

$$\hat{v}_{\eta,w}(A) = \max_{B \subseteq A} v_{\eta,w}(B) = \max_{B \subseteq A} \sum_{i=1}^{|B|} w_i = \sum_{i=1}^{|A|} w_i. \qquad \square$$

In accordance with the previous remarks, instead of using the games $v_{p,w}^U$ we will use the capacities associated with them.

Definition 11. *Let p and w be two weighting vectors, let $U \in \mathcal{U}^{1/n}$, and let $v_{p,w}^U$ be the game associated to p, w and U. The capacity $\hat{v}_{p,w}^U$ associated to the game $v_{p,w}^U$ will be called the capacity associated to p, w and U.*

Notice that, by definition, $v_{p,w}^U(A) \geq 0$ for all $A \subseteq N$. Therefore, when $|A| = 1$ we have $\hat{v}_{p,w}^U(A) = v_{p,w}^U(A)$.

Once we know how to obtain capacities, our next goal is to get normalized capacities. According to 2) of Remark 3 and Proposition 1, in order to obtain a normalized capacity on N satisfying the conditions given by (1) it is sufficient to find a game $v_{p,w}$ on N satisfying these conditions and such that $v_{p,w}(A) \leq 1$ for all $A \subseteq N$ and $v_{p,w}(N) = 1$. However, the game $v_{p,w}^U$ may not satisfy the condition $v_{p,w}^U(A) \leq 1$ for all $A \subseteq N$, as we show in the following example.

Example 2. Let $p = (0.5, 0.2, 0.1, 0.1, 0.1)$ and $w = (0.6, 0.2, 0, 0, 0.2)$. Consider the semi-uninorm (see Calvo et al. [1, p. 11]) given by

$$U(x, y) = \max\left(0, \min(1, x + y - 0.2)\right).$$

It is easy to check that $U \in \mathcal{U}^{0.2}$. If $A = \{1, 2\}$ we have

$$v_{p,w}^U(A) = 2\,U(0.35, 0.4) = 2 \cdot 0.55 = 1.1 > 1.$$

Nevertheless, as we show in the following proposition, idempotent semi-uninorms allow us to guarantee the condition $v_{p,w}^U(A) \leq 1$ for all weighting vectors p and w and for all $A \subseteq N$.

Proposition 2. *Let $U \in \mathcal{U}^{1/n}$. If U is idempotent, then $v_{p,w}^U(A) \leq 1$ for all weighting vectors p and w and for all $A \subseteq N$.*

Proof. Given $\boldsymbol{p}, \boldsymbol{w}$ two weighting vectors and a non-empty set A of N, we have

$$v_{\boldsymbol{p},\boldsymbol{w}}^U(A) = |A|\, U\left(\sum_{i \in A} p_i \frac{\sum_{i=1}^{|A|} w_i}{|A|}, \frac{\sum_{i=1}^{|A|} w_i}{|A|}\right) \leq |A|\, U\left(\frac{1}{|A|}, \frac{1}{|A|}\right) = |A|\frac{1}{|A|} = 1. \qquad \square$$

We will denote by $\mathcal{U}_i^e$ the set of idempotent semi-uninorms with neutral element $e \in [0,1]$. It is worth noting that this class of functions has been characterized by Liu [9].

Proposition 3. *Let* $U \in \mathcal{U}^e$. U *is idempotent if and only if*

$$U(x,y) = \begin{cases} \min(x,y) & \text{if } (x,y) \in [0,e]^2, \\ \max(x,y) & \text{if } (x,y) \in [e,1]^2 \setminus \{(e,e)\}, \\ P(x,y) & \text{otherwise,} \end{cases}$$

where $P : [0,e) \times (e,1] \cup (e,1] \times [0,e) \longrightarrow [0,1]$ *is monotonic and* $\min(x,y) \leq P(x,y) \leq \max(x,y)$ *for all* $(x,y) \in [0,e) \times (e,1] \cup (e,1] \times [0,e)$.

Obviously, the smallest and the greatest idempotent semi-uninorm are, respectively, the following uninorms (which were given by Yager and Rybalov [17]):

$$U_{\min}(x,y) = \begin{cases} \max(x,y) & \text{if } (x,y) \in [1/n,1]^2, \\ \min(x,y) & \text{otherwise,} \end{cases}$$

$$U_{\max}(x,y) = \begin{cases} \min(x,y) & \text{if } (x,y) \in [0,1/n]^2, \\ \max(x,y) & \text{otherwise.} \end{cases}$$

In the next subsection we formally define the SUOWA operators.

3.2   SUOWA Operators

We now introduce SUOWA operators as the Choquet integrals with respect to the capacities $\hat{v}_{\boldsymbol{p},\boldsymbol{w}}^U$.

Definition 12. *Let* $\boldsymbol{p}$ *and* $\boldsymbol{w}$ *be two weighting vectors and let* $U \in \mathcal{U}_i^{1/n}$. *The semi-uninorm based ordered weighted averaging (SUOWA) operator associated to* $\boldsymbol{p}, \boldsymbol{w}$ *and* U *is the function* $S_{\boldsymbol{p},\boldsymbol{w}}^U : \mathbb{R}^n \longrightarrow \mathbb{R}$ *given by*

$$S_{\boldsymbol{p},\boldsymbol{w}}^U(\boldsymbol{x}) = \sum_{i=1}^n s_i x_{[i]},$$

where $s_i = \hat{v}_{\boldsymbol{p},\boldsymbol{w}}^U(A_{[i]}) - \hat{v}_{\boldsymbol{p},\boldsymbol{w}}^U(A_{[i-1]})$, *with* $\hat{v}_{\boldsymbol{p},\boldsymbol{w}}^U$ *the capacity associated to* $\boldsymbol{p}, \boldsymbol{w}$ *and* U, $A_{[i]} = \{[1], \ldots, [i]\}$ *and, by convention,* $A_{[0]} = \varnothing$.

According to Remak 1, and since $\hat{v}^U_{\boldsymbol{p},\boldsymbol{w}}$ are normalized capacities, SUOWA operators are continuous, monotonic, idempotent, compensative and homogeneous of degree 1 functions. In the sequel we show an example to illustrate these operators (the weighting vectors $\boldsymbol{p}$ and $\boldsymbol{w}$ are taken from Torra [13]).

Example 3. Let us to consider the weighting vectors $\boldsymbol{p} = (0.4, 0.1, 0.2, 0.3)$ and $\boldsymbol{w} = (0.125, 0.375, 0.375, 0.125)$. Besides $U_{\min}$ and $U_{\max}$, we are also going to use U_{am}, the idempotent semi-uninorm obtained by means of the arithmetic mean:

$$U_{\mathrm{am}}(x,y) = \begin{cases} \min(x,y) & \text{if } (x,y) \in [0, 0.25]^2, \\ \max(x,y) & \text{if } (x,y) \in [0.25,1]^2 \setminus \{(0.25, 0.25)\}, \\ (x+y)/2 & \text{otherwise.} \end{cases}$$

In Table 1 we show the games and the capacities associated to these idempotent semi-uninorms. Note that all the values of the games coincide with those of the capacities; that is, the games $v^{U_{\min}}_{\boldsymbol{p},\boldsymbol{w}}$, $v^{U_{\mathrm{am}}}_{\boldsymbol{p},\boldsymbol{w}}$ and $v^{U_{\max}}_{\boldsymbol{p},\boldsymbol{w}}$ are actually capacities.

Table 1. Games and capacities associated to $U_{\min}$, U_{am} and $U_{\max}$

| Set | $U_{\min}$ | | U_{am} | | $U_{\max}$ | |
	$v^{U_{\min}}_{\boldsymbol{p},\boldsymbol{w}}$	$\hat{v}^{U_{\min}}_{\boldsymbol{p},\boldsymbol{w}}$	$v^{U_{\mathrm{am}}}_{\boldsymbol{p},\boldsymbol{w}}$	$\hat{v}^{U_{\mathrm{am}}}_{\boldsymbol{p},\boldsymbol{w}}$	$v^{U_{\max}}_{\boldsymbol{p},\boldsymbol{w}}$	$\hat{v}^{U_{\max}}_{\boldsymbol{p},\boldsymbol{w}}$
$\{1\}$	0.125	0.125	0.2625	0.2625	0.4	0.4
$\{2\}$	0.1	0.1	0.1	0.1	0.1	0.1
$\{3\}$	0.125	0.125	0.125	0.125	0.125	0.125
$\{4\}$	0.125	0.125	0.2125	0.2125	0.3	0.3
$\{1,2\}$	0.5	0.5	0.5	0.5	0.5	0.5
$\{1,3\}$	0.6	0.6	0.6	0.6	0.6	0.6
$\{1,4\}$	0.7	0.7	0.7	0.7	0.7	0.7
$\{2,3\}$	0.3	0.3	0.3	0.3	0.3	0.3
$\{2,4\}$	0.4	0.4	0.4	0.4	0.4	0.4
$\{3,4\}$	0.5	0.5	0.5	0.5	0.5	0.5
$\{1,2,3\}$	0.7	0.7	0.7875	0.7875	0.875	0.875
$\{1,2,4\}$	0.875	0.875	0.875	0.875	0.875	0.875
$\{1,3,4\}$	0.9	0.9	0.9	0.9	0.9	0.9
$\{2,3,4\}$	0.6	0.6	0.7375	0.7375	0.875	0.875
N	1	1	1	1	1	1

When $\boldsymbol{x} = (7, 6, 4, 3)$, the values returned by the SUOWA operators by using the capacities $v_{\boldsymbol{p},\boldsymbol{w}}^{U_{\min}}$, $v_{\boldsymbol{p},\boldsymbol{w}}^{U_{\mathrm{am}}}$ and $v_{\boldsymbol{p},\boldsymbol{w}}^{U_{\max}}$ are

$$S_{\boldsymbol{p},\boldsymbol{w}}^{U_{\min}}(7, 6, 4, 3) = 0.125 \cdot 7 + 0.375 \cdot 6 + 0.2 \cdot 4 + 0.3 \cdot 3 = 4.825,$$

$$S_{\boldsymbol{p},\boldsymbol{w}}^{U_{\mathrm{am}}}(7, 6, 4, 3) = 0.2625 \cdot 7 + 0.2375 \cdot 6 + 0.2875 \cdot 4 + 0.2125 \cdot 3 = 5.05,$$

$$S_{\boldsymbol{p},\boldsymbol{w}}^{U_{\max}}(7, 6, 4, 3) = 0.4 \cdot 7 + 0.1 \cdot 6 + 0.375 \cdot 4 + 0.125 \cdot 3 = 5.275.$$

However, when $\boldsymbol{x} = (6, 7, 3, 4)$, the three functions take the same value:

$$S_{\boldsymbol{p},\boldsymbol{w}}^{U_{\min}}(6, 7, 3, 4) = S_{\boldsymbol{p},\boldsymbol{w}}^{U_{\mathrm{am}}}(6, 7, 3, 4) = S_{\boldsymbol{p},\boldsymbol{w}}^{U_{\max}}(6, 7, 3, 4)$$
$$= 0.1 \cdot 7 + 0.4 \cdot 6 + 0.375 \cdot 4 + 0.125 \cdot 3 = 4.975.$$

4   Conclusion

In some practical cases it is necessary to combine values by using both a weighting mean and a OWA type aggregation. Although there exist in the literature a large number of aggregation operators, WOWA operators are the only ones that possess desirable properties for aggregation and allow us to deal with this kind of situations. As WOWA operators, the functions introduced in this paper are obtained from Choquet integrals with respect to normalized capacities. Therefore, SUOWA operators are continuous, monotonic, idempotent, compensative and homogeneous of degree 1 functions, and, consequently, they constitute an alternative to WOWA operators to deal with this kind of aggregation problems.

Acknowledgments. This work is partially supported by the Spanish Ministry of Economy and Competitiveness (Project ECO2012-32178).

References

1. Calvo, T., Kolesárová, A., Komorníková, M., Mesiar, R.: Aggregation operators: properties, classes and construction methods. In: Calvo, T., Mayor, G., Mesiar, R. (eds.) Aggregation Operators, pp. 3–104. Physica-Verlag, Heidelberg (2002)
2. Choquet, G.: Theory of capacities. Ann. Inst. Fourier 5, 131–295 (1953)
3. Fodor, J., Marichal, J.L., Roubens, M.: Characterization of the ordered weighted averaging operators. IEEE Trans. Fuzzy Syst. 3(2), 236–240 (1995)
4. Fodor, J., De Baets, B.: Uninorm basics. In: Wang, P.P., Ruan, D., Kerre, E.E. (eds.) Fuzzy Logic: A Spectrum of Theoretical & Practical Issues. STUDFUZZ, vol. 215, pp. 49–64. Springer, Berlin (2007)
5. Fodor, J.C., Yager, R.R., Rybalov, A.: Structure of uninorms. Int. J. Uncertain. Fuzziness Knowl.-Based Syst. 5(4), 411–427 (1997)
6. Grabisch, M.: Fuzzy integral in multicriteria decision making. Fuzzy Sets Syst. 69(3), 279–298 (1995)
7. Grabisch, M.: On equivalence classes of fuzzy connectives - the case of fuzzy integrals. IEEE Trans. Fuzzy Syst. 3(1), 96–109 (1995)

8. Grabisch, M., Marichal, J., Mesiar, R., Pap, E.: Aggregation Functions. Cambridge University Press, New York (2009)
9. Liu, H.W.: Semi-uninorms and implications on a complete lattice. Fuzzy Sets Syst. 191, 72–82 (2012)
10. Llamazares, B.: An analysis of some functions that generalizes weighted means and OWA operators. Int. J. Intell. Syst. 28(4), 380–393 (2013)
11. Murofushi, T., Sugeno, M.: A theory of fuzzy measures. Representation, the Choquet integral and null sets. J. Math. Anal. Appl. 159(2), 532–549 (1991)
12. Sugeno, M.: Theory of Fuzzy Integrals and its Applications. Phd thesis, Tokyo Institute of Technology (1974)
13. Torra, V.: The weighted OWA operator. Int. J. Intell. Syst. 12(2), 153–166 (1997)
14. Torra, V.: On some relationships between the WOWA operator and the Choquet integral. In: Proceedings of the Seventh International Conference on Information Processing and Management of Uncertainty in Knowledge-Based Systems (IPMU 1998), Paris, France, pp. 818–824 (July 1998)
15. Torra, V., Narukawa, Y.: Modeling Decisions: Information Fusion and Aggregation Operators. Springer, Berlin (2007)
16. Yager, R.R.: On ordered weighted averaging operators in multicriteria decision making. IEEE Trans. Syst., Man, Cybern. 18(1), 183–190 (1988)
17. Yager, R.R., Rybalov, A.: Uninorm aggregation operators. Fuzzy Sets Syst. 80(1), 111–120 (1996)

Attitude-Driven Web Consensus Support System for Large-Scale GDM Problems Based on Fuzzy Linguistic Approach

Iván Palomares * and Luis Martínez

University of Jaén, Computer Science Department,
Campus Las Lagunillas s/n, 23071 Jaén, Spain
{ivanp,martin}@ujaen.es

Abstract. In real-life Group Decision Making problems defined under uncertainty, it is usually necessary to carry out a consensus reaching process to achieve a solution that is accepted by all experts in the group. Additionally, when a high number of experts take part in such processes, it may sometimes occur that some subgroups of them with similar interests try to bias the collective opinion, which makes it more difficult to reach a collective agreement. The consensus reaching process could be optimized if the group's attitude towards consensus were integrated in it, and the complexity of dealing with large groups of experts could be reduced with the adequate automation of such a process. This paper presents a Web-based Consensus Support System for large-scale group decision making problems defined under uncertainty, that integrates the group's attitude towards consensus and allows experts to provide their preferences by means of linguistic information. The underlying consensus model of the proposed system carries out processes of Computing with Words to deal with linguistic preferences effectively.

Keywords: Linguistic Group Decision Making, Consensus Reaching, Consensus Support System, Attitude.

1 Introduction

Decision making is a usual mankind process in daily life. In a group decision making (GDM) problem, a group of decision makers or experts try to reach a common solution to a problem consisting of a set of possible alternatives [3]. Real GDM problems are often defined under an uncertain environment, so that experts may prefer in some occasions to provide information (preferences about alternatives) in a domain closer to human natural language, e.g. by means of linguistic information [1, 10].

An increasingly important aspect in many real GDM problems is the need for a common solution which is accepted by all experts in the group, which can be achieved if Consensus Reaching Processes (CRPs) are introduced as part of the

---

* Corresponding author.

C. Bielza et al. (Eds.): CAEPIA 2013, LNAI 8109, pp. 91–100, 2013.

GDM problems resolution process [7]. Nowadays computational advances make it possible the participation of larger groups of experts in CRPs. However, some challenges arise in CRPs during the resolution of large-scale GDM problems:

- The possible existence of subgroups of experts with an own-group interest, who try to deviate the solution of the GDM problem to a solution according to their aims forgetting about the CRP, so that it is much more difficult to achieve an agreed solution. In such cases, the integration of the group's attitude towards consensus, i.e. experts' capacity to modify their own preferences during the CRP, becomes an important aspect to optimize CRPs involving large groups [5].
- Despite CRPs are classically guided and supervised by a human moderator [7], the management of large groups not only turns his/her tasks more complex, but also complicates physical meetings. The design of a Consensus Support System (CSS) that automates the moderator's tasks and facilitates non-physical meetings becomes then necessary.

This paper presents a web-based CSS that supports consensus processes for large-scale GDM problems defined under uncertainty. The underlying consensus model of such a system integrates the group's attitude towards consensus in the CRP, and it allows experts the use of linguistic information to provide their preferences. In order to facilitate computations on linguistic information across the CRP, the methodology of Computing with Words (CW) [6,11] is considered, by utilizing the 2-tuple linguistic model [2] to carry out such computations.

This paper is structured as follows: Section 2 revises some basic concepts. Section 3 presents the proposed CSS and its underlying consensus model. Section 4 shows an example of the CSS performance, and Section 5 concludes the paper.

2 Basic Concepts

In this section, some preliminary concepts used in our proposal about linguistic GDM, the 2-tuple linguistic model and attitude integration in CRPs are reviewed.

2.1 Linguistic Group Decision Making

GDM problems are formally defined as decision situations in which a set $E = \{e_1, \ldots, e_m\}$, $(m \geq 2)$, of decision makers or *experts* must express their preferences over a finite set of *alternatives* $X = \{x_1, \ldots, x_n\}$, $(n \geq 2)$ by using a preference structure, for instance a *linguistic preference relation* P_i [1]:

$$P_i = \begin{pmatrix} - & \cdots & p_i^{1n} \\ \vdots & \ddots & \vdots \\ p_i^{n1} & \cdots & - \end{pmatrix}$$

where each assessment $p_i^{lk} = s_u \in S$ represents e_i's degree of preference of alternative x_l over x_k, $(l \neq k)$, expressed as a linguistic term s_u in a term set

$S = \{s_0, \ldots, s_g\}$ with granularity g. Without loss of generality, it is assumed in this paper that S is chosen by considering that linguistic terms s_u $(u = 0, \ldots, g)$, are symmetrically distributed in an ordered scale, with odd cardinality, $|S| = g + 1$. It is also assumed here that the semantics of a term $s_u \in S$ will be represented by a triangular fuzzy number in the unit interval [4].

2.2 2-tuple Linguistic Computational Model for CW

Classical resolution schemes for linguistic GDM [1], showed the necessity of using models to operate with linguistic information accurately and obtain understandable results [6]. The methodology of CW was proposed by L. Zadeh in [11] to facilitate reasoning, computational and decision making processes on linguistic information. In the field of CW, there exist multiple linguistic computational models that define different operations on linguistic information, such as aggregation, comparison, etc. One of the most extended models of CW in linguistic decision making is the so-called 2-tuple linguistic model [2], which avoids the loss of information and guarantees accurate and understandable results.

The 2-tuple linguistic model represents the information by means of a pair (s, α), where $s \in S$ is a linguistic term and $\alpha \in [-0.5, 0.5)$ is a *symbolic translation* that supports the "difference of information" between a counting of information β assessed in the interval of granularity of S, $[0, g]$, and its closest value in $\{0, \ldots, g\}$, which indicates the index of the closest linguistic term in S. Some functions were defined to facilitate computational processes on 2-tuples by transforming them into numerical values. A bijective function $\Delta : [0, g] \rightarrow S \times [-0, 5, 0.5)$ is defined as follows [2]:

$$\Delta(\beta) = (s_i, \alpha), \text{ with } \begin{cases} i = \text{round}(\beta), \\ \alpha = \beta - i, \end{cases} \tag{1}$$

where *round* assigns β its closest value $i \in \{0, \ldots, g\}$. An inverse function $\Delta^{-1} : S \times [-0, 5, 0.5) \rightarrow [0, g]$ which, given a linguistic 2-tuple, returns its equivalent numerical value β, is also defined as:

$$\Delta^{-1}(s_i, \alpha) = i + \alpha = \beta \tag{2}$$

The 2-tuple linguistic computational model defined different operations on 2-tuples [2]. The consensus approach proposed (see Sect. 3.1) considers the use of 2-tuple aggregation operators across the CRP [4,6].

2.3 Attitude Integration in Consensus Reaching

The integration of the group's attitude towards consensus in situations in which several subgroups of experts with different interests take part in a large-scale GDM problem, might help optimizing CRPs according to their needs and the characteristics of each particular problem. A model that integrates such an attitude was recently proposed in [5], where the following two types of group's attitudes were presented:

- *Optimistic attitude*: Achieving an agreement is more important for experts than their own preferences. Therefore, more importance is given to positions in the group with higher agreement.
- *Pessimistic attitude*: Experts prefer to preserve their own preferences. Therefore, positions in the group with lower agreement are given more importance.

Here, we also introduce the possibility of adopting a neutral attitude:

- *Neutral attitude*: Experts consider that both achieving an agreement and preserving their own preferences are equally important. Therefore, positions in the group with an intermediate degree of agreement attain a greater importance.

In order to integrate the attitude of experts in CRPs, it is used an aggregation operator, so-called Attitude-OWA, which extends OWA aggregation operators [8] and is specially suitable for dealing with large groups of experts [5]. Attitude-OWA uses two *attitudinal parameters* provided by the decision group:

- $\vartheta \in [0,1]$ represents the group's attitude, which can be optimistic ($\vartheta > 0.5$), pessimistic ($\vartheta < 0.5$) or neutral ($\vartheta = 0.5$). It is equivalent to the *orness* measure that characterizes OWA operators [8].
- $\varphi \in [0,1]$ indicates the amount of agreement positions that are given non-null weight in the aggregation. The higher φ, the more values are considered.

Attitude-OWA operator is then defined as follows:

Definition 1. *[5] An* Attitude-OWA operator *on a set* $A = \{a_1, \ldots, a_h\}$, *based on attitudinal parameters* ϑ, φ, *is defined by:*

$$Attitude - OWA_W(A, \vartheta, \varphi) = \sum_{j=1}^{h} w_j b_j \tag{3}$$

being $W = [w_1 \ldots w_h]^\top$ *a weighting vector, with* $w_i \in [0,1], \sum_i w_i = 1$, *and* b_j *the* j*-th largest of* a_i *values.*

Weights w_i are computed based on ϑ and φ, so that they reflect the attitude adopted by experts. The following scheme was proposed to compute them [5]:

i) The values of ϑ, φ are determined, based on the interests of experts in the group and/or the nature of the GDM problem.
ii) A *Regular Increasing Monotone* quantifier with membership funcion $Q(r)$,

$$Q(r) = \begin{cases} 0 & \text{if } r \leq \gamma, \\ \frac{r-\gamma}{\delta-\gamma} & \text{if } \gamma < r \leq \delta, \\ 1 & \text{if } r > \delta. \end{cases} \tag{4}$$

is defined, being $r \in [0,1]$, $\gamma = 1 - \vartheta - \frac{\varphi}{2}$ and $\delta = \gamma + \varphi$.
iii) Yager's method is applied to compute weights w_i [9]:

$$w_i = Q\left(\frac{i}{h}\right) - Q\left(\frac{i-1}{h}\right), i = 1, \ldots, h \tag{5}$$

3   Consensus Support System

This section presents an attitude-based Web CSS aimed to solve large-scale linguistic GDM problems. Its main novelty is the consensus model implemented, which extends the one proposed in [5], by introducing the necessary steps to manage linguistic information based on the 2-tuple linguistic model, and improving the feedback mechanism applied during the CRP to avoid generating an excessive amount of advice for experts. The Web-based CSS architecture is also presented.

The CSS description is divided into two parts: (i) a detailed scheme of the consensus model; and (ii) an overview of the architecture and functionalities of the system.

3.1   Consensus Model

A scheme of the proposed consensus model is depicted in Fig. 1. Its phases are described in detail below:

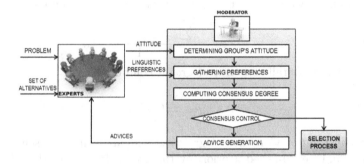

Fig. 1. Consensus model scheme

1. *Determining Group's Attitude*: The group's attitude towards consensus is determined by gathering attitudinal parameters ϑ, φ.
2. *Gathering Preferences*: Each e_i provides his/her preferences on X by means of a linguistic preference relation $P_i = (p_i^{lk})^{n \times n}$, $p_i^{lk} \in S$ (see Sect. 2.1).
3. *Computing Consensus Degree*: The degree of collective agrement is computed as a value in $[0,1]$ (inspired by Kacprzyk's notion of "soft consensus" [3]). This paper introduces the use of the 2-tuple linguistic model in this phase to carry out processes of CW on linguistic information. Additionally, the group's attitude towards consensus is integrated during this phase:
   (a) For each linguistic assessment $p_i^{lk} = s_u$ $(u = 0, \ldots, g)$, its corresponding β value (which will be denoted as β_i^{lk}) is computed as follows:

$$\beta_i^{lk} = \Delta^{-1}\left((s_u, 0)_i^{lk}\right) = u \tag{6}$$

   being $(s_u, 0)_i^{lk}$ the 2-tuple associated to an assessment $p_i^{lk} = s_u \in S$ and Δ^{-1} the transformation function shown in Eq. (2) [2].

(b) For each pair e_i, e_t, $(i < t)$, a *similarity matrix* $SM_{it} = (sm_{it}^{lk})^{n \times n}$, $sm_{it}^{lk} \in [0, 1]$, is computed:

$$sm_{it}^{lk} = 1 - \left| \frac{\beta_i^{lk} - \beta_t^{lk}}{g} \right| \tag{7}$$

(c) A *consensus matrix* $CM = (cm^{lk})_{n \times n}$ is obtained by aggregating similarity values, by means of Attitude-OWA operator, which integrates the group's attitude in the CRP (see Sect. 2.3) [5]. This aggregation step is the main novelty, with respect to other previous consensus models, for the management of large groups in CRPs:

$$cm^{lk} = Attitude - OWA_W (SIM^{lk}, \vartheta, \varphi) \tag{8}$$

where the set $SIM^{lk} = \{sm_{12}^{lk}, \ldots, sm_{1m}^{lk}, \ldots, sm_{(m-1)m}^{lk}\}$ represents all pairs of experts' similarities in their opinion on (x_l, x_k), and cm^{lk} is the degree of consensus achieved by the group in their opinion on (x_l, x_k).

(d) Consensus degrees ca^l on each alternative x_l, are computed as

$$ca^l = \frac{\sum_{k=1, k \neq l}^{n} cm^{lk}}{n - 1} \tag{9}$$

(e) Finally, an overall consensus degree is computed:

$$cr = \frac{\sum_{l=1}^{n} ca^l}{n} \tag{10}$$

4. *Consensus Control*: Consensus degree cr is compared with a consensus threshold $\mu \in [0, 1]$, established a priori by the group. If $cr \geq \mu$, the CRP ends and the group moves on the selection process; otherwise, the process requires further discussion. A parameter $Maxrounds \in \mathbb{N}$ can be also defined to limit the maximum number of discussion rounds.

5. *Advice Generation*: When $cr < \mu$, experts must modify their preferences to make them closer to each other and increase the consensus degree in the following CRP round. Despite a human moderator has been traditionally responsible for advising and guiding experts during CRPs [7], the proposed CSS automates his/her tasks, most of which are conducted in this phase of the CRP. Two novelties are introduced in this phase: the use of the 2-tuple linguistic model to carry out computations on linguistic assessments, and a threshold parameter that will improve the feedback generation mechanism.

(a) Compute a collective preference and proximity matrices: A 2-tuple-based collective preference $P_c = (p_c^{lk})^{n \times n}$, $p_c^{lk} \in S \times [-0.5, 0.5)$, is computed for each pair of alternatives by aggregating experts' preference relations:

$$p_c^{lk} = (s_u, \alpha)_c^{lk} = \nu((s_u, \alpha)_1^{lk}, \ldots, (s_u, \alpha)_m^{lk}) \tag{11}$$

where $s \in S$ and ν is a 2-tuple aggregation operator [2, 4, 6]. Afterwards, a proximity matrix PP_i between each e_i's preference relation and P_c

is obtained. Proximity values $pp_i^{lk} \in [0,1]$ are computed for each pair (x_l, x_k) as follows:

$$pp_i^{lk} = 1 - \left| \frac{\beta_i^{lk} - \beta_c^{lk}}{g} \right| \tag{12}$$

being $\beta_c^{lk} = \Delta^{-1}\left((s,\alpha)_c^{lk}\right)$.

(b) Identify preferences to be changed (CC): Assessments on pairs (x_l, x_k) whose consensus degrees ca^l and cp^{lk} are not enough, are identified:

$$CC = \{(x_l, x_k) | ca^l < cr \wedge cp^{lk} < cr\} \tag{13}$$

Based on CC, the model identifies those experts who should change their opinions on each of these pairs, i.e. those e_is whose assessment p_i^{lk} on $(x_l, x_k) \in CC$ is furthest to p_c^{lk}. To do so, an average proximity $\overline{pp}^{lk}$ is calculated, by using an aggregation operator λ:

$$\overline{pp}^{lk} = \lambda(pp_1^{lk}, \ldots, pp_m^{lk}) \tag{14}$$

Experts e_i whose $pp_i^{lk} < \overline{pp}^{lk}$ are advised to modify their assessments p_i^{lk} on (x_l, x_k).

(c) Establish change directions: Some direction rules are checked to suggest the direction of changes proposed to experts on their linguistic assessments. Here, we propose a novel mechanism that optimizes the performance of this step in large-scale GDM, by introducing an acceptability threshold $\varepsilon \geq 0$, to allow a margin of acceptability in the cases that β_i^{lk} and β_c^{lk} are close to each other. This approach prevents generating an excessive number of unnecessary advice for experts in such cases.

  – DIR.1: If $(\beta_i^{lk} - \beta_c^{lk}) < -\varepsilon$, then e_i should *increase* his/her assessment p_i^{lk} on (x_l, x_k).
  – DIR.2: If $(\beta_i^{lk} - \beta_c^{lk}) > \varepsilon$, then e_i should *decrease* his/her assessment p_i^{lk} on (x_l, x_k).
  – DIR.3: If $-\varepsilon \leq (\beta_i^{lk} - \beta_c^{lk}) \leq \varepsilon$ then e_i should not modify his/her assessment p_i^{lk} on (x_l, x_k).

3.2   System Architecture

The CSS is based on a client/server architecture with a Web user interface, so that users do not have to install any specific software to use the CSS in their computer. Figure 2 depicts the architecture of the CSS and the communication between the client and server sides, which will be explained in further detail below.

The main advantage of the system is the automation of the human moderator, thus eliminating any biasness caused by his/her possible subjectivity, and it facilitates ubiquitous CRPs amongst large groups of experts. The CSS functions are divided into two categories: client and server functions.

Client. On the client side, the following four interfaces have been designed to communicate the CSS with experts participating in a GDM problem:

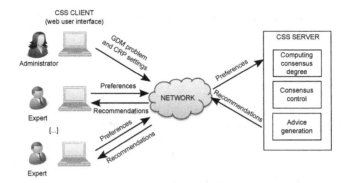

Fig. 2. CSS architecture and client-server communication

- *Authentication*: An expert introduces his/her username and password to authenticate in the CSS.
- *Problem selection*: The expert is shown information about the GDM problem/s to which he/she has been invited to take part.
- *Preferences elicitacion* (Fig. 3): Experts provide their preferences by means of a linguistic preference relation (Sect. 3.1, phase 2), whose assessments are linguistic terms in a term set defined a priori by the administrator of the CSS, as will be explained below.
- *Checking advice received during the CRP*: At the end of a discussion round (after phase 5 in Sect. 3.1), the application shows each expert the advice to modify his/her preferences.

Id Problem: p001

Description: Budget investment by city council

Round current: 1

Alternatives:
    x1: Tram line
    x2: Indoor shopping center
    x3: Green areas and parks
    x4: Leisure and sport facilities

Domain: {n=none, vl=very low, l=low, a=average, h=high, vh=very high, p=perfect}

INSERT NEW PREFERENCES:

	x1	x2	x3	x4
x1	-	l	l	a
x2	h	-	vh	vh
x3	l	vl	-	a
x4	a	vl	n	-

Insert opinion

Consult problem

Go out

Fig. 3. Expressing preferences

Additionally, some users can log in the system under the role of administrator to define the initial GDM problem settings, including: the GDM problem description and alternatives, experts invited to take part in the problem, parameters of the CRP and the linguistic term set to be used by experts.

Server. The server communicates with the client interfaces to send/receive information to/from experts by means of the Internet. Some modules that correspond with different phases of the consensus model described in Sect. 3.1 are implemented here to automate the human moderator tasks during the CRP: (i) computing the consensus degree (Sect. 3.1, phase 3), (ii) consensus Control (Sect. 3.1, phase 4) and (iii) advice Generation (Sect. 3.1, phase 5).

4 System Performance

In this section, a large-scale GDM problem is introduced and solved by using the proposed CSS. The problem is formulated as follows: a group of 41 students from Computer Science M.Sc. Degree, $E = \{e_1, \ldots, e_{41}\}$, must make an agreed decision about choosing a place to celebrate their graduation dinner. The set of proposed restaurants is $X = \{x_1 : $ 'Santa Catalina' castle, $x_2 : $ 'Los Caballos' ranch, $x_3 : $ 'Pegalajar' caves, $x_4 : $ 'Juleca' complex$\}$.

The following linguistic term set is defined to allow students provide their preferences, $S = \{s_0 : None(n), s_1 : Very\ low(vl), s_2 : Low(l), s_3 : Average(a), s_4 : High(h), s_5 : Very\ high(vh), s_6 : Perfect(p)\}$.

The group stated that they preferred to achieve a collective agreement as fast as possible, rather than preserving their own individual preferences. The CRP was first applied without considering the group's attitude (the arithmetic mean operator was used instead of Attitude-OWA to compute cm^{lk} in Eq. (8)). Afterwards, the CRP was carried out again twice, by defining two different attitudes: an optimistic and a pessimistic attitude. Table 1 shows the parameters defined for the CRP, including the two attitudes considered.

Table 1. Parameters defined at the beginning of the CRP

Attitudinal param.	Optimistic $\vartheta = 0.65, \varphi = 0.6$
	Pessimistic: $\vartheta = 0.35, \varphi = 0.6$
Consensus threshold	$\mu = 0.85$
Max. #rounds	$Maxrounds = 10$
Accept. threshold	$\varepsilon = 0.2$

Once all experts logged in the system, selected the GDM problem to take part in it and submitted their initial preferences by means of the Web user interface (see Fig. 3), the CRP began. Table 2 shows the convergence towards consensus, i.e. the consensus degree achieved at each round, for each case defined above. Students were most satisfied with the solution achieved when an optimistic attitude was adopted, because a fewer number of discussion rounds was required in this case to reach a consensus.

The proposed CSS facilitated the resolution of the large-scale GDM problem defined, taking into account the attitude of experts towards consensus and letting them provide their preferences by means of linguistic terms. The 2-tuple linguistic model made it possible to make the necessary computations of the CRP on linguistic information without any loss of information.

Table 2. Global consensus degree for each round

Consensus round:	1	2	3	4	5	6	7	8
Without attitude	0.695	0.743	0.772	0.805	0.823	**0.855**		
Pessimistic	0.512	0.587	0.656	0.707	0.749	0.801	0.839	**0.868**
Optimistic	0.793	0.828	**0.851**					

5   Concluding Remarks

In this paper, we have presented a Web-based Consensus Support System to deal with large-scale linguistic group decision making problems. The presented system, which incorporates a client-server architecture that automates the consensus reaching process to a high degree, is characterized by integrating the group's attitude towards consensus. The consensus model carries out processes of Computing with Words based on the 2-tuple linguistic model to deal with linguistic information provided by experts, thus preventing any loss of information.

Acknowledgements. This work is partially supported by the Research Project TIN-2012-31263 and ERDF.

References

1. Herrera, F., Herrera-Viedma, E.: Linguistic decision analysis: Steps for solving decision problems under linguistic information. Fuzzy Sets and Systems 115(1), 67–82 (2000)
2. Herrera, F., Martínez, L.: A 2-tuple fuzzy linguistic representation model for computing with words. IEEE Transactions on Fuzzy Systems 8(6), 746–752 (2000)
3. Kacprzyk, J.: Group decision making with a fuzzy linguistic majority. Fuzzy Sets and Systems 18(2), 105–118 (1986)
4. Martínez, L., Ruan, D., Herrera, F.: Computing with words in decision support systems: An overview on models and applications. International Journal of Computational Intelligence Systems 3(4), 382–395 (2010)
5. Palomares, I., Liu, J., Xu, Y., Martínez, L.: Modelling experts' attitudes in group decision making. Soft Computing 16(10), 1755–1766 (2012)
6. Rodríguez, R.M., Martínez, L.: An analysis of symbolic linguistic computing models in decision making. International Journal of General Systems 42(1), 121–136 (2013)
7. Saint, S., Lawson, J.R.: Rules for Reaching Consensus. A Modern Approach to Decision Making. Jossey-Bass (1994)
8. Yager, R.R.: On orderer weighted averaging aggregation operators in multi-criteria decision making. IEEE Transactions on Systems, Man and Cybernetics 18(1), 183–190 (1988)
9. Yager, R.R.: Quantifier guided aggregation using OWA operators. International Journal of Intelligent Systems 11, 49–73 (1996)
10. Zadeh, L.A.: The concept of a linguistic variable and its applications to approximate reasoning. Information Sciences, Part I, II, III, 8, 8, 9, 199–249, 301–357, 43–80 (1975)
11. Zadeh, L.A.: Fuzzy logic equals computing with words. IEEE Transactions on Fuzzy Systems 4(2), 103–111 (1996)

Decidability of a Logic for Order of Magnitude Qualitative Reasoning with Comparability and Negligibility Relations

Alfredo Burrieza

Dept. Filosofía, Universidad de Málaga, Spain
`burrieza@uma.es`

Abstract. Qualitative Reasoning is a branch of Artificial Intelligence that automates the reasoning about the behavior of physical systems by using qualitative rather than precise quantitative information. An approach in this field is Order-of-magnitude Reasoning which deals with coarse values of different orders of magnitude which are abstractions of precise values. Several multimodal logics has been introduced to deal with Orders-of-magnitude systems proving their correctness and completeness although their decidability has been scarcely studied. In this paper we focus our attention on this problem showing that a pioneering logic in this area has the strong model property.

Qualitative Reasoning (QR) is a branch of Artificial Intelligence that automates the reasoning about the behavior of physical systems by using qualitative rather than precise quantitative information. QR offers a representation of real world close to human patterns where quantitative reasoning is not so important to make decisions. An approach in this field is Order-of-magnitude Reasoning (OMR) which deals with coarse values of different orders of magnitude which are abstractions of precise values. Two approaches to order of magnitude reasoning can be identified: Absolute Order of Magnitude (AOM) and Relative Order of Magnitude (ROM) models. In AOM reasoning each element belongs to a qualitative class. It is usual to consider some specific real numbers as landmarks to divide the real line into equivalence classes. For instance, in [7] these classes are denoted by "negative large" (NL), "negative medium" (NM), "negative small" (NS), "zero" ([0]), "positive small" (PS), "positive medium" (PM) and "positive large"(PL). On the other hand, ROM reasoning introduces a family of binary order of magnitude relations which establish different comparison relations between numbers. The seminal work was the formal system introduced in [8], based on three basic relations, used to represent the intuitive concepts "negligibility", "closeness" and "comparability". However, both approaches AOM and ROM reasoning have been integrated in [9, 10], where an absolute partition is combined with a set of comparison relations between real numbers.

The first logic to deal with order of magnitude reasoning was introduced in [1], a multimodal logic considered in the context of a mixed approach where the set of values is merely a subset of the real numbers and with a designed number α so that $-\alpha$ and $+\alpha$ serves to delimit the qualitative classes:

C. Bielza et al. (Eds.): CAEPIA 2013, LNAI 8109, pp. 101–110, 2013.

In the picture, $-\alpha$ and $+\alpha$ are used to build the qualitative classes of "positive observable" (OBS$^+$), "negative observable" (OBS$^-$) and "non-observable" (also called infinitesimal) numbers (INF). This choice makes sense, in particular, when considering physical metric spaces in which we always have a smallest unit which can be measured; however, it is not possible to identify a least or greatest non-observable number. We can make comparisons between these sets of numbers by using binary relations such as x *is less than* y ($x < y$) and x *is less than and comparable to* y ($x \sqsubset y$). This approach was extended in [2] by introducing a negligibility relation x *is negligible w.r.t.* y ($x \prec y$). The notion of negligibility used in that paper is directional, that is, negligible numbers are always to the left, so a negligible number with respect to a given number x is smaller than x. Later on, a multimodal logic with a notion of bidirectional negligibility (where the sign of the numbers is not taken into account) was introduced in [4] and others magnitude relations as non-closeness and distance were introduced in [5]. In [4] neglibility relation is defined exclusively in terms of qualitative classes. Thus a number x is negligible with respect to a number y if and only if either $x = 0$ or both x is small and y is large (independently of their signs). In contrast, in [2] neglibility relation may even exist between two numbers of the same class unless both belong to INF.

Much work has been done on the completeness of this kind of logics but little in the study of their decidability. Until very recently the only work appeared on this subject was [3], where a decision procedure based on tableau calculus was developed but only for a fragment of the logic proposed in [1]. After that, the first result about the decidability of an entire logic on order-of-magnitude reasoning is [6]. In that paper the decidability of the logic proposed in [4] has been proved showing that it has the strong finite model property. In this paper we focus our attention on the decidability of the logic proposed in [2] proving that it has the same property.

1   Logic $\mathcal{L}(MQ)^N$

In our syntax we will consider the connectives $\overrightarrow{\square}$ and $\overleftarrow{\square}$ to deal with the usual ordering $<$, the connectives $\overrightarrow{\blacksquare}$ and $\overleftarrow{\blacksquare}$ to deal with $\sqsubset$ and the connectives $\overrightarrow{\boxdot}$ and $\overleftarrow{\boxdot}$ to deal with $\prec$. The intuitive meanings of each modal connective is as follows:

$\overrightarrow{\square}A$: *A is true for all number greater than the current one.*
$\overrightarrow{\blacksquare}A$: *A is true for all number greater than and comparable to the current one.*
$\overleftarrow{\square}A$: *A is true for all number less than the current one.*
$\overleftarrow{\blacksquare}A$: *A is true for all number less than and comparable to the current one.*
$\overrightarrow{\boxdot}A$: *A is true for all number from which the current one is negligible.*
$\overleftarrow{\boxdot}A$: *A is true for all number which is negligible from the current one.*

The alphabet of the language of $\mathcal{L}(MQ)^N$ is defined by using a stock of atoms or propositional variables, $\mathcal{V}$, the classical connectives $\neg, \wedge, \vee$ and $\rightarrow$, the constants $\top$ and $\bot$, the unary modal connectives $\overrightarrow{\Box}, \overleftarrow{\Box}, \overrightarrow{\blacksquare}, \overleftarrow{\blacksquare}, \overrightarrow{\boxed{m}}$ and $\overleftarrow{\boxed{m}}$, the constants α^+ and α^- and the auxiliary symbols: (,). $\mathcal{L}(MQ)^N$-*formulas* are generated from $\mathcal{V} \cup \{\alpha^+, \alpha^-, \top, \bot\}$ by the construction rules of classical propositional logic by adding the following rule: If A is a formula, then so are $\overrightarrow{\Box}A$, $\overleftarrow{\Box}A$, $\overrightarrow{\blacksquare}A$, $\overleftarrow{\blacksquare}A$, $\overrightarrow{\boxed{m}}A$ and $\overleftarrow{\boxed{m}}A$. The *mirror image* of A is the result of replacing in A each occurrence of $\overrightarrow{\Box}, \overleftarrow{\Box}, \overrightarrow{\blacksquare}, \overleftarrow{\blacksquare}, \overrightarrow{\boxed{m}}, \overleftarrow{\boxed{m}}, \alpha^+, \alpha^-$ by $\overleftarrow{\Box}, \overrightarrow{\Box}, \overleftarrow{\blacksquare}$, $\overrightarrow{\blacksquare}, \overleftarrow{\boxed{m}}, \overrightarrow{\boxed{m}}, \alpha^-, \alpha^+$, respectively. We will use the symbols $\overrightarrow{\Diamond}, \overleftarrow{\Diamond}, \overrightarrow{\blacklozenge}, \overleftarrow{\blacklozenge}, \overrightarrow{\boxed{\lozenge}}$ and $\overleftarrow{\boxed{\lozenge}}$ as abbreviations respectively of $\neg\overrightarrow{\Box}\neg, \neg\overleftarrow{\Box}\neg, \neg\overrightarrow{\blacksquare}\neg, \neg\overleftarrow{\blacksquare}\neg, \neg\overrightarrow{\boxed{m}}\neg$ and $\neg\overleftarrow{\boxed{m}}\neg$.

Definition 1. *An $\mathcal{L}(MQ)^N$-frame is a tuple $\Sigma = (\mathbb{S}, +\alpha, -\alpha, <, \prec)$, where*

1. *$\mathbb{S}$ is a non empty set of points and $<$ a binary relation of strict linear order on $\mathbb{S}$ [1].*
2. *$+\alpha$ and $-\alpha$ are designated points in $\mathbb{S}$ (called frame constants) and allow to form the sets OBS^+, INF, and OBS^- that are defined as follows:*
$$\mathrm{OBS}^- = \{x \in \mathbb{S} \mid x \leq -\alpha\}, \qquad \mathrm{INF} = \{x \in \mathbb{S} \mid -\alpha < x < +\alpha\},$$
$$\mathrm{OBS}^+ = \{x \in \mathbb{S} \mid +\alpha \leq x\}.$$
3. *$\prec$ is a restriction of $<$, i.e. $\prec \subseteq <$, and satisfies:*
   (i) *If $x \prec y < z$, then $x \prec z$.*
   (ii) *If $x < y \prec z$, then $x \prec z$.*
   (iii) *If $x \prec y$, then either $x \notin \mathrm{INF}$ or $y \notin \mathrm{INF}$.*

We will use $x \sqsubset y$ as an abbreviation of "$x < y$ and $x, y \in \mathrm{QC}$", where $\mathrm{QC} \in \{\mathrm{INF}, \mathrm{OBS}^+, \mathrm{OBS}^-\}$".

Definition 2. *Let Σ be an $\mathcal{L}(MQ)^N$-frame, we define an $\mathcal{L}(MQ)^N$- model on Σ as an ordered pair $\mathcal{M} = (\Sigma, h)$, where h is a meaning function (or, interpretation) $h: \mathcal{V} \longrightarrow 2^{\mathbb{S}}$. Any interpretation can be uniquely extended to the set of all formulas in $\mathcal{L}(MQ)^N$ (also denoted by h) by means of the usual conditions for the classical boolean connectives and the constants $\top$ and $\bot$, and the following conditions for the modal operators and frame constants:*

$$h(\overrightarrow{\Box}A) = \{x \in \mathbb{S} \mid y \in h(A) \text{ for all } y \text{ such that } x < y\}$$
$$h(\overrightarrow{\blacksquare}A) = \{x \in \mathbb{S} \mid y \in h(A) \text{ for all } y \text{ such that } x \sqsubset y\}$$
$$h(\overrightarrow{\boxed{m}}A) = \{x \in \mathbb{S} \mid y \in h(A) \text{ for all } y \text{ such that } x \prec y\}$$
$$h(\overleftarrow{\Box}A) = \{x \in \mathbb{S} \mid y \in h(A) \text{ for all } y \text{ such that } y < x\}$$
$$h(\overleftarrow{\blacksquare}A) = \{x \in \mathbb{S} \mid y \in h(A) \text{ for all } y \text{ such that } y \sqsubset x\}$$
$$h(\overleftarrow{\boxed{m}}A) = \{x \in \mathbb{S} \mid y \in h(A) \text{ for all } y \text{ such that } y \prec x\}$$
$$h(\alpha^+) = \{+\alpha\}$$
$$h(\alpha^-) = \{-\alpha\}$$

---

[1] That is, $<$ is a relation on $\mathbb{S}$: *irreflexive* (for all $x \in \mathbb{S}$: $x \not< x$), *transitive* (for all $x, y, z \in \mathbb{S}$: if $x < y$ and $y < z$, then $x < z$) and *connected* (for all $x, y \in \mathbb{S}$: either $x < y$ or $x = y$ or $y < x$).

The concepts of satisfiability, truth and validity of an $\mathcal{L}(MQ)^N$-formula are defined as usual in modal logics.

2   Axiomatization of $\mathcal{L}(MQ)^N$

In this section we present a Hilbert-style axiomatization of $\mathcal{L}(MQ)^N$. In what follows we will use the following abbreviations:

$$\mathsf{obs}^- =_{def} \overrightarrow{\Diamond}\alpha^- \vee \alpha^-, \ \mathsf{inf} =_{def} \overleftarrow{\Diamond}\alpha^- \wedge \overrightarrow{\Diamond}\alpha^+ \text{ and } \mathsf{obs}^+ =_{def} \alpha^+ \vee \overleftarrow{\Diamond}\alpha^+.$$

In our axiomatization we consider all the tautologies of classical propositional logic together with the following axiom schemata and rules:

Axiom schemata for white connectives:

K1 $\overrightarrow{\Box}(A \to B) \to (\overrightarrow{\Box}A \to \overrightarrow{\Box}B)$
K2 $A \to \overrightarrow{\Box}\overleftarrow{\Diamond}A$
K3 $\overrightarrow{\Box}A \to \overrightarrow{\Box}\overrightarrow{\Box}A$
K4 $(\overrightarrow{\Box}(A \vee B) \wedge \overrightarrow{\Box}(\overrightarrow{\Box}A \vee B) \wedge \overrightarrow{\Box}(A \vee \overrightarrow{\Box}B)) \to (\overrightarrow{\Box}A \vee \overrightarrow{\Box}B)$

Axiom schema for $\overrightarrow{\blacksquare}$:

C1 $\overrightarrow{\blacksquare}(A \to B) \to (\overrightarrow{\blacksquare}A \to \overrightarrow{\blacksquare}B)$

Mixed axiom:

M1 $\overrightarrow{\Box}A \to \overrightarrow{\blacksquare}A$

Axiom schemata for constants, where $\xi \in \{\alpha^+, \alpha^-\}$

c1 $\overleftarrow{\Diamond}\xi \vee \xi \vee \overrightarrow{\Diamond}\xi$
c2 $\xi \to (\overleftarrow{\Box}\neg\xi \wedge \overrightarrow{\Box}\neg\xi)$
c3 $\alpha^- \to \overrightarrow{\Diamond}\alpha^+$
c4 $\alpha^- \to \overrightarrow{\blacksquare}A$
c5 $\overrightarrow{\Diamond}\alpha^- \to \overrightarrow{\blacksquare}\mathsf{obs}^-$
c6 $\overrightarrow{\blacksquare}A \to \overrightarrow{\Box}(\mathsf{obs}^- \to A)$
c7 $\mathsf{inf} \to \overrightarrow{\blacksquare}\mathsf{inf}$
c8 $(\mathsf{inf} \wedge \overrightarrow{\blacksquare}A) \to \overrightarrow{\Box}(\mathsf{inf} \to A)$
c9 $(\mathsf{obs}^+ \wedge \overrightarrow{\blacksquare}A) \to \overrightarrow{\Box}A$

Axiom schemata for neglibility

N1 $\overrightarrow{\boxed{n}}(A \to B) \to (\overrightarrow{\boxed{n}}A \to \overrightarrow{\boxed{n}}B)$
N2 $A \to \overrightarrow{\boxed{n}}\overleftarrow{\Diamond}A$
N3 $\overrightarrow{\Box}A \to \overrightarrow{\boxed{n}}A$
N4 $\overrightarrow{\boxed{n}}A \to \overrightarrow{\Box}\overrightarrow{\boxed{n}}A$
N5 $\overrightarrow{\boxed{n}}A \to \overrightarrow{\boxed{n}}\overrightarrow{\Box}A$
N6 $\mathsf{inf} \to \overrightarrow{\boxed{n}}\mathsf{obs}^+$

We also consider as axioms the corresponding mirror images of all the axioms.

Rules of inference:

(MP) Modus Ponens for $\to$.
(N$\overrightarrow{\Box}$) If $\vdash A$ then $\vdash \overrightarrow{\Box}A$,   (N$\overleftarrow{\Box}$)] If $\vdash A$ then $\vdash \overleftarrow{\Box}A$.

Theorem 1. *Every $\mathcal{L}(MQ)^N$-formula A is $\mathcal{L}(MQ)^N$-valid iff it is $\mathcal{L}(MQ)^N$-provable.*

For the proof see [2].

3   Decidability

In this section we focus our attention on decidability of $\mathcal{L}(MQ)^N$ logic. For this end, we will follow the strategy of [6]. First, we have to show the soundness and completeness of the axiomatization of $\mathcal{L}(MQ)^N$ with respect to a class of models weaker than the $\mathcal{L}(MQ)^N$-models defined above, called "quasi $\mathcal{L}(MQ)^N$-models". Then applying the *filtration method*, we show that each formula satisfiable in a quasi $\mathcal{L}(MQ)^N$-model is satisfiable also in a finite quasi $\mathcal{L}(MQ)^N$-model with at most a given size. This means that $\mathcal{L}(MQ)^N$ logic has the strong finite model property which imply its decidability.

Definition 3. *A quasi $\mathcal{L}(MQ)^N$-frame is a tuple $\Sigma = (\mathbb{S}, +\alpha, -\alpha, <, \prec)$, where $\mathbb{S}$ is a non empty set of points, $<$ is a transitive and connected relation on $\mathbb{S}$, $+\alpha$ and $-\alpha$ are designated points in $\mathbb{S}$ with the properties: $+\alpha \not< +\alpha$, $-\alpha \not< -\alpha$ and $-\alpha < +\alpha$. With the help of these points we build the sets OBS^-, INF and OBS^+ as in Definition 1. Finally, the relation $\prec$ satisfies the conditions of item 3 of the Definition 1. A quasi $\mathcal{L}(MQ)^N$-model on Σ is an ordered pair $\mathcal{M} = (\Sigma, h)$, where h is a meaning function defined as in Definition 2.*

The notions of satisfiability, truth and validity of an $\mathcal{L}(MQ)^N$-formula are the same as in $\mathcal{L}(MQ)^N$-models. In what follows quasi $\mathcal{L}(MQ)^N$-models are referred to as $\mathcal{L}(MQ)^N_*$-models. Now we have the following proposition:

Proposition 1. *For every $\mathcal{L}(MQ)^N$-formula A, the following conditions hold:*

1. *If A is $\mathcal{L}(MQ)^N_*$-valid, then it is $\mathcal{L}(MQ)^N$-valid.*
2. *If A is $\mathcal{L}(MQ)^N$-provable, then it is $\mathcal{L}(MQ)^N_*$-valid.*

Proof. Item 1 is a consequence of the fact that every $\mathcal{L}(MQ)^N$-model is an $\mathcal{L}(MQ)^N_*$-model. With respect to item 2 it is sufficient to prove that all the axioms are valid in $\mathcal{L}(MQ)^N_*$-models and all the rules preserve $\mathcal{L}(MQ)^N_*$-validity. For space reasons we omit the proof.

As a result of Theorem 1 and Proposition 1 we have the following theorem:

Theorem 2. *For every $\mathcal{L}(MQ)^N$-formula A, the following conditions are equivalent: (i) A is $\mathcal{L}(MQ)^N$-valid, (ii) A is $\mathcal{L}(MQ)^N_*$-valid, and (iii) A is $\mathcal{L}(MQ)^N$-provable.*

Theorem 2 allows us to focus our attention on the $\mathcal{L}(MQ)^N_*$-models. Next we show that all $\mathcal{L}(MQ)^N_*$-satisfiable formula A is satisfiable in a finite $\mathcal{L}(MQ)^N_*$-model. As a preliminary question we will eliminate black operators rewriting $\mathcal{L}(MQ)^N$-formulas. To do this we establish the following proposition:

Proposition 2. *The following $\mathcal{L}(MQ)^N$-formulas are $\mathcal{L}(MQ)^N$-valid:*

1. $\blacksquare \overrightarrow{} A \leftrightarrow \left((\overrightarrow{\lozenge}\alpha^- \wedge \overrightarrow{\square}(obs^- \to A)) \vee \alpha^- \vee (inf \to \overrightarrow{\square}(inf \to A)) \vee (obs^+ \wedge \overrightarrow{\square}A) \right).$
2. $\blacksquare \overleftarrow{} A \leftrightarrow \left((obs^- \wedge \overleftarrow{\square}A) \vee (inf \to \overleftarrow{\square}(inf \to A)) \vee \alpha^+ \vee (\overleftarrow{\lozenge}\alpha^+ \wedge \overleftarrow{\square}(obs^+ \to A)) \right).$

In what follows we will consider a language containing only primitive operators (without black squares) and the constants obs$^-$, inf and obs$^+$. We start with the following definition:

Definition 4. *Let A be an $\mathcal{L}(MQ)^N$-formula written only in terms of the primitive operators (without black squares). Define*

$$A^* =_{def} A \wedge \left(\textbf{obs}^- \vee \textbf{inf} \vee \textbf{obs}^+\right) \wedge \bigwedge_{\xi \in \{\alpha^-, \alpha^+\}} (\xi \rightarrow \overrightarrow{\square}\neg\xi)$$

Because $(\textbf{obs}^- \vee \textbf{inf} \vee \textbf{obs}^+) \wedge \bigwedge_{\xi \in \{\alpha^-, \alpha^+\}}(\xi \rightarrow \overrightarrow{\square}\neg\xi)$ is an $\mathcal{L}(MQ)^N_*$–valid formula, then A is $\mathcal{L}(MQ)^N_*$–satisfiable if and only if A^* is $\mathcal{L}(MQ)^N_*$-satisfiable. This allows us to prove for a given $\mathcal{L}(MQ)^N_*$–satisfiable formula A that it is satisfiable in a finite $\mathcal{L}(MQ)^N_*$-model by proving that A^* is. In what follows we use Γ to denote a set closed under subformulas for some formula A^* as described above. Consider any $\mathcal{L}(MQ)^N_*$-model $\mathcal{M} = (\mathbb{S}, +\alpha, -\alpha, <, \prec, h)$. Take $x \sim_\Gamma y$ iff $\{B \in \Gamma: x \in h(B)\} = \{B \in \Gamma: y \in h(B)\}$. Clearly $\sim_\Gamma$ is an equivalence relation on $\mathbb{S}$. So, for every $x \in \mathbb{S}$ we define $[x] = \{y \in \mathbb{S}: y \sim_\Gamma x\}$, that is, $[x]$ is the equivalence class of x determined by $\sim_\Gamma$. Now we define the filtration model.

Definition 5. *Let $\mathcal{M} = (\mathbb{S}, -\alpha, +\alpha, <, \prec, h)$ be an $\mathcal{L}(MQ)^N_*$-model. We define a filtration model of $\mathcal{M}$ through Γ (a Γ-filtration of M, for short) as a structure of the form $\mathcal{M}_\Gamma = (\mathbb{S}_\Gamma, +\alpha_\Gamma, -\alpha_\Gamma, <_\Gamma, \prec_\Gamma, h_\Gamma)$, where:*

1. $\mathbb{S}_\Gamma = \{[x]: x \in \mathbb{S}\}$.
2. $+\alpha_\Gamma = [+\alpha]$ *and* $-\alpha_\Gamma = [-\alpha]$.
3. $<_\Gamma \subseteq \mathbb{S}_\Gamma \times \mathbb{S}_\Gamma$, *so that for every* $[x], [y] \in \mathbb{S}_\Gamma$ *we have* $[x] <_\Gamma [y]$ *iff:*
   - *for every* $\overrightarrow{\square}A \in \Gamma$: *if* $x \in h(\overrightarrow{\square}A)$, *then* $y \in h(A) \cap h(\overrightarrow{\square}A)$;
   - *for every* $\overleftarrow{\square}A \in \Gamma$: *if* $y \in h(\overleftarrow{\square}A)$, *then* $x \in h(A) \cap h(\overleftarrow{\square}A)$;
   - *for every* $\overrightarrow{\boxed{m}}A \in \Gamma$: *if* $x \in h(\overrightarrow{\boxed{m}}A)$, *then* $y \in h(\overrightarrow{\boxed{m}}A)$;
   - *for every* $\overleftarrow{\boxed{m}}A \in \Gamma$: *if* $y \in h(\overleftarrow{\boxed{m}}A)$, *then* $x \in h(\overleftarrow{\boxed{m}}A)$.
4. $\prec_\Gamma \subseteq \mathbb{S}_\Gamma \times \mathbb{S}_\Gamma$, *so that for every* $[x], [y] \in \mathbb{S}_\Gamma$ *we have* $[x] \prec_\Gamma [y]$ *iff:*
   - *for every* $[+]A \in \Gamma$: *if* $x \in h([+]A)$, *then* $y \in h(A) \cap h(\overrightarrow{\square}A)$;
   - *for every* $[-]A \in \Gamma$: *if* $y \in h([-]A)$, *then* $x \in h(A) \cap h(\overleftarrow{\square}A)$;
   - *if* $x \in h(\textbf{inf})$, *then* $y \in h(\textbf{obs}^+)$;
   - *if* $y \in h(\textbf{inf})$, *then* $x \in h(\textbf{obs}^-)$;

   being $[+] \in \{\overrightarrow{\square}, \overrightarrow{\boxed{m}}\}$ *and* $[-] \in \{\overleftarrow{\square}, \overleftarrow{\boxed{m}}\}$.
5. $h_\Gamma(p) = \{[x]: x \in h(p)\}$, *for every atom* $p \in \Gamma$ *(if* $p \notin \Gamma$, $h_\Gamma(p) = \varnothing$).

Remark 1. Observe that every element in an equivalence class of the filtration model belongs to the same qualitative class, that is, given $x, y \in \mathbb{S}$ such that $y \in [x]$ we have: $x \in QC$ iff $y \in QC$. For instance, take $QC = \text{OBS}^-$. It is easy to see that $x \in \text{OBS}^-$ iff $x \in h(\textbf{obs}^-)$. Since $\textbf{obs}^- \in \Gamma$ and $y \sim_\Gamma x$, hence $x \in \text{OBS}^-$ iff $y \in \text{OBS}^-$.

Remark 2. From the construction of the model $\mathcal{M}_\Gamma$ we obtain that the size of $\mathbb{S}_\Gamma$ is bounded by $2^{|A^*|}$, where $|A^*|$ is the length of the formula A^*.

Proposition 3. *Let* $\mathcal{M}_\Gamma = (\mathbb{S}_\Gamma, +\alpha_\Gamma, -\alpha_\Gamma, <_\Gamma, \prec_\Gamma, h_\Gamma)$ *be a* Γ*-filtration of an* $\mathcal{L}(MQ)_*^N$*-model* $\mathcal{M} = (\mathbb{S}, -\alpha, +\alpha, <, \prec, h)$. *Then for every* $x, y \in \mathbb{S}$:

1. *If* $x < y$, *then* $[x] <_\Gamma [y]$.
2. *If* $x \prec y$, *then* $[x] \prec_\Gamma [y]$.

Proof. For 1. Let $x < y$ be. Consider $\overrightarrow{\Box} A \in \Gamma$ and $x \in h(\overrightarrow{\Box} A)$, then $y \in h(A)$ and by the validity of $\overrightarrow{\Box} A \to \overrightarrow{\Box}\overrightarrow{\Box} A$ (axiom K3), we obtain also $x \in h(\overrightarrow{\Box}\overrightarrow{\Box} A)$, hence $y \in h(\overrightarrow{\Box} A)$. Similarly, if $\overleftarrow{\Box} A \in \Gamma$ and $y \in h(\overleftarrow{\Box} A)$ we obtain $x \in h(A) \cap h(\overleftarrow{\Box} A)$. On the other hand, if $\overrightarrow{\boxed{m}} A \in \Gamma$ and $x \in h(\overrightarrow{\boxed{m}} A)$, because $\overrightarrow{\boxed{m}} A \to \overrightarrow{\Box}\,\overrightarrow{\boxed{m}} A$ (axiom N4) is valid, then $x \in h(\overrightarrow{\Box}\,\overrightarrow{\boxed{m}} A)$ and so $y \in h(\overrightarrow{\boxed{m}} A)$. If $\overleftarrow{\boxed{m}} A \in \Gamma$ and $y \in h(\overleftarrow{\boxed{m}} A)$, we obtain in a similar way $x \in h(\overleftarrow{\boxed{m}} A)$. This completes the proof of $[x] <_\Gamma [y]$.

For 2. Let $x \prec y$ be. Then $x < y$, since $\prec \subseteq <$. So, as in the previous case, if $\overrightarrow{\Box} A \in \Gamma$ and $x \in h(\overrightarrow{\Box} A)$ then $y \in h(A) \cap h(\overrightarrow{\Box} A)$. A similar result is obtained for $\overleftarrow{\Box} A \in \Gamma$. On the other hand, assume $\overrightarrow{\boxed{m}} A \in \Gamma$ and $x \in h(\overrightarrow{\boxed{m}} A)$. Then $y \in h(A)$; moreover, since $\overrightarrow{\boxed{m}} A \to \overrightarrow{\boxed{m}}\overrightarrow{\Box} A$ (axiom N5) is valid, then $x \in h(\overrightarrow{\boxed{m}}\overrightarrow{\Box} A)$, hence $y \in h(\overrightarrow{\Box} A)$. We proceed in a similar way if $\overleftarrow{\boxed{m}} A \in \Gamma$. Let $x \in h(\mathsf{inf})$ be, since the formula $\mathsf{inf} \to \overrightarrow{\boxed{m}}\mathsf{obs}^+$ is valid (axiom N6), then $x \in h(\overrightarrow{\boxed{m}}\mathsf{obs}^+)$ and so $y \in h(\mathsf{obs}^+)$. Finally, if $y \in h(\mathsf{inf})$ we can obtain in a similar way that $x \in h(\mathsf{obs}^-)$. This completes the proof of $[x] \prec_\Gamma [y]$. QED

Proposition 4. *If* $\mathcal{M}_\Gamma = (\mathbb{S}_\Gamma, +\alpha_\Gamma, -\alpha_\Gamma, <_\Gamma, \prec_\Gamma, h_\Gamma)$ *is a* Γ*-filtration of an* $\mathcal{L}(MQ)_*^N$*-model* $\mathcal{M} = (\mathbb{S}, +\alpha, -\alpha, <, \prec, h)$, *then* $\mathcal{M}_\Gamma$ *is an* $\mathcal{L}(MQ)_*^N$*-model.*

Proof. (1)   First we have to prove that $<_\Gamma$ is a transitive and connected relation. The transitivity is an immediate consequence of the definition of $<_\Gamma$ and the connectedness comes from the fact that $<$ is connected and Proposition 3(1).
(2) $+\alpha_\Gamma$ $(= [-\alpha])$ and $-\alpha_\Gamma$ $(= [+\alpha])$ are designated points in $\mathbb{S}_\Gamma$. For these we have:

(a) $[-\alpha] <_\Gamma [+\alpha]$,   (b) $[-\alpha] \not\prec_\Gamma [-\alpha]$,   (c) $[+\alpha] \not\prec_\Gamma [+\alpha]$.

(a) is an immediate consequence of $-\alpha < +\alpha$ and the Proposition 3(1). With respect to (b) assume the contrary, that is, $[-\alpha] <_\Gamma [-\alpha]$. Now, given $-\alpha \in h(\alpha^-)$ and the validity of $\alpha^- \to \overrightarrow{\Box}\neg\alpha^-$, we obtain $-\alpha \in h(\overrightarrow{\Box}\neg\alpha^-)$. So, taking into account that $\overrightarrow{\Box}\neg\alpha^- \in \Gamma$ and the assumption, then $-\alpha \in h(\neg\alpha^-)$, that is, $-\alpha \notin h(\alpha^-)$, a contradiction. The proof of (c) is similar. So we can build the sets OBS_Γ^-, INF_Γ and OBS_Γ^+ as follows:

$$\mathrm{OBS}_\Gamma^- = \{[x] \in \mathbb{S}_\Gamma \colon [x] \leq_\Gamma [-\alpha]\}, \quad \mathrm{INF}_\Gamma = \{[x] \in \mathbb{S}_\Gamma \colon [-\alpha] <_\Gamma [x] <_\Gamma [+\alpha]\},$$
$$\mathrm{OBS}_\Gamma^+ = \{[x] \in \mathbb{S}_\Gamma \colon [+\alpha] \leq_\Gamma [x]\}. \,^2$$

---

[2] It should be noticed that the symbol $\leq_\Gamma$ does not denote necessarily an antisymmetric relation. It is used as an abbreviation for $<_\Gamma$ and $=$ in an standard way, where $<_\Gamma$ is only a transitive and connected relation. Moreover, in the context of $\mathcal{L}(MQ)_*^N$-models $\leq$ is used with the same meaning.

Now we prove that this definition is well established, that is:

(a) For every $[x] \in \mathbb{S}_\Gamma$: $[x] \in \text{OBS}_\Gamma^- \cup \text{INF}_\Gamma \cup \text{OBS}_\Gamma^+$.
(b) The sets $\text{OBS}_\Gamma^-, \text{INF}_\Gamma$ and OBS_Γ^+ are pairwise disjoint.
(c) For every $[x] \in \text{OBS}_\Gamma^-$, $[y] \in \text{INF}_\Gamma$ and $[z] \in \text{OBS}_\Gamma^+$, hold $[x] <_\Gamma [y] <_\Gamma [z]$.

The condition (a) is a consequence of the Proposition 3(1) and the fact: $x \in \text{OBS}^- \cup \text{INF} \cup \text{OBS}^+$. For condition (b) assume $[x] \in \text{OBS}_\Gamma^- \cap \text{INF}_\Gamma$ in order to reach a contradiction. From this assumption we have both $[x] \leq_\Gamma [-\alpha]$ and $[-\alpha] <_\Gamma [x] <_\Gamma [+\alpha]$. If $[x] = [-\alpha]$, then $[-\alpha] <_\Gamma [-\alpha]$, a contradiction. If $[x] <_\Gamma [-\alpha]$, we obtain the same result by transitivity of $<_\Gamma$. In a similar way we can prove that $\text{INF}_\Gamma \cap \text{OBS}_\Gamma^+$ and $\text{OBS}_\Gamma^- \cap \text{OBS}_\Gamma^+$ are empty sets. The condition (c) is an immediate consequence of transitivity of $<_\Gamma$.

(3)   Next we prove $\prec_\Gamma \subseteq <_\Gamma$. Assume $[x] \prec_\Gamma [y]$. Let $\overrightarrow{\square}A \in \Gamma$ and $x \in h(\overrightarrow{\square}A)$ be; then it is immediate that $y \in h(A) \cap h(\overrightarrow{\square}A)$. The case for $\overleftarrow{\square}A \in \Gamma$ is analogous. On the other hand, if $\overrightarrow{\boxdot}A \in \Gamma$ and $x \in h(\overrightarrow{\boxdot}A)$, then $y \in h(\overrightarrow{\square}A)$, and by the validity of $\overrightarrow{\square}A \to \overrightarrow{\boxdot}A$ (N3), we obtain $y \in h(\overrightarrow{\boxdot}A)$. The case for $\overleftarrow{\boxdot}A \in \Gamma$ is analogous. Hence $[x] <_\Gamma [y]$.

In what follows will be useful take into account the following properties about the sets OBS_Γ^-, INF_Γ and OBS_Γ^+. For any $x \in \mathbb{S}$ we have:

$$(\dagger_1) \quad [x] \in \text{OBS}_\Gamma^- \text{ iff } x \in h(\mathbf{obs}^-), \qquad (\dagger_2) \quad [x] \in \text{INF}_\Gamma \text{ iff } x \in h(\mathbf{inf}),$$
$$(\dagger_3) \quad [x] \in \text{OBS}_\Gamma^+ \text{ iff } x \in h(\mathbf{obs}^+).$$

To prove these properties we can prove first the conditions listed below. For every $x \in \mathbb{S}$:

$(*_1)$ If $[x] \leq_\Gamma [-\alpha]$, then $x \leq -\alpha$, $\qquad (*_3)$ If $[x] <_\Gamma [+\alpha]$, then $x < +\alpha$,
$(*_2)$ If $[-\alpha] <_\Gamma [x]$, then $-\alpha < x$, $\qquad (*_4)$ If $[+\alpha] \leq_\Gamma [x]$, then $+\alpha \leq x$.

For $(*_1)$. Suppose that $[x] \leq_\Gamma [-\alpha]$ and $-\alpha < x$ in order to reach a contradiction. By Proposition 3(1) we get $[-\alpha] <_\Gamma [x]$, and from this and the assumption we easily obtain $[-\alpha] <_\Gamma [-\alpha]$, which is impossible. The remaining cases are proved in a similar way.

Now consider $(\dagger_1)$ as an example: $[x] \in \text{OBS}_\Gamma^-$ iff $[x] \leq_\Gamma [-\alpha]$ iff $x \leq -\alpha$ (by using Proposition 3(1) and $(*_1)$) iff $x \in h(\mathbf{obs}^-)$.

(4)   Next we prove that if $[x] \prec_\Gamma [y] <_\Gamma [z]$, then $[x] \prec_\Gamma [z]$. Assume $[x] \prec_\Gamma [y] <_\Gamma [z]$. Now, since $[x] \prec_\Gamma [y]$, if $\overrightarrow{\square}A \in \Gamma$ and $x \in h(\overrightarrow{\square}A)$, then $y \in h(\overrightarrow{\square}A)$, and since $[y] <_\Gamma [z]$ then $z \in h(A) \cap h(\overrightarrow{\square}A)$. The case for $\overleftarrow{\square}A \in \Gamma$ is similar. Now consider $\overrightarrow{\boxdot}A \in \Gamma$ and $x \in h(\overrightarrow{\boxdot}A)$, then, given $[x] \prec_\Gamma [y]$, we obtain $y \in h(\overrightarrow{\square}A)$ and, given $[y] <_\Gamma [z]$, we get $z \in h(A) \cap h(\overrightarrow{\square}A)$. We proceed similarly if $\overleftarrow{\boxdot}A \in \Gamma$. Now, given $[x] \prec_\Gamma [y]$, if $x \in h(\mathbf{inf})$, then $y \in h(\mathbf{obs}^+)$, so by $(\dagger_3)$ above we have $[y] \in \text{OBS}_\Gamma^+$, and given $[y] <_\Gamma [z]$, then $[z] \in \text{OBS}_\Gamma^+$, and so by $(\dagger_3)$ again we get $z \in h(\mathbf{obs}^+)$. Moreover, if $z \in h(\mathbf{inf})$, we can also obtain $x \in h(\mathbf{obs}^-)$. Thus $[x] \prec_\Gamma [z]$.

(5) Next we prove that if $[x] <_\Gamma [y] \prec_\Gamma [z]$, then $[x] \prec_\Gamma [z]$. Assume $[x] <_\Gamma [y] \prec_\Gamma [z]$. Now, because $[x] <_\Gamma [y]$, if $\overrightarrow{\Box} A \in \Gamma$ and $x \in h(\overrightarrow{\Box} A)$, then $y \in h(\overrightarrow{\Box} A)$ and, since $[y] \prec_\Gamma [z]$, we obtain $z \in h(A) \cap h(\overrightarrow{\Box} A)$. The case for $\overleftarrow{\Box} A \in \Gamma$ is similar. Now, since $[x] <_\Gamma [y]$, if $\overrightarrow{\boxdot} A \in \Gamma$ and $x \in h(\overrightarrow{\boxdot} A)$, then we have $y \in h(\overrightarrow{\boxdot} A)$ and, since $[y] \prec_\Gamma [z]$, we obtain $z \in h(A) \cap h(\overrightarrow{\boxdot} A)$. If $\overleftarrow{\boxdot} A \in \Gamma$, we proceed in a similar way. If $x \in h(\mathsf{inf})$, then by $(\dagger_2)$ $[x] \in \mathrm{INF}_\Gamma$, and given $[x] <_\Gamma [y]$ we get $[y] \in \mathrm{INF}_\Gamma \cup \mathrm{OBS}_\Gamma^+$, thus $y \in h(\mathsf{inf}) \cup h(\mathsf{obs}^+)$ by $(\dagger_2)$ and $(\dagger_3)$. In this case, if $y \in h(\mathsf{inf})$, as $[y] \prec_\Gamma [z]$, then $z \in h(\mathsf{obs}^+)$. If $y \in h(\mathsf{obs}^+)$, then by $(\dagger_3)$, $[y] \in \mathrm{OBS}_\Gamma^+$ and as $[y] \prec_\Gamma [z]$, then $[y] <_\Gamma [z]$ (since $\prec_\Gamma \subseteq <_\Gamma$), thus $z \in \mathrm{OBS}_\Gamma^+$, and by $(\dagger_3)$ $z \in h(\mathsf{obs}^+)$. On the other hand, we can also prove that if $z \in h(\mathsf{inf})$, then $x \in h(\mathsf{obs}^-)$. Thus $[x] \prec_\Gamma [z]$.

(6) Finally we prove that $[x] \prec_\Gamma [y]$ implies either $[x] \notin \mathrm{INF}_\Gamma$ or $[y] \notin \mathrm{INF}_\Gamma$. Assume $[x] \prec_\Gamma [y]$ and $[x] \in \mathrm{INF}_\Gamma$, that is, $x \in h(\mathsf{inf})$, by $(\dagger_2)$. So, given $[x] \prec_\Gamma [y]$, we have $y \in h(\mathsf{obs}^+)$, then $y \notin h(\mathsf{inf})$ and, by $(\dagger_2)$, we finally get $[y] \notin \mathrm{INF}_\Gamma$.   QED

Proposition 5. Let $(\mathbb{S}_\Gamma, +\alpha_\Gamma, -\alpha_\Gamma, <_\Gamma, \prec_\Gamma, h_\Gamma)$ be a Γ-filtration of an $\mathcal{L}(MQ)_*^N$-model $(\mathbb{S}_\Gamma, +\alpha, -\alpha, <, \prec, h)$. Then, for every $A \in \Gamma$ and for every $x \in \mathbb{S}$ we have:

$$x \in h(A) \text{ if and only if } [x] \in h_\Gamma(A).$$

Proof. The proof is by induction on the lenght of A. As a way of example, let A be of the form $\overrightarrow{\boxdot} B$. Suppose that the proposition holds for B (induction hypothesis). Now assume $x \in h(\overrightarrow{\boxdot} B)$ and consider $[y] \in \mathbb{S}_\Gamma$ such that $[x] \prec_\Gamma [y]$. Then, as $\overrightarrow{\boxdot} B \in \Gamma$, $y \in h(B)$ and, by the induction hypothesis, $[y] \in h_\Gamma(B)$. Hence $[x] \in h_\Gamma(\overrightarrow{\boxdot} B)$. Reciprocally, assume $[x] \in h_\Gamma(\overrightarrow{\boxdot} B)$ and let $y \in \mathbb{S}$ be such that $x \prec y$. Thus, by Proposition 3(2), $[x] \prec_\Gamma [y]$. Now by the assumption, $[y] \in h_\Gamma(B)$, and by the induction hypothesis, $y \in h(B)$. Thus $x \in h(\overrightarrow{\boxdot} B)$. QED

The proof of the following proposition is straightforward.

Proposition 6. Let A be an $\mathcal{L}(MQ)^N$- formula satisfied in an $\mathcal{L}(MQ)_*^N$-model $\mathcal{M}$ by a point x in $\mathcal{M}$. Let Γ be the set of subformulas of A^* and $\mathcal{M}_\Gamma$ a Γ-filtration of $\mathcal{M}$, then A is satisfied in the $\mathcal{L}(MQ)_*^N$-model $\mathcal{M}_\Gamma$ by $[x]$.

Recall that a logic L has the *strong finite model property* whenever an L- formula A is satisfiable in an in an L-model, then there is a computable function f such that A is satisfiable in an L-model of size at most $f(|A|)$. Now we can state the following result:

Theorem 3 (Strong Finite Model Property). *The logic* $\mathcal{L}(MQ)^N$ *has the strong finite model property.*

Proof. From Remark 2 and Proposition 6.   QED

Finally, taking into account that, for all $\mathcal{L}(MQ)^N$-formula A, we can generate all finite $\mathcal{L}(MQ)_*^N$-models with size at most $2^{|A^*|}$, then by a standard argument using the previous theorem we finally get:

Theorem 4 (Decidability). *The logic* $\mathcal{L}(MQ)^N$ *is decidable.*

4   Conclusions and Future Work

In this paper we have proved the decidability of a multimodal logic for order-of-magnitude qualitative reasoning introduced in [2] called $\mathcal{L}(MQ)^N$. This result is achieved by using the filtration method proving that this logic has the finite strong model property. As future task we will develop a decision procedure for $\mathcal{L}(MQ)^N$ based on tableau method and a study of the complexity of this logic. Moreover, there are other logics than $\mathcal{L}(MQ)^N$ dealing with order-of-magnitude reasoning whose decidability is not solved and our intention is to tackle this problem also in next works.

References

1. Burrieza, A., Ojeda-Aciego, M.: A multimodal logic approach to order of magnitude qualitative eeasoning. In: Conejo, R., Urretavizcaya, M., Pérez-de-la-Cruz, J.-L. (eds.) CAEPIA/TTIA 2003. LNCS (LNAI), vol. 3040, pp. 431–440. Springer, Heidelberg (2004)
2. Burrieza, A., Ojeda-Aciego, M.: A multimodal logic approach to order of magnitude qualitative reasoning with comparability and negligibility relations. Fundamenta Informaticae 68, 21–46 (2005)
3. Burrieza, A., Ojeda-Aciego, M.: On the modal logic of order-of-magnitude qualitative reasoning: a tableau calculus. In: Bento, C., Amilcar C., Dias, G. (eds.) 12th Portuguese Conference on Artificial Intelligence, EPIA 2005, Covilha (Portugal), pp. 33–37. IEEE (2005)
4. Burrieza, A., Muñoz, E., Ojeda-Aciego, M.: Order of magnitude qualitative reasoning with bidirectional negligibility. In: Marín, R., Onaindía, E., Bugarín, A., Santos, J. (eds.) CAEPIA 2005. LNCS (LNAI), vol. 4177, pp. 370–378. Springer, Heidelberg (2006)
5. Burrieza, A., Muñoz-Velasco, E., Ojeda-Aciego, M.: A logic for order of magnitude reasoning with negligibility, non-closeness and distance. In: Borrajo, D., Castillo, L., Corchado, J.M. (eds.) CAEPIA 2007. LNCS (LNAI), vol. 4788, pp. 210–219. Springer, Heidelberg (2007)
6. Golińska-Pilarek, J.: On decidability of a logic for order of magnitude qualitative reasoning with bidirectional negligibility. In: Fariñas del Cerro, L., Herzig, A., Mengin, J. (eds.) JELIA 2012. LNCS, vol. 7519, pp. 255–266. Springer, Heidelberg (2012)
7. Missier, A., Piera, N., Travé, L.: Order of magnitude algebras: A survey. Revue d'Intelligence Artificielle 4(3), 95–109 (1989)
8. Raiman, O.: Order of magnitude reasoning. Artificial Intelligence 51, 11–38 (1991)
9. Sánchez, M., Prats, F., Piera, N.: Una formalización de relaciones de comparabilidad en modelos cualitativos. Boletín de la AEPIA (Bulletin of the Spanish Association for AI) 6, 15–22 (1996)
10. Travé-Massuyès, L., Prats, F., Sánchez, M., Agell, N.: Consistent relative and absolute order-of-magnitude models. In: Proc. Qualitative Reasoning 2002 Conference (2002)

Applying Resampling Methods for Imbalanced Datasets to Not So Imbalanced Datasets

Olatz Arbelaitz, Ibai Gurrutxaga, Javier Muguerza, and Jesús María Pérez

Computer Science Faculty, University of the Basque Country (UPV/EHU),
Manuel Lardizabal 1, 20018 Donostia, Spain
{olatz.arbelaitz,i.gurrutxaga,j.muguerza,txus.perez}@ehu.es
http://www.sc.ehu.es/aldapa

Abstract. Many efforts have been done recently proposing new intelligent re-sampling methods as a way to solve class imbalance problems; one of the main challenges of the machine learning community nowadays. Usually the purpose of these methods is to balance the classes. However, there are works in the literature showing that those methods can also be suitable to change the class distribution of not so imbalanced and even balanced databases, to a distribution different to 50% and significantly improve the outcome of the learning process. The aim of this paper is to analyse which resampling methods are the most competitive in this context. Experiments have been performed using 29 databases, 8 different resampling methods and two learning algorithms, and have been evaluated using AUC performance metric and statistical tests. The results show that SMOTE, the well-known intelligent resampling method, is one of the best candidates to be used, improving the results obtained by some of its variants that are successful in the context of class imbalance.

Keywords: Optimal class distribution, class imbalance problems, resampling methods, SMOTE.

1 Introduction

Class imbalance problem is considered one of the emerging challenges in the machine learning area [11, 17, 23]. In class imbalance problems, the number of examples of one class (minority class) is much smaller than the number of examples of the other classes, with the minority class being the class of greatest interest and that with the biggest error cost from the point of view of learning.

One of the approaches used to deal with class imbalance problems, called data approach, consists of resampling (subsampling or oversampling) the data in order to balance the classes before building the classifier. This approach is independent of the learning algorithm used and most of the research has been done in this direction [5, 9, 18]. One of the most popular data approaches is SMOTE [6]: an intelligent oversampling technique to synthetically generate more minority class examples. A broad analysis and comparison of some variants can be found in [4, 13].

C. Bielza et al. (Eds.): CAEPIA 2013, LNAI 8109, pp. 111–120, 2013.

Although resampling methods are usually addressed to solve class imbalance problems, Weiss and Provost [20] showed that there is usually a class distribution different to that appearing in the data set, with which better results are obtained.

Based on Weiss and Provost's work, Albisua et al. [1] confirmed that changes in the class distribution of the training samples improve the performance of the classifiers. However, in contrast to what Weiss and Provost pointed out in their work, they found that the optimal class distribution depends on the learning algorithm used (even if there are decision tree learners using the same split criteria, such as C4.5 and CTC) and also on whether or not the trees are pruned. Later, the same authors proposed in [2] an approach for enhancing the effectiveness of the learning process that combines the use of resampling methods with the optimal class distribution (instead of balancing the classes). It should be noted that the use of this approach is not restricted to imbalanced data sets but can be applied to any data set (imbalanced or not) in order to improve the results of the learning process. The authors demonstrated that 50% is not always the optimal class distribution even when intelligent resampling methods are used. The authors proposed a methodology able to find a class distribution that obtains better results than the balanced one with statistically significant differences (in many cases) for eight resampling methods and two learning algorithms. The experiments described in their work confirm that an optimal class distribution exists, but that it depends not only on the data's characteristics but also on the algorithm and on the resampling method used.

However, in the mentioned work there is a question that remains unanswered and we will try to answer in this work: when using C4.5 and PART to solve a real world problem, which of the 8 evaluated resampling methods and class distribution are the best for the concrete problem?

The work presented in this paper tries to answer the previous question based on experiments performed with 29 real problems (balanced and imbalanced ones) extracted from the UCI Repository benchmark [3] using 8 different resampling methods, C4.5 and PART algorithms and the AUC performance measure. For estimating performance we used a 10-fold cross-validation methodology executed five times (5x10CV). Finally, we used the non-parametric statistical tests proposed by Demšar in [8] and García et al. in [14] and [15] to evaluate the statistical significance of the results.

Section 2 provides a brief description of the resampling methods, algorithms and performance metric to be used. In Section 3 we describe the experimental methodology used to corroborate the previously mentioned hypothesis and in Section 4 we present an analysis of the experimental results. Finally, in Section 5 we summarize the conclusions and suggest further work.

2   Resampling Methods, Algorithms and Performance Metrics

In this section we briefly describe some of most popular and interesting resampling methods used to tackle the class imbalance problem found in bibliography, the two algoritms (C4.5 and PART) and the performance metric used to evaluate the classifiers.

According to resampling methods, random subsampling and random oversampling can be considered as baseline methods because they are the simplest methods and they do not use any kind of knowledge about the data set. In contrast, the rest of the methods can be considered as intelligent methods. Random subsampling (SUB) consists of erasing randomly selected examples from the majority class whereas random oversampling (OVER) consists usually in replicating randomly selected examples of the minority class to balance the training data [4].

SMOTE (SMT) (Synthetic Minority Oversampling TEchnique) [6] is an oversampling algorithm where the minority class is oversampled to generate new synthetic examples. The basic idea is to generate new synthetic examples that are located between each of the minority class examples and one of its k nearest neighbours combining their feature vectors.

In Borderline-SMOTE1 (SMT1) and Borderline-SMOTE2 (SMT2) [16] only the borderline minority examples are oversampled. The minority class examples will be considered to be in the borderline if more than half of their m nearest neighbours belong to the majority class. The Borderline-SMOTE1 option uses just the minority class neighbours of the borderline examples to generate the synthetic examples, whereas the Borderline-SMOTE2 option uses all the neighbours (minority and majority class).

Wilsons Edited Nearest Neighbour Rule (ENN) [21] is a cleaning algorithm that removes an example if it could be misclassified by its three nearest neighbours, erasing those examples having at least two of their three nearest neighbours belonging to the other class. The class distribution of the final sample cannot be chosen.

SMOTE-ENN (SMTN) is a combination of the oversampling method SMOTE and the cleaning algorithm ENN to be applied to the oversampled training set. The aim is to reduce the overfitting risk in the classifier. This method achieve very good results for data sets with few minority examples and it is considered as a reference method by some authors [4, 13].

ENN-SMOTE (NSMT) is a variant of SMOTE-ENN proposed in [2] where the cleaning process is done before applying SMOTE, and, as a consequence, it has a lower computational cost.

The resampling methods have been tested in two algorithms: C4.5 [19], one of the top 10 algorithms in data mining in the IEEE International Conference in Data Mining held in 2006 [22], and PART [12], a supervised learning algorithm that builds a rule set designed with the aim of combining the capacities of C4.5 and Ripper [7].

Finally, since accuracy (Acc) and error rate (Err = 1-Acc) are strongly biased in favour of the majority class, we used a metric based on the confusion matrix: AUC (Area Under ROC Curve), a graphical representation to compare TP rate and FP rate while changing the decision threshold of an example to belong to a class. The AUC metric [10] is one of the most used metrics in the bibliography for class imbalance problems.

3   Experimental Methodology

Inspired by the work presented by Albisua et al. in [2], the aim of this work is to find the best resampling method and class distribution to solve a concrete real problem. The authors presented in their paper a methodology able to find a class distribu-tion that obtains better results than the balanced one for 29 databases with eight resampling methods and two learning algorithms and we experimented with the same databases, class distributions, resampling methods and algorithms they proposed.

Experiments were performed with 29 two-class (all databases with more than two classes were transformed to two-class problems) real problems, all belonging to the UCI Repository benchmark [3]. The 29 databases have different class distribution ranges. There are 4 databases where the minority class examples are less than 10%, 9 databases where they are between 10% and 25%, 10 databases between 25% and 40% and 6 databases with more than 40%.

A 10-fold cross-validation methodology was used five times (5x10CV) to estimate the generalization capacity of the classifiers based on the AUC performance metric. The proposals were evaluated for 8 different resampling methods: the 7 resampling methods described in Section 2, (SUB, OVER, SMT, SMT1, SMT2 and SMTN and NSMT) and an additional version of SUB, SUBo. In SUBo the size of the samples is limited by the number of examples of the minority class (in average 27.64% of the training samples) based on Weiss and Provost's methodology [20]. In this work the size was limited to be able to evaluate a wide range of different values of the minority class distribution, from 2% to up 98%, and to make the comparison as fair as possible. Moreover, SUB was also used without size limitations i.e. randomly erasing selected examples from one of the classes only until the desired class distribution is achieved. When it is used to balance the sample, the size is the double of the size obtained with SUBo, i.e. 55.28%, in average.

On the other hand, for each of the folds and resampling methods, samples were generated for the three class distributions proposed in [2]:

- *ocd*: optimal class distribution, i.e., the class distribution obtaining the best results when samples were generated with SUBo, as Weiss and Provost did.
- *orm*: optimal class distribution for each of the resampling methods. Obtained exploring values around *ocd*: the next value (*ocd*+10%) and the previous value (*ocd*-10%).
- *bal*: balanced class distribution.

Aware of the important role randomness plays in every resampling method, from each training sample in the 5x10CV, 50 samples for each method and class distribution were generated.

The SMOTE-ENN method is an exception; in this case we generated a single sample, instead of 50. In order to apply this method 50 times, we had to recalculate a new distance matrix for each sample generated with SMOTE and then apply ENN. This caused problems with disk space and extended the experimental time.

These samples were used to build C4.5 and PART classifiers. When testing them, the corrector (oversampling ratio) proposed by Weiss & Provost to adapt the induced model to the distribution expected in reality was used.

As we previously indicated AUC was the performance metric selected to determine the best classifiers in the experiments. Moreover, the nonparametric tests proposed by Demšar in [8] and García et al. in [14] and [15] were used to evaluate the statistical significance of the results.

4   Experimental Results

Table 2 shows the results, as AUC average values of the 29 datasets, for the two algorithms (PART in the upper part and C4.5 in the lower one), for the eight resampling strategies (by columns) and for the three class distribution values considered, *bal*, *ocd* and *orm* (by rows). Besides, the first column is added, ORIG, which contains the results obtained using the whole training sample to build the classifiers; i.e. without any resampling method (because of this the value is the same for the three rows). This is a reference value to evaluate whether or not it is worth using any resampling method. For each row (combination of an algorithm and a class distribution value), the results related to the best resampling method are marked in bold, while all the results that do not improve the results for ORIG have a grey background.

Table 1. Mean values of AUC for each of the evaluated algorithms, resampling methods and class distributions used (*orm, ocd* and *bal*)

		ORIG	SUBo	SUB	OVER	SMT	SMT1	SMT2	SMTN	NSMT
PART	orm	79.92	84.27	85.54	85.37	85.23	85.11	**85.68**	83.46	83.61
	ocd	79.92	84.23	**85.20**	85.09	84.76	84.69	84.67	82.09	83.50
	bal	79.92	84.11	**85.52**	84.84	84.44	84.48	84.78	83.97	83.45
C4.5	orm	83.47	84.19	**85.69**	84.63	85.13	84.91	85.44	83.82	83.82
	ocd	83.47	84.17	**85.28**	84.17	84.84	84.47	85.12	82.63	83.55
	bal	83.47	83.97	**85.62**	84.18	84.80	84.42	84.96	84.15	83.29

As it can be observed in Table 1, most of the results obtained using some resampleng method are better than those obtained when any resampling method was used, ORIG (only for two cases the results were worse). On the other hand, in the most of the comparisons, the random subsampling method, SUB, was the strategy that obtained the best results, except to for the case of the PART algorithm and the *orm* class distribution, where the best results were obtained by Bordeline-SMOTE1.

However, if we calculate the average ranks for each combination of algorithm and class distribution value, the conclusion about what resampling method is better is different. This is because there are some datasets (e.g. abalone and sick_euthyroid, in the case of C4.5) which obtain much better GM values with SUB than with SMT but, however, SMT improves SUB in many more datasets. Fig. 1 shows graphically the average ranks obtained in order to be able to appreciate the distance between the obtained values associated to each resampling method for each comparison. As can be observed, in four out of six cases, SMT is the method that achieved the best rank and only when the balanced class distribution was used, SUB achieved the first position.

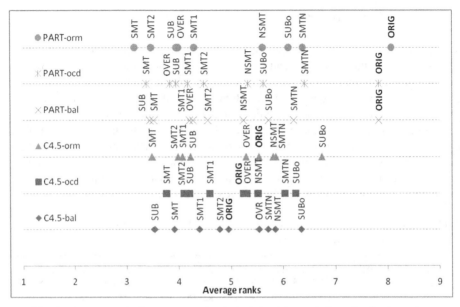

Fig. 1. Average ranks for each combination of algorithm and class distribution value

Observing the results of Fig. 1, we want to notice the difference between the results of the two algorithms. On the one hand, the position obtained by ORIG (no resampling method) always is the last for PART whereas it is an intermediate value (fourth or fifth rank) for C4.5, achieving better results than some resampling techniques as random subsampling (Weiss and Provost's size) and oversampling; and the combinations of SMOTE and ENN. On the other hand, the distance between the values of the average ranks is bigger for PART than for C4.5. As it is known, this will be crucial to find statistically significant differences in the performance of the compared resampling strategies based on the modern non-parametric tests.

We performed the statistical tests proposed by Demšar in [8] and García et al. in [14] and [15] in order to discover whether there are statistically significant differences among the resampling strategies applied to each comparison. Iman-Davenport test reported significant differences in the 6 comparisons. Then, we carried out a powerful post-hoc procedure, Shaffer test, to discover between which pairs of methods the significant differences appeared with a 95% significant level. Due to space limitation, we only will notice that, in the six comparisons, significant differences were found at least between the first and the last two options. In the case of PART, all resampling methods, except for SUBo and SMOTE-ENN (SMTN), achieved significant differences when comparing with the reference value, ORIG. However, for C4.5, any resampling method achieved differences with ORIG. Besides, it is worth noticing that, referred to the two algorithms, more pairs of methods achieved significant differences when we used the *ocd* class distribution than when we used the *bal* value, and even more when we used the *orm* class distribution value.

Anyway, in order to simplify the empirical study and to focus on the methods and the class distribution values with better behaviour, we used a methodology based on hierarchical comparisons. In this way, associated to each algorithm, first we selected the three best resampling strategies for each value of class distribution (*bal*, *ocd* and *orm*) and, adding the option without using any resampling technique, ORIG, we performed an analysis of statistically significant differences in order to determine which strategy has the best performance in this context.

Table 2 shows the average ranks (and the rank position) obtained among all datasets for the selected resampling strategies in each algorithm. As it can be observed, SMOTE (SMT) when *orm* class distribution is used, is the best option (in bold) for the two algorithms, and, in this case, the option without using any resampling method, ORIG, is the worst (the 10th position) for the two algorithms.

Table 2. Average ranks of the best resampling strategies related to each class distribution value and algorithm

	bal				*ocd*			*orm*		
	ORIG	SUB	SMT	SMT1	SMT	OVR	SUB	SMT	SMT2	SUB
PART	9.34	5.44	5.28	6.31	4.69	5.40	5.97	**3.50**	4.14	4.93
	(10)	(7)	(5)	(9)	(3)	(6)	(8)	**(1)**	(2)	(4)
			5.68			5.35			4.19	
			(3)			(2)			(1)	
	bal				*ocd*			*orm*		
	ORIG	SUB	SMT	SMT1	SMT	SMT2	SUB	SMT	SMT2	SMT1
C4.5	6.74	5.50	5.91	6.21	5.69	5.90	5.84	**3.97**	4.69	4.55
	(10)	(4)	(8)	(9)	(5)	(7)	(6)	**(1)**	(3)	(2)
			5.87			5.81			4.40	
			(3)			(2)			(1)	

Besides, in the second row associated to each algorithm, the mean of the three average ranks belonging to each class distribution value. As it can be observed, for the two algorithms, the resampling techniques for the *orm* value are the best ones, then the obtained ones with *ocd*, and, finally, the obtained ones with the balanced class distribution, *bal*.

Following with the analysis, we performed the previous mentioned statistical test in order to determine whether there are statistically significant differences between the results for each algorithm. Checking for significant differences using Iman-Davenport, the p-value is near to zero, and so, we can proceed with a Shaffer test. Table 3 shows the results associated to a Shaffer test for the two algorithms where the adjusted p-value (APV) related to each pair of the comparison appears. Besides, a "+" implies that the option in the row is statistically better than the one in the column; whereas "-" implies the contrary; and "=" means that there are not significant differences. Results with significant differences appear with a grey background. Due to space limitation, Table 3 shows the results of the multiple comparison test but only for those options that achieved significant differences (the p-value of the remaining of the compared pairs is 1.0 or near).

Table 3. Shaffer test for the best resampling strategies for each class distribution value and algorithm

PART		bal			ocd			orm		
	ORIG	SUB	SMT	SMT1	SMT	OVR	SUB	SMT	SMT2	SUB
ORIG	x	- 3.4×10^{-5}	- 1.1×10^{-5}	- 0.0048	- 1.7×10^{-7}	- 2.4×10^{-5}	- 7.6×10^{-4}	- 8.8×10^{-12}	- 2.1×10^{-9}	- 1.0×10^{-6}
orm SMT	+ 8.8×10^{-12}	= 0.4138	= 0.7399	+ 0.0147	= 1.0	= 0.4948	= 0.0559	x	= 1.0	= 1.0
orm SMT2	+ 2.1×10^{-9}	= 1.0	= 1.0	= 0.1824	= 1.0	= 1.0	= 0.6243	= 1.0	x	= 1.0
C4.5		bal			ocd			orm		
	ORIG	SUB	SMT	SMT1	SMT	SMT2	SUB	SMT	SMT2	SMT1
ORIG	x	= 1.0	= 1.0	= 1.0	= 1.0	= 1.0	= 1.0	- 0.0216	= 0.3552	= 0.2119
orm SMT	+ 0.0216	= 1.0	= 0.5137	= 0.1734	= 1.0	= 0.5455	= 0.6515	x	= 1.0	= 1.0

First, we can see the poor behaviour of the no-resampling method, ORIG, for the PART algorithm, since it is significantly outperformed by all analysed resampling strategies. On the other hand, in general terms, Table 3 suggests that SMOTE (SMT), when used with the *orm* class distribution value, is the only resampling strategy that achieves significant differences comparing with not using any resampling method, ORIG.

Finally, although beyond the context of this work, with regard to the differences between behaviour of the two algorithms, no significant differences were found by the Iman-Davenport test using the three best strategies for each algorithm (with a p-value equal to 0.6012).

5   Conclusions and Further Work

cIn this work we used resampling techniques, which were designed to deal with class imbalance problems, to be applied to datasets we can consider they are not so imbalanced or even balanced. These resampling techniques are often used to balance the unbalance in the representation in the classes since this makes the learning process a more complex problem. In this work we used an approach proposed in [2] in order to estimate the (near-)optimal class distribution for a given resampling method, the *orm* value, whatever the original class distribution may be, being applied on 29 datasets, 8 different resampling methods and two learning algorithms. The main aim of this work was to determine which was the best resampling method to solve a concrete classification problem in a context where the datasets are not so imbalanced.

Although random subsampling, one of the simplest and fastest methods, achieved competitive results, especially when used with balanced class distribution, the well-known SMOTE, an intelligent oversampling method, used with the estimated optimal class distribution, was the only one which achieved statistically significant differences comparing with the option without using any resampling strategy. Besides, in this context, SMOTE outperformed some its variants, as strategies based on the borderline minority examples or based on the combination with editing techniques, which have showed better results in the literature in the context of class imbalanced datasets. These results were confirmed by the two used algorithms: C4.5 and PART.

As further work, we think it would be interesting to extend the experimentation with more resampling techniques and to confirm the results with more learning algorithms. On the other hand, we are conscious that the quest of the optimal class distribution for each dataset and selected resampling method could be improved. The use of optimization techniques would be of interest in order to improve the results to deal with a concrete learning problem.

Acknowledgments. This work was funded by the University of the Basque Country, general funding for research groups (Aldapa, GIU10/02), by the Science and Education Department of the Spanish Government (ModelAccess project, TIN2010-15549), by the Basque Government's SAIOTEK program (Datacc2 project, S-PE12UN064) and by the Diputación Foral de Gipuzkoa. We would like to thank Iñaki Albisua for his support in the development of this work. Also, we would like to thank Francisco Herrera for his advice and his research group, SCI^{2}S, for making available the tools for analysis of statistically significant differences.

References

1. Albisua, I., Arbelaitz, O., Gurrutxaga, I., Martín, J.I., Muguerza, J., Pérez, J.M., Perona, I.: Obtaining optimal class distribution for decision trees: Comparative analysis of CTC and C4.5. In: Meseguer, P., Mandow, L., Gasca, R.M. (eds.) CAEPIA 2009. LNCS, vol. 5988, pp. 101–110. Springer, Heidelberg (2010)
2. Albisua, I., Arbelaitz, O., Gurrutxaga, I., Lasarguren, A., Muguerza, J., Pérez, J.M.: The Quest for the Optimal Class Distribution: an Approach for Enhancing the Effectiveness of Learning via Resampling Methods for imbalanced data sets. Progress in Artificial Intelligence 2(1), 45–63 (2013)
3. Bache, K., Lichman, M.: UCI Machine Learning Repository. University of California, School of Information and Computer Science, Irvine, CA (2013), http://archive.ics.uci.edu/ml
4. Batista, G.E.A.P.A., Prati, R.C., Monard, M.C.: A study of the behavior of several methods for balancing machine learning training data. ACM SIGKDD Explorations Newsletter 6, 20–29 (2004)
5. Berry, M.J.A., Linoff, G.: Astering Data Mining. The Art and Science of Customer Relationship Management. Willey (2000)
6. Chawla, N.V., Bowyer, K.W., Hall, L.O., Kegelmeyer, W.P.: SMOTE: Synthetic Minority Over-sampling Technique. Journal of Artificial Intelligence Research 16, 321–357 (2002)
7. Cohen, W.W.: Fast effective rule induction. In: Proc. of the Twelfth International Conference on Machine Learning, pp. 115–123 (1995)
8. Demšar, J.: Statistical Comparisons of Classifiers over Multiple Data Sets. Journal of Machine Learning Research 7, 1–30 (2006)

9. Estabrooks, A., Jo, T.J., Japkowicz, N.: A Multiple Resampling Method for Learning from Imbalanced Data Sets. Computational Intelligence 20(1), 18–36 (2004)
10. Fawcett, T.: ROC Graphs: Notes and Practical Considerations for Researchers. HP Laboratories (2004)
11. Fernández, A., García, S., Herrera, F.: Addressing the Classification with Imbalanced Data: Open Problems and New Challenges on Class Distribution. In: Corchado, E., Kurzyński, M., Woźniak, M. (eds.) HAIS 2011, Part I. LNCS, vol. 6678, pp. 1–10. Springer, Heidelberg (2011)
12. Frank, E., Witten, I.: Generating accurate rule sets without global optimization. In: Shavlik, J. (ed.) Proc. of the 15th Int. Conference on Machine Learning, pp. 144–151 (1998)
13. García, S., Fernández, A., Herrera, F.: Enhancing the effectiveness and interpretability of decision tree and rule induction classifiers with evolutionary training set selection over imbalanced problems. Applied Soft Computing 9, 1304–1314 (2009)
14. García, S., Herrera, F.: An Extension on "Statistical Comparisons of Classifiers over Multiple Data Sets" for all Pairwise Comparisons. Journal of Machine Learning Reserarch 9, 2677–2694 (2008)
15. García, S., Fernández, A., Luengo, J., Herrera, F.: Advanced nonparametric tests for multiple comparisons in the design of experiments in computational intelligence and data mining: Experimental Analysis of Power. Information Sciences 180, 2044–2064 (2010)
16. Han, H., Wang, W.-Y., Mao, B.-H.: Borderline-SMOTE: A New Over-Sampling Method in Imbalanced Data Sets Learning. In: Huang, D.-S., Zhang, X.-P., Huang, G.-B. (eds.) ICIC 2005. LNCS, vol. 3644, pp. 878–887. Springer, Heidelberg (2005)
17. He, H., Garcia, E.: Learning from imbalanced data. IEEE Trans. Knowl. Data Eng. 21(9), 1263–1284 (2009)
18. Japkowicz, N., Stephen, S.: The Class Imbalance Problem: A Systematic Study. Intelligent Data Analysis Journal 6(5), 429–449 (2002)
19. Quinlan, J.R.: C4.5: Programs for Machine Learning. Morgan Kaufmann Publishers Inc., San Mateo (1993)
20. Weiss, G.M., Provost, F.: Learning when Training Data are Costly: The Effect of Class Distribution on Tree Induction. Journal of Artificial Intelligence Research 19, 315–354 (2003)
21. Wilson, D.R., Martínez, T.R.: Reduction Techniques for Exemplar-Based Learning Algorithms. Machine Learning 38(3), 257–286 (2000)
22. Wu, X., Kumar, V., Quinlan, J.R., Ghosh, J., Yang, Q., Motoda, H., McLachlan, G.J., Ng, A., Liu, B., Yu, P.S., Zhou, Z.-H., Steinbach, M., Hand, D.J., Steinberg, D.: Top 10 algorithms in data mining. Knowledge and Information Systems 14, 1–37 (2008)
23. Yang, Q., Wu, X.: 10 challenging problems in data mining research. International Journal of Information Technology & Decision Making 5(4), 597–604 (2006)

Scaling Up Feature Selection: A Distributed Filter Approach

Verónica Bolón-Canedo, Noelia Sánchez-Maroño, and Joana Cerviño-Rabuñal

Laboratory for Research and Development in Artificial Intelligence (LIDIA),
Computer Science Dept., University of A Coruña, 15071 A Coruña, Spain
{veronica.bolon,noelia.sanchez,joana.cervino}@udc.es

Abstract. Traditionally, feature selection has been required as a preliminary step for many pattern recognition problems. In recent years,
distributed learning has been the focus of much attention, due to the
proliferation of big databases, in some cases distributed across different
nodes. However, most of the existing feature selection algorithms were
designed for working in a centralized manner, i.e. using the whole dataset
at once. In this research, a new approach for using filter methods in a distributed manner is presented. The approach splits the data horizontally,
i.e., by samples. A filter is applied at each partition performing several
rounds to obtain a stable set of features. Later, a merging procedure is
performed in order to combine the results into a single subset of relevant features. Five of the most well-known filters were used to test the
approach. The experimental results on six representative datasets show
that the execution time is shortened whereas the performance is maintained or even improved compared to the standard algorithms applied
to the non-partitioned datasets.

1   Introduction

In the past 20 years, the dimensionality of the datasets involved in data mining
has increased dramatically, as can be seen in [1]. This fact is reflected if one analyzes the *dimensionality* (samples × features) of the datasets posted in the UC
Irvine Machine Learning Repository [2]. In the 1980s, the maximal dimensionality of the data was about 100; then in the 1990s, this number increased to more
than 1500; and finally in the 2000s, it further increased to about 3 million. The
proliferation of this type of datasets with very high (> 10000) dimensionality
had brought unprecedented challenges to machine learning researchers. Learning
algorithms can degenerate their performance due to overfitting, learned models
decrease their interpretability as they are more complex, and finally speed and
efficiency of the algorithms decline in accordance with size.

Machine learning can take advantage of feature selection methods to be able
to reduce the dimensionality of a given problem. *Feature selection* (FS) is the
process of detecting the relevant features and discarding the irrelevant and redundant ones, with the goal of obtaining a small subset of features that describes
properly the given problem with a minimum degradation or even improvement

C. Bielza et al. (Eds.): CAEPIA 2013, LNAI 8109, pp. 121–130, 2013.

in performance [3]. Feature selection, as it is an important activity in data pre-processing, has been an active research area in the last decade, finding success in many different real world applications [4,5,6,7].

FS methods usually come in three flavors: *filter*, *wrapper*, and *embedded* methods [8]. The *filter* model relies on the general characteristics of training data and carries out the FS process as a pre-processing step with independence of the induction algorithm. On the contrary, *wrappers* involve optimizing a predictor as a part of the selection process. Halfway these two models one can find *embedded* methods, which perform FS in the process of training and are usually specific to given learning machines. By having some interaction with the predictor, wrapper and embedded methods tend to obtain higher prediction accuracy than filters, at the cost of a higher computational cost. When dealing with high dimensional data, as in this research, filters are preferable even when the subset of features is not optimal, due to their computational and statistical scalability [9].

Traditionally, FS methods are applied in a centralized manner, i.e. a single learning model to solve a given problem. However, when dealing with large amounts of data, distributed FS seems to be a promising line of research since allocating the learning process among several workstations is a natural way of scaling up learning algorithms. Moreover, it allows to deal with datasets that are naturally distributed, a frequent situation in many real applications (e.g. weather databases, financial data or medical records). There are two common types of data distribution: (a) horizontal distribution wherein data are distributed in subsets of instances; and (b) vertical distribution wherein data are distributed in subsets of attributes. The great majority of approaches distribute the data horizontally, since it constitutes the most suitable and natural approach for most applications [10,11,12,13]. While not common, there are some other developments that distribute the data vertically [14,15,16]. When the data come distributed in origin, vertical distribution is solely useful where the representation of data could vary along time by adding new attributes.

In this research, and in order to deal with large databases, we will distribute the data horizontally. In this manner, several rounds of FS processes will be performed, whose outputs will be combined into a single subset of relevant features. Experimental results on six benchmark datasets demonstrate that our proposal can maintain the performance of original FS methods, providing a learning scalable solution.

The rest of the paper is organized as follows: Section 2 presents our distributed filter approach, Section 3 depicts the experimental setup, and Sections 4 and 5 report the experimental results and the conclusions, respectively.

2   Distributed Feature Selection

In this paper we present a distributed filter approach by partitioning the data horizontally. The methodology consists of applying filters over several partitions of the data, combined in the final step into a single subset of features. The idea of distributing the data horizontally builds on the assumption that combining the output of multiple experts is better than the output of any single expert. There are three main stages: (i) partition of the datasets; (ii) application of the filter to the subsets; and (iii) combination of the results.

The feature selection algorithm (see pseudo-code in Algorithm 1) is applied to all the datasets in several iterations or rounds. This repetition ensures capturing enough information for the combination stage. At each round, the first step is the partition of the dataset, which consists of randomly dividing the original training dataset into several disjoint subsets of approximately the same size that cover the full dataset (see Algorithm 1, line 3). As mentioned above, the partition will be doing horizontally . Then, the filter algorithm chosen is applied to each subset separately and the features selected to be removed receive a vote (Algorithm 1, lines 5 - 8). At that point, a new partition is performed and another round of votes is accomplished until reaching the predefined number of rounds. Finally, the features that have received a number of votes above a certain threshold are removed. Therefore, a unique set of features is obtained to train a classifier C and to test its performance over a new set of samples (test dataset).

To determine the threshold of votes required to remove a feature is not an easy-to-solve question, since it depends on the given dataset. Therefore, we have developed our own automatic method which calculates this threshold, outlined in Algorithm 1, lines 9-19. The best value for the number of votes is estimated from its effect on the training set, but due to the large size of the dataset, not the complete training set was used, only 10% was employed.

Following the recommendations exposed in [17], the selection of the number of votes must take into account two different criteria: the training error and the percentage of features retained. Both values must be minimized to the extent possible, by minimizing the fitness criterion $e[v]$ (see Algorithm 1, line 18). To calculate this criterion, a term α is introduced to measure the relative relevance of both values and was set to $\alpha = 0.75$ as suggested in [17], giving more influence to the classification error. Because of performing a horizontally partition of the data, the maximum number of votes is the number of rounds r times the number of subsets s. Since in some cases this number is in the order of thousands, instead of evaluating all the possible values for the number of votes we have opted for delimiting into an interval $[minVote, maxVote]$ computed used the mean and standard deviation (see lines 9-12 in Algorithm 1).

3   Experimental Setup

This section presents the datasets chosen for testing the distributed approach and the concrete filters which will carry out the feature selection process. For testing the adequacy of our proposal, four well-known supervised classifiers, of different conceptual origin, were selected: C4.5, naive Bayes, IB1 and SVM. All the classifiers and filters are executed using the Weka tool [18], with default values for their parameters. Notice that the C4.5 classifier, widely-used in the FS literature, performs its own embedded selection of features so it might be using a smaller number of features than the other ones.

Algorithm 1: Pseudo-code for distributed filter

Data: $d_{(m \times n+1)} \leftarrow$ labeled training dataset with m samples and n input features

> $X \leftarrow$ set of features, $X = \{x_1, \dots, x_n\}$
> $s \leftarrow$ number of submatrices of d with p samples
> $r \leftarrow$ number of rounds
> $\alpha \leftarrow 0.75$

Result: $S \leftarrow$ subset of features $\backslash S \subset X$

`/* Obtaining a vector of votes for discarding features        */`

1 initialize the vector votes to 0, $|vector| = n$
2 **for** *each round* **do**
3 | Split d randomly into s disjoint submatrices
4 | **for** *each submatrix* **do**
5 | | apply a feature selection algorithm
6 | | $F \leftarrow$ features selected by the algorithm
7 | | $E \leftarrow$ features eliminated by the algorithm $\backslash E \cup F = X$
8 | | increment one vote for each feature in E
   | **end**
   end

`/* Obtain threshold of votes, `Th`, to remove a feature        */`

9   $avg \leftarrow$ compute the average of the vector votes
10 $std \leftarrow$ compute the standard deviation of the vector votes
11 $minVote \leftarrow$ minimum threshold considered (computed as $avg - 1/2std$)
12 $maxVote \leftarrow$ maximum threshold considered (computed as $avg + 1/2std$)
13 $z \leftarrow$ submatrix of d with only 10% of samples
14 **for** $v \leftarrow mixVote$ *to* $maxVote$ *with increment 5* **do**
15 | $F_{th} \leftarrow$ subset of selected features (number of votes $< v$)
16 | $error \leftarrow$ classification error after training z using only features in F_{th}
17 | $featPercentage \leftarrow$ percentage of features retained $\left(\frac{|F_{th}|}{|X|} \times 100 \right)$
18 | $e[v] \leftarrow \alpha \times error + (1 - \alpha) \times featPercentage$
    end
19 $Th \leftarrow min(e)$, Th is the value which minimizes the error e
20 $S \leftarrow$ subset of features after removing from X all features with a number of votes $\geq Th$

3.1   Datasets

In order to test our distributed filter approach, we have selected six benchmark datasets which are reported in Table 1, depicting their properties (number of features, number of training and test instances and number of classes). These datasets can be considered representative of problems from medium to large size, since the horizontally distribution is not suitable for small-sample datasets. All of them can be free downloaded from the UCI Machine Learning Repository [2]. Those datasets originally divided into training and test sets were maintained, whereas, for the sake of comparison, datasets with only training set were randomly divided using the common rule 2/3 for training and 1/3 for testing. The number of packets (s) to partition the dataset in each round is also displayed in the last column of Table 1. This number was calculated with the constraint of having, at least, three packets per dataset.

Table 1. Dataset description

Dataset	Features	Training	Test	Classes	Packets
Connect4	42	45038	22519	3	45
Isolet	617	6238	1236	26	5
Madelon	500	1600	800	2	3
Ozone	72	1691	845	2	11
Spambase	57	3067	1534	2	5
Mnist	717	40000	20000	2	5

3.2 Filter Methods

The distributed approach proposed herein can be used with any filter method. In this work, five well-known filters, based on different metrics, were chosen. While three of the filters return a feature subset (CFS, Consistency-based and INTERACT), the other two (ReliefF and Information Gain) are ranker methods, so it is necessary to establish a threshold in order to obtain a subset of features. In this research we have opted for retaining the c top features, being c the number of features selected by CFS. It is also worth noting that although most of the filters work only over nominal features, the discretization step is done by default by Weka, working as a black box for the user.

- **Correlation-based Feature Selection** (CFS) is a simple filter algorithm that ranks feature subsets according to a correlation based heuristic evaluation function [19]. Theoretically, irrelevant features should be ignored and redundant features should be screened out.
- The **Consistency-based Filter** [20] evaluates the worth of a subset of features by the level of consistency in the class values when the training instances are projected onto the subset of attributes.
- The **INTERACT** algorithm [21] is based on symmetrical uncertainty (SU). The authors stated that this method can handle feature interaction, and efficiently selects relevant features. The first part of the algorithm requires a threshold, but since the second part searches for the best subset of features, it is considered a subset filter.
- **Information Gain** [22] is one of the most common attribute evaluation methods. This filter provides an ordered ranking of all the features and then a threshold is required.
- **ReliefF** [23] is an extension of the original Relief algorithm that adds the ability of dealing with multiclass problems and is also more robust and capable of dealing with incomplete and noisy data. This method may be applied

in all situations, has low bias, includes interaction among features and may capture local dependencies which other methods miss.

4   Experimental Results

In this section we present and discuss the experimental results over six benchmark datasets. Our distributed approach is compared with the centralized standard approach of each method. To distinguish between both approaches, a "C" (centralized) or a "D" (distributed) was added to the name of the filter. In the case of the distributed approach, three rounds (r in Algorithm 1) have been executed.

Table 2 reports the test classification accuracies of C4.5, naive Bayes, IB1 and SVM over the six datasets. The best result for each dataset and classifier is highlighted in bold face, while the best result for dataset is also shadowed.

As expected, the results are very variable depending on the dataset and the classifier. However, in terms of average (last column), the best result for each classifier is obtained by a distributed approach, except for SVM. In particular, ReliefF-D combined with C4.5 achieves the highest accuracy, outperforming in at least 4% the best results for the remaining classifiers.

For datasets *Connect4* and *Isolet*, the highest accuracies are obtained by centralized approaches, although these results improve only in 0.90% and 2.19%, respectively, the best mark achieved by a distributed method. For Ozone dataset, both distributed and centralized approaches obtain the highest precision when combined with SVM classifier.

For the remaining datasets (*Madelon*, *Spambase* and *Mnist*), the best results are accomplished by a distributed method. It is worth mentioning the case of *Spambase*, where ReliefF distributed combined with naive Bayes reports 91.79% of classification accuracy whilest the same filter method in the standard centralized approach achieves a poor 41.85% of accuracy. The results for *Mnist* dataset are also remarkable, where the highest accuracy (96.31%) outperforms the best mark of a centralized method in more than 6%.

Table 3 reports the runtime of the feature selection algorithms, both in centralized and distributed manners. In the distributed approach, considering that all the subsets can be processed at the same time, the time displayed in the table is the average of the times required by the filter in each subset generated in the partitioning stage. In these experiments, all the subsets were processed in the same machine, but the proposed algorithm can be executed in multiple processors. Please note that this filtering time is independent of the classifier chosen.

As expected, the advantage of the distributed approach in terms of execution time over the standard method is significant. The time is reduced for all datasets and filters. It is worth mentioning the important reductions as the dimensionality of the dataset grows. For *Mnist* dataset, which has 717 features and 40000 training samples, the reduction is more than notable. For ReliefF filter, the processing time is reduced from almost 8 hours to 15 minutes, proving the adequacy of the distributed approach when dealing with large datasets.

Table 2. Test classification accuracy. Best results are highlighted.

		Connect4	Isolet	Madelon	Ozone	Spambase	Mnist	Average
C4.5	CFS-C	61.22	81.59	80.50	97.63	81.16	86.99	81.51
	CFS-D	61.25	**82.23**	76.88	95.86	79.27	88.65	80.69
	INT-C	60.48	78.96	80.63	96.92	78.16	87.24	80.40
	INT-D	61.66	79.03	82.38	94.79	80.83	88.62	81.22
	Cons-C	60.49	56.00	80.63	**98.70**	84.62	87.00	77.90
	Cons-D	61.66	77.10	82.63	96.33	79.34	**90.46**	81.25
	IG-C	**63.90**	81.40	72.75	98.22	83.83	87.83	81.32
	IG-D	62.34	81.08	79.63	97.87	**85.33**	87.88	82.36
	ReliefF-C	63.49	79.54	73.88	98.11	78.81	87.34	80.19
	ReliefF-D	63.00	80.56	**87.50**	98.46	84.75	87.95	**83.70**
NB	CFS-C	60.28	**75.05**	**71.75**	78.22	57.69	71.88	69.15
	CFS-D	58.83	73.89	70.13	76.69	57.24	73.34	68.35
	INT-C	53.85	71.26	70.00	78.22	57.95	70.94	67.04
	INT-D	59.16	70.75	70.13	75.03	74.77	71.06	70.15
	Cons-C	54.12	42.78	70.00	**98.70**	91.00	72.78	71.56
	Cons-D	59.16	69.92	70.38	73.25	**92.89**	**75.74**	**73.56**
	IG-C	60.42	69.34	70.38	74.08	76.53	70.74	70.25
	IG-D	60.28	67.54	70.63	77.63	89.70	68.09	72.31
	ReliefF-C	60.42	62.67	68.63	71.36	41.85	69.82	62.46
	ReliefF-D	**60.50**	56.51	71.50	60.95	91.79	70.93	68.70
IB1	CFS-C	53.90	56.00	85.63	96.45	79.14	87.93	76.51
	CFS-D	57.61	54.78	65.63	96.57	77.31	91.65	73.93
	INT-C	58.27	52.92	88.75	94.44	79.73	86.87	76.83
	INT-D	57.61	49.84	71.75	95.27	76.86	91.79	73.85
	Cons-C	58.06	49.90	88.75	**98.70**	80.83	87.36	77.27
	Cons-D	57.61	58.31	71.63	95.27	77.38	**96.31**	76.09
	IG-C	51.29	54.78	74.25	95.98	78.62	89.63	74.09
	IG-D	57.01	**59.72**	86.13	95.50	78.42	90.77	77.92
	ReliefF-C	**61.81**	59.14	75.25	95.98	76.99	89.97	76.52
	ReliefF-D	57.01	57.09	**90.88**	96.80	80.70	91.35	**78.97**
SVM	CFS-C	**60.42**	83.45	66.50	**98.70**	**85.85**	79.58	**79.08**
	CFS-D	**60.42**	82.42	67.13	**98.70**	82.27	**81.52**	78.74
	INT-C	**60.42**	73.83	66.38	**98.70**	80.31	78.54	76.36
	INT-D	**60.42**	78.00	**68.50**	**98.70**	81.49	80.84	77.99
	Cons-C	**60.42**	31.17	66.38	**98.70**	81.88	75.14	68.95
	Cons-D	**60.42**	68.12	66.50	**98.70**	81.94	80.85	76.09
	IG-C	**60.42**	82.94	67.13	**98.70**	83.83	78.28	78.55
	IG-D	**60.42**	79.67	67.13	**98.70**	83.38	79.30	78.10
	ReliefF-C	**60.42**	**84.61**	67.50	**98.70**	81.94	75.43	78.10
	ReliefF-D	**60.42**	82.36	67.50	**98.70**	83.57	75.72	78.04

For the distributed approach, there exist also the time required to find the threshold to build the final subset of features. This time highly depends on the classifier, as can be seen in Table 4. In this table it is visualized the average runtime for each filter and classifier. It is easy to note that the classifier which

Table 3. Runtime (hh:mm:ss) for the FS methods tested. Lowest times highlighted in bold font.

Method	Connect4	Isolet	Madelon	Ozone	Spambase	Mnist
CFS-C	00:02:25	00:05:49	00:00:55	00:00:12	00:00:16	00:44:55
CFS-D	00:00:06	00:01:12	**00:00:13**	00:00:04	**00:00:04**	00:05:24
INT-C	00:02:57	00:04:55	00:00:56	00:00:12	00:00:16	00:42:13
INT-D	**00:00:05**	00:00:54	00:00:14	00:00:04	**00:00:04**	00:04:50
Cons-C	00:13:36	00:07:03	00:01:01	00:00:12	00:00:19	03:22:21
Cons-D	**00:00:05**	00:01:02	00:00:14	00:00:04	00:00:05	00:09:37
IG-C	00:02:19	00:04:32	00:00:55	00:00:12	00:00:16	00:38:17
IG-D	**00:00:05**	**00:00:49**	**00:00:13**	**00:00:03**	**00:00:04**	**00:04:46**
ReliefF-C	00:31:40	00:13:04	00:01:23	00:00:14	00:00:29	07:54:40
ReliefF-D	00:00:06	00:00:57	00:00:17	**00:00:03**	**00:00:04**	00:15:59

requires more execution time is SVM whilst the one which requires the shortest time is naive Bayes. In any case, this is usually in the order of seconds (2 minutes in the worst case) so it is insignificant when compared with the time required by any of the centralized algorithms showed above. Moreover, if the user would rather save this time, it is possible to establish a fixed threshold and not performing this specific calculation.

Table 4. Average runtime (hh:mm:ss) for obtaining the threshold of votes. Lowest times highlighted in bold font.

Method	C4.5	NB	IB1	SVM
CFS-D	00:00:36	00:00:26	00:00:48	00:01:36
INT-D	00:00:31	00:00:24	00:00:50	**00:01:23**
Cons-D	**00:00:29**	**00:00:23**	00:00:46	00:01:41
IG-D	00:00:38	00:00:28	00:00:46	00:01:43
ReliefF-D	00:00:33	00:00:26	**00:00:41**	00:02:02

In light of the above, we can conclude that our distributed proposal performs successfully, since the running time is considerably reduced and the accuracy does not drop to inadmissible values. In fact, our approach is able to match and in some cases even improve the standard algorithms applied to the non-partitioned datasets.

5   Conclusions

In this work, we have proposed a new method for scaling up feature selection: a distributed filter approach. The proposed method has been able to successfully distribute the feature selection process, shortening the execution time and maintaining the classification performance.

An experimental study was carried out on six datasets considered representative of problems from medium to large size. In terms of classification accuracy, our distributed filtering approach obtains similar results to the centralized methods, even with slight improvements for some datasets. Furthermore, the most important advantage of the proposed method is the dramatically reduction in computational time (from the order of hours to the order of minutes). As future work, we plan to distribute other FS techniques, such as wrapper or embedded methods, and to try the vertical partition instead of the horizontal one.

Acknowledgements. This research has been economically supported in part by the Secretaría de Estado de Investigación of the Spanish Government through the research project TIN 2012-37954; and by the Consellería de Industria of the Xunta de Galicia through the research projects CN2011/007 and CN2012/211; all of them partially funded by FEDER funds of the European Union. V. Bolón-Canedo acknowledges the support of Xunta de Galicia under *Plan I2C* Grant Program.

References

1. Zhao, Z., Liu, H.: Spectral Feature Selection for Data Mining. Chapman & Hall/Crc Data Mining and Knowledge Discovery. Taylor & Francis Group (2011)
2. Frank, A., Asuncion, A.: UCI Machine Learning Repository (2010), http://archive.ics.uci.edu/ml (accessed April 2013)
3. Guyon, I., Gunn, S., Nikravesh, M., Zadeh, L.A.: Feature extraction: foundations and applications, vol. 207. Springer (2006)
4. Yu, L., Liu, H.: Redundancy based feature selection for microarray data. In: Proceedings of the Tenth ACM SIGKDD International Conference on Knowledge Discovery and Data Mining, pp. 737–742. ACM (2004)
5. Bolón-Canedo, V., Sánchez-Maroño, N., Alonso-Betanzos, A.: Feature selection and classification in multiple class datasets: An application to kdd cup 99 dataset. Expert Systems with Applications 38(5), 5947–5957 (2011)
6. Forman, G.: An extensive empirical study of feature selection metrics for text classification. The Journal of Machine Learning Research 3, 1289–1305 (2003)
7. Saari, P., Eerola, T., Lartillot, O.: Generalizability and simplicity as criteria in feature selection: application to mood classification in music. IEEE Transactions on Audio, Speech, and Language Processing 19(6), 1802–1812 (2011)
8. Liu, H., Motoda, H.: Feature selection for knowledge discovery and data mining. Springer (1998)
9. Saeys, Y., Inza, I., Larrañaga, P.: A review of feature selection techniques in bioinformatics. Bioinformatics 23(19), 2507–2517 (2007)
10. Chan, P.K., Stolfo, S.J., et al.: Toward parallel and distributed learning by meta-learning. In: AAAI Workshop in Knowledge Discovery in Databases, pp. 227–240 (1993)
11. Ananthanarayana, V.S., Subramanian, D.K., Murty, M.N.: Scalable, distributed and dynamic mining of association rules. In: Prasanna, V.K., Vajapeyam, S., Valero, M. (eds.) HiPC 2000. LNCS, vol. 1970, pp. 559–566. Springer, Heidelberg (2000)

12. Tsoumakas, G., Vlahavas, I.: Distributed data mining of large classifier ensembles. In: Proceedings Companion Volume of the Second Hellenic Conference on Artificial Intelligence, pp. 249–256 (2002)
13. Das, K., Bhaduri, K., Kargupta, H.: A local asynchronous distributed privacy preserving feature selection algorithm for large peer-to-peer networks. Knowledge and Information Systems 24(3), 341–367 (2010)
14. McConnell, S., Skillicorn, D.B.: Building predictors from vertically distributed data. In: Proceedings of the 2004 Conference of the Centre for Advanced Studies on Collaborative Research, pp. 150–162. IBM Press (2004)
15. Skillicorn, D.B., McConnell, S.M.: Distributed prediction from vertically partitioned data. Journal of Parallel and Distributed Computing 68(1), 16–36 (2008)
16. Rokach, L.: Taxonomy for characterizing ensemble methods in classification tasks: A review and annotated bibliography. Computational Statistics & Data Analysis 53(12), 4046–4072 (2009)
17. de Haro García, A.: Scaling data mining algorithms. Application to instance and feature selection. PhD thesis, Universidad de Granada (2011)
18. Hall, M., Frank, E., Holmes, G., Pfahringer, B., Reutemann, P., Witten, I.H.: The weka data mining software: an update. ACM SIGKDD Explorations Newsletter 11(1), 10–18 (2009)
19. Hall, M.A.: Correlation-based feature selection for machine learning. PhD thesis, Citeseer (1999)
20. Dash, M., Liu, H.: Consistency-based search in feature selection. Artificial Intelligence 151(1-2), 155–176 (2003)
21. Zhao, Z., Liu, H.: Searching for interacting features. In: Proceedings of the 20th International Joint Conference on Artifical Intelligence, pp. 1156–1161. Morgan Kaufmann Publishers Inc. (2007)
22. Hall, M.A., Smith, L.A.: Practical feature subset selection for machine learning. Computer Science 98, 181–191 (1998)
23. Kononenko, I.: Estimating attributes: Analysis and extensions of relief. In: Bergadano, F., De Raedt, L. (eds.) ECML 1994. LNCS, vol. 784, pp. 171–182. Springer, Heidelberg (1994)

Experiments on Neuroevolution and Online Weight Adaptation in Complex Environments

Francisco José Gallego-Durán,
Rafael Molina-Carmona, and Faraón Llorens-Largo

Departamento de Ciencia de la Computación e Inteligencia Artificial
Universidad de Alicante
{fgallego,rmolina,faraon}@dccia.ua.es

Abstract. Neuroevolution has come a long way over the last decade. Lots of interesting and successful new methods and algorithms have been presented, with great improvements that make the field become very promising. Concretely, HyperNEAT has shown a great potential for evolving large scale neural networks, by discovering geometric regularities, thus being suitable for evolving complex controllers. However, once training phase has finished, evolved neural networks stay fixed and learning/adaptation does not happen anymore. A few methods have been proposed to address this concern, mainly using Hebbian plasticity and/or Compositional Pattern Producing Networks (CPPNs) like in Adaptive HyperNEAT. This methods have been tested in simple environments to isolate the effectiveness of adaptation from the Neuroevolution. In spite of this being quite convenient, more research is needed to better understand online adaptation in more complex environments. This paper shows a new proposal for online weight adaptation in neuroevolved artificial neural networks, and presents the results of several experiments carried out in a race simulation environment.

Keywords: Neuroevolution, Online Adaptation, Complex Environments.

1 Introduction

Artificial Intelligence is always seeking to mimic human brain processes in one way or another. The more powerful and developed computers and algorithms are, the more we appreciate the intrinsic complexity and inherent generality of the human brain and its learning capabilities. Attempting to replicate the unique capabilities of the brains into software algorithms, the field of Artificial Neural Networks (ANNs) [13] came into live. The initial euphoria about what ANNs would be able to do soon vanished as the intrinsic complexities of neurons came along. Training ANNs is a difficult task, but even more difficult is finding effective and efficient topologies.

Neuroevolution [12,7] (i.e. the use of evolutive algorithms to search for ANNs topologies and weights) is one of the best known ways to generate and train complex, recurrent ANNs. One of the most prominent Neuroevolutive (NE) algorithms of the past decade was Neuroevolution of Augmenting Topologies

C. Bielza et al. (Eds.): CAEPIA 2013, LNAI 8109, pp. 131–138, 2013.

(NEAT) [9,7,10]which proposed a way of minimizing the problem of Competing Conventions and the use of complexification to traverse the search space looking for effective and efficient ANNs topologies. Yet, it remained very difficult to find and train large scale topologies of ANNs, which are believed to be necessary for complex tasks. Then Compositional Pattern Producing Networks (CPPNs) and Hyper-cube Based NEAT (HyperNEAT) [8,1,5] discovered a way to use NEAT as a form of indirect encoding for producing large scale ANNs with topological regularities (as in the human brain). Then on, HyperNEAT has shown great ability to produce large scale Neural Networks able to perform efficiently in complex domains where an intelligent controller is required.

However, as ANNs increase in complexity and capabilities, an important subject remains unsolved. Neuroevolution algorithms have shown as a great way to discover topologies and weight sets that exhibit complex behaviours but, once the training phase is over, the produced ANNs stay fixed from then on. This greatly limits the use of resulting ANNs to static domains or domains where variance is not a problem. In contrast, our brains show what is called Neural Plasticity, which enables them to learn and adapt constantly to changing situations. This means that further research on online learning and adaptation for ANNs is required, to let us develop systems able to perform well on changing domains. In this sense, adaptive Evolving-Substrate HyperNEAT (Adaptive ES-HyperNEAT) [6,5] has done a first step by adding Hebbian ABC Plasticity [3] as patterns of local rules to ANNs, and also using CPPNs to continuously adapt weights over time. Nevertheless, there is no theoretical or empirical evidence about the performance of these approaches in complex environments.

Our contribution in this paper is focused on two points: presenting a new proposal for online adaptation of previously evolved ANNs, and giving some empirical evidence on how these approaches perform in a complex environment. In section 2, a succinct background on previous developments that conform the base for our contribution is presented. Section 3 describes our proposal for online adaptation and its motivation. Experimental results are shown in section 4, along with a description of the simulation environment used. Finally, section 5 summarizes our conclusions and further work.

2   Background

Our contribution represents one more step in the way that has been followed by lots of researches previous to us. Next we describe some previous work on which our contribution is based.

2.1   Neuroevolution of Augmenting Topologies (NEAT)

NEAT is a direct-encoding neuroevolution algorithm with speciation that evolves populations of ANNs starting from the most simple possible topologies and increasingly complexifying them. This way of traversing the search space is aimed at getting the simplest possible ANNs that solve a given task (i.e. the topologies with least possible hidden neurons). It does so by adding new neurons and links by means of mutation and protecting innovations through speciation (i.e. different species have their own evolutive niche, not competing with each other). The key concept that makes NEAT a powerful algorithm is innovations tracking. The algorithm maintains a registry of all the innovations that have happened across all the populations of the different epochs. Each new link or neuron that appears in a new position is given a registration Id. and, from then on, each individual that gets a neuron in the same position is referred with the same Id. This mechanism effectively tracks innovations and permits the creation of an effective crossover operator that overcomes part of the consequences of the Competing Conventions problem.

Although NEAT represented a great breakthrough, it suffered from the same problem that all direct-encoding algorithms suffer: they are inherently not scalable and not modular. For instance, closely observing the human brain, there are lots of regularities and patterns that repeat everywhere. If a direct encoding was to discover that topology, it should repeatedly discover each one of the regularities again and again. Direct Encoding has no mechanism for replicating structures or patterns of structures across the phenotype, because it is a direct low-level map between genes and neurons/links.

2.2   Compositional Pattern Producing Networks (CPPN)

Compositional Pattern Producing Networks (CPPNs) [11] were created as an indirect encoding scheme to overcome the impossibility of modularization and pattern repetition that NEAT had due to its direct encoding. CPPNs are a kind of networks similar to ANNs, but with an important difference: each node, instead of being a neuron, represents a mathematical function (e.g. sine, cosine, gaussian...). Therefore, a CPPN is a composition of functions that can produce outputs full of symmetries, patterns and regularities.

Describing this composition of functions as a network instead of a formal math composition, the model can profit from existing neuroevolutive algorithms to produce CPPNs. In particular, a modification of NEAT, called CPPN-NEAT can evolve increasingly complex CPPNs that are suitable for indirectly encoding links and weights of ANNs.

2.3   Hypercube-Based NeuroEvolution of Augmenting Topologies

HyperNEAT[1] takes NEAT and CPPNs as indirect encoding scheme and produces large scale ANNs with regularities, patterns and symmetries. HyperNEAT takes a population of CPPNs as genotypes of the final large-scale ANNs, and uses CPPN-NEAT to evolve these genotypes. For a CPPN to produce an ANN, a geometric *substrate* is required. A substrate is a collection of nodes (i.e. neurons) placed in a N-dimensional space, thus having a vector of coordinates $\mathbf{x^i} = (\mathbf{x_1^i}, \mathbf{x_2^i}, ..., \mathbf{x_n^i})$ for each node i. Typically, in a 2D-space neurons would be scattered in $[-1, 1] \times [-1, 1]$. Once a substrate is defined, the next step is to add links and weights between neurons. This is done iteratively querying the

CPPN with the coordinates of each possible pair of neurons $(\mathbf{x^i}, \mathbf{x^j}) \forall i, j$, where the output value from the CPPN represents the weight of the link from $\mathbf{x^i}$ to $\mathbf{x^j}$.

Taking into account that links and their weights are produced as a function of the relative location of neurons in space, it follows that the resulting topology of the ANN is related to the actual geometry of the substrate. This is an interesting characteristic of HyperNEAT, because it can produce ANNs with the ability of understanding geometry relations in their inputs. For instance, if we think of a chess controller with 64 inputs (one for each square of the board), the CPPNs will produce ANNs with intrinsic knowledge of the board structure. This characteristic is not present in traditional ANNs, which have to discover this information by themselves during training phase.

2.4   Adaptive, Evolvable-Substrate HyperNEAT

The two most recent improvements on HyperNEAT address two important issues. On the one hand, HyperNEAT requires the user to design an a priori substrate. While this could be very interesting in some problem domains, it normally is a matter of concern. Most of the time there are no clues on how to design the substrate, how many neurons to use, how to distribute them, etc. For this issue, Evolvable Substrate HyperNEAT (ES-HyperNEAT) [5,6] has developed a way to automatically configure a suitable substrate. The main idea behind is to measure variance in the function that the CPPN encodes: spatial areas of high variance in the function are considered to encode more information and, therefore, to require more density of nodes. On the other hand, HyperNEAT produces trained ANNs that, like almost any other neuroevolution algorithm, do not learn and/or adapt outside the evolution phase. Therefore, produced ANNs have a sort of fixed, hardcoded behaviour that will not change even if it is required. In order to address this issue, weight adaptation has been added to HyperNEAT, encoded as a pattern of local rules that modulate each weight. Concretely, three alternatives have been explored in [4]: Hebbian plasticity, Hebbian ABC plasticity and a modification of CPPN to make them able to update weights at each iteration. These three approaches were tested in a T-Maze where there were two rewards that switched position sometimes. Two different experiments were set up: in the first one, there was one big reward and a small one that sometimes switched positions. In the second one, rewards were relative to a color graduation scheme, which was designed explicitly to be non linearly-separable. Simulated agents were required to traverse the T-Maze and find the best reward repeatedly, thus requiring online adaptation to the different reward schemes and changes. They found that standard Hebbian Plasticity was not able to adapt, whereas there was a trade-off between the other two alternatives, considering bests results for the modification of CPPNs but with higher computational costs, as CPPNs needed to be queried every time-step for each weight.

3   Proposed Method for Online Weight Adaptation

The approaches for ANNs online weight adaptation proposed by [4] are quite interesting and open up a new field for discussion. Results shown up to date encouraged us to further test with these approaches but in a more complex scenario, where online adaptation and learning is required. For our experiments we used a modification of The Open Racing Car Simulator (TORCS) game, as in the annual car racing competition [2]. The experimental setup and results are discussed in section 4.

The results in [4] have shown that the most promising approach seams to be the modification of CPPNs to accept pre and post synaptic activation information in order to output a new weight at each time-step. Thinking of this approach, it seams a reasonable hypothesis that good weight adaptation comes from non-linear functions (and, most probably, from continuous and derivable ones). However, thinking of the human brain, it is also reasonable to think that delays between activations, frequency and strength seam to be the most important factors in the modulation of neural connections. Therefore, adding up all these ideas, we hypothesized and constructed a new prospective model for weight adaptation. Our model considers that the updated weight of a link connecting neuron i to neuron j depends on the activations of i and j on the n previous time-steps. From these n previous time-steps we will consider the post-synaptic activity O of i and j (namely O^i and O^j) and the pre-synaptic activity I of j (I^j). The updated weight is the result of a relation between all these values at the n-th step (the latest one) and the mean of their previous values, pre-processed by three modulation functions $\psi_{\mathbf{m}}, m \in \{1, 2, 3\}$ and post-processed by the update-strength function ζ. This relation is expressed in equation 1.

$$\mathbf{w_{ij}} = \zeta_n \left(\frac{(n-1)\psi_1(O_n^i)\psi_2(I_n^j)\psi_3(O_n^j)}{\psi_1(\sum_{k=1}^{n-1} O_k^i)\psi_2(\sum_{k=1}^{n-1} I_k^j)\psi_3(\sum_{k=1}^{n-1} O_k^j)} \right) \tag{1}$$

This equation is the same for each link, with the exception of the parameter n, the modulation functions $\psi_{\mathbf{m}}$ and the update-strength function ζ. All this functions will be created by the CPPN as a weighted average of a pre-defined subset of the functions that the CPPN uses as internal nodes $\Omega = \{F_i\}$, at the time the phenotype is created. For this approach to work properly, CPPNs have been modified to include $4M$ new outputs, being $M = |\Omega|$. Each $M_k = \{m_{k1}, m_{k2}, ...m_{kM}\}$ set of parameters is used as coefficients to construct a weighted function, as in equation 2.

$$\psi_{\mathbf{k}}(\mathbf{x}) = \frac{\sum_{q=1}^{M} m_{kq} F_q(x)}{\sum_{q=1}^{M} m_{kq}} \tag{2}$$

4   Experimentation and Results

One of our main aims in this work was to do empirical tests in complex environments in order to give more evidence on the previously existing methods, and have initial measures and evidence to give us a hint on what to expect from our hypothesis (i.e. whether it has a probability of being good or it is plainly wrong). As we stated before, we have used a modification on the TORCS racing game as environment (see figure 1). We have set up a population of 200 individuals and have trained them to be able to drive alone in the circuit "CG Speedway number 1", which comes with the original game package. Drivers are evolved to drive alone until they drive fine enough to finish the track, and then no more evolution is carried and they enter the adaptive test phase. In this second phase, drivers are asked to drive the same circuit but with lots of opponents and starting from the last position. The problem requires the drivers to be able to adapt not to crash against opponents, just by using the local weight adaptation rules.

Fig. 1. A screenshot during a test of a previously trained driver. The driver receives 180.000 inputs (600 × 300) one from each pixel from the viewport in front.

Standard HyperNEAT was the algorithm chosen to evolve the ANNs, and a virtual first person camera, with a resolution of 600 × 300 pixels and 32 bits of color per pixel, was used as main input. The ANNs also had as input a status vector with this information: amount of damage done, current gear, current RPM, speed in x and y axis, and the 4 wheel rotation speeds. ANNs were required to output the values of acceleration, brake, gear up/down, and steer left/right. Therefore, the substrate was configured with 180.009 input neurons and 4 outputs. Based on experimental research, we set up 540.000 hidden nodes with recurrent connections enabled for CPPNs, and sine, gaussian, sigmoid, absolute value and linear as available activation functions. Neuron output range was set to $[-1, 1]$ and a CPPN output value less than 0.2 was considered 0 (no link). The functions contained in the Ω set where sine, gaussian and sigmoid. The compatibility threshold was set to 5.5, and the compatibility modifier to 0.3. Survival threshold within species was set to 20%, whereas drop-off age was set to 18 and target number of species to 7. There was a 4% chance of adding either a node or a link, and links had 50% chance of mutation.

After approximately 2500 epochs of evolution, drivers were able to satisfactory drive their cars to the finish line (just 1 lap) when asking them to drive alone. From then on, evolution was finished and drivers were put in the same track, but together with 37 other drivers (standard fuzzy logic drivers coming with the TORCS package). Each driver was repeatedly tested 1500 times with each online adaptation method and population averages were taken (see figure 2). Final results depicted in figure 2 show that our proposal has a decent level

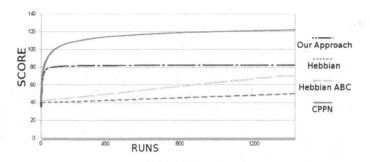

Fig. 2. Comparison of average results over 1500 runs of the track against 37 opponents. 100 points mark means that the driver arrived to the finish line in 70 seconds, more than 100 points means the driver arrived earlier

of adaptation, whereas CPPN shows the greatest performance. Interestingly, Hebbian approaches show some kind of linear improvements, what seems quite unnatural. We tested both Hebbian approaches with more than 1500 repetitions of the track, (actually, up to 3500 repetitions) and both of them reached a top in the intervals [47.54, 56.5] for standard Hebbian and [69.9, 75.6] for ABC Hebbian.

Despite the fact that CPPN clearly outperforms our approach in learning results, our approach has the advantage of being much more efficient computationally. For each single decision, CPPN has to query the entire network, whereas our method only has to do a simplified math calculation. Measured in CPU cycles of a Intel Core i7 920, CPPN takes a mean of 2.22Mpf (Million cycles per frame), whereas our approach takes only 1.25Mpf, which represents a 44% improvement.

5   Conclusions and Futher Work

In this paper we have considered Neuroevolution and HyperNEAT algorithms for Machine Learning and, in concrete, we have focused on the addition of different kinds of local adaptation rules (sometimes called neuro-plasticity) to enable the evolved individuals to continue learning online after training.

We also have presented a new proposal for online learning based on a combination of continuous and derivable functions to update weights each time-step. Our approach shows interesting results, as it shows some nice level of adaptation. Despite not achieving the same level of performance than CPPN-based approach, our approach is less computationally expensive, as it does not require to query the CPPN for each link at each time-step.

The first most interesting question to continue this research would be why our approach seams to reach a top so fast. It is our belief that more work on this approach could offer more interesting results, as there is still much room for new approaches on online learning through weight updating or even creation/destruction of neurons and links.

References

1. Gauci, J., Stanley, K.O.: Autonomous evolution of topographic regularities in artificial neural networks. Neural Computation 22(7), 1860–1898 (2010),
   http://eplex.cs.ucf.edu/publications/2010/gauci-nc10
2. Loiacono, D., Cardamone, L., Luca Lanzi, P.: Simulated car racing championship: Competition software manual (April 2013), http://arxiv.org/abs/1304.1672
3. Niv, Y., Joel, D., Meilijson, I., Ruppin, E.: Evolution of reinforcement learning in uncertain environments: A simple explanation for complex foraging behaviors. Adapt. Behav. 10(1), 5–24 (2002),
   http://dx.doi.org/10.1177/10597123020101001
4. Risi, S.: Towards Evolving More Brain-Like Artificial Neural Networks. Ph.D. thesis, Department of Electrical Engineering and Computer Science, University of Central Florida (2012)
5. Risi, S., Lehman, J., Stanley, K.O.: Evolving the placement and density of neurons in the hyperneat substrate. In: Proceedings of the 12th Annual Conference on Genetic and Evolutionary Computation, GECCO 2010, pp. 563–570. ACM, New York (2010), http://eplex.cs.ucf.edu/publications/2010/risi-gecco10
6. Risi, S., Stanley, K.O.: An enhanced hypercube-based encoding for evolving the placement, density and connectivity of neurons. Artificial Life, 54 (2012),
   http://eplex.cs.ucf.edu/publications/2012/risi-alife12
7. Stanley, K.O.: Efficient Evolution of Neural Networks Through Complexification. Ph.D. thesis, Department of Computer Sciences, The University of Texas at Austin (2004), http://nn.cs.utexas.edu/?stanley:phd04
8. Stanley, K.O., D'Ambrosio, D.B., Gauci, J.: A hypercube-based encoding for evolving large-scale neural networks. Artificial Life 15(2), 185–212 (2009),
   http://eplex.cs.ucf.edu/publications/2009/stanley-alife09
9. Stanley, K.O., Miikkulainen, R.: Evolving neural networks through augmenting topologies. Evolutionary Computation 10(2), 99–127 (2002),
   http://nn.cs.utexas.edu/?stanley:ec02 (The pdf file is made available by MIT Press)
10. Stanley, K.O., Miikkulainen, R.: Competitive coevolution through evolutionary complexification. Journal of Artificial Intelligence Research 21, 63–100 (2004),
    http://nn.cs.utexas.edu/?stanley:jair04
11. Stanley, K.: Compositional pattern producing networks: A novel abstraction of development. Genetic Programming and Evolvable Machines 8(2), 131–162 (2007),
    http://dx.doi.org/10.1007/s10710-007-9028-8
12. Wagner, G.P., Altenberg, L.: Complex adaptations and the evolution of evolvability. Evolution (1996),
    http://citeseerx.ist.psu.edu/viewdoc/summary?doi=10.1.1.28.1524
13. Yao, X.: Evolving artificial neural networks. PIEEE: Proceedings of the IEEE 87, 1423–1447 (1999), ftp://www.cs.adfa.edu.au/pub/xin/yao_ie3proc_online.pdf/knowledge-extracted-from-trained.pdf

Learning Conditional Linear Gaussian Classifiers with Probabilistic Class Labels

Pedro L. López-Cruz, Concha Bielza, and Pedro Larrañaga

Computational Intelligence Group, Departamento de Inteligencia Artificial
Facultad de Informática, Universidad Politécnica de Madrid
pedro.lcruz@upm.es, {mcbielza,pedro.larranaga})@fi.upm.es

Abstract. We study the problem of learning Bayesian classifiers (BC) when the true class label of the training instances is not known, and is substituted by a probability distribution over the class labels for each instance. This scenario can arise, e.g., when a group of experts is asked to individually provide a class label for each instance. We particularize the generalized expectation maximization (GEM) algorithm in [1] to learn BCs with different structural complexities: naive Bayes, averaged one-dependence estimators or general conditional linear Gaussian classifiers. An evaluation conducted on eight datasets shows that BCs learned with GEM perform better than those using either the classical Expectation Maximization algorithm or potentially wrong class labels. BCs achieve similar results to the multivariate Gaussian classifier without having to estimate the full covariance matrices.

Keywords: Bayesian classifiers, probabilistic class labels, partially supervised learning, belief functions.

1 Introduction

A classification problem consists of assigning a class label to an object based on a set of characteristic features. Traditionally, machine learning research has focused on two problems: supervised and unsupervised learning. In supervised learning, the true class label of a set of training instances is known. In unsupervised learning settings, on the other hand, the true class label of the training instances is not available. It can be both hard and expensive to identify the true class label of all training instances. However, it is often easier to locate partial or incomplete information about the true class labels, and more sophisticated methods have been proposed for incorporating that information. Semi-supervised learning deals with the problem of learning classifiers when the true class labels of only a few training instances are known, and the rest of the training set is unlabeled. In partially supervised learning, a subset of possible class labels (including the true class) is given for each instance.

A general framework for learning multivariate Gaussian classifiers (MGC) is provided in [1], where the class information is modeled as belief functions [2], and a generalized expectation maximization (GEM) algorithm is proposed.

C. Bielza et al. (Eds.): CAEPIA 2013, LNAI 8109, pp. 139–148, 2013.

This approach includes supervised, unsupervised, semi-supervised and partially supervised learning as particular cases. Here we particularize the GEM algorithm to a specific scenario, where the information about the class for each instance is given as a probability distribution over the class labels. This is motivated by a problem in which it is hard to identify the true class labels of the training instances, perhaps because each label is not clearly defined, and a set of experts is asked to label the (same) training set to gain information about how the labels are assigned. Then, we summarize the information about the experts' classifications as probability distributions over the class labels.

Bayesian networks [3] are probabilistic graphical models which encode a factorization of the joint probability distribution over a set of variables, allowing for different kinds of reasoning and efficient computations. Bayesian classifiers (BC) [4] adapt Bayesian networks to classification problems. Here we adapt the GEM algorithm to fit BCs with different structures when the class information for each instance is given as a probability distribution.

In Sect. 2 we particularize the GEM algorithm to the case where the class information is given as probability distributions. Section 3 shows the use of the GEM algorithm to learn BCs. Section 4 includes the evaluation of the classifiers over eight datasets. Section 5 ends with conclusions and future work.

2   The GEM Algorithm for Probabilistic Class Labels

Our problem domain is modeled using n predictive univariate variables $\mathbf{X} = (X_1, \ldots, X_n)$ and a class variable C. The domain of each variable X_j is continuous and denoted as Ω_{X_j}. The class variable is discrete with $\Omega_C = \{1, \ldots, K\}$. We have a training dataset with N instances: $D = \{(\mathbf{x}_1, \boldsymbol{\pi}_1), \ldots, (\mathbf{x}_N, \boldsymbol{\pi}_N)\}$, where $\mathbf{x}_i = (x_{i,1}, \ldots, x_{i,n})$ are the values of the predictive variables for the ith instance, and $\boldsymbol{\pi}_i = (\pi_{i,1}, \ldots, \pi_{i,k})$ is the class information, i.e., a probability distribution over Ω_C so that $\pi_{i,k}$ is the probability of instance i belonging to class k, with $0 \leq \pi_{i,k} \leq 1$ and $\sum_{k=1}^{K} \pi_{i,k} = 1$. For instance, imagine that we ask 20 experts to classify each instance of a two-class problem and, for the ith instance, 15 experts classify it as belonging to class 1 and the rest assign the instance to class 2. We model that information as the probability distribution: $\boldsymbol{\pi}_i = (0.75, 0.25)$.

In [1], the information about the class of each instance $\mathbf{x}_i$ is modeled as a basic belief assignment (bba), which is a function $m_i^{\Omega_C} : 2^{\Omega_C} \to [0, 1]$ over the powerset 2^{Ω_C}, verifying $\sum_{\omega \subseteq \Omega_C} m_i^{\Omega_C}(\omega) = 1$. Table 1 shows an example of a general bba (top) from [5]. Using the belief function theory in the context of the transferable belief model [2], a generalization of the Expectation Maximization (EM) algorithm [6] is derived in [1] for fitting a finite mixture of multivariate Gaussian distributions with K components

$$f_{\mathbf{X}}(\mathbf{x}) = \sum_{k=1}^{K} p_C(k; \boldsymbol{\theta}_C) f_{\mathbf{X}|k}(\mathbf{x}; \boldsymbol{\mu}_{\mathbf{X}|k}, \boldsymbol{\Sigma}_{\mathbf{X}|k}) \ , \tag{1}$$

which is used as a MGC, where $p_C(k; \boldsymbol{\theta}_C)$ is the prior probability of $C = k$ and $f_{\mathbf{X}|k}(\mathbf{x}; \boldsymbol{\mu}_{\mathbf{X}|k}, \boldsymbol{\Sigma}_{\mathbf{X}|k})$ is the conditional multivariate Gaussian density function of

Table 1. Example of a general bba $m_i^{\Omega_C}(\omega)$ taken from [5] (top) and a Bayesian bba (bottom). The class variable C has three values $\Omega_C = \{1, 2, 3\}$.

	$\emptyset$	$\{1\}$	$\{2\}$	$\{3\}$	$\{1,2\}$	$\{1,3\}$	$\{2,3\}$	Ω_C
General bba	0	0.1	0	0.3	0.2	0.3	0	0.1
Bayesian bba	0	0.3	0.2	0.5	0	0	0	0

the predictive variables $\mathbf{X}$ given $C = k$. The GEM algorithm finds the parameters $\Theta = \{\theta_C\} \cup \{\mu_{\mathbf{X}|k}, \Sigma_{\mathbf{X}|k}\}_{k=1,\dots,K}$ that maximize a generalized log-likelihood (LL) criterion

$$\ln(pl^{\Theta}(\Theta|D)) = \sum_{i=1}^{N} \ln \left(\sum_{k=1}^{K} pl_{i,k} p_C(k; \theta_C) f_{\mathbf{X}|k}(\mathbf{x}_i; \mu_{\mathbf{X}|k}, \Sigma_{\mathbf{X}|k}) \right) + \nu , \quad (2)$$

where ν is a constant and $pl_{i,k} = pl_i^{\Omega_C}(\{k\})$ are the plausibilities of the ith instance for the set $\{k\}$, with $pl_i^{\Omega_C}(\omega) = \sum_{\gamma \subseteq \Omega_C, \gamma \cap \omega \neq \emptyset} m_i^{\Omega_C}(\gamma), \forall \omega \subseteq \Omega_C$.

In our scenario, each bba is a probability distribution over Ω_C, so all the focal sets (subsets ω with $m_i^{\Omega_C}(\omega) > 0$) are singletons, and the bba is called a Bayesian bba (bottom row in Table 1). Since our $m_i^{\Omega_C}$ are Bayesian, the plausibility functions $pl_i^{\Omega_C}$ are probability measures: $pl_{i,k} = pl_i^{\Omega_C}(\{k\}) = m_i^{\Omega_C}(\{k\}) = \pi_{i,k}$. Then, the generalized LL criterion (2) is rewritten as

$$LL = \ln(p(\Theta|D)) = \sum_{i=1}^{N} \ln \left(\sum_{k=1}^{K} \pi_{i,k} p_C(k; \theta_C) f_{\mathbf{X}|k}(\mathbf{x}_i; \mu_{\mathbf{X}|k}, \Sigma_{\mathbf{X}|k}) \right) + \nu . \quad (3)$$

The GEM algorithm is then particularized to maximize the LL criterion (3) by alternating the two steps:

- Expectation step in iteration q: compute the expected posterior probabilities

$$t_{i,k}^{(q)} = \frac{\pi_{i,k} p_C(k; \theta_C) f_{\mathbf{X}|k}(\mathbf{x}_i; \mu_{\mathbf{X}|k}, \Sigma_{\mathbf{X}|k})}{\sum_{k'=1}^{K} \pi_{i,k'} p_C(k'; \theta_C) f_{\mathbf{X}|k'}(\mathbf{x}_i; \mu_{\mathbf{X}|k'}, \Sigma_{\mathbf{X}|k'})} , \quad (4)$$

- Maximization step in iteration q: find the parameters which maximize the expected LL of the complete data

$$\theta_{C=k}^{(q+1)} = \frac{1}{N} \sum_{i=1}^{N} t_{i,k}^{(q)} , \mu_{\mathbf{X}|k}^{(q+1)} = \frac{1}{\sum_{i=1}^{N} t_{i,k}^{(q)}} \sum_{i=1}^{N} t_{i,k}^{(q)} \mathbf{x}_i ,$$

$$\Sigma_{\mathbf{X}|k}^{(q+1)} = \frac{1}{\sum_{i=1}^{N} t_{i,k}^{(q)}} \sum_{i=1}^{N} t_{i,k}^{(q)} \left(\mathbf{x}_i - \mu_{\mathbf{X}|k}^{(q+1)} \right) \left(\mathbf{x}_i - \mu_{\mathbf{X}|k}^{(q+1)} \right)^T . \quad (5)$$

Like the EM algorithm, the GEM algorithm guarantees that the generalized LL (3) increases in each iteration q up to a local maximum. To avoid local maxima, several runs of the algorithm are usually performed with different randomized initializations of the parameters Θ, and the model with the highest LL is returned. Instead, we consider the $\pi_{i,k}$ as initial values for $t_{i,k}^{(1)}$ in the first expectation step (4) of the algorithm. Therefore, the algorithm is only run once. The stopping criterion used to check the convergence of the algorithm is $(LL^q - LL^{q-1})/|LL^{q-1}| < \epsilon$. We set $\epsilon = 10^{-6}$.

3   Learning Bayesian Classifiers with GEM

Multivariate Gaussian classifiers, such as the ones used in [1], need to estimate a full covariance matrix $\Sigma_{\mathbf{X}|k}$ for each class label. When the number of training instances N is low or a high number of predictive variables n are available in the dataset, the estimated covariance matrices might not be very accurate. BCs are able to exploit the conditional independence relationships between the predictive variables given the class variable, reducing the number of parameters for estimation. We focus on BCs which conform with the conditional linear Gaussian (CLG) network' structure [7], i.e., discrete variables cannot have continuous parents. Therefore, the class variable is a parent of all the predictive variables and the predictive variables can only have other (continuous) predictive variables as parents. In a BC with a CLG structure, the conditional density function for a continuous variable X_j having parents $\mathbf{Pa}(X_j) = (\mathbf{Y}_j, C)$, where $\mathbf{Y}_j$ is continuous, is defined as $f_{X_j|\mathbf{y}_j,k}(x_j) = \mathcal{N}(x_j \; ; \; \beta_{0,X_j|\mathbf{Y}_j,k} + \beta_{X_j|\mathbf{Y}_j,k}^T \mathbf{y}_j, \sigma^2_{X_j|\mathbf{Y}_j,k})$, with

$$\beta_{0,X_j|\mathbf{Y}_j,k} = \mu_{X_j|k} - \Sigma_{X_j,\mathbf{Y}_j|k}\Sigma_{\mathbf{Y}_j|k}^{-1}\mu_{\mathbf{Y}_j|k} \; ,$$
$$\beta_{X_j|\mathbf{Y}_j,k} = \Sigma_{\mathbf{Y}_j|k}^{-1}\Sigma_{\mathbf{Y}_j,X_j|k} \; , \tag{6}$$
$$\sigma^2_{X_j|\mathbf{Y}_j,k} = \Sigma_{X_j|k} - \Sigma_{X_j,\mathbf{Y}_j|k}\Sigma_{\mathbf{Y}_j|k}^{-1}\Sigma_{\mathbf{Y}_j,X_j|k} \; ,$$

where $\mu_{X_j|k}$ and $\mu_{\mathbf{Y}_j|k}$ are the mean values of variables X_j and $\mathbf{Y}_j$ given the class label k. Therefore, we only need to estimate, for each class label k, the covariances of each variable with its parents ($\Sigma_{X_j,\mathbf{Y}_j|k}$), and the covariances between the parents of the same variables ($\Sigma_{\mathbf{Y}_j|k}$) in the maximization step (5).

In this paper, we consider four BCs with different structures, and fit their parameters with GEM:

- The naive Bayes (NB) classifier [8] assumes that all the predictive variables are conditionally independent given the class variable. Therefore, the covariance matrices for each component are reduced to diagonal matrices, so only the main diagonal of $\Sigma_{\mathbf{X}|k}$ has to be estimated for each class label k in GEM (5). The updating equations for the mean values $\mu_{\mathbf{X}|k}$ of the conditional densities in (5) are unchanged.
- The averaged one-dependence estimators (AODE) classifier [9] learns n BCs with a tree-augmented naive Bayes (TAN) structure [4]. The variable X_j is a parent of all the other predictive variables in the jth BC. When classifying a new instance, we compute the posterior probability of each class label as the mean of the posterior probabilities yielded by each TAN classifier.

- The structural EM (SEM) algorithm [10] is used to find the structure of the BC. Since we want to find the conditional (in)dependence relationships between the predictive variables given the class variable, we search for the structure in the space of the predictive variables. The SEM algorithm alternates between a structural search step and a parameter search step. The structural search starts with a NB structure and greedily evaluates all the possible structures that can be obtained by adding, deleting or reversing an arc between two predictive variables. The arcs from the class variable C to each predictive variable X_j are fixed. In the parametric search, the GEM algorithm finds the maximum likelihood estimates of the parameters. The process is iterated until there is no further increase in the BIC score. We implemented a BIC score which uses the generalized LL (3): $BIC(\mathcal{M} : D) = \ln(p(\boldsymbol{\Theta}|D)) - 0.5 dim(\mathcal{M}) \ln N$, where $\mathcal{M}$ represents a classifier and $dim(\mathcal{M})$ is the number of free parameters in the classifier.
- The performance of BCs is known to suffer when irrelevant or redundant variables are not removed from the problem. Therefore, we have also considered including feature subset selection in the structural search step of the SEM algorithm. We call this algorithm the feature subset selected structural EM (FSSSEM). FSSSEM includes the class variable in the structural search step and introduces some restrictions to ensure that the BC structure is valid. First, arcs including the class variable have to be directed towards the predictive variables and cannot be reversed. Second, if an arc from the class variable to a predictive feature is deleted, we consider that the variable has been erased and we delete all the arcs including the predictive variable. Like SEM, the search procedure alternates between the structural search and the parameter search steps until the generalized BIC score does not increase.

When classifying a new instance $\mathbf{x}$, any BC yields a posterior probability $p(C = k|\mathbf{X} = \mathbf{x})$ for each class label k. We use the maximum a posteriori decision rule, so that $\mathbf{x}$ is assigned to the class with maximum posterior probability $k^* = \arg\max_{k \in \Omega_C} p(C = k|\mathbf{X} = \mathbf{x})$.

4   Experiments

This section includes the evaluation of the classifiers on eight datasets taken from the UCI[1] and KEEL[2] repositories (see Fig. 1). Each variable in the datasets was standardized by subtracting the mean and dividing by the standard deviation. We erased the eighth variable in the glass dataset because 82.24% of the values were zero and the estimated covariance matrices were not positive definite in some runs. Also, we erased the first variable in the ion dataset because it was discrete.

Five classifiers (MGC, NB, AODE, SEM and FSSSEM) were learned in four different scenarios according to the available data and the algorithm used:

---

[1] Available at: http://archive.ics.uci.edu/ml/
[2] Available at: http://keel.es

- GEM: The parameters of the BCs were found using the probability distribution for the class labels with the GEM algorithm.
- EM: The parameters of the BCs were found with the classical EM algorithm [6]. The probability distributions for the class labels were used to initialize $t_{i,k}^{(1)}$ in the E-step of the first iteration of the algorithm.
- Wrong labels (WL): The BCs were fitted as in a common supervised classification problem, but the class labels of some instances were flipped to a wrong label (see Sect. 4.1).
- True labels (TL): The BCs were fitted using the true class labels of the instances. This corresponds to an utopian scenario where the class labels of the instances are known to be correct.

4.1   Dataset Generation and Stratified l-Fold Cross-Validation

We artificially modified the real datasets by transforming the true class label of each instance into a probability distribution over the class labels. For each instance, we sampled a value b_i from a beta distribution with mean μ_B and standard deviation σ_B. If the true class label for the ith instance was k, then we set $\pi_{i,k} = 1 - b_i$ and $\pi_{i,k'} = b_i/(K-1), k' \neq k$. The beta distribution models the mistakes made by the experts when classifying the instances. The probability of the true class label was high with low values of μ_B, whereas high values of μ_B yielded probability distributions where the true class label did not have the maximum probability. Similarly, in the WL setting, we randomly modified the class label for some instances in the dataset. For each instance, we drew a value u_i from a uniform distribution in $[0, 1]$. If $u_i < b_i$, then the true class label was changed to any other class label in Ω_C with equal probability.

Stratified l-fold cross-validation was used to honestly estimate the classification error of the models. We assumed that the true class label of the instances was not available, so we based the stratified cross-validation on the probability distributions over the class labels. We proposed a simple greedy algorithm for generating the folds in the cross-validation process. The goal was to generate folds with the same mean probabilities as the complete dataset. First, for each class label k, the instances were ranked in decreasing order using the probabilities $\pi_{i,k}$. Then, a mean rank was computed for each instance using $K - 1$ rankings. We ordered the instances according to the mean rank and assigned each instance to the fold with the lowest sum of mean ranks at any time. The proposed stratified l-fold cross-validation algorithm yielded folds with similar proportions to the complete dataset, even when the class labels were unbalanced (not shown). Once the folds were generated, we proceeded as in a classical stratified cross-validation setting. Each fold was considered once to test the classifier learned using the other $l - 1$ folds. The estimated error of the classifier was the mean of the errors of the classifiers learned for each fold.

4.2   Results

Figure 1 shows the mean classification error achieved in each dataset for different values of $\mu_B = \{0.1, 0.2, 0.3, 0.4\}$ in the beta distribution used to generate

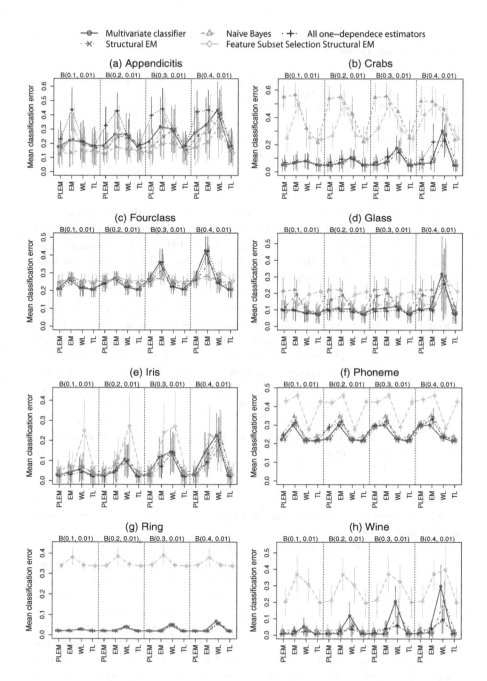

Fig. 1. Mean classification error and standard deviation bars in ten repetitions of a 10-fold stratified cross-validation procedure. The probability distributions for the class labels $\boldsymbol{\pi}_i$ were generated from beta distributions $B(\mu_B, 0.01)$ with $\mu_B = \{0.1, 0.2, 0.3, 0.4\}$.

Table 2. Comparison between algorithms considering the results for all the classifiers (5), datasets (8) and values of μ_B (4).

H_0	W/T/L	Binomial test		Bergmann-Hommel test	
		H_1	p-value	H_1	p-value
GEM = EM	141/1/18	> *	0.0000	$\neq$ *	0.0000
GEM = WL	104/0/56	> *	0.0000	$\neq$ *	0.0000
GEM = TL	32/5/123	< *	0.0000	$\neq$ *	0.0000
EM = WL	80/0/80	$\neq$	1.0000	$\neq$	0.1530
EM = TL	20/0/140	< *	0.0000	$\neq$ *	0.0000
WL = TL	16/0/144	< *	0.0000	$\neq$ *	0.0000

the artificial datasets. The value $\sigma_B = 0.01$ was used in all experiments. We performed ten repetitions of 10-fold stratified cross-validation and computed the classification error with respect to the true class labels of the instances. The GEM algorithm frequently outperformed the classical EM algorithm, the only exception being the `ring` dataset, where EM and GEM algorithms won 10 times each. Interestingly, GEM achieved better results than TL in some experiments, e.g., MGC in `appendicitis` and `crabs` datasets, or NB in `appendicitis`, `iris`, `ring` and `wine` datasets ($\mu_B = 0.1$). A possible explanation is that GEM uses the information about an instance to estimate the parameters of the conditional probabilities for all the class labels where the probability $\pi_{i,k}$ is higher than zero. Therefore, more information was available to fit the classifiers and higher accuracies could be achieved. The accuracy in the WL scenario deteriorated as we increased the mean value of the beta distributions, e.g., in the `appendicitis`, `crabs`, `glass`, `iris` or `wine` datasets. On the contrary, the accuracy of GEM remained rather stable or decreased slightly (e.g., `fourclass` or `phoneme`) when increasing μ_B. These behaviors could be observed for all but the classifiers learned with FSSSEM. In general, MGC, SEM and AODE were the classifiers that performed better for the different algorithms and datasets. NB yielded poor results in the `crabs` and `glass` datasets but seemed to outperform the other classifiers in `appendicitis`. FSSSEM's performance was not very good across all the datasets.

Table 2 compares the four learning algorithms (GEM, EM, WL and TL). The number of times the first algorithm wins, ties or loses against the second are shown. The binomial test checks whether or not the number of wins is equal to the number of losses. The non-parametric Bergmann-Hommel post-hoc test [11] checks whether or not the mean accuracy of the methods is the same. The p-value and the alternative hypothesis (H_1) are reported for each test. Statistically significant results at $\alpha = 0.05$ are shown with an asterisk. We found that GEM significantly outperformed both EM and WL. Not surprisingly, we found significant differences between TL and all the other learning scenarios. On the other hand, no significant differences were found between EM and WL.

Similarly, Table 3 compares the five BCs. We did not find significant differences between the pairwise performances of AODE, MGC and SEM. All the

Table 3. Comparison between classifiers considering the results for all the algorithms (4), datasets (8) and values of μ_B (4)

H_0	W/T/L	Binomial test		Bergmann-Hommel test	
		H_1	p-value	H_1	p-value
MGC = NB	80/0/48	> *	0.0030	≠ *	0.0022
MGC = AODE	49/17/62	<	0.1273	≠	1.0000
MGC = SEM	57/7/64	<	0.2928	≠	1.0000
MGC = FSSSEM	108/1/19	> *	0.0000	≠ *	0.0000
NB = AODE	41/0/87	< *	0.0000	≠ *	0.0003
NB = SEM	39/14/75	< *	0.0005	≠ *	0.0008
NB = FSSSEM	89/0/39	> *	0.0000	≠ *	0.0000
AODE = SEM	59/5/64	<	0.3593	≠	1.0000
AODE = FSSSEM	108/0/20	> *	0.0000	≠ *	0.0000
SEM = FSSSEM	100/1/27	> *	0.0000	≠ *	0.0000

classifiers significantly outperformed FSSSEM according to both tests. The feature subset selection method in FSSSEM is rather naive and uninformative and the number of selected variables in the final classifiers was usually low. This could explain FSSSEM's poor performance. Also, NB was outperformed by MGC, AODE and SEM.

5   Conclusions

In this paper we have adapted the GEM algorithm [1] to the particular scenario where the information about the class of the training instances is given as probability distributions over the class labels. We used this particularization of the GEM algorithm to learn Bayesian network classifiers with different structural complexities: multivariate Gaussian classifiers, naive Bayes, AODE or conditional linear Gaussian classifiers. We evaluated the classifiers on eight real datasets. BCs learned with GEM outperform others learned with the classical EM algorithm or with potentially wrong labels. We found no significant differences between the performances of MGC, AODE and CLG classifiers learned with SEM. In general, both AODE and SEM require a lower number of parameters than MGC to be estimated from data. Therefore, these classifiers might be more appropriate when the number of instances in the training datasets are low with respect to the number of variables.

Future work includes the extension to other BCs, e.g., TAN, k-DB, selective NB, etc. These methods are far more efficient than SEM or FSSSEM because the structural search uses the conditional mutual information between the predictive variables to find interrelationships. However, estimating the conditional mutual information between two variables when the class values are provided as probability distributions or belief functions is a matter of research. Other more informative methods could be used for feature subset selection. Adapting classical measures of the information that a variable (or a set of variables) provides about the class, such as the mutual information or correlation-based measures, to work with uncertain class labels is also challenging. In this paper, we have only considered score+search methods for learning BCs. However, there are approaches which are based on statistical tests for conditional independence between the variables. To the best of our knowledge, how to adapt conditional independence tests to work with probabilistic class labels is also an open question.

Finally, the GEM algorithm does not explicitly model class uncertainty, i.e., the probabilities $\pi_{i,k}$ remain constant throughout the whole algorithm and they do not appear in the final model (1). Other approaches that explicitly model these probabilities (e.g., using Dirichlet distributions) would be useful for studying and considering the interactions between the different class values.

Acknowledgments. This work has been partially supported by the Spanish Ministry of Economy and Competitiveness through Cajal Blue Brain (C080020-09) and TIN2010-20900-C04-04 projects. PLLC is supported by a Fellowship (FPU AP2009-1772) from the Spanish Ministry of Education, Culture and Sport.

References

1. Côme, E., Oukhellou, L., Denoeux, T., Aknin, P.: Learning from partially supervised data using mixture models and belief functions. Pattern Recognit. 42, 334–348 (2009)
2. Smets, P., Kennes, R.: The transferable belief model. Artif. Intell. 66, 191–243 (1994)
3. Pearl, J.: Probabilistic Reasoning in Intelligent Systems. Morgan Kaufmann (1988)
4. Friedman, N., Goldszmidt, M., Lee, T.J.: Bayesian network classification with continuous attributes: Getting the best of both discretization and parametric fitting. In: Shavlik, J.W. (ed.) Proceedings of the 15th ICML, pp. 179–187. Morgan Kaufmann (1998)
5. Vannoorenberghe, P., Smets, P.: Partially supervised learning by a credal EM approach. In: Godo, L. (ed.) ECSQARU 2005. LNCS (LNAI), vol. 3571, pp. 956–967. Springer, Heidelberg (2005)
6. Dempster, A.P., Laird, N.M., Rubin, D.B.: Maximum likelihood from incomplete data via the EM algorithm. J. R. Stat. Soc. Ser. B-Stat. Methodol. 39, 1–38 (1977)
7. Lauritzen, S.L., Wermuth, N.: Graphical models for associations between variables, some of which are qualitative and some quantitative. Ann. Stat. 17, 31–57 (1989)
8. Minsky, M.: Steps toward artificial intelligence. Proc. Inst. Radio Eng. 49, 8–30 (1961)
9. Webb, G.I., Boughton, J.R., Wang, Z.: Not so naive Bayes: Aggregating one-dependence estimators. Mach. Learn. 58, 5–24 (2005)
10. Friedman, N.: Learning belief networks in the presence of missing values and hidden variables. In: Fisher, D.H. (ed.) 14th ICML, pp. 125–133. Morgan Kaufmann (1997)
11. García, S., Herrera, F.: An extension on "Statistical comparisons of classifiers over multiple data sets" for all pairwise comparisons. J. Mach. Learn. Res. 9, 2677–2694 (2008)

Exact Incremental Learning for a Single Non-linear Neuron Based on Taylor Expansion and Greville Formula

David Martínez-Rego, Oscar Fontenla-Romero, and Amparo Alonso-Betanzos

Laboratory for Research and Development in Artificial Intelligence (LIDIA)
Department of Computer Science, Faculty of Informatics,
University of A Coruña,
Campus de Elviña s/n, 15071 A Coruña, Spain
{dmartinez,ofontenla,ciamparo}@udc.es

.

Abstract. Traditional machine learning algorithms are focused on batch learning from a static data set or from a well-known distribution. However, these algorithms take a considerable amount of time to learn a large amount of training data and besides many of them are not able to deal with nonstationary distributions. Recent machine learning challenges require the capability of online learning in nonstationary environments. Thus, in this work we propose a new learning method, for single-layer neural networks, that introduces a forgetting function in an incremental learning algorithm. The algorithm employs a recursive formula in order to obtain the solution of a weighted least squares problem. The performance of the method is experimentally checked over different data sets. The proposed algorithm has demonstrated high adaptation to changes while maintaining a low consumption of computational resources.

Keywords: Neural Networks, Incremental Learning, Nonstationary Learning.

1 Introduction

Nowadays, data analysis methods in machine learning play an important role in industry and science. The growth of the World Wide Web and improvements in data collection technology lead to a rapid increase in the magnitude and complexity of the analysis tools. This growth is driving the need for scalable and incremental algorithms that can handle the learning task on "Big Data". Moreover, recent machine learning challenges require the capability of adaptable learning in nonstationary environments. This implies the development of new algorithms that are also able to deal with changes in the underlying problem to be learnt.

In this scenario, the well-known Recursive Least Squares (RLS) [1,2] is a popular adaptive algorithm for solving Least Squares problems that has been extensively studied and applied in the last decades to problems such as signal processing, communications and control. In each iteration of the algorithm the

C. Bielza et al. (Eds.): CAEPIA 2013, LNAI 8109, pp. 149–158, 2013.

parameters are updated using recursive equations. The complexity of the RLS method is $O(I^2)$, being I the dimension of the data points. The algorithm minimizes the total squared error between the desired signal and the output of the system, from the beginning to the current data point. Therefore, the RLS has infinite memory as all errors are given the same consideration in the total error. In cases where the function to be modeled by the system comes from a nonstationary distribution, the use of a forgetting factor allows the RLS to reduce the value of older error data multiplying by an exponential weighting factor, and thus to adapt the optimal parameters in changing scenarios. In this algorithm there are two variables which have to be provided with initial values to start the recursions: the parameters of the model ($\mathbf{w}$) and a matrix ($\mathbf{P}$), that is proportional to the inverse of the covariance matrix of the parameters. The most commonly-used approximate initialization scheme consists of setting $\mathbf{w} = \mathbf{0}$ and $\mathbf{P} = \delta\mathbf{I}$, where $\delta \gg 0$ is a suitable chosen constant with a high value. In order to avoid the approximate initialization of the RLS, in [3] the authors present an order-recursive formula for the Moore-Penrose pseudoinverse of a matrix that extended the classical Greville formula [4]. This new version not only reduces almost half memory locations of Greville formula at each recursion, but also is very useful to derive recursive formulas for the optimization solutions involving the pseudoinverses of matrices. As applications, using the new formulas, the authors derive Recursive Least Squares procedures which coincide exactly with the batch Least-Squares (LS) solution, including a simple and exact initialization. This formulation has the advantage, compared to the RLS, that no initialization parameters must be established and then its performance does not depend on those values.

2   The Rationale of the Approach

Recently, a new convex objective function for single-layer neural networks has been presented in [5] which can be used to adjust the parameters of the network using nonlinear output functions. In that work it was remarked that the presented approach opens the opportunity to incrementally learn that kind of neural networks without the necessity of saving previous data. However, this incremental capacity involves the computation of a $I \times I$ system of linear equations for each new data point, leading to instabilities for ill-posed problems and with a complexity of $O(M * I^2)$ being M a heavy constant. In [6], the incremental learning capabilities of the model presented in [5] were explored and extended to nonstationary scenarios, obtaining good results. That model weights the importance of each data sample taking into account whether it is recent or not, giving exponentially more importance to recent data points. Although it demonstrates that it is an effective algorithm for concept drift problems, it still has to solve a new system of equation for each new data sample and has to reset the weighting of the data samples periodically leading to a cumbersome algorithm. Afterwards, the work in [7] extended the previous research using an initialization scheme which is equivalent to introducing a Tikhonov regularization term in the training objective function. This last property makes the proposed algorithm suitable for complex high-dimensional or noisy problems which are typically ill-posed.

In this work we derive a recursive algorithm that extends the later models to train exactly a single-layer neural network with a nonlinear output function in case this function is differentiable and invertible. Most of the the output functions used in Artificial Neural Networks [8] comply with these condition, so it can be used as basic build block for more complex models. The derivation of the algorithm is based on the global optimum theorem demonstrated in [5] and the variations of Greville formula for pseudoinverse computing developed in [3]. Depending on the values given to the hyperparameters and the selected output function, it can be demonstrated that RLS and the model in [5] are all special cases of the proposed algorithm.

3   Description of the Proposed Method

In the work presented in [5] a new convex objective function for the supervised learning of single-layer neural networks (see Figure 1) was presented. The function is based on the minimization of the mean squared error before the nonlinear activation functions, instead of after them, as is usually the case. In that research it was proved that the minimization of this function is approximately equivalent, up to first order of a Taylor series, to the minimization of the regular Mean Squared Error (MSE). Figure 1 contains the nomenclature employed in that work and in the rest of the paper, where I is the number of inputs and J is the number of outputs. For the sth pattern $\mathbf{x}_s = (1, x_{1s}, x_{2s}, \ldots, x_{Is})$ its associate desired output $\mathbf{d}_s$ is propagated backwards using the inverse of the output function for each neuron f_j^{-1} and the minimization of the error between the internal network value z_{js} and $f_j^{-1}(d_{js})$ is considered.

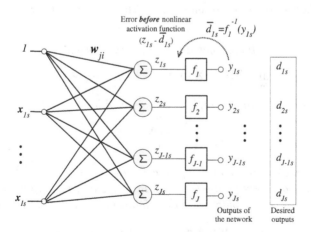

Fig. 1. Topology of a single-layer feedforward neural network

Specifically, the following theorem was demonstrated in [5]:

Theorem 1. *Let* $\mathbf{x} \in \mathbb{R}^{I+1}$ *be the column vector containing the input of a single-layer feedforward neural network,* $\mathbf{d}$; $\mathbf{y} \in \mathbb{R}^{J}$ *be the desired and real outputs,* $\mathbf{W} \in \mathbb{R}^{J \times (I+1)}$ *be the weight matrix, and* f ; f^{-1}; f' : $\mathbb{R}^{J} \to \mathbb{R}^{J}$ *be the non linear function, its inverse and its derivative. Then, the minimization of the MSE between* $\mathbf{d}$ *and* $\mathbf{y}$ *at the output of the non linearity*

$$\min_{\mathbf{W}} \frac{1}{S} \sum_{s=1}^{S} \|\mathbf{y}_s - \mathbf{d}_s\|^2, \tag{1}$$

where S *is the number of data points and* $\mathbf{y} = f(\mathbf{Wx})$, *is equivalent, up to first Taylor order, to minimizing the MSE before the non linearity, i.e., between* $\mathbf{z} = \mathbf{Wx}$ *and* $\bar{\mathbf{d}} = f^{-1}(\mathbf{d})$ *weighted depending on the value of the derivative of the non linearity at the corresponding operating point. Mathematically, this property can be written as*

$$\min_{\mathbf{W}} E[(\mathbf{d} - \mathbf{y})^T (\mathbf{d} - \mathbf{y})] \approx \min_{\mathbf{W}} E[(f'(\bar{\mathbf{d}}) \cdot \bar{\epsilon})^T (f'(\bar{\mathbf{d}}) \cdot \bar{\epsilon})] \tag{2}$$

where $(\cdot)$ *denotes the element-wise Hadamard product of vectors* $f'(\bar{\mathbf{d}})$ *and* $\bar{\epsilon} = \bar{\mathbf{d}} - \mathbf{z}$.

□

The details of the proof of this theorem can be consulted in [5]. Using the previous result, a method that uses a system of $I \times I$ linear equations to obtain the optimal parameters of the network was proposed. Therefore, the network, containing nonlinear activation functions, can be trained using a linear procedure which can be incrementally updated. The approaches to solve these systems of equations have a complexity, in the best case, of $O(M * I^2)$ being M a heavy constant.

Furthermore, in the research presented in [3] the following theorem was demonstrated:

Theorem 2. *Consider the weighted least squares problem:*

$$\min_{\mathbf{w}} (\mathbf{d}_N - \mathbf{X}_N \mathbf{w})^T \Lambda_N^2 (\mathbf{d}_N - \mathbf{X}_N \mathbf{w}) \tag{3}$$

where the weighting diagonal matrix Λ_N *is defined by*

$$\Lambda_N = \begin{pmatrix} \lambda_{N-1} \Lambda_{N-1} & 0 \\ 0 & 1 \end{pmatrix}, \tag{4}$$

$\mathbf{X}_N = (\mathbf{x}_1 \mathbf{x}_2 \cdots \mathbf{x}_N)$ *is the matrix of data points and* $\mathbf{d}_N = (d_1, d_2, ..., d_N)^T$ *is the column vector of desired outputs at instant* N. *Then, for any* $N = 0, 1, ...$ *the optimal parameters can be obtained by the following recursive equation:*

$$\mathbf{w}_{N+1} = \mathbf{w}_N + \mathbf{k}_{N+1}(d_{N+1} - \mathbf{x}_{N+1}^T \mathbf{w}_N) \tag{5}$$

where $\mathbf{k}_{N+1}$ *is defined by (using an auxiliar matrix* $\mathbf{Q}_N$*):*

1. *If* $\mathbf{x}_{N+1}^T \mathbf{Q}_N = \mathbf{0}$ *then*

$$\mathbf{k}_{N+1} = \mathbf{P}_N \mathbf{x}_{N+1} / (\lambda_N^2 + \mathbf{x}_{N+1}^T \mathbf{P}_N \mathbf{x}_{N+1}) \tag{6}$$

$$\mathbf{P}_{N+1} = \lambda_N^{-2} (\mathbf{I} - \mathbf{k}_{N+1} \mathbf{x}_{N+1}^T) \mathbf{P}_N \tag{7}$$

$$\mathbf{Q}_{N+1} = \mathbf{Q}_N \tag{8}$$

2. *If* $\mathbf{x}_{N+1}^T \mathbf{Q}_N \neq \mathbf{0}$ *then*

$$\mathbf{k}_{N+1} = \mathbf{Q}_N \mathbf{x}_{N+1} / (\mathbf{x}_{N+1}^T \mathbf{Q}_N \mathbf{x}_{N+1}) \tag{9}$$

$$\mathbf{P}_{N+1} = \lambda_N^{-2} (\mathbf{I} - \mathbf{k}_{N+1} \mathbf{x}_{N+1}^T) \mathbf{P}_N (\mathbf{I} - \mathbf{k}_{N+1} \mathbf{x}_{N+1}^T)^T \tag{10}$$

$$+ \mathbf{k}_{N+1} \mathbf{k}_{N+1}^T \tag{11}$$

$$\mathbf{Q}_{N+1} = (\mathbf{I} - \mathbf{k}_{N+1} \mathbf{x}_{N+1}^T) \mathbf{Q}_N \tag{12}$$

and the initial values are always fixed as $\mathbf{w}_0 = \mathbf{0}$, $\mathbf{P}_0 = \mathbf{0}$ *and* $\mathbf{Q}_0 = \mathbf{I}$. *The forgetting values* λ_N *can be established, as usual, in the interval* $(0, 1]$.

□

Applying the previous result, a set of recursive formulas (equations (5)-(12)) can be used to determine the optimal parameters, with a complexity of $O(I^2)$, instead of a system of linear equations. However, this scheme is restricted to be employed for networks with linear activation functions. If nonlinear functions are utilized in the output layer of the single-layer neural network then it prevents the use of this linear formulation.

In the following we present a new result that allows to extend the previous approach for the general case of any activation function (linear/nonlinear) in the neurons of the network. We center the attention in a single output neuron, in order not to make the presentation cumbersome, but the presented result can be applied in a neuron-by-neuron manner for a multi-output network.

Theorem 3. *Consider the weighted minimization problem of a single-layer neural network:*

$$\min_{\mathbf{w}} \ (\mathbf{d}_N - f(\mathbf{X}_N \mathbf{w}))^T \mathbf{\Lambda}_N^2 (\mathbf{d}_N - f(\mathbf{X}_N \mathbf{w})) \tag{13}$$

in which the diagonal matrix $\mathbf{\Lambda}_N$ *weights the error committed for each data point.*

For any $N = 0, 1, ...,$ *the exact solution, up to first Taylor order, to this optimization problem is given recursively by the following algorithm:*

$$\mathbf{w}_N = \mathbf{w}_N + f'(\bar{d}_{N+1}) \mathbf{k}_{N+1} (d_{N+1} - \mathbf{x}_{N+1}^T \mathbf{w}_N) \tag{14}$$

where $\mathbf{k}_{N+1}$ *is defined by:*

1. *If* $f'(\bar{d}_{N+1}) \mathbf{x}_{N+1}^T \mathbf{Q}_N = \mathbf{0}$ *then*

$$\mathbf{k}_{N+1} = \left(\mathbf{P}_N \mathbf{x}_{N+1} f'(\bar{d}_{N+1}) \right) / \left(\lambda_N^2 + f'(\bar{d}_{N+1})^2 \mathbf{x}_{N+1}^T \mathbf{P}_N \mathbf{x}_{N+1} \right) \tag{15}$$

$$\mathbf{P}_{N+1} = \lambda_N^{-2} (\mathbf{I} - f'(\bar{d}_{N+1}) \mathbf{k}_{N+1} \mathbf{x}_{N+1}^T) \mathbf{P}_N \tag{16}$$

$$\mathbf{Q}_{N+1} = \mathbf{Q}_N \tag{17}$$

2. If $f'(\bar{d}_{N+1})\mathbf{x}_{N+1}^T\mathbf{Q}_N \neq \mathbf{0}$ then

$$\mathbf{k}_{N+1} = \mathbf{Q}_N\mathbf{x}_{N+1}/\left(f'(\bar{d}_{N+1})(\mathbf{x}_{N+1}^T\mathbf{Q}_N\mathbf{x}_{N+1})\right) \tag{18}$$

$$\mathbf{P}_{N+1} = \lambda_N^{-2}(\mathbf{I} - \mathbf{k}_{N+1}\mathbf{x}_{N+1}^Tf'(\bar{d}_{N+1}))\mathbf{P}_N(\mathbf{I} - \mathbf{k}_{N+1}\mathbf{x}_{N+1}^Tf'(\bar{d}_{N+1}))^T \tag{19}$$

$$+\mathbf{k}_{N+1}\mathbf{k}_{N+1}^T \tag{20}$$

$$\mathbf{Q}_{N+1} = (\mathbf{I} - \mathbf{k}_{N+1}\mathbf{x}_{N+1}^Tf'(\bar{d}_{N+1}))\mathbf{Q}_N \tag{21}$$

and the initial values are

$$\mathbf{P}_0 = \mathbf{0}, \ \mathbf{Q}_0 = \mathbf{I}, \ \lambda_N \in (0,1].$$

Proof. The problem in equation (13) can be restated, using theorem 1, in the following manner:

$$\min_{\mathbf{w}} \ (\mathbf{d}_N - \mathbf{X}_N\mathbf{w})^T \mathbf{F}_N\mathbf{\Lambda}_N^2\mathbf{F}_N \ (\mathbf{d}_N - \mathbf{X}_N\mathbf{w}) \tag{22}$$

where $\mathbf{F}_N = \mathbf{diag}(f'(\bar{d}_1),\ldots,f'(\bar{d}_N))$. Therefore, if we multiply each element of $\mathbf{d}_N$ and each data point vector $\mathbf{x}_i$, $i = 1,\ldots,N$ by $\mathbf{F}_i$ we arrive to the problem,

$$\min_{\mathbf{w}} \ (\mathbf{d}_N^\star - \mathbf{X}_N^\star\mathbf{w})^T\mathbf{\Lambda}_N^2(\mathbf{d}_N^\star - \mathbf{X}_N^\star\mathbf{w}) \tag{23}$$

where $\mathbf{d}_N^\star = \mathbf{d}_N\mathbf{F}_N$ and $\mathbf{X}_N^\star = \mathbf{X}_N\mathbf{F}_N$. This problem, by theorem 2, can be solved by the same recursive procedure, but substituting d_{N+1} and $\mathbf{x}_{N+1}$ by $d_{N+1}^\star$ and $\mathbf{x}_{N+1}^\star$.

□

Using the previous result, a single-layer neural network, with nonlinear activation functions, can be trained in an incremental fashion using the recursive equations in (14)-(21). This allows us to use this scheme for either the learning of big data sets that must be processed online, due to memory limitations, or streaming data scenarios where samples arrive continuously. Regarding complexity analysis, the proposal has a complexity of $O(I^2)$, where I is the number of input neurons, due to the matrix-vector multiplications involved in the recursive formulas. Finally, the following issues can be discussed:

Remark 1: If $\lambda_N = 1, \forall N$ then the method works in a stationary learning mode, and it arrives to the same solution than in [5] but using an updating recursive formula instead of a system of linear equations.

Remark 2: If $\lambda_N = 1, \forall N$ and the output function f is the linear function, this model includes Exact Recursive Least Squares in [3] as a special case.

Remark 3: If $0 < \lambda_N < 1, \forall N$ then we can use this algorithm for learning in non stationary enviroments like in [6] and [7].

4   Experimental Results

Several simulations were carried out to verify the performance of the proposed method in incremental and nonstationary environments. Firstly, the behavior of the proposed model was checked for the prediction of the Mackey-Glass [9] chaotic time series. In order to test the adaptation ability of the method in nonstationary environments, the data set was generated changing the parameter of the Mackey-Glass equations (every 900 data points) using the following order $\tau = \{10, 15, 10, 14, 10, 13\}$. The task was to predict the value 85 steps ahead using an embedding input dimension of 8 values. In this case the forgetting parameter (λ_N) was set to 0.99. Figure 2 shows the Mean Squared Error (MSE), for the test, obtained in each step of the online learning. As can be observed, the error is monotonically decreased from the starting point and each 900 samples it grows due to the changes in the function to be learned. Despite this, the method is able to adapt its parameters to get quickly the solution for each new context. Therefore, in this complex identification task, the proposed model presents a fast convergence to the optimal and a good accuracy.

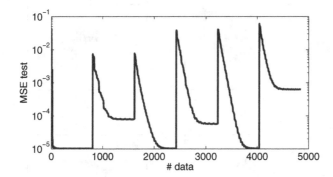

Fig. 2. MSE for the test set, of the Mackey data set, in each step of the online learning process

Secondly, the proposed method was applied to the Nebraska Weather Prediction Data. This data set is formed by the weather measurements compiled by the U.S. National Oceanic and Atmospheric Administration from over 9000 weather stations worldwide [10]. Records date back to the 1930s, providing a wide scope of weather trends. Daily measurements include a variety of features (temperature, pressure wind speed, etc.) and indicators for precipitation and other weather-related events. Following the methodology in [11] the Offutt Air Force Base in Bellevue, Nebraska, was chosen for this experiment due to its extensive range of 50 years (1949-1999) and diverse weather patterns, making it a longterm precipitation classification/prediction drift problem. In this case the experimental setting was as follows: the model is sequentially updated for each new pattern and next 300 patterns were used as test set. Class labels are based on the binary indicator provided for each daily reading of rain or not rain. Figure 3 contains the test accuracy for this classification problem using a λ_N value equal to 0.99. The results are comparable to those graphically obtained by the non linear approaches proposed in [11] but using a faster and simpler learning algorithm.

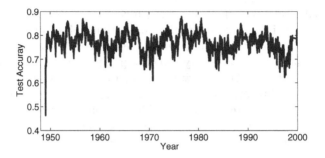

Fig. 3. Test accuracy for the Nebraska data set

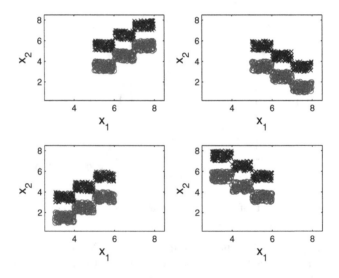

Fig. 4. Four subsets forming the Stairs data set. Each subset is obtained rotating 90 degrees the previous one.

Finally, an artificial data set, named Stairs data set, was employed for classification purposes. This 2D data set is the union of four subsets, each one forming two different stairs, one for each class (see Figure 4). In each subset the slope of the stairs is rotated 90 degrees with respect to the previous one. Each step of the stair is formed by 100 samples which are uniformly distributed in a unit square. The whole data set contains 2400 samples, 600 in each subset, divided in two classes. The class label is represented by a circle and a cross in the figure. In order to create a training and test set each subset was randomly divided in half, thus each set contains 1200 samples. As can be observed, this is a nonstationary data set as the optimal decision function for each subset varies and it is approximately a line with a slope of 45, 135, 225 and 270 degrees.

The data points of each subset were presented, sequentially, to the proposed method in a sample-by-sample manner and, thus, each 300 samples a change is produced in the problem to be learnt. Figure 5 contains the accuracy ratio, obtained by the proposed method for the corresponding test set at each epoch of the training process, using two different forgetting factors (λ_N=0.99 and λ_N=0.9). As can be seen, the first factor lead to a more conservative scenario whereas the second one allows a faster adaptation to changes.

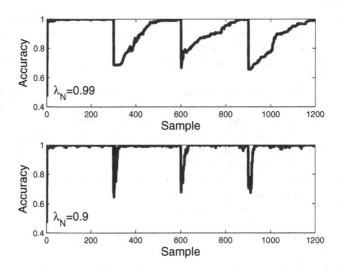

Fig. 5. Test accuracy for the Stairs data set using different forgetting factors (λ_N)

5   Conclusions

In this work we have presented a new incremental learning algorithm, with forgetting capability, for a single-layer neural network with non linear output functions. For practical purposes, it avoids the necessity of solving a system of linear equations at each step of the learning process, as in [5] and [6], thus making it an easier and more efficient algorithm for online and nonstationary scenarios. This is achieved using a new version of the classical Greville formula to derive recursive equations for the optimization process avoiding the pseudoinverses of matrices. In addition, for its application to large-scale learning scenarios, the proposed algorithm complies with the property of incremental learning, making it also a suitable method for batch learning from data sets which need to be considered by parts (chunks).

Acknowledgements. This work was supported by Secretaría de Estado de Investigación of the Spanish Government under project TIN2012-37954, and by the Xunta de Galicia through projects CN2011/007 and CN2012/211, all partially supported by the European Union ERDF. David Martínez Rego would like to thank the support by Spanish Ministry of Education FPU Grant Program.

References

1. Haykin, S.: Adaptive Filter Theory. Prentice-Hall, Englewood Cliffs (1996)
2. Kailath, T., Sayed, A., Hassibi, B.: Linear Estimation. Prentice-Hall, Englewood Cliffs (2000)
3. Zhou, J., Zhu, Y., Li, X.R., Zhisheng, Y.: Variants of the greville formula with applications to exact recursive least squares. SIAM Journal on Matrix Analysis and Applications 24(1), 150–164 (2002)
4. Greville, T.: Some applications of pseudoinverse of a matrix. SIAM Review 2, 578–619 (1960)
5. Fontenla-Romero, O., Guijarro-Berdiñas, B., Pérez-Sánchez, B., Alonso-Betanzos, A.: A new convex objective function for the supervised learning of single-layer neural networks. Pattern Recognition 43, 1984–1992 (2010)
6. Martínez-Rego, D., Fontenla-Romero, O., Alonso-Betanzos, A., Pérez-Sánchez, B.: A robust incremental learning method for non-stationary environments. Neurocomputing 74(11), 1800–1808 (2011)
7. Martínez-Rego, D., Fontenla-Romero, O., Alonso-Betanzos, A.: Nonlinear single layer neural network training algorithm for incremental, nonstationary and distributed learning scenarios. Pattern Recognition 45, 4536–4546 (2012)
8. Bishop, C.M.: Pattern Recognition and Machine Learning. Springer (2006)
9. Mackey, M., Glass, L.: Oscillation and chaos in physological control systems. Science 197, 287 (1977)
10. U.S. National Oceanic and Atmospheric Administration: Federal Climate Complex Global Surface Summary of Day Data, ftp.ncdc.noaa.gov/pub/data/gsod
11. Elwell, R., Polikar, R.: Incremental learning of concept drift in nonstationary environments. IEEE Transactions on Neural Networks 22(10), 1517–1531 (2011)

Augmented Semi-naive Bayes Classifier

Bojan Mihaljevic, Pedro Larrañaga, and Concha Bielza

Computational Intelligence Group, Departament de Inteligencia Artificial
Facultad de Informática, Universidad Politécnica de Madrid
{bmihaljevic,pedro.larranaga,mcbielza}@fi.upm.es

Abstract. The naive Bayes is a competitive classifier that makes strong conditional independence assumptions. Its accuracy can be improved by relaxing these assumptions. One classifier which does that is the semi-naive Bayes. The state-of-the-art algorithm for learning a semi-naive Bayes from data is the backward sequential elimination and joining (BSEJ) algorithm. We extend BSEJ with a second step which removes some of its unwarranted independence assumptions. Our classifier outperforms BSEJ and five other Bayesian network classifiers on a set of benchmark databases, although the difference in performance is not statistically significant.

Keywords: semi-naive Bayes, tree augmented naive Bayes, Bayesian network classifiers.

1 Introduction

A classifier is a function which uses a set of features of an object to assign it to a class. The naive Bayes classifier [1,2] is an effective probabilistic classifier. It assumes that the features are independent given the class. This assumption is violated in many domains and more accurate classification can often be obtained by avoiding unwarranted independence assumptions [3]. A common approach to this is to augment naive Bayes by accounting for interactions between features, obtaining an augmented naive Bayes model [3]

Semi-naive Bayes [4] is one such augmented naive Bayes classifier. It assumes that correlations exist only inside disjoint subsets of features. No independence assumptions are made within a feature subset, i.e., each feature directly depends on every other. The best-known algorithm for learning a semi-naive Bayes is the backward sequential elimination and joining (BSEJ) algorithm [4]. This algorithm tends to capture few correlations among the features [3].

We set out to extend the BSEJ algorithm with a second step which removes some of its independence assumptions that are not warranted by the data. We use tests of conditional independence to identify the unwarranted independences. We augment the semi-naive Bayes model with a restricted set of interactions. This procedure is inspired by the selective tree augmented naive Bayes algorithm [5].

We report an empirical comparison of our proposal with the BSEJ algorithm and with five other reference Bayesian network classifiers.

C. Bielza et al. (Eds.): CAEPIA 2013, LNAI 8109, pp. 159–167, 2013.
© Springer-Verlag Berlin Heidelberg 2013

This paper is organized as follows. Sections 2 introduces Bayesian network classifiers. Section 3 explains the backward sequential elimination and joining (BSEJ) algorithm. Section 4 describes the selective tree augmented naive Bayes algorithm. Section 5 explains the proposed extension of BSEJ. Section 6 reports the empirical evaluation of our proposal. Section 7 sums the paper up.

2   Bayesian Network Classifiers

We use upper-case letters to denote variables (X) and lower-case letters (x) to denote variable values. We use boldface letters to denote multidimensional vectors. A problem domain is described with n predictive variables or features $\mathbf{X} = (X_1, \ldots, X_n)$ and a class variable C. In our setting, all variables are discrete with $x_i \in \{1, \ldots, r_i\}$ and $c \in \{1, \ldots, r_c\}$. A *Bayes classifier* assigns a vector of feature values $\mathbf{x}$ to the most probable class, i.e.

$$c^* = \arg \max_c p(c|\mathbf{x}).$$

A Bayesian network classifier [3] uses a Bayesian network [6] to encode $p(c, \mathbf{x})$. A Bayesian network consists of two components: a directed acyclic graph G and a set of parameters $\mathbf{\Theta}$. Each node V in the graph corresponds to a random variable and the arcs represent direct dependencies between the variables. G encodes the conditional independence assumptions about the variables: a variable V is independent of its nondescendants given $\mathbf{Pa}(V)$, its parents in G. The parameters $\mathbf{\Theta}$ quantify the network by specifying the local probability distribution for each V, $p(v|\mathbf{pa}(v))$, where $\mathbf{pa}(v)$ is a value of the set of variables $\mathbf{Pa}(V)$. A Bayesian network classifier assigns $\mathbf{x}$ to the class that maximizes $p(c, \mathbf{x})$ since $\arg \max_c p(c, \mathbf{x}) = \arg \max_c p(c|\mathbf{x})$.

The best-known Bayesian network classifier is the naive Bayes. It assumes that the features are conditionally independent given the class (see Fig. 1a for its network structure), factorizing $p(c, \mathbf{x})$ as

$$p(c, \mathbf{x}) = p(c) \prod_{i=1}^n p(x_i|c).$$

This assumption is violated in many domains and more accurate classification can often be obtained by avoiding unwarranted independence assumptions [3]. A common approach to this is to augment naive Bayes' structure with arcs between features, obtaining an augmented naive Bayes model [3].

3   Semi-naive Bayes

The semi-naive Bayes (SB) is an augmented naive Bayes classifier. It assumes that correlations exist only inside disjoint subsets of features. No independence assumptions are made within a feature subset, i.e., each feature depends directly on every other. This means that the structure of a naive Bayes is augmented with

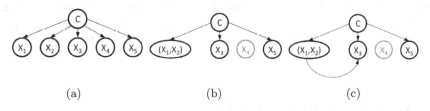

Fig. 1. Examples of Bayesian network classifier structures. Naive Bayes (a), semi-naive Bayes (b), and augmented semi-naive Bayes (c)

an arc between every pair of features in the same feature subset. For simplicity of representation, we depict the dependencies within a feature subset with a compound node corresponding to the Cartesian product of the features within the subset (see Fig. 1b). Unlike naive Bayes, the semi-naive Bayes model does not necessarily include all the features of a domain. According to the semi-naive Bayes,

$$p(c, \mathbf{x}) = p(c) \prod_{j \in Q} p(\mathbf{x}_{S_j} | c), \qquad (1)$$

where $S_j \subseteq \{1, \ldots, n\}$ is the j-th feature subset, $Q = \{1, \ldots, K\}$ is the set of indices of feature subsets, and the following conditions hold: $\cup_{j \in Q} S_j \subseteq \{1, 2, \ldots, n\}$ and $S_j \cap S_l = \emptyset$, $j \neq l$.

The number of possible partitions of the feature set into disjoint subsets grows faster than exponential in n. That justifies the use of heuristics for learning a semi-naive Bayes from data. The backward sequential elimination and joining (BSEJ) [4] algorithm is the state-of-the-art algorithm for this purpose. It uses a greedy search which, starting from the structure of a naive Bayes (where each feature is a singleton feature subset), chooses between two operations in each step:

– Removing a feature X_i from the model
– Creating a new feature subset $\mathbf{X}_{S_k}$ by merging two subsets, $\mathbf{X}_{S_j}$ and $\mathbf{X}_{S_j}$

A cross-validation estimate of predictive accuracy is used to evaluate the candidate operations. If no operation improves the accuracy of the current structure, the search stops.

4   Selective Tree Augmented Naive Bayes

The tree augmented naive Bayes (TAN) augments the naive Bayes with a tree over the features. That is, it conditions every feature except one (the root of the tree) on exactly one other feature. The augmenting tree which maximizes the likelihood of the TAN can be efficiently found using Chow-Liu's algorithm.

The selective tree augmented naive Bayes (STAN) may remove less than $n-1$ conditional independence assumptions of the naive Bayes. Before learning the augmenting tree, STAN discards dependencies that are not statistically significant. It may occur that a subset of features has no warranted conditional dependencies on other features. In that case there can be no arcs between this feature subset and the other features, and the augmenting structure will be a forest (a set of trees) rather than a tree.

5   Augmented Semi-naive Bayes

We would like to know if correlating some of the disjoint (and conditionally independent) feature subsets of a semi-naive Bayes can improve its predictive accuracy. Just before outputting the final semi-nave Bayes model, the BSEJ algorithm considers correlating each pair of feature subsets and finds that no correlation improves its estimate of accuracy. We consider correlating a pair of feature subsets if their conditional dependency is statistically significant. We augment the semi-naive Bayes with a tree or a forest over the feature subsets (see Fig. 1c), removing at most $K - 1$ unwarranted independence assumptions, where K is the number of feature subsets. We select the augmenting edges that maximize the likelihood of the model. Although correlating any feature subset pair of the final semi-naive Bayes did not improve the accuracy estimate of BSEJ, it is possible that removing several, unwarranted independence assumptions at once can improve prediction. In any case, augmenting the semi-naive Bayes in this way is fast compared to BSEJ's time complexity.

The augmented semi-naive Bayes (ASB) factorizes $p(c, \mathbf{x})$ as

$$p(c, \mathbf{x}) = p(c) \prod_{i \in R} p(\mathbf{x}_{S_i} | c) \prod_{i \in Q \setminus R} p(\mathbf{x}_{S_i} | \mathbf{x}_{j(i)}, c),$$

where Q and S_i are defined as in Equation (1), $R \subseteq Q$ is the set of indices of feature subsets that are conditioned only on the class variable (root(s) of the trees(s)), and $\{X_{j(i)}\} = \mathbf{Pa}(X_{S_i}) \setminus C$.

To test if two sets of features, $\mathbf{X}_{S_i}$ and $\mathbf{X}_{S_j}$, are conditionally independent given the class we use the χ^2 test of conditional independence (see, e.g., [7]). If the null hypothesis of conditional independence holds, then $2NI(\mathbf{X}_{S_i}; \mathbf{X}_{S_j} | C)$ asymptotically follows the χ^2 distribution with $(r_{S_i} - 1)(r_{S_j} - 1)r_c$ degrees of freedom, where N is the number of cases in our data sample, and $r_{S_i} = \prod_{k \in S_i} r_i$. The χ^2 approximation is not reliable when there are little cases in the contingency table over $\mathbf{X}_{S_j}$, $\mathbf{X}_{S_j}$, and C [8]. Following [9], we consider the χ^2 approximation to be reliable if the average cell count in the contingency table is at least 5. Also following [9], we assume conditional independence when this condition is not fulfilled. That is, we do not remove the independence assumption for a pair of feature subsets if the test of their conditional independence is unreliable.

The procedure for finding the augmenting structure is based on Chow-Liu's algorithm. First, we build a complete undirected graph $G = (K, A)$. Each vertex $j \in K$ corresponds to $\mathbf{X}_{S_j}$, a subset of features correlated in the semi-naive Bayes, and there is an edge between every two nodes i and j such that corresponding feature subsets, $\mathbf{X}_{S_i}$ and $\mathbf{X}_{S_j}$, are not conditionally independent according to the χ^2 test. As G is not necessarily a complete graph it is possibly not connected. In this case, the augmenting structure that maximizes the likelihood is not necessarily a tree but a maximum weighted forest (MWF) [10]. The MWF is given by the union of the maximum weighted spanning trees (MWST) for each connected component of G. This union of MWSTs can be found by applying Kruskal's algorithm on G (there is no need to run it separately for each connected component of G) [10].

Our procedure for augmenting the semi-naive Bayes is similar to the STAN algorithm for augmenting the naive Bayes. The differences are that ASB can remove independence assumptions between non-singleton sets of features and that it uses the standard procedure for testing for conditional independence (the one described in [7]). Namely, it seems that the authors of STAN were not aware of the test for conditional independence and therefore they developed and used a heuristic based on the χ^2 test of independence.

The full augmented semi-naive Bayes algorithm is specified more formally in Algorithm 1.

Algorithm 1. Augmented semi-naive Bayes

---

1. $B \leftarrow$ a semi-naive Bayes model
2. $\mathbf{S} \leftarrow$ a partition of features such that $\cup_{j=1}^{K} S_j = \mathbf{S}$ and $\mathbf{X}_{S_j}$ is a set of features correlated in B
3. $r_{S_j} \leftarrow \prod_{l \in S_j} r_l, j \in \{1, \ldots, K\}$
4. $G \leftarrow (K, E)$, a complete undirected graph with nodes K and edges E
5. **for all** $i, j = 1, \ldots, K, i < j$ **do**
6.   **if** $\frac{N}{r_{S_j} r_{S_i} r_c} \geq 5$ and $2NI(X_{S_i}; X_{S_j}|C)$ passes the $X^2_{(r_{S_i}-1)(r_{S_j}-1)r_c}$ test at significance level α **then**
7.   weight of edge i—j in $E \leftarrow I(\mathbf{X}_{S_i}; \mathbf{X}_{S_j}|C)$
8.   **else**
9.   remove edge i—j from E
10.   **end if**
11. **end for**
12. $\mathbf{T} \leftarrow$ maximum weighted forest obtained by applying Kruskal's algorithm on G
13. $\mathbf{T}' \leftarrow$ for each $T \in \mathbf{T}$ choose a root node at random and direct edges away from it
14. **for all** i, j such that arc $i \to j \in \mathbf{T}'$ **do**
15.   augment B with arcs from each X_l in $\mathbf{X}_{S_i}$ to every X_k in $\mathbf{X}_{S_j}$
16. **end for**

---

6 Experimental Evaluation

6.1 Setup

We compare the augmented semi-naive Bayes (ASB) algorithm to six reference algorithms for learning Bayesian network classifiers. Two of those algorithms learn a selective naive Bayes (SNB) [11] model. The forward sequential selection (FSS) algorithm [11] performs a greedy search guided by predictive accuracy while the filter forward sequential selection (FFSS) omits from the model the features that are deemed independent of the class by the χ^2 independence test. Besides SNB, we consider the naive Bayes (NB), the tree augmented naive Bayes (TAN), the selective tree augmented naive Bayes (STAN), and the backward sequential elimination and joining (BSEJ) algorithm.

We compare the classifiers over 14 natural domains from UCI repository [12] (see Table 1). Prior to classifier comparison, we removed incomplete rows and discretized numeric features with the MDL method [13].

For the BSEJ and the FSS, we used 5-fold stratified cross-validation to estimate predictive accuracy. For statistical tests of (conditional) independence we used a significance level of 0.05 and applied the criterion of χ^2 approximation reliability. In FFSS, if a test of independence of X_i and C is not reliable, then independence is assumed and X_i is omitted from the model. For STAN, we used the same test of conditional independence as for ASB. Laplace's correction of maximum likelihood was used to estimate parameters. We estimated predictive accuracy of the classifiers with 5 repetitions of 5-fold stratified cross-validation.

The Bayesian network classifiers are implemented in the `bayesClass` [14] package for the R statistical environment [15]. We used the `caret` [16] package for R to estimate predictive accuracy with cross-validation.

Table 1. Data sets. #Instances column displays the number of complete instances

No.	Data set	#Features	#Instances	#Classes
1	Balance Scale	4	625	3
2	Breast Cancer (Wisconsin)	9	683	2
3	Car	6	1728	4
4	Chess (kr vs. kp)	36	3196	2
5	Dermatology	34	358	6
6	Ecoli	7	336	8
7	House Voting 84	16	232	2
8	Ionosphere	34	351	2
9	Lymphography	18	148	4
10	Molecular Biology (Promoters)	57	106	2
11	Molecular Biology (Splice)	61	3190	3
12	Primary Tumor	17	132	22
13	Tic-tac-toe	9	958	2
14	Wine	13	178	3

6.2   Results

Following [17], we performed Friedman's test [18,19] and Iman and Devenport's correction [20] to compare the classifiers over all the data sets. Our proposal outperforms the other methods (see Table 2 for Friedman's ranks) although the difference is not statistically significant[1].

---

[1] The p-value from both Friedman's and Iman and Davenport's test was 0.2.

Table 2. Average Friedman's ranks. Lower ranking means better performance. ASB = augmented semi-naive Bayes, STAN = selective tree augmented Bayes, FSS = forward sequential selection, BSEJ = backward sequential elimination and joining, FFSS = filter forward sequential selection, NB = naive Bayes, TAN = tree augmented naive Bayes.

Algorithm	Friedman's ranks
ASB	3.11
STAN	3.96
FSS	5.21
BSEJ	3.57
FFSS	4.35
NB	3.53
TAN	4.25
p-value$_{Friedman}$	0.20
p-value$_{Iman-Davenport}$	0.20

Table 3. Estimated accuracies (in %) of the compared classifiers. The best performing classifiers on a data set are marked in bold. Some data set names are shorter than in Table 1 but the order is the same. ASB = augmented semi-naive Bayes, STAN = selective tree augmented Bayes, FSS = forward sequential selection, BSEJ = backward sequential elimination and joining, FFSS = filter forward sequential selection, NB = naive Bayes, TAN = tree augmented naive Bayes.

No.	Data set	ASB	STAN	FSS	BSEJ	FFSS	NB	TAN
1	Balance Scale	72.9±2.5	73.2±2.9	**73.6±2.2**	72.8±2.3	73.3±2.3	73.3±2.3	73.2+-2.9
2	Breast Cancer	97.1±1.1	97.1±1.1	96.9±1.4	**97.5±1.0**	**97.5±1.0**	97.5±1.0	97.1±1.1
3	Car	93.3±1.6	93.5±1.5	70.0±0.1	90.0±1.8	85.1±1.7	85.3±1.4	**94.1±1.6**
4	Chess	**94.1±1.1**	92.6±0.8	**94.1±1.0**	92.2±1.1	87.8±1.4	87.8±1.4	92.4±0.9
5	Dermatology	**98.2±1.5**	98.0±1.6	95.1±3.4	**98.2±1.5**	98.0±1.6	98.0±1.6	97.1±1.7
6	Ecoli	**85.7±3.4**	**85.7±3.4**	83.4±2.8	**85.7±3.4**	**85.7±3.4**	**85.7±3.4**	84.5±3.2
7	House Voting 84	94.3±2.8	92.9±2.8	**97.0±2.4**	91.2±4.5	91.3±4.5	91.2±4.4	93.6±2.7
8	Ionosphere	92.0±3.7	91.9±3.7	90.7±3.6	90.7±3.8	90.7±4.1	90.7±4.1	**92.2±3.1**
9	Lymphography	**85.4±6.1**	82.7±5.6	78.4±7.3	85.0±6.5	82.7±7.1	84.6±6.2	83.4±6.0
10	Promoters	89.8±6.4	90.5±5.0	84±11.2	89.8±6.4	90.5±5.0	**91.7±6.2**	48.7±1.2
11	Splice	94.9±0.7	95.0±0.8	93.5±0.8	**95.5±0.8**	95.4±0.9	95.5±0.8	52.5±0.3
12	Primary Tumor	46.5±9.4	21.3±2.0	42.5±7.7	46.5±9.4	21.3±2.0	**48.3±9.3**	41.6±8.0
13	Tic-tac-toe	75.3±3.2	74.8±2.9	69.6±3.4	71.7±3.7	70.4±3.9	70.4±3.8	**75.8±2.9**
14	Wine	98.7±1.6	98.7±1.6	95.4±2.9	**98.9±1.4**	**98.9±1.4**	**98.9±1.4**	96.9±2.6

The ASB significantly[2] improves on BSEJ on four data sets (car, chess, ionosphere, and tic-tac-toe. See Table 3 for accuracies.). The BSEJ outputs a model similar to the NB on those data sets (e.g. on ionosphere it removes a single feature and accounts for one interaction) while the ASB heavily augments the BSEJ (e.g. on ionosphere it builds a full tree among feature groups). This shows that useful interactions missed by BSEJ can be recovered by ASB.

There is no significant difference between ASB and BSEJ on the remaining data sets. The ASB degrades BSEJ on only three data sets and the degradation is

---

[2] According to Wilcoxon's signed rank test at 5% significance level.

minor (by at most 0.6% accuracy). On four data sets the ASB model is identical to the BSEJ. One of those data sets - primary tumor - has many classes (22) and not many cases (132). This yields the conditional independence test unreliable for every pair of features and therefore no arcs are be added. On the other three data sets, lowering the significance threshold would have would have produced augmented BSEJ models (i.e. arcs would have been added).

7   Concluding Remarks

We have presented the augmented-semi naive Bayes (ASB) algorithm, a method for removing some of the unwarranted independence assumptions of a semi-naive Bayes model. The ASB is computationally inexpensive compared to the BSEJ, the algorithm used for learning a semi-naive Bayes. Our experiments show that ASB improves BSEJ in some domains without degrading it others. The ASB outperformed BSEJ and five other Bayesian network classifiers on 14 benchmark data sets, although the improvement in performance is not statistically significant. Further experiments, over more data sets, might give more conclusive results. Since ASB seems to improve BSEJ, it might be interesting to extend the approach to augmenting other Bayesian network classifier learned by maximizing predictive accuracy, such as the forward sequential selection algorithm for learning a selective naive Bayes.

Acknowledgements. This work has been partially supported by the Spanish Economy and Competitiveness Ministry through Cajal Blue Brain (C080020-09) and TIN2010-20900-C04-04 projects. The authors thank Rubén Armañanzas and anonymous reviewers for useful comments.

References

1. Minsky, M.: Steps toward artificial intelligence. Transactions on Institute of Radio Engineers 49, 8–30 (1961)
2. Duda, R., Hart, P.: Pattern Classification and Scene Analysis. John Wiley and Sons (1973)
3. Friedman, N., Geiger, D., Goldszmidt, M.: Bayesian network classifiers. Machine Learning 29, 131–163 (1997)
4. Pazzani, M.: Constructive induction of Cartesian product attributes. In: Proceedings of the Information, Statistics and Induction in Science Conference (ISIS 1996), pp. 66–77 (1996)
5. Blanco, R., Inza, I., Merino, M., Quiroga, J., Larrañaga, P.: Feature selection in Bayesian classifiers for the prognosis of survival of cirrhotic patients treated with TIPS. Journal of Biomedical Informatics 38(5), 376–388 (2005)
6. Pearl, J.: Probabilistic Reasoning in Intelligent Systems. Morgan Kaufmann (1988)
7. Koller, D., Friedman, N.: Probabilistic graphical models: principles and techniques. MIT Press (2009)
8. Agresti, A.: Categorical Data Analysis. Wiley (1990)

9. Yaramakala, S., Margaritis, D.: Speculative Markov blanket discovery for optimal feature selection. In: ICDM 2005: Proceedings of the Fifth IEEE International Conference on Data Mining, pp. 809–812. IEEE Computer Society, Washington, DC (2005)

10. Murphy, K.P.: Machine learning: a probabilistic perspective. The MIT Press (2012)

11. Langley, P., Sage, S.: Induction of selective Bayesian classifiers. In: Proceedings of the 10th Conference on Uncertainty in Artificial Intelligence (UAI 1994), pp. 399–406. Morgan Kaufmann (1994)

12. Bache, K., Lichman, M.: UCI machine learning repository (2013), http://archive.ics.uci.edu/ml

13. Fayyad, U., Irani, K.: Multi-interval discretization of continuous-valued attributes for classification learning. In: Proceedings of the 9th International Joint Conference on Artificial Intelligence (IJCAI 1993), pp. 1022–1029. Morgan Kaufmann (1993)

14. Mihaljevic, B., Larrañaga, P., Bielza, C.: BayesClass: A package for learning Bayesian network classifiers (2013), R package version 1.0

15. R Core Team: R: A Language and Environment for Statistical Computing. R Foundation for Statistical Computing, Vienna, Austria (2012)

16. Kuhn, M., Wing, J., Weston, S., Williams, A., Keefer, C., Engelhardt, A., Cooper, T.: Caret: Classification and Regression Training (2013) R package version 5.15-052

17. García, S., Fernández, A., Luengo, J., Herrera, F.: Advanced nonparametric tests for multiple comparisons in the design of experiments in computational intelligence and data mining: Experimental analysis of power. Information Sciences 180(10), 2044–2064 (2010)

18. Friedman, M.: The use of ranks to avoid the assumption of normality implicit in the analysis of variance. Journal of the American Statistical Association 32(200), 675–701 (1937)

19. Friedman, M.: A comparison of alternative tests of significance for the problem of m rankings. The Annals of Mathematical Statistics 11(1), 86–92 (1940)

20. Iman, R., Davenport, J.M.: Approximations of the critical region of the friedman statistic. Communications in Statistics 9(6), 571–595 (1980)

Automatic Ontology User Profiling
for Social Networks from URLs Shared

Paula Peña, Rafael Del Hoyo, Jorge Vea-Murguía,
Carlos González, and Sergio Mayo

Aragon Institute of Technology
C/ María de Luna n°7, Zaragoza, Spain
{ppena,rdelhoyo,jvea,cgonzalez,smayo}@ita.es

Abstract. User profiling, defined as the inference of user interests, intentions, characteristics, behaviors and preferences, is nowadays one of the most important keys in personalized services on Internet, such as segmented target advertisements. In this paper, we propose a scalable and automated technique for user ontology profiling in social networks by extracting URL content shared by users in tweets. The new approach models a user profile as a semantic ontology where user interests and intentions are represented. OpenDNS and DBpedia collective knowledge databases are utilized in order to find the interests and intentions categories of the user profile ontology, enhancing the performance of our method and taking the collective categorization of the websites. User profile ontology evolves constantly and is populated with assertions of individuals and relationships of interest and intention from these collective knowledge repositories. Experimental results indicate strongly that the proposed method automatically generates, correctly, the interests and intentions of a user profile.

Keywords: Twitter, Social Networks, Ontology, RDF, OWL, NoSQL.

1   Introduction

User profiling, defined as the inference of user interests, intentions, characteristics, behaviors and preferences, is the new tool for Internet services expansion. For example, profiling a user's location, buy items or topic interests (which we will focus) enables new services to provide personalized search results, news sites to recommend buy items, and advertisers to serve targeted ads. To profile a user, the traditional approaches leverage limited user-centric data (e.g., search log or purchase history), mining values of various user attributes such as demographic characteristics (e.g., age, gender, origin), intentions (looking items to buy, e.g. TV LCD 32"), interests (e.g. politics, sports, TV programs). Scalable algorithms for mining big data in order to generate user profiles can help also in new advanced services on Internet such as: discovering danger users for a target topic like terrorism or looking for new specific customers. Twitter, LinkedIn, Google+, Facebook and other similar services study the users' posted content and their interactions with others. The real business of these companies is to know about their users to shell advertisements and to improve the quality of experience of them. Beyond this techniques, other methods try to generate

C. Bielza et al. (Eds.): CAEPIA 2013, LNAI 8109, pp. 168–177, 2013.
© Springer-Verlag Berlin Heidelberg 2013

online digital footprints [1] for disambiguating the users. A repository of improved user profiles may significantly generate better and new Internet business. Ontologies can play an important role in user profiling [2]. Ontologies are a formal description and specification of concepts. They provide a well-defined and constructed method to provide a standard format to define user interests.

In this work, we propose a scalable and automated technique for user profiling by extracting his URLs from publicly available tweets information, enhancing the performance of our method and taking the collective categorization of the websites from DBPedia[1] and OpenDNS[2]. In other words, we generate a concise, yet descriptive semantic ontology user profile using Twitter streams. With a semantically ontology user profile generated, one can easily identify and reasoning the exact topics of interest a user has. In contrast to bag of word approaches, we generate semantically enhanced user profiles that quantify the users' interests and intentions in a set of specific categories. Ultimately, our profiling method outputs a semantically enhanced user profile that reflects the real user interest.

The remainder of this paper is structured as follows: In section 2 we discuss related work on modeling expertise of social media users. Section 3 describes the architecture used and presents a high level description of the algorithm. In section 4 we describe the ontology used. We discuss our results in section 5 and highlight implications and of our work. Finally, section 6 describes conclusions of our work and discusses ideas for future work.

2   Social Network Analysis

Online social network services such as Twitter, LinkedIn, Google+ and Facebook become important platforms for users to connect with friends as well as share information. For example, Twitter, a social network for users to follow each other and publish tweets[3], now has almost 500 million active users and generates 50 million tweets daily. On one hand, those services need to "understand" their users better, because old tasks (e.g., targeted ads) now become even more challenging (e.g., serving ads without queries), and new tasks (e.g., recommending "friends") arise in the context of social network. How are people connected on Twitter? Who are the most influential people? What do people talk about? How does information diffuse via retweet? On the other hand, those services generate additional information to leverage, because not only user-centric data (e.g., tweets) is available, but also information from others can be propagated through users' social connections. Profile information including name, age, location in Twitter services, although it can be incomplete (a user may choose not to post bio details) or misleading (a user may choose to list a wrong place). As a micro-blogging site, Twitter is supposed to hold less personal information than sites like Facebook. Despite this, we wondered if it is possible to reconstruct the profiles of Twitter [3] users from only publicly available

---

[1]   DBpedia is a crowd-sourced community effort to extract structured information from Wikipedia (http://dbpedia.org).

[2]   OpenDNS cloud websites tagging.
http://community.opendns.com/domaintagging/

[3]   Twitter stats from http://www.statisticbrain.com/twitter-statistics/

information on their profile. However, other relevant attributes, such as explicit and implicit interests or political preferences are usually omitted. Different approaches can be obtained in the literature like automatic user classification and profiling politics interests [4]. For example, the problem to discover interest by casting it as a user classification task and leveraging two types of information: user-centric information reflecting the linguistic content of the user's tweets, his social behaviors and likes, and; social graph information in the form of the distribution of the possible target class values for the people connected to the user by a social graph link. Machine learning approach has been used in several occasions like in [5], where is described a general machine learning framework for social media user classification which relies on four general feature classes: user profile, user tweeting behavior, linguistic content of user messages and user social network features. It has been proposed the use of wavelet based on clustering method to group users for discovering regular and consistent behavioral patterns in topical tweeting [6] into different groups that exhibit behavioral similarity. According to [7], it is explored the usefulness of different types of user-related data (tweets, retweets, bio and list data) for making sense of the domain expertise of Twitter users. Also, there are papers working on the identification of the personality of the users [8]. Different works like [9, 10] develop tools and services to allow the end-users to inspect Twitter-based profiles and enables other applications to reuse these profiles. People can overview their personal Twitter activities or profiles of other users to explore the topics those users were concerned with in the past. Different methods (entity-based, topic-based and hashtag-based tag) are used to visualize profiles.

Another topic explored in Social network analysis is to use Twitter as a social virtual sensor [11, 12]. The large number of Twitter updates results in numerous reports related to events, including social events such as parties, baseball games, and presidential campaigns. Also, disastrous events such as storms, fires, traffic jams, riots, heavy rainfall, earthquakes or the last bomb attack in Boston can be used as event detector or sensor detector. User profiling or Twitter system event detection classifies events that are visible through tweets such as earthquakes, terrorist attacks or fires.

Different works exist in the literature to study the topological characteristics of Twitter and its power as a new medium of information sharing [12, 13]. Twitter has explicit social structures among users and can be viewed as a time-series which records the activity volumes of a user at different intervals over an extended time period [12]. In order to identify influences on Twitter, it is possible to rank users by the number of followers or ranking by retweets [14].

User profiling is taking place within the project Novared. It aims to find scalable methods to find users with specific interests and intentions to target advertising more tailored to the interests of the people.

3   Architecture and Algorithm

How to model user interests and intentions through user profiling is a key for providing personalized service. In our domain, a user profile is modeled by ontology based on OWL (*Ontology Web Language*) or RDF (*Resource Description Framework*)/XML format. For this reason, initial definition of user profile ontology has been created and completed with concepts extracted from additional sources such as advertisement taxonomies, OpenDNS taxonomy and DBpedia ontology. In addition, our taxonomy defined adheres to the Friend-Of-A-Friend (FOAF) ontology, allowing reuse its classes, properties and individual definitions. OpenDNS offers a free domain service, *Domain Tagging*, to filter web sites based on several categories. Domains or URLs has been tagged into these categories and voted on the accuracy of submitter's tag by Domain Tagging community members. According to the community, a domain can be *awaiting votes* (community is voting on this domain's tags), *approved* (domain is confirmed in the category by the community) or *rejected* (domain does not belong in the category). DBpedia extracts structured data from Wikipedia and make it available as RDF (*Resource Description Framework*). Data can be accessed using an SQL-like query language called SPARQL. OpenDNS and DBpedia knowledge bases play an important role in enhancing the performance of our method. Both cover many domains.

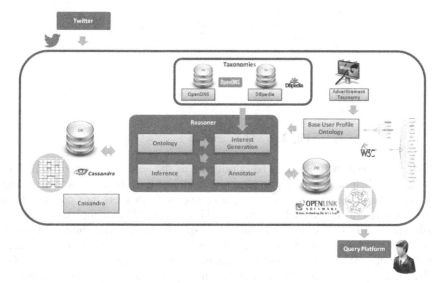

Fig. 1. Novared Architecture

Over the past few years, trends such as concurrency, connectivity, peer-to-peer, mobility and cloud computing have created the need to store large amount of data in distributed databases that provide high availability and scalability. New varieties of non-relational databases, commonly references as NoSQL, have emerged. The loss of flexibility or rigid schemes, the inability to scale data, the high latency or low performance and cost, are some of the major data management problems leading to the adoption of these technologies, nowadays widely used by companies such Amazon or Google. In this context and in order to support the ability to process large amounts of real-time information, NoSQL database become a crucial requirement in our application domain. After conducting a deep analysis of NoSQL technology and solutions current state, according to several features, *Cassandra*[4] and *Virtuoso*[5] non-relational databases, were the best suited to the desired application domain within the project.

---

[4] The Apache Cassandra database http://cassandra.apache.org/
[5] Virtuoso is an grade multi-model data server http://virtuoso.openlinksw.com/

The high level Novared architecture (Fig. 1) is focused on extracted URLs posted by users in tweets, user profile ontology, OpenDNS, DBpedia, NoSQL databases and Reasoner, seen as an intelligent component that implements the logic and key algorithm to populate user profiles with information about their interests and intentions.

In order to implement the algorithm, we have developed a set of sub-processes that allows adding new functionalities, defining and executing a workflow through an own library for semantic analysis of information inspired in UIMA[6] philosophy, called Moriarty. It works as server processes with BPEL interpreter engine (jBPMN).

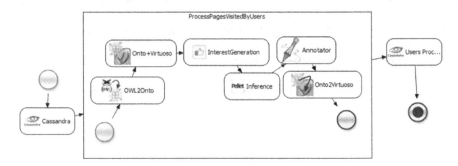

Fig. 2. Workflow and sub-processes

URLs contained in tweets can be considered as the seed for our approach. This information is helpful for identifying interests and intentions of a user and providing advanced Internet services. In our solution, tweets from users are crawled from Twitter in order to extract URL content, which cover different topics. URLs that people share on Twitter show their interests in specific topics. The ability to classify these URLs allows a first approximation to analyze their interests or their purchase intentions. This information posted by users in tweets is stored in Cassandra NoSQL database. Cassandra is a column oriented distributed storage system, designed to handle very large amount of data spread out across many servers while providing a highly available service with no single point of failure. This allows that the system to be scalable to support from hundred to millions of tweets.

In a batch mode, user tweets information gathered in Cassandra database is constantly analyzed. Basically, new information from all users is searched in Cassandra database through *Cassandra* sub-process. User-to-user, with its identification, *OWL2Onto* and *Onto+Virtuoso* sub-processes perform a search of its existing user profile ontology or a predefined ontological model within Virtuoso NoSQL database of RDF triples. Based on the extracted information, the aim of *InterestGeneration* sub-process is to generate new interest and intention relationships and concepts in user profile ontology. Over these relationships and concepts, *Inference* sub-process deduces new information about interests and intentions by means of a reasoner called Pellet[7] (e.g. if the property *hasIntent* is transitive, and the property relates individual A to individual B, and also individual B to individual C,

---

[6] UIMA Project http://uima.apache.org
[7] Pellet reasoning server http://clarkparsia.com/pellet/

then it can be inferred that individual A is related to individual C via property). Finally, *Onto2Virutuoso* sub-process allows saving the updated user profile with the new information inferred in Virtuoso NoSQL database. Once generated or updated the ontological profile for all users, *UserProcessedCassandra* sub-process set in the Cassandra database that users have been processed.

We propose a new user profiling algorithm which takes place in several steps and is described as follows:

User Profiling Algorithm

Input: url, userId, ontology

Output: user profile ontology with assertions

1.   Check if url is interesting (/*not a search engines, a url shortened by services or a generalist social networks */);
2.   **If** url is interesting **then**
3.   **If** url exists in ontology **then**
4.   *hasIntent* or *hasInterest* relationship is generated in user profile ontology;
5.   **Else**
6.   **Search** url **in** OpenDNS;
7.   **If** url exits in OpenDNS **then**
8.   **For each** categoryOpenDNS associated to the url **in** approved (by the community)
9.   categoryOpenDNS is added to user profile ontology;
10.   *hasIntent* or *hasInterest* relationship is generated in user profile ontology;
11.   **Search** url **in** DBpedia (/* whether the url exists or not in OpenDNS */);
12.   **If** url exits in DBpedia **then**
13.   **For each** categoryDBpedia associated to the url **in** the result of a query against DBpedia SPARQL endpoint
14.   categoryDBpedia is added to user profile ontology;
15.   *hasIntent* or *hasInterest* relationship is generated in user profile ontology;
16.   **Search** sameAs **in** categoryDBpedia
17.   **For each** categoryDBpediaSameAs associated to categoryDBpedia **in** the result of a SPARQL query
18.   *categoryDBpediaSameAs* is added to user profile ontology like *equivalent class* to c*ategoryDBpedia;*
19.   *hasIntent* or *hasInterest* relationship is generated in user profile ontology;
20. **return** ontology (/* with assertions of relationships and new concepts */);

Fig. 3. User Profiling Algorithm

Our algorithm discriminates between interesting and uninteresting URL. An uninteresting URL includes search engines (such as Google, Yahoo or Bing), URL shortened by services is resolved (such as Bitly, Goo or Su) and generalist social networks (such as Facebook, Twitter or Tuenti). User profiles are enriched with concepts and topics extracted from OpenDNS and DBpedia knowledge bases enhancing the performance of our approach. An extraction process of Domain Tagging data from OpenDNS has been implemented through Web-Harvest, an Open Source Web Data Extraction tool, in order to obtain URLs categorized by concepts. In addition, with concepts obtained as a result of a query against the DBpedia SPARQL endpoint[8], user profile ontology is populated with RDF assertions of URLs, concepts and relationships of interest and intention. As new concepts and relationships are defined and inferred, user profile ontology keeps alive.

---

[8] Sparlql query end point - `http://dbpedia.org/sparql`

4   Ontology

We use ontology to investigate how domain knowledge can help in the acquisition of user preferences. Artificial intelligence literature contains several definition of ontology, many of which contradict each other. Ontology is a term borrowed from philosophy that refers to the science describing the kinds of entities in the world and how they are related. On the other hand the OWL Web Ontology Language is a language for defining and instantiating Web Ontologies. We assume that ontology is a format explicit description of concepts in a particular domain ("class" sometimes called "concepts"), properties of each concept describing various features and attributes of the concept ("slots", sometimes called "roles" or "properties"), and restrictions on slots ("facets", also called "role restrictions").

Ontology together with a set of individuals of classes constitutes a knowledge base. Actually, there is a fine line where the ontology ends and the knowledge base begins. Classes are the focus of most ontologies and describe concepts in a domain. The profile Ontology inside Novared project is constructed based on standard advertisements taxonomy for user profile, OpenDNS taxonomy, and FOAF and DBpedia ontologies. The top class is "Thing" (profile) as the domain to build Novared ontology. Our ontology is always alive, as it may define new classes from the online update with additional concepts from other sources. The main classes are described as follows:

- *Person*: class that contains user identification.
- *URL*: class that includes URLs posted in tweets.
- *Interest:* class that hosts concepts related to relationships with user interests URLs.
- *Intention:* class that holds classes dedicated to relationships involving URLs user purchase intentions.
- *Unknown:* class that contains URLs that do not exists in OpenDNS and DBpedia.
- *UnknownCategory*: class of categories that do not exist in OpenDNS and DBpedia.

The main subclasses defined for intentions (Fig. 4) are *Auctions, AutoBuyers, Ecommerce/Shopping, Services* and *Travel;* the subclasses for interests (Fig. 5) are *Academia, Adult_Themes, Business_Services, Events, Government, GreenLiving, Health, Hobbies, Humor, JobSeekers, News/Media, Non-profits, Parenting, Politics, Religious, Sports, TechEnthusiasts* and *TravelEnthusiasts.*

The URL obtained for one user in the tweets is incorporated as exemplary of the class URL and associated to user entity. The topology of the ontology built can be showed in Fig. 6. Initial definition of advertisement with DBpedia categories was completed with new concepts (or synonyms) from the OpenDNS categories.

The basic relationships defined in ontology are "hasInterest" and "hasIntent" and their corresponding reflexive "isOfInterestTo" or "isOfIntent". Thus, each user classes are related to those of "Interest" by the relation "hasInterest", and are related to those of "Intention" by the relation "hasIntention". Obviously, URLs can have a relationship of belonging to one or more concepts from the categories of interest and intentions. Therefore, inference is done to obtain the interests and intentions of each user from de URLs posted in tweets.

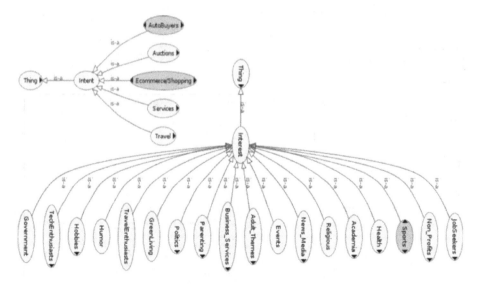

Fig. 4. and **Fig. 5.** Intent and interest first level branch of the ontology

5   Results

To evaluate our approach for generating user profiles, 18,000 tweets from 8,000 users are been crawled from Twitter in order to extract URL content.

We present an example of the results from an experiment conducted about how the user profiling is generated. From a URL, the topology of the inferred model is illustrated in Fig. 6 and Fig. 7. User profile ontology is populated with information (new concepts and relationships) about their interest and intentions.

In our experiment some URLs are only in OpenDNS, other are in both (OpenDNS and DBPedia) and other URLs are neither. In this case, the URL *www.avis.com* extracted in tweets is an exemplar of URLs that are in OpenDNS and in DBpedia.

Filtered the URL *www.avis.com* by OpenDNS, it can be observed that user profile ontology is populated with new concepts related to "Travel" category such as "Companies_based_in_Detroit,_Michigan", "Car_rental_companies", "Transportation_companies_of_the_United_States", "Companies_established_in_1946", "Companies_based_in_Morris_County,_New_Jersey", "Franchises", "Companies_based_in_Nassau_County,_New_York", and their "sameAs" provided by searches in DBpedia knowledge base. Moreover, as "Travel" belongs to "Intent" category of initial user profile ontology, "hasIntent" relationships have been generated between user and URL, URL and these categories and consequently, inferred intention relationships between user and sameAs categories are added. Finally, the "big" number of relationships generated was stored and can be queried in Virtuoso database, where billions of relationships can be asserted without performance problems.

Based on experimental results it can be confirmed that the method improves the automatic acquisition of interests and intentions of a user profile.

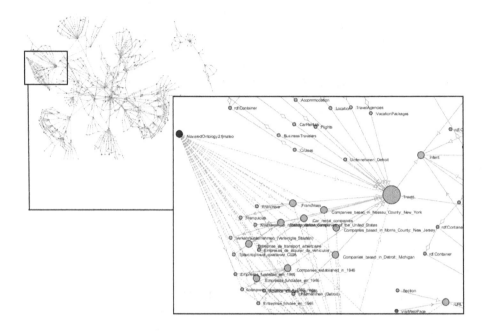

Fig. 6. and **Fig. 7.** Topology of inferred model generated

6   Conclusions and Future Work

Services on Internet are trying to adapt to the interests and intentions of users, providing them a more personalized attention. In this paper, a method based on the generation of user profiles is proposed in order to provide advertisements that really interest.

The results obtained allow us to face new tests and analysis of results with optimism. Our approximation allows obtaining automatically the interests and intentions of users through the URLs they share. They also show that the help of additional knowledge bases such as OpenDNS and DBpedia plays an important role and has a significant positive effect in user profiling. Social Networks and therefore Big Data have created the need to store, analyze and process large amount of data in distributed databases that provide high availability and scalability. Our ambition for the future work is to further investigate in massive data processing and clustering, allowing the implementation of scalable algorithms. We are currently working on analyzing the performance and scalability of the system presented, seeing the possibilities of massive data and user processing. On the other hand, we are working on including the categorization and opinion analysis of the Twitter text and the incorporation of new knowledge repositories such as DMOZ[9] or SUMO[10] in order to improve and enrich the user profiling.

---

[9] Open Directory Project http://www.dmoz.org/
[10] Suggested Upper Merged Ontology (SUMO) http://www.ontologyportal.org/

Acknowledgements. This work has been partly financed by the Mechatronics and Systems Group (SISTRONIC) of the Aragon Institute of Technology and by the Spanish "Ministerio de economía y competitividad" in the context of the *NOVARED: Sistema para Distribuir e Incrementar el Valor Creado en Internet* project.

References

1. Malhotra, A., Totti, L., Meira Jr., W., Kumaraguru, P., Almeida, V.: Studying User Footprints in Different Online Social Networks. In: 2012 IEEE/ACM International Conference on Advances in Social Networks Analysis and Mining, pp. 1065–1070 (2012)
2. Tao, X., Li, Y., Lau, R.Y.K., Geva, S.: Ontology-based Specific and Exhaustive User Profiles for Constraint Information Fusion for Multi-agents. In: 2010 IEEE/WIC/ACM International Conference on Web Intelligence and Intelligent Agent Technology, pp. 264–271 (2010)
3. Aïmeur, E., Brassard, G., Molins, P.: Reconstructing Profiles from Information Disseminated on the Internet. In: 2012 ASE/IEEE International Conference on Social Computing and International Conference on Privacy, Security, Risk and Trust, pp. 875–883 (2012)
4. Pennacchiotti, M., Popescu, A.: Democrats, Republicans and Starbucks Afficionados: User Classification in Twitter. In: Proceedings of the 17th ACM SIGKDD, pp. 430–438 (2011)
5. Pennacchiotti, M., Popescu, A.: A Machine Learning Approach to Twitter User Classification. In: Proceedings of the Fifth International AAAI Conference on Weblogs and SocialMedia, pp. 281–288 (2011)
6. Dey, L., Gaonkar, B.: Discovering regular and consistent behavioral patterns in topical tweeting. In: 21st International Conference on Pattern Recognition (ICPR 2012), pp. 3464–3467 (2012)
7. Wagner, C., Liao, V., Pirolli, P., Nelson, L., Strohmaier, M.: It's not in their tweets: Modeling topical expertise of Twitter users. In: 2012 ASE/IEEE International Conference on Social Computing and 2012 ASE/IEEE International Conference on Privacy, Security, Risk and Trust, pp. 91–100 (2012)
8. Quercia, D., Kosinski, M., Stillwell, D., Crowcroft, J.: Our Twitter Profiles, Our Selves: Predicting Personality with Twitter. In: 2011 IEEE International Conference on Privacy, Security, Risk, and Trust and IEEE International Conference on Social Computing, pp. 180–185 (2011)
9. Siehndel, P., Kawase, R.: TwikiMe! - User profiles that make sense. In: 11th International Semantic Web Conference (ISWC 2012) (2012)
10. Tao, K., Abel, F., Gao, Q., Houben, G.-J.: TUMS: Twitter-Based User Modeling Service. In: García-Castro, R., Fensel, D., Antoniou, G. (eds.) ESWC 2011. LNCS, vol. 7117, pp. 269–283. Springer, Heidelberg (2012)
11. Sakaki, T., Okazaki, M., Matsuo, Y.: Earthquake Shakes Twitter Users: Real-time Event Detection by Social Sensors. In: 19th International World Wide Web Conference Committee (IW3C2), pp. 851–860 (2010)
12. Lee, B., Hwang, B.-Y.A.: Study of the Correlation between the Spatial Attributes on Twitter. In: 28th International Conference on Data Engineering Workshops, pp. 337–340 (2012)
13. Li, R., Wang, S., Deng, H., Wang, R., Chen-Chuan, C.K.: Towards Social User Profiling:Unified and Discriminative Influence Model for Inferring Home Locations. In: ACM International Conference on Knowledge Discovery and Data Mining, pp. 1023–1031 (2012)
14. Lauschke, C., Ntoutsi, E.: Monitoring User Evolution in Twitter. In: 2012 IEEE/ACM International Conference on Advances in Social Networks Analysis and Mining, pp. 972–977 (2012)

A Common-Recipe and Conflict-Solving MAP Approach for Care Planning in Comorbid Patients

Gonzalo Milla-Millán, Juan Fdez-Olivares, and Inmaculada Sánchez-Garzón

Dpto. de Ciencias de la Computación e I.A., Universidad de Granada, Spain
{gmillamillan,faro,isanchez}@decsai.ugr.es

Abstract. The knowledge for managing diseases is usually compiled in single-disease clinical guidelines (CG). These CGs are not directly reusable for managing comorbid patients, who suffer from more than one disease. This is because some interactions may exist between the different involved CGs. However, some common high-level activities can be found in the different CGs. In this work we present a Multi-Agent Planning (MAP) approach which encodes these common activities in a *common recipe* used by planning agents to firstly obtain local solutions and then applying a conflict solving procedure over them. An experimental evaluation has been carried out to test the validity of the approach.

1 Introduction

Clinical Guidelines (CGs) are used in Clinical Decision Making to build care plans (the strategy to treat a patient). CGs unify criteria according to the best scientific evidence, encapsulating the knowledge to assist clinicians about appropriate health care for managing a single disease, which prevent CGs to be directly reusable when tailoring a care plan for a comorbid patient, who suffers from more than one disease [1]. That is because diseases (and their corresponding treatments) are not completely independent when they are present in the same patient. Therefore, if the integral care plan for a comorbid patient is built by just joining the separated care plans for each disease, some undesirable interactions might arise. An ontology with these interactions can be found in [2], including *drug interactions* (two different drugs which must not be administered together may be prescribed by different CGs); *redundant actions* (different CGs may prescribe the same intervention - e.g. a blood test - which should be practiced just once to the patient); and *timing interactions* (different CGs may prescribe different interventions which should be time constrained between them - e.g. two different X-rays, each one prescribed by a different CG for a different disease, should be scheduled in the same session). These interactions have to be avoided in order to not damage the patient, to make the most of each visit of the patient, and to improve the efficiency in the use of available resources.

On the other hand, the knowledge encoded in single-disease CGs is in the form of operating procedures which can be formalized in the so-called *Computer Interpretable Guidelines* using a representation based on "*Task-Network Models*"

C. Bielza et al. (Eds.): CAEPIA 2013, LNAI 8109, pp. 178–187, 2013.

[3], from which care plans must be tailored to specific patients. Hierarchical Task Network (HTN) planning with temporal capabilities has already been demonstrated to be a suitable approach for it in single-disease scenarios [4]. Moreover, *Computer Interpretable Guidelines* written in domain-specific languages can be translated to the HTN planning formalism [5]. The required inputs for such HTN planning processes are (1) a planning domain encoding the operating procedures of a single-disease CG, (2) the context relevant data (including patient information), (3) a set of high-level goal tasks, and (4) a start date for the care plan. The HTN planning process decomposes the high-level goal tasks using the knowledge in the planning domain until a set of basic actions is obtained, which corresponds to the required care plan for the patient.

Given the effort required to build a CG and to formalize it, it is all but realistic to manually create a new CG (and to formalize it) for every potential combination of diseases. On the other hand, the operating procedures in CGs usually follow a sequential schema composed of high-level activities such as diagnosis, pharmacological treatment, evaluation, etc. These high-level activities can be seen as sequential stages which a care plan must comply with for a single disease. Therefore, adherence to these stages needs to be also maintained when several diseases are present. In this work, we take advantage of these stages, common to different CGs, to obtain a care plan for a comorbid patient from single-disease CGs. This allows for the reuse of the knowledge already gathered in the single-disease CGs, saving modeling and implementation efforts. A MAP approach is implemented where the knowledge of each single-disease CG is formalized as a separated planning domain; a *common recipe* is created to represent the high-level stages which the integral care plan must adhere to; and the potential interactions between the different CGs are stored in a database. Each agent encodes the local knowledge for a single disease and is in charge of (1) computing a local care plan for each one of the stages of that disease, (2) communicating its local solutions to the rest of agents, and (3) carrying out a conflict solving process which uses the interactions database to detect and manage the potential interactions. These steps are carried out for each high-level stage of the common recipe. In order to allow for consistency between partial care plans, the context data and start time are updated at the beginning of the process and after a partial care plan is obtained for each stage. This approach allows for the distribution of the computation in both the local planning and conflict solving processes[1].

In the next section the concept of *common recipe* and the conflict solving process are introduced. In section 3, the MAP approach is explained. An experimental evaluation follows in section 4. The related work is exposed in section 5 and our conclusions finish the paper.

---

[1] In this work, the following adjectives are used with these meanings: **"local"** for entities within the scope of a single disease/agent; **"global"** for entities involving all the agents/diseases; **"partial"** for entities within the scope of a single stage of the care plan; and **"integral"** for entities involving all the stages. Thus, the approach presented in this paper can be seen as a way to obtain a **global integral** care plan from the **local partial** solutions proposed by several agents.

2   A Common Recipe and Conflict Solving Approach

In this section we introduce the concept of *common recipe* as a way to split the integral care planning process in different stages, and a conflict solving process to detect and manage the intra-stage interactions between local solutions. The way that these elements are used will be extended in section 3.

2.1   Common Recipe

A *Common Recipe* encodes the main high-level activities of a CG such as diagnosis, pharmacological treatment, evaluation, etc. These high-level activities can be seen as sequential stages according to which care plans must be planned and scheduled. These stages are specified as a set of planning goals to be achieved sequentially[2]. Some additional information is needed to allow the agents to correctly manage this common recipe. Next, these elements are enumerated.

Goals. There is a planning goal in the common recipe for each high-level stage of the care plan. Each planning goal is a high-level activity which needs to be decomposed until a set of basic actions is obtained. An example of goal would be *Diagnosis*, which is the high-level activity. An example of basic actions which this high-level activity could be decomposed in is: {*blood-test, chest-X-ray*}. Time constraints and causal dependencies might hold between different stages and inside each one of them. The intra-stage dependencies are encoded in the formal CGs (the local planning domains) and managed by each agent separately by the local planning processes. Managing inter-stage dependencies requires to store information about the partial solutions, as it is shown next.

Start Time of the care plan. This is needed as a reference to schedule the care plan actions. In order to comply with inter-stage constraints, this *Start Time* is updated after a global solution is found for each goal of the common recipe.

Context Data. The context data contains the relevant information about the patient and the available resources. In order to comply with inter-stage constraints, the *Context Data* needs to be updated after each goal of the common recipe is solved.

Selection Criterion. In case that several global solutions are found (by different agents) for a goal of the common recipe, a single one needs to be selected. This is the purpose of this selection criterion, which acts as an utility function assigning a numeric value to each global care plan.

2.2   Conflict Solving

The local planning processes within each stage do not have information about the potential interactions with other (external) local solutions. Therefore, a conflict solving process is implemented in each agent to detect and manage these

---

[2] In HTN planning, goals are specified as high-level activities which need to be decomposed by the planning algorithm.

interactions at planning time, before any care plan is given as output, so there is no chance for any interaction to happen at execution time (unless any deviation from the expected care plan takes place during its execution, which is something out of the scope of this paper). The conflict solving process is similar in all the agents and is also based in HTN planning like the local planning processes[3]. Each conflict solving process takes as inputs: (1) the context relevant data, **where the information about interactions is added**; (2) the start time for the current stage of the common recipe; (3) a set of conflict solving procedures encoded as task networks; and (4) the local partial solutions from each agent for the current goal of the common recipe. With this data, each conflict solver dynamically builds a new HTN planning problem whose output is a global partial solution for the current goal of the common recipe. The conflict solving process in each agent is responsible to accommodate the local proposals from the rest of agents to its own local solution in order to find an interaction-free global solution (i,e,. each agent explores different global solutions, namely those where its own local solutions remain unaltered). Next we explain the kind of interactions that this conflict solving process is able to detect and the processes used to manage them.

Drug Interactions occur between two different drugs when they must not be administered together. If each drug is intended to treat a different disease, they might be prescribed together by the respective local CGs for a patient suffering from both diseases. The process for managing this interactions consists of (1) storing in the planning state every drug prescribed by a local solution to the patient; (2) checking this information when a new drug administration is found in a different local solution; and (3) if a drug interaction is found, substitute the new drug by any other applicable and non-interacting drug.

Redundant Actions are those similar interventions prescribed by different guidelines (e.g. a blood test) which should be made just once to the patient. Redundant actions should be merged in order to make the most of each visit of the patient and to improve the efficiency in the use of resources. To avoid redundant actions: (1) the first time that an action susceptible to be redundant is found in a local solution, it is added to the global plan, and a fact is added to the planning state reflecting this addition; and (2) for subsequent appearances of this action in different local solutions, it is not added to the plan but the corresponding local constraints are adjusted accordingly (i.e., if an X-ray is scheduled after a blood test in a local solution, but another blood test was already scheduled by a different local solution, then the *new* blood test is not added to the global plan, but the X-ray should be scheduled after the already existing blood test).

Timing Interactions occur when different CGs prescribe different actions and a time constraint between them should be added in the global plan (e.g.: two different X-rays, prescribed by different CGs for different diseases, should be

---

[3] Though both the local planning and conflict solving processes are based in HTN planning, they are different processes used for different purposes. In order to not confuse them, the term "planning" is always used only for the local planning processes (except in the current subsection).

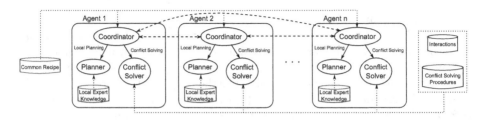

Fig. 1. Multi-agent architecture

scheduled in the same session). The reasons to manage these interactions are the same as for redundant actions. To manage timing interactions: (1) the first time that an action susceptible of a timing interaction is found in a local solution, it is added to the global care plan, and a fact is added to the planning state reflecting this addition; and (2) for subsequent appearances of timing-interacting actions in other local solutions, their schedules are adjusted with the first one, so timing interactions are complied and local constraints are not broken.

The formalism used for conflict solving is based on temporal HTN planning and allows for the representation and managing of these complex constraints via a hierarchy of compositional activities[4].

3   Multi-Agent Planning

In this section the MAP approach which makes use of the common recipe and conflict solving processes previously explained is detailed.

3.1   Agent Configuration and Architecture

Figure 1 depicts the configuration of each agent and the multi-agent architecture of our approach. The modules in each agent are: (1) a **coordinator**, which is in charge of managing the overall process of the agent and communicating with the rest of agents; (2) a **planner**, which uses the expert local knowledge of a single-disease CG to find local solutions; and (3) a **conflict solver**, which tries to resolve the interactions between local solutions. Each agent encapsulates the local expert knowledge about a single disease (distribution of the local partial planning), and explores different global solutions by its conflict solver module as explained in section 2 (distribution of the searching for global partial solutions). All the agents have access to the common recipe and the interaction information (both the interactions themselves and their related conflict solving procedures). The common recipe is used by the coordinator module to guide the overall process within each agent, and the interaction information is used by the conflict solvers to detect and manage interactions between local solutions at each stage of the common recipe. This is explained in detail next.

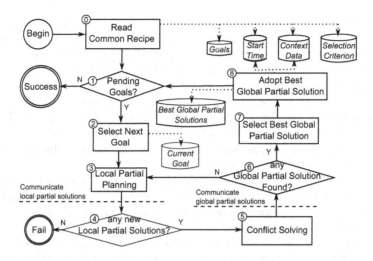

Fig. 2. Overall process. Solid lines represent the control flow. Dashed lines have been drawn where communication between agents takes place. Dotted lines depict the data flow which modify the data sources (it is explained in the text how and where these data sources are used, referring them in *italic* type).

3.2 Overall Process

The coordinator of each agent is responsible for the agent behavior, which is drawn in figure 2. The control flow elements are referred here by the numbers which label them in the figure. The process begins (step 0) by each agent reading the common recipe, which contains: the high-level *Goals* representing the sequential stages of the care plan, the earliest *Start Time* for the integral plan, the *Context Data* holding at that time, and the *Selection Criterion* for evaluating global solutions. Afterward, all the agents enter in an iterative cycle where:

1. Each agent checks if there are still pending *Goals* to process.
2. Each agent selects the next goal from the common recipe (if at least one is still pending) and set it as the *Current Goal*.
3. A local planning process is carried out in each agent for the *Current Goal*, the *Start Time*, the *Context Data*, and the encapsulated expert knowledge about a single-disease CG (see figure 1). Afterward, all the agents communicate their local partial solutions to the rest of agents (an empty message is sent by the agents who have not found any solution in this step). The local planning process is kept in a *stand-by* mode, so a controlled backtracking can be triggered in case that further local solutions are needed.
4. Each agent checks if there are new local partial solutions.
5. If at least a new local partial solution has been found by any of the local planning processes, a conflict solving process is carried out by each agent, taking as input the new proposals plus the information about interactions and conflict resolution procedures (see figure 1). Each solution found by a

conflict solving process is a global partial solution for the *Current Goal*, and is free of interactions. Afterward, all the agents communicate the global partial solutions that they have found to the rest of agents (an empty message is sent by agents who have not found any solution in this step).

6. Each agent checks if there are global partial solutions to evaluate for the *Current Goal*. If no global partial solution has been found by any agent, then each agent goes back to 3 and repeat the steps 3 to 6. As stated in step 3, the local planning process was kept in a *stand-by* mode so it can trigger a controlled backtracking in order to give a new (not already discovered) local partial solution for the *Current Goal*.

7. When at least a global partial solution is found, each agent selects the best one, according to the *Selection Criterion* read from the common recipe. This criterion is the same for all the agents, so all of them will select the same solution for the *Current Goal*.

8. The best global partial solution from the previous step is adopted by each agent, which means that: (1) the *Start Time* is updated with the latest end time of an action in the solution plan; (2) the *Context Data* is updated with the data holding at that time (end planning state of the solution); and (3) the solution is stored with the rest of *Best Global Partial Solutions*.

This whole process ends either with **Success** when a global partial solution has been found for every goal in the common recipe, or with **Fail** when no new local solutions are found by any agent while trying to solve any of the *Goals*. In case that the **Success** state is reached, the global integral solution (which represents an interaction-free care plan for the comorbid patient) is built up from the *Best Global Partial Solutions*. Updating the *Start Time* and the *Context Data* in step 8 allows for partial global solutions to comply with the sequentiality constraint between stages and for inter-stage interaction detection, respectively.

4   Experimental Evaluation

An experimental evaluation of the ideas presented in this work has been carried out. Two synthetic CGs for fictitious diseases X and Y have been encoded as local HTN planning domains[4]. The recommendations of each CG are divided in three different sequential stages: (1) *Diagnosis*, (2) *Pharmacological Treatment*, and (3) *Evaluation*. These stages are depicted in figure 3. A *Common Recipe* is created as explained in section 2, consisting of these sequential stages as goals, a start time for the care plan, the context data (of a unique fictitious patient), and a (random) selection criterion. Finally, the following interactions are encoded. **Drug interactions:** $X1$ and $Y1$ are known to interact between them. **Redundant actions:** *blood-test* and *information-gathering* must not be repeated in the global integral plan. **Timing interactions:** X-rays actions (*chest-X-ray* and *head-X-ray*) should be scheduled together.

---

[4] These synthetic CGs are not intended to reflect any real diseases but the kind of interactions that could be found between them.

Diagnosis stage for disease X

| information-gathering ⟶ blood-test ⟶ chest-X-ray |

Diagnosis stage for disease Y

| blood-test ⟶ head-X-ray |

(a) Diagnosis stages. The left frame is read: "*The* Diagnosis *stage for disease X consists of an information gathering about patient relevant data, a blood test and a chest X-ray*".

Drug	Required doses	Delay b/t doses
X1	2	24h
X2	4	12h

Drug	Required doses	Delay b/t doses
Y1	2	24h
Y2	6	8h

(b) Possible pharmacological treatments for diseases X (left) and Y (right). First row of the left table is read: "*the dosage of X1 drug consists of a total of 2 doses with a delay of 24 hours between them*".

Evaluation stage for disease X

| evaluate-evolution(X) |

Evaluation stage for disease Y

| information-gathering ⟶ evaluate-evolution(Y) |

(c) Evaluation stages. The right frame is read: "*The* Evaluation *stage of disease Y consists of an information gathering and an evaluation of the evolution of disease Y*".

Fig. 3. Modeling of the different stages for single-disease CGs

Two agents (named X and Y) are created according to figures 1 and 2. Each agent encapsulates the expert knowledge about a single disease (X and Y, respectively). The two shaded boxes most on the top of figure 4 represent the local integral solution plans, obtained by running agents X and Y separately. There it can be seen how just joining them would come up with several undesirable interactions, i.e.: (1) both $X1$ and $Y1$ drugs (which are known to interact) would be prescribed together; (2) the blood test would be repeated (times 1 and 2), as well as the information gathering action (times 1 and 11); and (3) two X-ray actions would be scheduled at different times (times 2 and 3). Furthermore, different stages would overlap along time (times 3 and 11). The bottom shaded box contains the result of running both X and Y agents together following the approach presented in sections 2 and 3[5]. There it can be seen how $Y1$ drug is replaced by $Y2$ which does not interact with $X1$. The correct drug dosage for $Y2$ is scheduled by the conflict solver as in figure 3(b). A single blood test is scheduled at time 2. Both the *chest-X-ray* and *head-X-ray* are scheduled together at time 3. Also the repetition of the gathering information action is avoided, which requires a special mention: the information gathering action for disease X (which remains in the global care plan) belongs to the *Diagnosis* stage, though the information gathering action for disease Y (which is removed in the global care plan) belongs to the *Evaluation* stage. This inter-stage and inter-agent interaction is correctly managed thanks to the inclusion of information about planned actions in the *Context data* (see section 2.2) and the consistent updating of the *Context Data* with the end state of each partial global solution (step 8 of figure 2).

---

[5] No alternative local proposals where needed in this experiment, where a global solution was always found with the first local proposals of each agent for each high-level goal.

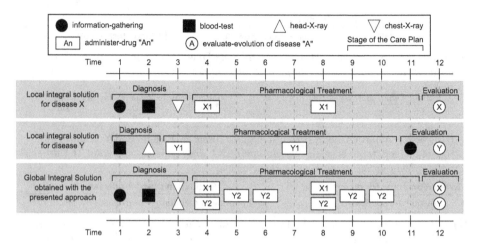

Fig. 4. Experiment results. The top frame contains the legend of the different icons in the timed frame below. Time is represented along the horizontal axis of the timed frame, which contains the experimental results. Equally-distributed and discrete time points have been used for the sake of clarity, but they correspond to real dates (and times) not necessarily separated by the same time interval.

5   Related Work

Some other approaches in the literature make distributed planning for a centralized plan as in ours. In [6], process planning for machined parts is divided into three different stages which look similar to the common recipe goals presented here. However, a single agent is responsible for each stage, while in our approach each stage is distributed and tackled in parallel by several agents. In [7], coordination is done at execution time between different agents to face possible context variances from a original plan previously computed in a centralized way. These features does not match our problem requirements, where the interactions which need for coordination are known *a priori* and must be managed at planning time. In the work of [8], the impact of any local decision is ultimately due to particular resources which cannot be committed to different agents. Redundant actions and timing interactions are not considered, and the drug interactions that we need to manage relate to the use of different resources by different agents.

Regarding the problem of care planning for comorbid patients, it has already been addressed from different single-agent perspectives in works as [9,10]. The GLINDA project [2] exploits the strength of agent-based representations for detecting and repairing interactions and consolidating treatment recommendations. Though there is not much information about this last approach, it seems that the HTN planning technology used in the present work allows for many more tailoring capabilities from CGs specifications to the specific patient features and available resources. The interaction ontology of [2] has been used here to categorize different kind of interactions.

6   Conclusions

A MAP approach is presented to tackle the problem of care planning for comorbid patients. Three types of interactions and their management processes have been characterized. The main contribution of this work is the implementation and management of a common recipe with the common high-level activities for several diseases, together with the conflict resolution processes based on HTN planning. All this in the frame of a MAP architecture which allows for the distribution of the local planning and conflict solving processes among the different agents. Our main objective for future work is to encode real clinical guidelines and try the approach in a more realistic scenario.

Acknowledgments. This work is supported by the Spanish MICINN project TIN2011-27652-C03-03.

References

1. Boyd, C.M., Darer, J., Boult, C., Fried, L.P., Boult, L., Wu, A.W.: Clinical practice guidelines and quality of care for older patients with multiple comorbid diseases. JAMA: the Journal of the American Medical Association 294(6), 716–724 (2005)
2. GuideLine INteraction detection architecture, http://glindaproject.stanford.edu/
3. Peleg, M., Tu, S., Bury, J., Ciccarese, P., Fox, J., Greenes, R.A., Hall, R., Johnson, P.D., Jones, N., Kumar, A., et al.: Comparing computer-interpretable guideline models: a case-study approach. Journal of the American Medical Informatics Association 10(1), 52–68 (2003)
4. Fdez-Olivares, J., Castillo, L., Cózar, J.A., García Pérez, O.: Supporting clinical processes and decisions by hierarchical planning and scheduling. Computational Intelligence 27, 103–122 (2011)
5. González-Ferrer, A., ten Teije, A., Fdez-Olivares, J., Milian, K.: Automated generation of patient-tailored electronic care pathways by translating computer-interpretable guidelines into hierarchical task networks. Artificial Intelligence in Medicine 57, 91–109 (2012)
6. Kambhampati, S., Cutkosky, M., Tenenbaum, M., Lee, S.H.: Combining specialized reasoners and general purpose planners: A case study. In: Proceedings of the Ninth National Conference on Artificial Intelligence (1991)
7. Durfee, E.H., Kenny, P.G., Kluge, K.C.: Integrated premission planning and execution for unmanned ground vehicles. Autonomous Robots 5(1), 97–110 (1998)
8. Conry, S.E., Kuwabara, K., Lesser, V.R., Meyer, R.A.: Multistage negotiation for distributed constraint satisfaction. IEEE Transactions on Systems, Man and Cybernetics 21(6), 1462–1477 (1991)
9. Abidi, S.R.: A conceptual framework for ontology based automating and merging of clinical pathways of comorbidities. In: Riaño, D. (ed.) K4HelP 2008. LNCS, vol. 5626, pp. 55–66. Springer, Heidelberg (2009)
10. Hing, M.M., Michalowski, M., Wilk, S., Michalowski, W., Farion, K.: Identifying inconsistencies in multiple clinical practice guidelines for a patient with co-morbidity. In: 2010 IEEE International Conference on Bioinformatics and Biomedicine Workshops (BIBMW), pp. 447–452. IEEE (December 2010)

An Argumentation-Based Multi-agent Temporal Planning System Built on t-DeLP

Pere Pardo and Lluís Godó

Institut d'Investigació en Intel·ligència Artificial (IIIA - CSIC)
Campus UAB s/n, E-08193 Bellaterra, Catalonia, Spain
{pardo,godo}@iiia.csic.es

Abstract. In this contribution, we study a system for argumentation-based backward planning built on t-DeLP, a temporal extension of Garcia and Simari's argumentation system known as defeasible logic programming framework (DeLP). In t-DeLP programs, temporal facts and defeasible temporal rules combine into arguments, which compare against each other to decide which of their conclusions are to prevail. We present a planning system by introducing actions (as in temporal planning) into this logical framework, and then study centralized algorithms for backward planning in scenarios involving multiple executing agents.

1 Introduction

A general assumption on the representation of actions in most planning systems (be it for actions with deterministic, conditional or disjunctive effects) is that the action encapsulates all the possible effects of its execution. While this assumption enables a quite simple update function, it also forbids reasoning about propositions, between states or even within a state. In the literature, reasoning about actions' preconditions or indirect effects is partially obtained by extending classical planning with (monotonic) conditional effects or rules.

The motivation for the present approach is to combine actions with more flexible and complex causal inferences; this is to allow modeling the indirect effects of actions (the ramification problem), or qualifications on their preconditions as well (the qualification problem). We use to this end a non-monotonic temporal logic programming framework t-DeLP based on defeasible argumentation [4], following the initial work in abstract argumentation [2] and logical argumentation (e.g. [9]). The use of temporal arguments allows to split the representation of a real-world action into: (i) a simple planning action, encapsulating its direct, incontestable effects; and (ii) a set of temporal defeasible rules, which combine with the former into arguments for indirect or context-dependent effects. By combining the t-DeLP notion of logical consequence (called warrant) with classical update, one can define a t-DeLP-based planning system. While t-DeLP planning problems for multiple executing agents can easily be solved by forward planning, we focus on the less trivial case of backward planning. In either case, Breadth First Search, BFS for short, (and other well-known search methods in OR-graphs) can be shown to be sound and complete for t-DeLP planning.

C. Bielza et al. (Eds.): CAEPIA 2013, LNAI 8109, pp. 188–198, 2013.

The paper is structured as follows. In Section 2 we briefly review first the t-DeLP temporal defeasible logic programming framework. Then in Section 3, we adapt the basic concepts of planning systems to the present case, including an appropriate update function for t-DeLP, and notions of planning domain and plan. In section 4 we present BFS algorithms for t-DeLP plan search. Finally, in Section 5, we show that BFS is sound and complete in the space of plans for a given planning domain.

Notation. We make use of the following conventions. Sequences are denoted $\langle x_0, \ldots, x_n \rangle$ (general case) or $[x_0, \ldots, x_n]$ (for argumentation lines) or $(x_0, \ldots, x_n)$ (for plans and update). Given a sequence $\boldsymbol{x} = \langle x_0, \ldots, x_n \rangle$ and an element x, we denote by $\boldsymbol{x} \cap \langle x \rangle$ the concatenation of $\boldsymbol{x}$ with x, i.e. the sequence $\langle x_0, \ldots, x_n, x \rangle$ or $[x_0, \ldots, x_n, x]$. If f is a function $f : X \to Y$ and $X' \subseteq X$, we define $f[X'] = \{f(a) \in Y \mid a \in X'\}$.

2 Preliminaries: Temporal Defeasible Logic Programming

In this Section, we briefly review the argumentation-based temporal logic programming framework t-DeLP used later in the planning system. For a detailed description and motivation for t-DeLP, the reader is referred to [7]. t-DeLP is indeed a temporal extension of Garcia and Simari's DeLP [4] and inherits from it a lot a features. The language of t-DeLP builds upon a set of temporal literals and temporal defeasible rules. *Temporal literals* are the form $\langle \ell, t \rangle$, where ℓ is a literal (expressions of the form p or $\sim p$ from a given set of variables $p \in \mathsf{Var}$) and t is a time point (we consider discrete time, so t will take values in the natural numbers), and will denote that ℓ *holds at time* t. Since the strong negation $\sim$ cannot be nested, we will use the following notation over literals: if $\ell = p$ then $\sim\ell$ will denote $\sim p$, and if $\ell = \sim p$ then $\sim\ell$ will denote p. Time is relevant to determine whether a pair of temporal literals $\langle \ell, t \rangle$ and $\langle \sim\ell, t' \rangle$ contradict each other: only when $t = t'$.

A *temporal defeasible rule* (or simply a *rule*) is an expression δ of the form

$$\langle \ell, t \rangle \ \prec\!\!\!- \ \langle \ell_0, t_0 \rangle, \ldots, \langle \ell_n, t_n \rangle \qquad \text{where } t \geq \max\{t_0, \ldots t_n\}$$

$\mathsf{body}(\delta)$ will denote the set of its conditions $\{\langle \ell_0, t_0 \rangle, \ldots, \langle \ell_n, t_n \rangle\}$ and $\mathsf{head}(\delta)$ its conclusion $\langle \ell, t \rangle$. A defeasible rule δ states that if the premises in $\mathsf{body}(\delta)$ are true, then there is a reason for believing that the conclusion (i.e. $\mathsf{head}(\delta)$) is also true. This conclusion, though, may be later withdrawn when further information is considered, as we will see later. t-DeLP only makes use of future-rules oriented rules: $\mathsf{head}(\delta)$ cannot occur earlier than any $\langle \ell, t \rangle \in \mathsf{body}(\delta)$. A special subset of defeasible rules is that of *persistence* rules, of the form $\langle \ell, t+1 \rangle \prec\!\!\!- \langle \ell, t \rangle$, stating that, unless there exist reasons to the contrary, ℓ is preserved from t to $t+1$ (if true at t). Such a rule will denoted as $\delta_\ell(t)$.

Given a set of temporal rules and literals Γ, we say a literal $\langle \ell, t \rangle$ *derives from* Γ, denoted $\Gamma \vdash \langle \ell, t \rangle$ or also $\langle \ell, t \rangle \in \mathrm{Cn}(\Gamma)$ iff $\langle \ell, t \rangle \in \Gamma$ or there exists $\delta \in \Gamma$ with $\mathsf{head}(\delta) = \langle \ell, t \rangle$, and such that $\mathsf{body}(\delta)$ is a set of literals that derive from Γ. We say Γ is *consistent* iff no pair $\langle \ell, t \rangle, \langle \sim\ell, t \rangle$ exists in $\mathrm{Cn}(\Gamma)$. In particular, a set of literals is consistent iff it does not contain any such pair. Note that derivability is monotonic: $\text{Cn}(\Gamma) \subseteq \text{Cn}(\Gamma')$ whenever $\Gamma \subseteq \Gamma'$.

Definition 1 (Program). *A t-DeLP program, or t-de.l.p., is a pair (Π, Δ) where Π is a consistent set of temporal literals (also called strict facts), and Δ is a set of temporal defeasible rules.*

Because of deafesible rules may be conflicting, the set of derivable literals in a t-DeLP program (Π, Δ) will not in general be consistent. To decide whether a literal can be accepted as a valid conclusion of the program, argumentation techniques can be used. In a sketch, DeLP-style argumentation techniques for logic programming formalisms work as follows: we start with a program or knowledge base (Π, Δ) with temporal facts in Π and defeasible rules in Δ, and a query $\langle \ell, t \rangle$; we combine facts and rules in (Π, Δ) into an argument $\mathcal{A}$ for $\langle \ell, t \rangle$, i.e. a consistent set $\mathcal{A} \subseteq \Pi \cup \Delta$ that entails $\langle \ell, t \rangle$ by applying only *modus ponens*. Once some such argument $\mathcal{A}$ for $\langle \ell, t \rangle$ is built, the argumentative process goes on by generating counter-arguments $\mathcal{B} \subseteq \Pi \cup \Delta$ defeating $\mathcal{A}$. Then arguments $\mathcal{C}$ defending $\mathcal{A}$ by way of defeating some such $\mathcal{B}$ are considered; and so on. The whole set arguments can be arranged in the form of a tree having $\mathcal{A}$ as its root and arcs denote the defeat relation. Finally, an iterative marking procedure starting from the leaf nodes of the tree determines whether the root argument $\mathcal{A}$ is undefeated, in which case its conclusion $\langle \ell, t \rangle$ is taken as a valid conclusion (or warrant) of the program. Below we provide formal defintions of all these notions.

Definition 2 (Argument). *Given a t-de.l.p. (Π, Δ), an argument for $\langle \ell, t \rangle$ is a set $\mathcal{A} = \mathcal{A}_\Pi \cup \mathcal{A}_\Delta$, with $\mathcal{A}_\Pi \subseteq \Pi$ and $\mathcal{A}_\Delta \subseteq \Delta$, such that:*

(1) $\mathcal{A}_\Delta \cup \Pi \vdash \langle \ell, t \rangle$,   *(3) $\mathcal{A}_\Delta$ is $\subseteq$-minimal satisfying (1) and (2).*
(2) $\Pi \cup \mathcal{A}_\Delta$ is consistent,   *(4) $\mathcal{A}_\Pi$ is $\subseteq$-minimal satisfying $\mathcal{A}_\Delta \cup \mathcal{A}_\Pi \vdash \langle \ell, t \rangle$*

Given an argument $\mathcal{A}$ for $\langle \ell, t \rangle$, we also define $\text{concl}(\mathcal{A}) = \langle \ell, t \rangle$, $\text{base}(\mathcal{A}) = \text{body}[\mathcal{A}] \smallsetminus \text{head}[\mathcal{A}]$ and $\text{literals}(\mathcal{A}) = (\bigcup \text{body}[\mathcal{A}]) \cup \text{head}[\mathcal{A}]$.

It can be shown that each $\langle \ell_0, t_0 \rangle \in \text{literals}(\mathcal{A})$ induces a unique sub-argument of $\mathcal{A}$, denoted $\mathcal{A}(\langle \ell_0, t_0 \rangle)$, i.e. a subset of $\mathcal{A}$ which is an argument for $\langle \ell_0, t_0 \rangle$.

Given a t-de.l.p. (Π, Δ), let $\mathcal{A}_0$ and $\mathcal{A}_1$ be arguments. We say $\mathcal{A}_1$ *attacks* $\mathcal{A}_0$ iff $\sim\text{concl}(\mathcal{A}_1) \in \text{literals}[\mathcal{A}_0]$, where we use the notation $\sim\langle \ell, t \rangle$ to denote $\langle \sim\ell, t \rangle$. In this case, we also say that $\mathcal{A}_1$ attacks $\mathcal{A}_0$ at the sub-argument $\mathcal{A}_0(\sim\text{concl}(\mathcal{A}_1))$.

Definition 3 (Defeat). *Let $\mathcal{A}_1$ attack $\mathcal{A}_0$ at $\mathcal{B}$, where $\text{concl}(\mathcal{A}_1) = \langle \sim\ell, t \rangle$. We say $\mathcal{A}_1$ is a proper defeater for $\mathcal{A}_0$, denoted $\mathcal{A}_1 \succ \mathcal{A}_0$, iff*

$$\text{base}(\mathcal{A}_1) \supsetneq \text{base}(\mathcal{B}) \quad or \quad \mathcal{B} = \mathcal{A}_1(\langle \ell, t' \rangle) \cup \{\delta_\ell(t'')\}_{t' \leq t'' < t}, \text{ for some } t' < t.$$

We say $\mathcal{A}_1$ is a blocking defeater for $\mathcal{A}_0$ when $\mathcal{A}_1$ attacks $\mathcal{A}_0$ but $\mathcal{A}_1 \not\succ \mathcal{A}_0$ and $\mathcal{A}_0 \not\succ \mathcal{A}_1$. Blocking defeat relations are denoted $\mathcal{A}_1 \prec\succ \mathcal{A}_0$. Finally, a defeater is a proper or a blocking defeater.

An argument $\mathcal{B}$ defeating $\mathcal{A}$ can in its turn have its own defeaters $\mathcal{C}, \dots$ and so on. This gives rise to *argumentation lines*, sequences of arguments where each

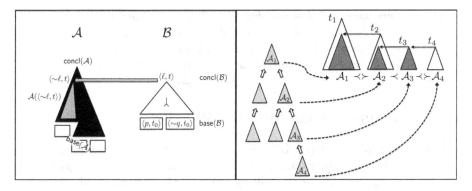

Fig. 1. (Left) Arguments $\mathcal{A}, \mathcal{B}$ are denoted with triangle-like figures. Strict facts from Π in $\mathsf{base}(\mathcal{A}), \mathsf{base}(\mathcal{B})$ are depicted as rectangles. Here, argument $\mathcal{B}$ attacks $\mathcal{A}$ at the sub-argument $\mathcal{A}(\langle \sim, \ell, t \rangle)$, depicted in grey. (Right) An argumentation line $\Lambda = [\mathcal{A}_1, \ldots, \mathcal{A}_4]$ in the dialectical tree for $\mathcal{A}_1$; defeated sub-arguments are depicted in grey. Notice that the time of these attacks is (non-strictly) decreasing: $t_1 > t_2 > t_3 = t_4$.

argument defeats its predecessor (among other conditions). More precisely, if $\mathcal{A}_1$ is an argument in a program (Π, Δ), an *argumentation line* for $\mathcal{A}_1$ is a sequence of arguments $\Lambda = [\mathcal{A}_1, \ldots, \mathcal{A}_n]$ such that:

(i) supporting arguments, i.e. those in odd positions $\mathcal{A}_{2i+1} \in \Lambda$ are jointly consistent with Π, and similarly for interfering arguments $\mathcal{A}_{2i} \in \Lambda$.

(ii) a supporting (interfering) argument is different from the attacked sub-arguments of previous supporting (interfering) arguments: $\mathcal{A}_{i+2k} \neq \mathcal{A}_i(\sim\mathsf{concl}(\mathcal{A}_{i+1}))$.

(iii) $\mathcal{A}_{i+1}$ is a proper defeater for $\mathcal{A}_i$ if $\mathcal{A}_i$ is a blocking defeater for $\mathcal{A}_{i-1}$.

The set of maximal argumentation lines for $\mathcal{A}_1$ can be arranged in the form of a tree, where all paths $[\mathcal{A}_1, \ldots]$ exactly correspond to all the possible maximal argumentation lines for $\mathcal{A}_1$. This *dialectical tree* for $\mathcal{A}_1$ is denoted $\mathcal{T}_{(\Pi, \Delta)}(\mathcal{A}_1)$.

The marking procedure of the arguments in a dialectical tree $\mathcal{T} = \mathcal{T}_{(\Pi, \Delta)}(\mathcal{A}_1)$ for $\mathcal{A}_1$ is defined as follows:

(1) mark all terminal nodes of $\mathcal{T}$ with a U (for undefeated);
(2) mark a node $\mathcal{B}$ with a D (for defeated) if it has a children node marked U;
(3) mark $\mathcal{B}$ with U if all its children nodes are marked D.

Definition 4 (Warrant). *Given a t-de.l.p. (Π, Δ), we say $\langle \ell, t \rangle$ is warranted in (Π, Δ) if there exists an argument $\mathcal{A}$ for $\langle \ell, t \rangle$ in (Π, Δ) such that $\mathcal{A}$ is marked undefeated (U) in the dialectical tree $\mathcal{T}_{(\Pi, \Delta)}(\mathcal{A}_1)$. The set of warranted literals is denoted $\mathsf{warr}(\Pi, \Delta)$.*

One can show t-DeLP enjoys the next logical properties, called Rationality Postulates [1,9], that prevent certain counter-intuitive results occur:

(P1) *Sub-arguments*: if $\mathcal{A}$ is undefeated in $\mathcal{T}_{(\Pi,\Delta)}(\mathcal{A})$, then any sub-argument $\mathcal{A}'$ of $\mathcal{A}$ is also undefeated in $\mathcal{T}_{(\Pi,\Delta)}(\mathcal{A}')$.

(P2) *Direct Consistency*: $\mathsf{warr}(\Pi,\Delta)$ is consistent.

(P3) *Indirect Consistency*: $\mathsf{warr}(\Pi,\Delta) \cup \Pi$ is consistent.

(P4) *Closure*: $\mathrm{Cn}(\mathsf{warr}(\Pi,\Delta) \cup \Pi) \subseteq \mathsf{warr}(\Pi,\Delta)$,

3 A Planning System for t-DeLP

After this brief review of t-DeLP, we proceed to introduce a planning system based on t-DeLP logic programming. In this paper, we study centralized planning with multiple agents: the plan is built by a central planner, endowed with goals, and knowledge of agents' abilities.

In order to simplify the description of the planning system, several assumptions are made on actions. An action e has a unique effect, denoted μ_e (or $\langle \mu_e, t_e \rangle$). The effect μ_e, which by default reads as *action e was just executed at t_e*, is exclusive to this action e (not found in nature, or other actions) and cannot be contradicted once it is made true. We also simplify the temporal aspects of these actions: the preconditions of e are all about some unique time-point t, and they need only be warranted at t, not during the full execution of e; this execution will take 1 time unit, so $t_e = t + 1$. These assumptions simplify proofs, but can be dropped out if necessary. Finally, agents are simplified as follows: (i) an action e can only be executed by an agent a, also denoted e_a; and its execution makes agent a busy during the interval $[t, t_e]$; (ii) we will also assume that there exist enough agents.

In what follows we will assume a t-DeLP language be given. Let us proceed with the basic definitions of action, planning domain and update.

Definition 5 (Action, Executability). *An action is a pair* $e = (\mathsf{pre}(e), \mathsf{post}(e))$, *where* $\mathsf{pre}(e) = \{\langle \ell, t \rangle, \ldots, \langle \ell', t \rangle\}$ *is a consistent set of temporal literals and* $\mathsf{post}(e) = \{\langle \mu_e, t_e \rangle\}$, *with* $t < t_e = t + 1$. *These are called the* preconditions *and the* (direct) effect *of* e.

An action e *is* executable *in a t-de.l.p. program* (Π, Δ) *iff* $\mathsf{pre}(e) \subseteq \mathsf{warr}(\Pi, \Delta)$. *Given a set of agents (or actuators)* $\mathsf{Ag} = \{a, b, \ldots\}$, *we denote an action* e *available to agent* a *by* e_a. *A set of actions* A *is* non-overlapping *wrt* Ag *iff for any two actions of a same agent* a *in* A, *say* e_a, f_a, *the effect of* e_a *is to occur strictly before the preconditions of* f_a, *or viceversa.*

Definition 6 (Planning Domain). *Given a set of agents* Ag, *we define a planning domain as a triple*

$$\mathbb{M} = ((\Pi, \Delta), A, G)$$

where (Π, Δ) *is a t-de.l.p. representing the domain knowledge[1], with* Π *representing (the facts holding true in) the initial state,* G *is a set of literals representing the goals, and* A *is a set of actions available to the agents in* Ag.

---

[1] The language of (Π, Δ) is assumed to contain a literal μ_e for each action $e \in A$. Moreover, temporal literals $\langle \mu_e, t_e \rangle$ can only occur in the body of the rules of Δ, while those of the form $\langle \sim\mu_e, t_e \rangle$ cannot occur anywhere in Π, Δ, A or G.

Definition 7 (Action Update). *The* update *of a t-de.l.p.* (Π, Δ) *by an action* e, *denoted* $(\Pi, \Delta) \diamond e$, *is another t-de.l.p. defined as follows:*

$$(\Pi, \Delta) \diamond e = \begin{cases} (\Pi \cup \mathsf{post}(e), \Delta), & \textit{if } \mathsf{pre}(e) \subseteq \mathsf{warr}(\Pi, \Delta) \\ (\Pi, \Delta), & \textit{otherwise.} \end{cases}$$

A *plan* π essentially contains a sequence of actions $\langle e_1, \ldots, e_n \rangle$. Actually, since actions are assigned an execution time by their preconditions, it can just be specified by a set of actions $\{e_1, \ldots, e_n\}$, rather than by a sequence. Indeed, it is not difficult to check that, given a t-de.l.p. (Π, Δ) and a pair of simultaneous actions e, f, i.e. $\mathsf{pre}(e) = \{\langle \ell, t \rangle, \ldots\}$ and $\mathsf{pre}(f) = \{\langle \ell', t \rangle, \ldots\}$, then $((\Pi, \Delta) \diamond e) \diamond f = ((\Pi, \Delta) \diamond f) \diamond e$. This enables the following definition.

Definition 8 (Plan update). *The* update *of a t-de.l.p.* (Π, Δ) *by a set of actions A is defined as follows:*

$$(\Pi, \Delta) \diamond A = \begin{cases} (\Pi, \Delta), & \textit{if } A = \varnothing \\ ((\Pi, \Delta) \diamond e_i) \diamond \{e_1, \ldots, e_{i-1}, e_{i+1}, \ldots, e_n\}, & \textit{if } A = \{e_1, \ldots, e_n\} \end{cases}$$

where the action e_i *is such that* $t_i \leq t_j$ *for any* $1 \leq j \leq n$, *with* t_j *denoting the time associated to the preconditions of the action* e_j *(for* $1 \leq j \leq n$).

A solution is then a plan whose actions make the goals warranted.

Definition 9 (Solution). *Given a set of agents* Ag *and planning domain* $\mathbb{M} = ((\Pi, \Delta), A, G)$ *and, a set of actions* $A' \subseteq A$ *is a* solution *for* $\mathbb{M}$ *and* Ag *iff*

$$G \subseteq \mathsf{warr}((\Pi, \Delta) \diamond A') \quad \textit{and} \quad A' \textit{ is non-overlapping w.r.t. } \mathsf{Ag}.$$

4   Backward Planning in t-DeLP

In this section we describe the plan space for a backward planning approach in t-DeLP. Actually one could also consider a forward search approach defined the cycle *add action-compute warrant in update-check if solution.* But this approach is straightforward in our setting: given a planning domain $\mathbb{M} = ((\Pi, \Delta), A, G)$, plans are simply sets of actions $A' \subseteq A$ which are obtained from the empty plan (i.e. the empty set of actions) by refinements of the form

$$A' \cup \{e\} \textit{ is a plan iff } \mathsf{pre}(e) \subseteq \mathsf{warr}((\Pi, \Delta) \diamond A')$$

and, for example, breadth-first search can easily be shown to be sound and complete for this forward approach. This simplicity derives from the fact that the planner always knows the "state" (warranted literals of a t-de.l.p.) given by the current plan. Therefore we will devote the rest of the paper to study the case of backward plan search.

The idea for t-DeLP backward planning is to start enforcing the goals with arguments and actions and iteratively enforce their undefeated status and, respectively, preconditions, with the help of more arguments (and actions). The

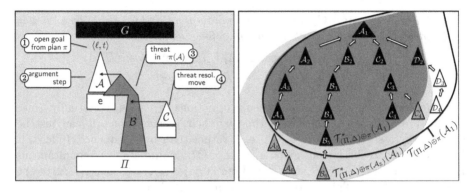

Fig. 2. (Left) An argument step $\mathcal{A}$ introduces an action e which triggers an argument threat $\mathcal{B}$ to $\mathcal{A}$. This threat is addressed by a further plan step $\mathcal{C}$. (Right) The dark-grey area represents the provisional tree for $\mathcal{A}_1$ in plan π, which is a sub-tree of the full dialectical tree (outlined area). After a refinement of π with $\mathcal{A}_5$, this plan step and new threats (the light grey area) occur in the new provisional tree for $\mathcal{A}_1$ in $\pi(\mathcal{A}_5)$.

plan construction, starting again from the empty plan and consisting of a sequence of (action+argument) refinement steps, stops when all these arguments and actions are, respectively, undefeated and executable. In our setting, we consider the following two types of refinement steps: *argument steps*, and *threat resolution moves* (the usual refinement steps in planning, namely actions, are just part of the former). An argument step is introduced to solve an open goal and consists of an argument for that goal, together with a set of actions whose effects (and facts from the initial state) support the base of this argument. A threat for an argument step $\mathcal{A}$ is an interfering argument in a maximal argumentation line for some dialectical (sub-)tree for $\mathcal{A}$. Finally a threat resolution move is like an argument step but defeating a threat rather solving a goal. Figure 2 (left) depicts examples of plan refinements: (1) a goal exists; (2) an argument step $\mathcal{A}$ (with an action e) is added; (3) the new action e plus the initial state Π enable a threat $\mathcal{B}$; this is an interfering argument in the (new) tree for $\mathcal{A}$; (4) this threat motivates another plan step $\mathcal{C}$, a threat resolution move.

A plan π for some planning domain $\mathbb{M} = ((\Pi, \Delta), A, G)$ will consist of a triple

$$(A(\pi), \mathsf{Trees}(\pi), \mathsf{goals}(\pi))$$

where $A(\pi)$ is the set of actions the plan involves, $\mathsf{Trees}(\pi)$ is a set of dialectical (sub-)trees (one for each argument step) and $\mathsf{goals}(\pi)$ is the set of open goals of π. $\mathsf{Trees}(\pi)$ is used to keep track of threats and threat resolution moves. To understand how these sub-trees are computed during the plan construction, note that a plan π does induce the *provisional* t-de.l.p.

$$(\Pi, \Delta) \oplus \pi = (\Pi \cup \mathsf{post}[A(\pi)], \Delta).$$

This t-de.l.p. results from considering that all the actions in $A(\pi)$ as being executable in (Π, Δ). At its turn, this t-de.l.p. induces a *provisional* dialectical tree $\mathcal{T}_{(\Pi,\Delta)\oplus\pi}(\mathcal{A})$. However this tree is not stored in Trees(π). Indeed, in order to avoid unnecessary threat resolution moves, the policy of the planner will be to address each threat $\mathcal{A}_k$ with a *single* defeater $\mathcal{A}_{k+1}$ for it. This results in a sub-tree of the former, denoted $\mathcal{T}^*_{(\Pi,\Delta)\oplus\pi}(\mathcal{A})$, that will be stored instead in Trees(π). All this makes each stored sub-tree in Trees(π) to be a sub-tree of the (corresponding) full tree in the same plan π, and also a sub-tree of the new sub-tree after any refinement $\pi(\mathcal{A})$.

Plans for a given a planning domain $\mathbb{M} = ((\Pi,\Delta), A, G)$ obtained by a sequence of refinement steps upon the empty plan. The initial *empty plan* for $\mathbb{M}$ is simply defined by the triple $\pi_\varnothing = (\varnothing, \varnothing, G)$. If π is the resulting plan after refining $\pi_\varnothing$ with n refinement steps $\mathcal{A}_1, \cdots, \mathcal{A}_n$, we will denote $\pi = \pi_\varnothing(\mathcal{A}_1, \ldots, \mathcal{A}_n)$. Moreover, for $1 \leq k \leq n$, we will write $\pi_k = \pi_\varnothing(\mathcal{A}_1, \ldots, \mathcal{A}_k)$, and a plan refinement of π by an refinement step $\mathcal{A}$ will be denoted $\pi(\mathcal{A}) = \pi_\varnothing(\mathcal{A}_1, \ldots, \mathcal{A}_n, \mathcal{A})$.

In the following, given a set of agents Ag and a planning domain $\mathbb{M} = ((\Pi,\Delta), A, G)$, we describe the two types of refinement steps.

Definition 10 (Argument Step Refinement). *Let $\pi = \pi_\varnothing(\mathcal{A}_1, \ldots, \mathcal{A}_k)$ be a plan for $\mathbb{M}$ and Ag. Let $\langle \ell, t \rangle \in$ goals(π) be an open goal in π. Let $\mathcal{A}$ be an argument for $\langle \ell, t \rangle$ in a t-de.l.p. $(\Pi \cup \Gamma, \Delta) \oplus \pi$, where Γ is a set of literals consistent with Π. If $\mathcal{A}$ satisfies:*

(i) base$(\mathcal{A}) \subseteq \Pi \cup$ post$[A^*]$*, for some $\subseteq$-minimal set $A^* \subseteq A$ of actions such that $A^* \cup A(\pi)$ is non-overlapping w.r.t. Ag.*
(ii) literals$(\mathcal{A}) \cup$ pre$[A^*]$ *is consistent with* $\bigcup_{1 \leq i \leq k}$ goals$(\pi^i) \cup \bigcup_{1 \leq i \leq k}$ literals$(\mathcal{A}_i)$

the refinement of π by $\mathcal{A}$, is the new plan $\pi(\mathcal{A})$ whose components are:

$A(\pi(\mathcal{A})) = A(\pi) \cup A^*$
goals$(\pi(\mathcal{A})) =$ *the previous goals* goals(π) *minus* $\langle \ell, t \rangle$ *and* Π*, plus preconditions for A^* not in Π or already solved in some π_i (with $1 \leq i \leq k$)*
Trees$(\pi(\mathcal{A})) =$ *the set of trees* Trees(π) *expanded with the new threats in $(\Pi,\Delta) \oplus \pi(\mathcal{A})$; and a new tree for $\mathcal{A}$ containing the arg. line $[\mathcal{A}]$ and each threat $[\mathcal{A},\mathcal{B}]$, for some arg. $\mathcal{B}$ from $(\Pi,\Delta) \oplus \pi(\mathcal{A})$*

Definition 11 (Threat resolution). *Let $\pi = \pi_\varnothing(\mathcal{A}_1, \ldots, \mathcal{A}_k)$ be a plan for $\mathbb{M}$ and Ag, and for some $1 \leq i \leq k$ let $\Lambda = [\mathcal{A}_i, \ldots, \mathcal{B}]$ be a threat in π (i.e. in $\mathcal{T}^*_{(\Pi,\Delta)\oplus\pi}(\mathcal{A}_i) \in$ Trees(π)). Further, let $\mathcal{C}$ be an argument in a t-de.l.p. $(\Pi \cup \Gamma, \Delta) \oplus \pi$, where Γ is a set of literals consistent with Π. If $\mathcal{C}$ satisfies:*

(i) base$(\mathcal{C}) \subseteq \Pi \cup$ post$[A^*]$*, for some $\subseteq$-minimal set $A^* \subseteq A$ of actions which is non-overlapping w.r.t. Ag*
(ii) $\Lambda^\frown[\mathcal{C}]$ *is an argumentation line in* $\mathcal{T}_{(\Pi\cup\text{post}[A^*],\Delta)\oplus\pi}(\mathcal{A})$

the refinement of π by $\mathcal{C}$, is the new plan $\pi(\mathcal{C})$ whose components are:

$A(\pi(\mathcal{C})) = A(\pi) \cup A^*$,
goals$(\pi(\mathcal{C})) =$ *the goals in* goals$(\pi) \setminus \Pi$*, plus preconditions of A^* which were not already solved in $\pi_1, \ldots, \pi_k$*
Trees$(\pi(\mathcal{C})) =$ *the trees from* Trees(π)*, each expanded with new threats in $(\Pi,\Delta) \oplus \pi(\mathcal{C})$*

Figure 2 (Right) illustrates a refinement by a threat resolution move $\mathcal{A}_5$ (the only newly added argument in a odd position in the dialectical sub-tree.

Definition 12 (Plan). π *is a* plan *for* $\mathbb{M}$ *and* Ag *iff it is obtained from* $\pi_\varnothing$ *after a finite number of refinement steps as defined in Definitions 10 and 11.*

5   Algorithms for t-DeLP Backward Planning

In t-DeLP backward planning, the *space of plans* for a planning domain $\mathbb{M}$ is the graph defined by the set of plans for $\mathbb{M}$ and the *"is a refinement of"* relation. In this graph, Breadth First Search is instantiated by the following algorithm:

Input : $\mathbb{M} = ((\Pi, \Delta), A, G)$.

LET   Plans $= \langle \pi_\varnothing \rangle$ and $\pi = \pi_\varnothing$
WHILE   goals$(\pi) \neq \varnothing$ OR threats$(\pi) \neq \varnothing$
        DELETE π FROM   Plans
        SET   Plans $=$ Plans $^\frown \langle \pi(\mathcal{A}) \mid \pi(\mathcal{A})$ is a refinement of $\pi \}$
        SET $\pi =$ the first element of Plans
        COMPUTE   threats(π)
Output : π (i.e. the set of actions $A(\pi)$); or fail, if Plans $= \varnothing$

Since G is a finite set of goals $\langle \ell, t \rangle$, these goals are bounded by some maximum value t^*, and so plan steps simply consist of arguments (and action) whose conclusions (resp. effects) are about some $t \leq t^*$. In consequence, only finitely-many plan step refinements (for any plan) can be obtained from (Π, Δ) and A, and so the space of plans is finite. Hence, the usual search methods BFS, DFS, etc are terminating, so the next proofs for BFS easily adapt to other methods.

Theorem 1 (Soundness of t-DeLP plan search.). *Let π be an output of the BFS algorithm in the space of plans for $\mathbb{M}$. Then π is a solution for $\mathbb{M}$.*

Proof sketch: The proof is by induction on the time instants (from $t = 0$ onwards) for the claim that the preconditions (open goals) required at t are warranted in the t-de.l.p. updated by the actions executed before t.   □

Theorem 2 (Completeness of t-DeLP plan search). *Let* $\mathbb{M} = ((\Pi, \Delta), A, G)$ *be a planning domain and assume some solution $A' \subseteq A$ exists. Then, the BFS search in the space of plans for $\mathbb{M}$ terminates with an output π.*

Proof sketch: Assume A' is $\subseteq$-minimal. From this set A', we extract undefeated arguments for each of their preconditions (to be used as argument steps), and a minimal set of defending arguments from their dialectical trees (to be used as threat resolution moves). Then it can be seen by induction (from $\pi_\varnothing$) that a refinement with an extracted argument exists, or the terminating condition goals$(\pi) = \varnothing =$ threats(π) is met.   □

Example. Imagine two agents desiring to move a table within a room, without breaking the jar lying upon the table. The table has two sides (north and south), which can be lifted by either action lift.N, lift.S. Consider the next abbreviations:

$b = \mathsf{broken}(\mathsf{jar})$ $h = \mathsf{horizontal}(\mathsf{table})$ $\mu_N = \mu_{\mathsf{lift.N}}$

$f = \mathsf{falls.off}(\mathsf{jar})$ $o = \mathsf{on}(\mathsf{jar},\mathsf{table})$ $\mu_S = \mu_{\mathsf{lift.S}}$

The indirect effects of lifting just one side of the table can indistinctly be represented with monotonic conditionals -as in standard temporal planning [5]- (up) or with t-DeLP defeasible rules (down):

$$\langle b, t+1\rangle \leftarrow \langle \mu_N, t\rangle, \langle \sim\mu_S, t\rangle, \langle o, t\rangle \qquad \langle b, t+1\rangle \leftarrow \langle \mu_S, t\rangle, \langle \sim\mu_N, t\rangle, \langle o, t\rangle$$

$$\langle \sim h, t\rangle \prec \langle \mu_N, t\rangle \qquad \langle \sim h, t\rangle \prec \langle \mu_S, t\rangle \qquad \langle h, t\rangle \prec \langle \mu_N, t\rangle, \langle \mu_S, t\rangle$$
$$\langle b, t\rangle \prec \langle f, t\rangle \qquad \langle \sim o, t\rangle \prec \langle f, t\rangle \qquad \langle f, t+1\rangle \prec \langle \sim h, t\rangle, \langle o, t\rangle$$

Note, though, that the conditionals require negative effects among their premises, e.g. the frame problem. This problem is aggravated by actions like *gluing the jar to the table*, since an extra premise $\langle \sim\mathsf{glued}(\mathsf{jar},\mathsf{table}), t\rangle$ must be added to each conditional, and so on. In contrast, t-DeLP planning domains can modularly expand Δ with the rule $\langle \sim f, t+1\rangle \prec \langle \sim h, t\rangle, \langle o, t\rangle, \langle \mathsf{glued}(\mathsf{jar},\mathsf{table}), t\rangle$.

6 Related Work and Conclusions

The literature on temporal planning is quite rich (see e.g. [5], Ch. 14), though most proposals are based on monotonic rules and hence they are unable to fully address the ramification problem. The combination of the temporal t-DeLP logic programming with planning techniques is largely inspired by the DeLP-based partial order planning (POP) system in [3]. While a POP planning system is more flexible than a linear planner, the underlying logic DeLP is less expressive given the implicit time approach and hence the absence of temporal reasoning. Distributed algorithms for this planning system can be found in [8,6].

In this paper we have presented a planning system which combines a classical update function for temporal planning with temporal defeasible logic programming t-DeLP logical system. This adds non-monotonic reasoning to temporal actions, thus allowing for complex indirect effects. The main contributions consist in showing that the usual plan search methods are sound and complete.

Acknowledgements. The authors acknowledge support of the Spanish CONSOLIDER-INGENIO 2010 project Agreement Technologies (CSD2007-00022) and the MINECO project EdeTRI (TIN2012-39348-C02-01).

References

1. Caminada, M., Amgoud, L.: On the evaluation of argumentation formalisms. Artificial Intelligence 171, 286–310 (2007)
2. Dung, P.: On the acceptability of arguments and its fundamental role in nonmonotonic reasoning, logic programming and n-person games. Artificial Intelligence 77(2), 321–357 (1995)

3. García, D., García, A., Simari, G.: Defeasible Reasoning and Partial Order Planning. In: Hartmann, S., Kern-Isberner, G. (eds.) FoIKS 2008. LNCS, vol. 4932, pp. 311–328. Springer, Heidelberg (2008)
4. García, A., Simari, G.: Defeasible logic programming: An argumentative approach, Theory and Practice of Logic Programming 4(1+2), 95–138 (2004)
5. Ghallab, M., Nau, D., Traverso, P.: Automated Planning: Theory and Practice. Morgan Kaufmann, San Francisco (2004)
6. Pajares, S., Onaindía, E.: Defeasible argumentation for multi-agent planning in ambient intelligence applications. In: Proc. AAMAS 2012, pp. 509–516 (2012)
7. Pardo, P., Godo, L.: t-DeLP: an argumentation-based Temporal Defeasible Logic Programming framework, Annals of Math. and Artif. Intel. (in press)
8. Pardo, P., Pajares, S., Onaindia, E., Godo, L., Dellunde, P.: Multiagent argumentation for cooperative planning in DeLP-POP. In: Proc. AAMAS 2011, pp. 971–978 (2012)
9. Prakken, H.: An abstract framework for argumentation with structured arguments. Argument & Computation 1(2), 93–124 (2010)

Engineering the Decentralized Coordination of UAVs with Limited Communication Range

Marc Pujol-Gonzalez[1], Jesús Cerquides[1], Pedro Meseguer[1],
Juan Antonio Rodríguez-Aguilar[1], and Milind Tambe[2]

[1] IIIA-CSIC, Campus de la UAB, Bellaterra, Spain
{mpujol,cerquide,pedro,jar}@iiia.csic.es
[2] University of Southern California, Los Angeles, CA
tambe@usc.edu

Abstract. This paper tackles the problem of allowing a team of UAVs with limited communication range to autonomously coordinate to service requests. We present two MRF-based solutions: one assumes independence between requests; and the other considers also the UAVs' workloads. Empirical evaluation shows that the latter performs almost as well as state-of-the-art centralized techniques in realistic scenarios.

1 Introduction

Unmanned Aerial Vehicles (UAVs) are an attractive technology for large-area surveillance. UAVs are fairly cheap, have many sensing abilities, exhibit a long endurance and can communicate using radios. Several applications can be efficiently tackled with a team of UAVs: power line monitoring, fire detection, and disaster response among others. The autonomous coordination of a UAV team to service a sequence of requests is an open problem receiving increasing attention. In our scenario the requests to be serviced are submitted by a human operator, and the surveillance area is larger than the UAVs' communication range. Most related work comes from robotics, where multi-robot routing [1] is identified as a central problem. But the usual version of multi-robot routing assumes that all robots can directly communicate with each other, which is not our case. Although some works drop this assumption [2,3], they are focused on exploration of locations, disallowing requests from operators. State-of-the-art research employs auctions to allocate requests to UAVs (robots bid on requests). Auctions are quite intuitive, and in some cases they provide quality guarantees [1]. However, the problem can also be modeled as a Markov Random Field (MRF) [4], or as a Distributed Constraint Optimization Problem (DCOP) [5], for which efficient and easy to distribute algorithms exist. Delle Fave *et. al.* [5] propose an encoding where each UAV directly selects which request it is going to service next. However their model disregards that UAVs can communicate with each other. In this paper we explore coordination solutions for a scenario in which each UAV can communicate with the neighboring UAVs in its range. First, we present an MRF-based solution where the cost of servicing each request is independent of

C. Bielza et al. (Eds.): CAEPIA 2013, LNAI 8109, pp. 199–208, 2013.
© Springer-Verlag Berlin Heidelberg 2013

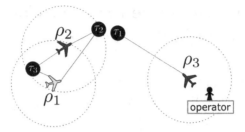

Fig. 1. Firefighting scenario: ρ_1, ρ_2, and ρ_3 are UAVs; dotted cicles around them are their communication ranges; τ_1, τ_2, and τ_3 are targets. A solid line between a target and a UAV means that the UAV is aware of the target.

the remaining requests assigned to the UAV. Thereafter, we introduce a second solution where UAVs adjust their estimations of the cost of servicing a task depending on their workload, with a slight increment in complexity. Empirical evaluation shows that this is a practical solution for realistic problems.

Motivating Example. In a firefighting context, consider a UAV team continuously monitoring a large natural park. A common approach is to adopt a centralized strategy: UAVs' routes are planned at a central commanding base that guarantees cooperation. However, if the natural park is significantly larger than the UAV communication range, performing centralized planning is unfeasible because the resulting plan can not be effectively transmitted to UAVs.

Figure 1 contains a snapshot of a possible firefighting scenario, with three UAVs, three targets, and a human operator. A good plan would send UAV ρ_1 to target τ_3 and UAV ρ_2 to targets τ_2 and τ_1. However, this plan of action can never be ascertained when assuming limited communication range. The only reasonable strategy to achieve cooperation with limited communication range is to make the UAVs directly coordinate between themselves, in a decentralised manner. Agents themselves must determine their best possible actions at each point in time so that the overall time to service requests is minimised.

Approach. This is a dynamic problem where UAVs move constantly and requests can be introduced at any time. In our approach, the operators send requests to some UAV in their range, which temporarily becomes its owner. Meanwhile, the UAVs use the algorithms detailed below to compute an allocation of all pending requests to some UAV. After each allocation cycle, each UAV becomes the owner of the requests that have been assigned to it, and a new allocation cycle begins. At every time, each UAV that owns some request flies towards the nearest of them, and each idle UAV tries to get in range of the closest operator.

2   Coordination Using Independent Valuations

Multi-agent coordination, and particularly task allocation, can be modeled as a MRF [4]. Despite the existance of very powerful algorithms for MRFs, this line of work has received much less attention than auction-based approaches.

2.1 Encoding the Problem as a Binary MRF

Let $R = \{\tau_1, \ldots, \tau_m\}$ be a set of requests, $P = \{\rho_1, \ldots, \rho_n\}$ be a set of UAVs, r and p are indexes for requests and UAVs respectively, $R_p \subseteq R$ be the set of requests that UAV p can service, and $P_r \subseteq P$ be the set of UAVs that can service request r. A naive encoding of the requests-to-UAVs allocation as an MRF is:

- Create a variable x_r for each request τ_r. The domain of this variable is the set of UAVs that can service the request, namely P_r. If x_r takes value ρ_p, it means that request τ_r will be serviced by UAV ρ_p.
- Create an n-ary constraint c_p for each UAV ρ_p, that evaluates the cost of servicing the requests assigned to ρ_p. We assume independence, so the cost of servicing a set of requests is the sum of the costs of servicing each request.

X_p is the set of variables that have ρ_p in their domains. An assignment of values to each of the variables in X_p is noted as $\mathbf{X_p}$. Solving the problem amounts to finding the combination of request-to-UAV assignments $\mathbf{X}^*$ that satisfies $\mathbf{X}^* = \arg\min_{\mathbf{X}} \sum_{p \in P} c_p(\mathbf{X_p})$.

Figure 2 shows an encoding of the motivating example. There is a variable for each request. The domain of x_1 is the set of UAVs that can service it. This is the set of all UAVs that are in communication range of the owner of τ_1. Hence, the domain of x_1 is just $\{\rho_3\}$. Likewise, the domain of x_2 and x_3 is $\{\rho_1, \rho_2\}$ because both UAVs can fulfill them. Next, we create a function c_p for each UAV ρ_p. Because ρ_3 can only service τ_1, the scope of function c_3 is x_1. As a result, c_3 is a unary function that specifies the cost for UAV ρ_3 to service τ_1, namely the distance between ρ_3 and τ_1 (hereafter δ_{pr} will be employed as a shorthand for the distance between ρ_p and τ_r). c_2's scope is $\{x_2, x_3\}$, because UAV ρ_2 can service both τ_2 and τ_3. Hence, c_2 has to specify four costs for ρ_2:

1. Both requests are allocated to ρ_1, which is 0.
2. τ_2 is allocated to ρ_1 but τ_3 is allocated to ρ_2, which is $\delta_{23} = 2$.
3. τ_2 is allocated to ρ_2, but τ_3 is allocated to ρ_1, which is $\delta_{22} = 2$.
4. Both requests are allocated to ρ_2, which is $\delta_{22} + \delta_{23} = 4$.

c_1 is similarly computed. From Figure 2 costs, $\mathbf{X}^* = \langle x_1 = \rho_3, x_2 = \rho_2, x_3 = \rho_1 \rangle$.

This encoding scales poorly. First, it does not exploit the fact that we assume independence when computing the cost of servicing a combination of requests in the constraints c_p. The number of entries in c_p is the product of the domain sizes

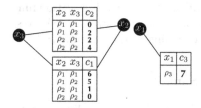

Fig. 2. Naive MRF encoding

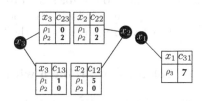

Fig. 3. Independent valuation

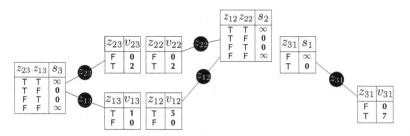

Fig. 4. Independent task valuation, binary encoding

of each of the variables in its scope. Hence, the number of entries in c_p scales exponentially with respect to the number of requests that UAV ρ_p can service. However, we can exploit the independence between requests by decomposing each cost function c_p into smaller cost functions, each one evaluating the cost of servicing a single request. That is, thanks to that independence between requests, we can represent c_p as a combination of cost functions c_{pr}, one per variable in the scope of c_p, such that $c_p(\mathbf{X_p}) = \sum_{x_r \in X_p} c_{pr}(\mathbf{x_r})$. Now the number of values to specify the cost of servicing a set of requests scales linearly with respect to the number of requests. Figure 3 represents the example in Figure 2 using this new encoding. Notice that for each UAV we specify the cost of servicing a given request when the request is assigned to it, or 0 when allocated to another UAV. However, the new encoding still suffers from redundancy. Say that another UAV ρ_4 is in the communication range of both ρ_1 and ρ_2. Since this UAV would be eligible to serve requests τ_2 and τ_3, the domain of x_2 and x_3 would become $\{\rho_1, \rho_2, \rho_3\}$. As a result, UAV ρ_1 must extend its cost function c_{12} to include a new entry where τ_2 is assigned to ρ_4, whose cost is obviously 0. Therefore, we must aim at an encoding such that a cost function c_{pr} contains only two values: δ_{pr} if τ_r is allocated to ρ_p, or 0 otherwise.

With this aim, we now convert the request variables into binary variables, replacing each original variable $x_r \in X$ by a set of binary variables z_{pr}, one per UAV in P_r. Previous c_{pr} cost functions now generate v_{pr} cost functions on these binary variables. In addition, for each r, z_{pr} are linked through a selection function s_r to ensure that a request can be only serviced by a single UAV. For instance, consider variable x_2 with domain $\{\rho_1, \rho_2\}$. We create two binary variables z_{12} and z_{22}. Intuitively, z_{12} being "on" means that request τ_2 is assigned to UAV ρ_1. A selection factor linked to both z_{12} and z_{22} would guarantee that only one of the two variables is set to "on". In our example, this selection function is a cost function s_2, which introduces an infinite cost whenever there is no single variable active. Figure 4 shows the binary encoding of the example in Figure 3.

2.2   Solving the Problem with Max-Sum

Now we optimize the max-sum algorithm to run on the last encoding of Section 2. Max-sum sends messages from factors to variables and from variables to factors.

However, our factor graph allows us some simplifications. Notice that each z_{pr} is only linked to cost function v_{pr} and selector function s_r. It is direct to observe that the message that z_{pr} must send to v_{pr} is exactly the one received from s_r, while the message that it must send to s_r is exactly the one received from v_{pr}. Then, since each variable simply relays messages between the cost function and selection function it is linked to, henceforth we will disregard variables' messages and instead we will consider that functions directly exchange messages.

The max-sum general message expression from function f to function g is

$$\mu_{f \to g}(\mathbf{Z_{f \cap g}}) = \min_{\mathbf{Z_{f-g}}} \left[f(\mathbf{Z_{f-g}}, \mathbf{Z_{f \cap g}}) + \sum_{g' \in N(f)-g} \mu_{g' \to f}(\mathbf{Z_{g' \cap f}}) \right], \qquad (1)$$

where $\mathbf{Z_{f \cap g}}$ stands for an assignment to the variables in the scope of f and g, $\mathbf{Z_{f-g}}$ stands for an assignment to the variables in the scope of f that are not in g, $N(f)$ stands for the set of functions f is linked to (its neighboring functions), and $\mu_{g' \to f}$ stands for the message from function g' to function f.

Observe in Figure 4 that selection and cost functions are connected by a single binary variable. Thus, the messages exchanged between functions in our problem will refer to the assignments of a single binary variable. In other words, the assignment $\mathbf{Z_{f \cap g}}$ will correspond to some binary variable z_{pr}. Therefore, a message between functions must contain two values, one per assignment of a binary variable. At this point, we can make a further simplification and consider sending the difference between the two values. Intuitively, a function sending a message with a single value for a binary variable transmits the difference between the variable being active and inactive. In general, we will define the single-valued message exchanged between two functions as

$$\nu_{f \to g} = \mu_{f \to g}(1) - \mu_{f \to g}(0). \qquad (2)$$

Next, we compute the messages between cost and selection functions.
(1) From cost function to selection function. This message expresses the difference for a UAV ρ_p between serving request τ_r or not, therefore

$$\nu_{v_{pr} \to s_r} = v_{pr}(1) - v_{pr}(0) = \delta_{pr} - 0 = \delta_{pr}. \qquad (3)$$

(2) From selection function to cost function. Consider selection function s_r and cost function v_{pr}. From equation 1, we obtain:

$$\mu_{s_r \to v_{pr}}(1) = 0, \quad \mu_{s_r \to v_{pr}}(0) = \min_{\rho_{p'} \in P_r - \rho_p} \delta_{p'r}$$

Then we can apply equation 2 to obtain the single-valued message $\nu_{s_r \to v_{pr}} = -\min_{\rho_{p'} \in P_r - \rho_p} \delta_{p'r}$. Moreover, this message can be computed efficiently. Consider the pair $\langle \nu^*, \nu^{**} \rangle$ as the two lowest values received by the selection function s_r. Then, the message that s_r must send to each v_{pr} is

$$\nu_{s_r \to v_{pr}} = \begin{cases} -\nu^* & \nu_{v_{pr} \to s_r} \neq \nu^* \\ -\nu^{**} & \nu_{v_{pr} \to s_r} = \nu^* \end{cases}. \qquad (4)$$

To summarize, each cost function computes and sends messages using equation 3; each selection function computes and sends messages using equation 4.

Max-Sum Operation. Max-sum is an approximate algorithm in the general case, but it is provably optimal on trees. Due to how we encoded the problem, the resulting factor graph contains a disconnected, tree-shaped component for each request r (see Figure 4). Thus, Max-sum operates optimally in this case. The algorithm is guaranteed to converge after traversing the tree from the leaves to the root and then back to the leaves again. In our case, the tree-shaped component for each request is actually a star-like tree, with the selection function s_r at the center, and all others connected to it. We are guaranteed to compute the optimal solution in two steps if we pick s_r as the root node of each component.

Typically, Max-sum's decisions are made by the variable nodes after running the algorithm. However, we have no variables in our graph because we eliminated them. Thus, we have to let either the selector nodes s_r or the cost nodes v_{pr} make the decision. Letting selectors choose is better because it guarantees that the same task is never simultaneously assigned to two different UAVs. Because the decisions are made by the s_r nodes, there is no need for the second Max-sum iteration (messages from selector to cost functions) anymore. Instead, the selector nodes can directly communicate their decision to the UAVs.

The logical Max-sum nodes include: a cost function v_{pr} for each each UAV ρ_p; and a selection function s_r for each request, that runs in its current owner.

Max-sum runs on our motivating example as follows. First, each leaf cost function v_{pr} must send its cost to the root of its tree, s_r. That is, UAV ρ_1 sends 1 to s_3 (within UAV ρ_2), and 5 to s_2 (within itself). Likewise, UAV ρ_2 sends 2 to s_2 and 2 to s_3, whereas UAV ρ_3 sends 7 to s_1. Thereafter, the s_r nodes decide by choosing the UAV whose message had a lower cost. Hence, s_3 (running within UAV ρ_2) decides to allocate τ_3 to ρ_1, s_2 allocates τ_2 to ρ_2, and s_1 allocates τ_1 to ρ_3. Upon receiving the allocation messages, each UAV knows precisely which requests have been allocated to itself.

3 Coordination Using Workload-Based Valuations

In realistic scenarios, requests do not appear uniformly across time and space, but concentrated around one or several particular areas, namely the *hot spots*. In that case, the assumption of independence in the valuation of the requests provides an allocation that assigns a large number of requests to the UAVs close to the hot spot, leaving the remaining UAVs idle. In these scenarios, the independence assumption is too strong. Next, we show that it is possible to relax this assumption while keeping an acceptable time complexity for Max-Sum. We introduce a new factor for each UAV: a penalty that grows as the number of requests assigned to the UAV increases. Formally, let $Z_p = \{z_{pr} | \tau_r \in R_p\}$ be the set of variables encoding the assignment to UAV ρ_p. The number of requests assigned to UAV i is $\eta_p = \sum_{r \in R_p} z_{pr}$. The workload factor for UAV ρ_p is

$$w_p(\mathbf{Z}_p) = f(\boldsymbol{\eta}_p) = k \cdot (\boldsymbol{\eta}_p)^\alpha, \tag{5}$$

where $k \geq 0$ and $\alpha \geq 1$ are parameters that can be used to control the fairness in the distribution of requests (in terms of how many requests are assigned to each UAV). Thus, the larger the α and the k, the fairer the request distribution.

The direct assessment of Max-Sum messages going out of the workload factor takes $O(N \cdot 2^{N-1})$ time, where $N = |Z_p|$. Interestingly, the workload factor is a particular case of a *cardinality potential* as defined by Tarlow *et. al.* [6]. A cardinality potential is a factor defined over a set of binary variables (Z_p in this case) that does only depend on the number of active variables. That is, it does not depend on which variables are active, but only on how many of them are active. As described in [6], the computation of the Max-Sum messages for these potentials can be done in $O(N \log N)$. Thus, using Tarlow's result we can reduce the time to assess the messages for the workload factors from exponential in the number of variables to linearithmic.

In addition, we can add the workload factor the cost factors that describe the cost for UAV ρ_p to service each of the requests. The following result[1] shows that if we have a procedure for determining the Max-Sum messages going out of a factor over binary variables, say f, we can reuse it to determine the messages going out of a factor h that is the sum of f with a set of independent costs, one for each variable.

Lemma 1. *Let f be a factor over binary variables $Y = \{y_1, \ldots, y_n\}$. Let $g(\mathbf{Y}) = \sum_{i=1}^{n} \gamma_i \cdot \mathbf{y}_i$ be another factor defined as the addition of a set of n independent factors, one over each variable y_i. Let $h(\mathbf{Y}) = f(\mathbf{Y}) + g(\mathbf{Y})$ be the factor obtained by adding f and g. Let*

$$\mu_{f \to y_j}(\mathbf{y}_j, \nu_1, \ldots, \nu_n) = \min_{\mathbf{Y}_{-j}} \left[f(\mathbf{Y}) + \sum_{k \neq j} \nu_k \cdot \mathbf{y}_k \right]$$

and $\nu_{f \to y_j}(\nu_1, \ldots, \nu_n) = \mu_{f \to y_j}(1, \nu_1, \ldots, \nu_n) - \mu_{f \to y_j}(0, \nu_1, \ldots, \nu_n).$
We have that $\nu_{h \to y_j}(\nu_1, \ldots, \nu_n) = \nu_{f \to y_j}(\nu_1 + \gamma_1, \ldots, \nu_n + \gamma_n) + \gamma_j.$

Thus, we can define a single factor that expresses the complete costs of a UAV when assigned a set of requests, that is the sum of the independent costs for each of the requests assigned plus the workload cost for accepting that number of requests. Formally the cost factor for UAV ρ_p is:

$$w_p(\mathbf{Z}_p) + \sum_{\tau_r \in R_p} c_{pr}(z_{pr}). \tag{6}$$

Summarizing, by introducing workload valuations that do not only depend on each individual request, but also on the number of requests, we have shown that it is possible to relax the assumption of independence between valuations with a very minor impact on the computational effort required to assess the messages (from linear to linearithmic).

---

[1] Due to lack of space the proof is provided in a technical report [7].

4   Empirical Evaluation

Next, we empirically evaluate our decentralized algorithms: (i) *d-independent*, that uses independent valuations on tasks; and (ii) *d-workload*, that employs workload-based request valuations. Comparing their performance against the current state-of-the-art is difficult because most methods can not cope with the communication range limitation of our problem. Thus, we implemented a relaxed version of the problem to compare against them. In this relaxation, UAVs delegate the allocation to a centralized planner agent, disregarding any communication limits. However, no request can be assigned to a UAV that is not aware of its existence. The central agent employs one of two different request allocation algorithms. The *c-independent* algorithm runs a single-item auction per request to allocate it to some plane. Hence, this technique assumes independent valuations for requests. In contrast, the *c-ssi* algorithm employs state-of-the-art Sequential Single Item [8] auctions to compute the allocation of requests to planes. Because we want to minimize the average service time, our SSI auctions employ the *BidMinPath* bidding rule as specified in [1]. Notice that these centralized methods are solving a simplified (less constrained) version of the problem.

We tested the performance of *c-independent*, *d-independent*, *c-workload* and *d-ssi* on multiple problems. Each problem represents a time-span (T) of a month. During that time, 10 UAVs with a communication range of 2 km survey a square field of $100\,km^2$. We assume that the UAVs always travel at a cruise speed of $50\,km/h$. In these scenarios, a single operator submits requests at a mean rate of one request per minute. We introduce four crisis periods during which the rate of requests is much higher. The requests submission times are sampled from a mixture of distributions. The mixture contains four normal distributions $\mathcal{N}_i(\mu_i, 7.2\,h)$ (one per crisis period) and a uniform distribution for the non-crisis period. The u_i means themselves are sampled from a uniform distribution $\mathcal{U}(T)$.

Next, we introduce two scenarios that differ on the spatial distribution of requests. In the *uniform* scenario, the requests are uniformly distributed, whereas the *hot spot* scenario models a more realistic setting where crisis requests are localized around hot spots. These spatial hot spots are defined as bivariate Gaussian distributions with randomly generated parameters. Figure 5 depicts an example of such scenario, where we painted one dot for each request. The scattered dots correspond to non-related requests, whereas related requests form dot clouds around their hot spot. Finally, the strong dot represents the operator, and the light circle surrounding it represents its communication range.

To use our *d-workload* method we have to set the values of k and α. Hence, we performed an exploration on the space of these parameters to determine which values are suitable to the *hot spot* scenarios. Figure 6 shows the results we obtained after this exploration. The colors correspond to the median of the average service time that we obtained after running the algorithm in 30 different scenarios for each pair (k, α). For instance, when $k = 10^2$ and $\alpha = 1.12$ the algorithm achieved a median average service time of $137\,s$. Observe that the algorithm exhibits a smooth gradient for any fixed value of α or k. Hence, good combinations of k and α can be found by fixing one parameter to a reasonable

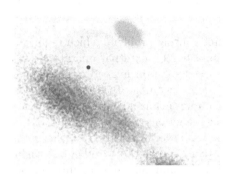

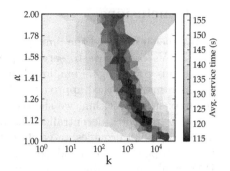

Fig. 5. Example task distribution in a Gaussian scenario

Fig. 6. Parameter exploration in the Gaussian scenario

value and performing a descent search on the other one. We chose $k = 1000$, and found the best corresponding α to be 1.36 with 0.01 precision.

Then we ran all the algorithms on a set of 30 new problems, to ensure that the parameters were not overfitted. In the *uniform* scenario, *c-independent* clearly obtains the best results. Figure 7 shows the results obtained by the other algorithms relative to *c-independent*'s performance (better algorithms appear lower in the graph). Surprisingly, dropping the independence assumption in these scenarios actually worsens performance instead of improving it. Nonetheless, the performance loss is much lower between *d-independent* and *d-workload* (5%) than between *c-independent* and *c-ssi* (17%).

In contrast, *c-ssi* obtains the best overall results in the *hot spot* scenarios. Figure 8 shows how the other algorithms fared in comparison. Our *d-workload* mechanism obtains very similar results than *c-ssi* (only 2% worse in median). Recall that *c-ssi* requires global communication between the agents, and can not be distributed without introducing major changes to the algorithm. Therefore, *d-workload* stands as the best algorithm when UAVs have limited communication ranges. These results show that, in the more realistic setting where there are request hot spots, relaxing the independence assumption provides significant gains in service time, both in the centralized and distributed algorithms.

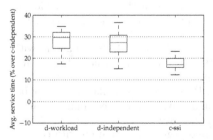

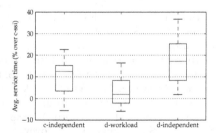

Fig. 7. *uniform* scenario results

Fig. 8. *hot spot* scenario results

5   Conclusions

This paper introduced the limited-range online routing problem, which requires that UAVs coordinate to serve requests submitted by external operators. To tackle this problem, we employed an MRF-based solution instead of the more common market-based approaches. Using a novel encoding of the problem and the max-sum algorithm, we showed that this approach can functionally mimic the operation of a decentralized parallel single-auctions approach. The MRF-based approach provides an easily extensible framework. In this case, we show that it is possible to introduce new factors to represent the workload of each UAV while maintaining low computational and communication requirements. Empirical evaluation shows that the improved version achieves 11% lower service times than the single-auctions approach. Moreover, the actual performance comes very close to that of employing state-of-the-art centralized SSI auctions. Because of the communication range limit, centralized SSI auctions can not be implemented in the real-world. Therefore, our workload-based mechanism is the method of choice for decentralized coordination with communication range limit.

Acknowledgments. Work funded by projects RECEDIT (TIN2009-13591-C02-02), AT (CSD2007-0022), COR (TIN2012-38876-C02-01), EVE (TIN2009-14702-C02-01), MECER (201250E053), the Generalitat of Catalunya grant 2009-SGR-1434, and the Spanish Ministry of Economy grant BES-2010-030466.

References

1. Lagoudakis, M., Markakis, E., Kempe, D., Keskinocak, P., Kleywegt, A., Koenig, S., Tovey, C., Meyerson, A., Jain, S.: Auction-based multi-robot routing. In: Robotics: Science and Systems, vol. 5. MIT Press (2005)
2. Sujit, P., Beard, R.: Distributed sequential auctions for multiple uav task allocation. In: IEEE American Control Conference, pp. 3955–3960 (2007)
3. Zlot, R., Stentz, A., Dias, M.B., Thayer, S.: Multi-robot exploration controlled by a market economy. In: Proceedings of IEEE International Conference on Robotics and Automation, ICRA 2002, vol. 3, pp. 3016–3023. IEEE (2002)
4. Butterfield, J., Jenkins, O., Gerkey, B.: Multi-robot markov random fields. In: Proceedings of the 7th International Joint Conference on Autonomous Agents and Multiagent Systems, vol. 3, pp. 1211–1214. International Foundation for Autonomous Agents and Multiagent Systems (2008)
5. Fave, F.M.D., Farinelli, A., Rogers, A., Jennings, N.: A methodology for deploying the max-sum algorithm and a case study on unmanned aerial vehicles. In: IAAI 2012, pp. 2275–2280 (2012)
6. Tarlow, D., Givoni, I.E., Zemel, R.S.: HOP-MAP: Efficient Message Passing with High Order Potentials. In: 13th International Conference on Artificial Intelligence and Statistics (AISTATS), vol. 9, pp. 812–819 (2010)
7. Pujol-Gonzalez, M., Cerquides, J., Meseguer, P., Rodriguez-Aguilar, J.A., Tambe, M.: Engineering the decentralized coordination of uavs with limited communication range. Technical report (2013), http://bit.ly/Xuo5yA
8. Koenig, S., Keskinocak, P., Tovey, C.: Progress on agent coordination with cooperative auctions. In: Proc. AAAI, vol. 10, pp. 1713–1717 (2010)

Concurrent CPU-GPU Code Optimization: The Two-Point Angular Correlation Function as Case Study

Miguel Cárdenas-Montes[1], Miguel Ángel Vega-Rodríguez[2], Ignacio Sevilla[1],
Rafael Ponce[1], Juan José Rodríguez-Vázquez[1], and Eusebio Sánchez Álvaro[1]

[1] Centro de Investigaciones Energéticas Medioambientales y Tecnológicas,
Department of Fundamental Research, Madrid, Spain
(miguel.cardenas,ignacio.sevilla,rafael.ponce,
jj.rodriguez,eusebio.sanchez)@ciemat.es
[2] University of Extremadura, ARCO Research Group,
Dept. Technologies of Computers and Communications, Cáceres, Spain
mavega@unex.es

Abstract. Nowadays many computational systems are endowed of multi-cores in the main processor units, and one or more many-core cards. This makes possible the execution of codes on both computational resources concurrently. The challenge in this scenario is to balance correctly both execution paths. When the scenario is simple enough, by-hand optimization can be affordable, otherwise metaheuristic techniques are mandatory. In this work, Differential Evolution algorithm is implemented to optimize a concurrent CPU-GPU code calculating the Two-Point Angular Correlation Function applied to the study of Large-Scale Structure of the Universe. The Two-Point Angular Correlation Function is a computationally intensive function, requiring the calculation of three histograms with different execution times. Therefore, this forces to implement a parameter for describing the percentage of computation in CPU per histogram, and the counterpart in GPU; and to use metaheuristic techniques to fit the appropriate values for these three percentages. As a consequence of the optimization process described in this article, a significant reduction of the execution time is achieved. This proof of concept demonstrates that Evolutionary Algorithms are useful for fairly balancing computational paths in concurrent computing scenarios.

Keywords: Code Optimization, Differential Evolution, Concurrent Computing, Two-Point Angular Correlation Function, GPU Computing.

1 Introduction

The maximization of the exploitation of the resources on an heterogeneous system, multi-core CPU and many-core GPU, requires an optimum balance between the execution time of the tasks assigned to CPU and to GPU. This forces to carefully select the amount of data analysed in each resource, which fairly balances both execution paths. Otherwise, an important penalization in the execution time might be produced.

In the previous version of this code, the amount of data analysed in CPU and GPU has been governed by a single parameter. This parameter governs the percentage of

C. Bielza et al. (Eds.): CAEPIA 2013, LNAI 8109, pp. 209–218, 2013.

galaxies analysed in CPU, while the remaining ones are analysed in GPU. This single parameter is applied to the three histograms that have to be built for the calculation of the Two-Point Angular Correlation Function (TPACF) when studying the Large-Scale Structure of the Universe. However, this strategy is quite naive and only partially satisfactory.

By measuring the execution time of each histogram construction when being executed completely in GPU, it has been proved that some of them take longer than others. These execution times are related to the nature of the data which the histogram analyses (positions of galaxies in the sky). The differences underlie on the data representation: on the one hand, galaxies randomly distributed on the sky, and on the other hand, galaxies distributed in clusters and superclusters following a particular cosmological model. These differences impact over the execution times through the construction of the histograms.

When histogramming galaxies with cosmological structure (clusters and superclusters of galaxies), most of the galaxies feed a reduced number of bins in the histogram. Then, the code must serialize a lot of increments in few bins. As a consequence, this produces an increment in the execution time. Oppositely, for random data the construction fairly distributes the counts in all bins, and therefore, less serialization is produced. In this case, the construction of the histogram operates with a higher degree of parallelism than in the previous case.

This scenario indicates that the strategy followed until this point —a single percentage for all the histograms— is quite naive. A single percentage does not balance correctly both execution paths in the histograms. Consequently, the most appropriate strategy is to propose independent percentages for each histogram. However, this increment in the number of parameters to optimize, in practice, impedes to fit the values by-hand, and makes necessary the use of evolutionary techniques for finding suitable values for them. It should be underlined that previous versions of this code have suffered from an intensive optimization process on the GPU part. Therefore, to produce an additional reduction of the execution time becomes a challenging task.

In spite of these efforts, the new astronomical surveys will largely increase the volume of data, and as a consequence, it will make necessary new developments and improvements. This motivates the present work, to evaluate the concurrent computing techniques to obtain an additional reduction of the execution time.

Due to its very simple and flexible implementation, Differential Evolution algorithm (DE) is usually proposed as first attempt to solve complex optimization problems. Moreover, DE is able to produce high-quality suboptimal solutions with a limited execution time budget. Python has been selected as programming language for the DE implementation.

The rest of the paper is organized as follows: Section 2 summarizes the Related Work and previous efforts done. A brief explanation of the underlying physics and the TPACF is presented in Section 3.1. In Sections 3.2 and 3.3, the most relevant details about the implementation are presented. The underpinning of the Statistical Inference is exposed in Section 3.4. The Results and the Analysis are displayed in Section 4. And finally, the Conclusions are presented in Section 5.

2   Related Work

The previous efforts done in the acceleration of the analysis of the distribution of galaxies can be classified in two categories. On the one hand, it can be mentioned the implementations of the TPACF problem into more powerful computing platforms: FPGA [1], GPU [2,3]. And, on the other hand, it can be cited the use of some tricky mechanism to reduce the complexity of the calculation without losing too much accuracy —i.e. kd-trees [4] or pixelization [5]—. The present work can be included in the first category; although no examples of concurrent implementation have previously been published.

No previous uses of Evolutionary Algorithms applied to the optimization of concurrent computing scenarios have been found in the scientific literature.

3   Methods and Materials

3.1   Underlying Physics

Recent progresses in observational cosmology have led to the development of the ΛCDM (Lambda Cold Dark Matter) model [6]. It describes a large amount of independent observations with a reduced number of free parameters. However, the model predicts that the energy density of the Universe is dominated by two unknown and mysterious components: the dark matter and the dark energy. These two components constitute the 96% of the total matter-energy density of the Universe.

Dark energy and dark matter have never been directly observed, and their nature remains unknown. Understanding the nature of the dark matter and the dark energy is one of the most important challenges of the current cosmology studies[1].

The distribution of galaxies in the Universe is one of the main probes of the ΛCDM cosmological model. The most important observable to study the statistical properties of this distribution is the Two-Point Angular Correlation Function (TPACF), which is a measure of the excess of probability, relative to a random distribution, of finding two galaxies separated by a given angular distance. By comparing different results in the correlation function, implicit comparisons between cosmological models are made.

The TPACF is a computationally intensive function. Taking into account that the astronomical surveys (Dark Energy Survey, the Kilo-Degree Survey or Euclid) expected for the forthcoming years will enlarge from dozens of thousands up to hundreds of millions of galaxies, and the number of accessible samples will also increase, then any improvement in the performance will be helpful to ameliorate the analysis capacity.

The TPACF, $\omega(\theta)$, is a measure of the excess or lack of probability of finding a pair of galaxies under a certain angle with respect to a random distribution. In general, estimators TPACF are built by combining the following quantities:

- DD(θ) is the number of pairs of galaxies for a given angle θ chosen from the data catalogue (D).

---

[1] The quantification of the budget between ordinary and dark components in the Universe is a major issue as proven by the recognition of the Science magazine in 1998 and 2003 as "Scientific Breakthrough of the Year".

- RR(θ) is the number of pairs of galaxies for a given angle θ chosen from the random catalogue (R).
- DR(θ) is the number of pairs of galaxies for a given angle θ taking one galaxy from the data catalogue (D) and another from the random catalogue (R).

Although diverse estimators for TPACF do exist, the estimator proposed by Landy and Szalay [7], (Eq. 1), is the most widely used by cosmologists due to its minimum variance. In this equation, N_{real} and N_{random} are the number of galaxies in data catalogue (D) and random catalogue (R).

$$\omega(\theta) = 1 + \left(\frac{N_{random}}{N_{real}}\right)^2 \cdot \frac{DD(\theta)}{RR(\theta)} - 2 \cdot \left(\frac{N_{random}}{N_{real}}\right) \cdot \frac{DR(\theta)}{RR(\theta)} \tag{1}$$

A positive value of $\omega(\theta)$ —estimator of TPACF— will indicate that galaxies are more frequently found at angular separation of θ than expected for a randomly distributed set of galaxies. On the contrary, when $\omega(\theta)$ is negative, a lack of galaxies in this particular θ is found. Consequently $\omega(\theta) = 0$ means that the distribution of galaxies is purely random.

3.2   Implementation of TPACF

Initially, the strategy for the GPU implementation pays attention to the use of shared memory for intermediary calculations and registers for frequently used data. Intermediary calculations are stored in shared memory, avoiding writing and reading operations in global memory, which is slower than shared memory.

Besides, the code is optimized by incrementing the data locality: frequently used data are stored in registers. Since each galaxy is analysed against all the rest, the coordinates of this galaxy are an excellent candidate to be stored in registers. Registers are closer to thread and faster than shared memory. Consequently, they are adequate to store this type of data. However, register storage is very limited (32 K registers per thread block), and an abuse of its use can lead to a depletion of this type of memory, and finally, to provoke a degradation of the performance.

By placing frequently used data or intermediate results in registers and shared memory, slow accesses to global memory are being replaced by fast accesses to these other types of memories.

The construction of the histograms: DD(θ), RR(θ) and DR(θ), is other potential bottleneck. Until this point, the sequence of commands in the kernel is: a multithreaded calculation has acted over the pairs of galaxies calculating the dot product, next the arc-cosine, and finally, the bin in the histogram where a count has to be added. Unfortunately, due to the multithreaded nature of the kernel, simultaneous updates of the same bin in the histogram can occur and must be avoided to do not loss any count. Therefore, the use of atomic operations becomes mandatory.

The use of atomic operations in global memory might cause a major performance degradation during the histogram construction. The alternative to overcome this drawback is a computational strategy where partial histograms are constructed in shared memory instead of a single histogram in global memory. Later, partial histograms are merged in a final histogram in global memory.

One of the most powerful abilities of the GPU is its capacity to parallelize a huge number of operations. For this reason, any operation tending to serialize them will provoke a performance degradation.

In the GPU architecture, a warp refers to a collection of 32 threads that are executed in a single time step. Each thread in a warp executes the same instruction on different data. This schema is extremely efficient if all the threads in the warp follow the same control flow path. However, if at least one thread follows a different control flow path — thread divergence—, then each path has to be serialized, and consequently the efficiency diminishes.

In reducing the thread divergence, the number of serialized threads is diminished, and an improvement of the performance is expected. For this reason, the if-conditionals in the kernel are substituted by *min()* function where possible.

On the other hand, the code implements a coalesced pattern access to the global memory. This is achieved by disposing the x-coordinates of all galaxies in a single array, and similarly for y-coordinates and z-coordinates. By implementing this data layout, adjacent threads in a block request contiguous data from global memory. Coalesced access maximizes the global memory bandwidth usage by reducing the number of bus transferences.

3.3 Differential Evolution Implementation

The evolutionary algorithm proposed in this work to fit the parameters governing the percentages of data analysed in CPU (%DD, %DR, and %RR) is Differential Evolution [8,9] under the schema DE/rand/1/bin [10]. The percentage of data analysed in GPU is $1 - \%$ of data analysed in CPU. The main features of this algorithm are its flexibility to deal with many different types of problems, and the speed in the implementation and in the execution, which allows quickly obtaining high-quality suboptimal solutions. The execution time of the whole process is, a priory, one of the most critical aspects of the problem. Due that each TPACF run takes around 250 seconds, the estimation of the execution time of the whole process (with a configuration of 10 vectors and 10 generations) will increase in two orders of magnitude in relation to a single TPACF run.

For the numerical experiments, a configuration of 10 cycles and 10 vectors have been established, although a very small production with 20 vectors is also performed. The initial values of the percentages are randomly selected in the range (0.03, 0.13). This range has been selected from the previous knowledge when executing the same problem with a single percentage.

In order to allow the manipulation of the CUDA code by other code, a Python implementation is proposed. This choice is based on the capacity of Python to handle pieces of text, to compose files with these pieces, to compile them, then to execute it, and finally to capture some output information. The output information is the fitness associated to the vector. By repeating this process, DE can make evolve the parameters: %DD, %DR, and %RR towards values which minimize the execution time.

As pseudorandom number generator, a subroutine based on Mersenne Twister [11] has been used in the Python implementation.

The numerical experiments have been executed in a machine with two Intel Xeon X5570 processors at 2.93 GHz and 8 GB of RAM, and a C2075 NVIDIA GPU card. CUDA release 5.0 and compute capability 2.0 have been used.

3.4   Statistical Inference

Statistical hypothesis is an essential method employed at the data analysis stage of a comparable experiment. For comparison purposes, two different types of tests can be applied: parametric or non-parametric. The difference between both types of tests rely on the assumption of a normal distribution for parametric tests, whereas non explicit conditions are assumed in non-parametric tests. For this reason, this type of tests is recommended when the statistical model of data is unknown [12].

The Wilcoxon signed-rank test belongs to the category of non-parametric tests. It is a pairwise test that aims to detect significant differences between two sample means [12,13]. The application of this test to our study will allow discern if the differences in the execution time when using different percentage values are significant.

In order to assess if the optimized parameters set performs better than the standard set, the sign test can be used. As well as the Wilcoxon signed-rank test, the sign test is a non-parametric test.

4   Results and Analysis

4.1   Single Percentage Implementation

Once the source code has been correctly assembled, Python implementation takes care about compiling the source code, to execute it, and finally, to capture the execution time. This last value corresponds to the fitness of each vector of the DE population. By repeating this process along the population and the generations, the code produces a set of optimized values for the three percentages.

Concurrent computation is possible because the construction of each histogram can be split in partial histograms. Firstly, input data are split in two chunks. These chunks are assigned to both computational resources: CPU and GPU, where the corresponding partial histograms are constructed. At the end of the process, both partial histograms are merged in the CPU. In the CPU part, a parallel implementation based on OpenMP is performed, whereas in GPU is based on CUDA.

When using a single percentage for the concurrent execution of the histograms, the fitness landscape presents a minimum in the range from 9% to 11% (Fig. 1). Unfortunately, the percentages that exhibit the lowest values (11%) and the lowest median (10%) do not coincide. This indicates the difficulty of the decision-making process about the most suitable percentage to minimize the execution time.

4.2   Multiple Percentages Implementation

By dividing the previous single percentage into three percentages, one per concurrent part of each histogram, a most suitable matching between the execution times of both

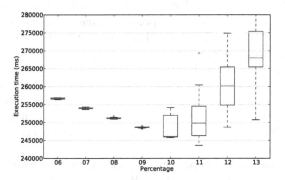

Fig. 1. Execution time (ms) of TPACF for concurrent execution by using a single percentage (12 executions per case)

computational paths is expected, and finally an extra reduction in the execution time. Although, the three parameters can be fitted separately, by freezing two histograms constructions and optimizing the remaining one, the relatively narrow time slot assigned to the optimization forces to run the optimization as a whole. Thus, each finished run produces a potential solution for later verification process.

When implementing the optimization process, each execution of the Differential Evolution code produces a candidate solution composed of three percentages which minimize the execution time (Fig. 2). The analysis of the results indicates a tendency towards larger values of %DD than for the other %RR and %DR. This result is consistent with the fact that DD histogram construction should take more time due to the galaxy clustering around low angles.

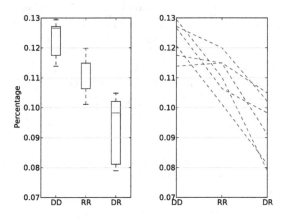

Fig. 2. Panel (a, left) shows the comparative box plots for the percentages of DD, RR and DR, while panel (b, right) shows the lines endorsing each particular realization.

Due that RR and DR histograms calculations involve random data, a lower number of serializations on the bins construction is expected. Therefore, these histograms should be faster than DD histogram calculation, and consequently to get lower percentage of data processed concurrently in the CPU.

By observing Fig. 2 and Table 1, it can be stated that a tendency towards graded values of the percentages:%DD >%RR >%DR is rawly achieved. The results mostly reproduce the structure expected for the percentages. However, an in-depth insight to the individual results (Right Panel in Fig. 2) demonstrated that the current implementation does not always produce sets with this schema, otherwise other schemas as %DD <%RR appear.

In order to check the quality of the achieved solutions, a new production with each particular percentage values set of %DD, %DR, and %RR obtained as optimizer so- lutions, is performed with 12 executions per case. In the two last columns of Table 1, the mean execution time (fitness) achieved, and the speed-up when comparing with the case of a single percentage with the lowest median (10%) are presented.

For some cases: R1, R3 and R4 the reduction of the execution time is relevant; whereas for other cases: R2 and R6 it is almost negligible. Finally, two cases: R5 and R7 do not produce any improvement in the execution time, even they take longer than the best case of single percentage (10%). These results underline the difficulty associated to

Table 1. Numerical results of the production with 10 vectors and 10 cycles: identifier, percentages of the best solution achieved, fitness (execution time of TPACF) of the best solution achieved, execution time of the optimizer run, mean and deviation standard of the fitness (execution time of TPACF) after 12 runs for this particular percentages set, and speed-up (compared when using a single percentage, 10%).

Id.	%DD	%RR	%DR	Best Fitness (ms)	Optimizer Execution Time	Mean Fitness (ms) 12 execution	Speedup
R1	12.66	10.64	9.82	241,888.5	1,029m11.296s	242,762.2±1,599.8	1.022
R2	11.39	11.49	10.49	242,691.7	1,026m41.409s	247,505.5±4,696.8	1.003
R3	12.94	11.01	7.90	242,810.7	1,043m30.935s	244,369.2±2,467.1	1.016
R4	12.06	10.12	8.11	244,090.9	1,053m57.763s	244,409.7±151.4	1.016
R5	12.72	12.00	10.21	242,427.0	1,041m49.962s	250,554.9±5,853.5	0.991
R6	11.75	11.49	9.10	243,011.7	1,041m46.596s	246,572.3±2,574.5	1.007
R7	10.40	11.60	9.37	244,596.7	1,043m14.309s	249,483.3±5,513.3	0.995

Table 2. Numerical results of the production with 20 vectors and 10 cycles: identifier, percentages of the best solution achieved, fitness (execution time of TPACF) of the best solution achieved, and execution time of the optimizer run.

Id.	%DD	%RR	%DR	Best Fitness (ms)	Optimizer Execution Time
R1	12.56	10.56	11.38	241,399.2	2,074m29.396s
R2	12.76	9.04	9.91	242,704.4	2,082m44.008s

obtain further reduction in the execution time of the optimized TPACF code. Moreover, the success cases demonstrate that the use of three percentages with the appropriate values face to a single percentage improves the productivity of the code.

In order to produce higher-quality solutions, diverse actions can be applied to the optimizer. Probably an increment in the number of cycles or in the population size might mitigate the adverse scenario, but at the same time, it will increment critically the optimizer execution time. Therefore, at this point a balance between the quality of the suboptimal solution and the execution time is mandatory.

As part of the production, two runs were executed doubling the population (Table 2). This increment results in an extra improvement of the fitness achieved, but unfortunately, a duplication of the execution time is produced too. This increment makes unfeasible to proceed with more improvements in the fitness through incrementing the population or the number of cycles.

When statistically analysing the numerical results of each production with the Wilcoxon signed-rank test, only the productions R1, R3 and R4 state that the differences are significant for a confidence level of 95% (p-value under 0.05). This means that the differences are unlikely to have occurred by chance with a probability of 95%.

Moreover, in order to assess if the performance is better than when using the best case of single percentage (10%), the sign test can be used. The analysis indicates that for the percentages obtained at R1, R3 and R4, the TPACF execution takes shorter than the previous best case, single percentage at 10%.

5   Conclusions

In this paper, the application of Differential Evolution algorithm to the optimization of a concurrent GPU-CPU code executing the Two-Point Angular Correlation Function is presented. This code has had a long track of successful optimizations in the past. Therefore, the achievement of any extra reduction in the execution time is a challenging task.

In the past, for distributing the computational tasks between the CPU and the GPU, a coarse-grained approach with a single percentage governing the whole concurrent part has been followed with satisfactory but limited results. By using multiple percentages —one percentage per histogram— an extra improvement in the productivity of the code is foreseen. However, the use of multiple percentages impedes by-hand optimization, and requires the implementation of an evolutionary technique to obtain suitable values for the percentages associated to the concurrent construction of each histogram.

As a result of applying Differential Evolution algorithm to the optimization of the three percentages, suitable percentages sets which produce a reduction of the execution time for the problem are achieved. This reduction reverberates in an increment of the productivity of the scientific collaborations where this code is used as analysis tool.

Beyond the particularities of the implementation presented, the work has demonstrated that evolutionary algorithms can be successfully applied to the correct balancing between multiple computational paths in concurrent computing.

Acknowledgements.   We thank the Spanish Ministry of Science and Innovation (MICINN) for funding support through grants AYA2009-13936-C06-03 and through the Consolider Ingenio-2010 program, under project CSD2007-00060. The research leading to these results has received funding from the European Community's Seventh Framework Programme (FP7/2007-2013) via the project EGI-InSPIRE under the grant agreement number RI-261323. We acknowledge the use of data from the MICE simulations, publicly available at http://www.ice.cat/mice

References

1. Kindratenko, V.V., Myers, A.D., Brunner, R.J.: Implementation of the two-point angular correlation function on a high-performance reconfigurable computer. Sci. Program. 17, 247–259 (2009)
2. Roeh, D.W., Kindratenko, V.V., Brunner, R.J.: Accelerating cosmological data analysis with graphics processors. In: Proceedings of 2nd Workshop on General Purpose Processing on Graphics Processing Units, GPGPU-2, pp. 1–8. ACM, New York (2009)
3. Cárdenas-Montes, M., Rodríguez-Vázquez, J.J., Ponce, R., Sevilla, I., Sánchez, E., Colino, N., Vega-Rodríguez, M.A.: New computational developments in cosmology. In: Ibergrid, pp. 101–112 (2012)
4. Moore, A., Connolly, A., Genovese, C., Gray, A., Grone, L., Kanidoris, N., Nichol, R., Schneider, J., Szalay, A., Szapudi, I., et al.: Fast algorithms and efficient statistics: N-point correlation functions. astroph0012333, 71 (2000)
5. Eriksen, H.K., Lilje, P.B., Banday, A.J., Górski, K.M.: Estimating n-point correlation functions from pixelized sky maps. The Astrophysical Journal Supplement Series 151(1) (2004)
6. Frieman, J., Turner, M., Huterer, D.: Dark Energy and the Accelerating Universe (2008)
7. Landy, S.D., Szalay, A.S.: Bias and variance of angular correlation functions. American Journal of Physics 412, 64–71 (1993)
8. Storn, R., Price, K.V.: Differential evolution – a simple and efficient heuristic for global optimization over continuous spaces. J. of Global Optimization 11(4), 341–359 (1997)
9. Price, K.V., Storn, R., Lampinen, J.: Differential Evolution: A practical Approach to Global Optimization. Springer, Berlin (2005)
10. Mezura-Montes, E., Velázquez-Reyes, J., Coello, C.A.C.: A comparative study of differential evolution variants for global optimization. In: GECCO, pp. 485–492 (2006)
11. Matsumoto, M., Nishimura, T.: Mersenne twister: A 623-dimensionally equidistributed uniform pseudorandom number generator. ACM Transactions on Modeling and Computer Simulation 8(1), 3–30 (1999)
12. García, S., Molina, D., Lozano, M., Herrera, F.: A study on the use of non-parametric tests for analyzing the evolutionary algorithms' behaviour: A case study on the cec'2005 special session on real parameter optimization. J. Heuristics 15(6), 617–644 (2009)
13. García, S., Fernández, A., Luengo, J., Herrera, F.: A study of statistical techniques and performance measures for genetics-based machine learning: Accuracy and interpretability. Soft Comput. 13(10), 959–977 (2009)

.Cloud: Unified Platform
for Compilation and Execution Processes in a Cloud

Fernando De la Prieta[1], Antonio Juan Sánchez[1],
Carolina Zato[1], Sara Rodríguez[1], and Javier Bajo[2]

[1] University of Salamanca, Deparment of Computer Science and Automation Control
Plaza de la Merced s/n, Salamanca, Spain
[2] Technical Univesity of Madrid, Department of Artificial Intelligence
Bloque 2, Despacho 2101, Campus Montegancedo, Boadilla del Monte, Madrid, Spain
{fer,anto,carol_zato,srg}@usal.es, jbajo@fi.upm.es

Abstract. Compiling is not only running a program that interprets a given
source file collection. In the compilation process, it is important the immediacy
and way of display the results, and the user interaction. In this research it
is proposed the creation of a unified platform (.Cloud) that supports editing,
compiling and running applications in multiple languages and that can execute
directly into the user's browser without installing any plugins, making it independent of the platform and operating system used. .Cloud will be independent
of the platform on which it runs, which will favor mainly to devices with limited resources, both hardware and platform software. The use of a Cloud tool
of this type also facilitates the work group within computing projects, allowing
multiple programmers working on the same data with optimized workflow.

Keywords: Cloud Computing, AI Applications, Cloud Storage, Utility
Computing, Cloud Compiling.

1 Introduction

The latest paradigm to emerge is Cloud computing [14, 2] which promises reliable
services delivered through next-generation data centers that are built on virtualized
compute and storage technologies. Although at first glance this may appear to be
simply a technological paradigm, reality shows that the rapid progression of Cloud
Computing is primarily motivated by economic interests that surround its purely
computational or technological characteristics [15]. As a result, the number of both
closed and open source platforms has been rapidly increasing [10].

The term "Cloud Computing" defined the infrastructure as a "Cloud" from which
businesses and users are able to access applications from anywhere in the world
on demand. Thus, the computing world is rapidly transforming towards developing
software for millions to consume as a service, rather than to run on their individual
computers.

To this end, it is necessary to take into account not only the underlying infrastructure, but also the services that are offered to the end user. Cloud computing platforms

C. Bielza et al. (Eds.): CAEPIA 2013, LNAI 8109, pp. 219–227, 2013.

has properties of clusters or grids environments, with its own special attributes and capabilities such strong support for virtualization, dynamically composable services with Web Service interfaces, value added services by building on Cloud compute, application services and storage. The infrastructure revolves around the concept of elasticity that autonomous, dynamic and automatic adaption, and learns from past experiences, with the aim of offering computational services of any type. The elasticity model constitutes the core of the system that, if correctly designed, will facilitate the remaining processes and their deployment in any environment independently of the physical features, operating system, etc. In conclusion, since user requirements for cloud services are varied, service providers have to ensure that they can be flexible in their service delivery while keeping the users isolated from the underlying infrastructure.

One of these new kinds of services and applications has to provide the capacity to develop software for cloud computing environments over the cloud itself. In this sense, this study presents .Cloud that is an IDE directly deployed over a Cloud Computing environment. This means, in fact, that .Cloud is an IDE that permit to develop software directly in the cloud (through the browser) without the need of install any kind of software in the user computer. Moreover, .Cloud allows to developers not only to program Web applications (HTML/CSS, PHP, Phyton, Perl an so on) but also traditional software (Java, C, etc.).

This paper is structured as follows, next section shows the state-of-the art of both Cloud Computing and cloud distributed compilation. Section 3 provides an overview of the .Cloud platform; and, finally, section 4 presents the results, conclusions and future work.

2   Compiling Software over the Cloud

The compilation can be defined as the process to translate a program written in a high level programming language into a machine code that the computer, where the program is going to be executed, is able to understand it. This definition has been accepted for a long time, however Cloud Computing is changed the traditional concept of computing environment and, for so, the compiling process has to evolve.

Cloud Computing can be considered as a metaphor for speaking about Internet. This technological paradigm helps to amplify the feeling of decentralization and obfuscation of the origin of information. Actually, Cloud is much more than Internet, or rather, it is over Internet and extends its services. So that, it can be consider as an abstraction of a complex mechanism that simplifies the services and provides a secure remote access to information (among other things).

A Cloud computing environment can be shown from two viewpoints [16]:

- At the *internal level*, the system consists of a set of physical machines (servers), which contribute to the system by means of their computational resources (processing capacity, volatile memory, etc.). These physical server forms the low layer of the infrastructure within the cloud environment. Over this physical layer, there is a virtual layer formed by units of hardware abstraction called virtual machines. This split of the infrastructure in two layers makes possible the external feel of unlimited resources, although obviously the infrastructure is limited to available resources.

• At the *external level*, a cloud computing system is composed of a set of services that are offered to the users. These services are commonly known as XaaS (XaaS: X as a Service) [17]. The most usual division consists in to split the services in three groups: Software, Platform, and Infrastructure. Software and platform services can be considered as web applications: the software layer know as SaaS (Software as a Service) provides a service with GUI (Graphical User Interface) to the end users similarity to the traditional software. the platform layer called PaaS (Platform as a Service) provides a set resources addressed to the developers. Infrastructure layer (IaaS, Infrastructure as a Service) is a layer that offers computational resources (Computational resources, storage, network, etc.) thanks to the virtualization layer described in the internal level.

Actually, the compilation and execution processes are very similar because the process of compiling consists of to act in a given set of files. The difference between executing and compiling is that in the compilation some parameters, such as the immediacy of generate and visualize the results, are less important. Besides, in compiling time, the interaction with the end-user is not import because the communication is only performed at starting and ending of the process.

Although, there are many examples of traditional IDEs (Integrated Developed Environment) such as Netbeans [13], Eclipse [6], JBuilder [12], .NET [1], App Cloud [3], etc. So far, there are few examples of compilation tools that are specific deployed for a Cloud Computing environment. Thus, it is possible to find the tool named Ideone [9] that offers a compiler and debugger for more than 40 programming languages through a web application. Other example is Compilify [5], which is similar to Ideone, and the first beta version allow to develop .NET applications writing in C#. And, finally, Cloud Compiler [4] which is framed under IBM operating systems OS/390 and z/OS, from the end user viewpoint works like a traditional compiler, but the compilation is done in a remote server..Cloud platform.

This section presents the .Cloud which is an IDE that allows to develop focus for and, also, in a Cloud Computing environment. This means that the developers do not have to install any software in computers and they only have to access to .Cloud deployed over a Cloud Computing environment.

.Cloud is deployed in the platform +Cloud [16, 7] that is a Cloud platform that makes it possible to easily develop applications in a cloud. This platform allows services to be offered at the PaaS (Platform as a Service) and SaaS (Software as a Service) levels. Both PaaS and SaaS layers are deployed using an internal layer, which provides a virtual hosting service with automatic scaling and functions for balancing workload. A more detailed description of each layer is provided below:

• **SaaS Layer.** This layer hosts a wide set of Cloud applications. +Cloud as environment offers a set of native applications to manage the complete Cloud environment: virtual desktop, user control panel and administration panel.

- **PaaS Layer.** The PaaS layer is oriented to offer services to the upper layer, and is supported by the lower IaaS layer. The PaaS layer provides services through RESTful web services [16] in an API format (i) the *File Storage Service* (FSS), which provides an interface for a container of files, emulating a directory structure in which the files are stored with a set of metadata, thus facilitating retrieval, indexing, search, etc; (ii) the *Object Storage Service* (OSS), which provides a simple and flexible schemaless database service oriented towards documents; and finally (iii), the IdentityManager (iM), which is the module of +Cloud in charge of offering authentication services to clients and applications;

2.1   +Cloud Architecture

.Cloud is divided into two main and independent components: the client application and the server application. This architecture is shown in Figure 1. Although, both client and server application can be deployed in the same remote server and the access from the end user can be done from an user agent, like a web browser. The advantage of this this splitting is that the client can be moved to another web server or infrastructure that is not directly supported by the Cloud environment; while the server is kept over +Cloud platform and it is in charge to perform the communications with other services within the cloud platform. The communication between them is done using web services.

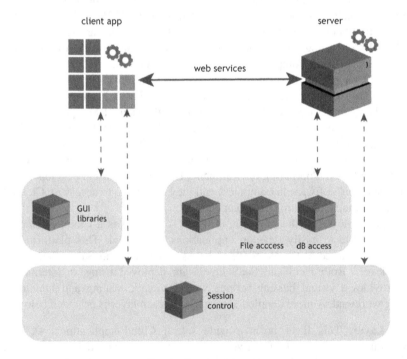

Fig. 1. Cloud architecture

A more detailed description of each layer is provided below

- The server application is in charge of manage the persistence of the data in the OSS and FSS. This server application can be framed in the PaaS layer of +Cloud. The access to OSS (object storage) is done through a specific entity classes called Compilator, Range, User and Project. The file storage is managed by the class Directory and it takes care of read/write operations.
- The client application includes the .Cloud GUI, this means, HTML for the visualization /CSS and Javascript for the control and generation of components. This client is deployed in the SaaS layer of the cloud architecture.

This division facilitates the execution of .Cloud in other user agent such as light clients for mobile device (smartphones, tablets, etc.), heavy desktop applications, etc. These new clients can be created without the need of changing the server side of the application.

2.2   .Cloud Services

Mainly, .Cloud provides two kind of services, one for program execution and another for compiling. Firstly, it is described the **programs' compiling** within the Cloud has to be modeled such as another kind of service (library, tool, etc.). To this end, the compiling process has to be structured such as black box where the end user invokes the service, the service execute the compilation process, and then the users gathers the results. This high level schema is shown in Figure 2.

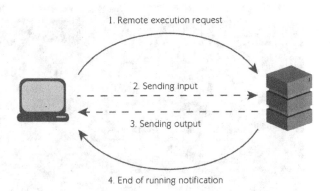

Fig. 2. Remote compiling process mechanism

As we said, the mechanism of **remote execution** is similar to the compiling process. It is shown in Figure 3. In the execution process, the client makes a remote execution request. This service creates two pipes within the system, one for read of data as input of the program, and the other one to write data as output of the program that is executed.

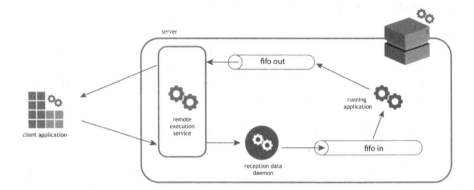

Fig. 3. Remote execution process mechanism

Both pipes are launched jointly with the program in execution, besides a daemon is launched and it is in charge of read the program output and send it to the execution service. This service, finally, returns this output to the client to be shown in the user agent, usually, a browser.

This daemon has a key role in the architecture, because it is in charge to keep the pipe open during the execution of the program. If it does not exist, the pipe will close

Fig. 4. Project editor

after the first output. This also triggers that the execution process will be canceled due to operating system restrictions. The writing daemon and the service exchange the information by means of a socket. This socket allows keeping open the communication during all the remote execution and avoiding busy-waiting.

With regards on the communication the first approach was to use RESTful web services, however there were some difficulties with this approach because it is not able to keep the session between the peers open. Finally, we have chosen to use an intermediate approach with REST service and PUSH technology. All services of .Cloud use JSON as exchange data language.

The server application has to provide a communication mechanism between the client and service, to gather and share the importation in execution time. This time depends on many factors (bandwidth, etc.); these factors also depend on the communication strategy (PUSH technologies). .Cloud has used long-polling mechanism in front of other strategies such as web-sockets, because long-polling offers a more reliable communication and more compatibility with the web browsers.

With the regards on the design of the GUI, it has been taken as reference other graphic features widely distributed web applications as Google Apps or iCloud, in which a simple and straightforward design helps the user to quickly guided by the interface. The interface is shown in Figure 4.

2.3   .Cloud Integration in +Cloud

.Cloud consider an environment with the following characteristics:

- +Cloud provide an object-oriented database (OSS) and storage files service (FSS).
- .Cloud has to allow the scalability of the system in terms of deployment of the system in many virtual machines.
- There is a virtual machine that centralized the information.

In order to allow that .Cloud can be executed in a Cloud environment, it is necessary to take into account that .Cloud can be executed in several virtual machines at the same time. If different end users are working with the same project at the same time, and this project is deployed in different virtual machines, .Cloud has to provide a process to update the information in execution time among all copies of the project (each of them used by a specific end user). To this end, there is a background program that ensure that every information is stored in the persistence layer (FSS and OSS) and at the same time this information is updated among all virtual machines that provide resources to .Cloud.

3   Results and Conclusions

This study presents .Cloud that is IDE specially developed to be deployed within a Cloud environment. .Cloud has been test in many traditional user agents (Internet Explorer 9, Safari, Google Chrome) as well as user agents of tablets and Smartphones

Table 1. Comparision between .Cloud and other similar platforms

	Netbeans	Eclipse	JBuilder	Visual Studio	App Cloud	Ideone	Cloud Compiler	Compilify	.Cloud
Projects	✓	✓	✓	✓	✓		✓		✓
Desktop version	✓	✓	✓	✓	✓		✓		
Browser version						✓		✓	✓
Debug tools	✓	✓	✓	✓	✓		✓		
Cloud storage					✓		✓	✓	✓
Multilingual	✓	✓	✓	✓					✓
Test tool	✓	✓	✓	✓	✓				
Workgroup tool	✓	✓	✓	✓			✓		✓
Additional complements.	✓	✓	✓	✓	✓				
Compiling and execution in a Cloud.					✓	✓	✓	✓	✓

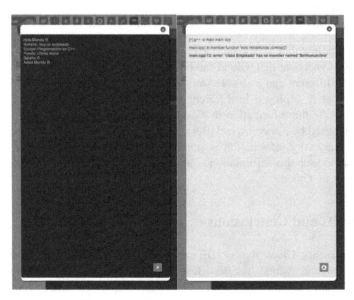

Fig. 5. Compiling and executing a Project

(Chrome Mobile and Safari for iOS) as shown in Figure 5. The forthcoming steps within the development of this platform will be the test the platform in a real environment with real end users.

As a conclusion, .Cloud presents a set of characteristics that are not provided for other IDES (traditional or cloud-based). Table 1 provides show a comparison between our platform and other platforms.

Acknowledgments. This research has been supported by the project SOCIEDADES HUMANO-AGENTE: INMERSION, ADAPTACION Y SIMULACION. TIN2012-36586-C03-03. Ministerio de Economía y Competitividad. Feder Funds.

References

1. .NET Framework, http://www.microsoft.com/net (Access: April 22, 2013)
2. Carolan, J., et al.: Introduction to Cloud Computing. Architecture. White Paper, 1st edn. Sun Microsystems (June 2009)
3. Cloud APP Studio, http://www.cloudappstudio.com/www/index.html (Access: April 22, 2013)
4. Cloud Compiling, http://www.cloudcompiling.com/ (Access: April 22, 2013)
5. Compilify, https://compilify.net/ (Access: April 22, 2013)
6. Eclipse, http://www.eclipse.org/ (Access: April 22, 2013)
7. De la Prieta, F., Rodríguez, S., Bajo, J., Corchado, J.M.: A multiagent system for resource distribution into a Cloud Computing environment. In: Demazeau, Y., Ishida, T., Corchado, J.M., Bajo, J. (eds.) PAAMS 2013. LNCS, vol. 7879, pp. 37–48. Springer, Heidelberg (2013)
8. (2008), http://www.gtsi.com/eblast/corporate/cn/09_09_2009/PDFs/Sun.pdfKLEMS
9. Ideone, http://ideone.com/ (Access: April 22, 2013)
10. Peng, J., Zhang, X., Lei, Z., Zhang, B., Zhang, W., Li, Q.: Comparison of several cloud computing platforms. In: 2nd In- ternational Symposium on Information Science and Engineering, ISISE 2009, pp. 23–27. IEEE Computer Society (2009)
11. Jacobson, I., Booch, G., Rumbaugh, J.: The united software development process. Addison Wesley (1999)
12. JBuilder, http://www.embarcadero.com/products/jbuilder (Access: April 22, 2013)
13. Netbeans IDE, https://netbeans.org/ (Access: April 22, 2013)
14. Mell, P., Grance, T.: The Nist Definition of Cloud Computing. In: NIST Special Publication 800-145. NIST, 1-3 (2011)
15. Buyya, R., Yeo, C.S., Venugopal, S.: Market-oriented cloud computing: Vision, hype, and reality for delivering it services as computing utilities. In: Department of Computer Science and Software Engineering (CSSE), The University of Melbourne, Australia. He, pp. 10–1016 (2008)
16. Heras, S., De la Prieta, F., Julian, V., Rodríguez, S., Botti, V., Bajo, J., Juan, M.: Corchado Agreement technologies and their use in cloud computing environments. Progress in Artificial Intelligence 1(4), 277–290 (2012)
17. Schaffer, H.E.: X as a Service, Cloud Computing, and the Need for Good Judgment. IT Professional 11(5), 4–5 (2009), doi:10.1109/MITP.2009.112

A SIR e-Epidemic Model for Computer Worms Based on Cellular Automata

Ángel Martín del Rey

Department of Applied Mathematics
E.P.S. de Ávila, University of Salamanca
C/Hornos Caleros 50, 05003-Ávila, Spain
delrey@usal.es

Abstract. In this work a mathematical model to simulate malware spreading is proposed. Specifically, it is an individual-based model whose dynamic is governed by means of a particular type of finite state machine called cellular automaton. Moreover, it is a SIR compartmental model, *i.e.* the population of hosts is divided into three classes: susceptible computers, infected computers and recovered computers, and the evolution between these states is ruled according to specific local transition functions involving boolean expressions. Several computer simulations are performed using different initial conditions.

Keywords: Malware propagation, Computer worms, Cellular automata, eEpidemic, SIR model, Computer networks.

1 Introduction and Preliminaries

Internet is probably one of the most important inventions of humans. It is a world-wide communication network that can be considered as an enormous digital library and publishing medium. People can share ideas and information (texts, images, videos, etc.) with a little more than a few keystrokes; Internet is open 24/7, and all users are able to instantly access all kinds of information from anywhere. However, this appealing scenario hides several dangers for the users and their computers: the malicious software is one of them.

Malicious software (malware in short) refers to software programs designed to damage or do other unwanted actions on a computer or network system. The worldwide economic and social impact of malware actions is high and consequently it is one of the most troubling security issues not only for large business but also for small ones and home environments. This problem has grown over the years along with the growth of the use of Internet. According to PandaLabs 2012 Annual Report 27 millions new strains of malware were detected during the year 2012 (the average number of new threats created every day had risen from 55.000 in 2009 to 74.000 in 2012).

The first malware software to gain public attention was computer viruses (a specific kind of malware); this term came about because of its similarities with

C. Bielza et al. (Eds.): CAEPIA 2013, LNAI 8109, pp. 228–238, 2013.

biological viruses that require a host organism to live and reproduce ([2,4]). Other types of malware are computer worms, Trojan horses, bots, logic bombs, spyware, adware, etc. A computer virus is a hidden and malicious program that infects a computer by copying itself to other programs or files. It is executed when the host program or the infected file is opened; subsequently it searches for uninfected files and tries to attach itself to them too. Unlike computer viruses, computer worms may not depend on other programs or victim actions for replication, dissemination or execution (a worm may replicate itself and, for example, send out a copy of itself to everyone listed in the contact/address book). Computer worms spread rapidly by taking advantage of file transport characteristics of the communication systems, and exploiting vulnerabilities exhibited by operating systems. Consequently, computer worms provide an efficient vehicle for the insertion of malicious payloads (if any) into network hosts on global scale. A computer worm basically consist of two modules: the spreading mechanism and the exploit mechanism.

The spreading mechanism transports the computer worm to the next target. It operates autonomously without an external assistance and is characterized by its spreading patterns in both space and time. This procedure can be either a topological or overlay spreading pattern. In the first case the spreading mechanism often ties to the IP addressing scheme: It commonly choses network addresses to probe and potentially infect in a sequential or random manner. In the second case the propagation is based on logical connections, relationships or knowledge existing in the environment (computer network, application-layer data, user data, etc.) Computer worms can be classified regarding to the speed of the spreading mechanism: fast spreading computer worms and slow spreading computer worms. In the first case when the computer worms reaches the host, immediately tried to probe other computer in the shortest way, then a great number of computer and bandwidth resources are consumed. On the other hand, slow spreading computer worm stays hidden in the host computer remaining dormant until certain trigger occurs; at this moment the computer worm is activated and try to propagate over the network usually proving a few number of machines.

The exploit mechanism takes advantage of the vulnerabilities (buffers overflows, vulnerable software, system services, weak passwords, etc.) of susceptible hosts in order to (unauthorized) access of the computer system. Many computer worms carry a malicious payload (that yields to the corruption of information contained in the hosts, the establishment of backdoors, the development of DDoS attacks, etc.) and may implement other functionality such as obfuscation techniques and learning abilities. Consequently, computer worms offers attackers an effective method to not only gain control but also to maintain it.

Taking into account this scenario, the analysis and design of mathematical and computational models that allow one to simulate the worm's spreading process is an important issue. In this sense, mathematical models provide theoretical foundation of control and forecast of malware. Several mathematical models related to this topic have been published in the scientific literature and the great majority are based on the use of differential equations (see, for example, [3,7] and references therein). Those are compartmental models since the population of hosts is divided into different classes: susceptible, exposed, infected, recovered, etc. In this sense SIR models (Susceptible-Infected-Recovered) play an important role when one try to simulate the dynamic of a fast spreading computer worm, whereas SEIR (Susceptible-Exposed-Infected-Recovered) models are suitable when slow spreading computer worms are considered (due to the existence of a latent period).

This work deals with fast spreading computer worms and consequently our attention will be focused on SIR models. There are few works published in the scientific literature introducing a SIR model for computer worm spreading and all of them are based on differential equations ([1,5,6,8,10]). Due to their own nature, these models based on differential equations present certain disadvantages such as the following: (1) They do not take into account interactions between hosts at the local level. Consequently, all the parameters involved are general and it is therefore impossible to observe the specificities of each computer. (2) They assume that the hosts are homogeneously distributed and that they are all connected with one another. When the spreading of the computer worm is macroscopically analyzed, results show a fairly accurate approximation to the real scene; nevertheless, it is not possible to obtain results at the microscopic scale (evolution of each computer), which are crucial to emergency management in situations of malware outbreaks.

These two deficiencies in the models based on differential equations may be addressed using cellular automata-based discrete models. These models allow for the contemplation of hosts' particular characteristics and of the different connection topologies, which may be changed over time. Cellular automata (CA for short) are finite state machines formed by a collection of n memory units called cells. At each step of time, they are endowed with a state from the state set given by a finite field (see, for example, [9]). The state of a particular cell is updated synchronously according to a specified rule function whose variables are the states of the neighbor cells at the previous time step. Unfortunately, as far we know, there is not any model based on cellular automata to study the spreading of computer worms on a computer network.

The main goal of this paper is to introduce a new mathematical model to simulate computer worm spreading. As this work deals with fast spreading computer worms that are mainly spreading by bulk e-mailing itself to those contacts existing in the address book of the infected hosts, the CA-based model proposed is a SIR compartmental model.

The rest of the paper is organized as follows: The basic theory of cellular automata on graphs is introduced in section 2; the mathematical model to simulate computer worm spreading is presented in section 3; in section 4 some simulations of the proposed model is given, and finally the conclusions are presented in section 5.

2   Cellular Automata on Graphs

A graph G is a pair (V, E) where $V = \{v_1, v_2, \ldots, v_n\}$ is an ordered non-empty finite set of elements called nodes and E is a finite family of pairs of elements of V called edges. The node v_j is said to be adjacent to the node v_i if there exists the edge $(v_j, v_i) \in E$. In this work we will consider undirected graphs, that is: $(v_i, v_j) = (v_j, v_i) \in E$ (v_j could be a adjacent to v_i, not vice-versa). The degree of a node v, d_v, is the number of its adjacent nodes.

A cellular automaton on a (directed) graph $G = (V, E)$ is a 4-uple $\mathcal{A} = (\mathcal{C}, \mathcal{S}, \mathcal{N}, f)$ where:

(1) The set $\mathcal{C}$ defines the cellular space of the CA such that every node stands for a cell of the cellular automaton.

(2) $\mathcal{S}$ is the finite set of states that can be assumed by the nodes at each step of time. In this sense, the state of the node v at time step t is denoted by $s[v, t] \in \mathcal{S}$.

(3) $\mathcal{N}$ is the neighborhood function which assigns to each node its neighborhood, that is: $\mathcal{N} \colon V \to 2^V$, $v \mapsto \mathcal{N}(v)$. Note that the neighborhoods of the nodes are, in general, different from others.

(4) The function f is the local transition rule that governs the dynamic of the cellular automaton. The local transition function f computes the state of every node at a particular time step $t + 1$ whose variables are the states of the neighbors cells at the previous step of time t, that is:

$$s[v_i, t+1] = f\left(s[v_{i_1}, t], s[v_{i_2}, t], \ldots, s[v_{i_{d_i}}, t]\right) \in \mathcal{S}, \tag{1}$$

where $\mathcal{N}(v_i) = \{v_{i_1}, v_{i_2}, \ldots, v_{i_{d_i}}\}$.

3   The SIR Model for Computer Worm Spreading

As is mentioned in Section 2 this work deals with fast spreading computer worms, *i.e.* there is not any dormant or latent period during the life cycle of the malware. Then, the computers of the network will be classified into the following three classes: (1) Susceptible computers, S: Those that have not been infected by the computer worm. (2) Infected computers, I: Those hosts that are reached by the computer worm. The malware is activated and it is able to propagate to another computer or file. (3) Recovered computers, R: Those that have been detected as infected by the computer worm and have been cleaned or quarantined.

Fig. 1. States of the computer where the computer virus is hosted

Consequently, the model is a SIR compartmental model where susceptible hosts becomes infected when the computer worm reaches them and infected hosts progress to recovered when the malware is detected and the countermeasures are successfully implemented. In Figure 1 a flow diagram with the evolution of the states of a computer is shown.

Moreover, in our model the following four assumptions are done: (1) The computer network is modeled as a directed graph $G = (V, E)$ with n nodes: $V = \{v_1, \ldots, v_n\}$ such that each node stands for a computer of the network. (2) There is an edge between the node v_j and the node v_i (i.e., $v_j v_i \in E$) if the email account associated to the node v_i is in the book address of the email account associated to the node v_j. (3) Any node computer is susceptible to be infected by the computer virus. (4) The number of nodes in the network remains constant throughout time and, as is mentioned above, at a particular step of time each node will be endowed with one of the following states: susceptible, infected or recovered.

The CA producing the dynamics of the system is defined as follows: The directed graph determining the computer network, $G = (V, E)$, gives the topology of the cellular space $\mathcal{C}$ (in this sense every cell stands for a node/computer). The state set is $\mathcal{S} = \{S, I, R\}$ and at every step of time the state of each cell is:

$$s[v, t] = \begin{cases} S, & \text{if the node } v \text{ is susceptible at time } t \\ I, & \text{if the node } v \text{ is infected at time } t \\ R, & \text{if the node } v \text{ is recovered at time } t \end{cases} \qquad (2)$$

The neighborhood of a cell v is formed by the cells/nodes of G adjacent to v.

Finally, the local transition functions that govern the transition between the cell's states are the following:

Transition from Susceptible to Infected: A susceptible computer v becomes infected when the computer worm reaches it, and it occurs when: the user has downloaded an infected software from a web page and/or the user opens an infected file attached to an incoming e-mail. The boolean function that model the transition from susceptible state to infected state is the following:

$$\mathtt{Inf}\left(\mathcal{N}\left(v\right), t\right) = \mathtt{d}[v] \oplus \bigoplus_{\substack{u \in \mathcal{N}(v) \\ s[u, t-1] = I}} \mathtt{m}[v, u], \qquad (3)$$

where d and m are random variables defined as follows:

$$\mathtt{d}[v] = \begin{cases} 1, & \text{with probability } \omega_v \cdot (1 - p_v) \\ 0, & \text{with probability } 1 - \omega_v \cdot (1 - p_v) \end{cases} \qquad (4)$$

$$\mathtt{m}[v, u] = \begin{cases} 1, & \text{with probability } \gamma_v \cdot \delta_{vu} (1 - p_v) \\ 0, & \text{with probability } \gamma_v \cdot \delta_{vu} \cdot (1 - p_v) \end{cases} \qquad (5)$$

where ω_v is the probability to visit a web page for downloading a file which could be suspect to be infected; p_v is the probability that the firewall installed in the computer detects the infected file; δ_{vu} is the probability that the user opens the attached file of an email from the neighbor node u, and γ_v the probability that the attached file will be infected.

Transition from Infected to Recovered: The computer worm can be detected by the antivirus software with probability $\tilde{p}_v$; as a consequence, if v is an infected node at time $t-1$ then:

$$\text{Rec}\,(v,t) = \begin{cases} 1, \text{with probability } \tilde{p}_v \\ 0, \text{with probability } 1 - \tilde{p}_v \end{cases} \tag{6}$$

Consequently the transition functions are as follows:

(1) $s[v,t] = S$ if $s[v,t-1] = S$ and $\text{Inf}\,(\mathcal{N}\,(v)\,,t) = 0$.
(2) $s[v,t] = I$ if $s[v,t-1] = I$ and $\text{Rec}\,(v,t-1) = 0$ or $s[v,t-1] = S$ and $\text{Inf}\,(\mathcal{N}\,(v)\,,t) = 1$.
(3) $s[v,t] = R$ if $s[v,t-1] = R$ or $s[v,t-1] = I$ and $\text{Rec}\,(v,t-1) = 0$.

4   Simulations and Discussion

In this section some simulations taking into account different scenarios will be performed and analyzed. The general assumptions are the following:

- A population of $n = 100$ hosts is considered in the simulations.
- The step of time is 1 hour.
- 168 iterations of the model are computed in every homogeneous simulation, that is, the evolution is computed for one week. In the case of heterogeneous simulations, 480 iterations are shown (20 days).
- The population of hosts is divided into four classes attending to the behavior of the user in regard with security awareness: Type I (experienced users), Type II (ordinary users awareness of security), Type III (ordinary users not awareness of security issues) and Type IV (novice users). Consequently, the values of the parameters involved in the model ($\omega_v, p_v, \delta_{vu}, \gamma_v$ and $\tilde{p}_v$) vary from one type to other.

Two scenarios will be considered. In the first one homogeneous conditions are stated, that is: (1) the topology of the cellular space is based on a complete graph (every host is connected with the rest of the hosts), and (2) the host belonging to the same category (Type I, Type II, Type III or Type IV) are endowed with the same parameters. Note that this scenario is similar to the ODE-based models. In the second one, we will consider heterogeneous (and more realistic) conditions: (1) the graph defining the cellular space will not be complete, that is, the neighborhoods are different from one to others, and (2) the values of the parameters are also different from one host to other (nevertheless, these values vary in the same range for every type).

Homogeneous Scenario. The values of the parameters used in these simulations are presented in the Table 1. Notice that all hosts of the same type have the same associated values and the following assumptions are made: (1) The parameter w_v is computed taking into account the number of downloads from a 'malicious" web page made in a period of time; (2) The parameters p_v and $\tilde{p}_v$ are computed taking into account the type of the user. In this sense, p_v (resp. $\tilde{p}_v$) will be higher for users of Type I (resp. Type IV) than others; (3) We will consider that all users open all e-mails independently of the sender (then $\delta_{uv} = 1$); and (4) The probability to send infected files also depends on the class of the host: this probability is higher in Type I than in other types.

Table 1. Values of the parameters depending on the host's class (homogeneous case)

Parameter	Type I	Type II	Type III	Type IV
w_v	1/720	1/360	1/168	1/24
p_v	0.5	0.4	0.25	0.1
δ_{vu}	1	1	1	1
γ_v	0.1	0.25	0.5	0.75
$\tilde{p}_v$	0.25	0.2	0.1	0.05

In Figure 2 two simulations with the evolution of the different classes of hosts (susceptibles, infected and recovered) are shown supposing that all hosts are susceptibles at time $t = 0$ and taking into account different sizes of the four types of hosts. In Figure 3 four simulations are introduced. In all of them the size of types is the same (Type I is 15%, Type II is 25%, Type III is 45% and Type IV is 15%) but there are infected hosts at time $t = 0$ which belong to different classes.

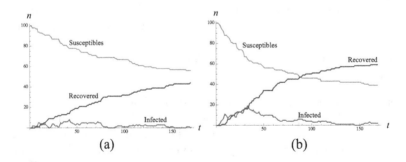

(a)   (b)

Fig. 2. Evolution of the number of the different compartments when homogeneous conditions are considered and different sizes of the types are used: (a) Type I (15%), Type II (25%), Type III (45%) and Type IV (15%). (b) Type I (15%), Type II (15%), Type III (35%) and Type IV (35%)

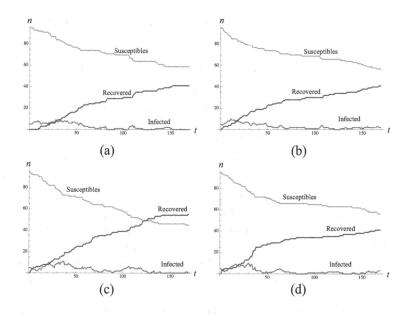

Fig. 3. The 5% of the population is infected at time $t = 0$ (a) The infected belong to Type I. (b) The infected belong to Type II. (c) The infected belong to Type III. (d) The infected belong to Type IV.

Although few simulations have been shown in this work, several have been done in laboratory. In all of them the trend is similar: there is an initial growth of the population of infected hosts whose speed and force depends on the following: (1) The size of the classes of users: the larger the sizes of the classes III and IV are, the more initial growing of infected compartment, and (2) The type of the infected hosts at $t = 0$: if initial infected hosts belong to types III and IV, there exists a notable growth of this compartment.

After the initial increasing of infected hosts, the evolutions shown by the simulations yield to a quasi-disease free equilibrium: the number of infected computers gradually decreases to reach a status close to the extinction, although some outbreaks appear periodically.

Heterogeneous Scenario. In this case the majority of the values of the parameters are not the same for all hosts belonging to the same type: they vary from a fixed range taking into account the main features of these classes (see Table 2). In this sense, the characteristics of the hosts are different from one to another. Nevertheless both the probability to download malware from web page, and the parameter representing the emails opening remain constants. The topology of the cellular space is defined by means of a graph with $n = 45$ nodes formed by three clusters of 15 elements which are joined across some of them (see Figure 4-(a)). In Figure 4-(b) a simulation of the global dynamic of the model is

Table 2. Values of the parameters depending on the host's class (heterogeneous scenario)

Parameter	Type I	Type II	Type III	Type IV
ω_v	1/720	1/360	1/168	1/24
p_v	[0.5,0.75]	[0.4,0.5]	[0.25,0.4]	[0.05,0.25]
δ_{vu}	1	1	1	1
γ_v	[0.05,0.25]	[0.25,0.5]	[0.5,0.75]	[0.75,0.95]
$\tilde{p}_v$	[0.75,0.95]	[0.5,0.75]	[0.25,0.5]	[0.05,0.25]

presented with the following distribution of classes: 7 hosts of Type I, 11 hosts of Type II, 20 hosts of Type III, and 7 hosts of Type IV. Moreover there is only one infected host at time $t = 0$ which is the union host between the left cluster (where hosts of Type IV are placed) and the middle cluster. The individual-based dynamic can also be computed due to the discrete nature of cellular automata. Some configurations of the system at steps of time $t = 0, 4, 13, 40$, and 90 are shown in Figure 5.

As in the previous case, the trend obtained from the simulations exhibits a quasi-disease free equilibrium. Nevertheless the force of the infection depends on the situation of the infected hosts at time $t = 0$ and the distribution of the types of host in the computer network. For example, if the hosts belonging to types III and IV are all concentrated in the same clusters (as is considered in the simulation of the Figure 5) the infection is mainly restricted to these clusters and it is reflected in the dynamic of the model. In this sense it is very important to pay special attention to these hosts that "join" clusters: the spreading of the malware could be contained if security countermeasures will be adopted in this nodes.

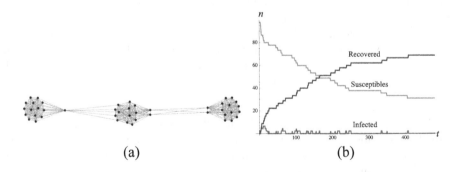

(a)   (b)

Fig. 4. (a) Graph topology of the computer network. (b) Evolution of the number of the different compartments when inhomogeneous conditions are considered.

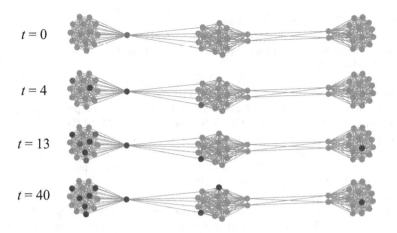

Fig. 5. Evolution of the state of every computer (green: susceptible computer, red: infected computer, blue: recovered computer)

5   Conclusions

A SIR mathematical model to simulate the propagation of a computer worm through a computer network is introduced. The mathematical tool used is a particular type of finite state machine called cellular automata on graphs and three classes of host are considered: susceptible, infected and recovered. By way of conclusions to this work, the following statements may be made: (1) The model is the first one based on cellular automata to simulate the behavior of a computer worm's spreading. (2) This model is an improvement on earlier ones (based on differential equations) since it allows for the contemplation of the specific characteristics of each of the hosts that make up the population, predicting both general and individual behavior. (3) It is crucial to accurately define the models parameters: topology, probabilities of infection and recovery, etc. (4) The model facilitates real-time predictions of the evolution of the malware spreading, making it possible to modify the different parameters and control measures.

Acknowledgments. This work has been supported by Ministry of de Economy and Competitiveness (Spain) and European FEDER Fund under project TUERI (TIN2011-25452).

References

1. Feng, L., Liao, X., Han, Q., Li, H.: Dynamical analysis and control strategies on malware propagation model. Appl. Math. Modelling (to appear, 2013)
2. Meisel, M., Pappas, V., Zhang, L.: A taxonomy of biologically inspired research in computer networking. Comput. Netw. 54, 901–916 (2010)

3. Mishra, B.K., Pandey, S.K.: Dynamic model of worms with vertical transmission in computer network. Appl. Math. Comput. 217(21), 8438–8446 (2011)
4. Murray, W.H.: The application of epidemiology to computer viruses. Comput. Secur. 7, 139–145 (1988)
5. Piqueira, J.R.C., Araujo, V.O.: A modified epidemiological model for computer viruses. Appl. Math. Comput. 213, 355–360 (2009)
6. Ren, J., Yang, X., Yang, L.-X., Xu, Y., Yang, F.: A delayed computer virus propagation model and its dynamics. Chaos Soliton Fract. 45, 74–79 (2012)
7. Toutonji, O.A., Yoo, S.M., Park, M.: Stability analysis of VEISV propagation modeling for network worm attack. Appl. Math. Model. 36(6), 2751–2761 (2012)
8. Wierman, J.C., Marchette, D.J.: Modeling computer virus prevalence with a susceptible-infected-susceptible model with reintroduction. Comput. Stat. Data An. 45, 3–23 (2004)
9. Wolfram, S.: A New Kind of Science. Wolfram Media Inc., Champaign (2002)
10. Zhu, Q., Yang, X., Ren, J.: Modeling and analysis of the spread of computer virus. Commun. Nonlinear Sci. 17, 5117–5124 (2012)

A Common Framework for Fault Diagnosis of Parametric and Discrete Faults Using Possible Conflicts

Noemi Moya Alonso, Anibal Bregon,
Carlos J. Alonso-González, and Belarmino Pulido

Depto. de Informática, Universidad de Valladolid, Valladolid, 47011, Spain
{noemi,anibal,calonso,belar}@infor.uva.es

Abstract. This work proposes a common framework for Fault Detection and Isolation of discrete and parametric faults in hybrid systems using Hybrid Possible Conflicts , HPCs. Fault detection is based on residual activation for the set of HPCs in the current mode. Using the structural information in each HPC we first search for discrete –related to actuators– fault candidates, because these faults introduce highly non-linear behaviors. To confirm or reject them, we track sets of HPCs in the current and potential faulty modes. We confirm the mode whose HPC residuals become zero, or start the fault isolation of parametric faults if every discrete fault is discarded. We test our approach in a hybrid four tank system.

1 Introduction

Hybrid systems can be found almost everywhere. Most of them are critical, so they must behave correctly, and in case of misbehavior, it should be detected quickly. Diagnosis systems allow accurate and fast fault detection and isolation.

The Model-based Artificial Intelligence community, known as DX, has approached hybrid systems modeling during the last 15 years. There are different proposals based on hybrid modeling [13,15], hybrid state estimation [10], or combination of online state tracking and residual evaluation [2,1]. All these solutions require to somehow model and eventually fully or approximately estimate the set of possible states, and to diagnose the current set of consistent modes. Both steps are computationally expensive or even infeasible for complex systems, but several solutions have been proposed [15,14].

The main source of hybrid behavior are discrete actuators, like discrete valves or switches in fluid or electrical systems, respectively. A fault in an actuator, that we will call a discrete fault, affects system dynamics, usually causing a mode change, thus modifying system behavior in a different way than a parametric fault [8].

Hybrid Possible Conflicts [4], HPCs, are an extension of Possible Conflicts [16], that rely upon Hybrid Bond Graphs, HBGs, [13] models to track hybrid systems behavior. HBGs are an extension of Bond Graphs (BG) [11] that model the discrete changes as ideal switching junctions which can be set to ON or OFF according to an automaton.

The main goal of this work is the definition and characterization of a common framework for Fault Detection and Isolation of discrete and parametric faults in hybrid systems. The new proposal uses Consistency-based Diagnosis, CBD, with HPCs for both, discrete and parametric faults. Once a fault is detected, and it can be related to a discrete fault, this kind of faults will be preferred candidates because they introduce highly non-linear behavior. We propose to track candidates for every possible new

C. Bielza et al. (Eds.): CAEPIA 2013, LNAI 8109, pp. 239–249, 2013.

mode, and reject those whose residuals do not become zero. Only if discrete faults are rejected, we start the parametric fault isolation stage.

The rest of the paper is organized as follows. Section 2 presents the case study used to illustrate our approach, and introduces HBG modeling. Section 3 summarizes HPCs. Section 4 describes the discrete fault diagnosis framework proposed in this work. Section 5 presents some results obtained in the case study. Section 6 discusses our approach against related work, and Section 7 draws some conclusions.

2   Case Study

The hybrid four-tank system in Figure 1(a) will be used to illustrate our proposal. The system has an input flow which can be sent to either tank 1, or tank 3 or both. Once the liquid in tank 1 reaches height h, tank 2 starts to fill. A symmetric configuration occurs for tanks 3 and 4.

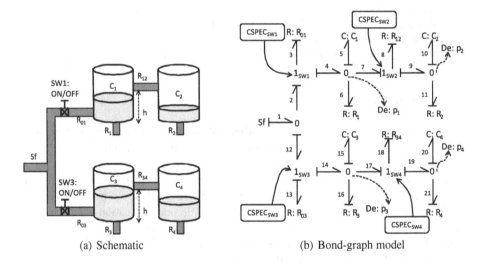

(a) Schematic   (b) Bond-graph model

Fig. 1. The four-tank hybrid system: schematic and associated bond-graph model

The methodology chosen to model the system in this work is Hybrid Bond Graphs, which are an extension of Bond Graphs. BGs are defined as a domain-independent energy-based topological modeling language for physical systems [11]. Several types of primitive elements are used to build BGs: storage elements (capacitances, C, and inductances, I), dissipative elements (resistors, R) and elements to transform energy (transformers, TF, and gyrators, GY). There are also effort and flow sources (Se and Sf), which are used to define interactions between the system and the environment. Elements in a BG are connected by 0 or 1 junctions (representing ideal parallel or series connections between components, respectively). Each bond has associated two variables (effort and flow). The rate of energy is defined as $effort \times flow$ for each bond. The SCAP algorithm [11] is used to assign causality automatically to the BG.

To model hybrid systems using BGs we need to use some kind of connections which allow changes in their state. HBGs [13] extend BGs by including those connections.

They are idealized switching junctions that allow mode changes in the system. If a switching junction is set to *ON*, it behaves as a regular junction. When it changes to *OFF*, all bonds incident on the junction are deactivated forcing 0 flow (or effort) for 1 (or 0) junctions. A finite state machine *control specification (CSPEC)* implements those junctions. Transitions between CSPEC states can be triggered by endogenous (autonomous) or exogenous (commanded) variables, called guards, as described in [18].

Figure 1(b) shows the HBG model of the four-tank system in Figure 1(a). The system has four switching junctions: SW_1, SW_2, SW_3 and SW_4. SW_1 and SW_3 are controlled *ON/OFF* transitions, while SW_2 and SW_4 are autonomous transitions. Both kinds of transitions are represented using a finite state machine. Figure 2(a) shows the automata associated with both kind of transition for SW_1 and SW_2. Automata for simmetric switches SW_3 and SW_4 are equivalent.

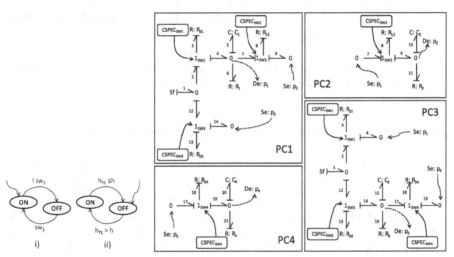

(a) Automata for commanded and autonomous transitions

(b) Bond graphs for the four PCs found for the four-tank system.

Fig. 2. On the left, automata associated with the commanded transition for SW_1, and for the autonomous transition in SW_2, respectively. On the right, the four HPCs found in the system.

3   Hybrid Possible Conflicts Background

The Possible Conflict, PC, approach is a model decomposition technique from the DX community [16], that have been successfully used for Consistency-based Diagnosis in continuous systems. PCs define minimal structurally overdetermined subsets of equations with minimal analytical redundancy to generate fault hypotheses from observed measurement deviations. In the original approach, only structural and causal information from the system model is used. PCs were originally computed using a hypergraph abstracting the structural model of the system. Recently, PCs can be directly computed from BG models [5].

The PC concept was recently extended to cope with hybrid system dynamics, modelled by means of HBGs [13], and it was named Hybrid Possible Conflicts [4]. Main advantage of HBG modelling is that does not require pre-enumeration of the system modes. However, using directly HBGs for fault diagnosis of hybrid systems [14] has the drawback of causality reassignment for the entire bond graph model, because during that process the diagnoser needs to stop tracking the behavior of the system, making it sensitive to miss faults that occur during (or immediately after) such reassignment process. HPCs simplify this process, because it has been shown [4] that if the HBG of the system has a valid causal assignment when all switching junctions are set to *ON*, then the set of HPCs can be uniquely determined from this configuration. For any given configuration, a transition of a switching junction from *ON* to *OFF*, or the other way around, have one of the following effects on an HPC:

- If the switching junction is not part of the HPC, the HPC remains the same.
- If the switching junction is part of the HPC and the transition induces a causality change in the HPC, new causality will be assigned and the HPC will be updated. If there is not a valid causal assignment, the HPC can not be used.
- If the switching junction is part of the HPC and the transition does not induce a change in causality, then either the HPC remains the same, or a subsystem of the HPC disappears or the whole HPC can not be used (because the discrepancy node disappears).

Hence, HPCs provide an efficient approach to hybrid systems fault diagnosis since:

- The set of HPCs is only computed in one configuration and does not need to be re-computed due to a transition in a switching junction. Also, HPCs that do not contain the switching junction can track and diagnose the system during the transition.
- The transition of a switching junction only requires to update causality on the HPCs that contain the switch, not in the whole system. This reassigment is efficiently performed online incorporating the proposal by Roychoudhury et al. [18]

For the case study we have found four HPCs, whose BG fragments are shown in figure 2(b). Each one of them estimates one of the measured variables (p_1, p_2, p_3, p_4).

For the system configuration where all the switches are *ON*, the relation between the HPCs and their related switching junctions can be seen in Table 1, which is called Hybrid Fault Signature Matrix (HFSM). This is an important information that we will use later in our proposal for discrete faults isolation.

For parametric faults, fault isolation is performed by means of the reduced qualitative fault signature matrix, RQ-FSM, shown in Table 2 for the mode where each switch is ON. Faulty parameters are represented as Θ. For a given mode, the Q-FSM can be online computed from the Temporal Causal Graph, TCG, associated to an HPC [13]. In Table 2 each column represents a measurement in the TCG obtained from the original HBG, which is also the source of a discrepancy for a HPC, and it shows the qualitative fault signatures as computed in TRANSCEND [13], except that it is minimal, i.e. each column represents the expected effect only in the measurement estimated by the HPC [6] for the set of faults, in rows, but do not propagate in the underlying TCG for any reachable measurement.

Table 1. Hybrid Fault Signature Matrix (HFSM) showing the relations between switching junctions and each HPC

Sw-j	HPC1	HPC2	HPC3	HPC4
1_{SW_1}	1		1	
1_{SW_2}	1	1		
1_{SW_3}	1		1	
1_{SW_4}			1	1

Table 2. Reduced Qualitative Fault Signature Matrix

Θ	HPC1	HPC2	HPC3	HPC4
C_1^+	-+			
C_2^+		-+		
C_3^+			-+	
C_4^+				-+
R_{01}^+	0-		0+	
R_{03}^+	0+		0-	
R_1^+	0+			
R_2^+		0+		
R_3^+			0+	
R_4^+				0+
R_{12}^+	0-	0-		
R_{34}^+			0+	0-

Table 3. Hybrid Qualitative Fault Signature Matrix

Sw-j	HPC1	HPC3
$1_{SW_1}(11)$	+	-
$1_{SW_1}(00)$	-	+
$1_{SW_1}(01)$	+	-
$1_{SW_1}(10)$	-	+
$1_{SW_3}(11)$	-	+
$1_{SW_3}(00)$	+	-
$1_{SW_3}(01)$	-	+
$1_{SW_3}(10)$	+	-

4 Discrete Fault Detection and Isolation

This section describes the proposed integration framework for fault detection and isolation in hybrid systems for both discrete and parametric faults. Prior to that, the meaning of discrete fault has to be clarified. Discrete faults in this work are defined as faults in discrete actuators, i.e. commanded mode switches that do not perform the correct action. Four faulty situations are considered (SW_i refers to switching junction i):

1. $SW_i = 11$: SW_i is stuck to ON (1).
2. $SW_i = 00$: SW_i is stuck to OFF (0).
3. $SW_i = 01$: Autonomous switch for SW_i from OFF (0) to ON (1).
4. $SW_i = 10$: Autonomous switch for SW_i from ON (1) to OFF (0).

Regarding faults profile, our current proposal works with single fault and abrupt fault assumptions. Abrupt faults appear instantaneously and its magnitude does not change afterwards (can be modelled as a step function).

For the sake of generality, we assume that the variable directly affected by a switching junction is not measured. Otherwise, discrete faults can be easily detected and isolated because they induce high non-linear changes in their governed system variables.

The main assumption in this work is that the operation mode of the system is known before a fault occurs. This assumption allows us to generalize the fault signature matrix method, usually applied to isolate parametric faults, to discrete faults. First, we define the Hybrid Qualitative Fault Signature Matrix (HQFSM): the signature matrix for the qualitative information about the effects of the discrete faults in the HPC residuals[1]. Qualitative signs represent the variation of the residual, which is built using the measured value in the actual system and the estimation for the measurement in the hypothetical mode we will be in if there is actually a fault. We just focus on the commanded mode changes. In our case study, there are only two commanded actuators: SW_1 and SW_3, we only build the HQFSM for SW_1 and SW_3, that can be seen

---

[1] Residuals are calculated as the actual value of the measurement - the estimated value.

in table 3. This HQFSM will allow rejecting those fault candidates whose residuals do not comply with the specification of the HQFS. Application of this rejection procedure requires knowing the system mode before a discrete fault occurs. Finally, since discrete faults generally have a bigger and potentially more dangerous influence in the system behavior, whenever possible, they will be considered as preferred fault candidates [9].

We will explain how we can track the hybrid system and how to perform fault isolation and identification for both discrete and parametric faults.

Tracking of hybrid systems can be performed using Hybrid PCs [4]. Initially, the set of HPCs is built assuming all switching junctions are set to *ON*. Afterwards, the set of models for the HPCs for the actual mode are efficiently built, and they start tracking the system. Whenever a mode change, commanded or autonomous is detected, a new set of models for the HPCs is computed online. In case a fault arises, some of the residuals must be activated, i.e. the HPC residuals must be significantly different from zero.

Based on the activated residuals for the set of active HPCs, the structural information in the HQFSM (table 3), and the QFSM (table 2), we build the current set of fault candidates. This set can contain both discrete and parametric faults. If there is no discrete fault as a fault candidate, we perform regular fault isolation and identification as described in [5]. Otherwise, we consider discrete faults as preferred candidates.

Discrete faults will be tested to confirm or discard them, hence we look at the HFSM (Table 1) to identify affected SW_i according to the activated PCs. Meanwhile, the HPCs tracking the system before the detection time will continue doing it to update the set of candidates in case of new activations.

We look at the QFSM of activated HPCs in Table 2. Those qualitative signatures that do not match observed signatures can be rejected. For each discrete fault whose qualitative signature matches the HQFSM (table 3), we build a new potential mode, i.e. a new configuration of HPCs, and we simulate them during a period σ_t. Eventually, during that σ_t period, the HPCs from the actual mode will converge. If all the HPCs of a candidate mode converge, their residuals are deactivated, the discrete fault is identified, so the initial HPCs are stopped and the HPCs from the new mode continue tracking the system. If none of the tested modes converges, their set of HPCs are deactivated, and the fault is assumed to be parametric, starting the common parametric fault detection and isolation procedure using the reduced QFSM (Table 2) to obtain an isolation as accurate as possible.

5   Results

Several scenarios have been tested to validate this approach: autonomous and commanded transitions that must not be detected, and fault injections (both discrete and parametric) that must be detected and isolated. We have run several experiments with different mode configurations and faults – varying the size, time of fault occurrence, even introducing faults immediately after the mode change–, obtaining satisfactory results in all of them. Due to space limitations, we explain here the results on two of those scenarios. Both experiments were run during 700 s using a sampling period of 1 s; the noise level is set to 5%.

Discrete Fault in SW_1. First experiment begins when all the tanks are empty, and we start filling the system. Values for the four switches are: $\{ON, OFF, ON, OFF\}$, respectively. After 500 s, we introduce a discrete fault in SW_1: the switch goes OFF. Figure 3(a) shows the evolution of the pressures in tanks 1, and 3, and their residuals for HPC_1, and HPC_3. Fault detection is done at $t = 502$ s, and looking at Table 1, we see that every discrete fault is a potential candidate.

At $t = 507$s, we can compute the fault signatures: a $0-$ signature is derived for HPC_1 residual, and a $0+$ signature is derived for HPC_3 residual. Looking at Table 3 and comparing with the actual fault signatures, we conclude that only four discrete faults are consistent with current observations: $1_{SW_1}(00), 1_{SW_1}(10), 1_{SW_3}(11)$, and $1_{SW_3}(01)$. Since we know that current state has every switch to ON, only two of them are possible (discrete faults $1_{SW_i}(1-)$): an autonomous transition to OFF in SW_1: $1_{SW_1}(10)$, and stuck ON in SW_3: $1_{SW_1}(11)$.

Our hybrid diagnosis framework creates two different instances of the HPCs in the system, one for each fault candidate. It quickly reassigns causality by running Hybrid SCAP for the mode transitions, and tracks the system for an empirically determined time interval σ_t(in this work, since system dynamics are quite fast we used $\sigma_t = 20$s) to isolate the fault. This tracking can be seen in Figure 3(b), and 3(c), for SW_1 and SW_3 fault candidates, respectively. As can be seen, only the HPCs estimations for hypothesized autonomous transition to OFF in SW_1 are able to track the current behavior (the residuals go to zero). Since the other hypothesized fault can not recover their residuals, it is rejected as a valid candidate.

Parametric Fault in R_{01}. Second experiment corresponds to a 20% blockage fault in R_{01} for the same initial configuration. The fault is introduced at time $t = 500$ s, leading to fault detection by HPC_1 and HPC_3 residuals at $t = 505$ s. Looking at Table 1, we see again that there are discrete fault candidates.

At time 511 s a $0-$ signature is derived for HPC_1 residual, and a $0+$ signature is derived for HPC_3 residual. These are the same signatures as in the previous experiment, then the set of candidates are the same.

The hybrid diagnosis framework creates two different instances of the HPCs in the system, Hybrid SCAP reassigns causality for the mode transitions, and tracks the system for the empirically determined time interval of 20 s. For this scenario none of the discrete fault candidates can be confirmed as the true fault in the system (all the residuals diverge); as a result, the isolation algorithm discards a discrete fault in the system. Next step in the algorithm is to hypothesize parametric faults. Looking at Table 2, we see that the fault signatures obtained for HPC_1 and HPC_3 only match the fault in R_{01}, thus confirming R_{01} as the true fault in the system, without further calculations.

6   Related Work

Only recently existing approaches have been able to cope with both parametric and discrete faults using a unique framework.

Initial works from the Control Theory community using parameterized ARRs [7] are not suitable for systems with high non-linearities or a large set of modes. Purely

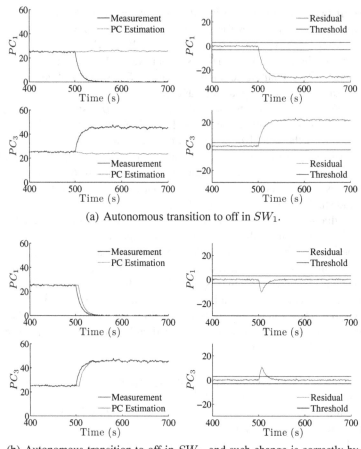

(a) Autonomous transition to off in SW_1.

(b) Autonomous transition to off in SW_1, and such change is correctly hypothesized.

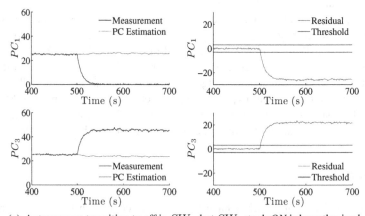

(c) Autonomous transition to off in SW_1, but SW_3 stuck ON is hypothesized.

Fig. 3. Measurements and estimations of HPC_1 and HPC_3, and their corresponding residuals, for an autonomous transition in SW_1

discrete models [12] are not feasible for the estimation of both continuous and discrete behavior.

In the DX community, most approaches regarding discrete faults require to follow every possible state [10,3]. Our approach assumes that we can identify the next state based on the estimation of the current one and the autonomous or commanded transitions. Recently, HyDe [15] deals with discrete faults, but in a generic framework that allows continuous, discrete and stochastic models. HyDe requires a model for the transition behavior of the system, which is not necessary in our approach.

Baydouh et al. [1] derive the set of ARRs for each mode, using a parity-space approach, avoiding the estimation of the continuous state. Our proposal also uses information of the HPC's residuals, but we do not need to build the set of HPCs for each mode. Additionally, we do not require an additional Discrete Event System for diagnosis.

Rienmuller et al. [17] couple the state estimator hME [10] with the framework proposed in [1]. Results of residuals from parameterized ARRs are analysed and used to focus the state-estimation process. Both steps work interleaved. Our framework just uses the result from the HPCs residuals of the most probable states, but not all of them are needed.

The HPCs approach elaborates on the TRANSCEND proposal for diagnosing hybrid systems using HBGs [14], and its extension to cope with discrete faults proposed by Daigle [8]. Main difference comes from using HPCs to focus the analysis of the switching junctions potentially responsible for the discrete fault, instead of analysing the whole model. Another difference is that we do not require the measurement of the flows related with the discrete fault. If that was the case, our proposal could obtain similar results and even lower response times.

7   Conclusions and Future Work

This work extends the HPCs framework [4] for fault detection and isolation of discrete and parametric faults. Assuming operation modes are related to changes in commanded and autonomous switches, we do not need to explicitly model changes in the configuration. We use structural information in the HPCs, the HFSM, to select candidates. Qualitative information in the HQFSM helps to reject conflicting candidates. We assume that HPCs in the correct state will provide rather quickly residuals close to zero. This proposal has been satisfactorily tested on several scenarios in a laboratory plant using simulation data.

We can conclude that using HPCs we deal with both parametric and discrete faults in a unified framework, by means of the fault signature matrix for both types of faults. We do not impose that the magnitude related to the SW_j modeling the discrete fault must be measured; instead, we use the HFSM to isolate discrete faults. The HQFSM, including qualitative information, speeds up the fault detection and isolation process.

Future work to improve this framework is to first include fault identification. We are also working on an integrated framework for hybrid systems fault detection, isolation, and identification using Dynamic Bayesian Networks to estimate the continuous behavior and also to identify parametric faults.

Acknowledgments. This work has been partially supported by the Spanish MCI TIN-2009-11326 grant and by the Regional Office of Education, and by the European Social Fund (ESF) through order EDU/1933/2008.

References

1. Bayoudh, M., Travé-Massuyès, L., Olive, X.: Towards Active Diagnosis of Hybrid Systems. In: Proc. of the 19th Int. WS on Pples. of Diagnosis, DX08, Blue Mountains, Australia (September 2008)
2. Benazera, E., Travé-Massuyès, L.: Set-theoretic estimation of hybrid system configurations. IEEE Trans. on Sys. Man Cyber. Part B 39, 1277–1291 (2009),
   http://portal.acm.org/citation.cfm?id=1656796.1656811
3. Benazera, E., Travé-Massuyès, L., Dague, P.: State Tracking of Uncertain Hybrid Concurrent Systems. In: Proc. of the 13th Int. WS on Pples. of Diagnosis, DX08, Austria (2002)
4. Bregon, A., Alonso, C., Biswas, G., Pulido, B., Moya, N.: Fault diagnosis in hybrid systems using possible conficts. In: Proc. of Safeprocess 2012, Mexico City, Mexico (2012)
5. Bregon, A., Biswas, G., Pulido, B.: A Decomposition Method for Nonlinear Parameter Estimation in TRANSCEND. IEEE Trans. Syst. Man, Cyber. Part A 42(3), 751–763 (2012)
6. Bregon, A., Pulido, B., Biswas, G., Koutsoukos, X.: Generating Possible Conflicts from Bond Graphs Using Temporal Causal Graphs. In: Proc. of the 23rd European Conference on Modelling and Simulation, ECMS 2009, Madrid, Spain, pp. 675–682 (2009)
7. Cocquempot, V., El Mezyani, T., Staroswiecki, M.: Fault detection and isolation for hybrid systems using structured parity residuals. In: 5th Asian Control Conference, vol. 2, pp. 1204–1212 (July 2004)
8. Daigle, M.: A qualitative event-based approach to fault diagnosis of hybrid systems. Ph.D. Thesis, Graduate School of Vandebilt University, Nashville, TN (May 2008)
9. Dressler, O., Struss, P.: The consistency-based approach to automated diagnosis of devices. In: Brewka, G. (ed.) Principles of Knowledge Representation, pp. 269–314. CSLI Publications, Standford (1996)
10. Hofbaur, M., Williams, B.: Hybrid estimation of complex systems. IEEE Trans. on Sys., Man, and Cyber. Part B 34(5), 2178–2191 (2004)
11. Karnopp, D., Margolis, D., Rosenberg, R.: System Dynamics: Modeling and Simulation of Mechatronic Systems. John Wiley & Sons, Inc., New York (2006)
12. Lunze, J.: Diagnosis of quantised systems by means of timed discrete-event representations. In: Lynch, N.A., Krogh, B.H. (eds.) HSCC 2000. LNCS, vol. 1790, pp. 258–271. Springer, Heidelberg (2000),
    http://portal.acm.org/citation.cfm?id=646880.710475
13. Mosterman, P., Biswas, G.: Diagnosis of continuous valued systems in transient operating regions. IEEE Trans. on Sys., Man, and Cyber. Part A 29(6), 554–565 (1999)
14. Narasimhan, S., Biswas, G.: Model-Based Diagnosis of Hybrid Systems. IEEE Trans. on Sys., Man and Cyber., Part A 37(3), 348–361 (2007)
15. Narasimhan, S., Brownston, L.: Hyde - a general framework for stochastic and hybrid model-based diagnosis. In: Proc. of the 18th Int. WS on Pples. of Diagnosis, DX07, Nashville, TN, USA, May 29-31 pp. 186–193 (2007)

16. Pulido, B., Alonso-González, C.: Possible Conflicts: a compilation technique for consistency-based diagnosis. IEEE Trans. on Sys., Man, and Cyber. Part B: Cybernetics 34(5), 2192–2206 (2004)

17. Rienmüller, T., Bayoudh, M., Hofbaur, M., Travé-Massuyès, L.: Hybrid Estimation through Synergic Mode-Set Focusing. In: Proc. of the 7th IFAC Symposium on Fault Detection, Supervision and Safety of Technical Processes, SAFEPROCESS 2009, Barcelona, Spain, pp. 1480–1485 (2009)

18. Roychoudhury, I., Daigle, M., Biswas, G., Koutsoukos, X.: Efficient simulation of hybrid systems: A hybrid bond graph approach. SIMULATION: Transactions of the Society for Modeling and Simulation International (6), 467–498 (June 2011)

Impact of the Production Mix Preservation on the ORV Problem

Joaquín Bautista, Alberto Cano, Rocío Alfaro, and Cristina Batalla

Universitat Politècnica de Catalunya
Avenida Diagonal 647, 7th floor, 08028 Barcelona, Spain
{joaquin.bautista,alberto.cano-perez,rocio.alfaro,
cristina.batalla}@upc.edu
http://www.prothius.com

Abstract. We present a sequencing problem given on *JIT* (Just In Time) manufacturing environments, with the objective of minimizing the variation of manufacturing rates (*ORV*: Output Rate Variation). Specifically, we propose an extension based on requiring to the sequences the preservation of the production mix throughout the products manufacturing. To solve the *ORV* and the extended problem, we propose algorithms based on *BDP* (Bounded Dynamic Programming) and we perform two computational experiments based on instances from the literature.

Keywords: Automobile industry, JIT manufacturing, Sequences, Scheduling algorithms, Dynamic programming, Heuristics.

1 Introduction

Mixed-products manufacturing lines are very common in *JIT* (Just In Time) and *DS* (Douki Seisan) environments and allow to manufacture variants of one or more products with same production system. These product units, despite having some degree of similarity (families), may require different use of resources (human resources, automated systems and tools) and components consumption in each of the workstations of the assembly line. Moreover, to obtain the final products, the parts that create each product (components), according to the *BOM* (Bill of Materials), are incorporated into the *WIP* (Work In Progress) following the line flow.

This flexibility of the line, due to the product variety, becomes necessary to determine the order in which the product units go through the line, according to three general principles: (I) a drastic reduction in component stock and semi-manufactured products, (II) efficient use of the available manufacturing time and (III) reduction of the work overload to the minimum. Thus, we find the sequencing problems, classified by [1] into three types (1) Mixed-model sequencing, (2) Car sequencing problem, and (3) Level scheduling.

This paper falls under the principle I and the problem type 3. Specifically, we focus on the study of the *ORVP* (Output Rate Variation Problem, a real problem) [2] and *PRVP* (Product Rate Variation Problem, an academic problem)

C. Bielza et al. (Eds.): CAEPIA 2013, LNAI 8109, pp. 250–259, 2013.
© Springer-Verlag Berlin Heidelberg 2013

[3] and we propose several approaches to treat both problems at once (desirable properties on the automobile industry). To solve the selected alternatives, in this paper we use a procedure based on Dynamic Programming using bounds [4].

2   *ORVP* and *PRVP*

2.1   The *ORV* Problem

The *ORVP* is described for the first time in a work by [2] dedicated to the Toyota production system, but its name comes from [5] and several heuristics ([2,4,6]) and exact procedures ([4,7]) have been proposed to solve it.

The problem focuses on sequencing, regularly, a total of D products, grouped into a set I of product types, of which d_i are of type $i(i = 1, ..., |I|)$. Moreover, the components are grouped into a set J. A product unit of type i requires $n_{j,i}$ units of component type $j(j = 1, ..., |J|)$. The objective is minimizing the variation in consumption rates of all components during the manufacturing of products. Thus, we can define the ideal consumption rate (constant over time) of component j as (1) and the ideal consumption of the component j when t products were manufactured as (2):

$$\dot{n}_j = \frac{1}{D}\sum_{i=1}^{|I|} n_{j,i} \cdot d_i \qquad j = 1, ..., |J| \qquad (1)$$

$$Y_{j,t}^* = \dot{n}_j \cdot t \qquad j = 1, ..., |J|; t = 1, ..., D \qquad (2)$$

Moreover, when t products were manufactured, of which $X_{i,t}$ are of type i $(i = 1, ..., |I|)$, the actual consumption of the component j $(j = 1, ..., |J|)$ is:

$$Y_{j,t} = \sum_{i=1}^{|I|} n_{j,i} \cdot X_{i,t} \qquad j = 1, ..., |J|; t = 1, ..., D \qquad (3)$$

The discrepancy or distance between the actual and ideal consumption of the component j when have passed through the line t product units is:

$$\delta_{j,t}(Y) = Y_{j,t} - Y_{j,t}^* \qquad j = 1, ..., |J|; t = 1, ..., D \qquad (4)$$

We can measure the non-regular consumption of components for D products through the discrepancies defined in (4); that is:

$$\Delta_R(Y) = \sum_{t=1}^{D}\sum_{j=1}^{|J|} |\delta_{j,t}(Y)|, \Delta_E(Y) = \sum_{t=1}^{D}\sqrt{\sum_{j=1}^{|J|} \delta_{j,t}^2(Y)}, \Delta_Q(Y) = \sum_{t=1}^{D}\sum_{j=1}^{|J|} \delta_{j,t}^2(Y) \qquad (5)$$

Where $\Delta_R(Y)$, $\Delta_E(Y)$ and $\Delta_Q(Y)$, are respectively the global rectangular, Euclidean and quadratic discrepancies of the components consumption.

Let $\Im_Y = \{\Delta_R(Y), \Delta_E(Y), \Delta_Q(Y)\}$ be the set of functions , then the resulting single-objective models for the $ORVP$ are:

M_ORV $Models$: $\qquad\qquad$ Min $f(f \in \Im_Y)$ $\qquad\qquad$ (6)

Subject to:

$$\sum_{t=1}^{D} x_{i,t} = d_i \qquad\qquad i = 1, ..., |I| \qquad\qquad (7)$$

$$\sum_{i=1}^{|I|} x_{i,t} = 1 \qquad\qquad t = 1, ..., D \qquad\qquad (8)$$

$$x_{i,t} \in \{0,1\} \qquad\qquad i = 1, ..., |I|; t = 1, ..., D \qquad\qquad (9)$$

Note that, constraints (7) satisfy the demand of all products; constraints (8) assign only one product unit to at each position in the sequence; and constraints (9) set the variables $x_{i,t} (i = 1, ..., |I|; t = 1, ..., D)$ as binary, taking the value 1 if a product unit of type i occupies the tth position of the sequence and 0 otherwise. Obviously, the link between the variables $x_{i,t}$ and $X_{i,t}$ is: $X_{i,t} = \sum_{\tau=1}^{t} x_{i,\tau}$ $(\forall i = 1, ..., |I|; \forall t = 1, ..., D)$.

2.2   The PRV Problem

The $PRVP$ is described for the first time in a work by [3] and its name comes from [5]. The problem focuses on sequencing, regularly, a total of D products, grouped into a set I of product types, of which d_i are of type i $(i = 1, ..., |I|)$ so that the production rates are maintained as constant as possible along the time in that the products are manufactured.

The $PRVP$ is a specific case of the $ORVP$ if we impose: (1) a bijective application between the sets I and J $(|I| = |J|)$ and (2) each product type requires one unit of component related through these application. In this case, we can define the following objective functions of non-regularity in production (X) between the actual and ideal productions over time:

$$\Delta_R(X) = \sum_{t=1}^{D}\sum_{i=1}^{|I|}|\delta_{i,t}(X)|, \Delta_E(X) = \sum_{t=1}^{D}\sqrt{\sum_{i=1}^{|I|}\delta_{i,t}^2(X)}, \Delta_Q(X) = \sum_{t=1}^{D}\sum_{i=1}^{|I|}\delta_{i,t}^2(X) \quad (10)$$

Where:

$$\delta_{i,t}(X) = X_{i,t} - X_{i,t}^* = \sum_{\tau=1}^{t} x_{i,\tau} - d_i \cdot t \qquad i = 1, ..., |I|; t = 1, ..., D \qquad (11)$$

Being $\dot{d}_i = d_i/D$ $(i = 1, ..., |I|)$ the ideal production rate of product type $i \in I$ and $\delta_{i,t}(X)$ the discrepancy or distance between the actual and ideal production of product i when t product units were manufactured.

If we define $\Im_X = \{\Delta_R(X), \Delta_E(X), \Delta_Q(X)\}$ as the set of functions, the resulting single-objective models for the $PRVP$ are:

$M\_PRV\ Models:$ $\qquad$ $Min\ f'(f' \in \Im_X)$ $\qquad$ (12)

Subject to: (7)-(9) from M_ORV Models.

2.3   Relation between the ORV and the PRV Problems

The $PRVP$ is a particular case of $ORVP$ when $I = J$ and $n_{j,i} = \delta_{j,i}$ (Kronecker delta). Furthermore, to establish a link between the solutions of both problems, we will use the properties derived from preserving a production mix when manufacturing product units over time.

Let $X_{i,t}^* = \dot{d}_i \cdot t$ be the number of units of product type i ($\forall i \in I$), of a total of t ($\forall t \in D$) units that should ideally be manufactured to maintain the production mix. And, let $\overrightarrow{X}^* = (X_{1,1}^*, ..., X_{|I|,D}^*)$ be the ideal point of cumulative production. Then, for the ideal point $\overrightarrow{X}^*$ the following is fulfilled: $\delta_{i,t}(X) = X_{i,t} - X_{i,t}^* = 0$ ($\forall i, \forall t$); and therefore, $\Delta_R(X), \Delta_E(X)$, and $\Delta_Q(X)$ are optimal and are equal to zero. In addition, the point $\overrightarrow{X}^*$ has the property of regularizing the consumption of components. In effect:

Theorem 1. For the ideal point $\overrightarrow{X}^*$: $\delta_{j,t}(Y) = Y_{j,t} - Y_{j,t}^* = 0$ ($\forall i, \forall t$).

Proof. We have: $Y_{j,t} = \sum_{i=1}^{|I|} n_{j,i} \cdot X_{i,t}^* \iff Y_{j,t} = \sum_{i=1}^{|I|} n_{j,i} \cdot \dot{d}_i \cdot t = t(\sum_{i=1}^{|I|} n_{j,i} \cdot \dot{d}_i) = t \cdot \dot{n}_j = Y_{j,t}^*$. Therefore, $\delta_{j,t}(Y) = Y_{j,t} - Y_{j,t}^* = 0$, ($\forall i \in I, \forall t \in D$).

Corollary 1: For point $\overrightarrow{X} = \overrightarrow{X}^*$, must be satisfied $\Delta_R(Y) = \Delta_E(Y) = \Delta_Q(Y) = 0$. Consequently, the functions of global discrepancies, rectangular, Euclidean and quadratic, of the components consumption are optimal.

3   Models for ORVP with Production Regularity

To address the $ORVP$ and $PRVP$ at once, we can use at least two ways of working: (1) Address the problems together as a multi-objective problem through the formulation and use of new models with bi-objective functions, and (2) add to the original $ORVP$ models a set of constraints that guarantee the preservation of production mix throughout the working day.

3.1   Bi-objective ORVP and PRVP Models

Based on Theorem 1 and the conclusions derived from it, we can state that the preservation of production mix is in line with the regularity of the consumption of components; so, if both properties are desirable, it is reasonable to formulate the following bi-objective models:

$M\_ORV\_PRV\ Models:$ $\quad$ $(Min\ f) \wedge (Min\ f')$ $\quad$ $(f \in \Im_Y, f' \in \Im_X)$ $\quad$ (13)

Subject to: (7)-(9) from M_ORV

3.2 *ORVP* Models with Production Mix Restriction (pmr)

From Theorem 1, we can also control the production regularity in sequences, if we limit the values of the variables of cumulative production, $X_{i,t}$ ($i = 1, ..., |I|$, $t = 1, ..., D$), to the integer values closest to the ideal values, $X_{i,t}^* = \dot{d}_i \cdot t$, because those variables must be whole integers. That is:

$$\lfloor \dot{d}_i \cdot t \rfloor \leqslant X_{i,t} \leqslant \lceil \dot{d}_i \cdot t \rceil \qquad\qquad i = 1, ..., |I|; t = 1, ..., D \qquad (14)$$

Where $\lfloor x \rfloor$ and $\lceil x \rceil$ are greatest integer less than or equal to x and smallest integer greater than or equal x, respectively.

If we impose the constraints (14) to the sequences, we can derive the following properties:

Theorem 2. If $\lfloor \dot{d}_i \cdot t \rfloor \leqslant X_{i,t} \leqslant \lceil \dot{d}_i \cdot t \rceil$, $(\forall i; \forall t)$, then $X_{i,t} - X_{j,t} \leqslant \lceil \dot{d}_i \cdot t \rceil - \lfloor \dot{d}_j \cdot t \rfloor$, $(\forall \{i, j\} \subseteq I; \forall t)$.

Proof. It is satisfied: $X_{i,t} \leqslant \lceil \dot{d}_i \cdot t \rceil$ and $\lfloor \dot{d}_j \cdot t \rfloor \leqslant X_{j,t}$, $(\forall \{i, j\} \subseteq I; \forall t)$.

Therefore, $X_{i,t} + \lfloor \dot{d}_j \cdot t \rfloor \leqslant \lceil \dot{d}_i \cdot t \rceil + X_{j,t} \iff X_{i,t} - X_{j,t} \leqslant \lceil \dot{d}_i \cdot t \rceil - \lfloor \dot{d}_j \cdot t \rfloor$, $(\forall \{i, j\} \subseteq I; \forall t)$.

Corollary 2: If $d_i < d_j$ then $X_{i,t} - X_{j,t} \leqslant 1$, $(\forall \{i, j\} \subseteq I; \forall t)$.

Using Theorem 2, we have $X_{i,t} - X_{j,t} \leqslant \lceil \dot{d}_i \cdot t \rceil - \lfloor \dot{d}_j \cdot t \rfloor$. Furthermore, $d_i < d_j \Rightarrow \lfloor \dot{d}_i \cdot t \rfloor \leqslant \lfloor \dot{d}_j \cdot t \rfloor$.

Therefore, we can write: $X_{i,t} - X_{j,t} \leqslant \lceil \dot{d}_i \cdot t \rceil - \lfloor \dot{d}_j \cdot t \rfloor \leqslant \lceil \dot{d}_i \cdot t \rceil - \lfloor \dot{d}_i \cdot t \rfloor \leqslant 1$ $(\forall \{i, j\} \subseteq I; \forall t)$.

Theorem 3. If $\lfloor \dot{d}_i \cdot t \rfloor \leqslant X_{i,t} \leqslant \lceil \dot{d}_i \cdot t \rceil$, $(\forall i; \forall t)$, then $X_{i,t} - X_{j,t} \geqslant \lfloor \dot{d}_i \cdot t \rfloor - \lceil \dot{d}_j \cdot t \rceil$, $(\forall \{i, j\} \subseteq I; \forall t)$.

Proof. $X_{i,t} \geqslant \lfloor \dot{d}_i \cdot t \rfloor$ and $\lceil \dot{d}_j \cdot t \rceil \geqslant X_{j,t}$, $(\forall \{i, j\} \subseteq I; \forall t)$ must be satisfied.

Therefore, $X_{i,t} + \lceil \dot{d}_j \cdot t \rceil \geqslant \lfloor \dot{d}_i \cdot t \rfloor + X_{j,t} \iff X_{i,t} - X_{j,t} \geqslant \lfloor \dot{d}_i \cdot t \rfloor - \lceil \dot{d}_j \cdot t \rceil$ $(\forall \{i, j\} \subseteq I; \forall t)$.

Corollary 3: If $d_i > d_j$ then $X_{j,t} - X_{i,t} \leqslant 1$, $(\forall \{i, j\} \subseteq I; \forall t)$.

From Theorem 3, we have $X_{i,t} - X_{j,t} \geqslant \lfloor \dot{d}_i \cdot t \rfloor - \lceil \dot{d}_j \cdot t \rceil$. Also, $d_i > d_j \Rightarrow \lceil \dot{d}_i \cdot t \rceil \geqslant \lceil \dot{d}_j \cdot t \rceil$.

Finally, we can write: $X_{i,t} - X_{j,t} \geqslant \lfloor \dot{d}_i \cdot t \rfloor - \lceil \dot{d}_j \cdot t \rceil \geqslant \lfloor \dot{d}_i \cdot t \rfloor - \lceil \dot{d}_i \cdot t \rceil \geqslant -1$ $\Rightarrow X_{j,t} - X_{i,t} \leqslant 1$, $(\forall \{i, j\} \subseteq I; \forall t)$.

Corollary 4: If $d_i = d_j$ then $|X_{i,t} - X_{j,t}| \leqslant 1$, $\forall \{i, j\} \subseteq I; \forall t)$.

From Theorem 2, $X_{i,t} - X_{j,t} \leqslant \lceil \dot{d}_i \cdot t \rceil - \lfloor \dot{d}_j \cdot t \rfloor \leqslant \lceil \dot{d}_i \cdot t \rceil - \lfloor \dot{d}_i \cdot t \rfloor \leqslant 1$.

From Theorem 3, $X_{i,t} - X_{j,t} \geqslant \lfloor \dot{d}_i \cdot t \rfloor - \lceil \dot{d}_j \cdot t \rceil \geqslant \lfloor \dot{d}_j \cdot t \rfloor - \lceil \dot{d}_j \cdot t \rceil \geqslant -1$.

Therefore: $-1 \leqslant X_{i,t} - X_{j,t} \leqslant 1 \Rightarrow |X_{i,t} - X_{j,t}| \leqslant 1$.

In this way, from M_ORV reference models, we have:

$$M\_ORV\_pmr Models: \qquad\qquad Min \ \ f(f \in \Im_Y) \tag{15}$$

Subject to: (7)-(9) from M_ORV and (14).

In this paper, we use the M_ORV and M_ORV_pmr models with the function $\triangle_Q(Y)$ as objective function f.

4   Use of *BDP* to Solve *ORVP* and *ORVP_pmr*

BDP (Bounded Dynamic Programming) is a procedure that combines features of dynamic programming with features of branch and bound algorithms related to the use of overall and partial bounds of the problem. The procedure determines an extreme path in a multistage graph with $D+1$ stages, explores some or all of the vertices at each stage $t(t = 0, ..., D)$ of the graph and uses overall bounds of the problem to remove, discard and select, stage by stage, the vertices most promising, then develop these, until the last stage D is reached.

To solve the *ORVP*, the algorithm *BDP* and the system of partial and overall bounds, *BOUND4*, designed for this problem [4], are used and the minimization of the function $\triangle_Q(Y)$ is fixed as objective.

Let be $q_{t,i}$ the minimum contribution of the product i situated at position t of the sequence (a procedure to calculate $q_{t,i}$ can be found at [4]). Then, the values of $q_{t,i}$ are ordered for fixed i in increasing order and, being $qo_{l,i}$ the value that occupies position l. The bound $BOUND4(t)$ is calculated as:

$$BOUND4(t) = \frac{1}{2} \cdot \sum_{i=1}^{|I|} \sum_{l=1}^{d_i - X_{i,t}} qo_{l,i} - \frac{1}{2} \cdot A(t) \tag{16}$$

Where $A(t)$ is the increment of $\triangle_Q(Y)$ of the product sequenced at stage t, and $d_i - X_{i,t}$ represents the pending demand of the product i. Finally the value used as guide in the *BDP* procedure is $LBZ = \triangle_Q(Y_{t-1}) + A(t) + BOUND4(t)$.

The procedure *BDP* is described following (see details on [8]):

BDP - ORVP_pmr

Input: $D, |I|, |J|, d_i(\forall i), n_{j,i}(\forall i, \forall j), Z_0, H$
Output: list of sequences obtained by *BDP*
0   *Initialization*: $t = 0$; $LBZ_{min} = \infty$
1   *While $t < D$ do*:
2                $t = t + 1$
3   *While* (list of consolidated vertices in stage t-1 **not empty**) *do*:
4   Select_vertex (t).
5   Develop_vertex (t).
6   Filter_vertex (Z_0, H, LBZ_{min}).
7   *End While*
8   End_stage ()
9   *End While*
End *BDP - ORVP_pmr*

To solve the ORV_pmr, the above procedure has been adapted for the $ORVP$ adding a mechanism to remove, at each stage ($t = 0, ..., D$), the vertices that do not satisfy the preservation conditions of production mix (14). This elimination rule reduces significantly the search space of solutions, because the number of vertices $H(t)$ to consider at each stage t of the graph is limited by the number of product types $|I|$ as follow:

$$H(0) = H(D) = 1; H(t) \leqslant \binom{|I|}{\lceil |I|/2 \rceil} \qquad t = 1, ..., D - 1 \qquad (17)$$

For example, in a set of instances with $|I| = 4$ for the $ORVP\_pmr$, a maximum window width of $H = 6$ will be sufficient to guarantee all optima.

The Theorems 2 and 3, and their corollaries, allowed us to incorporate to the BDP procedure different rules blocks, some of them with equivalent effect on the prune of the graph. In effect, when we reach stage t, $X_j(\forall j)$ is the satisfied demand of the vertex $J(t - 1)$ that is selected to be developed.

Let $J(t, i) = J(t - 1) \bigcup \{i\}$ be the new vertex to explore of stage t, built adding the product type i to the vertex $J(t - 1)$, then the following must be done: $X_i \leftarrow X_i + 1; X_j \leftarrow X_j$ ($\forall j$ if $j \neq i$). In these conditions, the following blocks of rules to discard vertices can be defined:

- $BLOCK\ 1$: Rules from (14)
  If $\exists j : (X_j < \lfloor \dot{d}_j \cdot t \rfloor) \vee (X_j > \lceil \dot{d}_j \cdot t \rceil) \rightarrow$ Discard vertex
- $BLOCK\ 2$: Rules from Theorem 2 and 3.
  $\forall j \neq i :$ if $\exists j : X_i - X_j > \lceil \dot{d}_i \cdot t \rceil - \lfloor \dot{d}_j \cdot t \rfloor \rightarrow$ Discard vertex
  $\forall j \neq i :$ if $\exists j : X_i - X_j < \lfloor \dot{d}_i \cdot t \rfloor - \lceil \dot{d}_j \cdot t \rceil \rightarrow$ Discard vertex
- $BLOCK\ 3$: Rules from Corollaries 2, 3 and 4.
  $\forall j \neq i :$ if $d_i < dj \wedge \exists j : X_i > X_j + 1 \rightarrow$ Discard vertex
  $\forall j \neq i :$ if $d_i = dj \wedge \exists j : |X_i - X_j| > 1 \rightarrow$ Discard vertex
  $\forall j \neq i :$ if $d_i > dj \wedge \exists j : X_j > X_i + 1 \rightarrow$ Discard vertex

5   Computational Experiment

5.1   Computational Experiment with ORV Reference Instances

The first computational experiment corresponds to 225 instances of reference [6] with 45 demand plans into 5 blocks (B), and 5 product-component structures (E), which represent the BOM. All instances have four product types ($|I| = 4$) and a total demand of 200 units ($D = 200$).

To obtain the optimal solutions from ORV and ORV_pmr models, the BDP was used under the following conditions: (1) BDP procedure programmed in C++, using gcc v4.2.1, running on an Apple Macintosh iMac computer with an Intel Core i7 2.93 GHz processor and 8 GB RAM using MAC OS X 10.6.7; (2) to reach the optima were used six windows width ($H = 1, 6, 64, 128, 512, 1024$), but to demonstrate all of them, $H = 2048$ and $H = 4096$ were necessary; (3) the initial solution, Z_0, for each window width was the solution obtained by BDP with the previous window width, except for $H = 1$, where $Z_0 = \infty$.

Given the models for ORV and ORV_pmr, the functions $\triangle_Q(Y)$, $\triangle_Q(X)$ and the set of instances E: (1) we determine the best solution for $\triangle_Q(Y)$ offered by both models for each instance $\epsilon \in$E, $S^*_{ORV}(\epsilon)$ and $S^*_{ORV\_pmr}(\epsilon)$; (2) from those best solutions we obtain the relative percentage deviations *(RPD)* for the values of the functions $f \in \{\triangle_Q(Y), \triangle_Q(X)\}$ as shown in (18). The main results of the experiment, using BDP, are collected in Tables 1 and 2.

$$RPD(f,\epsilon) = \frac{f(S^*_{ORV}(\epsilon)) - f(S^*_{ORV\_pmr}(\epsilon))}{f(S^*_{ORV}(\epsilon))} \cdot 100 \quad (f \in \{\triangle_Q(Y), \triangle_Q(X)\}; \epsilon \in E) \ (18)$$

The results show that that ORV_pmr is fifty times faster than ORV regarding the average CPU time required to demonstrate the optimal solutions $(\overline{CPU}_{ORV} = 11.32$ and $\overline{CPU}_{ORV_{pmr}} = 0.21)$ being the maximum $(CPU_{ORV} = 80.03; CPU_{ORV_{pmr}} = 0.22)$ and minimum $(CPU_{ORV} = 0.64; CPU_{ORV_{pmr}} = 0.17)$ lowest too. In addition, the CPU time, spent with ORV_pmr, does not depend on the instance solved. Other main results of the experiment, using BDP, are collected in Tables 1 and 2.

Table 1. Optima number reached[1] and demonstrated[2] for each window width (H)

H	1	6	64	128	512	1024	2048	4096
$ORV^{(1)}$	9	121	174	199	223	225	-	-
$ORV^{(1)}_{pmr}$	3	225	-	-	-	-	-	-
$ORV^{(2)}$	0	0	19	51	177	210	224	225
$ORV^{(2)}_{pmr}$	0	225	-	-	-	-	-	-

Table 2. Average values of $RPD(\triangle_Q(Y))$ and $RPD(\triangle_Q(X))$

	E1	E2	E3	E4	E5	Average
$RPD(\triangle_Q(Y))$	-5.02	-5.11	-1.60	-0.06	-10.92	-4.54
$RPD(\triangle_Q(X))$	39.24	19.03	5.11	0.17	37.03	20.11

In Table 1 we can see the optima reached and demonstrated for the window widths used. $H = 4096$ was necessary to demonstrate the optima of the 225 instances with ORV and $H = 1024$ was sufficient to reach them. For its part, ORV_pmr reached and demonstrated all the optima with a window width $H = 6$.

Finally, regarding the quality of the results, Table 2 shows: (1) an average worsening of 4.54% for optimal $\triangle_Q(Y)$ of ORV_pmr with regard to ORV; (2) the incorporation of the constraints (14) improves by an average of 20.11% the preservation of the production mix $(\triangle_Q(X))$; and (3) more radical average gains in $\triangle_Q(X)$ and average worsening in $(\triangle_Q(Y))$ in those product structures that move away from the possible equivalence between the $ORVP$ and the $PRVP$.

5.2 Computational Experiment with Instances from the *CSP*

The second computational experiment corresponds to 9 instances related to the *Car Sequencing Problem (prob001)* in the *CSPlib* library (www.csplib.org), without taking into account the constraints related to *the Car Sequencing Problem*. The total demand is $D = 100$ units in all instances and the number of components is $|J| = 5$, while the number of product types $|I|$ oscillates between 22 and 26. The maximum window width (H) required by *BDP* to demonstrate the optima, when the discard rules to preserve the production mix are incorporated, oscillates between $H \leqslant 705432$ (for $|I| = 22$) and $H \leqslant 10400600$ (for $|I| = 26$). However, in this computational experiment we used a maximum window width of $H = 1000$ taking as initial solutions those obtained with $H = 100$. We have compared the results obtained with *BDP* for the *ORV* and those obtained for the *ORV_pmr*, incorporating the constraints (14) or the rules to preserve the production mix. The main results are collected in Table 3.

Table 3. Values of $(\triangle_Q(Y))$, $(\triangle_Q(X))$, $RPD(\triangle_Q(Y))$, $RPD(\triangle_Q(X))$ and lower bound for $(\triangle_Q(Y))$ (LBZ_{min}) for the *ORV* and the *ORV_pmr*

	ORV		ORV_pmr		LBZ_{min}	RPD	RPD
Instance	$(\triangle_Q(Y))$	$(\triangle_Q(X))$	$(\triangle_Q(Y))$	$(\triangle_Q(X))$	$(\triangle_Q(Y))$	$(\triangle_Q(Y))$	$(\triangle_Q(X))$
4/72	48.7	1107.6	51.1	374.5	43.1	-4.8	66.2
6/76	47.2	1403.1	48.9	313.0	42.1	-3.7	77.7
10/93	47.1	1095.3	49.4	399.3	41.7	-4.9	63.5
16/81	44.5	1374.6	47.6	442.2	41	-7.1	67.8
19/71	45.8	762.9	49.5	410.3	41.7	-8.1	46.2
21/90	46.8	1176.0	49.7	393.4	42.0	-6.2	66.5
26/82	47.3	1300.9	49.4	401.9	42.0	-4.4	69.1
36/92	45.0	1089.9	48.3	376.0	40.7	-7.3	65.5
41/66	45.3	1233.0	49.5	320.6	40.5	-9.2	74.0
Average						-6.2	66.3

The solutions obtained for the *ORV* and *ORV_pmr* are not optimal. However, the bounds for $(\triangle_Q(Y))$ found through the *ORV_pmr* allowed us to find solutions for the *ORV* that are, on average for the nine instances, around 10.24% of the bound. The best solution obtained corresponds to the instance 16/81, whose value is located at a distance of 7.87% of his bound. The worst solution obtained corresponds to the instance 4/72, at a distance of 11.50% of his bound.

The average *CPU* times for each instance are 168s, for the *ORV*, and 96s for the *ORV_pmr*. The *CPU* time of the *ORV_pmr* is best in more than 40% compared with those of the *ORV*. Moreover, the improvement in the preservation of production mix $RPD(\triangle_Q(X))$ corresponds to a value of 66.3%, while the worsening in regular consumption of components $RPD(\triangle_Q(Y))$ corresponds to a value of 6.2%, when we incorporate to the *ORV* the rules related to the regularity on the production.

6   Conclusions

We have presented bi-objective and mono-objective models to the $ORVP$ with preservation of the production mix in the JIT and DS context.

From ORV and ORV_pmr models with quadratic function $(\triangle_Q(Y))$ for the consumption of components, we have realized two computational experiments using bounded dynamic programming as resolution procedure.

In the first experiment, with 225 reference instances from the literature, the incorporation of the restrictions to preserve the production mix into ORV, reduces to one fiftieth the average CPU time with BDP, being enough a window width of $H = 6$ to demonstrate all the optima. The component consumption regularity of ORV_pmr worsens by an average of 4.54 over ORV, but the gain of production mix preservation is 20.11%. In the second computational experiment, we have selected 9 instances from the Car $Sequencing$ $Problem$, corresponding to a high number of products. In this computational experiment, without reaching the optima, we obtained an average improvement of 66.3% in the preservation of production mix, and a worsening of 6.2% in regular consumption of components. The bounds obtained using BDP for the function $(\triangle_Q(Y))$ on the ORV_pmr problem improves to those obtained for the ORV, for all the instances.

Acknowledgments. The authors greatly appreciate the collaboration of Nissan Spanish Industrial Operations (NSIO). This work was funded by project PROTHIUS-III, DPI2010-16759, including EDRF funding from the Spanish government.

References

1. Boysen, N., Fliedner, M., Scholl, A.: Sequencing mixed-model assembly lines: survey, classification and model critique. European Journal of Operational Research 192(2), 349–373 (2009)
2. Monden, Y.: Toyota Production System. Industrial Engineering and Management Press, Norcross (1983)
3. Miltenburg, J.: Scheduling Mixed-Model Assembly Lines for Just-In-Time Production Systems. Management Science 35(2), 192–207 (1989)
4. Bautista, J., Companys, R., Corominas, A.: Heuristics and exact algorithms for solving the Monden problem. European Journal of Operational Research 88(1), 101–113 (1996)
5. Kubiak, W.: Minimizing variation of production rates in just-in-time systems: A survey. European Journal of Operational Research 66(3), 259–271 (1993)
6. Jin, M., Wu, S.D.: A new heuristic method for mixed model assembly line balancing problem. Computers & Industrial Engineering 44(5), 159–169 (2002)
7. Miltenburg, J.: Level schedules for mixed-model JIT production lines: characteristics of the largest instances that can be solved optimally. International Journal of Production Research 45(16), 3555–3577 (2007)
8. Bautista, J., Cano, A.: Solving mixed model sequencing problem in assembly lines with serial workstations with work overload minimisation and interruption rules. European Journal of Operational Research 210(3), 495–513 (2011)

Sustainable Internet Services
in Contributory Communities

Guillem Cabrera, Hebert Pérez-Rosés,
Angel A. Juan, and Joan Manuel Marquès

Internet Interdisciplinary Institute (IN3) - Universitat Oberta de Catalunya (UOC)
Roc Boronat, 117 7a planta, 08018 Barcelona
{gcabreraa,hperezr,ajuanp,jmarquesp}@uoc.edu

Abstract. The success of cloud computing services and the volunteer computing paradigm encouraged researchers to utilize user-donated resources for general purpose applications. The sustainability of this paradigm resides in making the most out of the existing under-utilized computer capabilities of Internet users. In this paper, we present a fast heuristic to determine which is the subset of hosts that consumes the minimum power while maintain a certain level of availability when a service is deployed on top of them in the framework of a large-scale contributory community. We evaluate our proposal by means of computer simulation in a stochastic environment.

1 Introduction

Cloud computing has become increasingly popular as a tool to outsource large computing infrastructures [2], which caused the data centers behind them to grow at an exponential rate. Those digital warehouses are usually made up by a significant amount of relatively homogeneous computing resources, stacked in racks inside cooled and secured server rooms. Strict administration and maintenance policies guarantee a certain level of service quality, and redundant ISP-managed network links connects them to the Internet. Maintaining these large infrastructures is neither cheap nor environmentally friendly [11]. Most of them consume vast amounts of energy not only to run active servers but also the network equipment, the cooling systems and idle servers. Hence, the *carbon footprint* [7] of these facilities is large enough to consider taking measures to reduce it.

Current trends [6, 8, 18] promote the use of non-dedicated resources for offering Internet services, as done in the Cloud Computing paradigm. Trying to go one step further in the use of non-dedicated resources than legacy Volunteer Computing systems and employing them for general-purpose computing, Lázaro proposed the contributory computing model [15], in which users contribute their resources to be used by anyone inside a community. Thus, a community-based cloud can be seized as a platform to deploy long-lived services. The uncertainty associated with these dynamic systems, where individual resources can fail or be disconnected at any time without previous notice, not only limits their use in practical applications but also restricts the complexity of the computations that

C. Bielza et al. (Eds.): CAEPIA 2013, LNAI 8109, pp. 260–268, 2013.

can be executed on them. In order to guarantee service availability over time in these scenarios, it becomes necessary to develop new methodologies that support efficient decision-making when selecting resources. These methodologies have to deal with large-scale networks, complex topologies and different host behaviors in order to support attractive services for the very end-user.

Besides the service availability, it would be profitable to reduce the energy consumption of every service deployed in a community. Energy consumption of every single host when supporting a given service could be combined with the availability when selecting the hosts to place service replicas and so obtain highly available and less energy-consuming service deployments. This paper presents a heuristic-based methodology to efficiently and automatically select the set of hosts that provide a given level of service availability while minimizing the energy consumption of the deployment.

The rest of this article is structured as follows. We briefly review the current literature related to this work in Section 2. We formally describe the problem addressed by this article in 3. We present our methodology in Section 4 and its evaluation by means of a numerical example by means of simulation in Section 5. We highlight the conclusions of our work in Section 6.

2 Related Work

Many recent studies focused on availability studies of distributed computing environments based on heterogeneous and non-dedicated resources [3, 12, 14]. These studies provided valuable information about the availability patterns of non-dedicated resources but they mainly focus on node-level availability, whereas our target is the system-level availability. Our work is focused on complex services, composed by several interconnected and intermittently available resources and aims to guarantee service availability and minimize the energy consumption.

The notion of collective availability [1] refers to making a service or a data object available by replicating it in several machines. It is considered to be available if at least k out of n computers are available [4, 9]. In [16], the authors studied the case of guaranteeing collective availability for computational services, considering n identical replicas of them and service availability only when at least k replicas are available.

In [19], the authors develop a reliability-aware task scheduling algorithm in which inter-dependencies among tasks are considered. The performance of their algorithm surpasses that of previous algorithms not considering reliability but some of their assumptions restrict the applicability of their model to large-scale systems.

Issues regarding the development of environmentally sustainable computing have been discussed since the emergence of the clouds. [10] designs, implements and evaluates a Green Scheduling Algorithm with a neural network predictor for optimizing power consumption in datacenters. They predict load demands from historical data and turns off or restarts servers according to it. *Green* task-scheduling algorithms are presented in [20]. After a simulation experiment, the authors conclude that heuristically assigning tasks to computers with lower energy is significantly more energy-efficient than doing it randomly. Borgetto *et al.* studied in [5] the problem of energy-aware resource allocation for long-term services or on-demand computing tasks hosted in clusters. They formalize the problem as an NP-hard constrained optimization problem, propose several heuristics and use simulation to validate their approaches by comparing their results in realistic scenarios.

3   Problem Description

Our goal is to deploy long-lived services on top of non-dedicated resources. We regard a service as any application, running on one or several computers, which is able to receive messages from other computers and send messages in response. A service is deployed for a period of time $\mathcal{T}$, after which some component re-assignment might be required. This is repeated until the service is explicitly stopped by an external agent. We assume all services are either stateless or has an internal procedure to maintain status amongst different replicas and a short processing time for queries, at least compared with time $\mathcal{T}$. Thanks to the former, service instances are easily replicable and many of them might be deployed simultaneously, offering some redundancy to the system.

We assume that a distributed service is a set $\mathcal{P}$ of interrelated processes that must run for a (usually long) period of time $(0, \mathcal{T})$. The processes communicate among themselves, which induces a *topology* in the service. This topology is described by logical conditions relating the various processes that make up the service. Let us assume that we have a pool $\mathcal{N}$ of n available hosts to deploy the service. Each of them is characterized by a certain availability behavior and an energy consumption.

The availability is obtained from historical behavior of every single host. It is possible to approximate the availability and unavailability intervals to a statistical function by observing their evolution. This way, the availability intervals would determine a failure distribution and the unavailability intervals a repair distribution. Many statistical functions may be considered to approximate the behavior of these intervals. From the expectancy of failure and the repair distributions, the mean availability can be obtained as $\bar{a}_{n_i} = \frac{E[failure_{n_i}()]}{E[failure_{n_i}()]+E[repair_{n_i}()]}$.

We consider the energy consumption of a host to be a variable with many factors that affect this value and its great variability over time. Despite this, some authors proposed to model the energy consumption of a computer as a linear function directly proportional to the load of the computer [17]. Therefore, it can be approximated as $e_{n_i}(t) = e_{n_i}^{min} + (e_{n_i}^{max} - e_{n_i}^{min}) \cdot s_{n_i}(t)$, where $e_{n_i}^{min}$ is the energy employed when there is no load in that computer, $e_{n_i}^{max}$ is the energy consumed at maximum load in the computer and $s_{n_i}(t)$ is the percentage load of the host n_i at time t. Consider $e_{n_i} \in [e_{n_i}^{min}, e_{n_i}^{max}]$ for $s_{n_i} \in [0, 1]$. This energy model is valid if we assume resources incorporate effective power-saving mechanisms, such as Dynamic Voltage and Frequency Scaling in the processors

Apart from their availability and energy consumption, we consider all nodes can host any process, but only one process at a given time. Clearly, a process is available at a given time t if and only if its host node is available at time t. A *deployment* of any distributed service is an injective function $D : \mathcal{P} \to \mathcal{N}$. For the sake of simplicity we use the expression D_j to indicate the service deployed over a set of given hosts. Another simplified description of the deployment is given by a set of binary variables $x_{n_i} \forall i \in \mathcal{N}$, where $x_{n_i} = 1$ if the node n_i was selected to host some process of the service, and $x_{n_i} = 0$ otherwise. The energy associated with the deployment is the sum of the individual energy consumptions of the selected hosts and this is the parameter that we want to minimize.

As services are something continuous on time, we attempt to provide a certain level of availability by guaranteeing the service will be available a percentage of the time $\mathcal{T}$. This percentage (a_{target}) must be one of the service requirements given when specifying the service itself. In summary, our problem can be formulate as a discrete optimization problem with a restriction:

$$
\begin{aligned}
&\text{Find} && D : \mathcal{P} \to \mathcal{N} \\
&\text{that minimizes} && \sum_{\forall i \in \mathcal{N}} x_{n_i} e_{n_i} \\
&\text{subject to} && \bar{a}_D \geq a_{target}
\end{aligned}
$$

The obtaining details of $\bar{a}_D$ are out of the scope of this work. We refer the reader to previous work on complex system availability estimation through discrete event simulator, for example the work in [13].

If $|\mathcal{P}| = m$, then the size of the search space is the number of different deployments, $\frac{n!}{(n-m)!}$. As we mainly deal with very large-scale systems, typically $n \gg m$, which makes $\frac{n!}{(n-m)!}$ very large, and rules out any form of brute-force search.

4   Methodology

Because of the size of the search space for service deployments in contributory communities, we developed a fast heuristic to determine pseudo-optimal deployments in restrained times. Assume we have historical information of the host availability and unavailability intervals; a mechanism to continuously monitor the load of the involved hosts at any given time; the target services are coherent (that is $\bar{a}_{D_j} > \bar{a}_{D_{j+1}}$); and a user service deployment request that indicates a desired availability level a_{target}. We developed a host selection methodology following the next steps:

1. Order the list of available hosts by mean availability in descending order, in such a way that $\bar{a}_{n_i} > \bar{a}_{n_{i+1}}$.
2. From the host ordered list, obtain a list of possible service deployments, considering only host subsets of consecutive elements in the host list. If service size is m and n hosts are available in the system, the obtained list

should contain $n - m + 1$ deployments. This step is possible due to the coherent traits of the studied systems (that is $\bar{a}_{D_j} > \bar{a}_{D_{j+1}}$).

3. Perform a binary search over the deployments list, keeping the immediate deployment in list such that $\bar{a}_{D_j} \geq a_{target}$. We named this deployment as D_{limit}.

4. Perform a linear search upwards the availability-sorted list of deployments. Since we consider the services to be coherent, all the deployments in this part of the list would have $a_{D_j} \geq a_{target}$, but the energy consumption associated to the selected hosts may be lower ($e_{D_{limit}} \geq e_{D_{limit-j}}$). Therefore, we seek for the deployment offering the lowest energy consumption only in that part of the list, since all deployments on it will fulfill the availability requirement.

Figure 1 shows a graphical chart of the operation of our proposal. The numbers in the figure are completely artificial, chosen to clarify the example. On it, D_{limit} is D_2, but the energy consumption of D_1 is lower, so the chosen deployment should be the latter (which still fulfills the availability requirements).

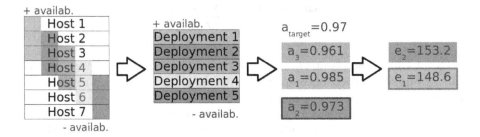

Fig. 1. Sketch of the proposed methodology in a reduced scenario: 3 component service and 7 available hosts in the community.

This methodology is flexible enough to adapt to very different service topologies and host behaviors. As well, it is ready to work either on large or small scale communities. Due to the stochastic nature of the load on the different hosts involved in a community, the pseudo-optimal deployments obtained by our heuristic might vary for a given service, since it depends on the system status at time the request was done.

5   Numerical Experiment

No real traces of availability and energy consumption are available for the intended systems in this work. For this reason, we artificially generated the information of 10,000 hosts by the parameters shown in Table 1. RandUniform(a,b) stands for a random number generation function following a Uniform distribution within the [a,b] range.

Table 1. Synthetically generated historical host information

Node ID		Node i
Failure Distribution	Type	Weibull
	Shape	`RandUniform(0.8, 2)`
	Scale	`RandUniform(0.5, 4)`
Repair Distribution	Type	Weibull
	Shape	`RandUniform(0.5, 1.75)`
	Scale	`RandUniform(0.2, 1.8)`
$\bar{a}_{n_i}$		$\frac{E[failure_i()]}{E[failure_i()]+E[repair_i()]}$
$\bar{e}_i$	e_{min_i}	`RandUniform(20, 50)`
	e_{max_i}	`RandUniform(350, 1000)`

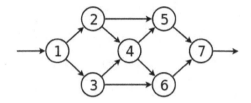

Fig. 2. Service topology description

We then considered an abstract service defined by the topology shown in the directed graph in Figure 2. The numbers indicate the arbitrary order in which the hosts are selected from the list ($\bar{a}_{n_i} \geq \bar{a}_{n_{i+1}}$).

We then built a computer simulator in Java to generate random behavior for the load in each of the involved hots if the service was placed on it. Our simulator generated random numbers in the range [0,1] as the load of each computer if the service was deployed on it every time a service deployment request was placed. From the expected load and the energy consumption information describing each host (previously obtained from Table 1), it was possible to determine the energy consumption for all the hosts. The energy consumption of a given service deployment can be then obtained by aggregating the energy consumption of all the selected hosts.

We ran the simulator for 100 lifetimes, as if 100 services were to be deployed in the community. In all cases, we fixed the availability requirement at 90% and we recorded the availability and the energy consumption of the most greedy deployment (selecting the most available hosts, as was D_1 in Figure 1) and the ones of the deployment found by our methodology. We show the mean results and the mean differences in Table 2 and we declare the mean execution time was 903.5 milliseconds in a desktop computer built of an Intel Core i5-2400 processor, 4 GBytes of RAM memory, running Ubuntu Linux 12.10 and the Oracle Java Virtual Machine 7u17-64bits.

We show in Figure 3 the result of four deployment search processes, selected randomly among the 100 performed in the experiment. The graphs depict the temporal process and the evolution of the service availability and energy

Table 2. Overview of the measured results

	$\bar{a}_D$	$\bar{e}_D$
Greedy deployments	0.992	4437.33
Our deployments	0.959	1938.35
$\varDelta$	3.31%	56.32%

consumption of the chosen hosts. The vertical dashed line indicates the time the binary search ends and the linear local search starts, while the horizontal one signals the availability threshold (a_{target}) imposed by the requester.

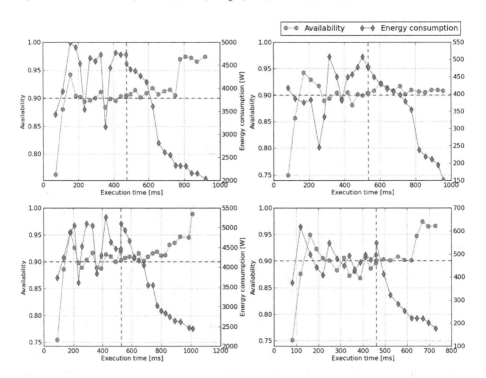

Fig. 3. Graphical evolution of four different service deployments

From the obtained results, we affirm our methodology outperforms the greedy approach in terms of energy consumption while maintains the availability above a given threshold. What is more, our method prove to work fast when dealing with a sizable pool of very different hosts. Thanks to this fact, it could be included in a user-interactive service deployment procedure within a real community.

6   Conclusions

Energy consumption of large-scale distributed computing infrastructures is a matter to be regarded by system administrators. As the scale of these systems grows, its environmental footprints also does.

We combined the environmental concern with the emerging computing concept of contributory communities. These communities are based on user-donated computers and require no large datacenters to offer long-lived services. However, its non-dedicated nature poses new challenges when guaranteeing service survival over time.

In this paper we proposed a simple and fast heuristic to determine a subset of hosts suitable to provide a given level of service availability. In addition, we included the energy consumption as a variable in the equation. The main goal of this research was to minimize the energy consumption of the deployed services while maintaining the service availability over the mentioned threshold.

We evaluated our heuristic by means of computer simulation and we found that investing very few time (less than a second) to perform a search among the available resources, it is possible to reduce the energy consumption up to a 56.32% while degrading the offered availability only a 3.31%.

References

1. Andrzejak, A., Kondo, D., Anderson, D.P.: Ensuring collective availability in volatile resource pools via forecasting. In: De Turck, F., Kellerer, W., Kormentzas, G. (eds.) DSOM 2008. LNCS, vol. 5273, pp. 149–161. Springer, Heidelberg (2008)
2. Armbrust, M., Fox, A., Griffith, R., Joseph, A., Katz, R., Konwinski, A., Lee, G., Patterson, D., Rabkin, A., Stoica, I., Zaharia, M.: A view of cloud computing. Commun. ACM 53, 50–58 (2010)
3. Bhagwan, R., Savage, S., Voelker, G.: Understanding Availability. In: Kaashoek, M.F., Stoica, I. (eds.) IPTPS 2003. LNCS, vol. 2735, pp. 256–267. Springer, Heidelberg (2003)
4. Bhagwan, R., Tati, K., Cheng, Y.C., Savage, S., Voelker, G.M.: Total recall: System support for automated availability management. In: NSDI, pp. 337–350 (2004)
5. Borgetto, D., Casanova, H., Da Costa, G., Pierson, J.: Energy-aware service allocation. Future Generation Computer Systems 28(5), 769–779 (2012), http://linkinghub.elsevier.com/retrieve/pii/S0167739X11000690
6. Chandra, A., Weissman, J.: Nebulas: using distributed voluntary resources to build clouds. In: Proceedings of the 2009 Conference on Hot Topics in Cloud Computing, HotCloud 2009, p. 2. USENIX Association, Berkeley (2009)
7. Commission, E., et al.: Carbon footprint: What it is and how to measure it (2007) (accessed on April 15, 2009)
8. Cunsolo, V., Distefano, S., Puliafito, A., Scarpa, M.: Cloud@home: bridging the gap between volunteer and cloud computing. In: Huang, D.-S., Jo, K.-H., Lee, H.-H., Kang, H.-J., Bevilacqua, V. (eds.) ICIC 2009. LNCS, vol. 5754, pp. 423–432. Springer, Heidelberg (2009)
9. Dimakis, A., Godfrey, P., Wu, Y., Wainwright, M., Ramchandran, K.: Network coding for distributed storage systems. IEEE Transactions on Information Theory 56(9), 4539–4551 (2010)
10. Duy, T., Sato, Y., Inoguchi, Y.: Performance evaluation of a green scheduling algorithm for energy savings in cloud computing. In: 2010 IEEE International Symposium on Parallel Distributed Processing, Workshops and Phd Forum (IPDPSW), pp. 1–8 (April 2010)

11. Glanz, J.: Power, pollution and the internet - the cloud factories. The New York Times (September 2012) (in press)
12. Javadi, B., Kondo, D., Vincent, J.M., Anderson, D.P.: Discovering statistical models of availability in large distributed systems: An empirical study of seti@home. IEEE Transactions on Parallel and Distributed Systems 22, 1896–1903 (2011)
13. Juan, A., Faulin, J., Serrat, C., Bargueño, C.: Predicting availability functions in time-dependent complex systems with saedes simulation algorithms. Reliability Engineering and System Safety 93, 1761–1771 (2008)
14. Kondo, D., Javadi, B., Iosup, A., Epema, D.: The failure trace archive: Enabling comparative analysis of failures in diverse distributed systems. In: 2010 10th IEEE/ACM International Conference on Cluster, Cloud and Grid Computing (CCGrid), pp. 398–407 (2010)
15. Lázaro, D.: A Middleware for Service Deployment in Contributory Computing Systems. Ph.D. thesis, Universitat Oberta de Catalunya (July 2011), http://dpcs.uoc.edu/lazaro/lazaro-thesis.pdf
16. Lázaro, D., Kondo, D., Marquès, J.M.: Long-term availability prediction for groups of volunteer resources. Journal of Parallel and Distributed Computing (2011), http://www.sciencedirect.com/science/article/pii/S0743731511002061
17. Lee, Y., Zomaya, A.: Energy efficient utilization of resources in cloud computing systems. The Journal of Supercomputing 60(2), 268–280 (2012)
18. Marinos, A., Briscoe, G.: Community cloud computing. In: Jaatun, M.G., Zhao, G., Rong, C. (eds.) Cloud Computing. LNCS, vol. 5931, pp. 472–484. Springer, Heidelberg (2009)
19. Tang, X., Li, K., Li, R., Veeravalli, B.: Reliability-aware scheduling strategy for heterogeneous distributed computing systems. J. Parallel Distrib. Comput. 70, 941–952 (2010), http://dx.doi.org/10.1016/j.jpdc.2010.05.002
20. Zhang, L., Li, K., Zhang, Y.: Green task scheduling algorithms with speeds optimization on heterogeneous cloud servers. In: Proceedings of the 2010 IEEE/ACM International Conference on Green Computing and Communications & International Conference on Cyber, Physical and Social Computing, pp. 76–80. IEEE Computer Society (2010)

A Study of the Combination of Variation Operators in the NSGA-II Algorithm

Antonio J. Nebro[1], Juan J. Durillo[2], Mirialys Machín[3],
Carlos A. Coello Coello[4], and Bernabé Dorronsoro[5]

[1] Department of Computer Science, University of Málaga, Spain
[2] Institute of Computer Science, University of Innsbruck, Austria
[3] Departamento de Computación, University of Informatic Sciences, Cuba
[4] CINVESAV-IPN, Mxico
[5] Computer Science Laboratory of Lille, Université Lille 1, France
antonio@lcc.uma.es, juan@dps.uibk.ac.at, mmachin@cav.uci.cu,
ccoello@cs.cinvestav.mx, bernabe.dorronsoro_diaz@inria.fr

Abstract. Multi-objective evolutionary algorithms rely on the use of variation operators as their basic mechanism to carry out the evolutionary process. These operators are usually fixed and applied in the same way during algorithm execution, e.g., the mutation probability in genetic algorithms. This paper analyses whether a more dynamic approach combining different operators with variable application rate along the search process allows to improve the static classical behavior. This way, we explore the combined use of three different operators (simulated binary crossover, differential evolution's operator, and polynomial mutation) in the NSGA-II algorithm. We have considered two strategies for selecting the operators: random and adaptive. The resulting variants have been tested on a set of 19 complex problems, and our results indicate that both schemes significantly improve the performance of the original NSGA-II algorithm, achieving the random and adaptive variants the best overall results in the bi- and three-objective considered problems, respectively.

Keywords: Multiobjective Optimization, Evolutionary Algorithms, Variation Operators, Adaptation.

1 Introduction

Evolutionary algorithms (EAs) are a family of stochastic search techniques within metaheuristics [1] widely used on optimization. Genetic Algorithms (GAs), Evolution Strategies (ES), Genetic Programming (GP), and Differential Evolution (DE), among others, are examples of EAs. Specialized versions of EAs to solve multi-objective optimization problems usually referred as to MOEAs.

Most of EAs and MOEAs operate under a common principle: one or several individuals undergo the effect of some variation operators. Examples of these operators are the crossover and mutation operators, in the context of GAs, or the differential evolution operator in DE methods.

C. Bielza et al. (Eds.): CAEPIA 2013, LNAI 8109, pp. 269–278, 2013.

Some researchers have shown that some operators are more suitable for some types of problems than others. If we focus on multi-objective optimization, we can find some examples. Deb *et al.* evaluated the behavior of a number of operators for solving problems with variable linkages [3], and observed that the SBX operator was unable to deal with these types of problems. Iorio and Li [7] discussed the suitability of a number of operators for solving rotated problems and those having epistatic interactions among decision variables.

To make things harder, there is no reason to think that a variation operator is equally effective, in terms of its *evolvability* or ability to produce better solutions, over the whole search space of a given problem. In fact, the search space of real-world optimization problems may not be free of variable-linkage, epistasis, rotation, or complex relationships among their decision variables. Under these circumstances, the use of methods that keep their variation operators invariant through the whole execution of the EA may not be the best alternative.

Our goal is to investigate, in the context of multi-objective optimization, whether the combined use of different variation operators during the search may improve the performance of classical MOEAs. Our hypothesis is that the variation operators used in most of these algorithms can be effective in the exploration of certain regions of the search space of a given problem, but not over the whole search space. We study this idea by endowing NSGA-II with the ability to select its variation operators from a set containing different alternatives. The resulting algorithms are evaluated by solving problems with difficult Pareto sets; in particular, the LZ09 [9] benchmark and problems of the CEC 2009 competition [12]).

In this paper we propose two new versions of the NSGA-II algorithm which are able to select from among different variation operators during the search. We have considered a set composed of three operators commonly used in multi-objective optimization metaheuristics: SBX crossover, polynomial-based mutation, and the variation operator used in DE. The first proposed version of NSGA-II, referred to as NSGA-IIr hereinafter, creates new solutions by randomly selecting an operator from the set. The second version, named NSGA-IIa from now on, uses a record of the contribution of each operator in the past for selecting the operator to apply. This second scheme is based on the one proposed in the AMALGAM algorithm [11], and the idea is to give to these operators a higher probability of being chosen when they are capable of producing solutions that survive from one generation to the next. Additionally, we include in the study a version of NSGA-II using only the DE operator.

The rest of this paper is organized as follows. Next section reviews related work. Section 3 details our proposals. The methodology used in this work is described in Section 4 and the obtained results are analyzed in Section 5. Finally, we present our main conclusions and some possible paths for future research.

2   Previous Related Work

In this section we review existing works related to ours. We focus only on multi-objective optimization aproaches.

In [10], Toscano and Coello dealt with the issue of selecting the best operator for solving a given problem. These authors proposed a micro genetic algorithm, called μGA2, which runs several simultaneous instances of μGA2 configured with different variation operators. Periodically, the instance with the poorest performance was replaced with the best performing one. Thus, after several generations, all the parallel instances worked only with the best performing operator. A disadvantage of this approach is that once an operator had been discarded, it could not be used again in the execution of the algorithm.

MOSaDE [5] combines the use of four different versions of the DE operator. This combination was made in an adaptive way: the version that contributes the most to the search was given a higher probability of being used for creating new solutions. This contribution was measured by considering the success, in terms of the non-dominated solutions that it produced in the last n iterations of the algorithm. An improved version of MOSaDE with object-wise learning strategies, called OW-MOSaDE [6], participated in the CEC2009 MOEA competition [13], obtaining an average rank of 9.39 among 13 algorithms.

Vrugt and Robinson proposed in [11] the AMALGAM algorithm, based on the idea of using a number of multi-objective algorithms within a master algorithm. By measuring the contribution of each method in the last iteration, each algorithm was adaptively used favoring those techniques exhibiting the highest reproductive success. The algorithms used were NSGA-II, a PSO approach, a DE approach, and an adaptive metropolis search (AMS) approach.

Relate works propose therefore new algorithms or the combination of several existing techniques using a master approach, like in AMALGAM. Additionally, all of them use an scheme based on the contribution of the different operators for considering their application. The main point of our work, however, is not to propose a new algorithm but to analyze whether the combination of operators can improve the performance of an existing algorithm such as NSGA-II, when dealing with difficult multi-objective optimization problems.

3   NSGA-II with Combined Operators

This section aims at describing NSGA-IIa and NSGA-IIr. For the sake of clarity, we first present the original technique and then our proposals.

3.1   NSGA-II

NSGA-II (Deb *et al.* [2]) is the most popular multi-objective metaheuristic by far. It is a generational GA, so it is based on a population P of size n which, at each iteration, is used to create another population of n new solutions as follows. For every solution in P, two parents are selected and combined using the recombination operator and the result is later altered by means of a mutation operator. We use SBX crossover and polynomial mutation, as done in NSGA-II when adopting real-numbers encoding. As a result of these two operations, a new individual is created and inserted into a temporal population Q. Finally, P and

Algorithm 1. Pseudocode of NSGA-IIr.

```
 1: Input: n // the population size
 2: P ← Random_Population() // P = population
 3: Q ← ∅                    // Q = auxiliar population
 4: while not Termination_Condition() do
 5:     for i ← 1 to (n) do
 6:         randValue←rand();
 7:         if (randValue ≤ 1/3) then
 8:             parent←Selection1(P); // only one parent is selected
 9:             offspring←PolynomialMutation(parent);
10:         else
11:             if (randValue ≤ 2/3) then
12:                 parents←Selection2(P); // two parents are selected
13:                 offspring←SBX(parents);
14:             else
15:                 parents←Selection3(P); // three parents are selected
16:                 offspring←DE(population[i], parents);
17:             end if
18:         end if
19:         Evaluate_Fitness(offspring);
20:         Insert(offspring,Q);
21:     end for
22:     R ← P ∪ Q
23:     Ranking_And_Crowding(R);
24:     P ← Select_Best_Individuals(R)
25: end while
26: Return P;
```

Q are merged in a single population R. The n best individuals, after applying the ranking and crowding procedures in R, will be selected to be the population P in the next generation of the algorithm. See further details in [2].

3.2   NSGA-IIr

NSGA-IIr is an extension of NSGA-II that makes use of three different variation operators: SBX crossover, polynomial mutation, and DE's variation operator. These operators are randomly selected whenever a new solution is to be produced. The pseudocode of this version is detailed in Algorithm 1.

The main difference with respect to the original NSGA-II lies in the parents selection mechanism and in the way in which offsprings are produced (lines 6-18). NSGA-IIr proceeds as follows. For each individual in P, it produces a random value in $[0, 1]$ (line 6). Depending of this value, one out of the three variation operators is selected, as shown in lines 7-18. Once the offspring is generated, the algorithm behaves as the original NSGA-II.

3.3   NSGA-IIa

NSGA-IIa applies the same variation operators as NSGA-IIr, but in an adaptive way, by taking into account their contribution, i.e., each operator selection probability is adjusted by considering that operator success in the last iteration.

The adaptive scheme considered for operator selection is based on the one used in AMALGAM [11]. Algorithm 2 describes such scheme. Assuming a number of *NumOperators* different operators, the method computes the contribution of

Algorithm 2. Computing the contribution of each operator.

```
 1: Input: P // population for the next iteration
 2: total_contribution ← 0
 3: for 1 ≤ operator ≤ NumOperators do
 4:     contribution_operator ← solutionsInNextPopulation(operator,P) ;
 5:     if contribution_operator ≤ threshold then
 6:         contribution_operator ← threshold;
 7:     end if
 8:     total_contribution ← total_contribution + contribution_operator;
 9: end for
10: for 1 ≤ operator ≤ NumOperators do
11:     probability_operator ← contribution_operator / total_contribution;
12: end for
```

all of them (loop between lines 3-9). The idea is to count how many solutions generated by each operator are part of the population P of the next generation (line 4). If an operator has contributed with less solutions than a minimum threshold, its contribution is set to this minimum threshold (lines 5-7); by doing so we avoid any operator to be discarded when producing no solutions in an iteration. Our motivation is that this operator may be useful later in a different phase of the search. In this work we have considered a threshold equal to 2, which was the value used in AMALGAM. Once the contribution of the operators have been computed, the probability of selecting them is updated (line 12). This way, the operators have a probability of being selected in the next generation which is proportional to their contribution.

3.4 NSGA-IIde

As we are using the DE operator in NSGA-IIr and NSGA-IIa, we consider interesting to include in the study another NSGA-II variant, where the mutation and crossover operators have been replaced by the DE operator. We have named this version NSGA-IIde. This way, we will have more information to determine if the performance improvements are not related to the use of a particular operator but to the combination of some of them.

4   Experimentation

Here we present the benchmark problems adopted for our tests, together with the parameter settings and the methodology followed in our experiments.

Benchmark Problems. We consider the LZ09 [9] benchmark and the problems defined for the CEC2009 competition [12]. The former is composed by nine problems (LZ09_F1 - LZ09_F9), all of which are bi-objective, except for LZ09_F6, which has three objectives. The latter contains problems with two, three, and five objectives, as well as constrained and unconstrained problems. We have selected the seven UF1- UF7 bi-objective and the UF8 - UF10 three-objective unconstrained problems.

Parameters Settings. For NSGA-II and its three variants we have used the same settings. The population size is 100, the SBX and polynomial mutation probabilities are 0.9 and $1/L$ (L is the number of decision variables of the problem being solved), respectively. Both operators share the same distribution index value, which is set to 20. The DE operator variant is current/1/bin, and the values of the CR and F control parameters are, respectively, 1.0 and 0.5. The stopping condition is $150,000$ function evaluations in the case of the LZ09 problems, and $300,000$ for the CEC 2009 problems.

Quality Assessment. To assess the performance of the algorithms we adopt two widely used indicators: additive epsilon [8]) and hypervolume [14].

Analysis of Results. For each combination of algorithm and problem we have made 30 independent runs, and we report the median, $\tilde{x}$, and the interquartile range, IQR, as measures of location (or central tendency) and statistical dispersion, respectively, for each considered indicator. When presenting the obtained values in tables, we emphasize with a dark gray background the best result for each problem, and a clear grey background is used to indicate the second best result; this way, we can see at a glance the most salient algorithms.

When comparing the values yielded by two algorithms on a given problem, we check if differences in the results are statistically significant. To cope with this issue, we have applied the unpaired Wilcoxon rank-sum test, a non-parametric statistical hypothesis test, which allows us to make pairwise comparisons between algorithms to analyze the significance of the obtained data [4]. A confidence level of 95% (i.e., significance level of 5% or p-value under 0.05) has been used in all cases, meaning that the differences were unlikely occurred by chance with a probability of 95%.

5   Comparison of Results

In this section, we analyze the obtained results when running the algorithms under the aforementioned experimental methodology. We first analyze the values yielded by the I_ϵ^+ indicator, and then the ones obtained by the I_{HV} one.

The values obtained by the I_ϵ^+ are summarized in Table 1. We start by analyzing the values obtained in the LZ09 family. As we can observe, the algorithm applying the adaptive combination of several operators, NSGAIIa, has led to an improvement of the results of the original version of NSGA-II in all the problems that are part of this benchmark, but it was outperformed, in turn, by the random variant, NSGA-IIr, in all the problems but two (LZ09_F4 and LZ09_F6). The NSGA-II variant using DE only achieved the best result in the first problem. Our wilcoxon analysis has releveaked that statistical significance has been found when comparing the the two extensions of NSGA-II algorithm with the original. Regarding to the comparison between our two proposals, there is no statistical significance in problems LZ09_F1 and LZ09_F4, NSGA-IIa outperforms NSGA-IIr in six problems, and NSGA-IIr improves NSGA-IIa in LZ09_F6, the only three-objective problem of the benchmark.

Table 1. LZ09 benchmark. Median and interquartile range of the I_ϵ^+ indicator.

	NSGA-II	NSGAII-r	NSGAII-a	NSGAII-de
LZ09_F1	$1.69e-02_{1.7e-03}$	$1.52e-02_{2.4e-03}$	$1.52e-02_{2.9e-03}$	$1.46e-02_{3.9e-03}$
LZ09_F2	$1.70e-01_{2.5e-02}$	$7.43e-02_{1.7e-02}$	$9.62e-02_{2.8e-02}$	$1.49e-01_{3.6e-02}$
LZ09_F3	$1.12e-01_{2.3e-02}$	$4.78e-02_{2.1e-02}$	$7.84e-02_{1.5e-02}$	$1.20e-01_{2.6e-02}$
LZ09_F4	$1.38e-01_{2.0e-02}$	$5.44e-02_{1.7e-02}$	$5.16e-02_{1.9e-02}$	$1.13e-01_{2.3e-02}$
LZ09_F5	$1.09e-01_{3.1e-02}$	$6.54e-02_{3.7e-02}$	$8.29e-02_{2.9e-02}$	$1.21e-01_{1.8e-02}$
LZ09_F6	$2.75e-01_{4.0e-02}$	$2.69e-01_{1.3e-02}$	$2.31e-01_{5.3e-02}$	$6.38e-01_{2.4e-02}$
LZ09_F7	$3.32e-01_{1.7e-01}$	$3.48e-02_{2.1e-02}$	$1.28e-01_{1.4e-01}$	$1.00e+00_{0.0e+00}$
LZ09_F8	$2.76e-01_{1.4e-01}$	$2.22e-01_{6.7e-02}$	$2.54e-01_{1.5e-01}$	$9.10e-01_{2.1e-01}$
LZ09_F9	$1.87e-01_{6.5e-02}$	$7.98e-02_{3.1e-02}$	$1.05e-01_{2.3e-02}$	$1.49e-01_{3.2e-02}$
UF1	$1.54e-01_{2.4e-02}$	$1.82e-02_{2.7e-03}$	$5.51e-02_{2.6e-02}$	$1.30e-01_{2.8e-02}$
UF2	$9.35e-02_{2.5e-02}$	$5.53e-02_{2.4e-02}$	$6.73e-02_{3.1e-02}$	$1.13e-01_{2.8e-02}$
UF3	$3.12e-01_{1.1e-01}$	$4.63e-02_{6.0e-02}$	$1.40e-01_{1.1e-01}$	$2.35e-01_{4.7e-02}$
UF4	$4.95e-02_{2.5e-03}$	$4.62e-02_{1.8e-02}$	$5.11e-02_{5.1e-03}$	$8.27e-02_{9.8e-03}$
UF5	$3.80e-01_{7.2e-02}$	$4.25e-01_{2.0e-01}$	$5.00e-01_{2.1e-01}$	$1.05e+00_{3.5e-01}$
UF6	$3.68e-01_{1.5e-01}$	$4.62e-01_{3.9e-01}$	$5.30e-01_{3.0e-01}$	$4.11e-01_{1.9e-01}$
UF7	$1.33e-01_{3.5e-01}$	$5.68e-02_{1.8e-01}$	$7.55e-02_{3.4e-02}$	$9.68e-02_{2.7e-02}$
UF8	$3.05e-01_{4.4e-01}$	$3.09e-01_{4.5e-01}$	$3.09e-01_{4.4e-01}$	$8.56e-01_{1.7e-01}$
UF9	$4.91e-01_{2.8e-01}$	$5.57e-01_{4.0e-01}$	$4.58e-01_{2.1e-01}$	$8.65e-01_{2.7e-01}$
UF10	$9.31e-01_{1.3e-01}$	$9.44e-01_{1.6e-01}$	$8.61e-01_{1.5e-01}$	$1.97e+00_{6.4e-01}$

Table 2. LZ09 benchmark. Median and interquartile range of the I_{HV} indicator.

	NSGA-II	NSGA-IIr	NSGA-IIa	NSGA-IIde
LZ09_F1	$6.53e-01_{1.1e-03}$	$6.55e-01_{6.9e-04}$	$6.55e-01_{7.2e-04}$	$6.56e-01_{7.6e-04}$
LZ09_F2	$5.53e-01_{1.3e-02}$	$6.35e-01_{9.6e-03}$	$6.25e-01_{2.1e-02}$	$5.66e-01_{3.6e-02}$
LZ09_F3	$6.24e-01_{8.1e-03}$	$6.46e-01_{3.5e-03}$	$6.41e-01_{6.6e-03}$	$5.85e-01_{1.6e-02}$
LZ09_F4	$6.34e-01_{4.7e-03}$	$6.44e-01_{2.8e-03}$	$6.48e-01_{3.8e-03}$	$5.89e-01_{1.4e-02}$
LZ09_F5	$6.28e-01_{1.1e-02}$	$6.43e-01_{1.0e-02}$	$6.41e-01_{8.5e-03}$	$5.96e-01_{1.2e-02}$
LZ09_F6	$2.08e-01_{3.4e-02}$	$2.51e-01_{2.7e-02}$	$2.89e-01_{2.9e-02}$	$4.35e-02_{4.7e-02}$
LZ09_F7	$4.80e-01_{4.3e-02}$	$6.50e-01_{4.5e-03}$	$6.37e-01_{2.9e-02}$	$0.00e+00_{0.0e+00}$
LZ09_F8	$4.62e-01_{4.8e-02}$	$5.33e-01_{3.8e-02}$	$5.00e-01_{4.4e-02}$	$0.00e+00_{0.0e+00}$
LZ09_F9	$2.25e-01_{4.1e-02}$	$2.99e-01_{1.7e-02}$	$2.88e-01_{1.8e-02}$	$2.31e-01_{2.9e-02}$
UF1	$5.73e-01_{1.9e-02}$	$6.53e-01_{8.9e-03}$	$6.47e-01_{7.7e-03}$	$5.78e-01_{2.9e-02}$
UF2	$6.34e-01_{8.9e-03}$	$6.47e-01_{4.4e-03}$	$6.46e-01_{6.0e-03}$	$5.99e-01_{1.3e-02}$
UF3	$4.74e-01_{4.8e-02}$	$6.38e-01_{2.1e-02}$	$6.00e-01_{5.7e-02}$	$3.43e-01_{5.4e-02}$
UF4	$2.64e-01_{1.4e-03}$	$2.68e-01_{6.5e-04}$	$2.66e-01_{2.1e-03}$	$2.34e-01_{1.4e-02}$
UF5	$1.87e-01_{8.1e-02}$	$1.53e-01_{2.1e-01}$	$1.98e-01_{1.5e-01}$	$0.00e+00_{0.0e+00}$
UF6	$2.43e-01_{6.7e-02}$	$2.34e-01_{1.6e-01}$	$2.39e-01_{1.6e-01}$	$5.42e-02_{2.2e-02}$
UF7	$4.41e-01_{8.8e-02}$	$4.81e-01_{7.1e-03}$	$4.77e-01_{4.7e-03}$	$4.51e-01_{1.9e-02}$
UF8	$1.96e-01_{9.6e-02}$	$1.08e-01_{1.4e-01}$	$1.87e-01_{1.6e-01}$	$0.00e+00_{3.9e-04}$
UF9	$3.21e-01_{1.6e-01}$	$1.78e-01_{3.7e-01}$	$3.94e-01_{2.0e-01}$	$3.53e-01_{6.9e-02}$
UF10	$1.73e-02_{2.3e-02}$	$0.00e+00_{2.7e-02}$	$3.63e-02_{6.3e-02}$	$0.00e+00_{0.0e+00}$

Regarding the problems of the CEC 2009 competition we can see that the random NSGA-II variant achieved the best values in five out the seven bi-objective problems and no best results in the tree-objective instances. The applied Wilcoxon Rank-sum test showed, however, that the differences with NSGA-II in problems UF5, UF6, and UF8 were not statistically significant. NSGA-IIa performed better that NSGA-II in problems UF4, UF5, and UF6, and it outperformed NSGA-IIr in UF9 and UF10 with confidence in all these instances.

The values for the I_{HV} are included in Table 2. A simple comparison with the convergence indicator results (Table 1) shows almost an identical performance of the algorithms for the LZ09 benchmark; however, the Wilcoxon ranks-sum test values showed some differences. According to the I_{HV}, NSGA-IIa obtained a better value in LZ09_F4 with statistical confidence and the differences in LZ09_F5 are non significant. Some values in Table 2 are 0; this means that the approximation front produced by the algorithm was beyond the limits of the Pareto front used to calculate the I_{HV} indicator, so none of the solutions contribute to the

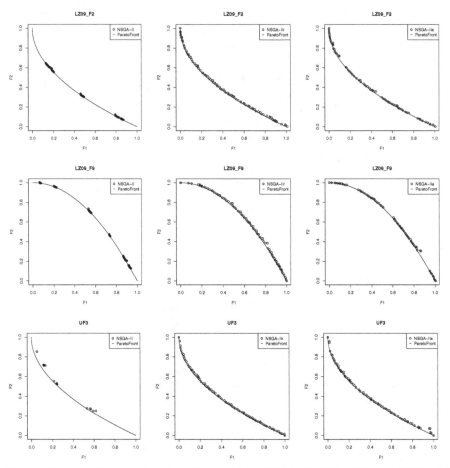

Fig. 1. Computed approximations for problems LZ09_F2, LZ09_F9, and UF3 with NSGA-II (left), NSGA-IIr (center), and NSGA-IIa (right)

hypervolume. In the case of the second evaluated benchmark, NSGA-IIr got again the best figures in most of the bi-objective problems, but it was outperformed by NSGA-II in the three-objective UF8, UF9, and UF10 instances by NSGA-II, being the differences significant according to the applied statistical methodoly. NSGA-IIa also yielded best results than NSGA-IIr in the same problems, although the differences are not significant in the UF8 problem. Compared with NSGA-II, NSGA-IIa obtained better values in six out the ten studied problems with confidence, being the differences in the rest of problems non significant.

To illustrate the performance of our proposals, we include the best Pareto front approximations found by the NSGA-II and its two variants according to the I_{HV} in Fig. 1 for problems LZ09_F2, LZ09_F9, and UF3. We can observe these problems posed a lot of difficulties to NSGA-II, which produced very poor approximation sets. The extensions of NSGA-II have generated better results in terms of the quality of the computed fronts, which can be visually stated.

6   Discussion

From the previous study we can infer some facts. First, it is clear that the combined used of the three chosen operators, in an adaptive or in a random way, lead to algorithms outperforming NSGA-II in most of the considered problems. Given that NSGA-IIde does not achieve better results compared with the original algorithm (with the exception of the LZ09_F1 problem) we conclude that the combination of the three operators is the reason of the performance improvements that are obtained by both the NSGA-IIr and NSGA-IIa variants.

The 19 evaluated problems have complex Pareto sets and most of state-of-the-art Pareto dominance-based MOEAs experiment troubles when solving them, so the enhancements illustrated by Fig. 1 are remarkable. Consequently, we infer that the combination of operators has a positive influence in the performance of the resulting algorithms, allowing a better exploration of the search space, thus supporting our initial hyphotesis of that the variation operators used in many MOEAs can be effective in the exploration of certain regions of the search space of a given problem but not over the whole search space.

Our analysis revealed that the random selection of operators provides overall better results than the adaptive version in bi-objective problems, while the latter outperforms the former in three-objective problems. This issue deserves further research.

7   Conclusions

We have studied two schemes for using variation operators in a combined way in the NSGA-II algorithm. The first one selects the operators at random, while the second one takes them in an adaptive way. The considered operators have been SBX crossover, polynomial mutation, and the DE operator. To assess the performance of the two combined strategies we have taken 19 multiobjective problems, two quality indicators, and we have statistically ensured the confidence of the obtained results. A version of NSGA-II using only the differential evolution operator has been included for completeness.

The experiments carried out revealed that the combinator of operators enhances the performance over the original NSGA-II algorithm. The random scheme was the most salient variant when solving the bi-objective problems, while the adaptive algorithm yielded the best results in the three-objective instances. The improvements achieved in many problems are remarkable; therefore, we conclude that the combined use of variation operators can improve classical MOEAs, as shown in the context of the experimentation carried out. It is worth noting that the modifications of the NSGA-II algorithm are kept in a minimum.

As future work, we plan the inclusion of a broader set of operators. The application of the analyzed variation schemes to other multi-objective evolutionary algorithms (e.g., MOEA/D), the study of potential benefits when applying it for solving scalable problems in the number of variables or objectives, and the investigation of why the random and adaptive schemes yield, respectively, the best Pareto front approximations in the bi- and three-objective selected problems are also a matter of future work.

Acknowledgments. Antonio J. Nebro is supported by projects TIN2011-25840 (Spanish Ministry of Education and Science) and P11-TIC-7529 (Innovation, Science and Enterprise Ministry of the regional government of the Junta de Andalucía). Juan J. Durillo acknowledges the Austrian Research Promotion Agency under contract nr. 834307 (AutoCore). Carlos A. Coello Coello acknowledges support from CONACyT project no. 103570. Bernabé Dorronsoro acknowledges that the present work is partially supported by the National Research Fund, Luxembourg, and cofunded under the Marie Curie Actions of the European Commission (FP7-COFUND).

References

1. Blum, C., Roli, A.: Metaheuristics in combinatorial optimization: Overview and conceptual comparison. ACM Computing Surveys 35(3), 268–308 (2003)
2. Deb, K., Pratap, A., Agarwal, S., Meyarivan, T.: A fast and elitist multiobjective genetic algorithm: NSGA-II. IEEE TEVC 6(2), 182–197 (2002)
3. Deb, K., Sinha, A., Kukkonen, S.: Multi-objective test problems, linkages, and evolutionary methodologies. In: GECCO 2006, pp. 1141–1148 (2006)
4. Demšar, J.: Statistical comparisons of classifiers over multiple data sets. J. Mach. Learn. Res. 7, 1–30 (2006)
5. Huang, V.L., Qin, A.K., Suganthan, P.N., Tasgetiren, M.F.: Multi-objective optimization based on self-adaptive differential evolution algorithm. In: Proceedings of the 2007 IEEE CEC, pp. 3601–3608 (2007)
6. Huang, V.L., Zhao, S.Z., Mallipeddi, R., Suganthan, P.N.: Multi-objective optimization using self-adaptive differential evolution algorithm. In: Proceedings of the 2009 IEEE CEC, pp. 190–194 (2009)
7. Iorio, A.W., Li, X.: Solving rotated multi-objective optimization problems using differential evolution. In: Australian Conference on Artificial Intelligence, pp. 861–872 (2004)
8. Knowles, J., Thiele, L., Zitzler, E.: A Tutorial on the Performance Assessment of Stochastic Multiobjective Optimizers. Technical Report 214, Computer Engineering and Networks Laboratory (TIK), ETH Zurich (2006)
9. Li, H., Zhang, Q.: Multiobjective optimization problems with complicated pareto sets, MOEA/D and NSGA-II. IEEE TEVC 2(12), 284–302 (2009)
10. Toscano Pulido, G., Coello Coello, C.A.: The micro genetic algorithm 2: Towards online adaptation in evolutionary multiobjective optimization. In: Fonseca, C.M., Fleming, P.J., Zitzler, E., Deb, K., Thiele, L. (eds.) EMO 2003. LNCS, vol. 2632, pp. 252–266. Springer, Heidelberg (2003)
11. Vrugt, J.A., Robinson, B.A.: Improved evolutionary optimization from genetically adaptive multimethod search. Proceedings of the National Academy of Sciences of the United States of America 104(3), 708–711 (2007)
12. Zhang, Q., Suganthan, P.N.: Special session on performance assessment of multi-objective optimization algorithms/cec 09 moea competition (May 2009)
13. Zhang, Q., Zou, A., Zhao, S., Suganthan, P.N., Liu, W., Tivari, S.: Multiobjective optimization test instances for the cec 2009 special session and competition. Technical Report CES-491, School of CS & EE, University of Essex (April 2009)
14. Zitzler, E., Thiele, L.: Multiobjective evolutionary algorithms: a comparative case study and the strength pareto approach. IEEE TEVC 3(4), 257–271 (1999)

A New Heuristic
for the Capacitated Vertex p-Center Problem

Dagoberto R. Quevedo-Orozco and Roger Z. Ríos-Mercado

Universidad Autónoma de Nuevo León, Graduate Program in Systems Engineering,
Cd. Universitaria, San Nicolás de los Garza, NL 66450, México
{dago,roger}@yalma.fime.uanl.mx

Abstract. A metaheuristic for the capacitated vertex p-center problem
is presented. This is a well-known location problem that consists of placing p facilities and assigning customers to these in such a way that the
largest distance between any customer and its associated facility is minimized. In addition, a capacity on demand for each facility is considered.
The proposed metaheuristic framework integrates several components
such as a greedy randomized adaptive procedure with biased sampling
in its construction phase and iterated greedy with a variable neighborhood descent in its local search phase. The overall performance of the
heuristic is numerically assessed on widely used benchmarks on location
literature. The results indicate the proposed heuristic outperforms the
best existing heuristic.

Keywords: Combinatorial optimization, discrete location, metaheuristics, GRASP, IGLS, VND.

1 Introduction

The vertex p-center problem can be defined as the problem of locating p facilities
and assigning customers to them so as to minimize the longest distance between
any customer and its assigned facility. The term *vertex* means that the set of
candidate facility sites and the set of customers are the same. In the capacitated
version (CpCP) it is required that the total customer demand assigned to each
facility does not exceeded its given capacity. The CpCP is $\mathcal{NP}$-hard [1]. Practical
applications of p-center problems can be found in school districting planning or
system design in health coverage, to name a few.

The uncapacitated version of the problem has been widely investigated from
both exact and approximate approaches. Elloumi et al. [2] provide an extensive
review of the literature. The CpCP has received less attention in the literature.
From an exact optimization perspective, Özsoy and Pınar [3] presented an exact
method based on solving a series of set covering problems using an off-the-shelf
mixed-integer programming (MIP) solver while carrying out an iterative search
over the coverage distances. More recently, Albareda-Sambola et al. [4] proposed
an exact method based on Lagrangian relaxation and a covering reformulation.
From the heuristic perspective, the work of Scaparra et al. [5] stands as the

C. Bielza et al. (Eds.): CAEPIA 2013, LNAI 8109, pp. 279–288, 2013.
© Springer-Verlag Berlin Heidelberg 2013

most significant. They developed a heuristic based on large-scale local search with a multiexchange neighborhood represented by an improved graph exploiting principles from network optimization theory. In this paper, we present a metaheuristic framework that integrates several components such as greedy randomized adaptive procedures with biased sampling in its construction phase and iterated greedy with a variable neighborhood descent in its local search phase. The empirical work indicates our heuristic outperforms the best existing method.

2 Problem Formulation

Let V be the set of nodes representing customers or potential locations for the p facilities. The integer distance between nodes i and j is represented for d_{ij}. Each node $j \in V$ has a demand or weight w_j and each node $i \in V$ has a capacity defined by s_i. For the combinatorial model, a p-partition of V is denoted by $X = \{X_1, ..., X_p\}$, where $X_k \subset V$ is called a subset of V. Each subset X_k is formed by a subset of nodes such that $\bigcup_{k \in K} X_k = V$ and $X_k \cap X_l = \varnothing$ for all $k, l \in K, k \neq l$ where $K = \{1, ..., p\}$. The set of centers is denoted by $P \subset V$ such that $P = \{c(1), ..., c(p)\}$ where $c(k)$ is the active location for subset X_k, i.e., the node that hosts the facility serving the customers in X_k. The problem can be represented by the following combinatorial model.

$$\min_{X \in \Pi} \; \max_{k \in K} f(X_k) \tag{1}$$

where Π is the collection of all p-partitions of V. For a given territory X_k its cost function, also called the bottleneck cost, is computed as $f(X_k) = \max_{j \in X_k} \{d_{j,c(k)}\}$ where the center $c(k)$, taking into account the capacity, is given by

$$c(k) = \arg \min_{i \in X_k} \left\{ \max_{j \in X_k} \left\{ d_{ij} : \sum_{j' \in X_k} w_{j'} \leq s_i \right\} \right\} \tag{2}$$

Here, by convention, if for a given X_k there is not any $i \in X_k$ such that $\sum_{j \in X_k} w_j \leq s_i$ then $f(X_k) = \infty$.

3 Proposed Heuristic

To solve the problem we propose a metaheuristic framework with several components such as a greedy randomized adaptive [6] procedure with biased sampling in its construction phase and Iterated Greedy Local Search (IGLS) with a Variable Neighborhood Descent (VND) in its local search phase. IGLS is a method related to the Iterated Local Search (ILS) originally proposed by Ruiz and Stützle [7]. IGLS takes a solution as an input and iteratively applies destruction and reconstruction phase, in a special way focusing on the space of solutions that are locally optimal. Instead of iterating over a local search as done in ILS, IGLS iterates over a greedy reconstruction heuristic.

The VND is a variant of Variable Neighborhood Search (VNS) proposed by Hansen and Mladenovic [8, 9]. VNS is a metaheuristic for solving combinatorial and global optimization problems whose basic idea is a systematic change of neighborhood both within a descent phase to find a local optimum and in a perturbation phase to get out of the corresponding valley. VND method is obtained if a change of neighborhoods is performed in a deterministic way. The proposed approach is presented in Algorithm 1. An initial solution is obtained on Steps 2–3. Within the main loop (Steps 5–14), the local search (Steps 6–7) is performed as long as the solution keeps improving. By improving we mean that either the new solution has a better objective function than the previous or if it reduces the number of bottleneck customers while not worsening the total cost, without creating new bottleneck subsets and new bottleneck customers. If the solutions does not improve, then a shake of the solution is applied, this is defined as removing several bottleneck subsets that meet a given criteria and reconstructing a new solution from the partial solution. These components are described next.

Algorithm 1. GVND

1: **procedure** GVND($V, p, \alpha, \beta, Iter_{max}, \mathrm{LB}$)
2:     $X \leftarrow$ Construction(α, p)
3:     $X \leftarrow$ VND(X)
4:     $X^{best} \leftarrow X$
5:     **while** ¬(stopping criteria) **do**
6:         $X \leftarrow$ IGLS(β, X)
7:         $X \leftarrow$ VND(X)
8:         **if** X is better that X^{best} **then**
9:             $X^{best} \leftarrow X$
10:        **else**
11:            $X \leftarrow$ Shake(α, X)
12:        **end if**
13:        $Iter_{max} \leftarrow Iter_{max} - 1$
14:    **end while**
15:    **return** X^{best}
16: **end procedure**

Construction: The construction phase is comprised of two sub-tasks: (a) center location and (b) customer allocation. First, p nodes are chosen as centers. The choice of these centers is made through a greedy randomized adaptive construction procedure, taking into account the distance factors and the capacity of each vertex $j \in V$. This phase is based on the greedy method proposed by Dyer [10] for the p-center problem. The location phase starts by choosing the first center randomly. Then, we iteratively choose the next center seeking a node whose weighted distance from its nearest center is relatively large. The motivation of this is to try to obtain centers that are as disperse as possible, but also to favor the choice of centers with large capacity such we can assign more customers to it in the allocation phase. Within a greedy randomized procedure method this is done as follows. Let P be a partial set of chosen centers. Then for each $j \in V \setminus P$, its nearest center is given by $i^* = \arg\min_{i \in P}\{d_{ij}\}$. The we compute the greedy function as

$$\gamma(j) = s_j d_{i^* j} \tag{3}$$

A restricted candidate list (RCL) is built by the elements whose greedy function evaluation falls, within $\alpha\%$ of the best value. RCL $= \{j : \gamma(j) \geq \gamma^{\max} - \alpha(\gamma^{\max} - \gamma^{\min})\}$, where $\alpha \in (0,1)$.

Instead of choosing the next candidate element to add to the partial solution uniformly at random, we introduce a biased selection mechanism. In the construction mechanism proposed by Bresina [11], a family of such probability distributions is introduced. First, a rank $r[j]$ assigned to each candidate element j, according to its greedy function value (3). The element with the largest greedy function value has rank 1, the second largest has rank 2, and so on. In this case, we defined the bias function using an exponential distribution as $b(r[j]) = e^{-r[j]}$. Once all elements of the RCL have been ranked, the probability $\pi(j)$ of selecting element $j \in$ RCL can be computed as $\pi(j) = b(r[j]) / \sum_{j' \in \text{RCL}} b(r[j'])$.

Once the centers are fixed, the second sub-task consists of allocating the customers to these centers. This phase is performed in a deterministic greedy manner. As some preliminary testing showed, performing this step under a randomized greedy strategy did not bring any value to the quality of the solution. In addition, the pure greedy approach in this phase is more efficient. The customers are defined by the remaining nodes $j \in V \setminus P$. To this end we define a greedy function that measures the cost of assigning a customer j to a center k located in $c(k)$ as follows:

$$\phi(j, k) = \max\left\{ \frac{d_{jc(k)}}{\bar{d}}, -\left(s_{c(k)} - \sum_{j' \in X_k} w_{j'}\right) + w_j \right\} \tag{4}$$

where $\bar{d} = \max_{i,j \in V}\{d_{ij}\} + 1$ is a normalization factor. If the capacity constraint is satisfied, the function only takes into account the distance factor, otherwise, the function returns an integer value that penalizes the assignment. Then assigns each node j to a nearest center, namely $X_{k^*} \leftarrow X_{k^*} \cup \{j\}$ where $k^* = \arg\min_{k \in K} \phi(j, k)$. Finally, once the assignment is done, the centers for the entire partition are updated using (2).

Local Search: Given an initial solution built by the construction phase, the improvement phase applies an IGLS followed by VND with two neighborhoods based on insertion and exchange. Each procedure is briefly described next.

1. *IGLS:* This method takes a solution as an input and iteratively applies destruction and reconstruction phases. In this specific case, deallocating the $\beta\%$ of nodes located in X_k, with high values of the function $\rho(j) = d_{jc(k)} / \sum_{j' \in X_k} d_{jc(k)}$. The choice of this function is motivated by the fact that the nodes farther from the center are the ones affecting more the dispersion function. The reconstruction phase reassigns each disconnected node

to a nearest center, namely $X_{k^*} \leftarrow X_{k^*} \cup \{j\}$ where $k^* = \arg\min_{k \in K} \phi(j,k)$. A priority assignment is given to the bottleneck nodes, i.e., nodes whose previous assignment matched the value of the objective function value.

2. *VND:* This method is formed by two neighborhoods based on reinsertion and exchange movements. It is presented in Algorithm 2, where neighborhoods are denoted as $\mathcal{N}_k, k = 1, ..., k_{max}$, in this case $k_{max} = 2$. For each of the two neighborhoods, the potential move takes into account the distance factors and the capacity. Each neighborhood is briefly described next.

Algorithm 2. Variable Neighborhood Descent

```
1: procedure VND(X)
2:     while k ≤ k_max do
3:         X' ← arg min_{y∈N_k(X)} f(y)
4:         if X' is better that X then
5:             X' ← X
6:             k ← 1
7:         else
8:             k ← k + 1
9:         end if
10:    end while
11:    return X
12: end procedure
```

$\mathcal{N}_1$) *Reinsertion:* This neighborhood considers moves where a node i (currently assigned to center of set X_q) is assigned to set X_k, i.e., given $X = (X_1, ..., X_p)$ $reinsertion(i,k) = \{X_1, ..., X_q \setminus \{i\}, ..., X_k \cup \{i\}, ..., X_p\}$ where i must be a bottleneck node for the move to be attractive.

$\mathcal{N}_2$) *Exchange:* This neighborhood considers moves where two nodes i and j in different subsets are swapped, i.e., given $X = (X_1, ..., X_p)$, $swap(i,j) = \{X_1, ..., X_q \cup \{j\} \setminus \{i\}, ..., X_k \cup \{i\} \setminus \{j\}, ..., X_p\}$, where either i or j must be a bottleneck node for the move to be attractive.

Improvement Criteria: We uses a effective improvement criteria propose in [5] which includes the reduction of bottleneck elements, this is defined as

$$f(X') < f(X) \vee (f(X') = f(X), \mathcal{B}(X') \subseteq \mathcal{B}(X), \mathcal{J}(X') \subset \mathcal{J}(X)) \qquad (5)$$

where $\mathcal{B}(X)$ denote the set of bottleneck subsets in X, i.e., $\mathcal{B}(X) = \{k \in K : f(X_k) = f(X)\}$ and $\mathcal{J}(X)$ contains the demand nodes with maximum distance from the active location in each subset X_k, i.e., $\mathcal{J}(X) = \{j \in X_k : d_{jc(k)} = f(X), k \in \mathcal{B}(X)\}$. This criteria is met if it decreases the objective function value or if it reduces the number of bottleneck customers while not worsening the total cost, without creating new bottleneck subsets and new bottleneck customers. The incumbent solution X^{best} is updated if a better feasible solution is found according to the criterion (5) otherwise a shake of the solution X is applied.

Shake: We define an auxiliary mechanism that performs a partial shake of the current solution through an aggressive removal and reconstruction of several subsets, which diversifies the structure of the solution. The selection criteria of subsets is

$$\mathcal{L} \leftarrow \{\eta^1(j), \eta^2(j), \eta^3(j) : \eta^1(j) = l(j), j \in \mathcal{J}(X)\} \tag{6}$$

where $\eta(j) = \arg\min_{k \in K} d_{jc(k)}$. Then $\eta^1(j)$, $\eta^2(j)$, and $\eta^3(j)$ are the first, second, and third nearest centers to j, respectively, under the distance criterion. $l(j)$ is the center serving customer j. Let $W \leftarrow \cup_{k \in \mathcal{L}} X_k$. We then now remove these sets from the current solution $X \leftarrow X \setminus W$. Now, using the construction phase, we construct a new solution X' by reassigning the nodes in W with $p = |\mathcal{L}|$. Finally $X \leftarrow X \cup X'$ is the new current solution.

Stopping criteria: The approach stops when the maximum number of iterations is met or if a relative deviation with respect to a known (if any) lower bound (LB) for the problem is less than a given ϵ. For our practical purposes a value of 1.0×10^{-8} is used for ϵ.

4   Computational Results

This section shows the overall performance of the heuristic which is empirically assessed on widely used benchmarks on location literature. The heuristic was coded in C++, compiled with gcc/g++ version 4.2 with the "-O3" optimization level. ILOG CPLEX 12.5 is used in exact method proposed in [3] and we imposed some resource limitation to every test: computation was halted after 1 hour or in case of memory overflow. Each of the experiments was carried out on a MacBook Pro 13" with Intel Core i5 2.4 GHz, 4 GiB RAM under OS X Lion 10.7.5. For the experiments, we used three different data sets generated for other location problems.

(Set A) Beasley OR-Library: Contains two groups of 10 instances, with 50 demand nodes and 5 facilities to be located, and 100 demand nodes and 10 facilities to be located, respectively. In all of the problems the capacity is assumed equal for every facility.

(Set B) Galvão and ReVelle: The set includes two networks that were randomly generated by for the maximal covering location problem. The set includes 8 instances with size of 100 and 150 customers, and range from 5 to 15 centers. In this case, the facility capacities are variable.

(Set C) Lorena and Senne: The set includes 6 large instances whose size ranges from 100 to 402 customers, and from 10 to 40 centers. Also in this case, all of the facility sites have equal capacity. This set is considered large scale and therefore more difficult to solve.

Recall from Section 3 that two important algorithmic parameters are α and β. In a preliminary phase, the heuristic was fine-tuned by running the algorithm 50 iterations for each possible combination $\alpha \times \beta \in \{0.0, 0.1, \ldots, 1.0\} \times \{0.0, 0.1, \ldots, 1.0\}$

on the three data sets. We choose the best combination (α, β) for each dataset based on an average of the objective function value for all executions and combinations (α, β). For the remaining experiments, the choices of (α, β) are set to (0.4, 0.3), (0.3, 0.3), and (0.3,0.3), for data sets A, B, and C, respectively.

For the next experiments every run of our heuristic was done using 30 repetitions with different random seeds and using 500 as iteration limit. No lower bound (LB) was used. We perform a comparison of the proposed approach (Heuristic QR) with the heuristic by Scaparra et al. [5] (Heuristic SP) and the exact method by Özsoy and Pınar [3] (Exact OP). These methods have been executed over the same machine, under the conditions specified for each method, to ensure a fair comparison.

Table 1. Comparison of methods on data set A

n	p	Instance	Optimal	OP		SP		QR		
				gap %	Time (s)	gap %	Time (s)	gap^1 %	gap^2 %	Time (s)
50	5	cpmp01	29	0.00	0.19	0.00	0.45	0.00	0.00	0.45
		cpmp02	33	0.00	1.13	0.00	0.72	0.00	0.00	0.49
		cpmp03	26	0.00	0.20	0.00	0.56	0.00	0.00	0.48
		cpmp04	32	0.00	0.53	0.00	0.61	0.00	0.00	0.53
		cpmp05	29	0.00	1.02	0.00	0.69	0.00	0.00	0.50
		cpmp06	31	0.00	1.62	3.23	0.75	2.90	0.00	0.49
		cpmp07	30	0.00	0.51	0.00	0.91	0.67	0.00	0.53
		cpmp08	31	0.00	0.61	0.00	0.73	0.00	0.00	0.49
		cpmp09	28	0.00	0.74	3.57	0.91	3.33	0.00	0.49
		cpmp10	32	0.00	2.14	12.50	1.74	13.75	0.00	0.48
		Average		0.00	0.87	1.93	0.81	2.07	0.00	0.49
100	10	cpmp11	19	0.00	2.91	21.05	5.4	8.25	0.00	1.41
		cpmp12	20	0.00	2.91	10.00	5.74	4.17	0.00	1.39
		cpmp13	20	0.00	3.46	5.00	5.46	0.33	0.00	1.36
		cpmp14	20	0.00	2.15	10.00	5.28	2.50	0.00	1.37
		cpmp15	21	0.00	4.06	9.52	5.9	3.49	0.00	1.41
		cpmp16	20	0.00	6.96	10.00	7.04	3.83	0.00	1.43
		cpmp17	22	0.00	30.14	9.09	6.03	4.55	4.55	1.41
		cpmp18	21	0.00	6.50	4.76	4.74	1.75	0.00	1.34
		cpmp19	21	0.00	9.30	9.52	6.25	5.40	0.00	1.42
		cpmp20	21	0.00	12.25	0.00	5.93	8.89	0.00	1.44
		Average		0.00	8.06	8.90	5.78	4.31	0.45	1.40
		Overall average		0.00	4.47	5.41	3.29	3.19	0.23	0.94

Tables 1–3 display the comparison of methods for each data set. In each table the first two columns represent the instance size measured by number of nodes n and number of partitions p. "Instance" is the name of the particular problem instance and "Optimal" indicates the optimal value of the instance. For each method column "gap (%)" expresses the percent of relative deviation or gap with respect to the optimal value and "Time (s)" gives the execution time in seconds. It should be noted that for the proposed method QR, we show the time average performance over the 30 independent repetitions, also "gap^1 %" and "gap^2 %" denote the average and best gap, respectively, over all repetitions. Table 4 summarizes the comparison among methods for the three data sets in terms of their average relative optimality gap, running time, and memory usage. The memory statistic indicates the maximum resident set size used [12], in bits, that is, the maximum number of bits of physical memory that each approach used simultaneously.

Table 2. Comparison of methods on data set B

n	p	Instance	Optimal	OP gap %	OP Time (s)	SP gap %	SP Time (s)	QR gap[1] %	QR gap[2] %	QR Time (s)
100	5	G1	94	0.00	4.49	3.19	4.71	1.88	1.06	1.39
100	5	G2	94	0.00	5.90	3.19	4.48	1.60	0.00	1.23
100	10	G3	83	0.00	121.44	9.64	8.01	8.72	4.82	1.58
100	10	G4	84	0.00	25.03	8.33	8.28	8.73	5.95	1.54
150	10	G5	95	0.00	190.95	5.26	22.61	4.95	3.16	2.70
150	10	G6	96	0.00	120.46	5.21	21.21	4.38	3.13	2.37
150	15	G7	89	0.00	60.62	8.99	28.31	8.35	5.62	3.53
150	15	G8	89	0.00	213.61	10.11	26.52	8.84	6.74	3.48
		Overall average		0.00	92.81	6.74	15.52	5.93	3.81	2.23

The first thing to notice is that for all instances tested, an optimal solution was found by the exact method, such that the "gap" column in all tables represents the true relative optimality gap found by any method. As far as data set A is concerned, the exact method was found very efficient for the smaller instance group (size 50×5), performing better than any heuristic. However, when attempting the larger group (size 100×10), there are a couple of instances for which the exact method struggled. The performance of both heuristics was more robust than that of the exact method as they both took less than 1.5 seconds to solve each instance. In terms of solution quality, the proposed heuristic found better solutions than the ones reported by the SP heuristic.

Table 3. Comparison of methods on data set C

n	p	Instance	Optimal	OP gap %	OP Time (s)	SP gap %	SP Time (s)	QR gap[1] %	QR gap[2] %	QR Time (s)
100	10	SJC1	364	0.00	195.16	26.67	8.79	23.24	7.478	0.68
200	15	SJC2	304	0.00	74.30	10.48	39.60	7.37	1.599	1.95
300	25	SJC3a	278	0.00	136.49	38.73	125.03	16.41	7.184	6.12
300	30	SJC3b	253	0.00	152.20	35.59	119.65	13.16	3.661	8.38
402	30	SJC4a	284	0.00	522.63	30.99	283.18	9.76	5.219	11.39
402	40	SJC4b	239	0.00	157.52	44.12	241.68	10.94	2.346	18.56
		Overall average		0.00	206.38	31.10	136.32	13.48	4.58	7.85

When analyzing data set B we can observe that the exact method takes considerably longer than both heuristics to reach an optimal solution. On average, the exact method takes about an order of magnitude longer. In terms of solution quality, again our heuristic obtains better solutions (average gap of 5.93 %) than the SP heuristic (average gap of 6.74%). Regarding data set C, we can observe that the exact method takes on average above 4 minutes while our heuristic takes less than 9 seconds. When comparing our heuristic with the SP heuristic, we can see that ours is faster and finds solutions of significantly better quality. Figure 1 shows a comparison of the methods in terms of their asymptotic running time and used memory resources with respect to the number of nodes. As can be seen, the resources used by the proposed approach are lower than those used by the other two methods.

There exist a recent data set added to the OR-Library that features values of p proportional to the number of nodes. This is regarded as a very hard set to

Table 4. Summary of comparison among methods on data sets A, B, and C

Dataset	Average gap (%)				Average time (s)			Average memory (bits)		
	OP	SP	QR^1	QR^2	OP	SP	QR	OP	SP	QR
A	0.00	5.41	3.19	0.23	4.47	3.29	0.94	2.59E+07	4.37E+07	5.12E+05
B	0.00	6.74	5.93	3.81	92.81	15.52	2.23	4.78E+07	2.12E+08	5.57E+05
C	0.00	31.10	13.48	4.58	206.38	136.32	7.85	1.38E+08	4.70E+08	7.96E+05

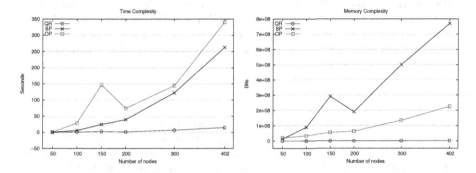

Fig. 1. Comparison of methods in terms of asymptotic running time and memory usage

solve for capacitated location problems such as p-median and p-center problems. In our preliminary experiments, we have observed that the exact method fails to find optimal solutions for some instances. Table 5 displays the results on this data set. As can be seen, the exact method is unable to find a feasible solution in all five instances either by reaching the time limit of 1 hr (instances 1 and 3) or by running out of memory (instances 2, 4, and 5). Heuristic SP fails in delivering an optimal solution in 3 out of 5 instances. Our heuristic finds a feasible solution in 4 out of 5 instances.

Table 5. Comparison of methods on data set D

Subset	Instance	n	p	OP		SP		QR	
				Best LB	Time (s)	Objetive	Time (s)	Objetive	Time (s)
D	27	150	60	10	3600.00	-	-	55	22.94
D	32	200	80	11	959.04	-	-	-	-
D	33	200	80	7	3600.00	10	49.72	14	47.95
D	35	200	80	8	964.56	12	59.91	16	41.18
D	40	200	80	8	2846.75	-	-	18	41.39

5   Conclusions

We have proposed a metaheuristic framework that integrates several components such as a greedy randomized adaptive procedure with biased sampling in its construction phase and iterated greedy with a variable neighborhood descent in its local search phase. The preliminary results are very promising. The results indicate the proposed heuristic outperforms the best heuristic in terms of both solution quality and running time. The performance of the proposed approach is more robust than that of the exact method, requiring less seconds and memory to solve each instance obtaining reasonably good objective values.

Acknowledgements. This work was supported by the Mexican National Council for Science and Technology (grant CONACYT CB-2011-01-166397) and Universidad Autónoma de Nuevo León (grant UANL-PAICYT CE728-11). We also thank Maria Scaparra for providing us with the source code of her heuristic.

References

[1] Kariv, O., Hakimi, S.L.: An algorithmic approach to network location problems, Part I: The p-centers. SIAM Journal on Applied Mathematics 37, 513–538 (1979)

[2] Elloumi, S., Labbé, M., Pochet, Y.: A new formulation and resolution method for the p-center problem. INFORMS Journal on Computing 16(1), 84–94 (2004)

[3] Özsoy, F.A., Pınar, M.Ç.: An exact algorithm for the capacitated vertex p-center problem. Computers & Operations Research 33(5), 1420–1436 (2006)

[4] Albareda-Sambola, M., Díaz-García, J.A., Fernández, E.: Lagrangean duals and exact solution to the capacitated p-center problem. European Journal of Operational Research 201(1), 71–81 (2010)

[5] Scaparra, M.P., Pallottino, S., Scutellà, M.G.: Large-scale local search heuristics for the capacitated vertex p-center problem. Networks 43(4), 241–255 (2004)

[6] Feo, T.A., Resende, M.G.C.: Greedy randomized adaptive search procedures. Journal of Global Optimization 6(2), 109–133 (1995)

[7] Ruiz, R., Stützle, T.: A simple and effective iterated greedy algorithm for the permutation flowshop scheduling problem. European Journal of Operational Research 177(3), 2033–2049 (2007)

[8] Hansen, P., Mladenović, N.: Variable neighborhood search: Principles and applications. European Journal of Operational Research 130(3), 449–467 (2001)

[9] Gendreau, M., Potvin, J.Y. (eds.): Handbook of Metaheuristics, 2nd edn. International Series in Operations Research & Management Science, vol. 146. Springer, New York (2010)

[10] Dyer, M.E., Frieze, A.: A simple heuristic for the p-center problem. Operations Research Letters 3(6), 285–288 (1985)

[11] Bresina, J.L.: Heuristic-biased stochastic sampling. In: Proceedings of the Thirteenth National Conference on Artificial Intelligence, AAAI 1996, Portland, USA, vol. 1, pp. 271–278. AAAI Press (1996)

[12] Loosemore, S., Stallman, R.M., McGrath, R., Oram, A., Drepper, U.: The GNU C Library Reference Manual: For version 2.17. Free Software Foundation, Boston, USA (2012)

Reducing Gas Emissions in Smart Cities by Using the Red Swarm Architecture

Daniel H. Stolfi and Enrique Alba

LCC, University of Málaga, Spain
{dhstolfi,eat}@lcc.uma.es

Abstract. The aim of the work presented here is to reduce gas emissions in modern cities by creating a light infrastructure of WiFi intelligent spots informing drivers of customized, real-time routes to their destinations. The reduction of gas emissions is an important aspect of smart cities, since it directly affects the health of citizens as well as the environmental impact of road traffic. We have built a real scenario of the city of Malaga (Spain) by using OpenStreetMap (OSM) and the SUMO road traffic microsimulator, and solved it by using an efficient new Evolutionary Algorithm (EA). Thus, we are dealing with a real city (not just a roundabout, as found in the literature) and we can therefore measure the emissions of cars in movement according to traffic regulations (real human scenarios). Our results suggest an important reduction in gas emissions (10%) and travel times (9%) is possible when vehicles are rerouted by using the Red Swarm architecture. Our approach is even competitive with human expert's solutions to the same problem.

Keywords: Application, Evolutionary Algorithm, Gas Emissions, Road Traffic, Smart City, Smart Mobility.

1 Introduction

The concept of Smart City is global, but it is related to six concrete characteristics: smart economy, smart people, smart governance, smart mobility, smart environment, and smart living [1]. There is an interplay between these domains as they are broadly related to future sustainable urban development.

The aim of the work presented here is to reduce greenhouse gas emissions and other gases which cause air pollution (smart environment). This is an important aspect of smart cities, since it directly affects the health of citizens (smart living) and represents the environmental impact of road traffic (smart mobility).

One of the European Union's objectives for the year 2020 is the reduction of greenhouse gas emissions [2]. Several countries have pledged to reduce these emissions by the year 2020 in sectors outside of carbon emission rights. While we wait for the electric car to become a mass reality, an effective system to manage road traffic will always mean to reduce the current gas emissions.

C. Bielza et al. (Eds.): CAEPIA 2013, LNAI 8109, pp. 289–299, 2013.

For example, carbon dioxide (CO_2) emissions from fuel combustion have been rising since 1971 [1] (the first year of pollution statistics) worldwide and this growing tendency will be hard to revert in the near future.

Carbon monoxide (CO) affects human health as well as the ability of the atmosphere to rid itself of polluting gases. Any combustion process has the potential to produce carbon monoxide gases, especially in vehicles. Furthermore, CO can be turned into CO_2 through chemical processes in the atmosphere. [3].

Our proposal directly relates to the strategy Europe 2020 and the Smart Cities initiative because we focus on the reduction of gas emissions and travel times. We have already presented a preliminary proposal of our Red Swarm [4] architecture for lowering travel times in Malaga (Spain) by rerouting vehicles using a globally distributed strategy that respects user destinations and is positive for travel times through the city. In the present work we state that this strategy can also be used to reduce the pollutant emissions from vehicles which move through the streets of a modern city.

This article is structured as follows. First, Section 2 reviews some other approaches related to the reduction of gas emissions. Then, Section 3 describes the methodology applied and the Red Swarm architecture while Section 4 focuses on the experiments conducted and the analysis of the results. Finally, Section 5 provides our conclusions and future work.

2   Related Work

There are several studies which focus on reducing gas emissions from vehicles in urban areas. In [5], the authors stated that an improvement in the traffic flow does not necessarily guarantee reduced emission levels and that a solution which focuses only on reducing travel times may result in higher emissions than others which also take emissions into account. We had also reached the same conclusion, so we decided to start the present work, taking gas emissions into account by including them in the optimization process.

Several route optimizations were performed in [6] using different metrics other than travel times. The authors observed that optimization seems to depend on the type of roads available in the area analyzed. Furthermore, a series of inter-dependencies between pollutant emissions and road network types were given. Although we have observed some of the dependencies mentioned in this paper, we will focus on reducing CO and check how the rest of the metrics behave.

Red Swarm is our proposal which concentrates on reducing traffic jams, so our solution is consistent with [7], where a linear and positive correlation between the occupancy of the network and the emissions criteria was demonstrated.

Finally, the necessity of using multiple metrics for evaluating Intelligent Transportation Systems (ITS) which include gas emissions as well as travel times was presented in [8]. The authors use an Inter-Vehicle Communication (IVC) system in order to inform vehicles of possible congestions or accidents. The results show

---

[1] CO_2 Emissions From Fuel Combustion - HighLights © OECD/IEA, (2012).

that metrics are usually in conflict with each other, which shows that we are attempting to solve a very complex problem.

These approaches have encouraged us to extend our previous proposal [4], which only focused on the optimization of travel times, and include here the reduction of gas emissions as an innovative solution in a smart city where communications between vehicles and the infrastructure (WiFi spots) is possible.

3   Methodology

Our architecture Red Swarm [4] is an affordable system for any modern city that only needs the utilization of already existing computers in traffic lights (which is true for most cities in Spain) plus a WiFi spot and our software solution based on bio-inspired algorithms. It consists of: *i)* Several spots distributed throughout the city, installed at traffic lights with the purpose of redirecting the traffic efficiently; *ii)* An Evolutionary Algorithm (EA) which calculates the configuration for the Rerouting Algorithm; and *iii)* The Rerouting Algorithm which runs in each spot and suggests alternative routes to vehicles by using a WiFi link between the spot and the On Board Unit (OBU) installed in each vehicle.

As we have successfully reduced travel times of vehicles in our afore mentioned previous approach, our next step is to address the reduction of gas emissions produced by vehicles in the city. In order to evaluate a configuration of the system, we use the microscopic traffic simulator SUMO (Simulator of Urban Mobility) [9] which interacts with TraCI (Traffic Control Interface) [10]. While SUMO simulates the traffic flow of each vehicle, TraCI allows our Rerouting Algorithm to control SUMO to obtain the state of the simulation and change it.

SUMO implements the car-following model developed by Stefan Krauß in [11] while pollutant emissions and fuel consumption are based on values of the HBEFA database [12]. At the end of the simulation, data from vehicles such as travel time, travel distance, fuel consumption, gas emissions, etc., can be collected from the log files generated.

Red Swarm is based on the principle of avoiding traffic jams. Each Red Swarm spot consists of a WiFi access point installed at a traffic light and a processing unit

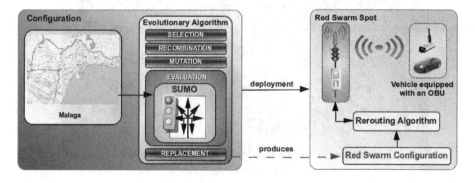

Fig. 1. Component Schema of Red Swarm

which communicates with the approaching vehicles (V2I) and informs them of the new itinerary to follow to their personal destination. This intelligent distribution of traffic is done by the Rerouting Algorithm which reads the configuration calculated previously by the EA according to the city's characteristics. Fig. 1 presents a schema with the relationship between components of Red Swarm.

3.1   Optimization Scenario and Technology

The scenario chosen for our study corresponds to an area of the city of Malaga (Spain). The analyzed square is bounded by Carretería Street to the north, the Mediterranean Sea to the south, Gutemberg Street to the east, and the Guadalmedina River to the west.

The characteristics of the scenario are:

– Eight inputs and eight outputs corresponding to real streets of the city.
– Sixty four flows (all possible journeys between input and output streets).
– Ten Red Swarm spots.
– Four different kinds of vehicles: sedan, van, wagon, and transport.

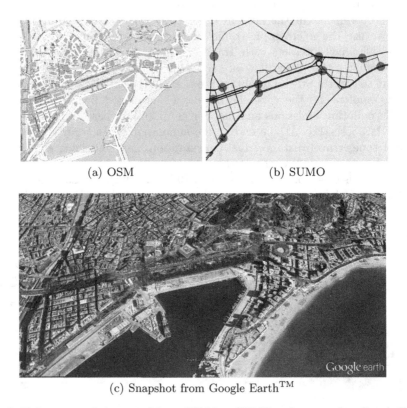

(a) OSM   (b) SUMO

(c) Snapshot from Google Earth[TM]

Fig. 2. Malaga scenario imported from OSM into SUMO and exported to Google Earth

First, we have imported the scenario from the OpenStreetMap (OSM) project in order to work with real streets of the urban area. Then, we can export this scenario from SUMO to Google Earth^{TM} with the vehicles, traffic lights and sensors which we have added to it, so that we can obtain a photorealistic snapshot of the simulation. In Fig. 2(a) we show a snapshot from OSM of the area analyzed, in Fig. 2(b) the same area imported into SUMO, and in Fig. 2(c) a snapshot exported from SUMO to Google Earth^{TM}. Note the ten Red Swarm spots placed in strategic junctions of the city (red circles).

3.2 Evolutionary Algorithm

We have designed an Evolutionary Algorithm (10+2)-EA to solve this problem.

Solution Encoding. The solution encoding consists of configuring the sensors related to each Red Swarm spot arranged into chunks of routes depending on the vehicles' destination. When a vehicle is rerouted, the Rerouting Algorithm gets a set of routes from the solution depending on the vehicle's destination and the street in which the vehicle is (determined by the sensor activated). Then, the new route for the vehicle is calculated based on the probabilities stored in the solution, thus the summation of all the probabilities which belong to the same destination chunk must be equal to 1.0. For example, if a vehicle v which is traveling to D_8 is detected by the sensor S_1, the Rerouting Algorithm will reroute it depending on the probabilities stored in the chunk D_8 which belongs to S_1. In Fig. 3 we illustrate the status vector of probabilities as well as their meaning. Note that the complete vector consists of 28 sensors with eight destination chunks included inside each one.

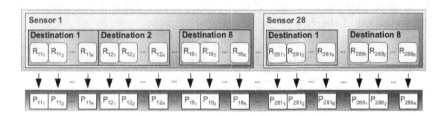

Fig. 3. Solution encoding

Fitness Function. We define the fitness function presented in Equation 1 in order to reduce only CO emissions and later evaluate the rest of the metrics (gas emissions, travel times, and route lengths) as a way of checking how robust our solution is and which correlations we can observe.

$$F = \omega_1(N - n_{trips}) + \omega_2 \frac{\sum CO_{trip}}{N} \qquad (1)$$

The fitness function contains two terms to be minimized. In the first one, N is the total number of vehicles in the scenario and n_{trips} is the number of vehicles which complete their trip during the simulation. This term guarantees that all vehicles arrive at their destination which is especially important as SUMO writes trip data in output files only for those vehicles which complete their itinerary. As a consequence, we need all the values to successfully calculate the fitness value. The second term represents the average CO emitted by the vehicles during the period of analysis. The weights ω_1 and ω_2 are required to normalize each term in the fitness value.

Operators. The selection strategy implemented in EA is nondeterministic. It selects two individuals from the population by using the uniform distribution provided by the pseudo-random number generator included in Python as it is the language in which we have developed the algorithm. We have used a standard two point crossover as the recombination operator and, ADOS (All Destinations - One Sensor) and ODOS (One Destination - One Sensor) [4] as specialized mutation operators. Finally, we have performed an elitist replacement, so that the worst individuals of the population are replaced if they have a fitness value higher than the offspring produced in the current generation.

Parameterization. We set a population size of ten individuals and, in each new generation, two new descendants are created according to the crossover (0.8) and mutation (0.6) probabilities. The mutation operator is selected depending on the mutation threshold. If the fitness value is over the threshold (8000) the ADOS mutation is applied and when the value is under the threshold, the ODOS mutation is used instead. The former allows a quick search of the data space while the latter performs a more careful exploration in order to improve the solution in small steps. These values, as well as the number of generations, were the best after performing a set of preliminary tests. Table 1 summarizes the parameterization of the EA.

Table 1. Parameters of the EA

Evaluation Time (s)	2000
Population Size	10
Offspring Size	2
Crossover Probability	0.8
Mutation Probability	0.6
Mutation Threshold	8000
Number of Generations	8000
(ω_1, ω_2)	(4096, 1)

Finally, the value of ω_1 (4096) corresponds to the average CO emissions from vehicles obtained from the experts' solution (included in Table 2), and the value of ω_2 (1) makes the CO emissions to be linearly related to the fitness value. Note that the first term of the fitness function is different from zero only when there exist vehicles which are still in the city at the end of the period analyzed, and hence penalizing these solutions.

3.3 Experimental Settings

We have performed 110 independent runs of the optimization algorithm on 16 machines which are part of the cluster belonging to the NEO (Networking and Emerging Optimization) group. Each one is equipped with an Intel Core2 Quad CPU (Q9400) @ 2.66GHz and 3.5 GB of RAM, running GNU/Linux 3.2.0-39. Each new generation lasted 40 seconds (we are dealing with a large number of streets, traffic lights and vehicles) and the average time spent in obtaining each final solution was about 50 hours. Such a long execution time is caused by the fact that we have optimized three different traffic scenarios simultaneously in order to find a robust solution for every single fitness evaluation.

4   Results

The optimization of the scenario was performed by using the EA previously defined. As a result, we have achieved the values shown in Table 2. We report the CO reduction as it is the metric which we focused on, but also the rest of the emissions obtained from the scenario are included as well as the travel time and the route length. Note that these values are the average of the 800 vehicles which have traveled through the city during the period analyzed.

Table 2. Results of the CO reduction and the effects on the rest of the metrics

Metric	Experts' Solution	Red Swarm	Improvement
CO (mg)	4095.7	**3950.7**	3.5%
CO_2 (g)	**518.6**	519.0	-0.1%
HC (mg)	175.5	**170.6**	2.8%
NO_x (mg)	**910.0**	912.9	-0.3%
Travel Time (s)	549.9	**544.5**	1.0%
Route length (m)	**1471.7**	1587.2	-7.9%

Results show a significant reduction (-3.5%) of carbon monoxide (CO) emitted by the vehicles and also 2.8% less in Hydro-Carbons (HC) when our Red Swarm system is used. Carbon dioxide emissions (CO_2) and Nitrogen oxides (NO_x) present a negligible increment of 0.1% and 0.3%, respectively, while the average travel time is still better (lower) than the experts' solution (-1.0%). This is an important fact for us, because Red Swarm was conceived as a method for reducing travel times in the city and we do not want to renounce this goal. Finally, route lengths are 7.9% longer, mainly because we are rerouting vehicles via alternatives streets which do not belong to the best path chosen by the experts.

Table 3. Results averaged over runs on 50 random instances and the best of them

Metric	Average			Best solution		
	Experts	R-S	Improv.	Experts	R-S	Improv.
CO (mg)	4161.4	**4080.0**	1.9%	4435.0	**3988.0**	10.1%
CO_2 (g)	**522.6**	533.0	-2.0%	549.7	**527.8**	4.0%
HC (mg)	178.9	**175.9**	1.7%	194.0	**173.2**	10.7%
NO_x (mg)	**914.6**	937.4	-2.5%	953.0	**927.0**	2.7%
Travel Time (s)	555.1	**552.4**	0.5%	597.4	**543.1**	9.1%
Route length (m)	**1459.4**	1617.3	-10.8%	**1467.5**	1616.1	-10.1%

Globally, we provide a very important reduction in pollution at the small and distributed cost of slightly longer journey for citizens. However, they are not spending more time in completing their journey, since we are explicitly computing the fastest routes for them.

Moreover, we have carried out 50 additional runs to evaluate different random seeds which affect the traffic distribution (vehicle order, flows, etc.) in order to test the robustness of our solution applied to this area of Malaga. We have calculated the average metrics of these runs and also selected the best of them to be analyzed as follows.

The results provided in Table 3 present a 10% (avg. 2%) reduction in carbon monoxide emissions, a 11% (avg. 2%) reduction in hydro-carbons emissions, and travel times are 9% (avg. 1%) shorter than the experts' solution. Although carbon dioxide emissions, nitrogen oxides emissions, and route lengths are not improved on average (2.0% and 2.5% higher, respectively), CO_2 and NO_x are actually reduced by our best solution (-4.0% and -2.7%, respectively). These average results were as expected because our main goal in this complex work was to reduce CO emissions of vehicles thus we have included only this metric in the fitness function.

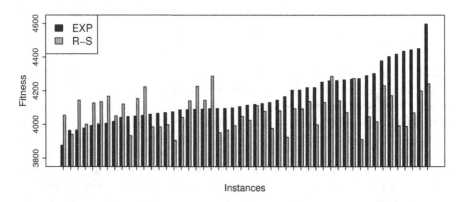

Fig. 4. Fitness from experts' solution and Red Swarm (50 instances)

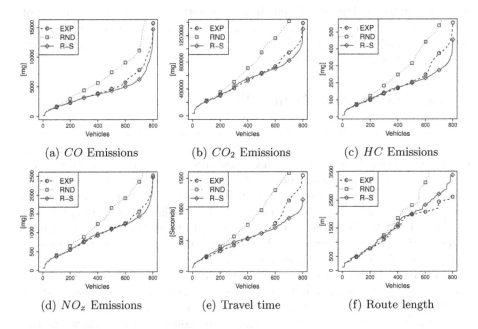

(a) CO Emissions   (b) CO_2 Emissions   (c) HC Emissions

(d) NO_x Emissions   (e) Travel time   (f) Route length

Fig. 5. Metrics for the experts' solution (EXP), RANDOM search (RND), and Red Swarm (R-S), for the best solution

The overall result is a positive one: we can reduce pollution and at the same time reduce travel times in the city. That will be what citizens and authorities will obtain as a net contribution towards a smart city. The small increments in route lengths are as we would all accept when using highways, for example.

Furthermore, the best result is satisfactory as is the average one, as we have tested it against 50 different instances in which Red Swarm outperforms the experts' solution in 34 of them (68%). Fig. 4 shows fitness values from the experts' solution (EXP) and Red Swarm (R-S) for each pair of instances evaluated. Note that they are sorted by the fitness value of the experts' solution and that the y axis does not start at zero.

We have also carried out a sanity check in order to validate our algorithm against a random search. Data from the experts' solution (EXP), RANDOM search (RND), and Red Swarm are shown in Fig. 5.

Figures 5(a), 5(b), 5(c) and 5(d) plot the graphs of gas emissions of the 800 vehicles sorted by value. We can observe that CO and HC emissions of Red Swarm (R-S) are in general, lower than the experts' values. Besides, CO_2 and NO_x emission values are not so different between the experts' solution and Red Swarm. Fig. 5(e) shows that the maximum travel time of vehicles in Red Swarm is lower than those observed in the experts' solution. And finally, Fig. 5(f) shows that routes in Red Swarm are longer than the experts' ones.

Additionally, values from RANDOM search (RND) shown in these figures are the worst of the comparison. These poor results of RANDOM search are mainly produced by the vehicles which remain into the city, moving in circles instead of being routed to their destination. This indicates that RANDOM search is not capable to produce a good configuration for Red Swarm, thus confirming that we need some smart guidance like the one provided by the EA used.

5 Conclusions and Future Work

In this paper we show how to reduce the gas emissions from vehicles during their journeys through the city of Malaga by using the Red Swarm architecture. To do this, we have defined an EA, a specialized fitness function, and carried out a great deal of complex experiments in order to obtain a solution which improves the experts' one implemented in SUMO. Results confirm that our approach is competitive not only in the best scenario (10.1% less in CO emissions) but also in 68% of the different traffic distributions tested (34 of 50). Moreover, we have observed that our work, based on Red Swarm, also reduces the travel time of vehicles as well as the rest of the emissions analyzed.

After studying the state of the art, especially [6,13], we have concluded that those works are based on a different model than our proposal because instead of setting the entire route of vehicles, we just send them to another Red Swarm spot or to their destination. Furthermore, our model does not restrict arrival times of vehicles to being fixed, so the comparative of results would not be fair.

As a matter of future work, we are currently extending the zone analyzed with the aim of including the whole city of Malaga in the optimization process. We are also testing different kinds of bio-inspired algorithms in order to reduce the computation time and the solution quality.

We should probably also try to have a more sophisticated problem definition, such as a multiobjective modeling; this is however difficult, since the high computing time and the realistic data we are using is quite different from standard benchmarks and will need a careful analysis in terms of metrics and Pareto fronts obtained (possibly with just a few points, for example).

Acknowledgments. Authors acknowledge funds from the Ministry of Economy and Competitiveness and FEDER under contract TIN2011-28194 roadME: (http://roadme.lcc.uma.es).

References

1. Giffinger, R., Pichler-Milanović, N.: Smart cities: Ranking of European Medium-sized Cities. Centre of Regional Science, Vienna University of Technology (2007)
2. European-Commission: Europe 2020: A Strategy for Smart, Sustainable and Inclusive Growth: Communication from the Commission. Publications Office (2010)
3. Wiedmann, T., Minx, J.: A Definition of 'Carbon Footprint'. Ecological Economics Research Trends (2007)
4. Stolfi, D.H., Alba, E.: Red Swarm: Smart Mobility in Cities with EAs. In: Proceeding of the Fifteenth Annual Conference on Genetic and Evolutionary Computation Conference, GECCO 2013, pp. 1373–1380. ACM (2013)

5. Zegeye, S.K., De Schutter, B., Hellendoorn, H., Breunesse, E.: Reduction of Travel Times and Traffic Emissions Using Model Predictive Control. In: 2009 American Control Conference, pp. 5392–5397 (2009)
6. Krajzewicz, D., Wagner, P.: Large-Scale Vehicle Routing Scenarios Based on Pollutant Emissions. In: Adv. Microsystems for Automotive Applications, pp. 237–246 (2011)
7. Sánchez Medina, J., Galán Moreno, M., Rubio Royo, E.: Study of Correlation Among Several Traffic Parameters Using Evolutionary Algorithms: Traffic Flow, Greenhouse Emissions and Network Occupancy. In: Moreno Díaz, R., Pichler, F., Quesada Arencibia, A. (eds.) EUROCAST 2007. LNCS, vol. 4739, pp. 1134–1141. Springer, Heidelberg (2007)
8. Sommer, C., Krul, R., German, R., Dressler, F.: Emissions vs. Travel Time: Simulative Evaluation of the Environmental Impact of ITS. In: 2010 IEEE 71st Vehicular Technology Conference, pp. 1–5 (2010)
9. Behrisch, M., Bieker, L., Erdmann, J., Krajzewicz, D.: SUMO - Simulation of Urban MObility: An Overview. In: The Third International Conference on Advances in System Simulation, SIMUL 2011, Barcelona, Spain, pp. 63–68 (October 2011)
10. Wegener, A., Hellbrück, H., Wewetzer, C., Lubke, A.: VANET Simulation Environment with Feedback Loop and its Application to Traffic Light Assistance. In: 2008 IEEE GLOBECOM Workshops, pp. 1–7. IEEE (2008)
11. Krauß, S.: Microscopic Modeling of Traffic Flow: Investigation of Collision Free Vehicle Dynamics. PhD thesis, Universitat zu Koln (1998)
12. Hausberger, S., Rexeis, M., Zallinger, M., Luz, R.: Emission Factors from the Model PHEM for the HBEFA Version 3. University of Technology, Graz, Report Nr. I-20/2009 Haus-Em 33(08), 679 (2009)
13. Gawron, C.: Simulation-based traffic assignment: Computing user equilibria in large street networks. PhD thesis (1999)

Heuristic Optimization Model
for Infrastructure Asset Management

Cristina Torres-Machí[1], Eugenio Pellicer[1], Víctor Yepes[2], and Alondra Chamorro[3]

[1] School of Civil Engineering, Universitat Politècnica de València, Spain
{critorma,pellicer}@upv.es
[2] ICITECH, Department of Construction Engineering, Universitat Politècnica de València
vyepesp@upv.es
[3] Departamento de Ingeniería y Gestión de la Construcción Escuela de Ingeniería,
Pontificia Universidad Católica de Chile
achamorro@ing.puc.cl

Abstract. In developed countries, the need of infrastructure maintenance is becoming an important issue because their infrastructures have been built up progressively over the last 100 years or longer. Moreover, users are increasingly demanding in terms of quality, comfort, and safety. Under this scenario, infrastructure managers seek to optimize each monetary unit invested in maintenance, thus ensuring that funds are allocated to the best alternative. This paper presents a heuristic model for solving the budget allocation problem with the implementation of a Simulated Annealing (SA) algorithm. An illustrative example is undertaken, analyzing the effect of budgetary restrictions in infrastructure performance. It can be concluded that infrastructure performance shows a good parabolic correlation with available budget.

Keywords: Asset management, optimization, budget allocation, maintenance, performance.

1 Introduction

Due to the fact that infrastructures are one of the main assets of countries, they need to be managed in such a way that they present an acceptable condition over their service lives. In developed countries, the need of maintenance management is especially important because their infrastructures have been built up progressively over the last 100 years or longer; the infrastructure network has tended to stabilize, reducing the funds requirements in new construction but increasing the requirements in preservation. At the same time, users are increasingly demanding in terms of quality, comfort, and safety. However, the current economic crisis is increasing the budgetary pressures on maintenance agencies. This leads to an important deterioration of infrastructures, making larger the gap between infrastructure needs and historical rates of investment.

Based on a report dealing with the current condition of American's infrastructures [1], the figures are worrisome: current spending ($1.1 trillion per year) amounts to only about a half of the investment needed to bring current condition to a good

C. Bielza et al. (Eds.): CAEPIA 2013, LNAI 8109, pp. 300–309, 2013.
© Springer-Verlag Berlin Heidelberg 2013

condition. In order to analyze a specific example: one-third of America's major roads are in poor or mediocre condition and the estimated budget needed annually to improve road conditions doubles the current spending ($70.3 billion per year). Other infrastructures currently present similar poor conditions and there is a clear trend of decreasing grades (Table 1).

Table 1. ASCE Report Card Grades [1]

	1988	1998	2001	2005	2009
Aviation	B-	C-	D	D+	D
Bridges	-	C-	C	C	C
Drinking water	B-	D	D	D-	D-
Hazardous waste	D	D-	D+	D	D
Inland waterways	B-	-	D+	D-	D-
Roads	C+	D-	D+	D	D-
Schools	D	F	D-	D	D
Solid waste	C-	C-	C+	C+	C+
Transit	C-	C-	C-	D+	D
Wastewater	C	D+	D	D-	D-
America's Infrastructure	*C*	*D*	*D+*	*D*	*D*

In this context, infrastructure managers seek to optimize each monetary unit invested in maintenance. For this purpose, managers undertake analysis at three levels [2]: project level, network level and strategic level. In broad terms, technical decisions on a specific asset are made at the project level; at the network level, the network maintenance programming is defined considering the available budget; and finally, at the strategic level, overall objectives are stated based on the organization's policies [3]. Previous works have dealt with the problem at the project [4] and strategic level [5]. This paper deals with the maintenance management problem at the network level.

At the network level, the problem is known as the "budget allocation problem" and it consists on defining the maintenance program by answering [6]: (a) which infrastructures should receive treatment?; (b) what treatment should be applied?; and (c) when should it be applied? However, the solution of the problem is not direct: S^{TxN} solutions are feasible for solving the maintenance program of a network with N infrastructures, S maintenance treatments and a planning horizon of T years [7] (Fig. 1).

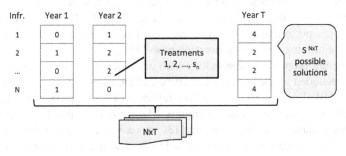

Fig. 1. Possible solutions to the budget allocation problem [7]

This kind of problem suffers from combinatorial explosion and it can be handle using different techniques. A recent review undertaken by the authors [8] reveals that the methods mainly used are mathematical optimization (i.e. linear, non-linear, integer programming, etc.) and heuristic optimization. However, reviewed applications using mathematical optimization show a trend of limiting the number of variables considered in the optimization [9-10]. Regarding heuristic methods, most studies have focused on evolutionary based optimization algorithms and, specifically, on genetic algorithms [11]. As far as the authors are aware, existing applications do not solve the problem at the network level considering local search heuristics.

Having stated this gap in the literature, this paper seeks to present a model that enables the optimization by local search heuristics of maintenance investments at the network level. Regarding the structure of the paper, after explaining the optimization problem, we present the heuristic algorithm implemented for the optimization. Finally, we apply it to an example for illustrative purposes, summarizing the findings and discussing the shortcomings of the study.

2   Optimization Problem Definition

The optimization problem proposed in this study consists of a single-objective optimization of long term effectiveness, measured by the infrastructures' performance over time (F, defined by Eq. (1)) satisfying both budgetary limitations and minimal performance level (g_j, defined by Eq. (2)).

$$Max\ F(x_1, x_2, \dots, x_m) \tag{1}$$

$$g_j(x_1, x_2, \dots, x_m) \leq 0 \tag{2}$$

In the expressions above, x_1, x_2, ..., x_m are the design variables of the problem.

2.1   Objective Function

The assessment of long term effectiveness proposed in this study is based on a life-cycle analysis, considering the evolution over time of infrastructure performance and maintenance treatments' costs. Infrastructure's performance (*IP*, hereafter) will assess the degree to which the infrastructure serves its users and fulfills the purpose to which it was built or acquired [6]. Performance indicators have been developed for different infrastructures: pavements [12-14], bridges [15], railroads [16], etc. The evolution of infrastructure's performance over time and the effect of treatment alternatives will be based on the infrastructure's deterioration model [17].

The measure proposed to assess long term effectiveness of maintenance alternatives is the area bounded by the performance curve and the threshold value of infrastructure's condition (ABPC, hereafter) (Fig. 2). The rationale of this approach is simple: a well-maintained infrastructure (having therefore a larger ABPC) provides greater benefits than a poorly maintained infrastructure [18]; moreover, as benefits derived from well maintained infrastructures are numerous and difficult to quantify in monetary terms, the ABPC can be used as a surrogate for overall user benefits [18-19].

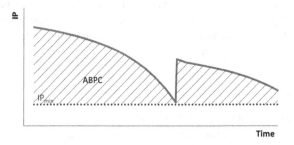

Fig. 2. Long-term effectiveness of a maintenance alternative

Therefore, the problem deals with the maximization of the long-term performance of maintenance alternatives at the network level. This study transforms constrained problems into unconstrained ones using a penalty function (*PF*) defined in Section 2.2.

$$\max F = max \left(\sum_{n=1}^{N} ABPC_n \right) - \sum_{n=1}^{N} PF_n \tag{3}$$

where $ABPC_n$ is the long-term effectiveness of infrastructure n, evaluated as the area bounded by the performance curve and the threshold value of infrastructure's condition ($IP_{min,n}$); and *PF* is the penalty function.

2.2   Constraints

Constraints in Eq. (2) include both an annual budgetary restriction (Eq. (4)) and a limitation of a minimum performance level for each of the infrastructures in the network (Eq. (5)).

$$\sum_{n=1}^{N} cost(x_n) \cdot \frac{1}{(1+i)^t} \leq B_t; \ \forall \, t \tag{4}$$

$$IP_{nt} \geq IP_{min,n} \ ; \ \forall \, t \ \text{and} \ \forall n \tag{5}$$

where t is the year in which the analysis is undertaken, where $t \leq T$; n is the infrastructure being analyzed, where $n \leq N$; $cost\,(x_n)$ is the unit cost of maintenance alternative x in infrastructure n; $\frac{1}{(1+i)^t}$ is the present worth factor for discount rate i, in year t; B_t is the available budget in year t; IP_{nt} is the performance level of infrastructure n in year t; and $IP_{min,n}$ is the minimum performance level allowed for infrastructure n.

In this problem, restrictions are relaxed to allow for solutions with unfulfilled restrictions. This procedure transforms the constrained problem into an unconstrained one by using penalty functions based on expressions of Yepes and Medina [20].

$$PF_{nj} = \begin{cases} 0, & (rv - av_j) \leq 0 \\ k_{1j} + k_{2j} \cdot (rv - av_j)^2, & (rv - av_j) > 0 \end{cases} ; \ \forall \, j \tag{6}$$

where k_{1j} is a fixed penalty for exceeding acceptable values for constraint equation j; k_{2j} is the penalty slope for exceeding acceptable values for constraint equation j; rv is the real value of the constraint function of the alternative being evaluated; and av_j is the acceptable value of the constraint function j.

2.3   Variables

A total of $m=NxT$ variables define a solution for the budget allocation problem of infrastructure maintenance at the network level (Fig. 1). Each of these variables can take S_n possible values, being S the number of treatment alternatives available for each infrastructure n. These variables define a sequence of maintenance treatments that can be implemented in the N infrastructures under study over the analysis period T. Given a set of values for the variables of the present problem, the evaluation of the ABPC and cost of a particular solution is straightforward.

2.4   Parameters

The parameters are all those magnitudes taken as data and therefore, remain constant in the optimization process. In the optimization problem proposed in this study, parameters are related to the analysis period (T), discount rate (i), performance models (IP_{nt}) and treatment costs $(cost (x_n))$.

3   Proposed Heuristic Strategy: Simulated Annealing

Simulated annealing algorithm (SA henceforth) is based on the analogy of crystal formation from masses melted at high temperature and let cool slowly [21]. This method presents the advantage of escaping from local optima by enabling, under some conditions, the degradation of a solution. Authors propose SA as it is a simple and efficient heuristic search in solving combinatorial optimization problems. Moreover, previous studies undertaken by the authors have compared SA to other heuristics and have conclude that SA provides very good results in different optimization problems [22-24]. The scope of the current paper is to analyze the viability of applying SA and therefore, local search heuristics, to the optimization problem. However, the suitability of this specific method (SA) towards other local search heuristics will need further analysis.

SA starts with a feasible solution randomly generated and a high initial temperature. This solution is gradually altered by applying moves to the values of the variables. Given a current solution, a move is applied obtaining a new solution, which is evaluated and it is adopted as the new current solution when is feasible and if it improves the objective function. Less effective solutions are accepted when a 0–1 random number is smaller than $\exp(-\Delta E/T)$, where ΔE is the decrease of long-term effectiveness of the new configuration and T is the temperature. The current solution is then checked against restrictions and if feasible, it is adopted as the new solution. The initial temperature is decreased geometrically ($T = kT$) by means of a coefficient of cooling k. A number of iterations called Markov chains is allowed at each step of temperature. The algorithm stops when the temperature is a small percentage of the initial temperature.

4   Numerical Application

A numerical application is developed in this section for illustrative purposes. This example analyzes the budget allocation problem in a network composed of five infrastructures, each of them having a deterministic deterioration model and a set of maintenance alternatives. In all cases, IP is rated between 0 and 100, being 100 a perfect performance and 0 a failure status. These five infrastructures, analyzed over a period of 25 years, lead to a problem with $m = NxT = 125$ variables.

The deterioration model considered assumes that the deterioration rate varies over time (Eq (7)): the first segment models the period after construction in which there is a lineal deterioration, while the second segment models the period during which deterioration rate is more significant, showing a parabolic relation over time.

$$
IP_{nt} = \begin{cases} IP_{n0} + \alpha_{n0} \cdot t, & t \le t_{ln} \\ IP_{n0} + \alpha_{n0} \cdot (t - t_{ln}) + \beta_{n0} \cdot (t - t_{ln})^2, & t > t_{ln} \end{cases} \tag{7}
$$

where IP_{nt} is the infrastructure's performance profile over time under no maintenance; IP_{n0} is the initial (i.e. t=0) infrastructure's performance; α_{n0} and β_{n0} are the initial deterioration rates of infrastructure n; t_{ln} is the time of initiation of parabolic deterioration; and t is the time. Table 2 shows the values of parameters considered.

Table 2. Parameters considered in the deterioration models

Parameter	Infr. 1	Infr. 2	Infr. 3	Infr. 4	Infr. 5
IP_{n0}	50	73	40	60	80
α_{n0}	0	-0.25	-0.01	-0.1	-0.3
β_{n0}	-0.7	-0.6	-0.4	-0.3	-0.9
t_{ln}	0	2	0	1	3

Table 3. Range of parameters' values considered in the maintenance models

Parameter	Infr. 1	Infr. 2	Infr. 3	Infr. 4	Infr. 5
S_n	21	5	10	15	10
ΔIP_{ns}	0-10	0-5	0-10	0-6	0-7
Δt_{ln}	0-3	0-1	0-0.5	0-2	0-0.75
$\Delta \alpha_{ns}$	0-0.05	0-0.05	0-0.04	0-0.01	0-0.001
$\Delta \beta_{ns}$	0-0.2	0-0.2	0-0.2	0-0.2	0-0.15
cost ($\in$)	0-200	0-150	0-160	0-185	0-200

Table 4. Parameters considered in the overall optimization problem

Parameter	Value
Analysis period (T)	25 years
Discount rate (i)	0.06
Minimum performance (IP_{min})	25
Available budget in € in year t ($B(t)$)	350-0.02·t
Fixed penalty (k_1)	2 000
Penalty slope (k_2)	100

The maintenance model in the example considers that each infrastructure (n) has a set of maintenance alternatives (s_n). Each of these alternatives can lead to one, several, or all of the following effects: an immediate increase of performance (ΔIP_{ns}); an increase of time in which the deterioration is lineal (Δt_{ln}); or a reduction of deterioration rates ($\Delta \alpha_{ns}$ and $\Delta \beta_{ns}$). The maintenance alternatives considered include both preservation and rehabilitation. Their application can, therefore, improve the initial value of *IP*. The range of parameters' values considered in the maintenance models is presented in Table 3. Finally, Table 4 shows parameters considered in the overall optimization problem.

4.1   Results

The algorithm was programmed in Matlab 12 on a PC AMD Phenom II X6 1055T Processor 2.80 GHz. The calibration of the algorithm recommended Markov chains of 10 000 iterations, a cooling coefficient of 0.99 and two Markov chains without improvements in the current solution as stop criterion. The initial temperature was adjusted following the method proposed by Medina [25].The most efficient move identified was a random variation of 2 or up to 2 variables of the 125 in the problem. 100 randomly generated initial solutions were tried to study the influence of the initial solution on the results. The statistical description of this sample is the following: the maximum and minimum values of long-term effectiveness are 6 659 and 6 168, respectively; the sample mean is 6 447, with a confidence interval of ±47.42 for a 0.05 level of significance; and the standard deviation of the sample is 132.5.

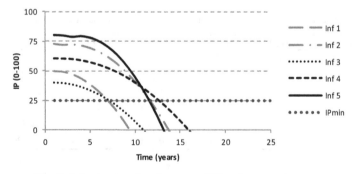

Fig. 3. Infrastructures' performance (*IP*) under no maintenance

In order to analyze the maintenance strategies, the optimal of the 100 solutions sample is analyzed in detail. Under no maintenance, the infrastructure network presents a poor performance at the end of the analysis period, with all infrastructures presenting a failure status (Fig. 3). As shown in Fig. 4 and Fig. 5, the optimization process improves the network performance while satisfying budgetary constraints. In fact, the average value of *IP* increases from failure ($IP_{average} < 0$) to a value of 80.75 in the optimal maintenance strategy. In the figures below, performance levels are evaluated as the percentage of time in which the infrastructures present a *IP* between the following intervals: A (*IP:* 75-100), B (*IP:* 50-75), C (*IP:* 25-50) and D (*IP:* 0-25).

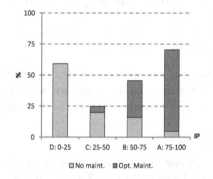
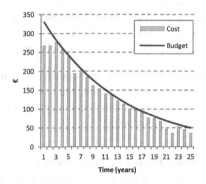

Fig. 4. Infrastructures' performance level before and after optimization

Fig. 5. Annual cost and budgetary restriction

Finally, a parametric study of budgetary restrictions was undertaken. This analysis would help infrastructure managers to evaluate the impact of budgetary limitations on infrastructure's performance. The analysis considered variations of ±20% and ±40% of the initial budgetary restriction (being the initial annual restriction $B(t) = 350-0.02 \cdot t$). These five budgetary scenarios were optimized, dealing to an optimal maintenance strategy for each scenario. Fig. 6 shows the variation of average infrastructures' performance with available budget. The results obtained have a good parabolic variation in terms of the total present budget: $IP = -2.96 \cdot TB^2 + 30.82 \cdot TB + 6.45$ with a regression coefficient of $R^2 = 0.981$, being *TB* the total present budget in k €.

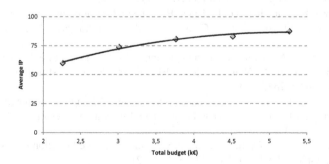

Fig. 6. Variation of average *IP* with budget restriction

5 Conclusions

In the light of the results obtained in this study, the following conclusions may be derived:

- Local search heuristics and more specifically the proposed SA algorithm is an efficient procedure for the design of maintenance strategies in terms of infrastructure performance under budget and technical restrictions, offering near-optimal solutions to the budget allocation problem.
- SA enables managers to undertake "what-if" analysis, evaluating the effect of budgetary restrictions in infrastructures' performance.
- From the parametric analysis, it can be concluded that near-optimal maintenance strategies show a good parabolic correlation with the available budget.

After having applied the algorithm in an illustrative example, two future research lines are defined: first, its application and validation in a real example; and second, the application of other local search heuristics in order to analyze the goodness of the proposed SA approach.

Acknowledgements. The authors would like to acknowledge the support of the Spanish Ministry of Science and Innovation (Research Project BIA2011-23602). Funding over Santander Universidades (Becas Iberoamérica Jóvenes Profesionales e Investigadores, 2013) to support this work is also gratefully appreciated.

References

1. American Society of Civil Engineers: 2009 Report Card for America's Infrastructure, Washington, D.C., USA (2009)
2. Remenyte-Prescott, R., Andrews, J.: Review of Infrastructure Asset Management Methods for Networked Systems. In: 19th AR2TS, Advances in Risk and Reliability Technology Symposium, U.K (2013)
3. Kerali, H., McMullen, D., Odoki, J.: Overview of HDM-4. Highway Development Management Series, vol. 1. International Study of Highway Development and Management (ISOHDM), World Road Association PIARC, Paris (2006)
4. Tsunokawa, K., Van Hiep, D., Ul-Islam, R.: True Optimization of Pavement Maintenance Options with What-If Models. Comput.-Aided Civ. Infrastruct. Eng. 21(3), 193–204 (2006)
5. Too, E.G., Betts, M., Arun, K.: A strategic approach to Infrastructure Asset Management. In: Sirikijpanichkul, A., Wai, S.H. (eds.) BEE Postgraduate Infrastructure Theme Conference, September 26 (2006)
6. Hudson, W.R., Uddin, W., Haas, R.C.: Infrastructure Management: Integrating Design, Construction, Maintenance, Rehabilitation and Renovation. McGraw-Hill Professional Publishing (1997)
7. Golroo, A., Tighe, S.: Optimum Genetic Algorithm Structure Selection in Pavement Management. Asian J. Appl. Sci. 5(6), 327–341 (2012)

8. Torres-Machí, C., Chamorro, A., Videla, C., Pellicer, E., Yepes, V.: Optimization and Prioritization Methods for Pavement Network Management. In: Transportation Research Board 92st Annual Meeting, Washington, D.C., USA, vol. 13-5057, pp. 1–14 (2013)

9. Gao, L., Xie, C., Zhang, Z., Waller, S.T.: Network-Level Road Pavement Maintenance and Rehabilitation Scheduling for Optimal Performance Improvement and Budget Utilization. Comput.-Aided Civ. Infrastruct. Eng. 27(4), 278–287 (2012)

10. Wang, F., Zhang, Z., Machemehl, R.: Decision-Making Problem for Managing Pavement Maintenance and Rehabilitation Projects. Transp. Res. Rec. 1853(1), 21–28 (2003)

11. Fwa, T.F., Chan, W.T., Tan, C.Y.: Genetic-algorithm programming of road maintenance and rehabilitation. J. Transp. Eng. 122(3), 246–253 (1996)

12. Chamorro, A., Tighe, S.: Development of a Management Framework for Rural Roads in Developing Countries. Transp. Res. Rec. 2093, 99–107 (2009)

13. Chamorro, A., Tighe, S., Li, N., Kazmierowski, T.: Validation and implementation of Ontario, Canada, network-level distress guidelines and condition rating. Transp. Res. Rec. 2153, 49–57 (2010)

14. Chamorro, A., Tighe, S., Li, N., Kazmierowski, T.J.: Development of distress guidelines and condition rating to improve network management in Ontario, Canada. Transp. Res. Rec. 2093, 128–135 (2009)

15. Neves, L.C., Frangopol, D.M.: Condition, safety and cost profiles for deteriorating structures with emphasis on bridges. Reliab. Eng. Syst. Saf. 89(2), 185–198 (2005)

16. El-Sibaie, M., Zhang, Y.J.: Objective Track Quality Indices. Transportation Research Record: Journal of the Transportation Research Board 1863, 81–87 (2004)

17. Chamorro, A., Tighe, S.: Condition performance models for network-level management of unpaved roads. Transp. Res. Rec. 2204, 21–28 (2011)

18. Khurshid, M.B., Irfan, M., Labi, S.: Comparison of methods for evaluating pavement interventions: Evaluation and case study. Transportation Research Record: Journal of the Transportation Research Board 2108, 25–36 (2009)

19. Haas, R.C., Tighe, S., Falls, L.C.: Determining Return on Long-Life Pavement Investments. Transportation Research Record: Journal of the Transportation Research Board 1974, 10–17 (2006)

20. Yepes, V., Medina, J.: Economic Heuristic Optimization for Heterogeneous Fleet VRPHESTW. J. Transp. Eng. 132(4), 303–311 (2006)

21. Kirkpatrick, S., Gelatt, C.D., Vecchi, M.P.: Optimization by Simulated Annealing. Science 220(4598), 671–680 (1983)

22. Martí, J.V., Gonzalez-Vidosa, F., Yepes, V., Alcalá, J.: Design of prestressed concrete precast road bridges with hybrid simulated annealing. Eng. Struct. 48, 342–352 (2013)

23. Perea, C., Alcala, J., Yepes, V., Gonzalez-Vidosa, F., Hospitaler, A.: Design of reinforced concrete bridge frames by heuristic optimization. Adv. Eng. Softw. 39(8), 676–688 (2008)

24. Carbonell, A., González-Vidosa, F., Yepes, V.: Design of reinforced concrete road vaults by heuristic optimization. Adv. Eng. Softw. 42(4), 151–159 (2011)

25. Medina, J.R.: Estimation of Incident and Reflected Waves Using Simulated Annealing. J. Waterw. Port Coast. Ocean Eng. 127(4), 213–221 (2001)

Learning more Accurate Bayesian Networks in the CHC Approach by Adjusting the Trade-Off between Efficiency and Accuracy

Jacinto Arias, José A. Gámez, and José M. Puerta

Department of Computing Systems - I3A
University of Castilla-La Mancha
Albacete, 02071
jacinto.arias@alu.uclm.es, {jose.gamez,jose.puerta}@uclm.es

Abstract. Learning Bayesian networks is known to be an NP-hard problem, this, combined with the growing interest in learning models from high-dimensional domains, leads to the necessity of finding more efficient learning algorithms. Recent papers propose constrained approaches of successfully and widely used local search algorithms, such as hill climbing. One of these algorithms families, called CHC (Constrained Hill Climbing), highly improves the efficiency of the original approach, obtaining models with slightly lower quality but maintaining its theoretical properties. In this paper we propose some modifications to the last version of these algorithms, FastCHC, trying to improve the quality of its output by relaxing the constraints imposed to include some diversification in the search process. We also perform an intensive experimental evaluation of the modifications proposed including quite large datasets.

Keywords: Bayesian Networks, Machine Learning, Local Search, Constrained Search, Scalability.

1 Introduction

Over the last decades, Bayesian Networks [7,9] have become one of the most relevant knowledge representation formalisms in the field of Data Mining. Due to its popularity and the increasing amount of data available it is not surprising that learning the structure of Bayesian Networks from data has become also a problem of growing interest.

This paper falls in the so-called *score+search* approach which poses learning as an optimization problem: A scoring metric function f ([6,8]) is used to score a network structure with respect to the training data, and a search method is used to look for the network with the best score. The majority of the proposed methods are based on heuristic and metaheuristic search strategies since this problem is known to be NP-hard [2]. If we add the necessity of dealing with massive datasets, local-search methods such as hill climbing, have achieved great

C. Bielza et al. (Eds.): CAEPIA 2013, LNAI 8109, pp. 310–320, 2013.

popularity due to its ease of implementation and its trade-off between their efficiency and the quality of the models obtained.

In order to deal with larger datasets, several scalable algorithms have been proposed, specifically based on local-search approaches. Those methods are usually based on restricting the search space in different ways performing a two-step process to first detect the constraints, and then perform an intensified and more efficient local search [10]. In [3], the CHC algorithm is introduced, which progressively restricts the search space when performing an iterated local search without needing a previous step. The development of this result leads to the FastCHC algorithm [4] which improves the performance of the original definition by reducing to one the number of iterations needed.

All the CHC algorithms provide an efficiency improvement when comparing them with most state of the art algorithms and especially with the unconstrained hill climbing approach, maintaining also its original theoretical properties. However, restricting the search space normally implies a loss of quality in the models obtained. In this paper, we propose some modifications to the FastCHC algorithm, as it has proven to be the most efficient of the CHC family, in order to balance the trade-off between efficiency and quality of the models, trying to provide better solutions without decreasing its efficiency advantage. These modifications relax the constraints imposed by the original algorithm in order to allow the algorithm visit additional solutions.

The rest of the paper is organized as follows: In Section 2 we review the necessary background on Bayesian Networks and the hill climbing approach to structural learning. In Section 3 we review the CHC algorithms family. In Section 4 we describe the modifications proposed to improve the FastCHC algorithm. Finally, in section 5 we evaluate the performance of the modifications proposed and compare them with the original algorithms. In section 6, we conclude with a discussion of the results obtained and future directions.

2   Learning the Structure of Bayesian Networks

Bayesian Networks (BNs) are graphical models than can efficiently represent and manipulate n-dimensional probability distributions [9]. Formally[1], a BN is a pair $B = \langle \mathcal{G}, \Theta \rangle$, where $\mathcal{G}$ is a graphical structure, or more precisely a Directed Acyclic Graph (DAG) whose nodes are in $\mathbf{V} = \{X_1, X_2, \ldots, X_n\}$ represent the random variables of the domain we wish to model, and the topology of the graph (the arcs in $\mathbf{E} \subseteq \mathbf{V} \times \mathbf{V}$) encodes conditional (in)dependence relationships among the variables (by means of the presence or absence of direct connections between pair of variables).

The second element of the pair, Θ, represents a set of numerical parameters, usually conditional probability distributions drawn from the graph structure

---

[1] We use standard notation, that is, bold font to denote sets and n-dimensional configurations, calligraphic font to denote mathematical structures, upper case for variables sets of random variables, and lower case to denote states of variables or configuration of states.

which quantifies the network: For each $X_i \in \mathbf{V}$ we have a conditional probability distribution $P(X_i \mid pa(X_i))$, where $pa(X_i)$ represents any combination of the values of the variables $Pa(X_i)$, and $Pa(X_i)$ is the parent set of X_i in $\mathcal{G}$.

From a BN $B = \langle \mathcal{G}, \boldsymbol{\Theta} \rangle$, we can recover the joint probability distribution over $\mathbf{V}$ given by:

$$P(X_1, X_2, \ldots, X_n) = \prod_{i=1}^{n} P(X_i \mid Pa(X_i))$$

The problem of learning the structure of a BN can be stated as follows: Given a training dataset $D = \{v^1, \ldots, v^m\}$ of instances of $\mathbf{V}$, find the DAG $\mathcal{G}^*$ such that

$$\mathcal{G}^* = \arg \max_{\mathcal{G} \in \mathcal{G}^n} f(\mathcal{G} : D)$$

where $f(\mathcal{G} : D)$ is a scoring metric which evaluates the merit of any candidate DAG. An important property of the metrics that are commonly used for BN structural learning is the decomposability in presence of full data, which evaluate a given DAG as the sum of its node family scores, i.e. the subgraphs formed by a node and its parents in $\mathcal{G}$ [7]. This provides an efficient neighbourhood evaluation for local search algorithms such as hill climbing, which evaluates local changes for a candidate solution, normally starting from the empty graph, and performs the one which maximizes the score function until it is not possible to find a better neighbour. By using local changes which only modify one arc at each step, we can reuse the computations carried out in previous stages and compute only the statistics corresponding to the variables whose parents have been modified. The most used operators are arc addition, deletion and reversal.

The popularity of HC is probably due to its ease of implementation as well as its good trade-off between efficiency and quality of the output, which is a local optimum. In addition, it has other theoretical properties which makes it interesting, e.g. under certain assumptions the algorithm guarantees that the resulting network is a minimal I-map[2] [3].

3   Constrained Hill Climbing Methods

The CHC algorithm [3] is based on a progressive restriction of the neighbourhood during the search process. The algorithm keeps what the authors call, *Forbidden Parents Sets (FP)* for each node, so in the neighbourhood generation step for the node X_i, any node $X_j \in FP(X_i)$ is not considered as a suitable parent of X_i and the algorithm avoids its evaluation, saving a large number of computations.

In order to include a node in the FP set, the algorithm uses the value of the score metric as a sort of conditional independence test when evaluating

---

[2] A DAG $\mathcal{G}$ is an I-map of a probability distribution p if all independences that $\mathcal{G}$ codifies are also present in the original p distribution and it is minimal if none of the arcs in the DAG can be deleted without violating the I-map condition.

local changes, so that when the difference $(diff)$ of score between the current structure and the one resulting of applying the considered operation does not reveal a gain in the structure, the FP sets are updated consequently:

- Adding $X_j \rightarrow X_i$. If $diff < 0$ then $\{X_j\}$ is added to $FP(X_i)$ and vice versa.
- Deleting $X_j \rightarrow X_i$. If $diff > 0$ then $\{X_j\}$ is added to $FP(X_i)$ and vice versa.
- Reversal of $X_j \rightarrow X_i$. Decompose as deleting$(X_j \rightarrow X_i)$+adding$(X_i \rightarrow X_j)$ and use the previous two rules to update the FP sets.

Although the initial CHC algorithm results in a much more efficient search process when compared with the unconstrained hill climbing it does not guarantee to return a minimal I-map and for that reason the CHC* algorithm is proposed, in which the output of the CHC algorithm is used as the initial solution of an unconstrained hill climbing to retain the theoretical properties.

An iterated version of the CHC algorithm is also proposed in [3], in which the algorithm performs several iterations by using the output of the previous one as the initial solution for the next restarting the FP sets to the empty set. The algorithm ends when it is unable to perform any change at the beginning of an iteration and, because no constraints are being used, it has the same stopping criterion as the hill climbing algorithm thus retains its theoretical properties: It guarantees a minimal I-map.

All the previous development lead to the most efficient version of the CHC algorithm, called FastCHC [4]. This algorithm guarantees a minimal I-map in just one iteration. To accomplish this, the algorithm tries to correct wrong discovered relationships in the graph by releasing some constraints every time it performs an addition operation to the network, i.e. after the algorithm adds the arc $X_i \rightarrow X_j$ it releases all the constraints from $FP(X_i)$ and $FP(X_j)$ respective neighbourhoods to allow the algorithm to correct the solution if needed to become an I-map.

4   Proposal

As mentioned before, constrained algorithms experiment a loss of quality for the sake of efficiency [4]. In this paper we propose two different strategies to relax the constraints present in the FastCHC algorithm to allow some diversification in the search process, thus it will visit additional solutions that otherwise would remain unexplored. All the following modifications maintain the theoretical properties of the original algorithm as we don't modify the required conditions.

4.1   Releasing Constraints in Variable Neighbourhood Levels

Our first proposal is a basic modification to FastCHC based on the aforementioned strategy [4] of releasing some of the constraints from the nodes involved in the change performed at each search step. Although this strategy was originally designed to correct wrong discovered relationships, we can also see it as a *diversification* technique, as it allows the search algorithm to explore additional solutions which could have a better score.

This modification, which we call FastCHC$_{Mod1}$, extends the described procedure to deletion and reversal operations. We also consider releasing constraints from a wider range of nodes in order to extend the unconstrained search space. To achieve this, we include a new parameter $L \in \mathbb{N}$ which represents levels of neighbourhood to release constraints from, i.e., for a value $L = 1$ when a change involving nodes X_i and X_j is performed any node adjacent to X_j $(adj^1(X_j))$ will be removed from $FP(X_i)$, and vice versa[3]; for a level $L = 2$, any node $X_{j'} \in adj^1(X_j)$ and its respective adjacent nodes $(adj^2(X_j))$ will be removed from $FP(X_i)$, and vice versa; for the general case $L = n$ any node in $adj^n(X_j)$ will be removed from $FP(X_i)$, and vice versa.

4.2   Limiting the FP Sets Size

The main disadvantage of the previous approach is that the behaviour of the modification is not much predictable and for that reason the new included parameter L could be difficult to set. Our second proposal tries to release constraints during the search procedure regarding the score metric value.

We add a limit S for the maximum number of FP constraints that can be simultaneously stored in the FP, so when the number of constraints reaches this limit some of them must be released in order to keep the number of constraints at S. As the constraints are added or released in pairs, i.e. if variable X_i is added to $FP(X_j)$ also X_j will be added to $FP(X_i)$, we count both directions as one so the parameter S refers to half the size of the sum of all the FP sizes:

$$\frac{1}{2} \sum_{i=1}^{n} \#FP(X_i) \leq S$$

This modification requires two design decisions to be defined: A suitable approximation S for the maximum number of FP constraints to be maintained and an update criteria to determine which constraints must be kept in the FP sets.

We should not use an absolute approximation to select an appropriate S value because the number of constraints that are discovered during a search procedure highly depends on the dataset number of attributes and other specific characteristics. For that reason, we ought to express a limitation parameter independently from the dataset that is being used. To make an approximate idea of the size that the FP sets reach when using different datasets, we carried out an experiment computing the maximum number of discovered constrains (S_{max}) for different datasets, which are described in Section 5. In Table 1 we can confirm how much this number varies from one dataset to another.

We can use this value S_{max} as a reference value that we can compute automatically and then express the size limitation as a reduction factor α which will

---

[3] The behaviour of the modification with $L = 1$ is similar to the original FastCHC, which releases constraints in the same way but only after performing addition moves.

Table 1. FP sets maximum size reached during a full execution of the original FastCHC and after the first iteration of the algorithm. The last column includes the ratio between these two values as a comparison.

Network	#vars	Full Execution (S_{max})	First Iteration (S_0)	Ratio
Mildew	35	556	474	85%
Barley	48	1053	841	80%
Hailfinder	56	1458	1243	85%
Pigs	441	96142	86912	90%

be applied to obtain S; having a parameter independent from the dataset. However, since obtaining S_{max} is not feasible without performing a full execution of the algorithm, we must find an approximate value that we could obtain using computations that the unmodified algorithm already performs. In Table 1, we show the size of the FP sets after the first iteration of the algorithm, S_0, and the ratio between this value and the one obtained after a full execution S_{max}, showing that there is no much difference between them, thus we can take the latter value as an optimistic approximation that should fit our requirements.

In summary, our modification performs the first iteration of the search process just as it does FastCHC, discovering and storing in the FP sets S_0 constraints, then a reduction of α is applied to the size of the FP sets and the algorithm releases all the constrains needed to fit this new maximum size: $S = \alpha \cdot S_0$. From that point, FastCHC algorithm is executed, with the difference that, when new FP constrains are discovered, the FP sets must be updated and some of the constraints need to be released in order to fit the imposed limit.

Regarding the update policy, we keep a list including all the constraints discovered ordered by their score at time of being included (as they are forbidden they will not be updated anymore). When the amount of constraints exceeds the limit, the one with the highest score will be released from the list.

In order to manually fix the parameter α we can interpret it as a balance between efficiency and quality of the models. As we can see in Figure 1, a value of α closer to 1.0 must keep an algorithm behaving much like FastCHC, but a value of α closer to 0.0 keeps the algorithm's behaviour closer to the Hill Climbing approach but retaining the speed up advantage of the first iteration of the original constrained algorithm.

5   Experimental Evaluation

In this section we examine the different modifications to the FastCHC algorithm proposed in this paper, we perform an empirical evaluation for each modification with different values of their parameters. We selected FastCHC$_{Mod1}$ with $L = 2$ and $L = 3$, as preliminary experiments revealed that larger values of L don't provide much difference, and FastCHC$_{Mod2}$ with $\alpha = 0.4$, $\alpha = 0.6$, and $\alpha = 0.8$ to evaluate α in a wide range. In addition, we include as reference algorithms the unmodified FastCHC and the standard hill climbing (HC).

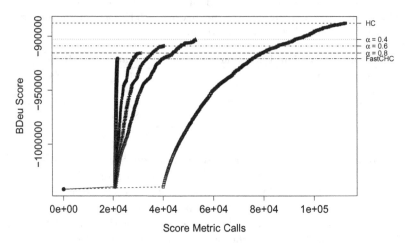

Fig. 1. Evolution of the search process of the HC, FastCHC and FastCHC$_{Mod2}$ with different values of α. Each point correspond to a complete search step representing the BDeu score metric value obtained (y-axis) and the score metric calls (x-axis). This execution corresponds to an single execution for a 5000 instances sample from one of the random *BN_200* networks, described in Section 5.

5.1   Implementation and Running Environment

All the algorithms have been implemented in Java using the ProGraMo library for dataset and graph structures management [5]. The score metric used is the Bayesian Dirichlet Equivalent Uniform (BDeu) [6] with an equivalent sample size of 10 and all other parameters set up as in [10]. We also take advantage of the internal cache described in [3] which saves the result of every score computation using the probability family as a hash key in order to re-use it later in the execution, achieving high computational savings especially in larger domains.

5.2   Performance Indicators

We consider two kind of factors as performance indicators to compare the different algorithms: the quality of the network obtained which is given by the value of the scoring metric (BDeu) and the efficiency of the algorithm which is given by the number of score function computations carried out by each algorithm (calls). As the execution time depends on both the implementation and the specification of the computer on which the algorithm is executed, we consider the score function calls for being independent of those factors and having direct correspondence with CPU time requirements.

5.3   Experiments

We have carried out a first set of experiments using a collection of *real worl networks* which are commonly referenced in the literature and varies from smaller

Table 2. Main characteristics of the real networks used in the experiments

Network	Alarm	Barley	Hailfinder	Insurance	Mildew	Munin1	Pigs
#vars	38	48	56	27	35	189	441
#arcs	46	84	66	52	46	282	592
Domain	Medicine	Agriculture	Meteorology	Insurance	Agriculture	Medicine	Genetics

to larger domains, the networks have been obtained from the Bayesian Network Repository[4]. Their main characteristics are shown in Table 2. In addition, a second set of more intensive experiments have been carried on using a set of synthetic databases sampled from a collection of *artificial networks*, which have been randomly generated with different degrees of difficulty based on the procedure described in [1]. We use a collection of 4 networks with 100 nodes and an average of 100 arcs and 4 networks with 200 nodes and an average of 400 arcs. We have sampled 5 datasets of 5000 instances for each network, the following results are obtained from the average of them.

5.4   Detailed Results

Table 3 shows the BDeu score metric value and calls for each algorithm and database. The results highlighted in bold are the best for the corresponding network. As we can confirm in the data, the algorithms perform consistently with their definition being hill climbing the one with highest scores and FastCHC the most efficient. Also, we can confirm the score improvements of the modifications, especially when comparing FastCHC$_{Mod2}$ for the three different values of α; FastCHC$_{Mod1}$ score improvement is more subtle but efficiency is hardly modified. As we can see, the score value an calls difference between the constrained and the unconstrained algorithms is more noticeable for the larger databases, supporting the scalability properties of the constrained algorithms.

5.5   Summary

Taking into account the two sets of experiments described above, a comprehensive performance comparison for each algorithm with hill climbing is shown in Figure 2, regarding the ratio between the score metric calls and the BDeu score; the later is computed using $\exp((\texttt{BDeu(Model}_i) - \texttt{BDeu(HC)})/m)$ in order to provide an estimation of the ratio between the probability that $\texttt{Model}_i$ and model HC assign to the next data sample. In this graphical comparison we can confirm the expected behaviour of the modifications, displaying the FastCHC algorithm in the bottom left corner as the most efficient but less accurate algorithm and the hill climbing in the upper right corner, being the less efficient algorithm which obtains the best solutions; the modifications are spread along the diagonal showing the desired balance between efficiency and quality according to their parameters values meaning.

---

[4] http://www.cs.huji.ac.il/site/labs/compbio/Repository/

Table 3. Score metric value (above) and calls (below) for each algorithm and network. BN_100 and BN_200 represent the average of the results obtained for the two collection of synthetic networks described.

Dataset	HC	FastCHC	FastCHC$_{Mod1}$ (L = 2)	FastCHC$_{Mod1}$ (L = 3)
Alarm	**-47999.3454**	-48045.1449	-48010.4824	-48009.5839
Barley	**-261888.6082**	-271658.9229	-269808.1994	-267565.7600
Hailfinder	**-250408.8787**	-251528.0754	-251417.5400	-251411.9393
Insurance	-67021.9905	-67317.2964	-67172.8644	-67131.2555
Mildew	**-232748.2202**	-243978.3822	-243444.3285	-243278.5567
Munin1	**-203005.5923**	-206639.3665	-205756.4947	-205235.2420
Pigs	-1673304.6600	-1673110.1193	-1672782.9907	**-1672522.5336**
BN_n100	**-328499.1000**	-334554.4000	-334223.4000	-333286.0000
BN_n200	**-667642.3000**	-682648.9000	-682081.4000	-680601.0000

		FastCHC$_{Mod2}$ (α = 40%)	FastCHC$_{Mod2}$ (α = 60%)	FastCHC$_{Mod2}$ (α = 80%)
Alarm		-48001.0012	-48001.0012	-48006.6924
Barley		-264254.3812	-266033.6374	-265699.4747
Hailfinder		-250346.7057	-250396.9589	-250472.7089
Insurance		**-67019.6496**	-67034.4770	-67058.0366
Mildew		-237832.5022	-243042.4006	-242635.9131
Munin1		-203452.6020	-204512.2889	-204837.3228
Pigs		-1673019.6149	-1672623.7133	-1672552.5238
BN_n100		-330526.2000	-331589.1000	-332992.9000
BN_n200		-673222.0000	-676501.1000	-678693.6000

Dataset	HC	FastCHC	FastCHC$_{Mod1}$ (L = 2)	FastCHC$_{Mod1}$ (L = 3)
Alarm	3444.2000	**1533.8000**	1673.4000	1848.0000
Barley	5680.8000	**1876.2000**	1993.4000	2123.8000
Hailfinder	7063.2000	**2401.0000**	2556.4000	2673.6000
Insurance	2230.0000	**1075.2000**	1266.0000	501.2000
Mildew	2460.4000	**906.4000**	960.0000	1041.4000
Munin1	102218.2000	**58598.8000**	62181.2000	67445.4000
Pigs	539248.6000	**125902.2000**	132401.0000	146048.2000
BN_n100	20712.2500	**6297.6000**	6712.9000	7658.3500
BN_n200	99766.6000	**22819.7500**	23591.9500	25775.7000

		FastCHC$_{Mod2}$ (α = 40%)	FastCHC$_{Mod2}$ (α = 60%)	FastCHC$_{Mod2}$ (α = 80%)
Alarm		2635.0000	2436.6000	2211.2000
Barley		3758.0000	3305.4000	2926.4000
Hailfinder		5031.2000	4427.2000	3698.8000
Insurance		1892.4000	1774.8000	1669.2000
Mildew		1695.8000	1418.8000	1217.8000
Munin1		94122.4000	91824.2000	88950.8000
Pigs		317561.4000	257212.0000	198098.6000
BN_n100		13831.8500	11059.7500	8753.0500
BN_n200		50421.9000	39880.6500	31093.2000

6   Conclusions

We have defined some modifications for constrained local search algorithms in order to obtain higher quality solutions closer to the state of the art algorithms when maintaining an efficient algorithm. The second modification proposed introduces a parameter which can be tuned in order to adjust the behaviour of the algorithm regarding the efficiency/quality tradeoff. Future works could lead to a parameters-free modification of the algorithm, in which the size of the FP sets

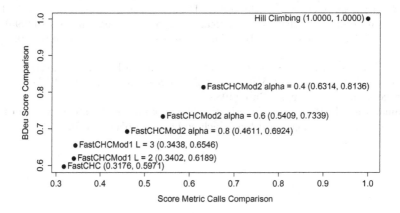

Fig. 2. Comparison between the different algorithms regarding score metric calls (x-axis) and score metric value (y-axis). The values displayed next to the algorithms names express the averaged ratios (calls, score) relative to the hill climbing algorithm from all datasets.

is reduced dynamically during the search process, trying to relax the constrains in the lasts steps of the search to take advantage of both constrained and unconstrained approaches. Preliminary experiments using a fixed rate reduction of the FP sets and statistical parameters such as the score variance between solutions have shown similar results to the parametrized modification.

Acknowledgments. This work has been partially funded by FEDER funds and the Spanish Government (MICINN) through project TIN2010-20900-C04-03.

References

1. Alonso-Barba, J.: delaOssa, L., Gámez, J., Puerta, J.: Scaling up the greedy equivalence search algorithm by constraining the search space of equivalence classes. International Journal of Approximate Reasoning (2013)
2. Chickering, D.M.: Learning bayesian networks is NP-complete. In: Learning from data, pp. 121–130. Springer (1996)
3. Gámez, J., Mateo, J., Puerta, J.: Learning bayesian networks by hill climbing: efficient methods based on progressive restriction of the neighborhood. Data Mining and Knowledge Discovery 22(1-2), 106–148 (2011)
4. Gámez, J., Mateo, J., Puerta, J.: One iteration CHC algorithm for learning Bayesian networks: an effective and efficient algorithm for high dimensional problems. Progress in Artificial Intelligence 1(4), 329–346 (2012)
5. Gámez, J., Salmerón, A., Cano, A.: Design of new algorithms for probabilistic graphical models. Implementation in Elvira. Programo Research Project (TIN2007-67418-c03) (2010)

6. Heckerman, D., Geiger, D., Chickering, D.M.: Learning bayesian networks: The combination of knowledge and statistical data. Machine Learning 20(3) (1995)
7. Jensen, F.V., Nielsen, T.D.: Bayesian networks and decision graphs. Springer (2007)
8. Neapolitan, R.E.: Learning bayesian networks. Pearson Prentice Hall (2004)
9. Pearl, J.: Probabilistic Reasoning in Intelligent Systems: Networks of Plausble Inference. Morgan Kaufmann Pub. (1988)
10. Tsamardinos, I., Brown, L., Aliferis, C.: The max-min hill-climbing bayesian network structure learning algorithm. Machine Learning 65(1), 31–78 (2006)

Approximate Lazy Evaluation
of Influence Diagrams

Rafael Cabañas[1], Andrés Cano[1],
Manuel Gómez-Olmedo[1], and Anders L. Madsen[2,3]

[1] Department of Computer Science and Artificial Intelligence
CITIC, University of Granada, Spain
{rcabanas,mgomez,acu}@decsai.ugr.es
[2] HUGIN EXPERT A/S
Aalborg, Denmark
anders@hugin.com
[3] Department of Computer Science
Aalborg University, Denmark

Abstract. Influence Diagrams are a tool used to represent and solve decision problems under uncertainty. One of the most efficient exact methods used to evaluate Influence Diagrams is Lazy Evaluation. This paper proposes the use of trees for representing potentials involved in an Influence Diagram in order to obtain an approximate Lazy Evaluation of decision problems. This method will allow to evaluate complex decision problems that are not evaluable with exact methods due to their computational cost. The experimental work compares the efficiency and goodness of the approximate solutions obtained using different kind of trees.

Keywords: Influence Diagram, Approximate computation, Lazy Evaluation, Deterministic algorithms, Context-specific independencies.

1 Introduction

An Influence Diagram (ID) [1] is a Probabilistic Graphical Model used for representing and evaluating decision problems under uncertainty. IDs can encode the independence relations between variables in a way that avoids an exponential growth of the representation. Several approaches have been proposed to evaluate IDs such as *Variable Elimination* [2,3] and *Arc Reversal* [4]. However, if the problem is too complex the application of these methods may become infeasible due to the high requirement of resources (time and memory). A technique that improves the efficiency of the evaluation is Lazy Evaluation (LE) [5]. The basic idea is to maintain a decomposition of the potentials and to postpone computation for as long as possible. Some other deterministic methods use alternative representations for the potentials, such as *trees* [6,7]. This representation supports the exploitation of *context-specific independencies* [8]. That is, identical values of the potential can be grouped. Moreover, if potentials are too large,

C. Bielza et al. (Eds.): CAEPIA 2013, LNAI 8109, pp. 321–331, 2013.

they can be pruned and converted into smaller trees, thus leading to approximate and more efficient algorithms. The potential representation as a numerical tree was already used for LE in Bayesian networks [9]. This paper proposes the use of trees for LE of IDs in order to obtain an approximate LE of Bayesian decision problems. The experimental work compares the computing time, memory requirements and goodness of approximations using tables, numerical and binary trees.

The paper is organized as follows: Section 2 introduces some basic concepts about IDs and Lazy Evaluation; Section 3 describes key issues about numerical and binary trees and and how they are used during the lazy evaluation of IDs; Section 4 includes the experimental work and results; finally Section 5 details our conclusions and lines for future work.

2 Preliminaries

2.1 Influence Diagrams

An ID [1] is a direct acyclic graph used for representing and evaluating decision problems under uncertainty. An ID contains three types of nodes: *chance nodes* (representing random variables), *decision nodes* (mutually exclusive actions which the decision maker can control) and *utility nodes* (representing decision maker preferences). We denote by $\mathcal{U}_C$ the set of chance nodes, by $\mathcal{U}_D$ the set of decision nodes, and by $\mathcal{U}_V$ the set of utility nodes. The decision nodes have a temporal order, $D_1, \ldots, D_n$, and the chance nodes are partitioned according to when they are observed: $\mathcal{I}_0$ is the set of chance nodes observed before to the first decision, and $\mathcal{I}_i$ is the set of chance nodes observed after decision D_i is taken and before decision D_{i+1} is taken. Finally, $\mathcal{I}_n$ is the set of chance nodes observed after D_n. That is, there is a partial temporal ordering: $\mathcal{I}_0 \prec D_1 \prec \mathcal{I}_1 \prec \cdots \prec D_n \prec \mathcal{I}_n$.

The *universe* of the ID is $\mathcal{U} = \mathcal{U}_C \cup \mathcal{U}_D = \{X_1, \ldots, X_m\}$. Let us suppose that each variable X_i takes values on a finite set $\Omega_{X_i} = \{x_1, \ldots, x_{|\Omega_{X_i}|}\}$. If I is a set of indexes, we shall write $\mathbf{X}_I$ for the set of variables $\{X_i | i \in I\}$, defined on $\Omega_{\mathbf{X}_I} = \times_{i \in I} \Omega_{X_i}$. The elements of Ω_{X_I} are called configurations of $\mathbf{X}_I$ and will be represented as $\mathbf{x}_I$. Each chance node X_i has a conditional probability distribution $P(X_i | pa(X_i))$ associated. In the same way, each utility node V_i has a utility function $U(pa(V_i))$ associated. In general, we will talk about potentials (not necessarily normalized). Let $\mathbf{X}_I$ be the set of all variables involved in a potential, then a *probability potential* denoted by ϕ is a mapping $\phi : \Omega_{\mathbf{X}_I} \to [0, 1]$. A *utility potential* denoted by ψ is a mapping $\psi : \Omega_{\mathbf{X}_I} \to \mathbb{R}$. The set of probability potentials is denoted by Φ while the set of utility potentials is denoted by Ψ.

When evaluating an ID, we must compute the best choice or *optimal policy* δ_i for each decision D_i, that is, a mapping $\delta_i : \Omega_{pa(D_i)} \to \Omega_{D_i}$ where $pa(D_i)$ are the informational predecessors or parents of D_i. To be well defined, informational predecessors of each decision in a ID must include previous decisions and informational predecessors of the previous decisions (*no-forgetting assumption*). The optimal policy maximizes the *expected utility* for each decision.

2.2 Lazy Evaluation

The principles of Lazy Evaluation (LE) were already used for making inference in BNs [10], so it can be adapted for evaluating IDs [5]. The basic idea of this method is to maintain the decomposition of the potentials for as long as possible and to postpone computations for as long as possible, as well as to exploit barren variables and independence relations introduced by evidence. LE is based on message passing in a *strong junction tree*, which is a representation of an ID built by moralization and by triangulating the graph using a strong elimination order. Nodes in the strong junction trees correspond to *cliques* (maximal complete subgraphs) of the triangulated graph. Each clique is denoted by C_i where i is the index of the clique. The root of the strong junction tree is denoted by C_1. Two neighbour cliques are connected by a separator which contains the intersection of the variables in both cliques. An example of a strong junction tree is shown in Fig. 1. The original IDs and details for building this strong junction tree are given in [2].

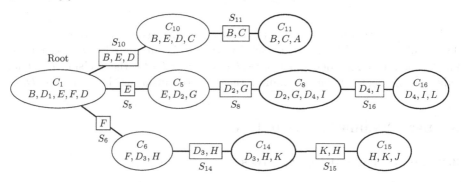

Fig. 1. Example of a Strong Junction Tree obtained from an ID

Propagation is performed by message-passing. Initially, each potential is associated to one clique containing all its variables. These potentials are not combined, so during propagation each clique and separator keeps two lists of potentials (one for probabilities and another for utilities). The message propagation starts by invoking the *Collect Message* algorithm in the root (Definition 1).

Definition 1 (Collect Message). *Let C_j be a clique where Collect Message is invoked, then:*

1. *C_j invokes Collect Message in all their children.*
2. *The message to the clique parent of C_j is built and sent by absorption (Definition 2).*

A clique can send the message to its parent (*Absorption*) if it has received all the messages from their children. Consider a clique C_j and its parent separator S. Absorption in C_j amounts to eliminating the variables of $C_j \backslash S$ from the list of probability and utility potentials Φ and Ψ associated with C_j and the separators of $ch(C_j)$ and then associating the obtained potentials with S. Algorithms for marginalizing a variable from a list of potentials are given in [5]. For example, when absorption is invoked in clique C_{14}, the variable K is removed from the list of potentials in C_{14} and in the child separator S_{15}. The resulting potentials are stored in the parent separator S_{14}.

Definition 2 (Absorption). *Let C_j be a clique, S be the parent separator and be $ch(C_j)$ the set of child separators. If Absorb Evidence is invoked on C_j, then:*

1. *Let $\mathcal{R}_S = \Phi_{C_j} \cup \Psi_{C_j} \cup \bigcup_{S' \in ch(C_j)}(\Phi^*_{S'} \cup \Psi^*_{S'})$.*
2. *Let $\mathbf{X} = \{X | X \in C_j, X \notin S\}$ the variables to be removed.*
3. *Choose an order to remove the variables in $\mathbf{X}$.*
4. *Marginalize out all variables in $\mathbf{X}$ from $\mathcal{R}_S$. Let Φ^*_S and Ψ^*_S the set of probability and utility potentials obtained. During this step, potential containing each variable are combined.*
5. *Associate Φ^*_S and Ψ^*_S to the parent separator S.*

The propagation finishes when the root clique has received all the messages. The utility potential from which each variable D_i is eliminated during the evaluation should be recorded as the *expected utility (EU)* for the decision D_i. The values of the decision that maximizes the expected utility is the policy for D_i.

3 Lazy Evaluation with Trees

3.1 Numerical and Binary Trees

Traditionally, potentials have been represented using tables. However, several alternative representations have been proposed in order to reduce the storage size of the potentials and improve the efficiency of the evaluation algorithms. An example are trees (numerical [6] and binary [7]) that will be denoted by NT and BT respectively. Figure 2 shows three different representations for the same utility potential: (a) table, (b) a NT and (c) a BT.

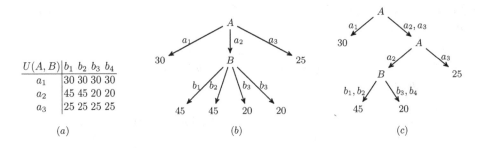

Fig. 2. Potential represented as a table (a), as a NT (b) and as BT (c)

The main advantage of trees is that they allow the specification of *context-specific independencies* [8]. For example, the table in Fig. 2 requires 12 values for representing the potential. When $A = a_1$, the potential will always take the value 30, regardless of the value of B. Similarly, when $A = a_3$, the utility value is also independent of B. Therefore, a NT representing the same utility potential requires 8 nodes. Moreover, the representation of the potential as a BT requires only 7 nodes since leaves labelled with 45 and 20 can be collapsed in two leaves. That is, BTs allow representing context-specific independencies which are finer-grained than those represented using NTs. These finer-grained independencies are also called *contextual-weak independencies* [11]. If trees are too large, they can be pruned and converted into smaller trees, thus leading to approximate algorithms. When a tree is pruned, leaves with a similar value are represented with a single leaf labelled with their mean. The prune is controlled with a threshold $\varepsilon \geq 0$. A low ε value will produce large trees with a low error, while a high ε value will produce small trees with a big error. When $\varepsilon = 0$, the exact prune is performed. That is, only identical values are grouped. When building a tree, variables are sorted in a way that the most informative variables must be situated in the highest nodes of the tree. This operation will reduce the error obtained when pruning a tree. More details for the building and pruning processes are given in [6,7].

3.2 Evaluation with Trees

LE algorithm for IDs can be easily adapted for working with trees (NTs or BTs). Evaluation algorithms for IDs require five operations with potentials: *restriction, combination, sum-marginalization, max-marginalization* and *division*. These operations must be implemented for operating with trees instead of tables. The general scheme of LE adapted for working with trees is shown below.

1. Initialization phase:
   (a) Build initial trees:
      − for each $\phi \in \Phi$ obtain $\mathcal{T}_\phi$.
      − for each $\psi \in \Psi$ obtain $\mathcal{T}_\psi$.
   (b) Prune all trees
   (c) Build the Strong Junction Tree from the ID.
2. Propagation phase:
   (a) Associate each potential (trees) in $\Phi \cup \Psi$ to only one clique containing all the variables in its domain.
   (b) Call the method *CollectMessage* in the root node. After removing each variable during the propagation, trees can be pruned again.

The main difference is that now it requires an initialization phase where initial trees are built from tables (1.a) and pruned in order to obtain smaller trees (1.b). After that, the Strong Junction Tree is built. Besides pruning initial potentials, an additional pruning can be performed after removing each variable during propagation. That is, after step 4 in Definition 2.

4   Experimentation

For testing purposes, two different families of IDs are used. First, a real world
ID used for the treatment of gastric NHL disease [12] with 3 decisions, 1 utility
node and 17 chance nodes. Second, a set of 20 randomly generated IDs with 2
decisions, 1 utility node, and a random number (between 6 and 17) of chance
nodes. All IDs are evaluated using different variations of the LE algorithm: using
tables (LET); using NTs and BTs pruning only initial potentials present in the
ID (LETNT and LETBT); and using NTs and BTs using the pruning operation
after removing each variable (LETNTPR and LETBTPR). The threshold used
for pruning is ranged in the interval $[0, 1.0]$. All the algorithms are implemented
in Java with the Elvira Software[1].

The graphics included in Fig. 3 show the storage requirement for storing all
the potentials during the NHL ID evaluation, that is, potentials associated to
the cliques and intermediate potentials used to compute the messages. For space
restrictions only results using the thresholds values 0 and 0.05 are shown. The
vertical axis indicate the storage size using a logarithmic scale: number of values
in the tables and number of nodes in the trees. The horizontal axis indicate the
evaluation stage when the storage size is measured. These measurements are
performed after combining potentials containing a variable to be removed, and
after pruning the resulting potentials of marginalization. It can be observed that
less space is needed for representing the potentials as BTs than using NTs or
tables. When the exact prune is performed (threshold $= 0$), differences are not
very significant, which become even less significant during the latest stages. This
is due to the combination of potentials during evaluation that makes the effect
of initial prune disappear. Moreover, at some stages of the evaluation tables
require less space for storing the potentials than trees, which need an additional
space for storing the internal nodes. However, with a higher threshold value, the
reduction of the size is more noticeable since the additional storage requirements
are compensated.

The reduction of the potential sizes should lead to more efficient algorithms:
operations with smaller potentials should be faster. In Figure 4 it is shown the
computation time for evaluating the NHL ID with different threshold values.
It can be observed that pruning after removing each variable (LENTPR and
LEBTPR) is not efficient when the exact prune is performed: the overhead introduced by pruning and sorting trees eats all the gain obtained with the smaller
potentials. The evaluation time with BTs (LEBT) is faster than the evaluation
with NTs (LENT). However, with higher threshold values, all variants of the
evaluation algorithm with trees obtain similar results. By contrast, worst results
are obtained using tables (LET).

Figure 5 includes six different graphics representing *root mean squared error*
calculated over all the configurations in the potential (horizontal axis) against
tree size (vertical axis) for the expected utilities corresponding to decisions 0,
1, and 2 for the NHL ID. Each point in the graphics corresponds to a different

---

[1] http://leo.ugr.es/~elvira

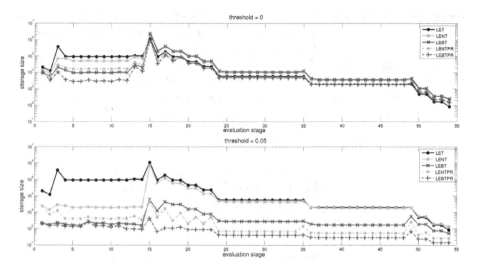

Fig. 3. Size of all potentials stored in memory during the NHL ID evaluation comparing tables, NTs and BTs with different threshold values

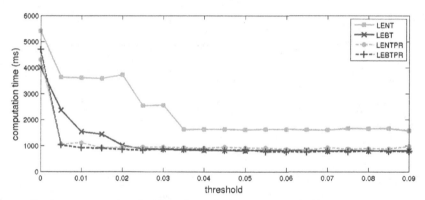

Fig. 4. Evaluation time for the NHL ID with different threshold values. The evaluation time using tables (LET) is approximately 15000 ms. and it is independent from the threshold value.

evaluation with a certain threshold value. Analyzing graphics corresponding to evaluations with a single initial prune (left column), it can be seen that in most of the evaluations the same error level is achieved using BTs of smaller size than the corresponding NTs. However, if the exact prune is performed (RMSE=0), the size is smaller using NTs. By contrast, if trees are also pruned after removing each variable (right column), NTs offer better approximate solutions than BTs. These conclusions can also be obtained with Table 1, which shows the hyper-volume indicators obtained from the evaluation of the NHL ID. The hyper-volume [13] is an unary indicator that measures the area of the dominated portion of the space. It is defined in the interval [0, 1], being 1 the optimal solution and 0 the worst. The hyper-volume indicator can be used to evaluate a set of different approximations of a potential if preferences about size and error are unknown. Each row corresponds to one of the expected utilities, whereas each column corresponds to the evaluation scheme. In case of a single prune, the hyper-volume values (H_{LEBT}) obtained using BTs are always larger (better) than the corresponding hyper-volume values (H_{LENT}) using NTs. In case of pruning after removing each variable (H_{LENTPR} and H_{LEBTPR}), the hyper-volume values obtained using BTs are lower for Decisions 2 and 1.

Table 1. Hyper-volume values of the approximate expected utilities

	H_{LENT}	H_{LEBT}	H_{LENTPR}	H_{LEBTPR}
Decision 2	0.7259	**0.7846**	**0.9756**	0.9673
Decision 1	0.6981	**0.7419**	**0.9758**	0.9645
Decision 0	0.2930	**0.5584**	0.9592	**0.9626**

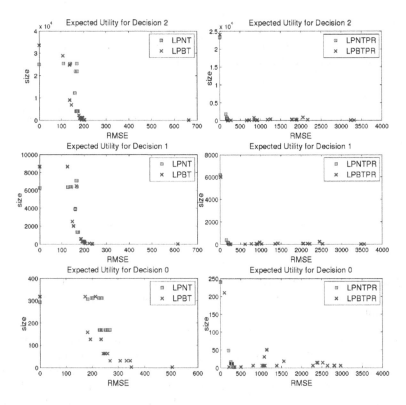

Fig. 5. Results of the expected utilities approximation for the NHL ID performing a single prune at the beginning (left) and pruning after removing each variable (right)

In order to get more solid conclusions in relation to the error obtained when approximating potentials with trees, a similar procedure can be done with random IDs. The hyper-volume values for the these IDs are shown in Table 2. Each row corresponds to a different random ID, whereas the columns indicate the evaluation scheme used and expected utility analyzed. Obtaining a 0 hyper-volume value means that the size of the expected utility is independent of threshold value used for pruning. This happen because the prune operation may reduce part of the trees which must be completely developed during posterior combinations. It can also be observed that the hyper-volume value H_{LEBT} is usually larger than the corresponding H_{LENT} value. By contrast there are less differences if H_{LEBTPR} and H_{LENTPR} are compared. Moreover, for Decision 0 H_{LENTPR} is usually larger than H_{LEBTPR}. To prove these hypothesis four Wilcoxon signed-rank are performed comparing H_{LENT} against H_{LEBT} and H_{LENTPR} againts H_{LEBTPR} for each decision. The results of these test are shown in Table 3. For each test, it shows the *p-value*, the percentage of IDs where the use of BTs give better results and whether the null hypothesis was rejected (NTs and BTs are not equal) with a significance level of 10%. For the comparison H_{LENT} and H_{LEBT} the hypothesis was rejected, then better approximate solutions are obtained using BTs than using NTs if only a single initial prune is performed. In case of pruning trees after removing each variable, the null hypothesis is not rejected for Decision 1. In case of Decision 0, the null hypothesis is rejected. Taking into account that H_{LENTPR} is usually larger than H_{LEBTPR}, it can be deduced that NTs offer better approximate solutions than BTs if trees are pruned after removing each variable.

Table 2. Hyper-volume values of utility trees comparing NTs and BTs

Decision 1		Decision 2		Decision 1		Decision 2	
H_{LENT}	H_{LEBT}	H_{LENT}	H_{LEBT}	H_{LENTPR}	H_{LEBTPR}	H_{LENTPR}	H_{LEBTPR}
0.28	**0.995**	0.296	**1**	**0.991**	0.989	**0.999**	0.999
0.745	0.671	0.177	**0.827**	**0.703**	0.665	**0.901**	0.844
0.26	**0.922**	0.261	**0.944**	0.981	**0.985**	**0.942**	0.937
0.447	0.393	0.613	**0.65**	0.364	**0.384**	**0.438**	0.277
0.529	0.341	**0.333**	0.163	**0.431**	0.341	0.548	**0.641**
0.671	0.635	0.369	**0.812**	0.606	**0.635**	**0.863**	0.809
0.0712	**0.168**	0.521	**0.747**	0.0695	**0.202**	0	**0.312**
0.8	**0.979**	0.605	**0.95**	0.95	**0.972**	**0.941**	0.937
0.891	**0.997**	0.395	**0.997**	0.99	**0.997**	**0.996**	0.995
0.443	**0.998**	0.334	**0.99**	0.994	**0.999**	0.926	**0.987**
0.178	**0.968**	0.283	**0.997**	**0.987**	0.972	**1**	0.999
0.259	0.259	0	0	0.247	**0.248**	**0.338**	0
0.577	0.571	0.445	**0.66**	**0.562**	0.559	**0.686**	0.631
0.456	0.378	0	**0.548**	**0.449**	0.376	**0.882**	0.856
0.319	**0.975**	0.253	**0.972**	**0.991**	0.968	**0.992**	0.96
0.533	0.524	0.34	**0.96**	0.507	**0.52**	**0.944**	0.94
0.278	**0.992**	0.295	**1**	**0.979**	0.975	0.988	**0.997**
0.413	0.388	0.411	**0.898**	0.334	**0.416**	**0.975**	0.892
0.686	0.656	0	**0.856**	**0.679**	0.648	**0.817**	0.816
0.746	**0.976**	0.45	**0.946**	**0.986**	0.979	**0.993**	0.982

Table 3. Results for the Willcoxon sign-rank test with the random ID

	H_{LENT} vs H_{LEBT}			H_{LENTPR} vs H_{LEBTPR}		
	p-value	% BT wins	rejected	p-value	% BT wins	rejected
Decision 1	0.0793	50	yes	0.94	50	no
Decision 0	$1.82 \cdot 10^{-4}$	95	yes	0.0859	20	yes

5   Conclusions and Future Work

This paper proposes to combine the use of trees for representing the potentials and Lazy Evaluation to evaluate IDs which allows to perform an approximate Lazy Evaluation of decision problems. It is explained how trees are used during the evaluation of IDs and compared the computing time, memory requirements and goodness of approximations using tables, NTs and BTs. The experiments shows that less space is used for storing potentials as a BT than as NT or as a table. Moreover, if potentials are approximated the reduction is more noticeable. In general, the evaluation with trees is faster than using tables. Concerning to the error level achieved, the experiments showed that BTs offer better approximate solutions than NTs if only initial potentials are pruned. If trees are pruned after removing each variable during evaluation NTs offer better results.

As regards future directions of research, we would like to study alternative heuristics or scores for triangulating the graph. The heuristics used until now consider that potentials are represented as tables, not as trees. Finally, another direction of research could be the integration of restrictions with binary trees. This would allow the treatment of asymmetric decision problems [14], where the set of legitimate states of variables may vary depending on different states of other variables.

Acknowledgments. This research was supported by the Spanish Ministry of Economy and Competitiveness under project TIN2010-20900-C04-01, the European Regional Development Fund (FEDER) and the FPI scholarship programme (BES-2011-050604). The authors have been also partially supported by " Junta de Andalucía" under projects TIC-06016 and P08-TIC-03717.

References

1. Howard, R.A., Matheson, J.E.: Influence diagram retrospective. Decision Analysis 2(3), 144–147 (2005)
2. Jensen, F., Jensen, F.V., Dittmer, S.L.: From Influence Diagrams to junction trees. In: Proceedings of the Tenth International Conference on Uncertainty in Artificial Intelligence, pp. 367–373. Morgan Kaufmann Publishers Inc. (1994)
3. Jensen, F., Nielsen, T.: Bayesian networks and decision graphs. Springer (2007)
4. Shachter, R.: Evaluating influence diagrams. Operations Research, 871–882 (1986)
5. Madsen, A., Jensen, F.: Lazy evaluation of symmetric Bayesian decision problems. In: Proceedings of the 15th Conference on Uncertainty in AI, pp. 382–390. Morgan Kaufmann Publishers Inc. (1999)

6. Gómez, M., Cano, A.: Applying numerical trees to evaluate asymmetric decision problems. In: ESCQARU, pp. 196–207 (2003)
7. Cabañas, R., Gómez, M., Cano, A.: Approximate inference in influence diagrams using binary trees. In: Proceedings of the 6th European Workshop on Probabilistic Graphical Models, PGM 2012, pp. 43–50 (2011)
8. Boutilier, C., Friedman, N., Goldszmidt, M., Koller, D.: Context-specific independence in Bayesian networks. In: Proceedings of the 12th International Conference on Uncertainty in AI, pp. 115–123. Morgan Kaufmann Publishers Inc. (1996)
9. Cano, A., Moral, S., Salmerón, A.: Penniless propagation in join trees. International Journal of Intelligent Systems 15(11), 1027–1059 (2000)
10. Madsen, A., Jensen, F.: Lazy propagation: a junction tree inference algorithm based on lazy evaluation. Artificial Intelligence 113(1-2), 203–245 (1999)
11. Wong, S., Butz, C.: Contextual weak independence in Bayesian networks. In: Proceedings of the 15th Conference on Uncertainty in AI, pp. 670–679. Morgan Kaufmann Publishers Inc. (1999)
12. Lucas, P., Taal, B.: Computer-based decision support in the management of primary gastric non-hodgkin lymphoma. UU-CS (1998-33) (1998)
13. Zitzler, E., Brockhoff, D., Thiele, L.: The hypervolume indicator revisited: On the design of pareto-compliant indicators via weighted integration. In: Obayashi, S., Deb, K., Poloni, C., Hiroyasu, T., Murata, T. (eds.) EMO 2007. LNCS, vol. 4403, pp. 862–876. Springer, Heidelberg (2007)
14. Bielza, C., Shenoy, P.: A comparison of graphical techniques for asymmetric decision problems. Management Science 45(11), 1552–1569 (1999)

Learning Recursive Probability Trees from Data

Andrés Cano[1], Manuel Gómez-Olmedo[1], Serafín Moral[1],
Cora Beatriz Pérez-Ariza[1], and Antonio Salmerón[2]

[1] Dept. Computer Science and Artificial Intelligence
CITIC-UGR, University of Granada, Spain
{acu,mgomez,smc,cora}@decsai.ugr.es
[2] Dept. Mathematics
University of Almería, Spain
antonio.salmeron@ual.es

Abstract. Recursive Probability Trees offer a flexible framework for representing the probabilistic information in Probabilistic Graphical Models. This structure is able to provide a detailed representation of the distribution it encodes, by specifying most of the types of independencies that can be found in a probability distribution. Learning this structure involves the search for context-specific independencies along with factorisations within the available data. In this paper we develop the first approach at learning Recursive Probability Trees from data by extending an existent greedy methodology for retrieving small Recursive Probability Trees from probabilistic potentials. We test the performance of the algorithm by learning from different databases, both real and handcrafted, and we compare the performance for different databases sizes.

Keywords: Bayesian networks learning, approximate computation, deterministic algorithms, probability trees, recursive probability trees.

1 Introduction and Previous Work

In general, inference algorithms become less efficient as the number of variables and general complexity of the model grow, as this implies operations with big structures that require large storage space and increase the computational processing time. A way of addressing this problem is by modelling the probabilistic information taking into account the existent patterns within the probability distributions that can compact the information, such as independencies that hold only for certain contexts, i.e. context-specific independencies (cs-independencies) [1] and different kinds of factorisations.

Recursive Probability Trees [3] (RPTs) were designed as an alternative to traditional data structures for representing probabilistic potentials, such as conditional probability tables (CPTs) or probability trees [6] (PTs). In this paper we present our approach for learning RPT structures from a database, extending an existent methodology based on detecting patterns within potentials [2].

The previous algorithm, developed by Cano et al. in [2], consists of building an RPT from another probabilistic potential (a CPT or a PT, for instance).

C. Bielza et al. (Eds.): CAEPIA 2013, LNAI 8109, pp. 332–341, 2013.

The problem of finding a minimal RPT is NP-hard as proven in [2]. Hence, this methodology focuses in obtaining an RPT in a greedy way, following a heuristic designed for selecting Split nodes that are likely to reduce the dependencies among the remaining variables. In this way it is intended to increase the possibilities of finding multiplicative factorisations, which constitute the basis for obtaining RPTs of small size.

In general, the methodology is oriented to the detection of cs-independencies and also multiplicative factorisations. Context-specific independencies are sought following a similar approach to the one used for building probability trees [6]. It is based on selecting variables for *Split* nodes according to their information gain, as it is done when constructing decision trees [5]. Regarding multiplicative decompositions, the idea is to detect groups of variables according to their mutual information. The obtained groups are later used to get the potentials making up the multiplicative decomposition. In this work, we adapt the general workflow of the algorithm to deal with the new problem: learning the structure from data.

The rest of the paper is organized as follows: Section 2 defines RPTs and describes their features; Section 3 describes our approach for learning an RPT from a database; Section 4 shows the experimental evaluation performed for testing the performance of the algorithm; and finally Section 5 presents conclusions as well as future research directions.

2   Recursive Probability Trees

Recursive Probability Trees [3] are a generalization of PTs. RPTs were developed with the aim of enhancing PTs' flexibility and so they are able to represent different kinds of patterns that so far were out of the scope of probability trees.

As an extension of a PT, an RPT is a directed tree, to be traversed from root to leaves, where the nodes (both inner nodes and leaves) play different roles depending on their nature. In the simplest case, an RPT is equivalent to a PT, where the inner nodes represent variables, and the leaf nodes are labelled by numbers. In the context of RPTs, we will call this type of inner nodes as *Split* nodes and this kind of leaves as *Value* nodes.

RPTs propose to include factorisations within the data structure by incorporating a type of inner node that lists together all the factors. Therefore, a *List* node represents a multiplicative factorisation by listing all the factors making up the division. If a *List* node stores a factorisation of k factors of a potential ϕ defined on $\mathbf{X_J}$, and every factor i (an RPT as well) encodes a potential ϕ_i for a subset of variables $\mathbf{X_{J_i}} \subseteq \mathbf{X_J}$, then ϕ corresponds to $\prod_{i=1}^{k} \phi_i(\mathbf{X_{J_i}})$.

When necessary, RPTs will include a fourth type of node denominated *Potential* node. This is a leaf node and its purpose is to encapsulate a full potential within the leaf in an internal structure. This internal structure usually will not be an RPT, but a probability tree or a probability table instead. In fact, as long as the internal structure of a Potential node supports the basic operations on potentials (namely marginalization, restriction and combination), it is accepted within the RPT representation.

In summary, an RPT can have four kind of nodes in total: *Split* or *List* nodes as inner nodes, and *Value* or *Potential* nodes as leaves. We can combine them in very different ways in order to find the structure that best fits the potential to be represented, making RPTs an extremely flexible framework to work with.

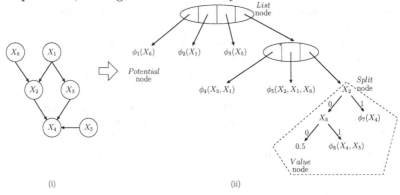

Fig. 1. An RPT representing a full Bayesian network

An RPT is able to represent a full model like a Bayesian network (BN) as it is shown in Fig. 1. The more straightforward way of representing a BN would be to join with a List node all the conditional probability distributions defined by the chain rule for Bayesian networks, as shown in the right part of Fig. 1. Every factor could be represented independently looking for patterns within it. In the figure, the conditional probability distribution associated to X_4 has been detailed using Split nodes.

3   Learning an RPT from a Database

The starting point is a database *cases* defined over a set of variables $\mathbf{X}$, and the aim of the algorithm is therefore to find a representation of the probability distribution encoded in *cases* as an RPT.

The proposed algorithm is defined in Alg. 1, and as it can be seen in the pseudocode, it is divided into four steps, iterating over them until finding a suitable representation for the encoded distribution of the data. The first step consists of building an auxiliary graph structure G_c with vertex set $\mathbf{X}$ where a pair of variables $X_i, X_j \in \mathbf{X}$ will be linked if there is probabilistic dependence between them. More precisely, a link $X_i - X_j$ is present in G_c if the weight of the link between X_i and X_j is bigger than 0. We use the Bayesian Dirichlet equivalent metric [4] to measure the relation between pairs of variables, and hence, a link $X_i - X_j$ will be included only if

$$W(X_i, X_j) = BDe(X_i|X_j) - BDe(X_i) > 0. \tag{1}$$

The second step of the algorithm consists of analysing the resultant graph G_c. A disconnected representation of G_c can be directly translated as a factorisation,

```
 1  learn(database cases)
    Input: A database cases
    Output: RT, an RPT for an approximation of the distribution in cases
 2  begin
 3  |    // Step 1: compute G_c
 4  |    G_c → graph for variables dependencies in cases
 5  |    // Step 2: graph analysis
 6  |    G_c analysis looking for connected components
 7  |    // Several scenarios are possible according to G_c
 8  |    if G_c is partitioned into components C = {C_1 ... C_n} then
 9  |    |    // Step 3: multiplicative factorisation
10  |    |    RT ← multiplicativeFactorisation(cases, C)
11  |    else
12  |    |    // Only one component: decomposition with Step 4
13  |    |    RT ← contextSpecificFactorisation(cases, G_c)
14  |    end
15  |    return RT
16  end
```

Algorithm 1. Main body of the learning algorithm

jumping into the third step of the algorithm, because the separation between the clusters mean that the dependence between their variables is weak. The fourth step of the algorithm corresponds to the case when the graph G_c remains as a single connected component, which means that the potential is not decomposable as a list of factors with disjoint variables. However, conditional decompositions are possible, so the algorithm looks for either factorisations that share variables, cs-independencies, or a combination of both.

3.1   Representing a Factorisation

If G_c is disconnected in n connected components $\mathbf{X}_1 \cup \cdots \cup \mathbf{X}_n = \mathbf{X}$. The factorisation is given by:

$$f(\mathbf{x}) = f_1(\mathbf{x}_1) \cdots f_n(\mathbf{x}_n), \tag{2}$$

where $f_i = f^{\downarrow \mathbf{X}_i}$, $i = 1, \ldots, n$. Each f_i is a potential with the absolute frequencies for all the variables in the correspondent connected component. Therefore, f corresponds to the joint probability distribution of all the variables in the G_c.

If the clusters do not share any variables (as it happens, for instance, when G_c is disconnected the first time that we compute it in Alg. 1), we can normalise each potential independently using the Laplacian correction to avoid dealing with zero probability values. If the clusters share variables, then we apply the Laplace correction taking into account all the variables only when normalising the first factor. The other factors are normalised using the Laplace correction but conditioned to the common variables, in order to avoid the introduction of normalising errors. This set of *conditioning variables* is associated to the cluster until the end of the algorithm, so further factorisations will be correctly normalised.

If any of the clusters contains more than 2 variables, we recursively apply the algorithm to try to learn a factorised substructure from the database for the correspondent subset of variables. Hence, the distribution for the current cluster can be represented as an RPT where the root node would be a List node containing the factors in Eq. 2.

3.2   Analysing Connected Components

This part of the algorithm will work with a subset of the variables of the database and will iteratively perform a series of steps: first, locate the variable within the cluster that present the highest *degree of dependence* with respect to the others, and remove it from the graph; second, recompute the links in the reduced graph by weighting the relations between every pair of the remaining variables; third, analyse the graph: if it becomes disconnected, we can represent the cluster as a factorisation, if it becomes too small (2 variables) it means that a factorisation is not possible, hence we represent the cluster as a Potential node, retrieving the parameters from the database. The third possibility is that after removing a variable, the graph continues being connected, in which case we iterate selecting a new variable to be removed, and so on.

The above mentioned *degree of dependence* between every variable X_i and those other variables belonging to its neighbourhood, $ne(X_i)$, is computed as:

$$V_{X_i} = \sum_{X_j \in ne(X_i)} W(X_i, X_j). \tag{3}$$

Every iteration of the loop selects the variable maximizing the degree of dependence in order to look for the context in which the underlying potential might be factorised:

$$X_{max} = \arg\max_{X_i} V_{X_i}. \tag{4}$$

Once X_{max} is selected it will be included in $\mathbf{S}_1$ or $\mathbf{S}_2$. These are auxiliary vectors that represent two types of variables: those that are closely related to all the others ($\mathbf{S}_1$) and those variables that are highly dependent of only a subset of the variables in the component ($\mathbf{S}_2$). Note that the ordering in which the variables are selected is very important, as every deletion is dependent on the previous one. The splitting of the tree with the variables of $\mathbf{S}_1$ will be performed using a first-in-first-out fashion.

Therefore, X_{max} will be included in $\mathbf{S}_1$ if it is completely connected to the rest of variables in G_c. Otherwise it will be included in $\mathbf{S}_2$. In both cases, X_{max} and its links will be removed from G_c producing a new graph $G_c^{X_{max}}$ that will be considered in further iterations.

Each remaining link $X_i - X_j$ is re-weighted according to the previously removed variables $\mathbf{X_S} = \mathbf{S}_1 \cup \mathbf{S}_2$, being only included the links that obtain a positive score: $W(X_i, X_j \mid X_s) = BDe(X_i \mid X_j, X_s) - BDe(X_i \mid X_s) > 0$.

3.3 Obtaining a Factorisation of a Cluster

If we disconnect the graph during the procedure explained above, we build the correspondent RPT as follows. If $\mathbf{S}_1$ has variables, we take the first variable X_i in $\mathbf{S}_1$ and build a List node with two children: one will be a Split node of X_i and the second a Potential node with the marginal probability distribution of X_i computed from the database, and normalised using Laplace but checking if X_i belongs to the conditioning set. Then, for every possible child of the Split node, we add the same structure for the next variable in $\mathbf{S}_1$, and so on until we represent all the variables in the set. We have to consider when learning the parameters both the Split nodes above and the possible list of conditioning variables in the Laplace normalisation.

Then for each branch of the Split nodes consistent with every possible configuration of the variables in $\mathbf{S}_1$, we store the factorisation at the leaves according to the variables in $\mathbf{S}_2$ and the resultant clusters $\mathbf{C} = \{c_1, ..., c_n\}$. The structure will be a factorisation computed as explained in Sec. 3.1, but considering that we include the variables in $\mathbf{S}_2$ to the set of variables of every subcluster:

$$f(\mathbf{c}_1, ..., \mathbf{c}_n, \mathbf{S}_2) := \prod_{i=1}^{n} f^h(\mathbf{c}_i, \mathbf{S}_2), \tag{5}$$

Once a decomposition is performed, the algorithm is recursively applied to each and every potential obtained successively, until no further decomposition can be computed.

As an example of the whole process, consider the situation represented in Fig. 2. After removing X_4 and X_3 we find a decomposition of the graph in two connected components, so we build an RPT with a Split chain of the variables in $\mathbf{S}_1$, in this example just X_4, and in the leaves we place the factorisation, that has a List node as a root, and one child per resultant connected component plus a normalisation factor. Each subfactor is analysed independently afterwards.

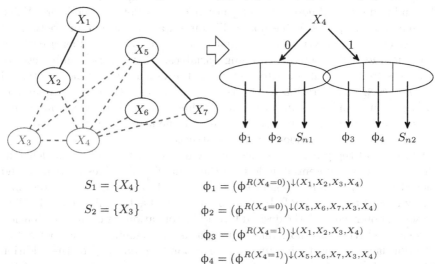

$$S_1 = \{X_4\} \qquad \phi_1 = (\phi^{R(X_4=0)})^{\downarrow(X_1, X_2, X_3, X_4)}$$

$$S_2 = \{X_3\} \qquad \phi_2 = (\phi^{R(X_4=0)})^{\downarrow(X_5, X_6, X_7, X_3, X_4)}$$

$$\phi_3 = (\phi^{R(X_4=1)})^{\downarrow(X_1, X_2, X_3, X_4)}$$

$$\phi_4 = (\phi^{R(X_4=1)})^{\downarrow(X_5, X_6, X_7, X_3, X_4)}$$

Fig. 2. Creation of a Split chain with a decomposition of the auxiliary graph

4   Experimental Evaluation

In this section we present the experimental evaluation carried out in order to analyse the performance of the proposed algorithm. We learned from different kind of databases, both handcrafted and real, and examined the results both in terms of accuracy (by analysing how well the learned models fit the data) and size of the obtained representation.

Generation of a Random RPT

Some of the RPTs used in the experiments were generated at random using the algorithm described below. We considered three parameters: a set of variables $\mathbf{X}$, a probability p_S for the generation of Split nodes as inner nodes, and a probability p_P for the generation of Potential nodes on the leaves.

The procedure is recursive, generating first the root node and going down to the leaves. If the size of $\mathbf{X}$ is less or equal than 2, we will generate a leaf node: if $\mathbf{X}$ is not empty, we generate a Potential node of its variables. If $\mathbf{X}$ is empty, then we incorporate a Value node labelled by a random value to the structure. If the number of remaining variables is between 3 and 5, the probability of generating an inner node (either Split or List node) is 0.2. If the number of variables is equal or greater than 5, then we will always generate an inner node.

When generating an inner node, a Split node of a random variable within the set will be created with probability p_S. For List nodes, a maximum of 5 children is allowed in order to bound the size of the factorisation. The choosing of the number of children for a List node follows a Poisson distribution. For each child of the List node, we randomly create a subset of variables to be represented. The intersection between the subsets does not have to be empty.

When building a leaf node, we will generate either a Potential node or a Value node according to p_P. A Value node will contain a random number between 0 and 1. To create a Potential node, we first randomly obtain a number n between 1 and the size of the set of remaining variables. Then we randomly retrieve n variables from the set and store them as the domain of the new Potential node. For each configuration of the new set of variables, we store a random value between 0 and 1, as its probability value. Potential nodes are internally represented as probability trees, with a small prune factor of 0.001, to avoid the storage of many similar values within the structure.

At the end of the process, we check if any of the variables of $\mathbf{X}$ was left out. If this is the case, a Potential node with the remaining variables is created, and attached to the previously generated RPT through a List node that becomes the new root of the final RPT. In this way it is possible to calibrate the RPT to represent a potential with the desired level of factorisations or cs-independencies. The generated RPTs are normalised afterwards by including at the root a normalisation factor equal to $1/sum_{RPT}$, corresponding sum_{RPT} to the addition of the probability values correspondent to every possible configuration of the variables in the RPT.

4.1   Detecting Factorisations and Context-Specific Independencies in the Data

The aim of this experiment was to check the accuracy and size of the learned RPTs. We sampled several RPTs with different degrees of factorisations and cs-independencies within them, and then learned a new structure with the proposed algorithm. Afterwards we compared the learned structure to the original one, both measuring the Kullback-Leibler divergence between them, and counting the number of probability values needed to represent the distribution.

To do so, we used the random RPT generator explained above to build RPTs of 10 binary variables, and varied the probability of generating a Split node (p_S) between 0 and 1, with intervals of 0.1. The probability of generating a Potential node (p_P) in the leaves was set to 0.8. For each combination of the parameters, the experiment was repeated 30 times. For each generated RPT we sampled a database of 100, 500, 1000, 2000 and 5000 entries.

Figure 3 shows the average of the 30 Kullback-Leibler divergence values obtained for each value of p_S. The Kullback-Leibler divergence shows generally reasonable accurate results, getting worse as the level of factorisations decrease in the original distributions. This means that the algorithm performs well at detecting clusters of highly dependent variables, and in general obtains good approximations of the distributions by detecting the patterns hidden within them. As for the number of samples in the database, we can see in Fig. 3 that small databases lead to poor representations, whilst too much data leads to overfitting. The best average results are obtained for the database of 2000 entries.

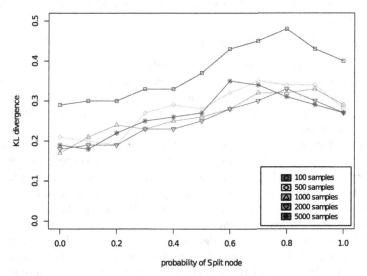

Fig. 3. Average Kullback-Leibler divergence between the original distribution and the learned, for different RPTs and for different database sizes

We also measured the sizes of both the original model and the learned structures for all the considered cases. In general, the learned RPTs are much more compact in all the cases. For instance, in Fig. 4 we see the averages of the 30 structures generated for each value of p_S, with the database of 2000 entries, where we can check how the approximations are much smaller and, as seen in Fig. 3, still reasonably accurate. We do not show the figures for all the database sizes due to lack of space, but the observed behaviour is constant for all the tested database sizes.

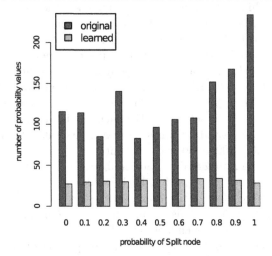

Fig. 4. Size of the learned RPTs for the database of 2000 instances

In general we can conclude from this experiment that the proposed algorithm returns compact structures representing good approximations of the original distributions.

4.2   Learning Bayesian Networks

In this experiment we learned the RPT models from 6 databases extracted from the UCI Machine Learning Repository[1].For each database, we learned the RPT with 80% of the data, and then computed the loglikelihood with the remaining 20%. We compared the resultant accuracy with the models obtained by the PC and K2 algorithms.

This procedure was repeated 30 times, every time varying the partition of the database. With the average of the loglikelihood and size (in terms of number of probability values stored) of the models we computed the Bayesian Information Criteria (BIC), that for small sample sizes penalizes more complex models. The results are shown in Fig.5, where we can see that RPTs get a better score than at least one of the other learned models with all the databases with the exception of Heart Disease, where all three algorithms obtain a very similar score. As an intuitive conclusion from the experiment, we have included horizontal lines in Fig. 5 detailing the average BIC for all the considered networks, where we can see how RPTs tie with the PC algorithm (with an average of -869,57 (s.d. 283,54) for RPTs and -866,51 (s.d. 452,09) for the PC), whilst K2 results fall far behind (with an average of -1090,98 and standard deviation of 389,64)).

---

[1] http://archive.ics.uci.edu/ml/

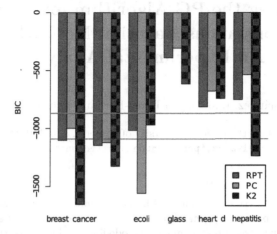

Fig. 5. Bayesian Information Criteria for the learned models

5 Conclusions

This paper presents an algorithm for learning RPTs from a database, looking for factorisations and cs-independencies within the data. The experiments suggest that the algorithm retrieves accurate and compact representations for the underlying distributions, being competitive against algorithms like PC and K2. In this work we have only considered the BDe metric for weighting the relations between variables, but other measures, like the mutual information, can be considered and tested against each other in future works. In fact, some preliminary experimentation (not included in this work due to lack of space) hints that the algorithm performs similarly changing the metric.

Acknowledgements. This research was supported by the Spanish Ministry of Economy and Competitiveness under projects TIN2010-20900-C04-01,02.

References

1. Boutilier, C., Friedman, N., Goldszmidt, M., Koller, D.: Context-specific independence in Bayesian networks. In: Horvitz, E., Jensen, F.V. (eds.) Proceedings of the 12th Conference on Uncertainty in Artificial Intelligence, pp. 115–123. Morgan Kaufmann (1996)
2. Cano, A., Gómez-Olmedo, M., Moral, S., Pérez-Ariza, C., Salmerón, A.: Learning recursive probability trees from probabilistic potentials. International Journal of Approximate Reasoning 53, 1367–13875 (2012)
3. Cano, A., Gómez-Olmedo, M., Moral, S., Pérez-Ariza, C., Salmerón, A.: Inference in Bayesian networks with recursive probability trees: data structure definition and operations. International Journal of Intelligent Systems 28 (2013)
4. Heckerman, D., Geiger, D., Chickering, D.: Learning bayesian networks: The combination of knowledge and statistical data. Machine Learning 20, 197–243 (1995)
5. Quinlan, J.: Induction of decision trees. Machine Learning 1, 81–106 (1986)
6. Salmerón, A., Cano, A., Moral, S.: Importance sampling in Bayesian networks using probability trees. Computational Statistics and Data Analysis 34, 387–413 (2000)

On Using the PC Algorithm for Learning Continuous Bayesian Networks: An Experimental Analysis

Antonio Fernández, Inmaculada Pérez-Bernabé, and Antonio Salmerón

Department of Mathematics, University of Almería, E-04120 Almería, Spain
{afalvarez,iperez,antonio.salmeron}@ual.es

Abstract. Mixtures of truncated basis functions (MoTBFs) have been recently proposed as a generalisation of mixtures of truncated exponentials and mixtures of polynomials for modelling conditional distributions in hybrid Bayesian networks. However, no structural learning algorithm has been proposed so far for such models. In this paper we investigate the use of the PC algorithm as a means of obtaining the underlying network structure, that is finally completed by plugging in the conditional MoTBF densities. We show through a set of experiments that the approach is valid and competitive with current alternatives of discretizing the variables or adopting a Gaussian assumption. We restrict the scope of this work to continuous variables.

Keywords: continuous Bayesian networks, PC algorithm, mixtures of truncated basis functions, structural learning.

1 Introduction

Mixtures of truncated basis functions (MoTBFs) [1] have been recently proposed as a general framework for handling hybrid Bayesian networks, i.e. Bayesian networks where discrete and continuous variables coexist. Previous hybrid models as the so-called mixtures of truncated exponentials (MTEs) [2] and mixtures of polynomials (MOPs) [3] can be regarded as particular cases of MoTBFs.

Unlike the conditional Gaussian (CG) model [4], where discrete variables are not allowed to have continuous parents, MoTBFs do not impose any structural restrictions to the network. Furthermore, they are closed under addition, multiplication, and integration and therefore inference in an MoTBF network can be performed efficiently using standard methods like the Shenoy-Shafer architecture [5] or the *variable elimination* algorithm [6].

The problem of learning marginal and conditional MoTBFs from data has been addressed from a general point of view [7] and also for the particular case of MTEs [8,9] and MOPs [10]. However, structural learning in this context has only been considered in the literature for the particular case of MTEs [11] where a score-and-search algorithm is proposed. The main difficulty in following a score-and-search approach is that it requires re-estimating conditional densities after

C. Bielza et al. (Eds.): CAEPIA 2013, LNAI 8109, pp. 342–351, 2013.
© Springer-Verlag Berlin Heidelberg 2013

each move is made, what is a specially time-consuming task in the particular case of MoTBFs, as we will discuss in Section 3.

In this paper we analyse a simple alternative to construct Bayesian networks with MoTBFs based on the PC algorithm. The idea is to obtain the structure using the PC algorithm over a discretized version of the data, and afterwards plugging in the conditional MoTBF densities. We carry out an experimental comparison of this strategy combined with MTEs and MOPs versus two other approaches: discretizing all the variables and assume that the joint distribution in the network is a multivariate Gaussian. We have not included methods based on kernel densities [12] in the comparison, since they do not admit exact inference algorithms. We only consider continuous variables in this work, leaving as a future task the inclusion of discrete ones. The implementations have been developed using the R statistical software [13] with the corresponding packages for supporting the PC algorithm [14] and the learning of Gaussian networks [15].

The paper continues with a description of the MoTBF framework in Section 2. The method used for learning MoTBFs from data is given in Section 3. The experimental analysis, which is the core of this work, is reported in Section 4. The paper ends with the conclusions in Section 5.

2   Mixtures of Truncated Basis Functions

The MoTBF framework [1] is based on the use of a set of real-valued *basis functions* $\psi(\cdot)$, which includes both polynomial and exponential functions as special cases. A *marginal MoTBF density* is defined as follows: Let X be a continuous variable with domain $\Omega_X \subseteq \mathbb{R}$ and let $\psi_i : \mathbb{R} \to \mathbb{R}$, for $i = 0, \ldots, k$, define a collection of real basis functions. A function $g_k : \Omega_X \mapsto \mathbb{R}_0^+$ is an MoTBF potential of level k wrt. $\Psi = \{\psi_0, \psi_1, \ldots, \psi_k\}$ if g_k can be written as

$$g_k(x) = \sum_{i=0}^{k} a_i \, \psi_i(x), \tag{1}$$

where a_i are real numbers. The potential is a density if $\int_{\Omega_X} g_k(x)\,dx = 1$. Note that as opposed to the MTE and MOP definitions [2,3], a marginal MoTBF potential does not employ interval refinement to improve its expressive power.

Example 1. By letting the basis functions correspond to polynomial functions, $\psi_i(x) = x^i$ for $i = 0, 1, \ldots$, the MoTBF model reduces to an MOP model for univariate distributions. Similarly, if we define the basis functions as $\psi_i(x) = \{1, \exp(-x), \exp(x), \exp(-2x), \exp(2x), \ldots\}$, the MoTBF model corresponds to an MTE model with the exception that the parameters in the exponential functions are fixed.

In a conditional MoTBF density, the influence a set of continuous parent variables $\mathbf{Z}$ has on their child variable X is encoded only through the partitioning of the domain of $\mathbf{Z}$, denoted as $\Omega_{\mathbf{Z}}$, into hyper-cubes, and not directly in the functional form of $g_k(x|\mathbf{z})$ inside each hyper-cube. More precisely, for a partitioning $\mathcal{P} = \{\Omega_{\mathbf{Z}}^1, \ldots, \Omega_{\mathbf{Z}}^m\}$ of $\Omega_{\mathbf{Z}}$, the conditional MoTBF is defined for $\mathbf{z} \in \Omega_{\mathbf{Z}}^j$, $1 \leq j \leq m$, as

$$g_k^{(j)}(x|\mathbf{z} \in \Omega_{\mathbf{Z}}^j) = \sum_{i=0}^{k} a_i^{(j)} \, \psi_i^{(j)}(x). \tag{2}$$

3   Learning MoTBFs

A procedure for fitting an MoTBF to any density function whose functional form is known is described in [1]. Roughly speaking, the procedure is based on assuming a set of orthonormal basis functions and using generalised Fourier series to estimate the parameters in Equation (1).

In what concerns learning marginal MoTBFs from data, we have used a modified version of the method in [7], based on fitting an MoTBF to the empirical distribution function of the data by least squares [16]. The empirical distribution function is defined for a sample $\mathcal{D} = \{x_1, \ldots, x_N\}$ as

$$G_N(x) = \frac{1}{N} \sum_{\ell=1}^{N} \mathbf{1}\{x_\ell \leq x\}, \quad x \in \mathbb{R}, \tag{3}$$

where $\mathbf{1}\{\cdot\}$ is the indicator function.

As an example, if we use polynomials as basis functions, $\Psi = \{1, x, x^2, x^3, \ldots\}$, the parameters can be obtained solving the optimization problem

$$\begin{aligned} \textbf{minimize} \quad & \sum_{\ell=1}^{N} \left(G_N(x_\ell) - \sum_{i=0}^{k} c_i \, x_\ell^i \right)^2 \\ \textbf{subject to} \quad & \sum_{i=1}^{k} i \, c_i \, x^{i-1} \geq 0 \quad \forall x \in \Omega, \\ & \sum_{i=0}^{k} c_i \, a^i = 0 \text{ and } \sum_{i=0}^{k} c_i \, b^i = 1, \end{aligned} \tag{4}$$

where the constraints ensure that the obtained parameters conform a valid density.

Conditional densities are also learnt using the algorithm in [7], which is based on splitting the domain of the parent variables, $\Omega_{\mathbf{Z}}$, as long as the BIC score is improved. As splitting criterium we use equal frequency binning. After splitting a variable Z, the algorithm fits a univariate MoTBF for each induced sub-partition $\Omega_{\mathbf{Z}}^1$ and $\Omega_{\mathbf{Z}}^2$. In order to decide whether or not to carry out a candidate partition $\Omega_{\mathbf{Z}'}$ we consider the potential improvement in BIC score [17] resulting from splitting that partition:

$$\text{BIC-Gain}(\Omega_{\mathbf{Z}}', Z) = BIC(f', \mathcal{D}) - BIC(f, \mathcal{D}),$$

where f' is the conditional MoTBF potential defined over the partitioning after splitting.

As we mentioned before, no structural learning algorithm for MoTBFs can be found so far in the literature. The only exception is the procedure described in [11], which is restricted to MTEs. We have decided not to take it as a basis for structural learning because of its computational complexity. The reason is that it is based on a score-and-search approach, and therefore it requires to re-estimate conditionals in each move. Notice that, unlike discrete conditionals, estimation of a conditional MoTBF can be a costly task, as it requires solving an optimisation problem in order to find the solution to the least squares equations employed to fit the parameters (see Eq. (4)). Hence, we have chosen a more simple alternative based on using the PC algorithm [18]. The procedure consists of the next three steps:

1. Discretise the variables in the database. In the experiments reported in Section 4 we used equal width binning with three resulting values.
2. Use the PC algorithm to obtain a Bayesian network structure from the discretised database. In the experiments reported in Section 4 we set a significance level $\alpha = 0.05$ and chose G^2 as the test statistic for the conditional independence tests.
3. Estimate a conditional MoTBF density for each variable given its parents in the network following the scheme given in [7].

4 Experimental Analysis

4.1 Algorithms Used in the Experiments

We have conducted a series of experiments aimed at testing the performance of the learning procedure described in Section 3. The idea is to determine whether or not the scheme based on PC + MoTBF conditionals is competitive with the simple application of the PC algorithm to obtain a discrete Bayesian network and with the construction of a continuous Bayesian network with CG distribution. All the experiments have been run on the R platform [13] using packages pcalg [14] and bnlearn [15]. More precisely, the algorithms used in the study are:

- MTEi, with $i = 2, 3, 4$. The algorithm described in Section 3 particularised for MTEs, by using exponentials as basis functions, and allowing the domain of the parent variables in conditionals to be split at most i times.
- MOPi, with $i = 2, 3, 4$. The same as above, but using polynomials instead of exponentials as basis functions.
- Discrete$i$, with $i = 3, 6, 8, 10$. The algorithm described in Section 3 dividing the domain of each variable into i pieces by equal frequency binning and adjusting a constant density into each interval.
- CG: The algorithm in [15] for obtaining a continuous Bayesian network with Gaussian joint distribution.

Table 1. Databases used in the experiments

dataset	#instances	#variables
diabetes	768	8
disclosure	662	4
ecoli	336	5
glass	163	7
iris	150	4
seeds	209	7
segmentation	210	16
slump	103	10
vertebral	310	6
waveform	5000	21

4.2   Experiments with Real-World Datasets

The first block of experiments consisted of testing the above mentioned algorithms over a set of databases taken from the UCI machine learning repository [19]. Most of the databases are oriented to classification, and therefore we removed the class variable in order to keep only the continuous features. The values for each variable were pre-processed by applying standardisation, in order to mitigate potential numerical errors when fitting the parameters of the exponential terms in MoTBFs. The description of the datasets is shown in Table 1. For each of the networks, we run the algorithms mentioned in Section 4.1 and computed the log-likelihood and the BIC score [17] of the training database given each learnt network. Notice that, as the likelihood is not comparable between discrete and continuous distributions due to the fact that continuous densities are not bounded above, we have represented the distribution of each discretised variable as a continuous density with a constant value in each of the regions corresponding to the discrete values. For instance, assume a variable X with support $[0,3]$ and discretised by equal width binning into three values 0, 1 and 2 corresponding to intervals $[0,1), [1,2)$ and $[2,3]$. Assume also that $P(X = 0) = 0.2$, $P(X = 1) = 0.5$ and $P(X = 2) = 0.3$. The distribution of X is then represented with a continuous density

$$f(x) = \begin{cases} 0.2 & \text{if } 0 \leq x < 1, \\ 0.5 & \text{if } 1 \leq x < 2, \\ 0.3 & \text{if } 2 \leq x \leq 3, \\ 0 & \text{otherwise.} \end{cases}$$

The results are displayed in Tables 2 and 3. Attending to the obtained results, the use of discrete variables and MOPs are the best choices in terms of likelihood while the CG model provides slightly better results in terms of BIC, which is not surprising as the CG model requires few parameters in general. It is worth pointing out that in two of the databases (seeds and vertebral) some of

Table 2. Average log-likelihood per record computed using the networks learnt by the tested algorithms. Boldfaced numbers indicate the best algorithm for each database.

Algorithm	diabetes	disclosure	ecoli	glass	iris	seeds	segmentation	slump	vertebral	waveform
MTE2	-8.43	-5.64	-6.50	-8.23	-4.69	-7.73	-11.59	**-10.38**	-7.40	-28.26
MTE3	-8.42	-5.64	-6.41	-8.36	-4.69	-7.70	-12.23	-10.38	-7.60	-28.50
MTE4	-8.53	-5.64	-6.54	-8.23	-4.69	-7.79	-12.09	-10.38	-7.95	-28.37
MOP2	-8.39	**-5.62**	-6.57	-7.86	-4.24	-7.59	**-10.29**	-10.44	-7.36	-27.37
MOP3	**-8.33**	-5.62	-6.17	-8.02	-5.80	-7.26	-11.67	-10.44	-7.42	-27.66
MOP4	-8.40	-5.62	-6.20	-7.66	-5.84	-7.49	-11.51	-10.44	-7.77	-27.94
CG	-10.98	-5.67	-6.54	-8.63	-4.35	-6.01	-15.05	-14.06	-7.42	**-26.75**
Discrete3	-13.78	-7.32	-7.25	-10.24	-4.26	-7.53	-19.23	-13.09	-9.00	-36.57
Discrete6	-13.00	-7.25	-6.27	-8.36	-3.95	-6.01	-15.55	-12.79	-8.10	-34.81
Discrete8	-12.54	-7.22	-5.98	-7.71	**-3.75**	-5.43	-14.28	-12.76	-7.57	-33.87
Discrete10	-12.22	-7.16	**-5.67**	**-7.56**	-3.83	**-4.92**	-13.48	-12.52	**-7.22**	-33.34

Table 3. Average BIC score per record computed using the networks learnt by the tested algorithms. Boldfaced numbers indicate the best algorithm for each database.

Algorithm	diabetes	disclosure	ecoli	glass	iris	seeds	segmentation	slump	vertebral	waveform
MTE2	-8.73	-5.79	-6.85	-9.18	-4.99	-8.72	-13.45	-11.60	-8.03	-28.59
MTE3	-8.77	-5.79	-6.83	-9.16	-4.99	-8.71	-14.29	-11.60	-8.27	-28.90
MTE4	-8.85	-5.79	-6.97	-9.18	-4.99	-8.92	-14.10	-11.60	-8.89	-28.76
MOP2	-8.73	-5.75	-6.88	**-8.72**	-4.69	-8.48	**-12.00**	**-11.56**	-7.92	-27.75
MOP3	**-8.71**	-5.75	-6.68	-8.99	-6.39	-8.50	-13.69	-11.56	-8.10	-28.02
MOP4	-8.79	-5.75	-6.76	-8.80	-6.48	-8.54	-13.72	-11.56	-8.61	-28.31
CG	-11.04	**-5.69**	**-6.61**	-8.81	**-4.45**	**-6.15**	-15.34	-14.33	**-7.51**	**-26.79**
Discrete3	-13.99	-7.38	-7.51	-10.84	-4.53	-8.06	-19.99	-13.72	-9.33	-36.82
Discrete6	-14.49	-7.47	-8.04	-11.41	-5.12	-9.53	-18.79	-15.04	-10.33	-37.68
Discrete8	-15.78	-7.60	-9.62	-11.76	-5.85	-12.32	-20.07	-16.38	-11.98	-38.96
Discrete10	-17.82	-7.73	-10.57	-12.62	-6.54	-15.50	-22.53	-17.79	-12.89	-40.03

the columns were linear functions of other columns. This kind of deterministic dependence is not taken into account by the algorithm for learning MoTBFs, while the CG model captures such dependencies in a natural way. In order to have a more precise picture of the significance of the difference among the tested algorithms, we run a Friedman's test ($\alpha = 0.05$) followed by a Nemenyi's post-hoc test in case of significant differences. In terms of likelihood, the outcome of the tests was that the only significant differences where found in favour of MOP2, 3, 4 and Discrete10 vs. the Discrete3 algorithm. For the BIC case, differences were reported by the statistical test indicating a superiority of the CG, MTE and MOP approaches vs. the discrete cases, except for Discrete3.

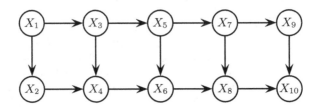

Fig. 1. Network used to generate the synthetic databases in the experiments

Table 4. Detail of the distributions in the synthetic network

$$X_1 \sim Be(0.5, 0.5) \qquad X_2|X_1 \sim Be(X_1, X_1)$$
$$X_3|X_1 \sim Exp(X_1 + 1) \qquad X_4|X_2, X_3 \sim \mathcal{N}(X_2 + X_3, 1)$$
$$X_5|X_3 \sim Exp(X_3 + 1) \qquad X_6|X_4, X_5 \sim Exp(|X_4 + X_4| + 1)$$
$$X_7|X_5 \sim \mathcal{N}(X_5, 2) \qquad X_8|X_6, X_7 \sim \chi^2_{\lfloor X_6 + X_7 \rfloor + 1}$$
$$X_9|X_7 \sim \mathcal{U}(0, |X_7| + 1) \qquad X_{10}|X_8, X_9 \sim \Gamma(X_8, X_9)$$

4.3   Experiments with Synthetic Databases

One of the advantages of MoTBFs with respect to other models is their ability to accurately approximate a wide variety of differently shaped probability densities [1]. Taking this into account, we designed an experiment in order to test the different algorithms in a setting where the variables in the network come from a range of densities with different shapes. With that aim, we constructed an artificial network with the structure depicted in Figure 1 and the conditional densities specified in Table 4. We randomly sampled five databases from the artificial network, with sizes 100, 500, 1000, 2500 and 5000 and run the algorithms over the generated databases, measuring the log-likelihood and the BIC score of each database given the learnt networks. The results are displayed in Tables 5 and 6. As expected, in this case the best option, both in terms of likelihood and BIC score, is the use of MoTBFs, and more precisely, MOPs. A more detailed analysis of the differences using Friedman's test plus Nemenyi's post-hoc reveals significant differences in terms of likelihood on the side of MOP3 vs. CG and of MOPs in general versus the discrete approaches (except Discrete10). In terms of BIC, the differences with respect to CG fade away whilst significant ones show up between MOPs and Discrete10.

Table 5. Average log-likelihood per record computed using the networks learnt from the synthetic datasets by the tested algorithms. Boldfaced numbers indicate the best algorithm for each database. The five rightmost columns correspond to the five databases used, of size 100, 500, 1000, 2500 and 5000.

Algorithm	100	500	1000	2500	5000
MTE2	-10.00	-9.74	-9.31	-9.46	-9.50
MTE3	-10.00	-9.52	-9.29	-9.47	-9.54
MTE4	-9.85	-9.56	-9.14	-9.62	-9.64
MOP2	**-9.79**	-9.57	-8.73	-8.85	-9.19
MOP3	-9.79	**-9.38**	**-8.55**	**-8.67**	**-9.03**
MOP4	-9.79	-9.48	-8.78	-8.94	-9.09
CG	-13.93	-13.65	-13.53	-13.65	-13.48
Discrete3	-13.82	-13.95	-14.93	-16.82	-16.20
Discrete6	-13.16	-12.62	-13.79	-15.73	-14.79
Discrete8	-12.91	-11.95	-13.28	-15.38	-14.20
Discrete10	-12.56	-11.08	-12.75	-15.03	-13.46

Table 6. Average BIC score per record computed using the networks learnt from the synthetic datasets by the tested algorithms. Boldfaced numbers indicate the best algorithm for each database. The five rightmost columns correspond to the five databases used, of size 100, 500, 1000, 2500 and 5000.

Algorithm	100	500	1000	2500	5000
MTE2	-11.19	-10.21	-9.67	-9.73	-9.66
MTE3	-11.19	-10.14	-9.76	-9.76	-9.69
MTE4	-11.28	-10.16	-9.63	-9.90	-9.81
MOP2	**-10.89**	-10.05	-9.20	-9.12	-9.36
MOP3	-10.89	**-9.98**	**-9.19**	**-8.98**	**-9.27**
MOP4	-10.89	-10.03	-9.33	-9.25	-9.32
CG	-14.23	-13.76	-13.59	-13.68	-13.50
Discrete3	-14.56	-14.37	-15.17	-16.93	-16.30
Discrete6	-16.04	-15.72	-15.50	-16.49	-16.11
Discrete8	-17.91	-18.74	-17.12	-17.14	-18.05
Discrete10	-20.22	-21.99	-19.71	-18.37	-20.35

5 Conclusions

In this paper we have analysed a simple way to induce continuous Bayesian networks from data using MoTBF densities. The idea, though simple, seems to have a valid practical value as shown by the experiments carried out. The models obtained in this way for the real-world databases tested are competitive with the CG model and superior to the discrete approach. For the synthetic databases, which represent a situation where the variables involved are of an heterogeneous nature, the MoTBF approach is superior in terms of likelihood an also in terms of BIC score. The conclusion is that, as long as no taylor-made structural learning algorithms for MoTBFs are developed, our simple approach can be a valid alternative for addressing practical applications. From the purely practical point of view, an important advantage is that no model assumptions have to be checked before using it (unlike, for example, the Gaussian case).

In what concerns future lines of work, the next immediate step is to extend the implementation of the learning algorithm to allow the inclusion of discrete variables, in which case the differences with respect to the CG approach should widen in favour of the MoTBF approach. More research is needed for developing taylor-made structural learning algorithms for MoTBFs, where a first way to explore can be to translate the use of the test statistics of the PC algorithm to the MoTBF framework.

Acknowledgments. This research has been partly funded by the Spanish Ministry of Economy and Competitiveness, through project TIN2010-20900-C04-02 and by Junta de Andalucía through project P11-TIC-7821 and by ERDF funds.

References

1. Langseth, H., Nielsen, T., Rumí, R., Salmerón, A.: Mixtures of truncated basis functions. International Journal of Approximate Reasoning 53, 212–227 (2012)
2. Moral, S., Rumí, R., Salmerón, A.: Mixtures of truncated exponentials in hybrid Bayesian networks. In: Benferhat, S., Besnard, P. (eds.) ECSQARU 2001. LNCS (LNAI), vol. 2143, pp. 156–167. Springer, Heidelberg (2001)
3. Shenoy, P., West, J.: Inference in hybrid Bayesian networks using mixtures of polynomials. International Journal of Approximate Reasoning 52, 641–657 (2011)
4. Lauritzen, S.: Propagation of probabilities, means and variances in mixed graphical association models. Journal of the American Statistical Association 87, 1098–1108 (1992)
5. Shenoy, P.P., Shafer, G.: Axioms for probability and belief function propagation. In: Shachter, R.D., Levitt, T.S., Lemmer, J.F., Kanal, L.N. (eds.) Uncertainty in Artificial Intelligence, vol. 4, pp. 169–198. North-Holland, Amsterdam (1990)
6. Zhang, N., Poole, D.: Exploiting causal independence in Bayesian network inference. Journal of Artificial Intelligence Research 5, 301–328 (1996)
7. Langseth, H., Nielsen, T., Salmerón, A.: Learning mixtures of truncated basis functions from data. In: Proceedings of the Sixth European Workshop on Probabilistic Graphical Models (PGM 2012), pp. 163–170 (2012)
8. Rumí, R., Salmerón, A., Moral, S.: Estimating mixtures of truncated exponentials in hybrid Bayesian networks. Test 15, 397–421 (2006)
9. Langseth, H., Nielsen, T., Rumí, R., Salmerón, A.: Parameter estimation and model selection for mixtures of truncated exponentials. International Journal of Approximate Reasoning 51, 485–498 (2010)
10. López-Cruz, P., Bielza, C., Larrañaga, P.: Learning mixtures of polynomials from data using B-spline interpolation. In: Proceedings of the 6th European Workshop on Probabilistic Graphical Models (PGM 2012), pp. 211–218 (2012)

11. Romero, V., Rumí, R., Salmerón, A.: Learning hybrid Bayesian networks using mixtures of truncated exponentials. International Journal of Approximate Reasoning 42, 54–68 (2006)
12. Monti, S., Cooper, G.F.: Learning hybrid Bayesian networks from data (1998)
13. R Development Core Team: R: A Language and Environment for Statistical Computing. R Foundation for Statistical Computing, Vienna, Austria (2011) ISBN 3-900051-07-0
14. Kalisch, M., Maechler, M., Colombo, D.: pcalg: Estimation of CPDAG/PAG and causal inference using the IDA algorithm (2011) R package version 1.1-4
15. Scutary, M.: Learning Bayesian networks with the bnlearn R package. Journal of Statistical Software 35(3), 1–22 (2010)
16. Langseth, H., Nielsen, T., Pérez-Bernabé, I., Salmerón, A.: Learning mixtures of truncated basis functions from data. International Journal of Approximate Reasoning (submitted)
17. Schwarz, G.: Estimating the dimension of a model. Annals of Statistics 6, 461–464 (1978)
18. Spirtes, P., Glymour, C., Scheines, R.: Causation, prediction and search. Lecture Notes in Statistics, vol. 81. Springer (1993)
19. Bache, K., Lichman, M.: UCI machine learning repository (2013)

Learning from Crowds in Multi-dimensional Classification Domains

Jerónimo Hernández-González, Iñaki Inza, and José A. Lozano

Intelligent Systems Group, University of the Basque Country UPV/EHU
{jeronimo.hernandez,inaki.inza,ja.lozano}@ehu.es

Abstract. Learning from crowds is a recently fashioned supervised classification framework where the true/real labels of the training instances are not available. However, each instance is provided with a set of noisy class labels, each indicating the class-membership of the instance according to the subjective opinion of an annotator. The additional challenges involved in the extension of this framework to the multi-label domain are explored in this paper. A solution to this problem combining a Structural EM strategy and the multi-dimensional Bayesian network models as classifiers is presented.

Using real multi-label datasets adapted to the crowd framework, the designed experiments try to shed some lights on the limits of learning to classify from the multiple and imprecise information of supervision.

Keywords: Multi-label classification, multi-dimensional classification, Learning from crowds, Structural EM method, Bayesian network models.

1 Introduction

The process of training a classifier in the standard supervised classification paradigm requires a training dataset of examples which are class-labeled by a domain expert, who establishes to which class each example belongs. Other related paradigms, under the general name of partially supervised classification, deal with datasets in which the expert is not able to label completely/certainly all the training examples. In one way or another, all these paradigms provide expert supervision of the training data. Moreover, the reliability of this information of supervision is a strong assumption, based on which most of the techniques taking part in the learning process have been developed (evaluation techniques, performance scores, learning methods, etc.). However, obtaining this kind of reliable supervision can be expensive and difficult, even for a domain expert.

In the last decades, the Web has emerged as a large source of information, providing a quick and easy way to collect data. Actually, the main drawback of the data collected in this way is its reliability. As it has been usually produced by non-expert annotators, this subjective data may involve incompleteness, impreciseness and/or incorrectness. Learning from noisy data (or labeled by an unreliable annotator) is a known problem [2,18]. However, these new technologies provide an easy and cheap way to obtain *not one but many* different personal

C. Bielza et al. (Eds.): CAEPIA 2013, LNAI 8109, pp. 352–362, 2013.

opinions about the class-membership of a given example. Thus, the idea of learning from data labeled by taking into account diverse and multiple (subjective) opinions has led to a new learning paradigm.

In the related literature, the problem of learning from multiple noisy labelers or annotators is known as *learning from crowds* [9]. In this problem, the real class-membership information of the training instances is not provided. However, a crowd of mainly non-expert labelers provides different subjective (noisy) opinions about the class-membership of the training instances. Note the differences with [6], where the opinions of a fixed number of *domain experts* have to be combined.

Learning to classify from this kind of data is possible and useful [12,14]. The learning algorithm has to cope with the individual unreliability of the annotators in order to build accurate classifiers from the consensus opinion. The ability to learn an accurate classifier from a given dataset of this type is largely influenced by two related factors: the quality of the annotators and the degree of consensus between them. Learning can be feasible even when the annotators do not have a high reliability if, for each instance, a subset of annotators agree in their predictions. Based on both concepts, we present our initial solution to the additional challenges which involves the application of the learning from crowds paradigm to multi-label classification (in a broader sense than [11]).

The rest of the paper is organized as follows. In the next section, a formal definition of the problem is presented, together with its adaptation to the multi-dimensional classification framework. Then, our method (an adaptation of a state-of-the-art algorithm) for learning multi-dimensional Bayesian network classifiers from this kind of data is described. Next, the experiments show some limits in the learning ability of our method (according to *noise rate* and *consensus degree*). And finally, some conclusions and future work are presented.

2   Learning from Crowds in Multi-label Domains

In the problem of multi-label learning from crowds, the examples are provided without the true labels (a.k.a. gold-standard), and only the label(s) assigned by multiple (non-expert) annotators are available. Here, an annotator assigns one or several labels to an instance according to their subjective opinion.

Like the classical multi-label (ML) learning paradigm, the problem is described by a set of n predictive variables $(X_1, \ldots, X_n)$ and a class variable C. Moreover, $\mathcal{X}$ denotes the instance space (all the possible value assignments to the n predictive variables) and $\mathcal{C} = \{c_1, \ldots, c_q\}$ denotes the label space (the set of q possible class labels). A ML dataset $D = \{(\mathbf{x}_1, \mathbf{c}_1), (\mathbf{x}_2, \mathbf{c}_2), \ldots, (\mathbf{x}_m, \mathbf{c}_m)\}$ consists of a set of m examples of the problem, where $\mathbf{x}_i \in \mathcal{X}$ is a n-tuple that assigns a value to each predictive variable and $\mathbf{c}_i \subseteq \mathcal{C}$ is the corresponding set of class labels, denoting the class-membership of the example.

Similarly, the dataset D in a multi-label learning from crowds framework is composed of m examples $D = \{(\mathbf{x}_1, \mathcal{A}_1), (\mathbf{x}_2, \mathcal{A}_2), \ldots, (\mathbf{x}_m, \mathcal{A}_m)\}$, which are assumed to have been sampled i.i.d. from some underlying probability distribution. Each instance $\mathbf{x}_i$ is provided together with a group $\mathcal{A}_i$, which contains the labels (annotations) provided by different annotators: $\mathcal{A}_i = \{\mathbf{c}_{i1}, \ldots, \mathbf{c}_{it}\}$, with $\mathbf{c}_{ij} \subseteq \mathcal{C}$

and t being the number of annotators. As a classical multi-label classification problem, the objective is to infer the class label(s) of new unseen instances.

A Transformation to Multi-dimensional Classification. In a multi-dimensional (MD) classification problem [1,10], there is more than one class variable $(C_1, \ldots, C_d)$, and each one has its own set of possible labels. In this case, the label space $\mathcal{C} = \mathcal{C}_1 \times \cdots \times \mathcal{C}_d$ denotes all the possible joint label assignments to the d class variables (label configurations). An example $(\mathbf{x}_i, \mathbf{c}_i)$ of a MD training dataset includes a d-tuple $\mathbf{c}_i \in \mathcal{C}$ that assigns a label to each class variable, apart from the instance predictive values $\mathbf{x}_i \in \mathcal{X}$. Given a new instance, the multi-dimensional classifier predicts a class label for each class variable.

In this paper, in order to deal with the presented multi-label problem, we transform it to the multi-dimensional classification framework. As explained in the related literature [1,10,17], the multi-label learning paradigm can be described as a multi-dimensional problem in which there are as many binary class variables as class labels in the multi-label problem ($d_{MD} = q_{ML}$). Thus, each binary class variable (MD) represents the presence/absence of a class label (ML).

The adapted dataset D of multi-dimensional learning from crowds is composed of m examples $D = \{(\mathbf{x}_1, \mathbf{A}^1), (\mathbf{x}_2, \mathbf{A}^2), \ldots, (\mathbf{x}_m, \mathbf{A}^m)\}$, where the information of supervision for each instance $\mathbf{x}_i$ is provided in a $(t \times d)$-matrix $\mathbf{A}^i$. Thus, the position A^i_{ac} indicates the class label predicted for the class variable C_c by the annotator L_a.

3   Learning from Crowds in Multi-dimensional Domains

The main characteristic of the learning from crowds framework is the availability of much and diverse information of supervision. A natural solution to this problem could be the transformation of the crowds information to some kind of probabilistic supervision. From this point of view, the problem is closely related with other problems with imprecise labels such as learning with partial labels [3], learning from probabilistic information [8], etc. Nevertheless, in the presence of imprecise or incorrect data, it is worth modeling the source of noise.

As explained previously, the crowd supervision consists of the class labels assigned to the instances according to the subjective opinion of several annotators. Certainly, each annotator can be considered as a source of noise. Based on this idea, Raykar et al. [9] proposed an EM-based algorithm to solve the learning from crowds problem in single-dimensional domains, using a set of weights to model the reliability of the annotators.

Under the realistic assumption that the annotators might show different reliability in different prediction tasks, we have extended the idea of Raykar et al. [9] to the multi-dimensional paradigm, independently modeling the reliability of each annotator predicting each class variable.

To sum up, we have reformulated the problem as searching the weights (w_{ac}) that better describe the ability of each annotator, L_a, to predict each class variable C_c, and leading to the generation of accurate classifiers. For solving both interrelated problems, we propose a learning algorithm based on the Structural

Expectation-Maximization (SEM) strategy, which iteratively alternates to improve the initially obtained reliability weights (several techniques are proposed) and to look for an improved fit of the model. A basic adaptation of a state-of-the-art local-search algorithm is used to learn the model, a multi-dimensional Bayesian network classifier (MBC [1]), from crowd data augmented with reliability weights. For the sake of simplicity, in this paper the number of annotators is fixed, i.e. all the instances are annotated by all the annotators.

3.1   Our Structural EM Strategy

A MBC [1] is a Bayesian network $\mathbb{M} = (G, \boldsymbol{\theta})$ defined over a set $\mathcal{V} = \{V_1, \ldots, V_v\}$ of random variables, where $G = (\mathcal{V}, \mathcal{R})$ is an acyclic directed graph and $\boldsymbol{\theta}$ its parameters. As a classifier, the set of variables can be divided in class variables, $\mathcal{V}_C = \{C_1, \ldots, C_d\}$, and predictive variables, $\mathcal{V}_X = \{X_1, \ldots, X_n\}$, where $v = n + d$. The graph of a MBC cannot contain arcs in $\mathcal{R}$ from the predictive ($\mathcal{V}_X$) to the class variables ($\mathcal{V}_C$).

The Structural EM strategy (SEM), proposed by Friedman [5], provides a suitable framework to infer both the graph structure and the model parameters of a Bayesian network model from missing data. The EM strategy, proposed by Dempster et al. [4], is used in our framework to obtain the maximum likelihood parameters from multiple weighted annotations. Iteratively, the method estimates the reliability weights of the annotators given the current fit of the model, and re-estimates the model parameters. Under fairly general conditions, the iterative increment of the likelihood has been proved to converge to a stationary value (most of the times, a local maximum) [7]. Additionally, the SEM strategy incorporates an outer loop to the parametric-convergence loop of the classical EM, and iteratively improves an initially-proposed structure.

In Algorithm 1, a pseudo-code of the SEM method developed in this paper is shown. In the following subsections, the different tasks of this method are explained in detail: the initialization of the reliability weights (line 3 in Algorithm 1) and their improvement (line 10); the structural learning (line 4) and structural improvement (line 14); and the parametric learning (line 9).

3.2   Reliability Weights of the Annotators

As previously mentioned, we use weights w_{ac} to indicate the reliability of the predictions of the annotator L_a for the class variable C_c. These weights are initialized in the first stage of the SEM method and updated iteratively.

Initializing Weights. Similar to [13], our SEM method initializes the weight w_{ac} as the ability of the annotator L_a to agree with other annotators (consensus) in the label assigned to class variable C_c, averaging over all the instances of the dataset. That is,

$$w_{ac} = \frac{1}{m} \sum_{i=1}^{m} \frac{1}{t-1} \sum_{a' \neq a} \mathbb{I}[A_{a'c}^i = A_{ac}^i] \tag{1}$$

where m is the number of instances, t is the number of annotators and $\mathbb{I}[condition]$ is a function that returns 1 when the *condition* is true, and 0 otherwise.

Algorithm 1 Pseudo-code of our Structural EM method.

1: **procedure** STRUCTURALEM($D, maxIt, \epsilon$)   ▷ D: dataset
2:    $i = 0$ ▷ $maxIt$: max. number of iterations
3:    $\mathbf{W} \leftarrow$ initializeWeights(D)   ▷ ϵ: threshold (stop condition)
4:    $G_i \leftarrow$ structuralLearning($D, \mathbf{W}$)
5:    **repeat**
6:       $j = 0$
7:       **repeat**
8:          $\hat{\mathbf{W}} \leftarrow \mathbf{W}$
9:          $\boldsymbol{\theta}_j \leftarrow$ parametricLearning($D, \mathbf{W}, G_i$)
10:          $\mathbf{W} \leftarrow$ estimateWeights($D, G_i, \boldsymbol{\theta}_j$)
11:          $j = j + 1$
12:       **until** (diff($\mathbf{W}, \hat{\mathbf{W}}$) $< \epsilon$) Or ($j = maxIt$)
13:       $i = i + 1$
14:       $G_i \leftarrow$ findMaxNeighborStructure($D, \mathbf{W}, G_{i-1}$)
15:    **until** ($G_i = G_{i-1}$) Or ($i = maxIt$)
16:    **return** $\mathbb{M} \equiv (G_i, \boldsymbol{\theta}_j)$
17: **end procedure**

Weights Updating. To update the reliability weights, four alternative procedures has been developed: two model-based procedures (using the most probable label configuration; or using the probabilities of all the possible label configurations), both of them combined or not with the consensus concept.

On the one hand, the information provided by the model $\mathbb{M}$ (learnt in the previous EM iteration) is used in two ways. In a first approach, the label configuration of maximum joint probability $\check{\mathbf{c}}$ given the instance is calculated. Then, each weight w_{ac} is updated as the mean accuracy of the annotator L_a over the class variable C_c, using each maximal configuration $\check{\mathbf{c}}_i$ as the golden truth:

$$w_{ac} = \frac{1}{m} \sum_{i=1}^{m} \mathbb{I}[\check{c}_{ic} = A^i_{ac}] \tag{2}$$

In the second approach, for each instance the marginal probability of each class variable is calculated using the model $\mathbb{M}$. Subsequently, these probabilities are used to update each weight of an annotator by averaging the probability of their predictions for the given class variable over the whole dataset,

$$w_{ac} = \frac{1}{m} \sum_{i=1}^{m} \sum_{j=1}^{|\mathcal{C}|} p^{\mathbb{M}}(\bar{\mathbf{c}}^j | \mathbf{c}_i) \cdot \mathbb{I}[\bar{c}^j_c = A^i_{ac}] \tag{3}$$

where $\mathcal{C}$ is the label space (set of all the label configurations) and $\bar{\mathbf{c}}^j \in \mathcal{C}$.

On the other hand, the weight-updating process can *remember* the mean degree of consensus. Thus, the reliability weights are updated according to the function, $w_{ac} = (w^{Cons}_{ac} + w^{\mathbb{M}}_{ac})/2$, where w^{Cons}_{ac} is the consensus weight (calculated by means of Eq. 1) and $w^{\mathbb{M}}_{ac}$ is the model-based weight (calculated with either Eq. 2 or Eq. 3). Therefore, as both model-based functions can be extended with the consensus idea, we finally have four weight-updating techniques.

3.3   Estimating the Model Parameters from Crowds in Multi-dimensional Domains

In this paper, the parameters of the MBC are estimated by frequency counts, as usual. In order to cope with the weighted and multi-labeled class information provided by the crowds, we have adapted the procedure to collect frequency counts. Thus, given an instantiation $(u_1, \ldots, u_j)$ of a set of variables $\mathcal{U}_\mathbf{u} = \{U_1, \ldots, U_j\} \subseteq \mathcal{V} = (\mathcal{V}_X, \mathcal{V}_C)$, the posterior probability is defined as,

$$p(u_1, \ldots, u_i | u_{i+1}, \ldots, u_j) = N(u_1, \ldots, u_i, u_{i+1}, \ldots, u_j)/N(u_{i+1}, \ldots, u_j)$$

where $N(\cdot)$ represents the counts obtained from the provided dataset. In this problem, they are calculated as follows:

$$N(\mathbf{u}) = \frac{1}{\sum_{a=1}^{t} \mathbf{W}_a^{\downarrow\mathbf{u}}} \sum_{a=1}^{t} \mathbf{W}_a^{\downarrow\mathbf{u}} \sum_{y \in \mathcal{X}(D, \mathbf{A}_a)} \mathbb{I}[y_{[U_1]} = u_1, \ldots, y_{[U_{|\mathbf{u}|}]} = u_{|\mathbf{u}|}]$$

where $[U_j]$ indicates the index of the variable $U_j \in \mathcal{U}_\mathbf{u}$ in the original set of variables $\mathcal{V}$ and $\mathcal{X}(D, \mathbf{A}_a)$ is the set of instances D labeled according to the annotations $\mathbf{A}_a$ of annotator L_a. In the specific count, the weight assigned to annotator L_a ($\mathbf{W}_a^{\downarrow\mathbf{u}}$) is calculated as the product of the weights per variable, taking into account only those variables in $\mathcal{U}_\mathbf{u}$:

$$\mathbf{W}_a^{\downarrow\mathbf{u}} = \prod_{U \in \mathcal{U}_\mathbf{u}} w_{a[U]} \tag{4}$$

As previously shown, our SEM method only estimates the weights w_{ac} of the class variables ($C_c \in \mathcal{V}_C$). Consequently, regarding Eq. 4, the weights of the predictive variables ($X_x \in \mathcal{V}_X$) are considered constant, $w_{ix} = 1$. In practice, the estimator implements the Laplacian correction in order to avoid zero counts.

3.4   Local Search for Structural Learning

Our method to learn the structure of a MBC B from the data (line 4 in Algorithm 1) is based on the wrapper algorithm of Larrañaga et al. [1]. Following their proposal, at each iteration of the local search, the arc inclusion/deletion (candidate change) that, respecting a fixed ancestral order, most improves the score of the current structure is chosen. The candidate changes are evaluated using the log K2 score:

$$\log P(B, D) = \sum_{i=1}^{v} \sum_{j=1}^{q_i} \log \frac{(r_i - 1)!}{(N_{ij} + r_i - 1)!} \sum_{k=1}^{r_i} \log N_{ijk}!$$

where v is the number of variables, r_i is the number of values that the variable V_i can take, and q_i is the number of possible configurations of the parents of V_i. As the log K2 score is decomposable, the arc inclusion/deletion can be evaluated only taking into account the arc-destination variable and its parents.

Structural MBC Improvement. The function at line 14 of the Algorithm 1 performs a single local-search step in the MBC structure space in order to find a better fit of the model. In practice, the structural improvement is chosen using the same procedure as the structural learning method presented before, but restricted to a single step.

4   Experiments

In this section, the two factors that we have used to describe the amount of information provided in the learning from crowds problem are tested. Due to the lack of time, we have not managed to obtain real crowd datasets[1]. However, we have designed a strategy to simulate multiple annotators controlling the noise rate and the consensus between them. Thus, three real multi-label datasets[2] have been adapted to simulate multiple-annotated datasets.

Generation of Annotators. We have implemented a strategy for generating annotators from the real class labels of the ML datasets. For each class variable, starting from the true labels, a user-specified percentage of these labels —randomly selected— are fixed (well-labeled instances). The rest of labels are swapped with probability 0.5 in order to introduce the characteristic noise of this kind of data.

The degree of consensus is controlled by sharing the same fixed set of well-labeled instances between a user-specified number of annotators. Then, an extra (small) rate of changes is applied to each annotator individually in order to generate low divergence between them.

In both experimental settings, 10 annotators have been generated (this selection is based on the discussion of Snow et al. [14]), and all of them annotate all the class variables and instances. By default, the method uses the provided indexation of variables as ancestral order (always respecting that the class variables appear before the predictive variables). Regarding the learned models, the MBC have been restricted to a maximum of $K = 3$ parents per variable.

4.1   Influence of the Noise Rate

The first set of experiments has been designed in order to test the ability of our learning method to cope with an increasing amount of noise in the annotations. In this way, the consensus degree has been fixed to four annotators [14] and different values (four) of mean noise rate have been tested for each dataset. Three real ML datasets (emotions, scene and yeast) have been used to simulate the information of crowds. Moreover, for each designed test, ten datasets have been generated, summing up to the total number of datasets, 120 (4 error rates, 3 datasets, 10 repetitions).

---

[1] For future work, Mechanical Turk (http://www.mturk.com) is an online platform that allows to easily collect data from crowds.

[2] Multi-label datasets available at: http://mulan.sourceforge.net/datasets.html

Table 1. Experiments developed to test the noise rate influence. The three datasets are evaluated in a 10 × 5-fold CV according to four measures [1], and the results are shown in terms of the mean value and the corresponding standard deviation (each experiment is repeated over 10 equal-generated crowd datasets).

Noise rate	10%	20%	30%	40%	10%	20%	30%	40%
microf1	0.59 ± 0.01	0.56 ± 0.02	0.50 ± 0.03	0.41 ± 0.03	0.44 ± 0.02	0.35 ± 0.02	0.24 ± 0.03	0.13 ± 0.03
macrof1	0.58 ± 0.02	0.54 ± 0.02	0.48 ± 0.03	0.41 ± 0.03	0.44 ± 0.02	0.35 ± 0.01	− − −	− − −
globalAcc	0.24 ± 0.01	0.22 ± 0.01	0.18 ± 0.02	0.11 ± 0.02	0.34 ± 0.02	0.26 ± 0.02	0.15 ± 0.02	0.07 ± 0.02
meanAcc	0.72 ± 0.01	0.70 ± 0.01	0.69 ± 0.02	0.69 ± 0.01	0.83 ± 0.01	0.82 ± 0.01	0.82 ± 0.00	0.83 ± 0.00
	emotions				scene			

Noise rate	10%	20%	30%	40%
microf1	0.59 ± 0.01	0.57 ± 0.01	0.56 ± 0.01	0.54 ± 0.01
macrof1	− − −	− − −	− − −	− − −
globalAcc	0.15 ± 0.01	0.13 ± 0.01	0.11 ± 0.01	0.09 ± 0.02
meanAcc	0.76 ± 0.02	0.75 ± 0.01	0.74 ± 0.01	0.74 ± 0.01
	yeast			

In Table 1, the results obtained from these experimental settings show the expected tendency of an increment of the degradation as the noise rate is larger. However, as a result of the transformation to the multi-dimensional framework, the resulting class variables tend to be strongly unbalanced (a class value is over-represented in the dataset). Among the problems that this generates, note that the accuracy-based evaluation measures become unfair. For example, in the tests with most noise of Table 1, some of the displayed mean accuracy values correspond to the label proportions of the dataset (which have macrof1 = '− − −'), i.e. the method is always predicting the majority class label. In this way, our weight updating procedure based on maximal-probability could be failing to capture the information of supervision as a combination of the multiple annotations.

4.2 Influence of the Consensus

In the second set of experiments, we show the behavior of our method when the consensus between the labelers increases. Thus, following the procedure described before, five groups of ten datasets were generated where the degree of consensus ranges from two to six annotators. The annotators in consensus have been generated with a noise rate of 10%, and the rest with 30%. Due to lack of space, only the ML dataset *emotions* is used in this experimental settings.

As a fundamental parameter in our approach, we wanted to show the reliability weights of the annotators obtained after the training process. As shown in Figure 1, all the weight updating procedures identify the reliable annotators (all of them are shown over 1). However, the weights produced by the approaches that incorporate the consensus idea are those which are most unbalanced. Surprisingly, larger consensus annotators' weights do not imply a notable gain in terms of global accuracy (nor other performance measures, not shown due to lack of space). Our method behaves as expected when it performs better as the degree of consensus is increased. However, the performances do not show

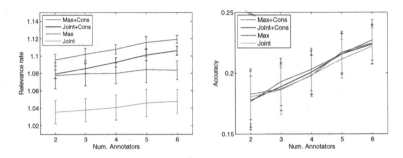

Fig. 1. Experiments developed to test the influence of the consensus degree. In the left figure, the relevance rate of the consensus annotators (mean of the weights of the consensus annotators divided by that of non-consensus annotators) according to different weight-updating approaches. In the right figure, the same experiments are evaluated in terms of global accuracy. All the results are shown by means of mean value and the corresponding standard deviation, evaluated in a 10×5-fold CV (repeated over 10 equal-generated crowd datasets).

notable differences whether the weight-updating approach considers the consensus information or not.

5   Conclusions

As shown, the current method does not seem to make the most of this kind of data, being unable to extract information from the consensus between annotators. It could be worth exploring other paradigms to weight the relevance of the annotators, according to other performance metrics (see, for example, [16]).

As explained before, our method implements four approaches for updating the weights of the annotators. Specifically, two of them only consider the model predictions in the update procedure, and the other two combine the model estimations and the consensus information, both with the same relevance. An interesting idea for future work could be to implement a simulated-annealing based technique that modifies the relevance of both factors (model predictions and consensus) throughout the iterative method every time that the weights are updated. In this way, in the first iterations we could rely more on the consensus information and, in the final iterations, relying on the model predictions.

Moreover, considering that the annotators can choose the instances that they label, we could skip the previous assumption that all the annotators label all the instances. Similarly, it could be also interesting to allow annotators not to assert the membership of every instance to all the classes [15]; that is, to consider a new state for the annotations (member, non-member, *unknown*). Skipping both assumptions would introduce new challenges to the learning process, mainly affecting the way in which we calculate the reliability weights of the annotators.

Acknowledgments. This work has been partially supported by the Saiotek and IT609-13 programs (Basque Government), TIN2010-14931 (Spanish Ministry of Science and Innovation), network in computational bio-medicine (Carlos III Health Institute), 2011-CIEN-000060-01 (Diputación Foral de Gipuzkoa) and CRC-Biomarkers project (6-12-TK-2011-014, Diputacióon Foral de Bizkaia). Jerónimo Hernández-González holds a grant (FPU) from the Spanish Ministry of Science and Innovation. Thanks to Aritz Pérez-Martínez for his helpful comments.

References

1. Bielza, C., Li, G., Larrañaga, P.: Multi-dimensional classification with Bayesian networks. International Journal of Approximate Reasoning 52(6), 705–727 (2011)
2. Brodley, C.E., Friedl, M.A.: Identifying mislabeled training data. Journal of Artificial Intelligence Research 11, 131–167 (1999)
3. Cour, T., Sapp, B., Taskar, B.: Learning from partial labels. Journal of Machine Learning Research 12, 1501–1536 (2011)
4. Dempster, A.P., Laird, N.M., Rubin, D.B.: Maximum likelihood from incomplete data via the EM algorithm. Journal of the Royal Statistical Society. Series B (Methodological) 39(1), 1–38 (1977)
5. Friedman, N.: Learning belief networks in the presence of missing values and hidden variables. In: Proceedings of the 14th ICML, pp. 125–133 (1997)
6. López-Cruz, P.L., Larrañaga, P., DeFelipe, J., Bielza, C.: Bayesian network modeling of the consensus between experts: An application to neuron classification. International Journal of Approximate Reasoning (in press, 2013)
7. McLachlan, G.J., Krishnan, T.: The EM Algorithm and Extensions (Wiley Series in Probability and Statistics). Wiley Interscience (1997)
8. Nguyen, Q., Valizadegan, H., Hauskrecht, M.: Learning classification with auxiliary probabilistic information. In: Proceedings of the 11th IEEE International Conference on Data Mining (ICDM 2011), pp. 477–486 (2011)
9. Raykar, V.C., Yu, S., Zhao, L.H., Valadez, G.H., Florin, C., Bogoni, L., Moy, L.: Learning from crowds. Journal of Machine Learning Research 11, 1297–1322 (2010)
10. Rodríguez, J.D., Martínez, A.P., Arteta, D., Tejedor, D., Lozano, J.A.: Using multidimensional bayesian network classifiers to assist the treatment of multiple sclerosis. IEEE Transactions on Systems, Man, and Cybernetics 42(6), 1705–1715 (2012)
11. Sellamanickam, S., Tiwari, C., Selvaraj, S.K.: Regularized structured output learning with partial labels. In: Proceedings of the 12th SDM, pp. 1059–1070 (2012)
12. Sheng, V.S., Provost, F.J., Ipeirotis, P.G.: Get another label? improving data quality and data mining using multiple, noisy labelers. In: Proceedings of the International Conference on Knowledge Discovery and Data Mining, pp. 614–622 (2008)
13. Smyth, P., Fayyad, U., Burl, M., Perona, P., Baldi, P.: Inferring ground truth from subjective labelling of venus images. In: Proceedings of the Advances in Neural Information Processing Systems (NIPS), pp. 1085–1092 (1994)
14. Snow, R., O'Connor, B., Jurafsky, D., Ng, A.Y.: Cheap and fast - but is it good? evaluating non-expert annotations for natural language tasks. In: Proceedings of the Conference on Empirical Methods in NLP, pp. 254–263 (2008)

15. Sun, Y.Y., Zhang, Y., Zhou, Z.H.: Multi-label learning with weak label. In: Proceedings of the 24th AAAI Conference on Artificial Intelligence, AAAI 2010 (2010)
16. Younes, Z., abdallah, F., Denœux, T.: Evidential multi-label classification approach to learning from data with imprecise labels. In: Hüllermeier, E., Kruse, R., Hoffmann, F. (eds.) IPMU 2010. LNCS, vol. 6178, pp. 119–128. Springer, Heidelberg (2010)
17. Zhang, M.L., Zhou, Z.H.: A review on multi-label learning algorithms. IEEE Transactions on Knowledge and Data Engineering (in press, 2013)
18. Zhu, X., Wu, X., Chen, Q.: Eliminating class noise in large datasets. In: Proceedings of the 20th ICML, pp. 920–927 (2003)

Learning Mixtures of Polynomials
of Conditional Densities from Data

Pedro L. López-Cruz[1], Thomas D. Nielsen[2],
Concha Bielza[1], and Pedro Larrañaga[1]

[1] Department of Artificial Intelligence, Universidad Politécnica de Madrid, Spain
pedro.lcruz@upm.es, {mcbielza,pedro.larranaga}@fi.upm.es
[2] Department of Computer Science, Aalborg University, Denmark
tdn@cs.aau.dk

Abstract. Mixtures of polynomials (MoPs) are a non-parametric density estimation technique for hybrid Bayesian networks with continuous and discrete variables. We propose two methods for learning MoP approximations of conditional densities from data. Both approaches are based on learning MoP approximations of the joint density and the marginal density of the conditioning variables, but they differ as to how the MoP approximation of the quotient of the two densities is found. We illustrate the methods using data sampled from a simple Gaussian Bayesian network. We study and compare the performance of these methods with the approach for learning mixtures of truncated basis functions from data.

Keywords: Hybrid Bayesian networks, conditional density estimation, mixtures of polynomials.

1   Introduction

Mixtures of polynomials (MoPs) [1,2], mixtures of truncated basis functions (MoTBFs) [3], and mixtures of truncated exponentials (MTEs) [4] have been proposed as density estimation techniques in hybrid Bayesian networks (BNs) including both continuous and discrete random variables. These classes of densities are closed under multiplication and marginalization, and they therefore support exact inference schemes based on the Shenoy-Shafer architecture. Also, the densities are flexible in the sense that they do not impose any structural constraints on the model, unlike, e.g., conditional linear Gaussian networks.

Only marginal and conditional MoTBFs appear during inference in hybrid BNs [5]. Learning MoP, MoTBF and MTE approximations of one-dimensional densities from data has been studied in [6,7]. Learning conditional density approximations has, however, only been given limited attention [7,8]. The main difficulty is that the classes of functions above are not closed under division. The general approach shared by existing methods for learning conditional densities is that the conditioning variables are discretized, and a one-dimensional approximation of the density of the conditional variable is found for each combination

C. Bielza et al. (Eds.): CAEPIA 2013, LNAI 8109, pp. 363–372, 2013.
© Springer-Verlag Berlin Heidelberg 2013

of the (discretized) values of the conditioning variables. Thus, the estimation of a conditional density is equivalent to estimating a collection of marginal densities, where the correlation between the variable and the conditioning variables is captured by the discretization procedure.

In this paper, we present two new approaches, based on conditional sampling and interpolation, respectively, for learning MoP approximations of conditional densities from data. Our approach differs from previous methods in several ways. As opposed to [1,2,3], we learn conditional MoPs directly from data without any parametric assumptions. Also, we do not rely on a discretization of the conditioning variables to capture the correlation among the variables [7,8]. On the other hand, our conditional MoPs are not proper conditional densities, hence posterior distributions established during inference have to be normalized so that they integrate to 1.

The paper is organized as follows. Section 2 briefly introduces MoPs and details the two new approaches for learning conditional MoPs. Experimental results and a comparison with MoTBFs are shown in Sect. 3. Section 4 ends with conclusions and outlines future work.

2   Learning Conditional Distributions

2.1   Mixtures of Polynomials

Let $\mathbf{X} = (X_1, \ldots, X_n)$ be a multi-dimensional continuous random variable with probability density $f_{\mathbf{X}}(\mathbf{x})$. A MoP approximation of $f_{\mathbf{X}}(\mathbf{x})$ over a closed domain $\Omega_{\mathbf{X}} = [\epsilon_1, \xi_1] \times \cdots \times [\epsilon_n, \xi_n] \subset \mathbb{R}^n$ [1] is an L-piece d-degree piecewise function of the form

$$\varphi_{\mathbf{X}}(\mathbf{x}) = \begin{cases} pol_l(\mathbf{x}) & \text{for } \mathbf{x} \in A_l, \, l = 1, \ldots, L, \\ 0 & \text{otherwise,} \end{cases}$$

where $pol_l(\mathbf{x})$ is a multivariate polynomial function with degree d (and order $r = d + 1$) and $A_1, \ldots, A_L$ are disjoint hyperrectangles in $\Omega_{\mathbf{X}}$, which do not depend on $\mathbf{x}$, with $\Omega_{\mathbf{X}} = \cup_{l=1}^{L} A_l$, $A_i \cap A_j = \emptyset, i \neq j$.

Following the terminology used for BNs, we consider the conditional random variable X as the child variable and the vector of conditioning random variables $\mathbf{Y} = (Y_1, \ldots, Y_n)$ as the parent variables. Given a sample $\mathcal{D}_{X,\mathbf{Y}} = \{(x_i, \mathbf{y}_i)\}, i = 1, \ldots, N$, from the joint density of $(X, \mathbf{Y})$, the aim is to learn a MoP approximation $\varphi_{X|\mathbf{Y}}(x|\mathbf{y})$ of the conditional density $f_{X|\mathbf{Y}}(x|\mathbf{y})$ of $X|\mathbf{Y}$ from $\mathcal{D}_{X,\mathbf{Y}}$.

2.2   Learning Conditional MoPs Using Sampling

The proposed method is based on first obtaining a sample from the conditional density of $X|\mathbf{Y}$ and then learning a conditional MoP density from the sampled values. Algorithm 1 shows the main steps of the procedure. First, we find a MoP representation of the joint density $\varphi_{X,\mathbf{Y}}(x, \mathbf{y})$ (step 1) using the B-spline interpolation approach proposed in [6]. Second, we obtain a MoP of the marginal density of the parents $\varphi_{\mathbf{Y}}(\mathbf{y})$ by marginalization (step 2). Next, we use a sampling algorithm to obtain a sample $\mathcal{D}_{X|\mathbf{Y}}$ from the conditional density of $X|\mathbf{Y}$ (step 3), where the conditional density values are obtained by evaluating the quotient $\varphi_{X,\mathbf{Y}}(x,\mathbf{y})/\varphi_{\mathbf{Y}}(\mathbf{y})$. More specifically, we have used a standard Metropolis-Hastings sampler for the reported experimental results. For the sampling process we generate uniformly distributed values over $\Omega_{\mathbf{Y}}$ for the parent variables $\mathbf{Y}$, whereas the proposed distribution for the child variable is a linear Gaussian distribution $\mathcal{N}(\boldsymbol{\beta}^T\mathbf{y}, \sigma^2)$, where $\boldsymbol{\beta}$ is an n-dimensional vector with all components equal to $1/n$. We used $\sigma^2 = 0.5$ in our experiments. Next, we find an (unnormalized) MoP approximation of the conditional density $X|\mathbf{Y}$ from $\mathcal{D}_{X|\mathbf{Y}}$ (step 4). Finally, we apply the partial normalization procedure proposed in [1] to obtain a MoP approximation $\varphi_{X|\mathbf{Y}}(x|\mathbf{y})$ of the conditional density (steps 5 and 6). The complexity of the algorithm is dominated by the complexity of the learning algorithm in [6].

This method has some interesting properties. The B-spline interpolation algorithm for learning MoPs in [6] guarantees that the approximations are continuous, non-negative and integrate to one. Therefore, the conditional MoPs obtained with Algorithm 1 are also continuous and non-negative. Continuity is not required for inference in BNs, but it usually is a desirable property, e.g., for visualization purposes. The algorithm provides maximum likelihood estimators of the mixing coefficients of the linear combination of B-splines when learning MoPs of the joint density $(\varphi_{X,\mathbf{Y}}(x,\mathbf{y}))$ and the marginal density $\varphi_{\mathbf{y}}(\mathbf{y})$, hence the quotient $\varphi_{X,\mathbf{Y}}(x,\mathbf{y})/\varphi_{\mathbf{Y}}(\mathbf{y})$ corresponds to a maximum likelihood model of the conditional distribution. It should be noted, though, that this property is not shared by the final learned model as the partial normalization (steps 5 and 6) does not ensure that the learned MoP is a proper conditional density. Therefore, the MoP approximations of the posterior densities should be normalized to integrate to 1.

Algorithm 1
Inputs:

- $\mathcal{D}_{X,\mathbf{Y}}$: *A training dataset* $\mathcal{D}_{X,\mathbf{Y}} = \{(x_i, \mathbf{y}_i)\}, i = 1, \ldots, N$
- r: *The order of the MoP*
- L: *The number of pieces of the MoP*

Output: $\varphi_{X|\mathbf{Y}}(x|\mathbf{y})$. *The MoP approximation of the density of* $X|\mathbf{Y}$
Steps:

1. *Learn a MoP* $\varphi_{X,\mathbf{Y}}(x,\mathbf{y})$ *of the joint density of* $(X,\mathbf{Y})$ *from the dataset* $\mathcal{D}_{X,\mathbf{Y}}$ *using polynomials with order* r *and* L *pieces* [6].
2. *Marginalize out* X *from* $\varphi_{X,\mathbf{Y}}(x,\mathbf{y})$ *to yield a MoP* $\varphi_{\mathbf{Y}}(\mathbf{y})$ *of the marginal density of the parent variables* $\mathbf{Y}$: $\varphi_{\mathbf{Y}}(\mathbf{y}) = \int_{\Omega_X} \varphi_{X,\mathbf{Y}}(x,\mathbf{y})dx$.
3. *Use a Metropolis-Hastings algorithm to yield a sample* $\mathcal{D}_{X|\mathbf{Y}}$ *with* M *observations from the conditional density* $\varphi_{X,\mathbf{Y}}(x,\mathbf{y})/\varphi_{\mathbf{Y}}(\mathbf{y})$.
4. *Learn an unnormalized conditional MoP* $\varphi_{X|\mathbf{Y}}^{(u)}(x|\mathbf{y})$ *from* $\mathcal{D}_{X|\mathbf{Y}}$ *using polynomials with order* r *and* L *pieces* [6].

5. *Compute the partial normalization constant:*

$$c = \int_{\Omega_X} \int_{\Omega_\mathbf{Y}} \varphi_\mathbf{Y}(\mathbf{y}) \varphi_{X|\mathbf{Y}}^{(u)}(x|\mathbf{y}) d\mathbf{y} dx \ .$$

6. *Find the partially normalized MoP of the conditional density:*

$$\varphi_{X|\mathbf{Y}}(x|\mathbf{y}) = \frac{1}{c} \varphi_{X|\mathbf{Y}}^{(u)}(x|\mathbf{y}) \ .$$

We show an example with two variables X and Y. We sampled a training dataset $\mathcal{D}_{X,Y}$ with $N = 5000$ observations from the two-dimensional Gaussian density $(X, Y) \sim \mathcal{N}\left(\begin{pmatrix} 0 \\ 0 \end{pmatrix}, \begin{pmatrix} 2 & 1 \\ 1 & 1 \end{pmatrix}\right)$. This two-dimensional density corresponds to a Gaussian BN, where $Y \sim \mathcal{N}(0,1)$ and $X|Y \sim \mathcal{N}(y,1)$. Next, we applied Algorithm 1 to learn the MoP approximation of the conditional density of $X|Y$. The domain of the approximation was set to $\Omega_{X,Y} = [-3, 3] \times [-2, 2]$, which includes 0.9331 of the total Gaussian density mass. Note that $\sigma_Y^2 = 1$ is smaller than $\sigma_X^2 = 2$, thus the domain $\Omega_Y = [-2, 2]$ is smaller than Ω_X. We used the BIC score to greedily find the number of pieces L and the order r of the MoP. The conditional MoP learned with Algorithm 1 is shown in Fig. 1(a). The conditional MoP had $L = 16$ pieces and order $r = 2$, i.e., 64 polynomial coefficients. The true conditional density of $X|Y$ is the linear Gaussian density $\mathcal{N}(y, 1)$ shown in Fig. 1(b). We can see that the conditional MoP in Fig. 1(a) is continuous and close to the true conditional density. We observe high peaks at the "corners" of the domain $\Omega_{X,Y}$. These are due to numerical instabilities when evaluating the quotient $\varphi_{X,Y}(x, y)/\varphi_Y(y)$, caused by both the joint and the marginal MoPs yielding small values (close to zero) at the limits of the approximation domain.

Next, we performed inference based on the conditional MoP learned with Algorithm 1. Figures 1(c), (d) and (e) show the MoPs (solid) and true (dashed) posterior densities for Y given three different values for X. The three values correspond to the percentiles 10, 50 and 90 of $X \sim \mathcal{N}(0, 2)$. Both the MoPs and the true posterior densities shown in Figs. 1(c), (d) and (e) were normalized in the domain Ω_Y so that they integrate to one. We can see that the MoPs of the posterior densities are also continuous and close to the true posterior densities; Kullback-Leibler divergence values are reported in Sect. 3.

2.3   Learning Conditional MoPs Using Interpolation

The preliminary empirical results output by Algorithm 1 show that the sampling approach can produce good approximations. However, it is difficult to control or guarantee the quality of the approximation due to the partial normalization.

This shortcoming has motivated an alternative method for learning a MoP approximation of a conditional probability density for $X|\mathbf{Y}$. The main steps of the procedure are summarized in Algorithm 2. First, we find MoP approximations of both the joint density of $(X, \mathbf{Y})$ and the marginal density of $\mathbf{Y}$ in the

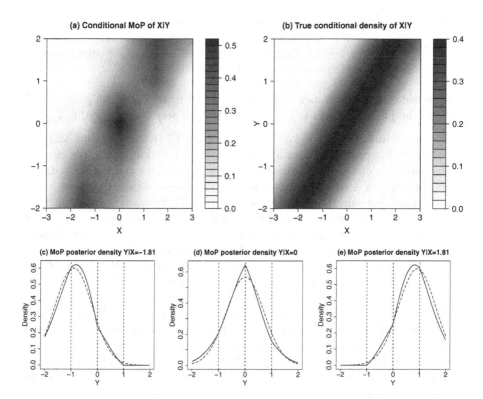

Fig. 1. (a) Conditional MoP of $X|Y$ learned with Algorithm 1. (b) True conditional density of $X|Y \sim \mathcal{N}(y, 1)$. (c,d,e) MoP approximations (solid) and true posterior densities (dashed) of $Y|X$ for three values of X.

same way as in Algorithm 1 (steps 1 and 2). Next, we build the conditional MoP $\varphi_{X|\mathbf{Y}}(x|\mathbf{y})$ by finding, for each piece $pol_l(x, \mathbf{y})$ defined in the hyperrectangle A_l, a multidimensional interpolation polynomial of the function given by the quotient of the joint and the marginal densities $\varphi_{X,\mathbf{Y}}(x, \mathbf{y})/\varphi_{\mathbf{Y}}(\mathbf{y})$.

Algorithm 2

Inputs:

- $\mathcal{D}_{X,\mathbf{Y}}$: *A training dataset* $\mathcal{D}_{X,\mathbf{Y}} = \{(x_i, \mathbf{y}_i)\}, i = 1, \dots, N$
- *r: The order of the MoP*
- *L: The number of pieces of the MoP*

Output: $\varphi_{X|\mathbf{Y}}(x|\mathbf{y})$. *The MoP approximation of the density of* $X|\mathbf{Y}$
Steps:

1. *Learn a MoP* $\varphi_{X,\mathbf{Y}}(x, \mathbf{y})$ *of the joint density of the variables* X *and* $\mathbf{Y}$ *from the dataset* $\mathcal{D}_{X,\mathbf{Y}}$ [6].
2. *Marginalize out* X *from* $\varphi_{X,\mathbf{Y}}(x, \mathbf{y})$ *to yield a MoP* $\varphi_{\mathbf{Y}}(\mathbf{y})$ *of the marginal density of the parent variables* $\mathbf{Y}$: $\varphi_{\mathbf{Y}}(\mathbf{y}) = \int_{\Omega_X} \varphi_{X,\mathbf{Y}}(x, \mathbf{y}) dx$.

3. *For piece $pol_l(x, \mathbf{y})$, defined in A_l, $l = 1, \ldots, L$, in the conditional MoP $\varphi_{X|\mathbf{Y}}(x|\mathbf{y})$:*

  Find a multi-dimensional polynomial approximation of function $g(x, \mathbf{y}) = \varphi_{X,\mathbf{Y}}(x, \mathbf{y})/\varphi_{\mathbf{Y}}(\mathbf{y})$ using an interpolation method.

We consider two multidimensional interpolation methods, which can be used to obtain the polynomials of the pieces $pol_l(x, \mathbf{y})$ in step 3 of Algorithm 2:

- The multidimensional Taylor series expansion (TSE) for a point yields a polynomial approximation of any differentiable function g. The quotient of any two functions is differentiable as long as the two functions are also differentiable. In our scenario, polynomials are differentiable functions and, thus, we can compute the TSE of the quotient of two polynomials. Consequently, we can use multidimensional TSEs to find a polynomial approximation of $g(x, \mathbf{y}) = \varphi_{X,\mathbf{Y}}(x, \mathbf{y})/\varphi_{\mathbf{Y}}(\mathbf{y})$ for each piece $pol_l(x, \mathbf{y})$. We computed these TSEs of $g(x, \mathbf{y})$ for the midpoint of the hyperrectangle A_l.
- Lagrange interpolation (LI) finds a polynomial approximation of any function g. Before finding the LI polynomial, we need to evaluate function g on a set of interpolation points. In the one-dimensional scenario, Chebyshev points are frequently used as interpolation points [9]. However, multidimensional LI is not a trivial task because it is difficult to find good interpolation points in a multidimensional space. Some researchers have recently addressed the two-dimensional scenario [9,10]. To find a conditional MoP using LI, we first find and evaluate the conditional density function $g(x, \mathbf{y}) = \varphi_{X,\mathbf{Y}}(x, \mathbf{y})/\varphi_{\mathbf{Y}}(\mathbf{y})$ on the set of interpolation points in A_l. Next, we compute the polynomial $pol_l(x, \mathbf{y})$ for the piece as the LI polynomial over the interpolation points defined in A_l. Note that other approaches, e.g., kernel-based conditional estimation methods, can also be used to evaluate the conditional density $g(x, \mathbf{y})$ on the set of interpolation points.

Compared with Algorithm 1, there are some apparent (dis)advantages. First, the conditional MoPs produced by Algorithm 2 are not necessarily continuous. Second, interpolation methods cannot in general ensure non-negativity, although LI can be used to ensure it by increasing the order of the polynomials. On the other hand, the learning method in Algorithm 2 does not need a partial normalization step. Thus, if the polynomial approximations are close to the conditional density $\varphi_{X,\mathbf{Y}}(x, \mathbf{y})/\varphi_{\mathbf{Y}}(\mathbf{y})$, then the conditional MoP using these polynomial interpolations is expected to be close to normalized. As a result, we can more directly control the quality of the approximation by varying the degree of the polynomials and the number of hyperrectangles.

We applied Algorithm 2 to the example in Fig. 1. We used the two-dimensional LI method over the Padua points in [10] to compute the polynomials $pol_l(x, \mathbf{y})$ of the conditional MoP, see Fig. 2(a). The conditional MoP with the highest BIC score had $L = 16$ pieces and order $r = 3$, i.e., 144 polynomial coefficients. We observe that the conditional MoP in Fig. 2(a) is not continuous. Also, the MoPs of the posterior density in Figs. 2(c), (d) and (e) are not continuous either; Kullback-Leibler divergence values are reported in Sect. 3.

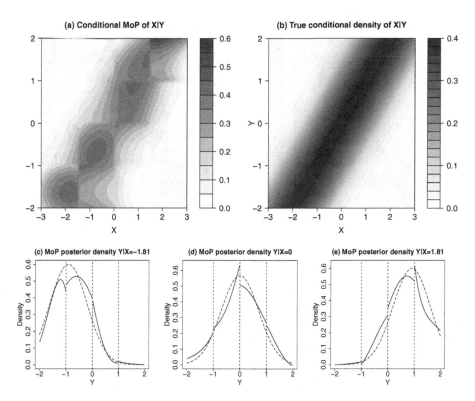

Fig. 2. (a) Conditional MoP of $X|Y$ learned with Algorithm 2. (b) True conditional density of $X|Y \sim \mathcal{N}(y, 1)$. (c,d,e) MoP approximations (solid) and true posterior densities (dashed) of $Y|X$ for three values of X.

3   A Comparison with MoTBFs

In this section, we compare the approaches proposed in this paper with the method proposed in [7] for learning conditional MoTBFs from data. Figure 3 shows the MoTBFs of the conditional (a) and the posterior (c,d,e) densities approximated using the data in Figs. 1 and 2. The conditional MoTBF had $L = 6$ pieces and each piece defined a MoP with at most six parameters. MoTBF approximations of conditional densities are obtained by discretizing the parent variables and fitting a one-dimensional MoTBF for each combination of the discrete values of the parents. Compared with the two learning methods proposed in Algorithms 1 and 2, the method in [7] captures the correlation between the parent variables and the child variable through the discretization instead of directly in the functional polynomial expressions.

   If there is a weak correlation between the child and parent variables, then the conditional MoTBF approach is expected to yield approximations with few pieces. On the other hand, as the variables become more strongly correlated,

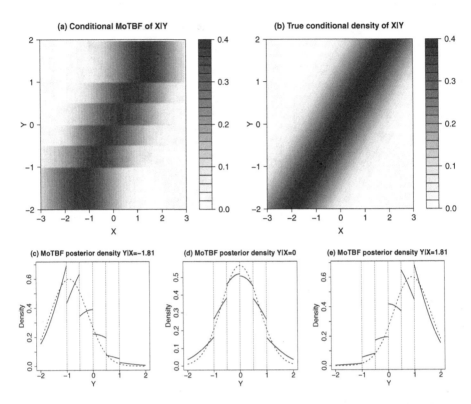

Fig. 3. (a) Conditional MoTBF of $X|Y$ learned with the approach in [7]. (b) True conditional density of $X|Y \sim \mathcal{N}(y,1)$. (c,d,e) MoTBF approximations (solid) and true posterior densities (dashed) of $Y|X$ for three values of X.

additional subintervals will be introduced by the learning algorithm. The MoTBF learning algorithm does not rely on a discretization of the child variable, but it rather approximates the density using a higher-order polynomial/exponential function. In contrast, Algorithms 1 and 2 yield conditional MoPs with more pieces because the domain of approximation $\Omega_{X,\mathbf{Y}}$ is split into hyperrectangles in all the dimensions. However, with the finer-grained division of the domain into hyperrectangles, the polynomial functions of the conditional MoPs will usually have a low order.

We empirically compared the results of Algorithm 1, Algorithm 2 (using both TSE and LI) and the method proposed in [7]. We sampled ten datasets for each sample size ($N = 25, 500, 2500, 5000$) from the Gaussian BN, where $Y \sim \mathcal{N}(0,1)$ and $X|Y \sim \mathcal{N}(y,1)$. We used Algorithms 1 and 2 as part of a greedy search procedure. We started by considering one interval for each dimension ($L = 1$) and order $r = 2$ (linear polynomials). Then, we increased either the number of intervals to 2 ($L = 4$) or the order of the polynomials to $r = 3$. Finally, we chose the MoP with the highest BIC score out of the two MoPs (increasing either L or r) and iterated until there was no further increase in the BIC score.

Table 1. Mean Kullback-Leibler divergences between the MoP approximations and the true posterior densities for ten datasets sampled from the BN, where $Y \sim \mathcal{N}(0,1)$ and $X|Y \sim \mathcal{N}(y,1)$. The best results for each sample size are highlighted in bold. Statistically significant differences at $\alpha = 0.05$ are shown with symbols $*, \dagger, \ddagger, \star$.

N	$Y|X = x$	Alg. 1 ($*$)		Alg. 2 TSE ($\dagger$)		Alg. 2 LI ($\ddagger$)		MoTBF ($\star$)	
	$X = -1.81$	0.5032	$\dagger\star$	0.7297		**0.3487**	$*\dagger\star$	0.7084	$\dagger$
25	$X = 0.00$	0.0746	$\ddagger\star$	**0.0745**	$*\ddagger\star$	0.1510		0.0939	$\ddagger$
	$X = 1.81$	**0.4952**	$\dagger\ddagger\star$	0.7297	$\ddagger$	1.4582		0.7084	$\dagger\ddagger$
	$X = -1.81$	0.4194		0.2321	$*\ddagger$	0.3161	$*$	**0.2191**	$*\ddagger$
500	$X = 0.00$	**0.0239**	$\dagger\ddagger\star$	0.0646	$\star$	0.0453	$\dagger\star$	0.0950	
	$X = 1.81$	0.4141		0.2311	$*\ddagger$	0.3701	$*$	**0.2170**	$*\ddagger$
	$X = -1.81$	0.1045		0.0850		0.1128		**0.0728**	$*\ddagger$
2500	$X = 0.00$	0.0387		0.0441		**0.0097**	$*\dagger\star$	0.0272	$*\dagger$
	$X = 1.81$	0.0984		0.0978		0.1041		**0.0695**	$*\ddagger$
	$X = -1.81$	0.0575		0.0413		0.0341	$*$	**0.0308**	$*$
5000	$X = 0.00$	**0.0196**		0.0262		0.0221		0.0210	
	$X = 1.81$	0.0556		0.0425		0.0383		**0.0322**	$*$

Table 1 shows the mean Kullback-Leibler divergences between the MoPs and the true posterior densities $Y|X$ for three values of X in the ten repetitions. We applied a paired Wilcoxon signed-rank test and report statistically significant differences at a significance level $\alpha = 0.05$. The null hypothesis is that the two methods perform similarly. The alternative hypothesis is that the algorithm in the column outperforms the algorithm shown with a symbol: $*$ for Alg. 1, $\dagger$ for Alg. 2 with TSE, $\ddagger$ for Alg. 2 with LI, and $\star$ for conditional MoTBFs. For instance, a $\star$ in the column corresponding to Alg. 1 in Table 1 shows that Alg. 1 significantly outperformed MoTBFs for a given value of N and X. Algorithms 1 and 2 yielded competitive results against conditional MoTBFs.

4   Conclusion

We have presented two methods for learning MoP approximations of the conditional density of $X|\mathbf{Y}$ from data. Both methods are based on finding MoP approximations of the joint density $\varphi_{X,\mathbf{Y}}(x, \mathbf{y})$ and the marginal density of the parents $\varphi_{\mathbf{Y}}(\mathbf{y})$. Thus, the first method obtains a sample from the conditional density $\varphi_{X,\mathbf{Y}}(x, \mathbf{y})/\varphi_{\mathbf{Y}}(\mathbf{y})$ using a Metropolis-Hastings algorithm, from which it learns the conditional MoP $\varphi_{X|\mathbf{Y}}(x|\mathbf{y})$. The second method obtains a MoP of the conditional density $\varphi_{X,\mathbf{Y}}(x, \mathbf{y})/\varphi_{\mathbf{Y}}(\mathbf{y})$ using a multidimensional interpolation technique. Multidimensional TSE and LI were considered and evaluated. The approaches were empirically studied and compared with MoTBFs using a dataset sampled from a Gaussian BN. As opposed to previous research on approximating conditional densities, the proposed approaches rely only on data without assuming any prior knowledge on the generating parametric density. Also, continuous parents do not need to be discretized.

In this paper, the same number of intervals were used for learning the MoPs of the joint and the conditional densities. Also, equal-width intervals $[\epsilon_i, \xi_i]$ are considered in each dimension, and the hyperrectangles A_l have the same size. In the future, we intend to study how to automatically find appropriate values for the order r, the number of pieces L, and the limits $[\epsilon_i, \xi_i]$ of the hyperrectangles defining each one of the MoPs. This should reduce the number of pieces required to find good MoP approximations. We also intend to use these approaches in more complex BNs. This involves considering other problems, e.g., BN structure learning. Finally, we intend to thoroughly compare these methods with MTE and MoTBF approaches.

Acknowledgments. This work has been partially supported by the Spanish Ministry of Economy and Competitiveness through Cajal Blue Brain (C080020-09) and TIN2010-20900-C04-04 projects. PLLC is supported by a Fellowship (FPU AP2009-1772) from the Spanish Ministry of Education, Culture and Sport.

References

1. Shenoy, P.P., West, J.C.: Inference in hybrid Bayesian networks using mixtures of polynomials. Int. J. Approx. Reason. 52, 641–657 (2011)
2. Shenoy, P.P.: Two issues in using mixtures of polynomials for inference in hybrid Bayesian networks. Int. J. Approx. Reason. 53, 847–866 (2012)
3. Langseth, H., Nielsen, T.D., Rumí, R., Salmerón, A.: Mixtures of truncated basis functions. Int. J. Approx. Reason. 53, 212–227 (2012)
4. Moral, S., Rumí, R., Salmerón, A.: Mixtures of Truncated Exponentials in Hybrid Bayesian Networks. In: Benferhat, S., Besnard, P. (eds.) ECSQARU 2001. LNCS (LNAI), vol. 2143, pp. 156–167. Springer, Heidelberg (2001)
5. Langseth, H., Nielsen, T.D., Rumí, R., Salmerón, A.: Inference in hybrid Bayesian networks with mixtures of truncated basis functions. In: Proceedings of the 6th European Workshop on Probabilistic Graphical Models, pp. 163–170 (2012)
6. López-Cruz, P.L., Bielza, C., Larrañaga, P.: Learning mixtures of polynomials from data using B-spline interpolation. In: Proceedings of the 6th European Workshop on Probabilistic Graphical Models, pp. 211–218 (2012)
7. Langseth, H., Nielsen, T.D., Rumí, R., Salmerón, A.: Learning mixtures of truncated basis functions from data. In: Proceedings of the 6th European Workshop on Probabilistic Graphical Models, pp. 163–170 (2012)
8. Langseth, H., Nielsen, T.D., Rumí, R., Salmerón, A.: Maximum likelihood learning of conditional MTE distributions. In: Sossai, C., Chemello, G. (eds.) ECSQARU 2009. LNCS, vol. 5590, pp. 240–251. Springer, Heidelberg (2009)
9. Harris, L.A.: Bivariate Lagrange interpolation at the Chebyshev nodes. Proc. Amer. Math. Soc. 138, 4447–4453 (2010)
10. Caliari, M., De Marchi, S., Sommariva, A., Vianello, M.: Padua2DM: Fast interpolation and cubature at the Padua points in Matlab/Octave. Numer. Algorithms 56, 45–60 (2011)

A Dynamic Bayesian Network Framework for Learning from Observation

Santiago Ontañón[1], José Luis Montaña[2], and Avelino J. Gonzalez[3]

[1] Drexel University, Philadelphia, PA, USA 19104
santi@cs.drexel.edu
[2] University of Cantabria, Santander, Spain
montanjl@unican.es
[3] University of Central Florida, Orlando, FL, USA
gonzalez@ucf.edu

Abstract. Learning from Observation (a.k.a. learning from demonstration) studies how computers can learn to perform complex tasks by observing and thereafter imitating the performance of an expert. Most work on learning from observation assumes that the behavior to be learned can be expressed as a state-to-action mapping. However most behaviors of interest in real applications of learning from observation require remembering past states. We propose a Dynamic Bayesian Network approach to learning from observation that addresses such problem by assuming the existence of non-observable states.

1 Introduction

Learning by watching others do something is a natural and highly effective way for humans to learn. It is also an intuitive and highly promising avenue for machine learning. It might provide a way for machines to learn how to perform tasks in a more natural fashion. This form of learning is known as *Learning from Observation* (LfO). Works reported in the literature also refer to *learning from demonstration*, *learning by imitation*, *programming by demonstration*, or *apprenticeship learning*, as largely synonymous to LfO.

This paper presents a new framework for LfO, based on *Dynamic Bayesian Networks* [7], called LfODBN. While there has been much work on LfO in the past (for a recent overview, see [1]), most proposed approaches assume that the behavior to be learned can be represented as a situation-to-action mapping (a policy). This assumes that, in the behavior to be learned, the choice of actions depends only on the current observable state. However, most behaviors of interest in the real world do not satisfy this restriction. For example, if we were to teach a robot how to automatically drive a car, the robot will need to remember past information that is not part of the current observable state, such as what was the last speed limit sign seen.

In general, the problem is that when learning from observation, the learning agent can observe the state of the world and the actions executed by the demonstrator or expert, but not the internal mental state of the expert (e.g. her

C. Bielza et al. (Eds.): CAEPIA 2013, LNAI 8109, pp. 373–382, 2013.

memory). The LfODBN model presented in this paper takes into account that the expert has a non-observable internal state, and, under some restrictions, can learn such behaviors.

Work in learning from observation can be traced back to the early days of AI. For instance, Bauer [2] proposed in 1979 to learn programs from example executions, which basically amounts to learning strategies to perform abstract computations by demonstration. This form of learning was especially popular in robotics [8]. Modern work on the more general LfO subject came from Sammut et al [15] and Sidani [17]. Fernlund et al. [5] used learning from observation to build agents capable of driving a simulated automobile in a city environment. Pomerleau [13] developed the ALVINN system that trained neural networks from observation of a road-following automobile in the real world. Although the neural network approach to learning from observation has remained popular with contributions such as the work of Moriarty and Gonzalez [9], LfO has been explored in the context of many other learning paradigms such as reinforcement learning [16], *case-based reasoning* (CBR) [6,11], and *Inverse Reinforcement Learning* (IRL) [10]. These approaches, however, ignore the fact that the expert might have internal state. For example, IRL assumes the expert is solving a Markov Decision Process (MDP), and thus has no additional internal state other than the observed state. For IRL to be applicable to the general problem of LfO, it needs to consider partially observable MDPs (POMDP), to account for the lack of observability of the expert's state.

The remainder of this paper is organized as follows. Sections 2 and 3 present some background on dynamic Bayesian networks and learning from observation respectively. Then, Section 4 presents our LfODBN model. After that, Section 5 empirically evaluates the LfODBN in a synthetic benchmark.

2   Background

A Bayesian Network (BN) is a modeling tool that represents a collection of random variables and their conditional dependencies as a directed acyclic graph (DAG). In this paper, we are interested in a specific type of BNs called *Dynamic Bayesian Networks* (DBN) [7]. In a DBN, the variables of the network are divided into a series of identical time-slices. A time-slice contains the set of variables representing the state of the process that we are trying to model at a given instant of time. Variables in a time-slice can only have dependencies with variables in the same or previous time-slices. DBNs can be seen as graphical representations of *stochastic processes*, i.e. random processes that depend on time [12].

The most common example of a DBN is the Hidden Markov Model [14], or HMM. There are only two variables in each time slice t in an HMM. A hidden variable C_t, typically called the *state*, and an observable variable Y_t, typical called the *output*. The output Y_t only depends on the state C_t, and the state C_t only depends on the state in the previous time slice, C_{t-1} (except in the first time slice). Moreover, the conditional probabilities $p(C_t|C_{t-1})$ and $p(Y_t|C_t)$ are assumed to be independent of t.

Although HMMs are the best known DBN and have many applications, such as speech recognition [14], there are other well-studied DBNs such as *Input-Output Hiden Markov Models* (IOHMM) [3]. In an IOHMM, in addition to the state and the output, there is an observable input variable, X_t upon which both the state C_t and the output Y_t depend. In the remainder of this paper we will use the following convention: if X is a variable, then we will use a calligraphic $\mathcal{X}$ to denote the set of values it can take, and lower case to denote the specific values it takes, i.e. $x_t \in \mathcal{X}$.

3   Learning from Observation

The goal of learning from observation (LfO) is to automatically learn a behavior by observing an expert perform a given task. The main difference between LfO and standard supervised learning is that the goal is to learn a behavior that might vary over time, rather than approximating a static function. The basic elements in LfO are the following:

- There is an *environment E*.
- There is one *actor* (or trainer, expert, or demonstrator), who performs a task in the environment E.
- There is a *learning agent A*, whose goal is to learn how to achieve the task in the environment E by observing the actions performed by the actor.

In learning from observation, the learning agent A first observes one or several actors performing the task to be learned in the environment, and records their behavior in the form of *traces*, from where behavior is learned. Some learning from observation approaches assume that the learner also has access to a reward signal R. In our framework we will assume such reward signal is not available, and that the goal is thus to just imitate the actor.

Specifically, the behavior of an agent can be captured by three different variables: its perception of the environment, X, its unobservable internal mental state C, and the perceptible actions it executes, Y. We will define $\mathcal{I} = \mathcal{X} \times \mathcal{C} \times \mathcal{Y}$, and interpret the actor behavior as a stochastic process $I = \{I_1, ..., I_n, ...\}$, with state space $\mathcal{I}$. $I_t = (X_t, C_t, Y_t)$ is the random variable where X_t and Y_t represent respectively the input and output variables at time t, and C_t represents the internal state of the actor at time t. The observed behavior of an actor in a particular execution defines a *learning trace*: $LT = [(x_1, y_1), ..., (x_n, y_n)]$ where x_t and y_t represent the specific perception of the environment and action of the actor at time t. The pair of variables X_t and Y_t represent the *observation* of the learning agent A, i.e.: $O_t = (X_t, Y_t)$. Thus, for simplicity, we can write a learning trace as $LT = [o_1, ..., o_n]$.

We assume that the random variables X_t and Y_t are multidimensional variables that can be either continuous or discrete. In our framework, thus, the LfO problem reduces to estimating the unknown probability measure that governs the stochastic process, taking as input a data set of k trajectories $\{LT_j : 1 \leq j \leq k\}$ of the stochastic process I.

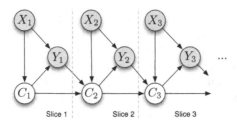

Fig. 1. The LfODBN Model. Grayed out variables are observable by the learning agent, white variables are hidden. X_t is the perception of the state, Y_t is the action, and C_t is the internal state of the agent.

As mentioned above, most work on LfO [1] assumes that the action Y_t depends exclusively on the state X_t (i.e. that the behavior is Markovian). Under this assumption, each of the entries (x_t, y_t) in a trace can be taken as individual examples in a supervised learning framework. Thus, if we assume that the action the expert executes at time t only depends on the perception at time t, then learning from observation is equivalent to supervised learning. However, in many real-life behaviors this assumption doesn't hold.

Consider the following example. When a driver in a highway sees a sign indicating the desired exit is approaching, the driver starts merging to the right lanes, even if she does not see the sign any more. Thus, the driver needs to remember that she has seen such sign (in her internal state C).

As a second example, imagine an agent wants to learn how to play Stratego by observation. Stratego is similar to Chess, but players do not see the types of the pieces of the opponent, only their locations. Thus, the perception of the state X_t contains only the locations of the pieces of the opponent (in addition to the player's piece locations and types). After certain movements, a player can temporally observe the type of one piece, and must remember this in order to exploit this information in the future. In this case, the internal state C_t of an actor should contain all the types of the opponent pieces observed up to time t.

The typical strategy to avoid this situation when designing a LfO system is to identify all of those aspects the expert has to remember, and include them in the set of input features. For example, we could add a variable to x_t representing "which is the last exit sign we saw in the highway". However, this requires manual "feature engineering", which is highly undesirable.

4 DBN-Based Learning from Observation

Using the DBN framework, we can represent the probability distribution of the stochastic process representing the behavior of an actor as the network shown in Figure 1, that we call the *LfODBN* model. The LfODBN model contains all the variables in LfO and their conditional dependencies (grayed out variables are observable, white variables are hidden). The internal state of the actor at time t, C_t, depends on the internal state at the previous instant of time, C_{t-1}, the

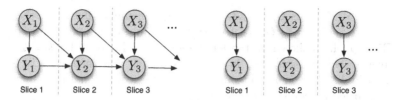

Fig. 2. Simplifications of the model in Figure 1 For assumptions 1 (right) and 2 (left)

previous action Y_{t-1} and of the current observation X_t. The action Y_t depends only on the current observation, X_t and the current internal state C_t.

Given the LfODBN model, if the learning agent wants to learn the behavior of the expert, it has to learn the dependencies between the variables C_t, X_t, and Y_t, i.e. it has to learn the following conditional probability distributions: $\rho(C_1)$, $\rho(Y_t|C_t, X_t)$, and $\rho(C_t|C_{t-1}, X_t, Y_{t-1})$. If the learning agent is able to infer the previous conditional probability distributions, it can replicate the behavior of the expert. In practice, the main difficulty is that the internal state variable C_t is not observable, which, although typically neglected in the LfO literature, plays a key role in many behaviors of interest.

Also, notice that the goal of LfO is just to learn to replicate the behavior (i.e. actions) of the actor. Thus, relations such as the dependency of X_t in X_{t-1} and Y_{t-1} (that captures the effect that actions have on the environment) are irrelevant. Those relations would be key, however, if the learning agent was learning a model of the world for planning purposes.

Let us now present three approaches to LfO based on making three different assumptions over the internal state of the actor C_t.

4.1   Assumption 1: No Internal State

The assumption that the expert has no internal state, i.e. that C_t is irrelevant, is equivalent to assuming the behavior is reactive, and thus the action Y_t only depends on the current observation (X_t). In this case, we can simplify the LfODBN model as shown on the right hand side of Figure 2. Under this assumption, we can just use standard supervised learning techniques to learn the conditional probability $\rho(Y_t|X_t)$.

In this approach, each entry in a learning trace can be treated independently, and any supervised learning algorithm such as decision trees, neural networks or SVMs can be used. This is the simplest approach to LfO, with the only drawback that it cannot learn any behavior that requires the agent to remember anything from past states. The next two approaches make less restrictive assumptions about the internal state of the expert, to alleviate this problem.

4.2   Assumption 2: Time Window

In this approach, we assume that the expert internal state is a time window memory that stores the last k observations (i.e., the current state X_t, and the last $k - 1$ observations $O_{t-1}, ..., O_{t-(k-1)}$). For example, if $k = 2$, the expert internal state is $C_t = (X_t, O_{t-1})$. Under this assumption we can reformulate the LfODBN model, as shown on the left hand side of Figure 2 for $k = 2$. Notice that given k, we can ignore C_t in the DBN model, and thus, we still have no hidden variables. In general, for any given k, the conditional probability that must be learned is: $\rho(Y_t | X_t, O_{t-1}, ..., O_{t-(k-1)})$.

In this approach, each subsequence of k entries in a learning trace can be treated independently as a training example, and we can still use supervised learning techniques. The main drawback of this approach is that, as k increases, the number of features in the training examples increases, and thus, the learning task becomes more complex.

4.3   Assumption 3: Finite Discrete Internal State

Using the time window assumption, it is possible to learn behaviors where the agent only needs to remember a fixed number of past states; however, in general, the agent might need to remember a past state that is arbitrarily far in the past.

In this more general assumption, we assume that the internal state of the expert is discrete and can take a finite amount l of different values. In this assumption, we need to consider the complete LfODBN model as shown in Figure 1. Under this assumption, the Expectation-Maximization (EM) algorithm [4] can be used to learn the parameters of the LfODBN.

A possible simplification assumes that the internal state C_t depends only on previous internal state C_{t-1} and observation X_t (i.e. that it does not depend on the past action). The resulting model corresponds to an *Input-Output Hidden Markov Model* (IOHMM), for which specialized algorithms are known [3].

5   Experimental Evaluation

This section presents an experimental validation of algorithms based on the three assumptions presented above, and compares them with other common LfO algorithms in the literature. Specifically, these experiments are designed to show that standard algorithms used in the literature of LfO (such as neural networks) can only learn a limited set of behaviors; algorithms based on the LfODBN model, however, make a less restrictive assumption on the internal state of the expert, and thus, can learn a wider range of behaviors.

The domain we used for our experiments simulates an automatic vacuum cleaner navigating a room, and removing dirt spots. The goal is to remove dirt spots in a grid map. For these experiments, all the obstacles are static, and the only moving object in the simulation is the vacuum cleaner. The simulation time is discreet, and at each time step, the vacuum cleaner can take one out of these 5 actions: up, down, left, right and stand still, with their intuitive effect (if the vacuum tries to move into an obstacle, the effect is equivalent to the stand still action). Actions are deterministic. Thus, the control variable Y can take 5 different values: $\{up, down, left, right, stand\}$.

The vacuum cleaner perceives the world through 8 different variables: two binary variables per direction (up, down, left, right), one of them identifying what can the vacuum cleaner see in each direction (dirt or obstacle), and the other determining whether the object being seen is close (touching) or far. For the experiments, we created a collection of 7 different maps, of different sizes, from 8x8 to 32x32 and with different configuration of obstacles and dirt (with between 2 to 8 dirt spots). We created several different experts to learn from:

RND: SmartRandom. This agent executes random actions, except if it sees dirt in one of the four directions, in which case it will move straight for it.

STR: SmartStraightLine. This agent picks a direction at random and moves in a straight line until collision. Then, it repeats its behavior. But if it sees dirt in one of the four directions, it will move straight for it.

ZZ: ZigZag. This agent moves in zig-zag: it moves to the right, until colliding, then moves down and starts moving to the left until colliding. When it cannot go down any further, it repeats the behavior, but going up, and so on.

SEQ: FixedSequence. This agent always repeats the same, fixed, sequence of actions (15 actions long). Once the sequence is over, it restarts from scratch.

EXP: SmartExplorer. This is a complex agent that remembers all the cells in which it has already been. With a high probability (0.75) it selects the action that will lead him closer to an unexplored cell. Once all the cells in the map have been explored, the agent stops. If it sees dirt in one of the four directions, it will move straight for the dirt. Notice that in order to perform this behavior, the agent needs to remember each cell it has visited before.

We generated a total of 35 learning traces (one per expert per map). Each learning trace is 1000 steps long. Therefore, the learning agents have 7 learning traces per expert. We compared the performance of the following algorithms:

Algorithms Making Assumption 1: We used NN (Neural Networks), widely used in the literature of LfO [13,9], and BN (Bayesian Networks), a direct implementation of the simplified Bayesian Network shown in Figure 2. Neural Networks in our experiments have one hidden layer with 10 nodes, and 5 output nodes (one per possible action).

Algorithms Making Assumption 2: We also experimented with two algorithms in this case: NNk2 (Neural Networks) and BNk2 (Bayesian Networks). For both algorithms, we used $k = 2$, i.e. they learn to predict the expert actions based on the current state of the world, and the state and action in the previous instant of time.

Algorithms Making Assumption 3: We experimented with using the EM algorithm[1] to learn the parameters of both our proposed LfODBN model (Figure 1), as well as an IOHMM. In both cases, we ran 20 iterations of EM, and limited the internal state to have 4 different values.

---

[1] Specifically, we used the EM implementation in the Matlab *Bayes Net Toolbox* using the *jtree_2TBN_inf_engine* inference engine.

Table 1. Output Evaluation of the different LfO algorithms consisting of the percentage of expert actions predicted correctly. The bottom row shows the average of all the other rows, showing that LfODBN obtains the highest accuracy overall.

	NN	BN	NNk2	BNk2	IOHMM	LfODBN
RND	32.0	30.9	32.0	31.0	31.0	31.1
STR	40.0	40.7	85.1	84.8	77.2	84.3
ZZ	41.3	40.9	73.7	91.6	65.2	83.4
SEQ	43.2	36.2	66.4	51.9	85.8	88.2
EXP	48.4	49.3	79.1	77.6	65.3	79.3
Avg.	41.0	39.6	67.26	67.38	64.9	72.3

We evaluated the performance of the algorithms by measuring their accuracy in predicting the actions executed by the experts. For this purpose, we performed a leave-one-out evaluation, where agents learned from 6 learning traces, and were asked to predict the actions in the 7th, test trace. Specifically, given a model M learned by one of the learning algorithms, and a test trace LT containing n entries, the predictive accuracy $Acc(M, LT)$ was measured as follows:

$$P(M, LT, t) = \begin{cases} 1 & \text{if } M(x_t, [o_{t-1}, ..., o_1]) = y_t \\ 0 & \text{otherwise} \end{cases}$$

$$Acc(M, LT) = \frac{1}{n} \sum_{t=1...n} P(M, LT, t)$$

where $M(x_t, [o_{t-1}, ..., o_1])$ represents the action predicted by the model M given the observation at time t, and the entire subtrace from time 1 to time $t - 1$. Since our traces have 1000 entries each, and we had 7 traces per expert, each reported result is the average of 7000 predictions.

Table 1 shows the predictive accuracy of each learning algorithm when learning from each of the experts. The best results for each expert are highlighted in bold (when more than one learning agent achieved statistically undistinguishable results, all of them are highlighted in bold). The easiest behavior to learn is the SmartRandom (RND) expert. All the learning agents were capable to perfectly learning this behavior. Notice that, even if the behavior is perfectly learned, they can only predict about a 31% of the actions of this expert, since the behavior of the expert involved randomness.

Next in difficulty is the SmartStraightLine (STR) expert. For this behavior, agents need to remember what was the last direction in which they moved. Thus, learning agents using assumption 1 (NN and BN) could simply not learn this behavior. All the other learning agents could learn this behavior perfectly (except IOHMM, which learned a pretty good approximation, but not exactly). The problem with IOHMM is that the relationship between Y_{t-1} and C_t is not present in the DBN, and thus, it has troubles learning behaviors that depend on the previous action. Again, no agent reached a 100% of prediction accuracy, since the expert would pick a random direction each time it hit a wall.

The ZigZag (ZZ) agent is even harder to learn, since, in addition to the last direction of movement, the agent must remember whether it is currently traveling down or up. No learning algorithm was able to learn this properly. All the algorithms making assumptions 2 and 3 properly learned the left-to-right behavior (and thus the high accuracy of BNk2), but none was capable of learning when to move down or up when changing directions. This was expected for algorithms making assumption 2, however, algorithms making assumption 3 are, in principle, capable of learning this. GEM was not capable of learning this from the training data provided though, and ended up learning only an approximate behavior, with some mistakes.

The FixedSequence (SEQ) expert is complex to learn, since, in order to learn the fixed sequence of 15 moves, agents must internally remember in which of the 15 states of the sequence they are. By using the past action as a reference, algorithms making assumption 2 (NNk2, BNk2) could better learn this behavior better that agents making assumption 1 (NN, BN) (increasing the value of k all the way up to 15 should let agents using assumption 2 learn this behavior, but with prohibitive number of features). However, only agents making assumption 3 could learn a good enough approximation.

Finally, the SmartExplorer (EXP) expert is very hard to learn, since it involves remembering every cell that has been visited. None of the agents was able to learn this behavior. Some algorithms, like LfODBN, have a high predictive accuracy (79.3%) just because they appropriately learn the probability of the expert to stop (the expert stops after exploring the whole room), and then they can predict correctly that the expert will just issue the *stand* action till the end of the trace. The bottom row of Table 1 shows the average predictive accuracy for all the learning algorithms we experimented with, showing that LfODBN obtains the highest accuracy overall.

6   Conclusions

This paper has presented a model of Learning form Observation (LfO) based on Dynamic Bayesian Networks (DBN), called LfODBN. The main contribution of this model is that it makes explicit the need for accounting for the unobservable internal state of the expert when learning a behavior from observation.

Additionally, we proposed three different approaches to learn from observation, based on three different assumptions on the internal state of the expert: 1) assume the expert has no internal state, 2) assume the internal state of the expert is a memory of the last k states, and 3) assume the expert has a finite discrete internal state. Each of the three assumptions leads to a different collection of algorithms: the first two can be addressed with supervised learning algorithms, but the last requires a different learning approach (for which we propose to use DBN learning algorithms that account for hidden variables).

Our experimental results show that algorithms making different assumptions can learn different ranges of behaviors, and that supervised learning approaches to LfO are not enough to deal with the general form of the LfO problem.

As part of our future work, we want to explore further less restrictive assumptions over the internal state of the expert, that allow learning broader ranges of behaviors, while still being tractable. Finally, we would also study better evaluation metrics for LfO, since, as observed in this paper, traditional classification accuracy is not very representative of the performance of LfO algorithms.

Acknowledgements. This work is partially supported by spanish grant TIN2011-27479-C04-04.

References

1. Argall, B.D., Chernova, S., Veloso, M., Browning, B.: A survey of robot learning from demonstration. Robot. Auton. Syst. 57, 469–483 (2009)
2. Bauer, M.A.: Programming by examples. Artificial Intelligence 12(1), 1–21 (1979)
3. Bengio, Y., Frasconi, P.: Input/output hmms for sequence processing. IEEE Transactions on Neural Networks 7, 1231–1249 (1996)
4. Dempster, A.P., Laird, N.M., Rubin, D.B.: Maximum likelihood from incomplete data via the em algorithm. Journal of the Royal Statistical Society, Series B 39(1), 1–38 (1977)
5. Fernlund, H.K.G., Gonzalez, A.J., Georgiopoulos, M., DeMara, R.F.: Learning tactical human behavior through observation of human performance. IEEE Transactions on Systems, Man, and Cybernetics, Part B 36(1), 128–140 (2006)
6. Floyd, M.W., Esfandiari, B., Lam, K.: A case-based reasoning approach to imitating robocup players. In: Proceedings of the Twenty-First International Florida Artificial Intelligence Research Society (FLAIRS), pp. 251–256 (2008)
7. Ghahramani, Z.: Learning dynamic Bayesian networks. In: Caianiello, E.R. (ed.) Adaptive Processing of Sequences and Data Structures, International Summer School on Neural Networks. Tutorial Lectures, pp. 168–197. Springer, London (1998)
8. Lozano-Pérez, T.: Robot programming. Proceedings of IEEE 71, 821–841 (1983)
9. Moriarty, C.L., Gonzalez, A.J.: Learning human behavior from observation for gaming applications. In: FLAIRS Conference (2009)
10. Ng, A.Y., Russell, S.: Algorithms for Inverse Reinforcement Learning. In: in Proc. 17th International Conf. on Machine Learning, pp. 663–670 (2000)
11. Ontañón, S., Mishra, K., Sugandh, N., Ram, A.: On-line case-based planning. Computational Intelligence Journal 26(1), 84–119 (2010)
12. Papoulis, A., Pillai, S.U.: Probability, Random Variables, and Stochastic Processes. McGraw-Hill Series in Electrical and Computer Engineering. McGraw-Hill (2002)
13. Pomerleau, D.: Alvinn: An autonomous land vehicle in a neural network. In: Touretzky, D.S. (ed.) Advances in Neural Information Processing Systems, vol. 1. Morgan Kaufmann (1989)
14. Rabiner, L.R.: A tutorial on hidden markov models and selected applications in speech recognition. Proceedings of the IEEE, 257–286 (1989)
15. Sammut, C., Hurst, S., Kedzier, D., Michie, D.: Learning to fly. In: Proceedings of the Ninth International Workshop on Machine Learning (ML 1992), pp. 385–393 (1992)
16. Schaal, S.: Learning from demonstration. In: NIPS, pp. 1040–1046 (1996)
17. Sidani, T.: Automated Machine Learning from Observation of Simulation. Ph.D. thesis, University of Central Florida (1994)

Approximate Counting of Graphical Models via MCMC Revisited

José M. Peña

ADIT, IDA, Linköping University, Sweden
jose.m.pena@liu.se

Abstract. In [6], MCMC sampling is applied to approximately calculate the ratio of essential graphs (EGs) to directed acyclic graphs (DAGs) for up to 20 nodes. In the present paper, we extend that work from 20 to 31 nodes. We also extend that work by computing the approximate ratio of connected EGs to connected DAGs, of connected EGs to EGs, and of connected DAGs to DAGs. Furthermore, we prove that the latter ratio is asymptotically 1. We also discuss the implications of these results for learning DAGs from data.

Keywords: Bayesian networks, Markov equivalence, MCMC.

1 Introduction

Probably the most common approach to learning directed acyclic graph (DAG) models[1] from data, also known as Bayesian network models, is that of performing a search in the space of either DAGs or DAG models. In the latter case, DAG models are typically represented as essential graphs (EGs). Knowing the ratio of EGs to DAGs for a given number of nodes is a valuable piece of information when deciding which space to search. For instance, if the ratio is low, then one may prefer to search the space of EGs rather than the space of DAGs, though the latter is usually considered easier to traverse. Unfortunately, while the number of DAGs can be computed without enumerating them all [9, Equation 8], the only method for counting EGs that we are aware of is enumeration. Specifically, Gillispie and Perlman enumerated all the EGs for up to 10 nodes by means of a computer program [3]. They showed that the ratio is around 0.27 for 7-10 nodes. They also conjectured a similar ratio for more than 10 nodes by extrapolating the exact ratios for up to 10 nodes.

Enumerating EGs for more than 10 nodes seems challenging: To enumerate all the EGs over 10 nodes, the computer program of [3] needed 2253 hours in a "mid-1990s-era, midrange minicomputer". We obviously prefer to know the exact ratio of EGs to DAGs for a given number of nodes rather than an approximation to it. However, an approximate ratio may be easier to obtain and serve as well as the exact one to decide which space to search. In [6], a Markov chain Monte Carlo (MCMC) approach was proposed to approximately

---

[1] All the graphs considered in this paper are labeled graphs.

C. Bielza et al. (Eds.): CAEPIA 2013, LNAI 8109, pp. 383–392, 2013.
© Springer-Verlag Berlin Heidelberg 2013

calculate the ratio while avoiding enumerating EGs. This approach consisted of the following steps. First, the author constructed a Markov chain (MC) whose stationary distribution was uniform over the space of EGs for the given number of nodes. Then, the author sampled that stationary distribution and computed the ratio R of essential DAGs (EDAGs) to EGs in the sample. Finally, the author transformed this approximate ratio into the desired approximate ratio of EGs to DAGs as follows: Since $\frac{\#EGs}{\#DAGs}$ can be expressed as $\frac{\#EDAGs}{\#DAGs}\frac{\#EGs}{\#EDAGs}$, [2] then we can approximate it by $\frac{\#EDAGs}{\#DAGs}\frac{1}{R}$ where $\#DAGs$ and $\#EDAGs$ can be computed via [9, Equation 8] and [10, p. 270], respectively. The author reported the so-obtained approximate ratio for up to 20 nodes. The approximate ratios agreed well with the exact ones available in the literature and suggested that the exact ratios are not very low (the approximate ratios were 0.26-0.27 for 7-20 nodes). This indicates that one should not expect more than a moderate gain in efficiency when searching the space of EGs instead of the space of DAGs. Of course, this is a bit of a bold claim since the gain is dictated by the average ratio over the EGs visited during the search and not by the average ratio over all the EGs in the search space. For instance, the gain is not the same if we visit the empty EG, whose ratio is 1, or the complete EG, whose ratio is $1/n!$ for n nodes. Unfortunately, it is impossible to know beforehand which EGs will be visited during the search. Therefore, the best we can do is to draw (bold) conclusions based on the average ratio over all the EGs in the search space.

In this paper, we extend the work in [6] from 20 to 31 nodes. We also extend that work by reporting some new approximate ratios. Specifically, we report the approximate ratio of connected EGs (CEGs) to connected DAGs (CDAGs), of CEGs to EGs, and of CDAGs to DAGs. We elaborate later on why these ratios are of interest. The approximate ratio of CEGs to CDAGs is computed from the sample as follows. First, we compute the ratio R' of EDAGs to CEGs in the sample. Second, we transform this approximate ratio into the desired approximate ratio of CEGs to CDAGs as follows: Since $\frac{\#CEGs}{\#CDAGs}$ can be expressed as $\frac{\#EDAGs}{\#CDAGs}\frac{\#CEGs}{\#EDAGs}$, then we can approximate it by $\frac{\#EDAGs}{\#CDAGs}\frac{1}{R'}$ where $\#EDAGs$ can be computed by [10, p. 270] and $\#CDAGs$ can be computed as shown in Appendix A. The approximate ratio of CEGs to EGs is computed directly from the sample. The approximate ratio of CDAGs to DAGs is computed with the help of Appendix A and [9, Equation 8].

The computer program implementing the MCMC approach described above is essentially the same as in [6] (it has only been modified to report whether the EGs sampled are connected or not).[3] The program is written in C++ and compiled in Microsoft Visual C++ 2010 Express. The experiments are run on an AMD Athlon 64 X2 Dual Core Processor 5000+ 2.6 GHz, 4 GB RAM and Windows Vista Business. The compiler and the computer used in [6] were Microsoft Visual C++ 2008 Express and a Pentium 2.4 GHz, 512 MB RAM and Windows 2000.

---

[2] We use the symbol $\#$ followed by a class of graphs to denote the cardinality of the class.

[3] The modified program will be made available after publication.

Table 1. Exact and approximate $\frac{\#EGs}{\#DAGs}$ and $\frac{\#EDAGs}{\#EGs}$

NODES	EXACT			OLD APPROXIMATE			NEW APPROXIMATE		
	$\frac{\#EGs}{\#DAGs}$	$\frac{\#EDAGs}{\#EGs}$	Hours	$\frac{\#EGs}{\#DAGs}$	$\frac{\#EDAGs}{\#EGs}$	Hours	$\frac{\#EGs}{\#DAGs}$	$\frac{\#EDAGs}{\#EGs}$	Hours
2	0.66667	0.50000	0.0	0.66007	0.50500	3.5	0.67654	0.49270	1.3
3	0.44000	0.36364	0.0	0.43704	0.36610	5.2	0.44705	0.35790	1.0
4	0.34070	0.31892	0.0	0.33913	0.32040	6.8	0.33671	0.32270	1.2
5	0.29992	0.29788	0.0	0.30132	0.29650	8.0	0.29544	0.30240	1.4
6	0.28238	0.28667	0.0	0.28118	0.28790	9.4	0.28206	0.28700	1.6
7	0.27443	0.28068	0.0	0.27228	0.28290	12.4	0.27777	0.27730	2.0
8	0.27068	0.27754	0.0	0.26984	0.27840	13.8	0.26677	0.28160	2.3
9	0.26888	0.27590	7.0	0.27124	0.27350	16.5	0.27124	0.27350	2.6
10	0.26799	0.27507	2253.0	0.26690	0.27620	18.8	0.26412	0.27910	3.1
11				0.26179	0.28070	20.4	0.26179	0.28070	3.8
12				0.26737	0.27440	21.9	0.26825	0.27350	4.2
13				0.26098	0.28090	23.3	0.27405	0.26750	4.5
14				0.26560	0.27590	25.3	0.27161	0.26980	5.1
15				0.27125	0.27010	25.6	0.26250	0.27910	5.7
16				0.25777	0.28420	27.3	0.26943	0.27190	6.7
17				0.26667	0.27470	29.9	0.26942	0.27190	7.6
18				0.25893	0.28290	37.4	0.27040	0.27090	8.2
19				0.26901	0.27230	38.1	0.27130	0.27000	9.0
20				0.27120	0.27010	40.3	0.26734	0.27400	9.9
21							0.26463	0.27680	17.4
22							0.27652	0.26490	18.8
23							0.26569	0.27570	13.3
24							0.27030	0.27100	14.0
25							0.26637	0.27500	15.9
26							0.26724	0.27410	17.0
27							0.26950	0.27180	18.6
28							0.27383	0.26750	20.1
29							0.27757	0.26390	21.1
30							0.28012	0.26150	21.6
31							0.27424	0.26710	47.3

The experimental settings is the same as before for up to 30 nodes, i.e. each approximate ratio reported is based on a sample of 10^4 EGs, each obtained as the state of the MC after performing 10^6 transitions with the empty EG as initial state. For 31 nodes though, each EG sampled is obtained as the state of the MC after performing 2×10^6 transitions with the empty EG as initial state. We elaborate later on why we double the length of the MCs for 31 nodes.

The rest of the paper is organized as follows. In Section 2, we extend the work in [6] from 20 to 31 nodes. In Section 3, we extend the work in [6] with new approximate ratios. In Section 4, we recall our findings and discuss future work. The paper ends with two appendices devoted to technical details.

2 Extension from 20 to 31 Nodes

Table 1 presents our new approximate ratios, together with the old approximate ones and the exact ones available in the literature. The first conclusion that we draw from the table is that the new ratios are very close to the exact ones, as well as to the old ones. This makes us confident on the accuracy of the ratios for 11-31 nodes, where no exact ratios are available in the literature due to the high computational cost involved in calculating them. Another conclusion that we draw from the table is that the ratios seem to be 0.26-0.28 for 11-31 nodes. This agrees well with the conjectured ratio of 0.27 for more than 10 nodes reported in [3]. A last conclusion that we draw from the table is that the fraction of EGs that represent a unique DAG, i.e. $\frac{\#EDAGs}{\#EGs}$, is 0.26-0.28 for 11-31 nodes, a substantial fraction.

Recall from the previous section that we slightly modified the experimental setting for 31 nodes, namely we doubled the length of the MCs. The reason is as follows. We observed an increasing trend in $\frac{\#EGs}{\#DAGs}$ for 25-30 nodes, and interpreted this as an indication that we might be reaching the limits of our experimental setting. Therefore, we decided to double the length of the MCs for 31 nodes in order to see whether this broke the trend. As can be seen in Table 1, it did. This suggests that approximating the ratio for more than 31 nodes will require larger MCs and/or samples than the ones used in this work.

Note that we can approximate the number of EGs for up to 31 nodes as $\frac{\#EGs}{\#DAGs}\#DAGs$, where $\frac{\#EGs}{\#DAGs}$ comes from Table 1 and $\#DAGs$ comes from [9, Equation 8]. Alternatively, we can approximate it as $\frac{\#EGs}{\#EDAGs}\#EDAGs$, where $\frac{\#EGs}{\#EDAGs}$ comes from Table 1 and $\#EDAGs$ can be computed by [10, p. 270].

Finally, a few words on the running times reported in Table 1 may be in place. First, note that the times reported in Table 1 for the exact ratios are borrowed from [3] and, thus, they correspond to a computer program run on a "mid-1990s-era, midrange minicomputer". Therefore, a direct comparison to our times seems unadvisable. Second, our times are around four times faster than the old times. The reason may be in the use of a more powerful computer and/or a different version of the compiler. The reason cannot be in the difference in the computer programs run, since this is negligible. Third, the new times have some oddities, e.g. the time for two nodes is greater than the time for three nodes. The reason may be that the computer ran other programs while running the experiments reported in this paper.

3   Extension with New Ratios

In [3, p. 153], it is stated that "the variables chosen for inclusion in a multi-variate data set are not chosen at random but rather because they occur in a common real-world context, and hence are likely to be correlated to some degree". This implies that the EG learnt from some given data is likely to be connected. We agree with this observation, because we believe that humans are good at detecting sets of mutually uncorrelated variables so that the original learning problem can be divided into smaller independent learning problems, each of which results in a CEG. Therefore, although we still cannot say which EGs will be visited during the search, we can say that some of them will most likely be connected and some others disconnected. This raises the question of

Table 2. Approximate $\frac{\#CEGs}{\#CDAGs}$, $\frac{\#CEGs}{\#EGs}$ and $\frac{\#CDAGs}{\#DAGs}$

NODES	NEW APPROXIMATE		
	$\frac{\#CEGs}{\#CDAGs}$	$\frac{\#CEGs}{\#EGs}$	$\frac{\#CDAGs}{\#DAGs}$
2	0.51482	0.50730	0.66667
3	0.39334	0.63350	0.72000
4	0.32295	0.78780	0.82136
5	0.29471	0.90040	0.90263
6	0.28033	0.94530	0.95115
7	0.27799	0.97680	0.97605
8	0.26688	0.98860	0.98821
9	0.27164	0.99560	0.99415
10	0.26413	0.99710	0.99708
11	0.26170	0.99820	0.99854
12	0.26829	0.99940	0.99927
13	0.27407	0.99970	0.99964
14	0.27163	0.99990	0.99982
15	0.26253	1.00000	0.99991
16	0.26941	0.99990	0.99995
17	0.26942	1.00000	0.99998
18	0.27041	1.00000	0.99999
19	0.27130	1.00000	0.99999
20	0.26734	1.00000	1.00000
21	0.26463	1.00000	1.00000
22	0.27652	1.00000	1.00000
23	0.26569	1.00000	1.00000
24	0.27030	1.00000	1.00000
25	0.26637	1.00000	1.00000
26	0.26724	1.00000	1.00000
27	0.26950	1.00000	1.00000
28	0.27383	1.00000	1.00000
29	0.27757	1.00000	1.00000
30	0.28012	1.00000	1.00000
31	0.27424	1.00000	1.00000
∞	?	?	≈ 1

whether $\frac{\#CEGs}{\#CDAGs} \approx \frac{\#DEGs}{\#DDAGs}$ where DEGs and DDAGs stand for disconnected EGs and disconnected DAGs. In [3, p. 154], it is also said that a consequence of the learnt EG being connected is "that a substantial number of undirected edges are likely to be present in the representative essential graph, which in turn makes it likely that the corresponding equivalence class size will be relatively large". In other words, they conjecture that the equivalence classes represented by CEGs are relatively large. We interpret the term "relatively large" as having a ratio smaller than $\frac{\#EGs}{\#DAGs}$. However, this conjecture does not seem to hold according to the approximate ratios presented in Table 2. There, we can see that $\frac{\#CEGs}{\#CDAGs} \approx 0.26\text{-}0.28$ for 6-31 nodes and, thus, $\frac{\#CEGs}{\#CDAGs} \approx \frac{\#EGs}{\#DAGs}$. That the two ratios coincide is not by chance because $\frac{\#CEGs}{\#EGs} \approx 0.95\text{-}1$ for 6-31 nodes, as can be seen in the table. A problem of this ratio being so close to 1 is that sampling a DEG is so unlikely that we cannot answer the question of whether

$\frac{\#CEGs}{\#CDAGs} \approx \frac{\#DEGs}{\#DDAGs}$ with our sampling scheme. Therefore, we have to content with having learnt that $\frac{\#CEGs}{\#CDAGs} \approx \frac{\#EGs}{\#DAGs}$. It is worth mentioning that this result is somehow conjectured by Kočka when he states in a personal communication to Gillispie that "large equivalence classes are merely composed of independent classes of smaller sizes that combine to make a single larger class" [2, p. 1411]. Again, we interpret the term "large" as having a ratio smaller than $\frac{\#EGs}{\#DAGs}$. Again, we cannot check Kočka's conjecture because sampling a DEG is very unlikely. However, we believe that the conjecture holds, because we expect the ratios for those EGs with k connected components to be around 0.27^k, i.e. we expect the ratios of the components to be almost independent one of another. Gillispie goes on saying that "an equivalence class encountered at any single step of the iterative [learning] process, a step which may involve altering only a small number of edges (typically only one), might be quite small" [2, p. 1411]. Note that the equivalence classes that he suggests that are quite small must correspond to CEGs, because he suggested before that large equivalence classes correspond to DEGs. We interpret the term "quite small" as having a ratio greater than $\frac{\#EGs}{\#DAGs}$. Again, this conjecture does not seem to hold according to the approximate ratios presented in Table 2. There, we can see that $\frac{\#CEGs}{\#CDAGs} \approx$ 0.26-0.28 for 6-31 nodes and, thus, $\frac{\#CEGs}{\#CDAGs} \approx \frac{\#EGs}{\#DAGs}$.

From the results in Tables 1 and 2, it seems that the asymptotic values for $\frac{\#EGs}{\#DAGs}$, $\frac{\#EDAGs}{\#EGs}$, $\frac{\#CEGs}{\#CDAGs}$ and $\frac{\#CEGs}{\#EGs}$ should be around 0.27, 0.27, 0.27 and 1, respectively. It would be nice to have a formal proof of these results. In this paper, we have proven a related result, namely that the ratio of CDAGs to DAGs is asymptotically 1. The proof can be found in Appendix B. Note from Table 2 that the asymptotic value is almost achieved for 6-7 nodes already. Our result adds to the list of similar results in the literature, e.g. the ratio of labeled connected graphs to labeled graphs is asymptotically 1 [4, p. 205].

Note that we can approximate the number of CEGs for up to 31 nodes as $\frac{\#CEGs}{\#EGs}\#EGs$, where $\frac{\#CEGs}{\#EGs}$ comes from Table 2 and $\#EGs$ can be computed as shown in the previous section. Alternatively, we can approximate it as $\frac{\#CEGs}{\#CDAGs}\#CDAGs$, where $\frac{\#CEGs}{\#CDAGs}$ comes from Table 2 and $\#CDAGs$ can be computed as shown in Appendix A.

Finally, note that the running times to obtain the results in Table 2 are the same as those in Table 1, because both tables are based on the same samples.

4   Discussion

In [3], it is shown that $\frac{\#EGs}{\#DAGs} \approx 0.27$ for 7-10 nodes. We have shown in this paper that $\frac{\#EGs}{\#DAGs} \approx 0.26\text{-}0.28$ for 11-31 nodes. These results indicate that one should not expect more than a moderate gain in efficiency when searching the space of EGs instead of the space of DAGs. We have also shown that $\frac{\#CEGs}{\#CDAGs} \approx 0.26\text{-}$ 0.28 for 6-31 nodes and, thus, $\frac{\#CEGs}{\#CDAGs} \approx \frac{\#EGs}{\#DAGs}$. Therefore, when searching the space of EGs, the fact that some of the EGs visited will most likely be connected does not seem to imply any additional gain in efficiency beyond that due to searching the space of EGs instead of the space of DAGs.

Some questions that remain open and that we would like to address in the future are checking whether $\frac{\#CEGs}{\#CDAGs} \approx \frac{\#DEGs}{\#DDAGs}$, and computing the asymptotic ratios of EGs to DAGs, EDAGs to EGs, CEGs to CDAGs, and of CEGs to EGs. Recall that in this paper we have proven that the asymptotic ratio of CDAGs to DAG is 1. Another topic for further research, already mentioned in [6], would be improving the graphical modifications that determine the MC transitions, because they rather often produce a graph that is not an EG. Specifically, the MC transitions are determined by choosing uniformly one out of seven modifications to perform on the current EG. Actually, one of the modifications leaves the current EG unchanged. Therefore, around 14 % of the modifications cannot change the current EG and, thus, 86 % of the modifications can change the current EG. In our experiments, however, only 6-8 % of the modifications change the current EG. The rest up to the mentioned 86 % produce a graph that is not an EG and, thus, they leave the current EG unchanged. This problem has been previously pointed out in [7]. Furthermore, he presents a set of more complex modifications that are claimed to alleviate the problem just described. Unfortunately, no evidence supporting this claim is provided. More recently, He et al. have proposed an alternative set of modifications having a series of desirable features that ensure that applying the modifications to an EG results in a different EG [5]. Although these modifications are more complex than those in [6], the authors show that their MCMC approach is thousands of times faster for 3, 4 and 6 nodes [5, pp. 17-18]. However, they also mention that it is unfair to compare these two approaches: Whereas 10^4 MCs of 10^6 transitions each are run in [6] to obtain a sample, they only run one MC of 10^4-10^5 transitions. Therefore, it is not clear how their MCMC approach scales to 10-30 nodes as compared to the one in [6]. The point of developing modifications that are more effective than ours at producing EGs is to make a better use of the running time by minimizing the number of graphs that have to be discarded. However, this improvement in effectiveness has to be weighed against the computational cost of the modifications, so that the MCMC approach still scales to the number of nodes of interest.

Appendix A: Counting CDAGs

Let $A(x)$ denote the exponential generating function for DAGs. That is,

$$A(x) = \sum_{k=1}^{\infty} \frac{A_k}{k!} x^k$$

where A_k denotes the number of DAGs of order k. Likewise, let $a(x)$ denote the exponential generating function for CDAGs. That is,

$$a(x) = \sum_{k=1}^{\infty} \frac{a_k}{k!} x^k$$

where a_k denotes the number of CDAGs of order k. Note that A_k can be computed without having to resort to enumeration by [9, Equation 8]. However, we do not know of any formula to compute a_k without enumeration. Luckily, a_k can be computed from A_k as follows. First, note that

$$1 + A(x) = e^{a(x)}$$

as shown by [4, pp. 8-9]. Now, let us define $A_0 = 1$ and redefine $A(x)$ as

$$A(x) = \sum_{k=0}^{\infty} \frac{A_k}{k!} x^k,$$

i.e. the summation starts with $k = 0$. Then,

$$A(x) = e^{a(x)}.$$

Consequently,

$$\frac{a_n}{n!} = \frac{A_n}{n!} - (\sum_{k=1}^{n-1} k \frac{a_k}{k!} \frac{A_{n-k}}{(n-k)!})/n$$

as shown by [4, pp. 8-9], and thus

$$a_n = A_n - (\sum_{k=1}^{n-1} k \binom{n}{k} a_k A_{n-k})/n.$$

See also [1, pp. 38-39]. Moreover, according to [12, Sequence A082402], the result in this appendix has previously been reported in [8]. However, we could not gain access to that paper to confirm it.

Appendix B: Asymptotic Behavior of CDAGs

Theorem 1. *The ratio of CDAGs of order n to DAGs of order n tends to 1 as n tends to infinity.*

Proof. Let A_n and a_n denote the numbers of DAGs and CDAGs of order n, respectively. Specifically, we prove that $(A_n/n!)/(a_n/n!) \to 1$ as $n \to \infty$. By [13, Theorem 6], this holds if the following three conditions are met:

(i) $\log((A_n/n!)/(A_{n-1}/(n-1)!)) \to \infty$ as $n \to \infty$,
(ii) $\log((A_{n+1}/(n+1)!)/(A_n/n!)) \geq \log((A_n/n!)/(A_{n-1}/(n-1)!))$ for all large enough n, and
(iii) $\sum_{k=1}^{\infty} (A_k/k!)^2/(A_{2k}/(2k)!)$ converges.

We start by proving that the condition (i) is met. Note that from every DAG G over the nodes $\{v_1, \ldots, v_{n-1}\}$ we can construct 2^{n-1} different DAGs H over $\{v_1, \ldots, v_n\}$ as follows: Copy all the arrows from G to H and make v_n a child in H of each of the 2^{n-1} subsets of $\{v_1, \ldots, v_{n-1}\}$. Therefore,

$$\log((A_n/n!)/(A_{n-1}/(n-1)!)) \geq \log(2^{n-1}/n)$$

which clearly tends to infinity as n tends to infinity.

We continue by proving that the condition (ii) is met. Every DAG over the nodes $V \cup \{w\}$ can be constructed from a DAG G over V by adding the node w to G and making it a child of a subset Pa of V. If a DAG can be so constructed from several DAGs, we simply consider it as constructed from one of them. Let $H_1, \ldots, H_m$ represent all the DAGs so constructed from G. Moreover, let Pa_i denote the subset of V used to construct H_i from G. From each Pa_i, we can now construct $2m$ DAGs over $V \cup \{w, u\}$ as follows: (i) Add the node u to H_i and make it a child of each subset $Pa_j \cup \{w\}$ with $1 \leq j \leq m$, and (ii) add the node u to H_i and make it a parent of each subset $Pa_j \cup \{w\}$ with $1 \leq j \leq m$. Therefore, $A_{n+1}/A_n \geq 2A_n/A_{n-1}$ and thus

$$\log((A_{n+1}/(n+1)!)/(A_n/n!)) = \log(A_{n+1}/A_n) - \log(n+1)$$

$$\geq \log(2A_n/A_{n-1}) - \log(n+1) \geq \log(2A_n/A_{n-1}) - \log(2n) = \log(A_n/A_{n-1}) - \log n$$

$$= \log((A_n/n!)/(A_{n-1}/(n-1)!)).$$

Finally, we prove that the condition (iii) is met. Let G and G' denote two (not necessarily distinct) DAGs of order k. Let $V = \{v_1, \ldots, v_k\}$ and $V' = \{v'_1, \ldots, v'_k\}$ denote the nodes in G and G', respectively. Consider the DAG H over $V \cup V'$ that has the union of the arrows in G and G'. Let w and w' denote two nodes in V and V', respectively. Let S be a subset of size $k-1$ of $V \cup V' \setminus \{w, w'\}$. Now, make w a parent in H of all the nodes in $S \cap V'$, and make w' a child in H of all the nodes in $S \cap V$. Note that the resulting H is a DAG of order $2k$. Note that there are k^2 different pairs of nodes w and w'. Note that there are $\binom{2k-2}{k-1}$ different subsets of size $k-1$ of $V \cup V' \setminus \{w, w'\}$. Note that every choice of DAGs G and G', nodes w and w', and subset S gives rise to a different DAG H. Therefore, $A_{2k}/A_k^2 \geq k^2 \binom{2k-2}{k-1}$ and thus

$$\sum_{k=1}^{\infty} (A_k/k!)^2/(A_{2k}/(2k)!) = \sum_{k=1}^{\infty} A_k^2 (2k)!/(A_{2k}k!^2)$$

$$\leq \sum_{k=1}^{\infty} ((k-1)!(k-1)!(2k)!)/(k^2(2k-2)!k!^2) = \sum_{k=1}^{\infty} (4k-2)/k^3$$

which clearly converges.

Acknowledgments. This work is funded by the Center for Industrial Information Technology (CENIIT) and a so-called career contract at Linköping University, by the Swedish Research Council (ref. 2010-4808), and by FEDER funds and the Spanish Government (MICINN) through the project TIN2010-20900-C04-03. We thank Dag Sonntag for his comments on this work.

References

1. Castelo, R.: The Discrete Acyclic Digraph Markov Model in Data Mining. PhD Thesis, Utrecht University (2002)

2. Gillispie, S.B.: Formulas for Counting Acyclic Digraph Markov Equivalence Classes. Journal of Statistical Planning and Inference, 1410–1432 (2006)
3. Gillispie, S.B., Perlman, M.D.: The Size Distribution for Markov Equivalence Classes of Acyclic Digraph Models. Artificial Intelligence, 137–155 (2002)
4. Harary, F., Palmer, E.M.: Graphical Enumeration. Academic Press (1973)
5. He, Y., Jia, J., Yu, B.: Reversible MCMC on Markov Equivalence Classes of Sparse Directed Acyclic Graphs. arXiv:1209.5860v2 [stat.ML]
6. Peña, J.M.: Approximate Counting of Graphical Models Via MCMC. In: Proceedings of the Eleventh International Conference on Artificial Intelligence and Statistics, pp. 352–359 (2007)
7. Perlman, M.D.: Graphical Model Search Via Essential Graphs. Technical Report 367, University of Washington (2000)
8. Robinson, R.W.: Counting Labeled Acyclic Digraphs. In: New Directions in the Theory of Graphs, pp. 239–273 (1973)
9. Robinson, R.W.: Counting Unlabeled Acyclic Digraphs. In: Proceedings of the Fifth Australian Conference on Combinatorial Mathematics, pp. 28–43 (1977)
10. Steinsky, B.: Enumeration of Labelled Chain Graphs and Labelled Essential Directed Acyclic Graphs. Discrete Mathematics, 266–277 (2003)
11. Steinsky, B.: Asymptotic Behaviour of the Number of Labelled Essential Acyclic Digraphs and Labelled Chain Graphs. Graphs and Combinatorics, 399–411 (2004)
12. The On-Line Encyclopedia of Integer Sequences (2010), published electronically at http://oeis.org
13. Wright, E.M.: A Relationship between Two Sequences. In: Proceedings of the London Mathematical Society, 296–304 (1967)

Multidimensional k-Interaction Classifier: Taking Advantage of All the Information Contained in Low Order Interactions

Aritz Pérez Martínes, José A. Lozano, and Iñaki Inza

University of the Basque Country
Computer Science and Artificial Intelligence Dept.

Abstract. This work presents a multidimensional classifier described in terms of interaction factors called multidimensional k-interaction classifier. The classifier is based on a probabilistic model composed of the product of all the interaction factors of order lower or equal to k and it takes advantage of all the information contained in them. The proposed classifier does not require a model selection step and its complexity is controlled by the regularization parameter k. Multidimensional k-interaction classifier is a generalization of the Kikuchi-Bayes classifier (Jakulin et al. 2004) to the multidimensional classification problem. The proposed multidimensional classifier is especially appropriate for small k values and for low dimensional domains. Multidimensional k-interaction classifier has shown a competitive behavior in difficult artificial domains for which the low order marginal distributions are almost uniform.

1 Multidimensional Supervised Classification

In the last years, a novel problem called *multidimensional supervised classification* has been proposed by the machine learning community. It is the natural generalization of the well known supervised classification problem, from a single class variable to multiple class variables. The interest in multidimensional supervised classification emerges naturally from the real world problems where, usually, more than one variable is needed to be predicted or diagnosed. Many of the methodological contributions to this novel problem consist of adapting techniques taken from supervised classification by taking advantage of the relations among the different class variables. This work generalizes the Kikuchi-Bayes classifier [7] to the multidimensional supervised classification problem by modeling the lower order interactions among the class variables. We propose an alternative interpretation of the probabilistic model in which the classifier is based: it is presented in terms of interaction factors instead of the Kikuchi approximation.

Formally, a multidimensional supervised classification problem consists of two types of random variables, the *features* denoted as $\boldsymbol{X} = (X_1, ..., X_n)$ and the *class* variables denoted as $\boldsymbol{C} = (C_1, ..., C_m)$ [1]. In this work we focus on *discrete random variables*, where X_i and C_j takes r_i and l_j possible categories (or labels) in the spaces Ω_{X_i} and Ω_{C_j}, respectively. The random variables $\boldsymbol{X}$ and $\boldsymbol{C}$ take values in $\Omega_{\boldsymbol{X}} = \Omega_{X_1} \times ... \times \Omega_{X_n}$ and $\Omega_{\boldsymbol{C}} = \Omega_{C_1} \times ... \times \Omega_{C_m}$, respectively. Given a set of indexes $\mathcal{S}$, we denote $\boldsymbol{X}_{\mathcal{S}}$ the $|\mathcal{S}|$-dimensional random variable $(X_i)_{i \in \mathcal{S}}$. We say that a function defined over

C. Bielza et al. (Eds.): CAEPIA 2013, LNAI 8109, pp. 393–401, 2013.

X_S has order $|S|$. We assume that the features and the class variables are distributed according to a joint probability distribution denoted as $p(\boldsymbol{x}, \boldsymbol{c})$, where $\boldsymbol{x} = (x_1, ..., x_n)$ and $\boldsymbol{c} = (c_1, ..., c_m)$ are instantiations of the random variables $\boldsymbol{X}$ and $\boldsymbol{C}$, respectively. A *multidimensional classifier* can be seen as a function $\psi(\boldsymbol{x})$ which maps $\Omega_{\boldsymbol{X}}$ onto $\Omega_{\boldsymbol{C}}$. The quality of the constructed classifier is usually measured in terms of (global) *classification error* defined as the probability of misclassification, and given by $\epsilon(\psi) = \sum_{\boldsymbol{x}} p(\boldsymbol{x})[1 - p(\psi(\boldsymbol{x})|\boldsymbol{x})]$.

One of the main approaches to construct a classifier consists of estimating the joint distribution $p(\boldsymbol{X}, \boldsymbol{C})$ from the available data $\mathcal{D} = \{(\boldsymbol{x}^1, \boldsymbol{c}^1), ..., (\boldsymbol{x}^N, \boldsymbol{c}^N)\}$, e.g. using maximum likelihood estimation. Thus, the classifier is given by an estimate of the joint distribution together with the *Bayes (classification) rule*:

$$\psi(\boldsymbol{x}) \equiv \arg_{\boldsymbol{c}} \max \hat{p}(\boldsymbol{x}, \boldsymbol{c}) \tag{1}$$

where $\hat{p}$ represents the estimated probability distribution. This approach is known as generative [8] and it is optimal in terms of classification error when the true distribution is used. The optimal classifier is known as the *Bayes classifier*. In the multidimensional classification literature stand out the use of generative classifiers based on Bayesian networks [1,2,4,14,16,17].

A closely related approach consists of using an estimate of the class conditional distribution $\hat{p}(\boldsymbol{c}|\boldsymbol{x})$, instead of the joint distribution, to define the classifier $\psi(\boldsymbol{x}) \equiv \arg_{\boldsymbol{c}} \max \hat{p}(\boldsymbol{c}|\boldsymbol{x})$. This alternative approach is known as *conditional* (or discriminative) [8]. The reader should note that any function $f(\boldsymbol{x}, \boldsymbol{c})$, fulfilling $f(\boldsymbol{x}, \boldsymbol{c}) \propto \hat{p}(\boldsymbol{x}, \boldsymbol{c})$ when $\boldsymbol{x}$ is fixed, produces a classifier equivalent to the one given by Equation 1. The multidimensional classifier proposed in this work is a conditional classifier. We consider this choice more appropriate because the conditional distribution requires the estimation of fewer parameters than the joint distribution, and because $\hat{p}(\boldsymbol{x})$ is irrelevant for classification purposes [5].

In Section 2 we propose the multidimensional k-interaction classifier. Section 3 presents the empirical results obtained in artificial domains, which highlight the benefits of our proposal compared to forward greedy classifier induction algorithms. Finally, in Section 4, we summarize the main contributions of this work and we point out the main future work lines.

2   Multidimensional k-Interaction Classifier

This section presents the *multidimensional k-interaction classifier* (MkIC). MkIC is a conditional classifier based on an approximation of the class conditional distribution $p(\boldsymbol{c}|\boldsymbol{x})$. The approximation is presented in terms of a product of interaction factors, which are closely related to the quantity of information theory called interaction information. A single regularization parameter k, fixed by the user, limits the order of the marginal distributions involved in the factorization of the approximation. This classifier is the generalization of Kikuchi-Bayes [7] to the multidimensional classification problem.

It is easy to prove that the joint distribution of $\boldsymbol{X}_S$ can be factorized as follows:

$$p(\boldsymbol{x}_S) = \prod_{\mathcal{R} \subseteq S} \phi(\boldsymbol{x}_{\mathcal{R}}) \tag{2}$$

where ϕ is called interaction factor. That is, the joint distribution of a set of discrete random variables is factorized into the product of the interaction factors of all of its subsets. The *interaction factor* for X_S is defined as

$$\phi(x_S) = \prod_{\mathcal{R} \subseteq S} p(x_{\mathcal{R}})^{(-1)^{|S|-|\mathcal{R}|}} \tag{3}$$

where $\phi(x_S) = 1$ when $p(x_S) = 0$. Besides, $\phi(x_S)$ can be alternatively defined as the quotient of the joint distribution for X_S divided by its Kirkwood approximation [10]. The expectation of the logarithm of an interaction factor $E[\log \phi(x)]$ is an information theory quantity called *interaction information* [6,11,12]. Krippendorff [11] indicates that it *is a unique dependency from which all relations of a lower order are removed*. The interaction information has been used in order to quantify the strength of the interaction among a set of random variable [6,12].

In the light of Equation 2 we can decompose the class conditional distribution as follows:

$$\begin{aligned} p(c|x) &= \frac{p(x, c)}{p(x)} \\ &= \frac{\prod_{S \subseteq \{1,\dots,m\}} \prod_{\mathcal{R} \subseteq \{1,\dots,n\}} \phi(x_{\mathcal{R}}, c_S)}{\prod_{\mathcal{R} \subseteq \{1,\dots,n\}} \phi(x_{\mathcal{R}})} \\ &= \prod_{\substack{S \subseteq \{1,\dots,m\} \\ S \neq \emptyset}} \prod_{\mathcal{R} \subseteq \{1,\dots,n\}} \phi(x_{\mathcal{R}}, c_S) \end{aligned}$$

Note that all the factors of the denominator in the second equality are included in the numerator and, thus, they have been removed for obtaining the last equality.

Our approach to the conditional distribution $p(c|x)$ is based on the interaction factors of order lower or equal to k:

$$f_k(c|x) = \prod_{\substack{S \subseteq \{1,\dots,m\} \\ 0 < |S| \le k}} \prod_{\substack{\mathcal{R} \subseteq \{1,\dots,n\} \\ |S|+|\mathcal{R}| \le k}} \phi(x_{\mathcal{R}}, c_S)$$

Higher order factors are ignored in order to control the complexity of the approximation, i.e. the number of parameters. The function f_k is known in the literature as a *hierarchical* structural model [11]. The approximation f_k to $p(c|x)$ for values of k higher than one is not a distribution except for special cases of $p(c|x)$. However, we can construct a classifier based on this approach using the Bayes rule because we are only interested in the maximum value of f_k given x. Moreover, the approximation can be easily normalized for each value x.

The function f_k can be expressed in terms of marginal distributions in a closed form as follows:

$$f_k(c|x) = \prod_{\substack{S \subseteq \{1,\dots,m\} \\ 0 < |S| \le k}} \prod_{\substack{\mathcal{R} \subseteq \{1,\dots,n\} \\ |S|+|\mathcal{R}| \le k}} p(x_{\mathcal{R}}, c_S)^{e_{\mathcal{R}}^{S}} \tag{4}$$

where the exponents are given by $e_{\mathcal{R}}^{\mathcal{S}} = \sum_{i=0}^{k-|\mathcal{S}|} \sum_{j=0}^{k-i-|\mathcal{S}|-|\mathcal{R}|} (-1)^{i+j} \binom{m-|\mathcal{S}|}{i} \binom{n-|\mathcal{R}|}{j}$.
For example, in a domain with $\boldsymbol{x} = (X_1, X_2)$ and $\boldsymbol{C} = (C_1, C_2)$ we have that
$f_2(\boldsymbol{c}|\boldsymbol{x}) = \phi(c_1)\phi(c_2)\phi(c_1, c_2)\phi(x_1, c_1)\phi(x_2, c_1)\phi(x_1, c_2)\phi(x_2, c_2)$ or, equivalently,
$f_2(\boldsymbol{c}|\boldsymbol{x}) = p(c_1, c_2)p(x_1, c_1)p(x_2, c_1)p(x_1, c_2)p(x_2, x_2)p(c_1)^{-2}p(c_2)^{-2}p(x_1)^{-2}$
$p(x_2)^{-2}$.

MkIC is defined as follows:

$$\psi_k(\boldsymbol{x}) \equiv \arg_{\boldsymbol{c}} \max f_k(\boldsymbol{c}|\boldsymbol{x})$$

2.1   Merits and Caveats of MkIC

MkIC depends on a single regularization parameter k which controls the number of parameters of the model and the maximum order of the marginal distributions. The model is completely determined by the marginal distributions of order k, because lower order marginal distributions can be obtained by marginalization. The approximation f_k given in Equation 4 models all the interactions of order lower or equal to k and, therefore, MkIC can take advantage of all the information contained in them. Clearly, since it models all the interactions of lower order there is not a model selection step and, once k is fixed the model can be given in a closed form.

The number of factors implied in f_k (see Equation 4) is $\sum_{i=1}^{k} \sum_{j=0}^{k-i} \binom{m}{i} \binom{n}{j}$ and it grows exponentially with k. As a consequence, the computational cost for classifying unlabeled instances for MkIC is $\mathcal{O}(\sum_{i=1}^{k} \sum_{j=0}^{k-i} \binom{m}{i} \binom{n}{j})$. Clearly, in order to control the number of factors and the time required for classifying an unlabeled instance, the use of a low value of k is advisable. Besides, due to its high computational complexity the model is recommendable for domains with a small number of random variables.

An important property of the factorization of probability distributions is described in term of a set of integer numbers called counting regions [9,15]. A counting region number express the strength of the contribution of a (multidimensional) random variable in a given factorization: its influence in the probability mass of the factorization increases as its counting region is higher. *Counting region* [9,15] is associated to *region based factorizations* [15], a family of factorizations of probability distributions given in terms of a product of marginal distributions powered to an integer. Thus, the approach to the conditional distribution $p(\boldsymbol{c}|\boldsymbol{x})$ given in Equation 4 can be seen as a region based approximation. In Equation 4, the counting region of a multidimensional variable $(X_{\mathcal{R}}, C_{\mathcal{S}})$ is given by the sum of the exponents of the marginal distributions defined over random variables $(X_{\mathcal{T}}, C_{\mathcal{U}})$ for which $\mathcal{R} \subseteq \mathcal{T}$ and $\mathcal{S} \subseteq \mathcal{U}$. A factorization of a probability distribution is said to be a *valid region-based decomposition* for a (multidimensional) random variable when its counting region is one. Intuitively, it can be said that a (multidimensional) random variable with the counting region equal to one contributes exactly once to the probability mass of the approached distribution.

Interestingly, the counting region associated to random variable $(X_{\mathcal{R}}, C_{\mathcal{S}})$ in the factorization given in Equation 4 is one if and only if $\mathcal{S} \neq \emptyset$ and $|\mathcal{S}| + |\mathcal{R}| \leq k$, and zero otherwise. Thus, the factorization f_k is a valid region-based approximation for every subset of the variables of order k or less, which contain at least one class variable. In other words, the multidimensional random variables which contain a class variable of order lower or equal to k contributes one time to the probability mass of the factorization.

3   Experimentation in Artificial Domains

The experimentation consists of a comparison of MkIC for $k \in \{2, 3, 4\}$ with the *wrapper multidimensional Bayesian classifier* [1] (*Wrapper*) and the Bayes classifier (*Bayes*). Details of Wrapper are shown in Appendix. Following the suggestions for model selection given in [13], we have used the stratified 5-fold cross validation error estimator in order to guide the search of Wrapper. The estimated probability distributions have been learned from data using the Laplace correction.

The experimentation is focused on artificial domains in order to illustrate the benefits of using MkIC in domains for which the lower order marginal distributions tend to have a small discriminative power. The domains are characterized by:

– Number of class variables: $m \in \{2, 3, 4, 5, 6, 7, 8\}$
– Number of features: $n \in \{4, 6, 8, 10, 12, 14, 16\}$

All the random variables are binary. The probability distribution of the different domains, $p(\boldsymbol{x}, \boldsymbol{c})$, has been randomly sampled using Dirichlet distributions with the following parameters:

– $p(\boldsymbol{c})$ is sampled from a Dirichlet with parameters $\alpha = 1$. These parameters do not favor balanced or unbalanced class probability distributions.
– $p(\boldsymbol{x}|\boldsymbol{c})$ is sampled from a Dirichlet distribution with parameters $\alpha = 1/n$. These parameters favor more unbalanced distributions $p(\boldsymbol{x}|\boldsymbol{c})$, as the number of features n increases.

The average Bayes error for the different type of the domains is shown in Table 1. Due to the selected parameters, the average Bayes error tends to increase as m increases, and it tends to decrease as n increases. For each combination of the parameters m and n, we have generated 25 probability distributions at random. For each probability distribution we have sampled a test set of size 1000, in order to reliably estimate the errors, and training sets of size $N \in \{10, 30, 100, 300, 1000, 3000, 10000\}$. The different training set sizes are used for analyzing the evolution of the behavior of MkIC as the training set size increases.

The randomly generated domains are unstructured, i.e. with a high probability they do not exhibit conditional independences among the implied random variables. Besides, the domains can be considered difficult because with a high probability the marginal distributions of low order are almost uniform and, thus, they tend have low discriminative power. By the aggregation property of the Dirichlet distribution, it can be demonstrated that $p(x_i, c_j)$ can be seen as sampled from a Dirichlet distribution with parameters $\alpha = \frac{2^{n-1}}{n} + 2^{m-1}$. A Dirichlet with these parameters samples distributions close to the uniform with a high probability.

Taken into account the low discrimination power of the low order marginals and the absence of conditional independences, we can say that the generated domains are difficult for supervised classification, and specially difficult for forward greedy algorithms based on graphical models [1], e.g. the Wrapper algorithm. We have selected the Wrapper algorithm due to its competitive classification behavior among a variety of forward greedy algorithms based on Bayesian networks [1]. The experimentation tries

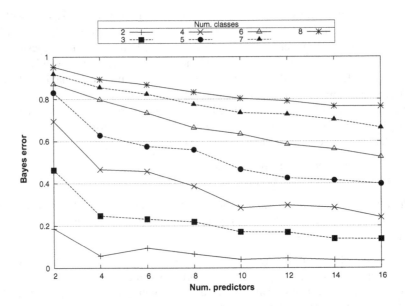

Fig. 1. Average Bayes error among the randomly sampled domains for the different values of m and n

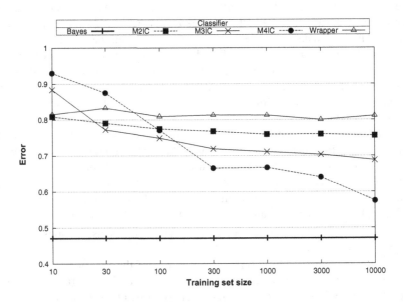

Fig. 2. Evolution of the average error among all the domains obtained by the different classifiers as the training set size increases

to illustrate the advantages of using MkIC and the difficulties of the popular family of the greedy heuristic in domains with the described particularities.

Figure 2 summarizes the obtained results. We have decided to present the average among the different domains because the same pattern appears for the domains with a different number of class variables. On one hand, Wrapper is not able to learn an appropriate joint distribution from data due to the low discriminative power of the marginal distributions of low order. It learns graphs with a very low number of edges and, thus, it can not take advantage of the larger training sets. On the other hand, MkIC reduces the error as the training set size increases because it is able to take advantage of all the discriminative information contained in the low order interactions. Besides, as k increases the reduction of the error with respect to the training set size seems to be higher because MkIC is able to learn more complex interactions. At low values of the training set size (100 or less) M4IC behaves worse than M2IC and M3IC because it needs more data to learn appropriate interaction factors of order 4. This result suggests that the optimal k value tends to be higher as the training set size increases.

4   Conclusions

the multidimensional k-interaction classifier is a conditional classifier based on an approach to the conditional class distribution $p(c|x)$ which takes into account all the interaction factors of order equal or lower than k. The approach does not require a model selection step and it is given in a closed form fixed a k value. The multidimensional k-interaction classifier is able to exploit all the information contained in low order interactions. This characteristic seems to be highly beneficial in domains for which the low order marginal distributions have a low discriminative power. In the performed experimentation, multidimensional k-interaction classifier has shown a competitive behavior in this type of domains.

The multidimensional k-interaction classifier has a computational cost for classifying an instance of $\mathcal{O}(\sum_{i=1}^{k} \sum_{j=0}^{k-i} \binom{m}{i}\binom{n}{j})$. Thus, it is advisable to choose low values of k (typically $k \in \{2,3,4\}$), and it is specially appropriate for domains with low dimensionality.

In the future, in order to reduce the number of factors implied in our approach, we will develop an interaction factor selection procedure based on the interaction information quantity [3]. Besides, a heuristic for the selection of an appropriate value of k will be proposed based on the particularities of the multidimensional supervised classification domain and the size of the available data.

Acknowledgements. This work has been possible due to the financial support of the research projects *Modelos Gráficos Probabilísticos en Aprendizaje Automático y Optimización: Implementaciones Eficientes y Aplicaciones (TIN2010-14931)* from the Ministry of Science and Innovation of Spain, *Inteligencia Computacional (IT609-13)* from the Basque Country and *Osadatu (Osasun Datuak Kudeatu) Gestión de Datos Sanitarios* from the University of the Basque Country.

Appendix: The Wrapper Classifier Induction Algorithm

The pseudocode of the wrapper classifier induction algorithm is shown in Algorithm 1. The parameters of the probability represented with Bayesian networks based on the constructed graphs are obtained from data using the Laplace's correction. The multidimensional Bayesian classifier associated to a graph $\mathcal{G}$ is denoted as $\psi_{\mathcal{G}}$. The estimated error is obtained with the stratified k-fold cross-validation and it is denoted as $\hat{e}$.

Algorithm 1 (The Wrapper algorithm)

Input: Data set, $D = \{(\boldsymbol{x}^1, \boldsymbol{c}^1), ..., (\boldsymbol{x}^N, \boldsymbol{c}^N)\}$, number of folds of the stratified k-fold cross-validation error estimation, k
Output: Multidimensional Bayesian classifier
Pseudocode:

```
- Initialization: assign all the possible arcs among the random variables x₁,...,xₙ,
  c₁,...,cₘ to addArcs, set remArcs to an empty set of arcs, set G to the empty graph,
  set minError to one and cont to true
- While(cont)
    • Obtain the error associated to all the classifiers obtained by adding each arc
      in addArcs which does not cause cycles to G, and select the best G⁺
    • Obtain the error associated to all the classifiers obtained by removing each
      arc in remArcs from G, and select the best G⁻
    • If ê(ψ_G) ≤ ê(ψ_G⁻)
        * If ê(ψ_G⁺) < minError
            · Add the arc in G⁺ not included in G to remArcs and remove it from
              addArcs
            · G = G⁺
            · minError = ê(ψ_G⁺)
        * Else cont = false
    • Else
        * If ê(ψ_G⁻) < minError
            · Remove the arc in G⁻ included in G from remArcs
            · G = G⁻
            · minError = ê(ψ_G⁻)
        * Else cont = false
- End While
- Return ψ_G
```

References

1. Bielza, C., Li, G., Larrañaga, P.: Multi-dimensional classification with Bayesian networks. International Journal of Approximate Reasoning 52(6), 705–727 (2011)
2. Borchani, H., Bielza, C., Larrañaga, P.: Learning CB-decomposable multi-dimensional Bayesian network classifiers. In: Proceedings of the 5th European Workshop on Probabilistic Graphical Models, pp. 25–32 (2010)
3. Brown, G.: Conditional likelihood maximisation: A unifying framework for information theoretic feature selection. Journal of Machine Learning Research 13, 27–66 (2012)
4. de Waal, P.R., van der Gaag, L.C.: Inference and learning in multi-dimensional bayesian network classifiers. In: Mellouli, K. (ed.) ECSQARU 2007. LNCS (LNAI), vol. 4724, pp. 501–511. Springer, Heidelberg (2007)
5. Friedman, N., Geiger, D., Goldszmidt, M.: Bayesian network classifiers. Machine Learning 29, 131–163 (1997)
6. Jakulin, A.: Attribute Interactions in Machine Learning. PhD thesis, University of Ljubljana (2005)

7. Jakulin, A., Rish, I., Bratko, I.: Kikuchi-Bayes: Factorized models for approximate classification in closed form. Internal Report RC23602 (W0505-053). IBM (2004)
8. Jebara, T.: Machine Learning: Discriminative and Generative. Kluwer Academic Publishers (2004)
9. Kikuchi, R.: A theory of cooperative phenomena. Physical Review 81(6), 988–1003 (1951)
10. Kirkwood, J.G.: Statistical mechanics of fluid mixtures. Journal of Chemical Physics 3, 300–313 (1935)
11. Krippendorff, K.: Information Theory. Structural models for Qualitative Data. Sage University (1986)
12. McGill, W.J.: Multivariate information transmission. Psychometrika 19(2), 97–116 (1954)
13. Rodríguez, J.D., Pérez, A., Lozano, J.A.: An unified framework for the statistical analysis of the sources of variance for classification error estimators. Pattern Recognition 46(3), 855–864 (2013)
14. van der Gaag, L., de Waal, P.: Muti-dimensional Bayesian network classifiers. In: Proceedings of the Third European Workshop in Probabilistic Graphical Models, pp. 107–114 (2006)
15. Yedidia, J.S., Freeman, W.T., Weiss, Y.: Constructing free energy approximations and generalized belief propagation algorithms. In: Garbow, B.S., Dongarra, J., Boyle, J.M., Moler, C.B. (eds.) Matrix Eigensystem Routines - EISPACK Guide Extension. LNCS (LNAI), vol. 51, pp. 2282–2313. Springer, Heidelberg (1977)
16. Zaragoza, J.C., Sucar, L.E., Morales, E.F., Bielza, C., Larrañaga, P.: Bayesian chain classifiers for multidimensional classification. In: IJCAI, pp. 2192–2197 (2011)
17. Zaragoza, J.C., En. Sucar, L., Morales, E.F.: A two-step method to learn multidimensional Bayesian network classifiers based on mutual information measures. In: FLAIRS Conference (2011)

Author Index

Alba, Enrique   289
Alfaro, Rocío   250
Alonso-Betanzos, Amparo   149
Alonso-González, Carlos J.   239
Arbelaitz, Olatz   111
Arias, Jacinto   310
Arias Gallego, Mario   12

Bajo, Javier   219
Batalla, Cristina   250
Bautista, Joaquín   250
Bellogín, Alejandro   22
Bielza, Concha   139, 159, 363
Bolón-Canedo, Verónica   121
Bragard, Jean   62
Bregon, Anibal   239
Burrieza, Alfredo   101

Cabañas, Rafael   321
Cabrera, Guillem   260
Campos, Pedro G.   22, 42
Cano, Alberto   250
Cano, Andrés   321, 332
Cantador, Iván   22, 42
Cárdenas-Montes, Miguel   209
Carmona, Neus   62
Cerquides, Jesús   199
Cerviño-Rabuñal, Joana   121
Chamorro, Alondra   300
Chenlo, Jose M.   32
Coello Coello, Carlos A.   269
Corcho, Oscar   12

De la Prieta, Fernando   219
Del Hoyo, Rafael   168
del Rey, Ángel Martín   228
Díez, Fernando   22, 42
Dorronsoro, Bernabé   269
Durillo, Juan J.   269

Elorza, Jorge   62

Fdez-Olivares, Juan   178
Fernández, Antonio   342
Fernández, Javier D.   12

Fernández-Tobías, Ignacio   42
Fontenla-Romero, Oscar   149

Galand, Lucie   1
Gallego-Durán, Francisco José   131
Gámez, José A.   310
Godó, Lluís   188
Gómez-Olmedo, Manuel   321, 332
Gonzalez, Avelino J.   373
González, Carlos   168
González-Hidalgo, Manuel   70
Gurrutxaga, Ibai   111

Hernández-González, Jerónimo   352

Inza, Iñaki   352, 393

Juan, Angel A.   260

Larrañaga, Pedro   139, 159, 363
Llamazares, Bonifacio   80
Llorens-Largo, Faraón   131
López-Cruz, Pedro L.   139, 363
Losada, David E.   32
Lozano, José A.   352, 393

Machín, Mirialys   269
Machuca, Enrique   1
Madsen, Anders L.   321
Mandow, Lawrence   1
Marquès, Joan Manuel   260
Martínez, Luis   91
Martínez-Prieto, Miguel A.   12
Martínez-Rego, David   149
Massanet, Sebastià   70
Mayo, Sergio   168
Meseguer, Pedro   199
Mihaljevic, Bojan   159
Milla-Millán, Gonzalo   178
Mir, Arnau   70
Molina-Carmona, Rafael   131
Montaña, José Luis   373

Moral, Serafín   332
Moya Alonso, Noemi   239
Muguerza, Javier   111

Nebro, Antonio J.   269
Nielsen, Thomas D.   363

Ontañón, Santiago   373

Palazuelos, Camilo   52
Palomares, Iván   91
Parapar, Javier   32
Pardo, Pere   188
Pellicer, Eugenio   300
Peña, José M.   383
Peña, Paula   168
Pérez, Jesús María   111
Pérez-Ariza, Cora Beatriz   332
Pérez-Bernabé, Inmaculada   342
Pérez Martínes, Aritz   393
Pérez-Rosés, Hebert   260
Ponce, Rafael   209
Puerta, José M.   310
Pujol-Gonzalez, Marc   199
Pulido, Belarmino   239

Quevedo-Orozco, Dagoberto R.   279

Recasens, Jordi   62
Ríos-Mercado, Roger Z.   279
Rodríguez, Sara   219
Rodríguez-Aguilar, Juan Antonio   199
Rodríguez-Vázquez, Juan José   209
Ruiz-Aguilera, Daniel   70

Salmerón, Antonio   332, 342
Sánchez, Antonio Juan   219
Sánchez Álvaro, Eusebio   209
Sánchez-Garzón, Inmaculada   178
Sánchez-Maroño, Noelia   121
Sevilla, Ignacio   209
Stolfi, Daniel H.   289
Suárez-Figueroa, Mari Carmen   12

Tambe, Milind   199
Torres-Machí, Cristina   300

Vea-Murguía, Jorge   168
Vega-Rodríguez, Miguel Ángel   209

Yepes, Víctor   300

Zato, Carolina   219
Zorrilla, Marta   52